A Telescope on Society

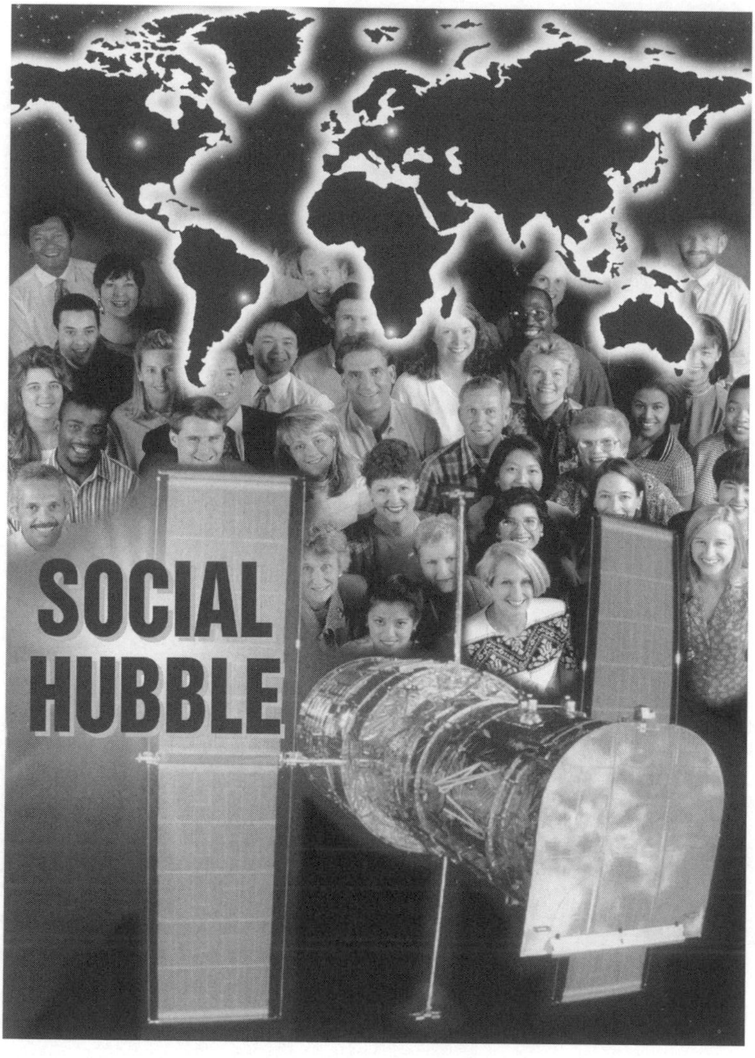

This image of the Hubble telescope and a diverse and multinational set of people was developed in conjunction with the effort of Institute for Social Research Director David Featherman and his international counterparts to create a set of Centers around the globe for comparative and cooperative survey-based social research: a telescope on the global society. (Image by Athos Russo Valério, courtesy of the Institute for Social Research.)

A Telescope on Society

Survey Research and Social Science at the University of Michigan and Beyond

James S. House, F. Thomas Juster, Robert L. Kahn, Howard Schuman, and Eleanor Singer, Editors

WITH A FOREWORD BY DAVID L. FEATHERMAN

The University of Michigan Press

Ann Arbor

Published in the United States of America by
The University of Michigan Press
Manufactured in the United States of America
♾ Printed on acid-free paper
2007 2006 2005 2004 4 3 2 1

A CIP catalog record for this book is available from the British Library.

Library of Congress Cataloging-in-Publication Data

A telescope on society : survey research and social science at the
University of Michigan and beyond / edited by James S. House . . .
[et al.] ; with a foreword by David L. Featherman.
p. cm.
Includes bibliographical references and index.
ISBN 0-472-09848-9 (cloth : alk. paper) —
ISBN 0-472-06848-2 (pbk. : alk. paper)
1. Social surveys—United States—History. 2. University of Michigan.
Survey Research Center—History. 3. University of Michigan. Institute
for Social Research—History. I. House, James s., 1944–

HM538 .T4 2004
300'.7'23—dc22 2003016341

This volume is dedicated to the memory of

Rensis Likert,
Angus Campbell,
George Katona,
Leslie Kish, and
Charles Cannell,

whose vision, creativity, and productivity contributed so much to making social science and survey research what they are today—scientifically and institutionally.

Contents

Foreword
David L. Featherman xi

Acknowledgments *xvii*

CHAPTER 1. The Development and Contribution of Survey Research as a Scientific Instrument and Social Institution
James S. House, Eleanor Singer, Robert L. Kahn, Howard Schuman, and F. Thomas Juster 1

CHAPTER 2. Survey Methodology
Robert M. Groves and Eleanor Singer, with James M. Lepkowski, Steven G. Heeringa, and Duane F. Alwin 21

PART 1. Political Behavior and Systems
Introduction by William Zimmerman 65

CHAPTER 3. Voting and Electoral Behavior
Philip E. Converse and Donald R. Kinder 70

CHAPTER 4. Survey Research and Political Socialization
M. Kent Jennings 98

PART 2. The Behavioral Study of Economics
Introduction by F. Thomas Juster 119

CHAPTER 5. Psychology and Macroeconomics
Richard T. Curtin 131

CHAPTER 6. Evolution and Change in Family Income, Wealth, and Health: The Panel Study of Income Dynamics, 1968–2000 and Beyond
Greg J. Duncan, Sandra L. Hofferth, and Frank P. Stafford 156

PART 3. From the Study of Organizations to the Study of Health
Introduction by Robert L. Kahn 195

CHAPTER 7. Survey Research in the Study of Organizations
Robert L. Kahn 201

CHAPTER 8. Understanding and Improving the Mental Health of Populations
Richard H. Price 222

CHAPTER 9. The Psychosocial Nature of Physical Health
James S. House and George A. Kaplan 248

PART 4. Developments in the Study of Family and the Life Course
Introduction by Duane F. Alwin 271

CHAPTER 10. The Social Demography of Fertility: Some Contributions of American Surveys
Arland Thornton and William G. Axinn 281

CHAPTER 11. Studying the Transition from Youth to Adulthood: Impacts on Substance Use and Abuse
Patrick M. O'Malley, Jerald G. Bachman, Lloyd D. Johnston, and John Schulenberg 305

CHAPTER 12. Research on Aging
A. Regula Herzog, Robert J. Willis, and David R. Weir 330

PART 5. Surveying the Subtleties and Complexities of Race
Introduction by Maria Krysan 355

CHAPTER 13. Racial Attitudes: Developments and Divisions in Survey Research
Donald R. Kinder and Howard Schuman 365

CHAPTER 14. Surveying the Black American Population
James S. Jackson and David R. Williams 393

CHAPTER 15. Survey Research and Social Science: Retrospect and Prospect
James S. House, Eleanor Singer, Robert L. Kahn, Howard Schuman, and F. Thomas Juster 439

Contributors 455
Index 467
Illustrations *following page* 172

Foreword

David L. Featherman
DIRECTOR OF THE INSTITUTE FOR SOCIAL RESEARCH

Survey research, based on ever more precise samples of populations, measurements of concepts, and methods of mental interrogation, is little more than a century old. This period—the late nineteenth through the twentieth centuries—also is the historical era in which social science redefined its raison d'être from societal reform to scientific inquiry. Both developments, of course, are intertwined, for the tools enabling any human enterprise are fashioned for their purpose. Conversely, refinements and embellishments of tools and instruments can alter or expand the tools' original instrumental purpose.

Such research methods as taking probability samples and interviewing representative individuals or households of a whole society advanced apace in America, especially after World War II. But earlier roots, both in the United States and Britain, of today's survey research were laid in the mid- to late nineteenth century by social reformers using less scientific methods. In both countries, the so-called settlement house movements (such as Hull House) used systematic observations and measurements or interviewed public health nurses or other "experts" about conditions of (usually poor) families in local communities. Their objective was to characterize the dimensions of social problems—mostly those attributed to rapidly expanding cities and industrialization—and to use this information as the basis of a liberal political agenda of change. While in Britain there were notable predecessors (Lewis Mayhew) and successors (Seebohm Rowntree), Charles Booth pioneered the use of in-home interviews and systematic data summarization in statistical form in his landmark studies of turn-of-the-century London's poor and the ramifications of poverty. Booth's influence extended into America. Florence Kelley within Hull House—examining child labor and unsavory housing environments of youth, as well as poverty per se—and W. E. B. Du Bois's classic *The Philadelphia Negro* mirrored Booth in scope and approach. These American developments were accelerated after World War I by the Social Survey Movement and later by the Department of Survey and Exhibits, funded and organized by the reformist Russell Sage Foundation in New York City. (For a succinct summary of this early history, see Bulmer 2001.)

Our modern probability sample surveys expanded rapidly just prior to and after World War II. The impetus came largely from the influences of statisticians, again in Britain (e.g., R. A. Fischer and Karl Pearson) as well as in America. Here, statisticians and sociologists such as Jerzy Neyman, Samuel Stouffer, and Paul Lazarsfeld and political scientists and psychologists such as Howard Gosnell and L. L. Thurstone advanced the statistical precision of sample designs and of the measurement of attitudes, opinions, and reports about behavior. During World War II, Rensis Likert—first at the U.S. Department of Agriculture and later at the Survey Research Center (SRC), which he founded at Michigan—advanced attitude measurement but also the case for probability (over quota) sampling. The coincident emergence of market research and opinion polling as a flourishing industry after 1930 reflected, perhaps, our American style of consumer-oriented capitalism, individualism, and liberal democracy. But this development, too, advanced the modern era in survey research. What distinguishes this era from its reformist ancestry is the premise that the mathematics of probability theory—statistical science—elevates survey methodology from the idiosyncrasies of local studies and individual observers' reports, the imprecision of qualitative assessments, and the political agenda of reformers. Social surveys after World War II made their claim as scientific tools in the hands of social scientists making objective assessments. Whereas in the earlier era the reformist Russell Sage Foundation promoted American advances, in the modern period institutional sponsorship of field development fell to scientific and scholarly organizations, for example, the Social Science Research Council (SSRC) in New York City and such offshoots as the Committee on Government Statistics and Information Services of the SSRC and the American Statistical Association. (For a succinct summary of this modern era, see Fienberg and Tanur 2001.)

And so the metaphor of survey research as a telescope on society draws our attention to this intensive interplay throughout the twentieth century between the creation and continual refinement of a scientific tool for social analysis, on the one hand, and of an empirically grounded description and understanding of human behavior and institutions, on the other. As the tool became more scientific—the telescope's optics and fidelity improved as the theory and means to do so advanced—so did the results of its application. Throughout the latter half of this seminal period, the SRC and the Institute for Social Research (ISR) of the University of Michigan have pioneered in the science of society. As the chapters of this book so ably demonstrate, the inquiring minds of the SRC's and the ISR's scientists—whether they were focused on poverty and income dynamics, electoral politics, health and well-being, or family formation, for example—constantly required and inspired improvements in sampling, interviewing, statistical analysis of data, and other survey methodologies. In a sense, the SRC itself became the telescope, a scientific institution at one and the same time refining a specific set of tools—survey research methodology, a burgeoning professional field as of the early twenty-first century—and, through their application, a scientific narrative of social life in America and in the wider world. And for most of the past half century, hundreds if not thousands of younger social scientists and graduate students from around the world have traveled to the SRC and to the ISR, to this unique telescope on society. They come, even to this day, principally to the SRC's renowned Summer Institute (and to a companion program administered at ISR by the Inter-university Consortium for Political and Social Research [ICPSR]), much as high-energy physicists might travel to the world's fastest supercollider at CERN in Switzerland for unique research or advanced training.

The history of survey research is first a story about the evolution of extensive and intensive scientific understanding of society. But it also is a history of democracy and some of its foundational principles. Especially in America, modern (random) sample surveys are characterized as giving voice to the people, to all elements of society—not just to its economic elite, to its urbane intellectuals, or to its long-standing citizens. As an objective, scientific tool in the hands of the "politically neutral" analyst, the social survey yields honest numbers for democracy. Since the principal centers of survey research are located at or are adjuncts to major research universities—historically, Columbia University, the University of Chicago, and, of course, ISR at the University of Michigan—the capacity of the telescope is distributed among institutions that promote informed debate, learn from intellectual disagreements, and test ideas against evidence. These institutional values of universities are the building blocks of a scientific as well as a democratic discourse. Surrounded by these values and institutional practices, the focusing and imaging of this telescope on society (i.e., what it looks at and what its revealed data are interpreted to mean) lie well beyond the effective control of government or of any particular partisan agenda. (For a summary of the theoretical relationships between the values and cultural institutions of democracy and science, and the link between the two in the case of social surveys, see Sztompka 1999.)

Reality, of course, is a little different from this principled narrative about surveys and popular democracy. For example, survey data, once in the public domain, are subject to many different analytical objectives—some partisan and political and some more driven by scientific curiosity. Governments, at first local but then increasingly national or federal, have collected "political arithmetic" from censuses and state-run surveys for hundreds of years. Also, the artfully purposive phrasing or sequencing of questions in interviews, whether in the hands of academics or partisans, can elicit different responses to nominally the same question or issue. Still, the legacy of survey research and of the accessibility of survey data as an informational tool is a powerful contribution to democratic debate. That legacy also speaks to the ongoing challenge in any democracy to hear the voices of its people and to empower that people with "honestly brokered" information. (For a historical account of the role of social science in social reform and policy-making in the American democracy, see Featherman and Vinovskis 2001.)

At the celebration of its fiftieth anniversary in 1997, ISR adopted a logo that claimed for its institutional mission "social science in the public interest." There is no better basis for this claim than *A Telescope on Society*. This volume brings into sharp focus the passion for deep inquiry, the quest for ever more precise measurement. It describes a collective, collaborative process of scientific discovery that draws upon many experiences and interdisciplinary expertise. And in its choice of social issues on which to focus this telescope, the book also reveals a legacy of social consciousness, of scientific responsibility, that harkens back to a much earlier era of social science and to its reformist past. This in no way diminishes its contributions as contemporary social science. Rather, it illustrates the dual motivations of scientists as citizens who make their intellectual work useful and accessible to others in this democratic society and beyond. Like ISR, this book is social science in the public interest.

REFERENCES

Bulmer, M. 2001. History of social survey. In *International encyclopedia of the social and behavioral sciences*, ed. N. J. Smelser and P. B. Baltes, 21:14469–73. Oxford: Elsevier.

Featherman, D. L., and M. Vinovskis, eds. 2001. *Social science and policy-making: A search for relevance in the twentieth century.* Ann Arbor: University of Michigan Press.
Fienberg, S., and J. Tanur. 2001. History of sample surveys. In *International encyclopedia of the social and behavioral sciences,* ed. N. J. Smelser and P. B. Baltes, 20:13453–58. Oxford: Elsevier.
Sztompka, P. 1999. Science and democracy. In *World social science report, 1999,* 256–65. Paris: UNESCO/Elsevier.

Acknowledgments

This volume seeks to convey a sense of the development of social science in the twentieth century through its interaction with a major new instrument for gathering data about society—survey research. The story is largely told by social scientists affiliated with the Survey Research Center (SRC) and Institute for Social Research (ISR) at the University of Michigan and is largely about work done there. But we have also sought to place the work at Michigan in the broader context of developments in survey-based social science in our nation and the world, to which many individuals and institutions beyond SRC, ISR, and Michigan have also greatly contributed. The Michigan case is probably the best single exemplar of these developments, but it is only one exemplar.

Thus, we hope the volume will speak and be useful to a wide audience of social science and survey research professionals and students interested in learning more about the broad content and history of survey-based social science and about its contributions to understanding scientific and social issues in the areas of politics, economics, organizations, health, human development and aging, and racial/ethnic diversity and relations. We also wish to convey how institutional and public support have been and will continue to be crucial to the development of social science and survey research, in the same way that this support has been crucial to developments in the natural, biomedical, and life sciences. In both regards the volume may be of special interest and use to those interested in the Michigan experience.

Creating this volume has been a collective labor of love, reflecting our joint delight in doing social science through survey research and in doing it within the very special and supportive institutional contexts of SRC, ISR, and the University of Michigan. From its inception at the end of the twentieth century and through the fiftieth anniversaries of the SRC and ISR, to its final completion, the volume has been a truly collective effort not only of the five editors and twenty-six contributors but of all of our colleagues, past and present, whose potential contributions could not be fully incorporated into a single volume of publishable size but whose work constitutes the substance of much of what is here and much more of what is not. This volume would also not have been possible without the financial support and efforts of multiple staff of SRC and ISR, only some of whom can be recognized by name. For all of this we are grateful.

It is only possible to do a volume like this because we stand, in the words of Newton, "on the shoulder of giants"—the founding quintet of SRC and ISR (Rensis Likert, Angus Campbell, George Katona, Leslie Kish, and Charles Cannell, now all deceased and to whom we dedicate this volume) and their contemporaries elsewhere such as George Gallup, Paul Lazarsfeld, Samuel Stouffer, and Herbert Hyman. Their foundational contributions to developing the science and institutional infrastructures for survey-based social science are evident throughout the volume. We have been made poignantly aware of these contributions over the course of this volume's writing by the deaths of Kish and Cannell, as well as of Elizabeth Douvan, the one female member of the founding ISR generation, and of another senior female colleague, A. Regula Herzog, who was the principal author of chapter 12 of this volume before her death.

The book and its content also would not have been possible without the forward-looking and sustained support of the University of Michigan and the major external sponsors of social science research at SRC, ISR, and beyond, including the National Institutes of Health, the National Science Foundation, major private foundations, and some private sector companies. This support underlies all of the lines of research described in the chapters that follow.

The University of Michigan Press has been a patient and supportive partner in bringing this volume to fruition. We especially appreciate the encouragement we received from the Press's then editor, Colin Day, and the sustained assistance we received from Ellen McCarthy, the Press's senior acquisitions editor for social science, and her staff throughout the review, editing, and production of the manuscript.

We owe a special debt to several individuals whose contributions have enhanced the quality of our work. Norman Bradburn's and David Featherman's frank and thoughtful comments on the first draft of the volume have substantially improved what has come after, as have those of two anonymous University of Michigan Press reviewers, who provided detailed and constructive feedback on a later draft. Patti Meyer provided clerical and administrative support in the initial stages of the project, and Cathy Doherty has shepherded the manuscript through its final two years of progression toward publication with great care, equanimity, and good humor. We hope these individuals and all whom we have worked with in the venture enjoy seeing the fruits of their labor as much as we do. None of it would have been possible without them or the original vision, creativity, and energy of Rensis Likert, Angus Campbell, George Katona, Leslie Kish, and Charles Cannell.

James S. House, F. Thomas Juster, Robert L. Kahn,
Howard Schuman, and Eleanor Singer
Ann Arbor, Michigan, and
Phippsburg, Maine
OCTOBER 2002

CHAPTER 1

The Development and Contribution of Survey Research as a Scientific Instrument and Social Institution

James S. House, Eleanor Singer, Robert L. Kahn, Howard Schuman, and F. Thomas Juster

Quantitative, empirical social science is largely a development of the twentieth century. The advent of the twenty-first century provides an apt moment for assessing its accomplishments and prospects. The present volume seeks to do this by examining the past contributions and future frontiers of one of the most significant developments of twentieth-century social science—the scientific sample survey. Our purpose is thus broad. Our examples and case studies, however, are drawn primarily from the work of the Survey Research Center (SRC) and the Institute for Social Research (ISR) of the University of Michigan, of which we are members (see the brief overview and history of SRC and ISR later in this chapter). Although we will always try to connect SRC/ISR research with research done elsewhere, readers should anticipate that much of what will be discussed here is based on work in the SRC and ISR.

We begin with the premise that social science is neither a misnomer nor an oxymoron; it is indeed a form of science, like the physical and biomedical sciences, in many of its defining characteristics. The conceptual vocabulary, the formal nature of theory, and the research methods of all the sciences vary with their subject matter. Among the natural sciences, for example, physics is arguably the oldest, having highly developed, distinct, but closely connected components of mathematical theory and largely experimental empirical research and utilizing highly sophisticated and expensive technology and apparatus. In contrast, ecological and evolutionary biology employs verbal as well as mathematical theory and heavily utilizes nonexperimental observation and measurement as well as laboratory experimentation. Chemistry and cellular/molecular biology lie in between, as do the sciences of particular natural phenomena such as astronomy, geology, meteorology, and the emerging earth/environmental sciences. All of them, however, share a respect for quantitative data; a search for general, if frequently contingent, truths; and an insistence on the continuous testing of theoretical ideas using data collected, analyzed, and interpreted as objectively as possible. All scientific disciplines develop via a complex interplay among the empirical realities and problems they seek to understand and the available theory and methods for achieving such understanding. Theory leads to new questions and hypotheses about the empirical world; empirical data lead to the revision of existing theories and the creation of new ones; and available methods and research instruments shape the limits and opportunities for empirical knowledge and theoretical development.

In the natural sciences the importance of innovations in methods and instruments is almost self-evident. For example, the telescope and its developments, from optical to radio to orbiting satellites and interplanetary probes, have continually transformed the nature of theory and data in astronomy and physics, such that we have begun to understand the origins of the universe itself. The microscope and its developments, from optical to electron to computerized imaging and genetic mapping, have similarly transformed our understanding of the nature of life, health, and disease in the life sciences, both natural (e.g., biology) and social (e.g., anthropology and psychology) (cf. Rasmussen 1997). The same can be said for particle accelerators in physics or for analytic tools in chemistry from spectroscopy to carbon dating, the latter also affecting the social science of anthropology. These innovations and their impact have also spread from science to the larger society, and many of them are now used routinely in both the private and public sectors for other than purely scientific purposes. Their broad societal impact is epitomized by the computer, first developed to address problems of basic science but now shaping all aspects of social life and much of our economy.

In the social sciences, the development of methods for scientific sample surveys constitutes perhaps the leading example of a comparable progression in methods and instrumentation, transforming both empirical knowledge and theoretical understanding. Survey methods comprise (1) precise techniques, deriving largely from the field of statistics, for selecting a relatively small sample of units from a total population (of people, organizations, or other elements) such that accurate estimates of the whole population can be derived from analysis of the sample; (2) valid and reliable measurement methods, deriving largely from psychology, for assessing attributes and behaviors of the constituent elements, usually individual people, of a population sample; and (3) methods of data processing and empirical analysis, deriving again from the field of statistics, and especially applications thereof in other social science disciplines such as economics, psychology, and sociology. Together, these methods make possible informative, descriptive, and causal understanding of social phenomena and processes from survey data.

As the title of this book suggests, we regard the sample survey as analogous to a telescope on human society (Converse 1987). The survey can provide empirical images of the populations of organizations, communities, societies, and even the world. Like a telescope, its focus can be broadened or narrowed to allow examinations of supra- and subpopulations of individuals or organizations and, ultimately, even individual communities, organizations, or persons. Prior to the development and refinement of survey methods, such comprehensive and systematic examination of social life was not possible, at least for populous and complex societies.

The chapters of this volume illustrate the impact that developments in survey research have had and continue to have on a broad range of social science disciplines and interdisciplinary areas ranging from political behavior and electoral systems to macroeconomics and individual income dynamics, mental and physical health, human development and aging, and racial/ethnic diversity and relationships. In the area of politics, survey research has drastically revised understanding of the causes and consequences of electoral attitudes and behaviors, both over the life course and across generations, and in the process has radically reshaped the discipline of political science (part 1, chaps. 3 and 4). In the area of economics, surveys have revealed the influence of psychological and behavioral factors in macroeconomic cycles of growth and recession and have also contributed to the growing understanding of the nature, extent, causes, and consequences of changes in income, welfare, and poverty (part 2, chaps. 5 and 6). The ability to systematically survey the thoughts, feelings, and behavior of members of organizations facilitated the development of theories of organization grounded in the actual rather than the assumed or imputed psychology of organizational members (part 3, chap. 7).

In the area of health, surveys first facilitated population epidemiology based on biomedical theories and then helped to transform theories of morbidity and mortality to recognize the role of social, psychological, and behavioral factors in both mental and physical health. Within SRC, ISR, and other places, the study of social aspects of health grew primarily out of studies of organizational members (part 3, chaps. 8 and 9). Systematic survey research also transformed knowledge and understanding of the causes and consequences of human fertility and family development, substance use and abuse among youth, and adolescent and early adult development more generally, and is increasingly transforming our understanding of the dynamics of aging in both individuals and society (part 4, chaps. 10–12). Since the work of Du Bois (1899) at the end of the nineteenth century, surveys have played an increasingly central role in delineating and understanding the racial/ethnic diversity of our society and the attitudes and relations among major racial/ethnic groups (part 5, chaps. 13 and 14), especially over the last sixty years. Continuing development of the methods of survey research undergird all of these developments and give promise of new approaches that will improve understanding of both human individuals and populations and of their relationship to the social and biological-physical-chemical environments in which they live and work (chaps. 1, 2, and 15).

In addition to their influence in these domains of social science, survey methods have also spawned or fundamentally transformed major enterprises in both the public and private sectors. Survey research has been the foundation of increasingly complex and sophisticated systems of government statistics within and across nations. For example, the monthly Current Population Survey (CPS) conducted by the Department of Commerce's Bureau of the Census is the source of official monthly estimates of employment and unemployment and thus of the changing state of the economy. Market research, political and public opinion polling, and organizational development and consulting have utilized survey methods to become major sectors of the economy and important influences on the behavior and decisions of leaders and groups in government and the private sector. All of this is now part of our routinely lived and assumed reality; yet almost none of it existed a century ago.

The Institutional Context of Scientific Methods and Instrumentation

Crucial to the development and maintenance of major innovations in scientific methods or instrumentation is their location within a nurturing institutional infrastructure. Smaller-scale methods and instruments (e.g., personal computers, small microscopes, and small telescopes) can be diffused across many individual offices and laboratories. However, more capital- or labor-intensive methods or instruments (e.g., mainframe or supercomputers, major telescopes, complex and expensive microscopes and other imaging devices, particle accelerators, and nuclear reactors) must be situated in larger institutional contexts, such as university- or organization-wide, regional, or even national or international facilities. Survey research can be conducted at any of these levels, but as science develops, larger-scale methods and instrumentation tend to be required for further progress. Thus with survey research, as with other major methods or instruments of science, advances in methodological, substantive, and theoretical knowledge increasingly require institutional arrangements that can sustain large-scale and long-term research programs, while allowing the broad scientific community both to influence their research designs and to utilize the resulting data. In this chapter, and again in the conclusion, we highlight ways in which supportive and innovative institutional contexts have been and continue to be necessary to the development of survey research and the scientific knowledge and innovations provided by it. Here we also acknowledge the enormous importance of broad public support for science in general and especially for survey research, which not only needs general public support but also the active cooperation and participation of the public as the respondents who are the ultimate source of survey data.

Historical Developments

Survey research in one sense has a long history—with elements present in the registration/taxation rolls of the Roman Empire, which the Bible tells us led Mary and Joseph from Nazareth to Bethlehem, where Christ was born. Censuses, which are really surveys of total national populations, were essential elements in the development of representative democratic political systems in the United States and elsewhere. Converse (1987, 88–90) and Bulmer (2001) trace the intellectual ancestry of modern survey research to the English social surveys by Karl Marx and others in the nineteenth century (see also the foreword to this volume by Featherman); the study of attitudes and their measurement in academic social psychology in the 1920s; methods pioneered by early market research firms; and the first sample surveys of large populations in the United States by three commercial polling firms established in the mid-

1930s: the Gallup Organization, the Roper Poll, and the Crossley Organization.

Several developments of importance for scientific survey methods occurred in the United States in the 1930s. Some were in the areas of measurement and the development of organizational capacity for survey research in government and academia. Rensis Likert, in his doctoral dissertation at Columbia University, demonstrated that the five-point Likert scale, as it came to be called, produced data almost identical to that generated by the theoretically elegant but cumbersome Thurstone method of paired comparisons. Likert then moved to head a research unit of the insurance industry, where he could try out both his methodological innovation and his emerging ideas about organizational leadership. In 1939 he moved to Washington, DC, to become the director of a small survey unit in the Department of Agriculture, whose mission was to conduct surveys into farmers' experiences and opinions about federal programs such as soil conservation and farmer resettlement (Converse 1987, 157). During the same decade, survey research made what is probably its earliest academic appearance in the United States. Paul F. Lazarsfeld, a Viennese émigré social psychologist, established at the University of Newark in 1935 a survey unit that, in 1940, he moved to Columbia University as the Bureau of Applied Social Research.

Even with the best and most extensive efforts at measurement, however, surveys still lacked the essential foundation of accurate and valid inferences to larger populations. This problem was epitomized by the infamous *Literary Digest* poll of 1936 concerning the presidential election, in which, despite a huge sample of some ten million mail questionnaires, the lists used for sampling were biased toward higher income people and the two million who mailed back their questionnaires were apparently even more biased in this direction. *Literary Digest* predicted victory for the Republican candidate, Alfred Landon, but Franklin Roosevelt won in the greatest landslide in American history. Gallup used a form of quota sampling that provided a better representation of the electorate and correctly predicted the Roosevelt win, providing some initial evidence of the value of the emerging science of sample surveys, though even Gallup underestimated the size of Roosevelt's victory. As noted later in this chapter and in chapter 3, the commercial pollsters proved inaccurate in the closer 1948 election, due to some combination of their quota sampling methods, the closeness of the election, and the timing of their last polls. Getting a sample of respondents to accurately represent a much larger population required the development of probability sampling, the foundations of which were also laid in the 1930s.

During the years of the Great Depression and the efforts of the Roosevelt administration to mitigate its effects, the actual number of unemployed persons became an issue of great political and economic importance. Several continuing series of unemployment estimates were published on a monthly basis, among them one by the AFL-CIO and another by the National Industrial Conference Board. Neither of these series was survey based, and their estimates were widely divergent, in directions that appeared to reflect their sponsorship. The labor unions' estimates numbered many millions; the estimates of the Conference Board were so modest that, a few years later when the economy improved, the Conference Board series began to show "negative unemployment."

Meanwhile, in the Division of Research and Statistics of the Works Progress Administration (WPA), the emerging methods of probability sampling and survey interviewing were brought to bear on the problem of estimating the national level of unemployment. In the late 1930s this new enterprise—variously titled the Nationwide Research Project, the Monthly Report on Unemployment, and the Monthly Report on the Labor Force—began to publish national estimates of employment and unemployment. In 1942 the project and its research staff moved from its home in the WPA to the Bureau of the Census, where it continues in vastly refined and expanded form as the CPS. Probably the most important early innovation in the WPA was the development of area probability sampling, largely the work of J. Stevens Stock, who later became the first sampling expert in Likert's group at the Department of Agriculture, and Lester Frankel, who moved with the WPA survey group to the Bureau of the Census. These developments built on earlier work by Keir in Norway and Neyman in England (Converse 1987, 41–45). The essential contribution was that *every* element of a population had a known, nonzero probability of inclusion in the sample. Statistical theory then allowed estimates (e.g., of voting intention, behavior, or employment status) for the entire population with an accurately estimable margin of error that rapidly diminished as samples increased in size from hundreds to thousands, regardless of the size of the total population (see chap. 2 for further details).

These several streams of work came together in Washington, DC, in the early 1940s, when the need for good, fast information to guide the wartime programs of various government agencies—such as the Office of War Information, the Office of Price Administration, and the Treasury

Department—suddenly put a premium on what this novel and relatively untried technology of survey research could accomplish. By the fall of 1942 there were over one hundred social scientists on the staff of the Division of Program Surveys (Hyman 1991, 4). Commitment to the war effort, a heady sense of excitement and innovation, and the intellectual stimulation of so many bright young people from a variety of disciplines and occupations all gathered together in one place spurred the invention of new survey methods and their application to a host of practical problems. The later chapters in this volume give a number of examples of the first accomplishments from this early period. "Likert's vision," writes Hyman (1991, 5), "was of a survey method distinct from and superior to both the commercial polling and academic attitude research of the period. That method would help solve the social problems of peacetime as well as wartime, and the theoretical problems of social science."

Origins of the University of Michigan Survey Research Center and Institute for Social Research

Like that at many other institutions, survey research at SRC and ISR developed as a result of the improvisations and special efforts made necessary by World War II and of the associations forged in the course of those efforts. Among those who worked in Washington during the war years with Rensis Likert were the psychologists Angus Campbell, Charles Cannell (who directed the field staff at the Division of Program Surveys and later at SRC), Daniel Katz, and Dorwin Cartwright (who later headed the Research Center for Group Dynamics [RCGD] at Michigan); the Gestalt psychologist turned economist George Katona; and the sampling statistician Leslie Kish. By 1946, with the end of World War II, however, there was pressure to again limit the surveys carried out by Likert's unit to the problems of farmers. The young scholars, who had experienced the heady excitement of inventing a discipline in the service of vitally important goals, were not ready for such restricted goals. "Likert must have seen the handwriting on the wall," writes Hyman (1991, 19), "and anticipated his fate. He had raised the Division from respectable but humble origins on the farm to its glorious wartime status. He would not end up back on the farm."

It was Likert who proposed a move to a university and the creation there of a new organization that would be devoted to the development of survey research and its application to important social problems—a continuation, as it were, of the ideals and ideas that had driven the development of the new discipline in the wartime years. The prospects for such a move were explored with several universities, including the University of Michigan, where in the 1920s Likert had been a student, first of engineering and then of sociology. By 1946 Michigan was at the beginning of a long developmental surge in the social sciences, and the relevant departments offered strong support for the proposed move of the Likert group. Thus, in 1946 the regents of the university agreed to establish the SRC on terms that protected the university general funds from any risk but that nonetheless gave the new center an academic home (Frantilla 1998).

The SRC was to be entirely self-supporting through grants and contracts. It would not be permitted to make any charge on the university budget, its staff would have no university tenure, and the whole experimental arrangement could be terminated at any time. However, to provide the SRC with some fiscal stability of its own, it would be allowed to retain all overhead or indirect funds included in its grants and contracts. On this basis, the "Washington émigrés"—Likert, Campbell, Cannell, Katona, and Kish—moved to Michigan. Two years later, the SRC, already growing rapidly, was joined by the RCGD, which Dorwin Cartwright and his colleagues brought from the Massachusetts Institute of Technology after the death of the RCGD's founder, Kurt Lewin. In 1949, the two centers, SRC and RCGD, were officially united as the ISR, with Likert as director of the ISR, Campbell as director of the SRC, and Cartwright as director of the RCGD (Cannell and Kahn 1984). From these promising but modest origins, the ISR had grown by 2001 to an organization with four centers, close to two hundred Ph.D. scientists, five hundred permanent support staff, over one thousand contingent employees (mostly interviewers) in Ann Arbor and around the country, and an annual research volume of over $70 million. Throughout the history of ISR, survey research has remained at its core, with the SRC constituting 60–70 percent of the total ISR in terms of both personnel and dollar volume of research and the other centers also utilizing its survey facilities.

Other Major Academic Survey Research Centers

Another important development in academically based survey research, this one arising from commercial origins, should also be noted. In 1941 Harry H. Field, a talented associate of George Gallup, established the National Opinion Research Center (NORC) at the University of Denver, and in 1942 it was already using the survey method to focus on an important social issue, race relations in America. In 1947 NORC moved to become affiliated with, though not be an integral part of, the University of Chicago, thus providing another major academically connected survey organization, parallel to those at Columbia University and the University of Michigan. The largely friendly competition among the three survey organizations—at Columbia, Chicago, and Michigan—promoted distinctive innovations in the development and application of the survey method, much as has occurred in other scientific fields. The histories of these organizations have been chronicled elsewhere (Converse 1987; Hyman 1991; Hackett 1992), and detailed consideration of them is beyond the scope of this volume, though we have tried at various points to reflect some of their most notable contributions. As with other major scientific instruments, such as telescopes, there is a collective interest in having multiple major research centers while avoiding inefficient proliferation and competition for scarce resources. Our interest is particularly in survey research focused on the advancement of basic science in an academic context—the model that has largely driven advances in the natural and life sciences. For these purposes, the Michigan case remains probably the most apt and enduring example.

The Development of Survey Research and Social Science at the University of Michigan and Beyond: An Overview

The remaining chapters of this volume provide a broad, though necessarily still selective, overview of major developments in survey research and social science at the University of Michigan SRC and ISR and beyond. It is a history not only of quantitative growth but also of qualitatively transformative contributions to our understanding of many major social phenomena. As such, survey research constitutes one of the foundation pillars of the development of social science in the twentieth century and its prospects for the twenty-first century.

Survey Methodology

To begin, it is necessary to understand the nature and development of the survey method itself, grounded in the basic theories of mathematics and statistics on the one hand and sociology and psychology on the other and continuously transformed by developments in information technology.

Chapter 2 by Groves and his colleagues considers the development of survey methods from the refinement of area probability sampling and face-to-face interviewing in the 1930s, 1940s, 1950s, and 1960s, through the emergence of telephone interviewing in the 1970s and 1980s, to the use of computer-assisted interviewing by telephone and in person in the 1980s and 1990s, and now to the Web survey. The authors focus on scientific research on the survey method itself, including issues of the representativeness of samples, nonresponse and missing data, the reliability and validity of the questions asked, the impact of the modes of administering questions, and statistical adjustment and analysis of survey data. As with all major scientific methods, it is a tale of advances and accomplishments, coupled with growing self-conscious understanding of the promise as well as problems of the method and of ways of addressing those problems.

The development of practical and effective area probability sampling and structured interviewing made it possible to quite accurately estimate and predict the characteristics of populations of hundreds of millions of people from samples of mere thousands and sometimes even hundreds. As noted earlier, commercial polls, using quota sampling methods, correctly predicted the 1936 landslide victory of Franklin Roosevelt over Alfred Landon, while the self-selected sample of millions of readers of the *Literary Digest* had predicted that Landon would win. In turn, a strict national probability sample of about six hundred voters by the SRC in 1948 correctly predicted Harry S. Truman's narrow victory over Thomas Dewey, which commercial pollsters had conceded to Dewey (although the confidence interval for the SRC prediction also included a Dewey win). In the succeeding fifty years we have come to understand much better, and to better compensate for, the full range of sources of survey error in sampling, interviewing, coding, and data processing and analysis. Indeed, survey methodology is now becoming an emergent new field, much as statistics and computer science before it, and is beginning to be recognized as such by the establishment of degree-granting graduate programs in survey methodology at the University of Michigan and other universities.

Political Behavior and Systems

The study of political, and especially voting and electoral, behavior and phenomena has been a major focus of survey research from its formative days. Of all the social sciences, political science has been most transformed by the data and theories emerging from survey research, as chronicled by Converse and Kinder in chapter 3. Political behavior became one of the earliest research programs of the SRC, based in part on the somewhat serendipitous success in predicting the 1948 presidential election. Before the advent of survey research, the academic and scientific study of politics and government had relied on normative theory and empirical analysis of the workings of government or aggregate evidence thereof such as voting records. The sample survey allowed interdisciplinary teams of social psychologists interested in politics and political scientists interested in social psychology to understand the social psychological nature of individual voting and electoral behavior and from this the more aggregate ebbs and flows in the fortunes of political candidates and parties. The Columbia and then Michigan studies found the nature and behavior of the candidates and parties much less important than political theory and analysis had assumed heretofore and found the psychology and social context of the individual voter, especially his or her political party identification, much more consequential. The first decade of Michigan election studies transformed political science into a heavily quantitative and behavioral science and led to the establishment of both the National Election Studies (NES) as the first National Science Foundation (NSF)–supported national data resource in the social sciences and the Inter-university Consortium for Political and Social Research (ICPSR) as the first major archive for computerized social science data.

The Michigan studies stimulated increasing interdisciplinary interchange among political science, psychology, and sociology. The latter disciplines were also using the new methods of survey research to transform theories of human development and aging that had previously been based largely on understanding childhood development from clinical practice or observation of small and selective populations. Survey research made possible studies of development over the full life course, based increasingly on representative general population samples. These developments led to major new lines of research in political science, especially at Michigan, on the transmission and development of political attitudes and behavior within and between generations, as discussed by Jennings in chapter 4. In politics as well as other domains (cf. chaps. 10–12), the influence of parents on their children proved more limited than previously believed. Rather, as children matured into adults, they were substantially influenced by broader patterns of social relations and events, producing continual evolution and change over their life course. However, adolescence and young adulthood were formative periods in which preexisting trajectories sometimes became disrupted and new lines of development were established, often to be strengthened in later adulthood.

Economic Behavior

Survey research also had major impacts on our understanding of economic phenomena, both at the macro- and microeconomic levels. However, the survey influence was not as transformative of the discipline of economics as it had been of political science, economics being arguably the best established social science discipline prior to the advent of survey research. Juster's introduction to part 2 overviews these developments and the important role of measurement methods in this process.

The longest running programs of research at the SRC are the Survey of Consumer Finances (SCF) and the Survey of Consumer Attitudes (SCA). The SCF has been through several stages of design evolution and of survey sponsorship (the main outlines of this history are described in Juster's introduction to part 2). As Curtin discusses in chapter 5, the SCA owes its existence to George Katona, who used a combination of theoretical acumen and pragmatic craftiness to make what began as a supposed throwaway set of introductory questions on the SCF into an empirical measure of consumer behavioral orientations and expectations that proved in the aggregate to be a robust predictor of cycles of growth and recession in the post–World War II U.S. economy. An index of these questions became one of the leading economic indicators of the U.S. Department of Commerce and has been increasingly emulated around the world. This work presaged a renaissance of interest in the psychology of expectations in economics that constitutes a major frontier for future research. The coming of age of behavioral economics was signaled by the 2002 Nobel prizes in this area, with some believing that Katona would have received a Nobel much earlier had he not died before it could be awarded.

The program of research on consumer attitudes addressed the post-Depression and post–World War II concern about business cycle recessions and depressions. By the 1960s, these concerns had receded and were superseded by the rediscovery of extensive poverty (Harrington 1962) in an increasingly affluent society (Galbraith 1958). The prevailing wisdom in social science and policy circles was that such poverty largely reflected peculiar and persistent disadvantage, passed down from generation to generation, in selected populations of people (e.g., in Appalachia or other areas of the rural South, urban ghettos, etc.) who were left behind either because of their personal deficiencies or because of the protracted structural economic problems of the areas in which they lived. But no one had ever studied the dynamics of income and poverty in microeconomic terms, examining the behavior of large and representative samples of the population over extended periods.

This is what James Morgan and his colleagues set out to do in the Panel Study of Income Dynamics (PSID), as discussed in chapter 6 by Duncan, Hofferth, and Stafford. Since 1968, Morgan and his colleagues have followed the economic fortunes of a probability sample of about five thousand American families, oversampling families below the poverty line and interviewing each family every year for over twenty-five years and now biennially. Their initial results confounded the conventional wisdom—poverty was not the isolated experience of a distinct underclass but rather a state into which many American individuals and families fall at least once. At any point in time, most people in poverty are there only transiently. But their data also suggested, and later research using new methods for analyzing longitudinal data confirmed, that a small but significant fraction of the poor at any one time are poor for longer spells. The subsequent and continuing research of PSID and other longitudinal panel studies such as the National Longitudinal Studies (NLS) has become the foundation for enhanced scientific understanding of the course and consequences of poverty and wealth and of social policies regarding them. Moreover, the PSID has been named by the NSF as one of its fifty most significant projects of the twentieth century—the only social science project to be so identified.

From Organizational Behavior to the Psychosocial Nature of Health

The study of organizations was the third major initial research program of the SRC, as discussed in Kahn's introduction to part 3 and in chapter 7, but evolved over several decades into a program on the effects of organizational and social environments on health. The SRC program of organizational research was a major force in developing the "human relations" approach to understanding organizational life and behavior, an approach that highlighted the importance of the relationships among individuals within and across organizational levels, aspects of organizational life that had been neglected in the more structural approach to organizational analysis pioneered by Max Weber (1947) and in the mechanistic approaches of time and motion studies deriving from Frederick Taylor (1915). The SRC program brought to this work careful survey assessment of individuals composing an organization and of their relationships. Initially, the focus was on the impact of individuals and their relationships on organizational functioning, but over time the focus shifted increasingly to the impact of work and organizations on individual well-being and health.

Bringing survey research to bear on the study of mental and physical health had major impacts on theory and research in what were previously deemed largely the domains of biomedical science. As discussed in chapter 8 by Price, the SRC played the major role in extending to a national level methods developed for surveying the subjective well-being and mental health of community populations. Where understanding of mental health had once derived almost entirely from the study of patients in outpatient or institutional treatment or from statistics about them, SRC studies in the 1950s, 1960s, and 1970s provided the first national data on the perceived mental health and psychological well-being of the population and how individuals sought to deal with their psychological problems and distress. This research complemented a growing body of surveys of community populations. In the 1980s, methods were developed for generating psychiatric diagnoses from interviews by lay interviewers, and these were first applied on a national scale by SRC in the early 1990s. The results helped to confirm a much greater prevalence of psychological distress and psychiatric disorder in the population than had been previously recognized, with consequent implications for science and policy. For example, depression has now been recognized nationally and internationally as the leading cause of days lost from work and normal functioning (Murray and Lopez 1996).

In the area of physical health, House and Kaplan document in chapter 9 the central role that survey methods have come to play in clinical and field trials of drugs or other therapies, epitomized by the SRC's major role in the field trials establishing the efficacy of the Salk polio vaccine. Survey research was also the foundation of a new model of epidemiological research—the prospective study of organizational and community populations to establish and discover risk factors for chronic disease. As the number of organizations and communities so studied increased, as national prospective studies were added, and as the range of potential risk factors widened, the set of identified risk factors for mortality and morbidity grew from traditional biomedical variables such as blood pressure and blood lipids to include (1) individual behaviors such as smoking, immoderate consumption of food and alcohol, and lack of exercise; (2) more social environmental variables such as acute and chronic stress in work and life or social relationships and supports; and (3) individual dispositions such as anger, hostility, and distrust and low self-efficacy or sense of control. Concurrent and related developments in theory and laboratory research suggested plausible psychophysiological mechanisms for these effects. Thus, between the 1950s and 1990s, psychosocial phenomena became recognized as increasingly important factors in the etiology and course of almost all forms of physical and mental health and disease. As we enter the twenty-first century, socioeconomic and racial disparities in health, and the psychosocial sources of these, have become one of the top priorities for health research policy of the Public Health Service and the National Institutes of Health (NIH). All of these developments were almost unimaginable at the middle of the twentieth century and could not have happened without survey research, used as a key instrument for studying population health.

The Life Course of Individuals and Families

As already noted, the developing capability of survey research over the last half of the twentieth century to study representative samples of the members of any population as they developed and aged across the full human life course transformed our ability to understand human development and aging from birth to death. As the United States has evolved from a rapidly growing and young population with relatively high fertility but declining mortality at midcentury to an increasingly aging population with low fertility and mortality at the end of the twentieth century, the study of human development has moved from a heavy focus on childhood toward an increasing focus first on adolescence and young adulthood and more recently on mature adulthood and old age. This evolution has been evident in the nature of survey studies of human development at the SRC and ISR and elsewhere.

The scientific sample survey revolutionized the study of demography and its social determinants and consequences, which had heretofore relied almost exclusively on governmental data from vital statistics, immigration records, and census data (the last, of course, being a survey of the entire population). With sample survey data, it became possible not only to model flows of fertility, mortality, and migration in relation to overall population size and density but also to study the biopsychosocial causes and consequences of fertility, mortality, and migration at the level of individuals. Such research has yielded new evidence and theories that have improved population science and policy locally, nationally, and internationally. Focusing on a long-term cooperative program of research at the Michigan Population Studies Center and SRC, chapter 10 by Thornton and Axinn reviews these developments in areas of fertility and (marital or other) union formation and dissolution, social processes that have evolved and changed rapidly over the past half century and will continue to do so in the future.

As O'Malley and his colleagues observe in chapter 11, the recognition of adolescence as a stage of the life course only emerged in the twentieth century, creating social and scientific needs to understand how youth transition through this life stage into adulthood. The SRC launched a major study of these issues in the late 1960s, as did a number of other research centers and institutes, most notably perhaps the National Longitudinal Studies of Youth (NLSY) conducted by Ohio State University through NORC, all of which identified the transitions from school to work and marriage (often via higher education or military service) as critical junctures influencing many aspects of later adult development. In response to emerging social and funding priorities, the SRC study, Monitoring the Future (MTF), came by the mid-1970s to focus on substance use and abuse and has continued as perhaps the leading social science study in this area ever since. Again survey research, and the theories deriving and resulting from it, confounded conventional wisdom (still clung to by many) that drug and substance use is principally a "supply" problem, the solution to which is controlling or interdicting the availability of the substance, whether tobacco, alcohol, or licit and illicit drugs. The repeated cross-sectional and increasingly longitudinal MTF surveys of high school students, some now followed into middle adulthood, showed that usage was driven much more heavily by "demand" rather than supply factors, most notably the social contexts (especially living arrangements and marital status) of potential users and their perceptions or understandings of the risks associated with substance use.

As the populations of the nation and world have aged, many of the aforementioned areas of research have focused increasingly on issues of aging, and new survey vehicles have been created to illuminate the increasingly important scientific and social issues associated with aging. In chapter 12, Herzog, Willis, and Weir describe these developments at Michigan and more broadly, culminating in the launching in the early 1990s of the major new longitudinal Health and Retirement Study (HRS), the unique features and findings of which are discussed in chapters 12 and 15 as well as in Juster's introduction to part 2. Longitudinal studies of aging have already greatly altered the common conception that aging is an inexorable process of physical and mental decline and resulting social withdrawal, driven by intrinsic biological processes. Rather, the studies at Michigan and elsewhere indicate that aging is a highly variable process, with the elderly often differing more among themselves than they do from younger people. Increasing numbers of people continue to remain physically and mentally healthy, active, and productive into their eighties and sometimes beyond, as a function not only of genetic constitution but also of the psychosocial contexts and conditions in which they live in older age and the decades leading up to it. The problem for science and society in the twenty-first century is how to adapt our institutions and policies to the evolving nature of our aging population.

Race and Ethnicity

W. E. B. Du Bois (1899), one of the earliest practitioners of sophisticated survey research and social science, declared the problem of the twentieth century to be the "color line," and the same may still be true in different ways for the twenty-first century. The twentieth century saw a continuous struggle of historically subordinated and colonized people of color for their political and social equality, both within and across nations, with the dismantling of Jim Crow segregation in the United States at midcentury and apartheid in South Africa in the 1990s as signal examples of the profound changes occurring as nations and the world moved toward an increasingly multiracial and multiethnic social order. In the United States, and also internationally, survey research has been a principal method for describing and understanding both the trends toward racial/ethnic equality and multiracial/multiethnic social orders and the continuing conflicts over, and resistance to, such change.

Kinder and Schuman show in chapter 13 how, despite the difficulties inherent in assessing individuals' attitudes and beliefs on a sensitive issue, survey research has accurately monitored not only dramatic changes toward interracial equality in terms of social norms and behavior, but also continuing resistance to much of what is probably required to make full equality a reality. Perhaps most importantly, a growing range of survey studies shows that massive declines in traditional racism (i.e., beliefs in the inherent inferiority of biological racial/ethnic groups) have been accompanied by persistence and even increase in new forms of "racism" (i.e., beliefs that many members of disadvantaged racial/ethnic groups are still not socially or morally deserving of full equality or further government assistance because their plight is attributable mainly to their own self-destructive behaviors or lack of motivation). However, the underlying social psychological bases of these new types of beliefs about disadvantaged groups remain contested. Importantly, research also suggests that changes in social policy and practice may lead as much as follow changes in attitudes and beliefs.

Du Bois (1899) carried out a pioneering survey study of the African-American community in Philadelphia at the turn of the century. However, the rest of social science, like the rest of society, was not ready or willing, at least in Du Bois's lifetime, to give equal priority to the study of social and ethnic minorities as to the broader majority population. New methods of survey research in the second half of the twentieth century, however, made possible the oversampling of members of minority populations in many studies and facilitated the development of research programs focused primarily or exclusively on minority populations, one of which—the Program for Research on Black Americans (PRBA)—has been centered in the RCGD and SRC of the ISR. Jackson and Williams chronicle in chapter 14 how that program fostered the development of innovative survey methods for studying the African-American and other minority populations, leading to novel and unexpected insights into the nature and variability of an African-American population that has become increasingly diverse within itself in terms of place of residence, socioeconomic position, and other factors.

The Breadth and Depth of Survey Research and Its Influence

This introductory chapter and the succeeding thirteen chapters suggest the breadth and depth of the impact that the development of the scientific sample survey has had on social science and society in the last half of the twentieth century, although our coverage remains necessarily highly selective. The chapters also convey the importance of creative, adaptive, and supportive institutional arrangements for fostering the continual development and productive application of the survey method, a theme to which we will return in the concluding chapter. The development and maintenance of major centers of high-quality survey research have benefited the national and international scientific communities, just as major telescopes, cyclotrons, and genome sequencing centers have done. All of this has occurred, and will continue to do so, through shared access to both the use of the facilities and the data generated by them.

Social science is sometimes seen as being small in scope and significance and obvious and redundant in its theoretical development and empirical findings. This volume suggests that social science is, in contrast, increasingly broad in scale, mature in its theory and methods, and able to generate important theoretical and empirical insights for advancing scientific understanding and social policy formation in the public and private sectors. This has surely been the case for survey research and for social science based in and on it. The transformative developments in theory and knowledge spawned by survey-based social science justify the significant institutional investments that have been made in it by government funding agencies, foundations, and research universities, without which these developments and contributions would not be possible. Continuing investments will be necessary as we address the frontiers and challenges of the twenty-first century, a topic to which we return in the concluding chapter.

REFERENCES

Bulmer, M. 2001. History of social survey. In *International encyclopedia of the social and behavioral sciences,* ed. N. J. Smelser and P. B. Baltes, 21:14469–73. Oxford: Elsevier.

Cannell, Charles F., and Robert L. Kahn. 1984. Some factors in the origins and development of the Institute for Social Research, the University of Michigan. *American Psychologist* 39 (11): 1256–66.

Converse, Jean M. 1987. *Survey research in the United States: Roots and emergence.* Berkeley: University of California Press.

Du Bois, W. E. B. 1899. *The Philadelphia Negro.* Philadelphia: Published for the University.

Frantilla, Anne. 1998. *Social science in the public interest: A fiftieth-year history of the Institute for Social Research.* Ann Arbor: Bentley Historical Library, University of Michigan.

Galbraith, John Kenneth. 1958. *The affluent society.* Boston: Houghton Mifflin.

Hackett, Jeff, ed. 1992. *National Opinion Research Center fiftieth anniversary report 1991: America by number.* Chicago: National Opinion Research Center.

Harrington, Michael. 1962. *The other America: Poverty in the United States.* New York: Macmillan.

Hyman, Herbert H. 1991. *Taking society's measure.* New York: Russell Sage.

Murray, Christopher J. L., and Alan D. Lopez, eds. 1996. *The global burden of disease: A comprehensive assessment of mortality and disability from diseases, injuries, and risk factors in 1990 and projected to 2020.* Cambridge: Harvard University Press.

Rasmussen, Nicolas. 1997. *Picture control: The electron microscope and the transformation of biology in America, 1940–1960.* Stanford: Stanford University Press.

Taylor, Frederick Winslow. 1915. *Scientific management.* New York and London: Harper and Brothers.

Weber, Max. 1947. *The theory of social and economic organizations.* New York: Free Press.

CHAPTER 2

Survey Methodology

Robert M. Groves and Eleanor Singer
with James M. Lepkowski, Steven G. Heeringa, and Duane F. Alwin

Introduction

The idea that humans can gain insight into their condition by standardized measurement yielding quantitative information was not novel to the twentieth century. However, the second half of the twentieth century witnessed an unprecedented expansion of the use of sample surveys to study diverse domains of human activity. The invention of the sample survey has had a pervasive influence on society because of its dual contributions to policy and science. Government statistical agencies use the tool as the most frequent way to acquire information needed by policymakers. The creation after World War II of major survey research centers at universities such as Michigan, Chicago, and Columbia placed surveys in an environment that used them not merely to describe fixed populations but also to test theories of social behavior. These dual uses of surveys, descriptive and analytical, form an energizing tension in the development of the field over its short history (Deming 1953; Hansen, Madow, and Tepping 1983).

The "invention" underwent continuous evolutionary change over the first decades of the Survey Research Center (SRC) (some of them well documented in Converse 1987). As is common in many emerging fields (e.g., medical imaging, supercollider design), the method of acquiring knowledge becomes its own target of study. "Survey methodology" is the phrase increasingly used to describe the field of inquiry into survey design, collection, and analysis. Fields that have an academic base tend to foster wide dissemination of these methodological studies, consistent with scientific norms of publication, and the need for replication. Fields with a commercial base (e.g., pharmaceuticals) use the studies for competitive advantage. Thus, siting the SRC in an academic environment led to a rich stream of methodological inquiries that benefited the entire survey community.

This chapter reviews alternative perspectives on survey methods that have contributed to the field and to present practice. To set the stage, it identifies and describes several ongoing themes or tensions in the science of surveys. They include (a) the extent of reliance on statistical models in inquiries about survey quality; (b) standardization versus flexibility in design, collection, and analysis of data; (c) quantitative versus qualitative approaches to inquiries in surveys; and (d) the need to construct inclusive paradigms describing survey quality.

Models and Survey Design

The explosion in the use of surveys in midcentury occurred in large part as a result of the development of practical methods of probability sampling (especially influenced by Neyman's 1934 work on stratified designs). These were largely taking place in Washington, DC, during the late 1930s and early 1940s. At this time young statisticians (e.g., Hansen, Deming, Stock, Frankel, Steinberg, and Kish) consumed the new statistical developments with a passion, often in self-guided night sessions in government offices (including that of the secretary of agriculture).

The work offered a comprehensive theoretical framework for drawing inference from probability samples to a population of fixed, finite size. The developments guaranteed that, if a sample were drawn from a sampling frame (e.g., a list of population members) such that each member of the frame had a known nonzero chance of selection, descriptive statistics (e.g., sample means and totals) would be unbiased estimates of the frame population and have measurable variance over all possible replications of the same design. The developments were attractive to those viewing the survey as a tool of science, not only because of replicability inherent in probability sampling but also because they supplied measures of quality.

The developments, however, lacked key features. They were based on statistics for fixed, finite populations; they ignored description of infinite processes. They were focused on descriptive statistics, but scientific questions (questions of "why" a phenomenon occurred) traditionally used other types of statistics (e.g., regression coefficients and other statistical measures of relationships). Finally, the theory applied to cases where all sampled cases were measured (i.e., there was no nonresponse), and there were no errors of measurement.

Within those constraints, the development of probability sampling led to inference to a population value with known levels of uncertainty in the conclusions. It was almost fully a model-free approach in that few assumptions about the nature of the population or the sampling frame were formalized. That is, the set of formal assumptions required of the analyst to support the description of the population was limited to theorems based on probability theory, not on an a priori set of assumed relationships among attributes of the population.

This model-free state of classical probability sampling lies in stark contrast to analytic statistics, which, more in tune with scientific reasoning itself, forms its inference about causal relationships within a set of constraints formalized by explicit assumptions. For example, if one is interested in the effects of education on lifetime earnings, one might posit a simple linear model with equal effects for each additional year of education, as $y_i = \beta_0 + \beta_1 x_i + \varepsilon_i$, where x_i is years of education completed and y_i is the lifetime earnings of the *i*th person. Under usual statistical estimation techniques, all of the desirable derived properties of the estimated β_0 and β_1 are dependent on the correct specification of the linear model. If, for example, the effects of education on earnings diminish at higher levels of education, these properties of the estimates are not attained. From time to time in the history of surveys, clashes between statistical approaches using models in the design or analysis of data and more model-free approaches have been fought out in the journals (e.g., Hansen, Madow, and Tepping 1983, comments, and rejoinder). A key issue between the two approaches is what aspects of the survey design (sample design, interviewer corps) need to be taken into account at the time of analysis.

Standardization versus Flexibility, Qualitative versus Quantitative

All social sciences using the survey method experience oscillations between quantitative and qualitative foci. The qualitative side focuses on ideas, conceptual frameworks, dialectic interplay, and argumentation. In the social sciences it is often linked with attention to the organic nature of social milieus, with fine-grained studies of individuals and small groups. The quantitative side emphasizes solutions to problems, extraction of principles that have wide applicability, generalization of results, and standardization of measurement. It often touts the advantages of the scientific method, with its formalistic steps of observation, hypothesis generation, testing, and inference. The use of surveys is common within this perspective in many of the social sciences.

The scientific and quantitative revels in the notion of standardization, permitting replication by any scientist following the same protocol. The flexible and qualitative often gives the freedom to invent attractive conceptual structures that become the basic theories of the field. It argues that standardized measurement is subject to untenable positivistic assumptions, that is, that the ability to generate survey measures is mistakenly viewed as evidence of their informational value. For example, a researcher may assume that the statistics based on standardized measurements are error-free indicators of the population, as if they aggregated perfect reflections of each individual measured.

When a critic can demonstrate that subsets of the population are subject to completely different conceptual frameworks in the area of study, then the antipositivist attack has merit. Such a situation is common when minority groups and subcultures are studied using surveys. For example, what is the utility of measuring the employment rate (a basic economic indicator of many societies) when economic activities are conducted largely without payment for labor or when some subgroup makes extensive use of bartering systems?

In a real way, the field of survey methodology falls between these two extremes. A central premise of survey methodology is that all survey-based estimates are flawed. (In this sense, survey methodology attacks the naive positivism of some practitioners of the survey method.) Its driving research focus, however, is to measure and reduce those errors. In that sense, the field is firmly part of the survey enterprise, committed to improving the informational value of surveys. At times survey methodology uses qualitative approaches to seek those improvements (focus groups, unstructured "cognitive" interviews), while at other times it uses statistical investigations of alternative standardized methods.

The Need for More Inclusive Conceptual Frameworks

The application of surveys to an expanding set of problems forced attention away from sampling error to other aspects of survey quality (Deming 1944).

The "total survey error" paradigm has utility for many of these inquiries. This framework identifies the following threats to the quality of survey statistics:

- Coverage error—reflecting the omission of distinctive sets of population members from the sampling frame, damaging the ability of survey statistics to describe the full population (e.g., omission of nontelephone households from household telephone surveys)
- Sampling error—reflecting the deliberate omission of some population elements from the sample
- Nonresponse error—reflecting the omission of some sampled persons/units from the respondent pool (e.g., because of their refusal to grant the survey request)
- Measurement errors—due to mismatches between the underlying construct and the measures, variation in how questions are comprehended, failure to reveal embarrassing personal attributes, and the influence of interviewers, questionnaires, and mode of data collection on respondent behavior
- Processing errors—reflecting damage to the quality of the data that occurs during coding, editing, construction of analytic variables, weighting, or imputation for missing data

This chapter reviews the progress in survey methodology within this general framework, with special emphasis on the role of SRC in its development.

Coverage of the Population

One visible success of the newly formed SRC and its emphasis on scientific methods was its estimate, using a relatively small national probability sample survey, that Truman would win the presidential election over Dewey in 1948. Although the standard error of that estimate (based on six hundred cases) was very large, the correct prediction drew attention to the contrast between the more rigorous methods of SRC and the methods of pollsters. The vast majority of sample surveys conducted by SRC attempt to obtain a representative sample of the U.S. household population. When face-to-face interviewing methods are used, the samples for those surveys use area probability sampling techniques. The attraction of area probability sampling methods is that the first stage selection units are areas of land, and assembly of a complete coverage of the United States is rather simple using mapping materials. If every resident of the United States can be associated with one and only one piece of land, then the area frame offers theoretically complete coverage of the U.S. population. Usually the method of association of persons to areas is the housing unit, the residence of the person.

While theoretically attractive, area probability sampling entails practical problems that lead to "coverage" error, the inadvertent omission of some persons from all samples that could be drawn using the technique. First, not all persons can be associated with a household. The homeless are missed in area probability sampling. This omission is true for almost all sample surveys but is of most concern for studies of low income and socially isolated subpopulations. The impact of coverage error on a simple statistic like a sample mean is

$$\bar{Y}_C = \bar{Y}_N + \frac{M}{N}(\bar{Y}_C - \bar{Y}_M)$$

where $\bar{Y}_C$ is the mean based on covered cases, $\bar{Y}_N$ is the mean based on the full target population (both covered and noncovered), M is the number of noncovered cases, and $\bar{Y}_M$ is the mean based on the noncovered cases.

The simple expression implies that noncoverage error is a function of the relative size of the noncovered population and of how distinctive it is on the survey variable of interest. Note also that coverage error will vary across different statistics (different Ys) in a single survey. (Similar expressions apply to other classes of statistics.)

Researchers at the SRC contributed to the understanding of coverage error at two significant time points. First, Kish and Hess (1958) studied the properties of missed housing units during the process of listing addresses prior to a sample survey. Their method was to compare listings from a set of blocks sampled for an SRC study with block statistics from the most recent census (1950). Their emphasis was on the term $(\bar{Y}_C - \bar{Y}_M)$, attempting to describe the differences between those successfully listed and those not. They found that there were few correlates that were systematically present. The method assumed that the census statistics were not subject to coverage error, but the exercise was hobbled by the passage of time between the census and the analysis.

As survey research matured, an alternative sampling frame for household surveys came into use—the set of telephone numbers assigned to the United States. In 1975 the SRC launched an experimental comparison of national face-to-face surveys (based on area frames) with a telephone survey (based on random digit dialing) (Groves and Kahn 1979). The study provided one of the first examinations of the characteristics of nontelephone households, yielding the now familiar result that these households tend to be lower in income, more transient, more rural, and smaller. At the time of the study, the *M/N* term was about 7 percent. For most of the comparisons of the study there appeared to be negligible differences between $\bar{Y}_C$ and $\bar{Y}_N$. (The comparison of telephone and nontelephone households was conducted within the face-to-face sample, in order to avoid confounding coverage effects with the effects of mode of data collection.)

The large-scale movement of survey practice from face-to-face interviewing to telephone surveying generated other investigations of coverage error—most of them focused on statistical issues of frame and sample design. Lepkowski and Groves, in a series of studies for the redesign of the National Crime Victimization Survey, addressed different ways of combining telephone and area probability sampling methods. They concluded that the cost savings from sampling, contact, and data collection tended to be sufficiently large in that case to argue for mixes of telephone and face-to-face methods, even though the nonresponse and measurement error characteristics may not favor telephone measurement. These "dual frame, mixed mode" designs permitted expansion of the coverage of telephone surveys to nontelephone households, without the full cost of a face-to-face survey (Groves and Lepkowski 1985; Lepkowski and Groves 1986).

Coverage of sample surveys is an area that was traditionally regarded very differently by those fitting causal models to survey data and those using surveys to describe populations. Traditional developments of analytic statistics treat the data as arising from some stochastic or random process of infinite duration, one whose products or outcomes the researcher observes to create his or her data set (e.g., the effect of vitamin C deficiency on scurvy). The statistics computed are used to draw inference to the process (e.g., whether and how the vitamin deficiency causes the disease). Any specific target population might be viewed as a convenient vehicle to study this process, but the researcher's analysis is meant to illuminate a more universal phenomenon. In contrast, researchers attempting to estimate the total number of women using contraceptives in the United States tend to be very concerned about whether those omitted from the sampling frame exhibit different behaviors from those included. While some of the early work of the SRC provided such basic prevalence estimates as these, it increasingly used surveys to test theories rather than simply estimating the size of different subpopulations. Perhaps because of this, SRC has not been active in research on coverage error, much of which has been done in the context of the U.S. decennial census.

Sampling

An early commitment of the founders of the SRC to probability sampling made the University of Michigan the center of its application to the social sciences. During this time theoretical developments were taking place throughout the world, notably at Iowa State and Harvard Universities and at the U.S. Bureau of the Census, but for SRC the repeated uses of the survey method demanded solutions to a continuous stream of practical problems of application. Many of these applied problems found their way into Leslie Kish's (1965b) text *Survey Sampling*.

Sampling methods were initially developed for descriptive uses of survey data. Theoretical developments followed methodological innovation, laying out theorems that underlie unbiased properties and uncertainty measures due to sampling error. These theorems identified the role of the four principal dimensions of sample design in the bias and variance properties of survey statistics. The Sampling Section of SRC innovated beginning in the 1950s on all four of these dimensions: size, stratification, clustering, and assignment of probabilities of selection.

Size and Stratification

In contrast to government surveys, SRC surveys, usually with limited funding from private or government agencies, were often based on one-time rather small designs. SRC found itself tackling issues of sample design constrained to have a small number of primary selections (e.g., a sample of business organizations). Constrained numbers of first stage selections inflate the standard errors of estimates and also produce unstable estimates of standard errors. Early work demonstrated the effectiveness of stratification as an antidote, but Goodman, Kish, and Hess faced many situations where the number of strata that could be effectively used exceeded the number of primary selections that could be afforded. This practical problem led to a long series of research efforts in the use of "controlled selection," which introduces multidimensional stratification (Goodman and Kish 1950; Groves and Hess 1975). The ingenious technique assures that each sample drawn will mirror marginal distributions on individual stratifying variables and most two-way joint distributions, while limiting the number of primary selections. Thus the positive effects of deep stratification are attained. In doing so, however, unbiased estimators of the sampling variance were lost; traditional variance estimators overestimated the standard errors of estimates. In a philosophy that maintains itself today, the SRC designers chose deep stratification to improve the precision of the estimates, even though standard error estimates would not reflect those gains.

The use of stratification was also employed to solve a persistent problem generated by imperfect knowledge about the size of units. In household sampling, selection of a block or other area unit is often based on data that may be as much as ten to twelve years out of date. When listing and data collection begin, planned interviewer workloads can be substantially altered if such units have grown significantly since the out-of-date information was obtained. SRC developed and employed a "surprise" stratification procedure that allowed the growth from such units to be spread over several surveys, reducing the impact on interviewer workload and survey efficiency.

Furthermore, the idea of growth of sampling units was addressed through the development of stratification procedures for selection methods to maximize overlap between samples. National sample surveys are often based on master samples in which the primary sampling units are selected once a decade (following the latest census of population). It is costly to select an entirely new set of primary sampling units each decade, abandoning trained interviewing staff in areas that were used in the master sample for a decade. Techniques for maximizing the overlap between decade-to-decade samples were devised by sampling statisticians outside of SRC (Keyfitz 1951), but SRC made significant contributions to the area by identifying improved methods for maximizing the overlap in the face of changing stratification.

Clustering

The loss of precision (inflation of standard errors) that accompanies clustered area probability samples was not generally acknowledged in the commercial and opinion polling surveys in the early 1950s. SRC statisticians thus faced the problem of how best to teach users of their surveys' statistics to reflect this added uncertainty. The problem in the first few decades was exacerbated by the large computing task required in calculating appropriate standard errors, especially with mechanical calculators lacking any memory function. The computation of the standard error of a single percentage estimate might require an entire day's labor. The problem was compounded by the fact that SRC surveys tended to be multipurpose, with large numbers of statistics computed from each one. In contrast, federal government surveys, which did indeed produce correct standard errors, were ordinarily single purpose (e.g., computing unemployment rates). A solution was needed, a mechanism to alert users to the inflation of variances affecting a specific survey while acknowledging the inability to compute standard errors for all possible statistics.

The creation of the concept of the "design effect" was a significant step. The design effect is the ratio of the sampling variance of a statistic reflecting all the design complexities to that expected from a simple random sample of the same number of elements. While standard errors are measured in the metric of the variable (e.g., dollars, years), design effects are metric free and are used as simple multipliers on the variances based on simple random assumptions. Furthermore, since design effects are a function of the number of sample elements per cluster and an intracluster correlation, they were found to be somewhat stable across sets of statistics in the same survey. Tables of approximate standard errors for percentages on the total sample and on key subclass differences accompanied final reports of SRC surveys. Later these were labeled "generalized variance functions" and became common to the field. As the field evolved, attempts to model generalized design effects were made (Kish, Groves, and Krotki 1976; Rust 1984).

Cluster sample selection and its consequences arise in multiple stages of sample selection, including small unequal-sized clusters such as households. Kish made within household selection a subject of study through his development of objective respondent selection (see, for example, Kish 1965a, section 11.3B). The procedure was a clever combination of practical methods and probability selection that made it possible for interviewers to make cluster sample selections in the field without the direct assistance of central office staff.

Assignment of Probabilities of Selection

A large-scale shift in the focus of social science sample surveys took place between the 1970s and the 1990s. While most surveys in the early decades of SRC were national equal probability samples, the focus of various fields turned to subpopulations, particularly those of disadvantaged minorities.

Thus in the late 1970s major national surveys of African-Americans and Mexican-Americans were mounted, some of which involved gross over-sampling of areas with higher densities of eligible persons and, correspondingly, large variation in selection weights. Novel screening techniques, which used neighborhood observations and proxy informants to identify households with eligible respondents, were attempted (see chap. 14).

Although Neyman's important 1934 paper laid the theoretical groundwork for the effects on standard errors of departing from equal probability sampling, stratification was introduced at SRC for other reasons. Many SRC surveys required separate estimates with controlled precision for minority subpopulations. It was Kish's research that investigated the various trade-offs of unequal probabilities of selection (Kish 1965a, 1969, 1976).

Statistical Computing for Complex Surveys

As the field moved from rotary calculators and counter-sorters for data cards to large-scale computers, it became feasible to develop general purpose software for the computation of sampling variances. Simultaneously, the use of analytic statistics (e.g., regression coefficients) from sample surveys became more prevalent, often involving rather large-scale computation for complex sample standard errors. SRC was at the forefront of developing methods to estimate variances for more and more complex estimators. As early as 1962, Kish (1962b) developed variance estimation procedures for indexes estimated from complex samples. Further advances required the development of statistical software that could handle the increasingly complicated estimation procedures.

Kish and Frankel simultaneously developed software for Taylor series approximation, balanced repeated replication, and jackknife repeated replication estimators of standard errors for basic estimators such as means and proportions as well as for much more complex estimators such as differences of subclass means and proportions, regression coefficients, and correlation coefficients (Kish and Frankel 1970, 1974). Furthermore, they applied the software to the assessment of the quality of these different variance procedures, providing guidance on which methods worked best for which statistical estimators. The software that resulted from this effort, Sampling Error Program Package, eventually was incorporated into the OSIRIS Statistical Software System developed at the Institute for Social Research (ISR). For many years, OSIRIS was the only statistical program package that incorporated variance estimation for complex sample surveys.

The purpose of the variance estimation for complex sample survey data was to provide tools for analysts to generate inferential statistics that properly accounted for the stratified multistage sample design, including weighted estimates. The OSIRIS software provided a platform for further expansion of the available routines. For example, analysis of large-scale contingency tables advanced to the formulation of models to explain variation in the factors used to form a cross-classification.

ISR ceased development of the OSIRIS system in the 1980s, but work on variance estimation at SRC continued. Recently, software has been developed (see the section "Processing and Analysis of Survey Data" later in this chapter) that incorporates the OSIRIS routines into a package that allows not only proper inference from complex samples but also correct inference for imputed data. The IVEWare package is used throughout SRC to impute for missing data and to estimate variances and provide inferential statistics, which account for stratification, weighting, multistage selection, and imputation simultaneously. IVEWare is freeware available through a publicly accessible Web site maintained by SRC: <http://www.isr.umich.edu/src/smp/ive/>. This work has some parallels at other software development organizations.

Sampling of Telephone Numbers

As the cost of face-to-face surveys rose and telephone coverage of the household population increased, many survey efforts moved to telephone sample frames. The sample designs for these were largely invented outside SRC by commercial users (Waksberg 1978). However, once SRC began their use, it also launched a program of evaluation of the techniques (Groves 1978), postsurvey adjustments that fit telephone sampling needs (Groves and Couper 1995), and later the development of new sampling techniques that optimized use of various properties of the frame.

Currently, the sampling of households through their telephone numbers is changing rapidly. The increasing prevalence of cellular and computer-related telephone numbers and the opening of local exchanges to competition for household and business service have led to an explosion of new area codes and prefixes. The proportion of all possible telephone numbers assigned to household numbers is declining, making random digit dialing as a sampling technique less efficient. Research continues at

SRC and elsewhere to find new telephone sample designs that accommodate the changes in the telephone number population.

Nonresponse

In contrast to other data collection mechanisms, surveys gain their greatest inferential power through assurance that "representative" subsets of a population are measured in a standardized fashion. Like coverage errors and some sampling errors, the failure to measure sample persons can bias survey results. Response rates for academic surveys have experienced a rather consistent downward trend in the United States (Steeh 1981; Steeh et al. 1999; Groves and Couper 1998). Temporal declines appear to be larger in urban areas and, in the United States, for telephone surveys versus other modes.

Methodological research into nonresponse has a long tradition at SRC. It can be classified into theory construction for understanding nonresponse behavior, efforts to reduce nonresponse rates, and adjustment procedures for nonresponse. Although the development of theoretical frameworks came relatively late, we use these frameworks to describe the contributions of SRC researchers.

Theory Construction to Explain Nonresponse Behavior

Groves and Couper (1998) provide a conceptual framework for understanding household survey nonresponse. They first present evidence that the process of "noncontact" needs to be distinguished from the process of "refusal" in household surveys. The influences on noncontact are simple (see figure 2.1) relative to those on refusals. If the researcher knew the times when one or more household members were at home and accessible, contact on a single visit would be possible. The absence of that knowledge leads designers to fashion call scheduling protocols, directing the time of calls over repeated efforts (Weeks et al. 1980; Weeks, Kulka, and Pierson 1987). Complicating the process is the fact that, especially in large urban areas and areas with expensive housing, households invest in devices to protect their privacy. For face-to-face surveys, locked apartment buildings (sometimes with security guards), walled subdivisions, intercom systems, locked gates, and a variety of other physical features

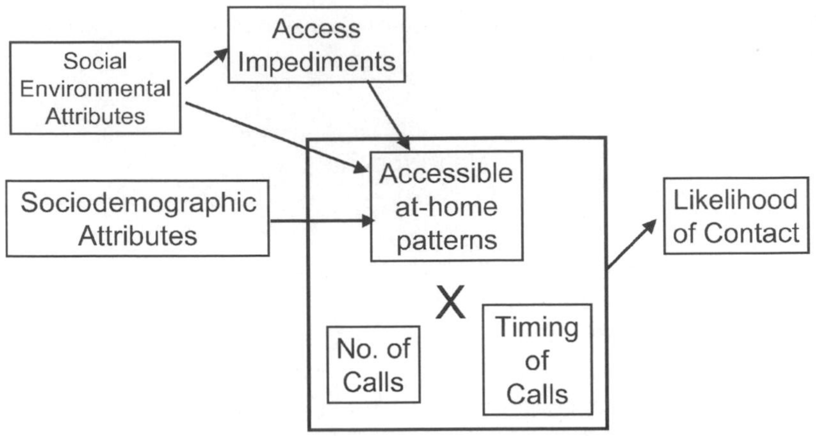

FIG. 2.1. Influences on the likelihood of contact with sample households

impede the ability of interviewers to contact the household. For telephone surveys, answering machines and "caller ID" features fulfill similar functions.

These influences on contactability produce systematic compositional differences in respondent pools across surveys that differ in contact rates. Households with one member, households with all adults employed out of the home, households without children, urban households, and households in large multiunit structures generally require more calls to contact. In surveys not investing in such efforts, these groups tend to be underrepresented among respondents. In telephone surveys, households with answering machines tend to require more calls to contact. This form of nonresponse appears to be consistent across different survey topics (indeed, it is generally not influenced by the topic of the survey) (Groves et al. 2000). Low contact rates produce high nonresponse error when the survey statistics are themselves related to these household characteristics (e.g., a time use survey with high noncontact rates would grossly underestimate out-of-home activities).

In contrast to the contact process in surveys, the decision-making process of contacted persons appears to be much more complex. This decision-making process, especially in telephone surveys, takes place in the few seconds during the introduction of a survey and the delivery of a request by an interviewer. On the phone, most refusals take place in less than thirty seconds (Oksenberg, Coleman, and Cannell 1986).

We now believe that such quick decisions are based on a set of heuristics that allow persons to make them rapidly with low risk of penalties. The heuristics themselves seem to be guided by a set of social environmental influences (e.g., predispositions regarding the openness to strangers based on local environmental patterns) and a set of personal attributes (e.g., roles played within the household regarding contact with those outside the household). Both of these are in large part outside the control of the researcher. The two sets of influences on the right-hand side of figure 2.2—prerequest features (e.g., advance letters, incentives) and attributes and behaviors of interviewers—are features of the survey protocol selected by the researcher that have impact on cooperation rates.

Householders spend the first few moments of interaction detecting cues that help them decide whether to prolong or terminate the encounter. Variations in interviewer behavior and attributes may make one or more of these concerns more salient than others. Groves, Singer, and Corning (2000) have proposed a "leverage-saliency" theory to describe this interactive process. Different features of the survey design are differentially effective in motivating response among sample persons (the leverage of the feature). In addition, different introductory utterances by interviewers make a design feature differentially salient. The theory asserts that any specific survey design feature (e.g., topic, length of interview, sponsorship) will be differentially important to different persons and will move them toward or away from participation. These variations among sample persons and survey protocols are used to explain the lack of replicability of many experiments to increase cooperation.

There is some optimism that impacts of noncontact nonresponse will be consistent over broad classes of surveys and that design options to minimize noncontact error will be articulated in the near future. Similar optimism does not exist for nonresponse error arising from refusals.

Reducing Refusal Rates through Interviewer Behavior

As shown in figure 2.2, the interviewer is the agent of the researcher who makes the survey request. There has been a persistent belief that interviewers are differentially successful at obtaining cooperation. In early face-to-face surveys, field managers had difficulty separating the effects of interviewers on response rates from the fact that they were assigned different populations (with different base tendencies to cooperate). But when centralized telephone surveys became more common, and a group of

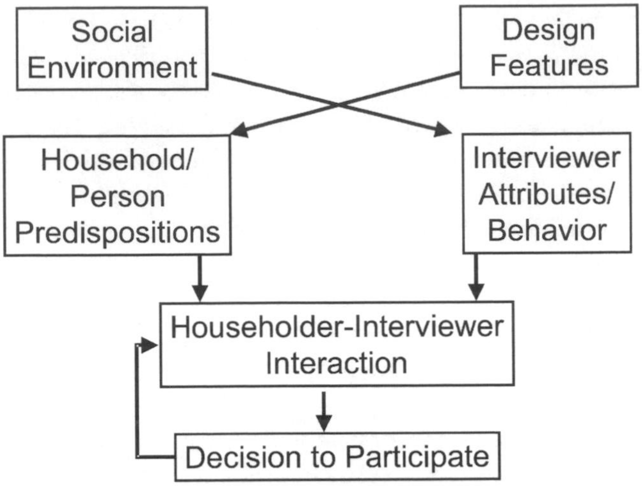

FIG. 2.2. Conceptual framework for survey participation (Groves and Couper 1998).

interviewers shared cases, it became obvious that the interviewer component of variation was large and pervasive.

ISR researchers have inquired into the role of the interviewer more as a source of measurement error (see the section "Research on Interviewing and Interviewer Effects" later in this chapter) than as a source of nonresponse. There are two important exceptions to this general rule, however. When centralized telephone interviewing began to show that refusals were taking place in the first few seconds of interaction, Oksenberg, Coleman, and Cannell (1986) showed that the pace, intonation, inflection, and tone of the interviewer's voice appeared to be related to the likelihood of cooperation. This helped build the case that voice characteristics were one of the heuristics respondents used to guide their decisions.

On the basis of focus group discussions and the monitoring of telephone interviewers, Groves and Couper (1998) argued that successful interviewers deliberately extended the conversation with sample persons prior to making the formal survey request. They report doing this by engaging in talk that is of apparent interest to the sample person even if it is not central to the survey request. This behavior, termed "maintaining interaction," was seen as a conversational device to enrich the information observed by interviewers about household concerns related to the survey request. Interviewers who had higher rates of cooperation appeared to customize their remarks to their perceptions of the householder's concerns. This behavior was called "tailoring."

In a set of interviewer training experiments, Groves and McGonagle (2001) showed that interviewers can be trained in tailoring behavior. The training protocol was based on qualitative investigations into common issues or concerns raised by sample persons, classified into themes. The protocol taught interviewers to classify different utterances of sample persons into the appropriate theme and instructed them in responses to these concerns found to be effective among a set of senior interviewers. The experiments showed that the training effectively decreased the variation in interviewer performance, bringing up the cooperation rates of the worse-performing interviewers. The overall cooperation rates of interviewers receiving the training increased by 12 to 16 percentage points, far exceeding any gains experienced by those not receiving the training.

Reducing Refusal Rates through Design Features

The theories of survey participation outlined previously suggest that there should be large numbers of interaction effects—what works for some householders may not work for others. Since first efforts to contact and interview respondents can often not be tailored, however, much research on reducing refusal rates has looked for survey design features with ubiquitous positive effects on cooperation.

Several experiments have examined whether sending an advance letter alerting the sample household to an upcoming call from the interviewer might act to increase response rates. There was evidence of an interaction effect with sponsorship: Brunner and Carroll (1969) found that letters from a marketing research firm generated lower cooperation rates while those from a university generated higher cooperation rates. In an experiment in an SRC telephone survey—sending letters to numbers with listed addresses—Traugott, Groves, and Lepkowski (1987) and Traugott and Goldstein (1993) found that sending advance letters to the household from the University of Michigan generated higher cooperation rates than did sending no letter. On the other hand, Singer, Van Hoewyk, and Maher (2000) found no such effect on the ongoing SRC Survey of Consumer Attitudes. Why the results differ is subject to speculation—the topics differ across surveys, the length of the data collection period differs, the base response rates differ. As response rates to surveys have declined, researchers have considered more seriously the use of monetary and noncash incentives. Such incentives were common for decades in market research but were never used in public opinion research or in government research. They became more prevalent with high burden and longitudinal economic surveys (Ferber and Sudman [1974] offered the first experimental evidence of their potential value in that domain). Church (1993) and Singer and her colleagues (Singer et al. 1999; Singer, Van Hoewyk, and Maher 2000; Singer 2002) showed that there appear to be general increases in response rates due to incentives across all mail, telephone, and face-to-face surveys. Sometimes, indeed, the total cost of the survey can be reduced by using incentives, as they save interviewer hours spent in callbacks and refusal conversion. Under the theories reviewed previously, we now suspect that incentives are most effective among those groups who have no other reason to cooperate. Leverage-saliency theory suggests that those interested in the topic of the survey or committed to community involvement (and who connect surveys to that commitment) show greatly diminished incentive effects, and indeed Groves, Singer, and Corning (2000) have demonstrated this. The theory also suggests that the biasing effects of refusals to cooperate arise from situations where the topic itself is a central cause of the participation decision (e.g., when interest in politics influences the decision to participate in an election survey). Sponsorship can also influence the decision to participate (e.g., support or opposition to the federal government as a reason to refuse or respond to a survey sponsored by a federal agency). When the topic of the survey is closely allied with the mission of the sponsor, refusal bias can result (e.g., if a farmer opposed to Department of Agriculture price subsidies refuses to participate in a survey sponsored by the Department of Agriculture).

Research on Measurement Error

"Measurement error" is a property of surveys that reflects either a lack of consistency within a respondent with respect to answers to survey questions over repeated administrations or a systematic tendency to answer questions one way in one situation and a different way in another. Measurement error includes mismatches between the underlying construct and its measures; variation in how questions are understood; failure to reveal embarrassing personal attributes; and the influence of interviewers, questionnaires, and mode of data collection on respondent behavior. When the measure reflects an observable trait of a respondent (e.g., "How many times did you visit a doctor in the last two weeks?"), survey methodologists have employed the notion of measurement bias to reflect the difference between the report and the "true" value. When the measure reflects a subjective phenomenon, the notion of bias is less useful. In these situations the field has studied measurement circumstances that produce distinctive responses (e.g., modes of data collection) or lack of consistency in response over repeated administrations.

Research on the Questionnaire

Early History. Most surveys attempt to obtain information by posing questions to a sample of respondents. The questions can be more or less structured; they can be posed in written form, via a self-administered questionnaire, or asked by an interviewer; they can attempt to elicit information directly from the respondent about himself or herself or can use the respondent as an informant about others. Although Likert developed the structured, closed-ended, five-point Likert scale for measuring attitudes as part of his doctoral dissertation at Columbia University in 1932, he became a passionate advocate of standardized open-ended questions and nondirective probes when he moved to the Department of Agriculture as the director of its Division of Program Surveys later in the 1930s and, still later, when he became the director of the Division of Intensive Surveys, under contract to the Office of War Information during World War II. Under the pressure of costs, however, closed questions began to be used selectively in conjunction with open questions and part-time interviewers were hired. The need for training a large national interviewing staff also put a premium on standardization. As a result, attitude research and questionnaire construction have been dominated for the last fifty years by Lazarsfeld's conclusion that the open-ended interview "is indispensable at the beginning of any study where it clarifies the structure of a problem in all its details," providing guidance in designing subsequent structured questions, and "it is also invaluable at the end of a study," to clarify, guide, and enrich the analysis (1944, 39).

Systematic Research on Question Wording. Experimentation on the effects of question wording has occurred in various places from the earliest days of survey research. But, as Converse (1987, 370) notes, "methodological research into question form . . . did not get off the ground at SRC in these years." It was with the work of Schuman and Presser (1981) that SRC became a leader in the methodological study of question wording and context effects in attitude measurement, following earlier research in this area by Sudman and Bradburn (1974; Bradburn, Sudman et al. 1979) at the National Opinion Research Center.

Schuman and Presser approached the problem of "response effects" (i.e., systematic changes in answers associated with different measurement circumstances) produced by variations in question wording and question order by systematically embedding randomized experiments into ongoing telephone as well as face-to-face surveys carried out at SRC and elsewhere with random national samples, thus enhancing the external validity of the results. Furthermore, they generally replicated between-subject randomized experiments over several surveys and with several different questions, thus assuring the stability and generality of the findings. Prior to this point such rigor was rare in research on questionnaire effects. And unlike the earlier analysts, Schuman and Presser concentrated on the consequences of response effects for relationships between variables and on the reasons for these effects.

Most of Schuman and Presser's experiments focus on structural features of survey questions. For example, a series of experiments investigated the effect that omitting or including an explicit "Don't Know" option had on the distribution of responses. In every case, the proportion of respondents answering "Don't Know" was substantially higher when this option was offered. The increment was fairly constant and seemed to be unrelated to the difficulty of the question. Schuman and Kalton (1985, 648) note that similar findings occur with the omission or inclusion of a "middle alternative" between two extreme positions (Kalton, Roberts, and Holt 1980) and with the omission or inclusion of an item on a checklist of possible responses. Schuman and Kalton interpret all of these phenomena as instances of "constraint"—that is, of the fact that responses are to some extent shaped or constrained by formal features of the questionnaire. Of considerable interest, however, is the finding that correlations with other items appeared to be little affected by whether or not a "filter" question was used to screen out respondents who had no opinions on an issue and that the division of substantive opinion was rarely, if ever, affected by whether or not a "Don't Know" option was offered. This and other findings related to questions about fictional or obscure objects have obvious implications for whether or not survey responses are to be interpreted as "nonattitudes" (Converse 1970).

Systematic variations in responses that are attributable to characteristics of the questions rather than characteristics of the respondents pose a dilemma for researchers since they call into question the validity (i.e., the relationship between the response to the measure and the unobservable underlying trait being measured) of the responses obtained. A similar dilemma is posed by research demonstrating variations in responses to the same question by different survey organizations. Sparked by an article by Turner and Krauss (1978), which demonstrated large discrepancies between the responses obtained by different survey organizations to the same question, the survey community mounted a program of research into measurement. The first fruit of that effort was Turner and Martin's *Surveying Subjective Phenomena* (1984), an edited book that grew out of an interdisciplinary National Academy panel, followed shortly by what has come to be known as the cognitive movement in survey research (Jabine et al. 1984).

Schuman and Presser (1981) demonstrated the response effects of certain variations in question wording and context without setting these in a single theoretical framework. But from the perspective of cognitive psychology, response effects are not unexpected outcomes but rather phenomena that can be understood and, more important, predicted on the basis of cognitive and social psychological theory. Schwarz (in Schwarz and Sudman 1992, 1994), in particular, has written extensively on the effects of question order and response alternatives from this perspective and has shown that variations in responses are predictable from certain features of the questions. For example, what other investigators have called "consistency" or "contrast" effects are shown by Schwarz to be interpretable as due to implicit instructions to respondents to include or exclude certain phenomena when answering the question. The constraining effects of response alternatives to a question can similarly be understood as reflecting the respondent's interpretation of the meaning of those categories as well as their socially desirable properties. For example, Schwarz shows that response distributions shift when response alternatives to a question about the amount of television the respondent watches are anchored in different endpoints. He interprets this as occurring because respondents do not have readily available a good estimate of how much television they actually watch and use the response alternatives themselves as cues.

Thus, there appears to be a relationship between the notion of "satisficing" (Simon 1957; Krosnick and Alwin 1987) and Schwarz's theory of how questionnaire effects come about, since presumably response alternatives will *not* affect estimates if respondents readily know how much television they watch or can be motivated to make the effort to estimate the amount accurately. Experiments by Cannell, Miller, and Oksenberg (1981), in which the respondent is asked to make a commitment to provide accurate data and interviewers are instructed to provide positive as well as negative feedback, have shown some success in reducing both underreporting and overreporting (Miller and Cannell 1977), though the effectiveness of these techniques in reducing the effect of response alternatives has not been tested in an experimental setting.

Recent Developments: Return to More Flexible Questioning? Showing that variations in responses based on variations in question wording are predictable does not, of course, solve the basic dilemma of how best to ask a question if one is interested in an accurate answer rather than in the cognitive processes by which an answer is arrived at. Thus, research by cognitive psychologists has improved the predictability of question-related behaviors without enabling us to reduce measurement error significantly. Schuman's response to this dilemma, common to a psychometric approach to measurement, is to call for using multiple indicators of a concept and correlations rather than marginal frequencies, since the former are more resistant to unwanted influences from the questionnaire itself. Another obvious solution is to reduce the influence of the questionnaire by going back to a more "open" format, thus minimizing the cues provided to the respondent; but Schuman notes there is evidence that the open question may also influence the range of answers that are given, presumably because it is framed by the rest of the questionnaire (Schuman and Presser 1981).

A related development has been criticism of the structured form of questioning used in large-scale surveys and proposals for a more conversational style of interviewing (Suchman and Jordan 1990). This can be viewed as a more recent occurrence of the tension between the qualitative and quantitative approaches to information acquisition that pervades survey research. Such criticism had been anticipated by Lazarsfeld in his 1935 article, "The Art of Asking Why."

> Traditional opinion is that a question should be so worded as always to insure the same reaction on the part of all those interviewed. We advocate a rather loose and liberal handling of a questionnaire by an interviewer. It seems to us much more important that the question be fixed in its *meaning* than in the *wording*. This . . . places the responsibility on the interviewer for knowing exactly what he is trying to discover and permits him to vary the wording in accordance with the experience of the respondent. (32)

Recent experiments (e.g., Schober and Conrad 1997) with a more "flexible" interviewing style, in which interviewers are encouraged to help respondents understand the meaning of a question and arrive at an accurate answer, even if this means departing from the standardized questionnaire, appear to show that this technique can produce more accurate answers, although there is some question whether the standardized version has been fairly represented in these experiments. It is possible, however, that for questions whose answer depends on a *shared* meaning of certain concepts—the definition of what constitutes a bathroom, for example, or just how the investigator wants the respondent to define "unemployment"—a more flexible interviewing style that permits more negotiation between the respondent and the interviewer than the standardized questionnaire normally does would yield better answers. Much more specification and testing are needed, however, to maximize the benefits from this approach and minimize its costs, especially for attitudinal questions. From a statistical perspective, there is concern that flexible interviewing will trade increased interviewer variance as the price for lower average response bias. So far, the research evidence has not been assembled to answer this point.

Research on Reliability and Validity. Another set of approaches to studying the questionnaire developed at SRC along a different dimension—that is, the use of formal modeling to evaluate the effects of specific question properties on the nature of their errors. This has involved two different design strategies: between subjects versus within-subjects designs. In the former case (the split-ballot randomized experiment) the more familiar approach to the study of response errors in surveys, two or more forms (or ballots) are devised that are hypothesized to evoke different responses in a given population.

There have been very few split-ballot study designs with multiple measures of social indicators that examined the correlational or covariance properties of survey questions; one exception is Alwin and Krosnick (1985), which used a split-ballot experiment to study differences in the properties of ratings and rankings in assessing values, that is, beliefs about desired outcomes. Using this strategy, they were able to show that the covariance properties of the two measurement forms were quite different and therefore produced quite different correlational patterns with criterion variables, that is, different types of predictive validity, suggesting that ratings and rankings generally measure different things.

With its roots in psychometric theory, the within-subjects design is a much more common approach to assessing measurement errors in surveys. The basic approach is to administer replicates of the same or similar question to the same respondents and evaluate the correlational or covariance information among the measures using a model that interprets that information in terms of the properties of their psychometric reliability and validity. These approaches have moved beyond the traditional focus on *internal consistency* to estimate the measurement properties of single survey questions (see Alwin 2003).

There are two basic strategies that have been employed within the within-subjects framework. There are those that present multiple indicators to respondents within the same interview; these are contrasted with those that use longitudinal, or panel data, to assess components of measurement error. The advantages and disadvantages of these two strategies have been debated (e.g., Alwin 1989; Saris and Andrews 1991), but it is generally agreed that both approaches provide useful information and should be compatible in their results. The main advantage of the cross-sectional approach is that it aspires to partition reliable variance into *valid* and *invalid* components. The main advantage of the longitudinal approach is that it avoids the problem of spurious consistency among measures contained within the same interview.

The cross-sectional approach relies on a *multitrait-multimethod* (MTMM) design, in which each of several traits or concepts are each measured within the same interview with different methods (e.g., with response formats that vary the number of response categories). Over the past few decades researchers have done extensive analyses of the quality of survey measures using this approach, one that has relied primarily, though not exclusively, on the analysis of cross-sectional data that incorporates method variation in measurement within the same survey (Alwin 1989, 1997; Andrews 1984; Andrews and Herzog 1986; Rodgers, Herzog, and Andrews 1988; Rodgers, Andrews, and Herzog, 1992; Saris and van Meurs 1990; Saris and Andrews 1991; Scherpenzeel and Saris 1997).

Frank Andrews (1984), a longtime member of the Survey Research Center, pioneered the application of the MTMM measurement design to large-scale survey data in order to tease out the effects of method factors on survey responses. His research suggested that substantial amounts of variation in measurement quality could be explained by seven survey design characteristics, here listed in order of their importance in his meta-analysis of effects on data quality: the number of response categories; explicit offering of a "Don't Know" option; battery length; absolute versus comparative perspective of the question; length of the introduction and of the question; position of the question in the questionnaire; and the full labeling of response categories.

A second approach to estimating reliability of single questions in survey data uses the multiple-wave re-interview (i.e., test-retest) or panel design (see O'Muircheartaigh 1991). Alwin (2003) has recently applied the longitudinal approach to more than 500 survey measures in six representative three-wave panel studies conducted at the Survey Research Center in which re-interviews were separated by two or more years. This project focused specifically on the conceptualization and estimation of the nature and extent of *measurement error* in surveys and established a rationale for the consideration of measurement errors when designing and conducting survey research.

Alwin's (2003) research also examined several formal properties of the questions in relationship to their tendency to generate measurement errors, specifically the *number of response options* provided in closed-form questions, the use of *unipolar* versus *bipolar* response formats, the use of *visual aids*, particularly the use of *verbal labeling* of response categories, the provision of an explicit *Don't Know option*, and the *length of questions* used in survey questionnaires. He found clear support for using verbal labeling in the measurement of nonfactual content to improve the quality of response, and strong and systematic support for increments in reliability for questions with fewer numbers of words.

Research on Questionnaire Development. Qualitative, open-ended interviewing has long been used in the early stages of developing a structured questionnaire and indeed was recommended by Lazarsfeld as "indispensable" in his 1944 article. In recent years, the related process of "cognitive interviewing," which attempts to elicit the respondent's associations and reactions to the questions in order to assure their comprehension, has come into frequent use (see, e.g., De Maio et al. 1993).

Cognitive interviews are ordinarily part of the process of developing an instrument. Once it has been developed, one or more pretests can be used to evaluate it in a field setting. But experience and systematic examination demonstrate that this procedure is frequently not adequate to assure a standard stimulus for each respondent. A more formal technique for evaluating the adequacy of a questionnaire is known as "behavior coding" (Oksenberg, Cannell, and Kalton 1991), originally developed as a technique for evaluating interviewer performance (Cannell, Lawson, and Hausser 1975).

The first use of behavior coding in survey research was for training interviewers in techniques of asking questions, probing, and other acceptable interaction techniques. This assumed that the questions themselves were problem free. Monitoring of interviewers' behavior by means of behavior coding, however, revealed that the problems were frequently not attributable to interviewers but rather to the questions themselves. This led to the use of behavior coding as a technique for evaluating questions.

In behavior coding, a sample of interviewer and respondent behaviors is coded for accuracy in asking questions and adequacy in providing answers. For example, interviewers' readings may be coded as "exact," "slight change (minor reorder, does not alter meaning)," or "major change (meaning is altered)." Respondents' answers may be coded as "adequate answer," "asks for clarification," "qualified answer," "inadequate answer," "don't know," or "refuses to answer." In a comparison of four methods of pretesting survey questions (conventional pretests, behavior coding, cognitive interviews, and expert panels), Presser and Blair (1994) found that conventional pretesting and behavior coding were especially good at identifying problems involving the reading and wording of the questions, whereas expert panels tended to be the most productive and least expensive in terms of the overall number of problems identified.

It has been assumed that a question that elicits a high rate of inexact readings and a high rate of inadequate answers is a problem question that needs improvement, but until recently evidence for this belief was lacking. In the last several years, empirical evidence has accumulated that questions that are problematic according to behavior coding criteria are also associated with lower validity (Belli and Lepkowski 1995; Dykema, Lepkowski, and Blixt 1997) as well as lower test-retest reliability (Hess, Singer, and Bushery 1999). Still in its early stages, however, is research demonstrating that the repairs made to problematic questions actually result in less missing data and more accurate answers (Presser et al. 2004).

Research on Interviewing and Interviewer Effects

With the exception of self-administered questionnaires, most surveys depend on interviewers to mediate between the written questionnaire and the respondent. They play two important roles in this process. First, as already noted, they must make contact with potential respondents and persuade them to participate. Second, they must communicate the researcher's intended meaning to respondents and elicit appropriate responses. In the process of doing so, they may also have a variety of *unin-*

tended effects on response rate and response quality. In this section, we review research bearing on all of these issues.

Improving the Quality of Response. In the SRC, research on interviewing and interviewer effects can be seen as an extension of the program of methodological research, much of it experimental in design, initiated by Charles Cannell and his colleagues in the 1960s. A number of the more innovative findings of this program group came from their work on cognitive aspects of the interviewer-respondent relationship. This emphasis, more complementary than conflicting, contrasted with the earlier research on interviewer-respondent rapport, as it was then called—the ability of the interviewer to convey a sense of understanding, of friendly but not intrusive interest in respondents and their answers. Experiments by Cannell and his colleagues demonstrated the effects of behavior balance—that is, the tendency of the length and detail of answers to be highly correlated ($r = .77$) with the amount of verbal activity by the interviewer in asking, probing, feeding back acceptance, and the like.

Related experiments showed the specific effect of the interviewer's feedback regarding the relevance and adequacy of responses throughout the interview process, although the success of such verbal reinforcement in increasing the completeness of the response depended on its appropriateness to the education and sophistication of the respondent. Other experiments involved the brief negotiation of respondents' commitment to their role in the interview process before it began. This was done by written agreement, read and signed by each respondent, to provide accurate and complete answers to the best of their ability. This modest contractual process had positive effects on completeness and accuracy of data, but given increased reliance on telephone interviewing, it has not been widely adopted.

Since research indicated that each of the several experimental techniques—explicit instructions to respondents, feedback, and commitment—was effective in improving completeness and precision of response, a final experiment in this series combined them. As predicted, the combination of the three provided the most consistent improvement in the completeness and quality of the interview data as assessed by performance measures and external comparisons. In combination, they generated an increase of about 20 percent in the amount of information provided and increases of 11 to more than 200 percent in seven "indices of precision." These indices included the reporting of illnesses of an intimate or embarrassing kind, the dates of visits to doctors, and the checking of outside information sources (Cannell, Oksenberg, and Converse 1977).

The technique of interviewing, note Cannell and Kahn (1968, 573), "comprises all spontaneous, unprogrammed behavior of the interviewer relevant to attaining the three basic conditions for successful measurement by interviewing—cognition, accessibility, and motivation." The dominant tendency among survey researchers has been to try to standardize interviewer behavior along with the questionnaire (Schuman and Kalton 1985, 683; Cannell, Miller, and Oksenberg 1981), but Cannell and Kahn noted as early as 1968 that the "universal tendency of interviewers to introduce flexibility into rigid procedures probably has the effect of saving some distant question writers from the fate they prescribe for themselves" (577).

That standardization is not necessarily achieved is shown in a study of interviewer reading errors (deviations from the standardized question wording) by Blair (Bradburn, Sudman, and Associates 1979, chap. 3). Blair found such errors in one out of every three questions and, more important, found that more experienced interviewers deviated more often. In early research Marquis and Cannell (1969) found that the most frequent unprogrammed interviewer behavior was positive feedback to the respondent, given indiscriminately to undesirable as well as desirable behavior. This finding led Cannell, Miller, and Oksenberg (1981) to try to specify such reinforcement so that positive feedback was given only for desirable behavior and negative feedback was given when a response was inadequate.

Unintended Effects of Interviewer Behaviors. Research on the interviewer as a source of variable error and bias thrived in the late 1940s and early 1950s (see, especially, Hyman et al. 1954), and then languished until the late 1960s. Hyman's early experimental work at NORC demonstrated that interviewers' expectations about the consistency of respondents' behavior did influence their categorization of ambiguous responses, depending on what answers had preceded them, but found little evidence for the operation of other kinds of expectation effects. Subsequent experiments by Sudman et al. (1977) and by Singer and Kohnke-Aguirre (1979) showed that interviewers' expectations concerning the ease or difficulty of asking certain kinds of questions had a demonstrable though small impact on item nonresponse but little if any effect on the overall response rate. However, Singer, Frankel, and Glassman (1983) found that, in a telephone survey with a much lower response rate than the two earlier face-to-face surveys, interviewer expectations had a strong effect on response rates but little additional effect on item nonresponse.

The civil rights movement of the late 1960s and associated civil disorders sparked a large number of studies of racial attitudes, and these in turn revived interest in the effect of interviewer characteristics, especially race, on the attitudes expressed by respondents. Such effects had been demonstrated by Stouffer et al. (1949) and Hyman et al. (1954) and were reported for black respondents by Schuman and Converse (1971) and for white respondents by Hatchett and Schuman (1975). In both cases, Schuman interprets the findings in terms of norms of politeness constraining the responses given to interviewers and is careful to point out that the answers given to same-race interviewers need be no more correct than those given to opposite-race interviewers. Effects attributable to other interviewer characteristics—for example, gender—have been found in some studies, although these effects have generally been small. However, as Schuman and Kalton note (1985, 686), such effects may be expected "whenever respondents classify the interviewer into a larger category and believe they know what would offend or please persons in that category." For example, they report an early study that shows fewer anti-Jewish responses to interviewers with Jewish-sounding names (Robinson and Rohde 1946).

In an interesting extension of research on the effects of interviewer characteristics on response, Krysan and Couper (2003) investigate whether video images of interviewers produce the same race-of-interviewer effects as live interviewers do, hypothesizing that the effect will be intermediate between those of live interviewers and self-administered questionnaires.

A completely different approach to measuring interviewer effects rests on statistical models of variation in results obtained by different interviewers, so-called interviewer variance. This source of variation is seen to increase the instability of survey statistics because responses on a particular survey are subject to variation depending on who the interviewers happen to be. Early work by Mahalanobis in India (1946) informed the approach of Hansen, Hurwitz, and Bershad (1961), creating practical survey designs that permitted measurement of the interviewer variance component. Kish (1962a) offered an alternative model based on a one-way analysis of variance. The basic finding from this line of work is that the interviewer variance component is larger when interviewers are unscripted and less well trained. Interviewer variance for sensitive questions appears to be higher than that for others. Unfortunately, the two approaches—randomized studies of how observable attributes of interviewers affect responses, on the one hand, and statistical measurement of interviewer variance, on the other—have not been well integrated over time.

Increasing reliance on telephone rather than face-to-face interviewing has divergent implications for interviewer effects. On the one hand, telephone interviewing greatly reduces the number of interviewers involved in any one survey and makes it possible to monitor and supervise their performance much more closely than can be done with a dispersed field staff. Thus, in principle, random variation between interviewers should be reduced; and indeed a study by Groves and Magilavy (1986) demonstrates that this is the case. The greater homogeneity of interviewer behaviors reduces measurement variability, but the tendencies to use a smaller staff in telephone surveys than in face-to-face surveys implies that interviewer effects can remain an issue in this mode.

Research on Mode of Questioning

Three considerations have driven the quest for alternative modes of obtaining information by means of surveys: cost, speed of data collection, and data quality.

The shift from face-to-face to telephone interviewing was driven primarily by cost considerations. As telephone coverage improved, the cost of reaching a national sample by telephone became increasingly attractive when compared with the costs of training and maintaining a national field staff. At the same time, questions arose concerning the comparability of the data obtained by telephone, because changes in mode of interviewing might result in changes in the composition of the sample as well as direct effects on the quality of responses. In 1979 Groves and Kahn published an exhaustive comparison of the two modes in national surveys, which confirmed the dollar cost advantages of telephone interviewing while providing reassuring evidence that the costs in terms of coverage, response rates, and data quality were acceptably small.

Subsequent research by Groves and Lepkowski (1985) demonstrated that dual-frame, mixed mode designs make it possible to combine the cost advantages of one method (typically, telephone) with the coverage advantages of another (typically, face-to-face). As the difficulties of contacting respondents and persuading them to be interviewed have increased, other mixed mode designs have become more common, for example, "list-assisted" telephone surveys, in which those members of a random-digit dialed (RDD) sample for whom an address can be found are sent a letter in advance (Traugott, Groves, and Lepkowski 1987), or people originally contacted by mail are followed up by telephone and face-to-face contact (e.g., Shettle and Mooney 1999).

It had been supposed that telephone interviewing, which appears to provide greater privacy, might lead people to give more candid responses. Although mode differences in responses to sensitive items are small, they tend to support that hypothesis (e.g., Aquilino 1992; Aquilino and LoSciuto 1990; De Leeuw 1992; Rogers 1976; but see Singer 1980).

Several early studies investigating the effects of mode on reports of undesirable behavior found that self-administration proved even more conducive to such reports than did telephone interviews (Locander, Sudman, and Bradburn 1976; Wiseman 1972). Since then, a large number of experiments have generally shown self-administered paper-and-pencil questionnaires to yield higher rates of reporting for undesirable or threatening behavior than interviewer-administered surveys, though none of these experiments has validated the self-reports (e.g., Hay 1990; Turner, Lessler, and Devore 1992; London and Williams 1990; Smith 1992). Other experiments have demonstrated a similar advantage for computer-assisted self-interviewing (CASI) versus interviewer-administered questionnaires (e.g., Locke et al. 1992; Robinson and West 1992). More recently, Tourangeau et al. (1997) attempted to unconfound interviewer administration and computerization. They found that self-administration, whether by computer or by paper and pencil, had the most consistent positive effect on the reporting of sensitive information and that computerization in itself had no consistent effect on levels of reporting.

The technique of audio computer-assisted self-interviewing (audio-CASI), in which a respondent hears the questions over headphones and enters his or her responses directly into the computer, shows further promise in reducing social desirability effects. Audio-CASI was a logical outgrowth of the early CASI work and was designed to further increase the privacy of the interview by preventing other persons present from knowing which question the respondent is answering. In addition, audio-CASI reduces the literacy requirements of traditional self-administered questionnaires. Turner et al. (1998) embedded an experimental comparison of a paper-and-pencil self-administered questionnaire with audio-CASI for the most sensitive items on the National Survey of Adolescent Males (NSAM). They reported an almost fourfold increase in the number of respondents reporting male-male sexual contact, from 1.5 percent for paper and pencil to 5.5 percent for audio-CASI. Tourangeau and Smith (1996), comparing computer-assisted personal interviewing (CAPI), CASI, and audio-CASI, found that across a wide variety of questions involving sexual behavior and drug use, audio-CASI and CASI generally yielded higher levels of reporting than did CAPI.

With two exceptions, however, none of these experiments has validated the self-reported behavior. Locander, Sudman, and Bradburn (1976) found an advantage for self-administration only with respect to reducing overreporting of socially desirable behavior, and Tourangeau et al. (1997) found that the reporting of abortion—the only behavior for which validation data were available—showed equal and substantial inaccuracy regardless of the method of administration. Clearly, there is need for more validation of these mode effects in future studies.

Survey-based studies of audio-CASI have focused on the increased privacy offered by audio-CASI vis-à-vis other people present in the interview setting and have largely ignored the potentially biasing effect of the voice used in the audio-CASI device. Studies in psychology and communication research, however, suggest that voice may well make a difference. Nass, Moon, and Green (1997), for example, conclude that the tendency to gender stereotype can be triggered by minimal gender cues, such as voice on a computer. Reeves and Nass (1996) posit that the presentation of minimal cues on a computer (such as the words used in a text-based tutoring task) can engender reactions from subjects that resemble those when interacting with people. Their central thesis is that people treat computers as social actors rather than as inanimate tools. If their claims are true, audio-CASI might produce *more,* not less, social desirability bias than text-CASI, because additional social cues are provided to the respondent in the form of the "interviewer's" voice. Recent experiments by Couper, Singer, and Tourangeau (2003) and Tourangeau, Couper, and Steiger (2003) provide no support for this hypothesis, however.

Computerized interviewing, whether by telephone or in person, has permitted much greater tailoring of the interview schedule to the individual respondent and has also changed the skills required of the interviewer. Early face-to-face surveys using complicated questionnaires tended to hire interviewers capable of following complex skip instructions who also possessed interpersonal skills. The shift to computerized interviewing instead put a premium on comfort with computers and reduced the skill required for adapting a questionnaire to a particular respondent. Indeed, computerization permits much greater tailoring than was possible even with a highly skilled staff and also permits the embedding of complex experimental designs into surveys conducted under normal field conditions. At the same time, it also creates a new set of problems having to do with constraints on the way questions can be presented to interviewers on the screen. Recent developments in Web-based surveys promise to increase the individualization of survey instruments even further and to eliminate the interviewer as an intermediary altogether. At the present time, however, both theory and research about the potential effects of these developments on coverage errors, sampling errors, and measurement errors are in their infancy.

Processing and Analysis of Survey Data

In contrast to the research administration model used in clinical trials research, ISR did not develop a group of statisticians who formed an independent analytic core of the organization, as occurred at major nonacademic survey organizations such as Westat and Research Triangle Institute. Statisticians did indeed guide sample design and estimation of sampling variances. However, ISR has historically been a place where social scientists performed the statistical analyses required to describe behaviors and attitudes being studied in the surveys.

From time to time in the history of ISR, innovations in the analysis of data have been spearheaded by ISR researchers. Some came from a group of data-oriented economists who joined the SRC early in its history, believing that direct measurement of humans was a key tool to test important components of microeconomic theory. For example, the existence of highly multivariate surveys and powerful computers led Morgan and Sonquist to develop a sequential method for identifying subgroups of a sample that had large differences in some dependent variable. Their technique—first called Automatic Interaction Detector (AID) and, through the assistance of Andrews and others, subsequently evolving to CHAID and SEARCH—was based on identifying groups associated with maximal *F* or chi-square statistics. This tool was quickly adopted by commercial survey researchers attempting to maximize predictive power in a multivariate model. It is the forerunner of regression trees and a large set of tools that come under the rubric of "data mining."

A related set of developments by Morgan and Sonquist led to the development of Multiple Classification Analysis (MCA), based on ordinary least squares regression methods using dichotomous dummy variables but presenting the effects of predictors as adjusted means of the dependent variable associated with categories of the predictors. This too had attractions for analysts who needed simple statistics to present to their readers, despite the fact that they may reflect complex modeling.

The decade of the 1990s saw many social sciences beginning to address issues of how influences on individual behavior might come from multiple levels of aggregation (i.e., the person, family, neighborhood, work organization, professional organization). Two ISR developments are notable in this regard. Achen and Shively (1995) addressed a key statistical issue faced by political scientists using aggregated data (e.g., voting precinct data)—how models based on such data might be informed by an understanding of influences operating on the individual level (e.g., how education affects voter behavior).

Bryk and Raudenbush (1992) developed a set of tools first motivated by the need to separate out the effects of school, teacher, family, and individual attributes on student performance. Such hierarchical linear models allow the researcher to fit alternative models specifying different ways in which such levels of influences might combine to influence individual behavior. The power of these models has led researchers to attempt the assembly of contextual data (from observations, administrative records, aggregated government statistics) matched to sample survey data. Survey design is thus pointed in the direction of mixed mode data collections at multiple levels.

Statisticians have developed a substantial literature on methods for adjusting data to compensate for unit and item nonresponse. These methods rely on implicit and explicit models that may be related to the underlying assumptions substantive research makes about the relationships of concepts measured in the data. Since most analysis at SRC is done by substantive researchers who prefer to develop their own models, there has been a reluctance to employ many of the adjustment methods to SRC data. SRC sampling statisticians have often provided to project teams weights that compensate for unequal probabilities of selection, unit nonresponse, or population control adjustments (that is, poststratification). Only recently have SRC surveys made compensation for item nonresponse a more widely applied adjustment, notably in surveys that collect large amounts of quantitative economic data.

In this regard, SRC has been slow to make postsurvey adjustment of survey data for unit and item nonresponse a part of SRC survey data. However, SRC researchers have been actively engaged in research on improving nonresponse compensation in surveys. For example, Kalton and his colleagues (see, e.g., Kalton, Lepkowski, and Lin 1985) examined unit nonresponse weights in the federal Income Survey Development Program in the early 1980s. Their work developed weighting and imputation schemes that later were adopted in the Survey of Income and Program Participation.

Little developed model-based procedures for handling missing data in analysis (Little and Rubin 1987). Employing conditional likelihood models and missing data patterns, Little and Rubin's methods have broken new ground in handling missing data in many forms of analysis. More recently, Raghunathan and his colleagues (2001) have developed software for multiple imputation of survey data. Multiple imputation is a method used in surveys to replace item missing values in such a way that the added contributions to variance of the imputation process itself can be estimated. It poses substantial burdens on survey data because it may increase significantly the size of the survey data set that must be analyzed. The IVEware software developed by Raghunathan directly implements multiple imputation using a sequential regression technique. It can be applied to large survey data sets that have mixtures of continuous, count, and categorical data. Furthermore, as noted previously, analysts can also obtain from the same software estimated variances and inferential statistics that account not only for stratified multistage sample design and weights but also for the added contribution to variance that the imputation itself makes.

Conclusion

Survey methodology is a field of inquiry addressing questions about what properties of measurement via surveys lead to useful information about attributes of a population. Like most fields of study, it contains theoretical frameworks (e.g., theorems regarding variance estimation in complex samples, social and communication theories of verbal comprehension) as well as practical operations (e.g., use of incentives to stimulate cooperation, poststratification to stabilize population estimates).

As a field, it has historically chosen to identify weaknesses in survey statistics as a first step and then, with later developments, to seek solutions. Indeed, new students of survey methodology often become disenchanted with its emphasis on weaknesses in survey statistics. However, this self-critical stance is common to all of science. As Russell (1962) notes, "It is characteristic in those matters in which something is known with exceptional accuracy that, in them, every observer admits that he is likely to be wrong, and knows about how much wrong he is likely to be" (65). In an updated version of this idea, Kish (1978, 2) notes, "To err is human, to forgive, divine, but to include errors in your design is statistical."

The evolution of the field has been complicated by two facts. First, necessary ingredients of the field come from multiple traditional disciplines. Second, some of the properties of survey measurement depend on the relationship between the topic of measurement and the population being measured. The ISR, with its diverse research programs, provided rich sets of design, collection, and analysis problems. While early methodological developments were motivated by solving these problems, the need for theoretical frameworks explaining how multiple features of a design together affect the quality of its statistics became clearer over the years. This stimulated the development, in 1992, of the Survey Methodology Program in SRC, combining statisticians, sociologists, psychologists, and computer scientists interested in uniting these various perspectives on survey measurement.

At this writing, it is clear that many of the unsolved measurement problems will not easily yield to solutions through standardized, rigid designs. Flexibility in designs to reduce nonresponse rates, in interviewer behavior to reduce measurement error, and in postsurvey adjustments appears to be a requisite step to improve the quality of survey statistics. Although the basic theorems derived from probability theory still have their role in survey inference, the use of statistical models, which formally incorporate sources of bias and variance, is required to improve estimation in surveys.

Finally, it appears that many of the causes of survey error lie in complicated interactions of human cognition, social norms, and social stratification. Qualitative investigations of ethnic and racial subgroups, for example, reveal how differently these groups may react to designs standardized with the majority population in mind. It is likely, therefore, that survey methodology, although necessarily devoted to the quality of statistical quantities, will retain a qualitative arm, productive of new theoretical insights into the field.

Survey methodology as a field is itself affected by survey practice. The last two decades have led to the unrivaled prominence of the survey as a tool to measure economic indicators, customer satisfaction, public opinion on political and social policy matters, environmental valuation, and a host of other matters. In achieving this central role in many societies, it has also become a commercial industry, but growth in the nonacademic sector has not, in general, been followed by corresponding infrastructure developments in the academic sector. On most campuses, survey methodology is not taught as a focus; rather, surveys are used as a technique of scientific inquiry adjunct to a given discipline. In the traditional disciplinary organization of universities in the United States, survey methodology has had no home. Thus, while there exists a vibrant and growing commercial sector, some of which is investing in methodological research and development, the relative share of this activity in the academic sector has probably shrunk in the last few decades. This stands as a challenge to the scientific orientation of survey methodology toward free dissemination of scientific findings and innovations and to the betterment of the field as a whole. Only recently have degree programs in survey methodology arisen at several universities in the United States and Europe. While currently they exist as fragile newborns, they offer the hope of continued theoretical and practical development to improve the invention of surveys as a tool to understand the human condition.

REFERENCES

Achen, Christopher H., and W. Phillips Shively. 1995. *Cross-level inference.* Chicago: University of Chicago Press.

Alwin, Duane F. 1974. Approaches to the interpretation of relationships in the multitrait-multimethod matrix. In *Sociological methodology 1973–74,* ed. H. L. Costnar 79–105. San Francisco: Jossey-Bass.

———. 1989. Problems in the estimation and interpretation of the reliability of survey data. *Quality and Quantity* 23:277–331.

———. 2003. The reliability of survey measures. Final report to the National Science Foundation, Division of Social and Behavioral Research. Research Grant number 9710403.

Alwin, Duane F., and D. J. Jackson. 1979. Measurement models for response errors in surveys: Issues and applications. In *Sociological Methodology 1980,* ed. K. F. Schuessler. San Francisco: Jossey-Bass.

Alwin, Duane F., and J. A. Krosnick. 1985. The measurement of values in surveys: A comparison of ratings and rankings. *Public Opinion Quarterly* 49:535–52.

Andrews, F. M. 1984. Construct validity and error components of survey measures: A structural modeling approach. *Public Opinion Quarterly* 48:409–42.

Andrews, F. M., and A. R. Herzog. 1986. The quality of survey data as related to age of respondent. *Journal of the American Statistical Association* 81:403–10.

Aquilino, W. S. 1992. Telephone versus face-to-face interviewing for household drug use surveys. *International Journal of the Addictions* 27:71–91.

Aquilino, W. S., and L. LoSciuto. 1990. Effects of interview mode on self-reported drug use. *Public Opinion Quarterly* 54:362–95.

Belli, Robert, and James M. Lepkowski. 1995. Behavior of survey actors and the accuracy of response. Paper presented at the annual meeting of the American Association for Public Opinion Research, Ft. Lauderdale, FL, May.

Bishop, George. 1999. Response order effects and question order effects: Is there any relationship between them? Paper presented at the annual meeting of the American Association for Public Opinion Research, Ft. Lauderdale, FL, May.

Bradburn, Norman M., Seymour Sudman, and Associates. 1979. *Improving interview method and questionnaire design.* San Francisco: Jossey-Bass.

Brunner, G. A., and S. J. Carroll. 1969. The effect of prior notification on the refusal rate in fixed address surveys. *Journal of Marketing Research* 9:42–44.

Bryk, Anthony S., and Stephen W. Raudenbush. 1992. *Hierarchical linear models.* Newbury Park, CA: Sage.

Cannell, Charles F., and Robert L. Kahn. 1968. Interviewing. In *Handbook of social psychology,* ed. G. Lindzey and E. Aronson, 2d ed. Reading, MA: Addison-Wesley.

Cannell, Charles F., Sally A. Lawson, and Doris L. Hausser. 1975. *A technique for evaluating interviewer performance.* Ann Arbor, MI: Survey Research Center.

Cannell, Charles F., Peter V. Miller, and Lois Oksenberg. 1981. Research on interviewing techniques. In *Sociological methodology,* 12:389–437, ed. S. Leinhardt. San Francisco: Jossey-Bass.

Cannell, Charles F., Lois Oksenberg, and Jean M. Converse. 1977. Striving for response accuracy: Experiments in new interviewing techniques. *Journal of Marketing Research* 14:306–15.

———. 1979. *Experiments in interviewing techniques.* Ann Arbor, MI: Survey Research Center.

Cantril, Hadley. 1944. *Gauging public opinion.* Princeton: Princeton University Press.

Church, Allan H. 1993. Estimating the effect of incentives on mail survey response rates: A meta analysis. *Public Opinion Quarterly* 57:62–79.

Converse, Jean M. 1987. *Survey research in the United States: Roots and emergence, 1890–1960.* Berkeley: University of California Press.

Converse, P. E. 1970. Attitudes and non-attitudes: Continuation of a dialogue. In *The quantitative analysis of social problems,* ed. E. R. Tufte. Reading, MA: Addison-Wesley.

Couper, M. P., R. M. Groves, and A. Spitz. 1989. Evaluation of post-survey noncoverage adjustment for fertility surveys by telephone. Paper presented at the annual meeting of the Population Association of America, Baltimore, April.

Couper, M. P., E. Singer, and R. Tourangeau. 2003. Understanding the effects of Audio-CASI on self-reports of sensitive behavior. *Public Opinion Quarterly* 67:385–95.

De Leeuw, Edith D. 1992. *Data quality in mail, telephone and face-to-face surveys.* Amsterdam: TT-Publikaties.

De Maio, Theresa, Nancy Mathiowetz, Jennifer Rothgeb, Mary Ellen Beach, and Sharon Durant. 1993. Protocol for pretesting demographic surveys at the Census Bureau. Washington DC: U.S. Bureau of the Census.

Deming, W. E. 1944. On errors in surveys. *American Sociological Review* 9 (4): 359–69.

———. 1953. On the distinction between enumerative and analytic surveys. *Journal of the American Statistical Association* 48:224–55.

Dykema, Jennifer, James M. Lepkowski, and Steven Blixt. 1997. The effect of interviewer and respondent behavior on data quality: Analysis of interaction coding in a validation study. In *Survey measurement and process quality,* ed. L. Lyberg et al. New York: Wiley.

Ferber, R., and S. Sudman.1974. Effects of compensation in consumer expenditure studies. *Annals of Economic and Social Measurement* 3 (2): 319–31.

Goodman, Roe, and Leslie Kish. 1950. Controlled selection—A technique in probability sampling. *Journal of the American Statistical Association* 45 (251): 350–72.

Groves, Robert M. 1978. An empirical comparison of two telephone sample designs. *Journal of Marketing Research* 15:622–31.

———. 1979. Actors and questions in telephone and personal interview surveys. *Public Opinion Quarterly* 43:190–205.

Groves, Robert M., Robert B. Cialdini, and Mick P. Couper. 1992. Understanding the decision to participate in a survey. *Public Opinion Quarterly* 56:475–95.

Groves, Robert M., and Mick P. Couper. 1995. Theoretical motivation for post-survey nonresponse adjustment in household surveys. *Journal of Official Statistics* 11 (1): 93–106.

———. 1998. *Nonresponse in household interview surveys.* New York: Wiley.

Groves, Robert M., and Irene Hess. 1975. An algorithm for controlled selection. In *Probability sampling of hospitals and patients,* ed. Irene Hess, Donald C. Riedel, and Thomas B. Fitzpatrick, 2d ed. Ann Arbor, MI: Health Administration Press.

Groves, Robert M., and Robert L. Kahn. 1979. *Surveys by telephone.* New York: Academic Press.

Groves, Robert M., and James M. Lepkowski. 1985. Dual frame, mixed mode survey designs. *Journal of Official Statistics* 1:263–86.

Groves, Robert M., and Lou J. Magilavy. 1986. Measuring and explaining interviewer effects in centralized telephone surveys. *Public Opinion Quarterly* 50:251–66.

Groves, Robert M., and Katherine A. McGonagle. 2001. A theory-guided interviewer training protocol regarding survey participation. *Journal of Official Statistics* 17:249–65.

Groves, Robert M., Eleanor Singer, and Amy Corning. 2000. Leverage-saliency theory of survey participation: Description and an illustration. *Public Opinion Quarterly* 64:299–308.

Groves, Robert M., Douglas Wissoker, L. Greene, D. Montemarano, and M. McNeeley. 2000. *Common influences across household surveys on noncontact nonresponse: Theory and data.* Ann Arbor: University of Michigan. Manuscript.

Hansen, M. H., W. N. Hurwitz, and M. A. Bershad. 1961. Measurement errors in censuses and surveys. *Bulletin of the International Statistical Institute,* 38 (2): 359–74.

Hansen, M. H., W. G. Madow, and J. Tepping. 1983. An evaluation of model-dependent and probability-sampling inferences in sample surveys. *Journal of the American Statistical Association* 78 (384): 776–93.

Hatchett, Shirley, and Howard Schuman. 1975. White respondents and race-of-interviewer effects. *Public Opinion Quarterly* 39:523–28.

Hay, D. A. 1990. Does the method matter on sensitive survey topics? *Survey Methodology* 16:131–36.

Hess, Jennifer, Eleanor Singer, and John Bushery. 1999. Predicting test-retest reliability from behavior coding. *International Journal of Public Opinion Research* 11:346–60.

Hyman, Herbert H. 1991. *Taking society's measure.* New York: Russell Sage.

Hyman, Herbert H., et al. 1954. *Interviewing in social research.* Chicago: University of Chicago Press.

Jabine, Thomas B., Myron Straf, Judith Tanur, and Roger Tourangeau, eds. 1984. *Cognitive aspects of survey methodology: Building a bridge between disciplines.* Washington, DC: National Academy Press.

Johnston, J., and C. Walton. 1995. Reducing response effects for sensitive questions: The computer-assisted self interview with audio. *Social Science Computer Review* 13:304–19.

Jöreskog. K. G. 1978. Structural analysis of covariance and correlation matrices. *Psychometrika* 43:443–77.

Kalton, Graham, James M. Lepkowski, and Ting Kwon Lin. 1985. Compensating for wave nonresponse in the 1979 ISDP Research Panel. Proceedings of the Survey Research Methods Section, American Statistical Association, 372–77.

Kalton, Graham, J. Roberts, and D. Holt. 1980. The effects of offering a middle response option with opinion questions. *Statistician* 29:65–78.

Keyfitz, Nathan. 1951. Sampling with probabilities proportional to size: Adjustment for changes in the probabilities. *Journal of the American Statistical Association* 46:105–9.

Kinsey, S. H., J. S. Thornberry, C. P. Carson, and A. P. Duffer. 1995. Respondent preferences toward audio-CASI and how that affects data quality. Paper presented at the annual meeting of the American Association for Public Opinion Research, Ft. Lauderdale, FL, May.

Kish, L. 1962a. Studies of interviewer variance for attitudinal variables. *Journal of the American Statistical Association* 57:92–115.

———. 1962b. Variances for indexes from complex samples. Proceedings of the Social Statistics Section, American Statistical Association, 190–99.

———. 1965a. Sampling organizations and groups of unequal sizes. *American Sociological Review* 30:564–72.

———. 1965b. *Survey sampling*. New York: Wiley.

———. 1969. Design and estimation for subclasses, comparisons, and analytical statistics. In *New developments in survey sampling*, ed. N. L. Johnson and H. Smith Jr., 416–37. New York: Wiley.

———. 1976. Optima and proxima in linear sample designs. *Journal of the Royal Statistical Society* (Series A) 139:80–95.

———. 1978. Chance, statistics, and statisticians. *Journal of the American Statistical Association* 73 (361): 1–6.

Kish, L., and M. R. Frankel. 1970. Balanced repeated replications for standard errors. *Journal of the American Statistical Association* 65:1071–94.

———. 1974. Inference from complex samples. *Journal of the Royal Statistical Society* (Series B) 36 (1):1–37.

Kish, L., R. M. Groves, and K. Krotki. 1976. Sampling errors for fertility surveys. *Occasional Papers, World Fertility Survey*. London: World Fertility Survey.

Kish, L., and I. Hess. 1958. On noncoverage of sample dwellings. *Journal of the American Statistical Association* 53:509–24.

Krosnick, Jon A., and Duane F. Alwin. 1987. An evaluation of a cognitive theory of response order effects in survey measurement. *Public Opinion Quarterly* 51:201–19.

Krysan, Maria, and Mick P. Couper. 2003. Using virtual and live interviewers to explore race of interviewer effects and features of inter-racial attitudes and interaction. *Social Psychology Quarterly*, forthcoming.

Lazarsfeld, Paul F. 1935. The art of asking why in marketing research. *National Marketing Review* 1:26–38.

———. 1944. The controversy over detailed interviews—An offer for negotiation. *Public Opinion Quarterly* 8:38–60.

Lepkowski, James M., Judy B. Bromberg, and J. Richard Landis. 1981. A program for the analysis of categorical data from complex sample surveys. Proceedings of the Statistical Computing Section, American Statistical Association, 8–15.

Lepkowski, James M., and Robert M. Groves. 1986. A mean squared error model for dual frame, mixed mode survey design. *Journal of the American Statistical Association* 81:930–37.

Lessler, Judith T., and J. M. O'Reilly. 1995. Literacy limitations and solution for self-administered questionnaires to enhance privacy. Seminar on New Directions in Statistical Methodology, Statistical Policy Working Paper 23, U.S. Office of Management and Budget, Part 2, 453–69.

Little, R. J. A., and D. B. Rubin. 1987. *Statistical analysis with missing data.* New York: Wiley.

Locander, William, Seymour Sudman, and Norman B. Bradburn. 1976. An investigation of interview method, threat, and response distortion. *Journal of the American Statistical Association* 71:269–75.

Locke, S. E., H. B. Kowaloff, R. G. Hoff, C. Safran, M. A. Popovsky, D. J. Cotton, D. M. Finkelstein, P. L. Page, and W. V. Slack. 1992. Computer-based interview for screening blood donors for risk of HIV transmission. *Journal of the American Medical Association* 268:1301–5.

London, K., and L. Williams. 1990. A comparison of abortion underreporting in an in-person interview and self-administered questionnaire. Paper presented at the annual meeting of the Population Association of America, Toronto, Canada, May.

Mahalanobis, P. C. 1946. Recent experiments in statistical sampling in the Indian Statistical Institute. *Journal of the Royal Statistical Society* (Series A)109:325–78.

Marquis, Kent H., and Charles F. Cannell. 1969. A study of interviewer-respondent interaction in the urban employment surveys. Ann Arbor: Survey Research Center, University of Michigan.

Miller, Peter V., and Charles F. Cannell. 1977. Communicating measurement objectives in the survey interview. In *Strategies for communication research,* ed. Paul M. Hirsch, Peter V. Miller, and F. Gerald Kline. Beverly Hills: Sage.

Miller, Peter V., and Robert M. Groves. 1985. Matching survey responses to official records: An exploration of validity in victimization reporting. *Public Opinion Quarterly* 49 (3): 366–80.

Nass, C., Y. Moon, and N. Green. 1997. Are computers gender neutral? Gender stereotypic responses to computers with voices. *Journal of Applied Social Psychology* 27:864–76.

Neyman, J. 1934. On the two different aspects of the representative method: The method of stratified sampling and the method of purposive selection. *Journal of the Royal Statistical Society* (Series A) 97:558–625.

Oksenberg, L., L. Coleman, and C. F. Cannell. 1986. Interviewers' voices and refusal rates in telephone surveys. *Public Opinion Quarterly* 50:97–111.

Oksenberg, L., C. F. Cannell, and G. Kalton. 1991. New strategies for pretesting survey questions. *Journal of Official Statistics* 7:349–65.

O'Muircheartaigh, C. A. 1991. Measurement error in surveys: A historical perspective. In *Survey measurement and process quality,* ed. L. Lyberg, P. Biemer, M. Collins, E. de Leeuw, C. Dippo, N. Schwarz, D. Trewin, 1–25. New York: John Wiley Interscience.

O'Reilly, J. M., M. Hubbard, J. T. Lessler, P. B. Biemer, and C. F. Turner. 1994. Audio and video computer assisted self-interviewing. *Journal of Official Statistics* 10:197–214.

Payne, Stanley. 1951. *The art of asking questions.* Princeton: Princeton University Press.

Presser, Stanley, and Johnny Blair. 1994. Survey pretesting: Do different methods produce different results? *Sociological Methodology* 24:73–104.

Presser, Stanley, Jennifer Rothgeb, Mick P. Couper, Judith T. Lessler, Elizabeth A. Martin, Jean Martin, and Eleanor Singer, eds. 2004. *Methods for testing and evaluating survey questionnaires.* New York: Wiley.

Raghunathan, T. E., J. M. Lepkowski, J. Van Hoewyk, and P. Solenberger. 2001. A multivariate technique for multiply imputing missing values using a sequence of regression models. *Survey Methodology* 29:85–95.

Reeves, B., and C. Nass. 1996. *The media equation: How people treat computers, television, and new media like real people and places.* Cambridge: Cambridge University Press.

Robinson, D., and S. Rohde. 1946. Two experiments with an anti-Semitism poll. *Journal of Abnormal and Social Psychology* 41:136–44.

Robinson, R., and R. West. 1992. A comparison of computer and questionnaire methods of history-taking in a genito-urinary clinic. *Psychology and Health* 6:77–84.

Rodgers, W. L., F. M. Andrews, and A. R. Herzog. 1992. Quality of survey measures: A structural modeling approach. *Journal of Official Statistics* 3:251–75.

Rogers, Theresa F. 1976. Interviews by telephone and in person: Quality of responses and field performance. *Public Opinion Quarterly* 40:51–65.

Russell, B. 1962. *The scientific outlook.* New York: W. W. Norton.

Rust, K. F. 1984. Techniques for estimating variances for sample surveys. Ph.D. diss., University of Michigan.

Saris, W. E., and F. M. Andrews. 1991. Evaluation of measurement instruments using a structural modeling approach. In *Measurement errors in surveys,* ed. P. B. Biemer, R. M. Groves, L. E. Lyberg, N. A. Mathiowetz, and S. Sudman, 575–97. New York: Wiley.

Saris, W. E., and A. van Meurs. 1990. *Evaluation of measurement instruments by meta-analysis of multitrait multimethod studies.* Amsterdam: North-Holland.

Scherpenzeel, A. C., and W. E. Saris. 1997. The validity and reliability of survey questions: A meta-analysis of MTMM studies. *Sociological Methods and Research* 25:341–83.

Schober, Michael F., and Frederick G. Conrad. 1997. Does conversational interviewing reduce survey measurement error? *Public Opinion Quarterly* 61:576–602.

Schuman, Howard. 1986. Ordinary questions, survey questions, and policy questions. *Public Opinion Quarterly* 50: 432–42.

Schuman, Howard, and Jean Converse. 1971. Effects of black and white interviewers on black responses in 1968. *Public Opinion Quarterly* 35:44–68.

Schuman, Howard, and Shirley Hatchett. 1974. *Black racial attitudes: Trends and complexities.* Ann Arbor: Institute for Social Research, University of Michigan.

Schuman, Howard, and Graham Kalton. 1985. Survey methods. In *Handbook of social psychology,* ed. Gardner Lindzey and Elliot Aronson, 3d ed., 1:635–97. New York: Random House.

Schuman, Howard, and Stanley Presser. 1981. *Questions and answers in attitude surveys.* New York: Academic Press. Reprint, with a new preface, Thousand Oaks, CA: Sage, 1996.

Schwarz, Norbert, and Seymour Sudman, eds. 1992. *Context effects in social and psychological research.* New York: Springer Verlag.

———. 1994. *Autobiographical memory and the validity of retrospective reports.* New York: Springer Verlag.
Shettle, Carolyn, and Geraldine Mooney. 1999. Monetary incentives in U.S. government surveys. *Journal of Official Statistics* 15:231–50.
Simon, Herbert A. 1957. *Models of man.* New York: Wiley.
Singer, Eleanor. 1980. Telephone interviewing as a black box. National Center for Health Survey Research, *Proceedings,* Third Biennial Conference, Seymour Sudman, ed., 124–27.
———. 2002. The use of incentives to reduce nonresponse in household surveys. In *Survey nonresponse,* ed. R. M. Groves et al. New York: Wiley.
Singer, Eleanor, Martin R. Frankel, and Marc B. Glassman. 1983. The effect of interviewers' characteristics and expectations on response. *Public Opinion Quarterly* 47:68–83.
Singer, Eleanor, John Van Hoewyk, Nancy Gebler, Trivellore Raghunathan, and Katherine McGonagle. 1999. The effects of incentives on response rates in face-to-face and telephone surveys. *Journal of Official Statistics* 15:217–30.
Singer, Eleanor, and Luane Kohnke-Aguirre. 1979. Interviewer expectation effects: A replication and extension. *Public Opinion Quarterly* 43:245–60.
Singer, Eleanor, John Van Hoewyk, and Mary P. Maher. 2000. Experiments with incentives in telephone surveys. *Public Opinion Quarterly* 64:171–88.
Smith, T. W. 1992. Discrepancies between men and women in reporting number of sexual partners. *Social Biology* 39:203–11.
Steeh, Charlotte. 1981. Trends in nonresponse rates, 1952–79. *Public Opinion Quarterly* 45:40–57.
Steeh, Charlotte, Nicole Kirgis, Brian Cannon, and Jeff DeWitt. 1999. Are they as bad as they seem? Nonresponse rates at the end of the twentieth century. Paper presented at the International Conference on Nonresponse, Portland, OR, October.
Stouffer, Sam A., E. A. Suchman, L. C. DeVinney, S. A. Star, and R. M. Williams Jr., eds. 1949. *The American soldier: Adjustment during army life.* Princeton: Princeton University Press.
Suchman, L., and B. Jordan. 1990. Interactional troubles in face-to-face survey interviews. *Journal of the American Statistical Association* 85:232–41.
Sudman, Seymour, and Norman M. Bradburn. 1974. *Response effects in surveys.* Chicago: Aldine.
Sudman, Seymour, Norman M. Bradburn, Ed Blair, and Carol Stocking. 1977. Modest expectations: The effects of interviewers' prior expectations on responses. *Sociological Methods and Research* 6:177–82.
Tourangeau, Roger, Mick P. Couper, and Darby Miller Steiger. 2003. Humanizing self-administered surveys: Experiments on social presence in web and IVR surveys." *Computers in Human Behavior* 1911–24.
Tourangeau, Roger, Kenneth Rasinski, Jared B. Jobe, Tom W. Smith, and W. F. Pratt. 1997. Sources of error in a survey on sexual behavior. *Journal of Official Statistics* 13:341–65.
Tourangeau, Roger, and Tom W. Smith. 1996. Asking sensitive questions: The impact of data collection mode, question format, and question context. *Public Opinion Quarterly* 60:275–304.
———. 1998. Collecting sensitive information with different modes of data collection.

In *Computer assisted survey information collection,* ed. M. P. Couper et al. New York: Wiley.

Traugott, Michael W., and K. Goldstein. 1993. Evaluating dual frame samples and advance letters as a means of increasing response rates. Proceedings of the Survey Research Methods Section, American Statistical Association, 1284–86.

Traugott, Michael W., Robert M. Groves, and James M. Lepkowski. 1987. Using dual frame designs to reduce nonresponse in telephone surveys. *Public Opinion Quarterly* 51:522–39.

Turner, Charles F., and Elissa Krauss. 1978. Fallible indicators of the subjective state of the nation. *American Psychologist* 33:456–70.

Turner, C. F., L. Ku, S. M. Rogers, L. D. Lindberg, J. H. Pleck, and F. L. Sonenstein. 1998. Adolescent sexual behavior, drug use and violence: Increased reporting with computer survey technology. *Science* 280 (May 8): 867–73.

Turner, Charles F., Judith T. Lessler, and J. Devore. 1992. Effects of mode of administration and wording on reporting of drug use. In *Survey measurement of drug use: Methodological studies,* ed. C. F. Turner, J. T. Lessler, and J. D. Gfroerer, USDHHS Pub. No. 92–1929. Rockville, MD: National Institute on Drug Abuse.

Turner, Charles F., and Elizabeth Martin, eds. 1984. *Surveying subjective phenomena.* New York: Russell Sage.

Waksberg, J. 1978. Sampling methods for random digit dialing. *Journal of the American Statistical Association* 73 (361): 40–46.

Weeks, M. F., B. L. Jones, R. E. Folsom, and C. H. Benrud. 1980. Optimal times to contact sample households. *Public Opinion Quarterly* 44 (1): 101–14.

Weeks, M. F., R. A. Kulka, and S. A. Pierson. 1987. Optimal call scheduling for a telephone survey. *Public Opinion Quarterly* 51:540–49.

Wiseman, Frederick. 1972. Methodological bias in public opinion surveys. *Public Opinion Quarterly* 36:105–8.

PART 1

Political Behavior and Systems

William Zimmerman

The chapters in this section illustrate two areas, American national elections and political socialization, where survey research has produced more than a generation of pathbreaking scholarship. The National Election Studies (NES), described by Philip E. Converse and Donald R. Kinder in chapter 3, constitute a remarkable time-series that now extends for more than a half century. Likewise, the political socialization study summarized by M. Kent Jennings in chapter 4 has entailed four waves of systematic surveys extending from 1965 to 1997. These surveys focused initially on high school seniors in 1965 and their parents. Repeated surveys have made it possible to analyze family units and to undertake aggregate-level generational analysis as well as panel analysis of individuals. In both instances, researchers have demonstrated the payoffs of survey research designs that permit the examination of long-term trends for addressing key empirical and normative questions about citizen attitudes and behavior.

Why do Americans vote as they do? Are the beliefs of mass publics sufficiently coherent so that the public can link their preferences with the policies, past and proposed, of political leaders? How stable is public opinion? Is there a rational public? Where do people get their beliefs? Are such views stable over the life course, or does aging or changes in the historical context alter persons' beliefs in systematic ways? Most Americans vote at least occasionally. But, who participates in political life in other ways? Why do relatively few people vote in the United States? Why, when educational level correlates highly with the propensity to vote, has electoral turnout diminished over time, even as educational levels have grown in the United States? As communications technologies have evolved, have mass publics become more subject to elite manipulation by appeals to their baser instincts? As levels of education have increased, has there been an accompanying broadening of that part of the public that is keenly attuned to the disputes among political leaders?

These are key empirical questions of enormous relevance to the normative case for democracy. Are the responses by mass publics to survey questions so scattered as to call in question whether it is appropriate to assert that mass publics have "attitudes?" Were that so, it would undermine the empirical basis for the normative argument that democracy provides citizens with the opportunity to choose leaders whose views will reflect citizen preferences. If the evolution of communications technologies has increased the ability of leaders to mobilize mass opinion by appeals to an expansionist nationalism, or by exclusionary racist or ethnic slogans, this too would constitute an empirically grounded challenge to the normative basis for democracy. Similarly, if party identification constitutes an overwhelming predictor of persons' attitudes and political behavior and if party identification in turn is imbibed with mother's milk, this would call into question assumptions core to classical democratic thought about reasoned choice on the part of voters.

If the public's views are unstable and highly volatile, then worries about the long-term viability of democracy would be justified. If public opinion is highly volatile and readily subject to manipulation by elites, leaders seeking a stable global environment would have to worry more about "making democracy safe for the world" (to borrow the felicitous title of a chapter by Theodore Lowi) rather than urging policies (in the words of a former president of both the United States and the American Political Science Association, Woodrow Wilson) designed to "make the world safe for democracy."

For these and many other major empirical issues about democracy and its long-term prospects, survey research has proved an enormously valuable instrument—the political scientist's telescope, to use the metaphor of this volume. As with other scientific instruments, the survey has evolved over the last sixty years. It has evolved in the sense that as an instrument it has been refined and improved. Specialists have come to have a better appreciation of the place of context in shaping respondents' answers or in understanding the interaction between, for instance, question wording and question order, on the one hand, and respondents' answers, on the other.

Like the telescope, surveys have gone from being a tool for specialists to being a widely diffused and by now conventional means for assessing individual behavior and attitudes. The acquisition of the skills requisite for utilizing surveys as a tool has occurred in large part through the training in statistics, sampling, questionnaire construction, and data analysis that persons from around the world have acquired at the University of Michigan, whether as graduate students in social science degree programs; as visiting scholars attached to the Institute for Social Research's Center for Political Studies (CPS), its Research Center for Group Dynamics, or its Survey Research Center (SRC); or as participants in the summer programs offered by SRC and the Inter-university Consortium for Political and Social Research.

That survey research has become a mainstream tool for social and behavioral scientists, especially but not exclusively political scientists, might be seen as constituting a challenge for something like the NES. I think not. The track record for the last decade is clear. Studies based in whole or in part on NES data have constituted a major fraction of the articles published in the *American Political Science Review* in the last decade, as well as in other prestigious political science and social science journals more broadly.

Moreover, I would argue that the pervasiveness of training in survey research represents an enormous opportunity for survey research in general and for studies of elections and political socialization in particular to generate important new knowledge about how democracies work. There have been developments in the world (as well as trends in the social sciences) that raise the prospect that we are on the cusp of a new era in the advancement of knowledge about electoral studies and political socialization. Both the political socialization project and the NES have focused exclusively on American data, though Converse and Kinder and Jennings in their chapters report on the diffusion of comparable studies, especially to Western Europe, and, in the case of NES, the development of a formal international Comparative Study of Electoral Systems.

The proliferation of free and partly free countries over the last fifteen years has created circumstances such that it may be possible to augment the rich findings of the Michigan electoral and political socialization studies with cross-national studies of countries whose cultures, histories, and institutions differ substantially from those of the United States or even from those of the countries of North America and Western Europe. What Samuel P. Huntington (1991) has called the "Third Wave" of democratization in Latin America, Southern and East Central Europe, and Eurasia holds forth the promise that we can achieve new understandings of the links between institutions and the origins of individual attitudes and political behavior. This development is the political scientist's explosion of a super nova with its concomitant birth of new stars, or, in this instance, new political systems. The instrumentation represented by the substantive and technical knowledge cumulated from over half a century of American national election studies and at least a generation of study of political socialization is our telescope. It provides scholars with the intellectual tools to study newly free and partly free polities and to compare them with relatively stable democracies such as the United States and the states of Western Europe. This in turn offers opportunities to study attitudes and behaviors while institutions emerge and stabilize as well as to compare, for instance, the effects of divergent electoral systems on individual political behavior.

Equally important, the telescope permits an assessment of the "portability" of insights drawn from stable democracies such as the United States. For example, is there a modest role for party identification in states such as Russia, where more than twenty parties—down from more than forty in 1995—competed in the 1999 Duma election? Timothy Colton (2000), drawing on a survey instrument utilizing, inter alia, a module emulating the NES, has argued for the affirmative. Similarly, I have found sharp between-cohort differences in Russians' disposition to the market and democracy (Zimmerman 2002). These are partly explained by age-related differences in opportunity structure, but much of the story turns on an understanding of differences across age groups in the political socialization experiences of Russian citizens.

The work of Ronald Inglehart (1990, 1997; Inglehart, Basañez, and Moreno 1998) has combined the contemporaneous comparison across nations of citizen attitudes and beliefs with efforts to understand cohort changes. Specifically, Inglehart has shown that, across many different nations, people born before World War II tend to have more material concerns—about economic security, for example—while later cohorts, who have had the benefit of greater economic prosperity, focus less on material concerns and more on quality-of-life goals.

In the process of comparing how emerging institutions shape citizen attitudes and behaviors in newly democratizing states, I would expect there to be important feedback for our understanding of the links between institutions and individual political attitudes and behaviors in more stable democracies. In settings where there is greater variance in the institutions, it is far more possible to distinguish between the role of political socialization and institutional and historical context than in settings like the United

States and Great Britain, where the institutions have been fundamentally stable, leaving little or no variance on a potentially major predictor variable. The globalization of democracy and the globalization of survey research (along with the new institutionalism in political science) offer the promise of new insights about political behavior in the United States, the prime exemplars of which for years have been the studies of electoral behavior, described by Converse and Kinder in chapter 3, and of political socialization, as reported by Jennings in chapter 4.

REFERENCES

Colton, Timothy. 2000. *Transitional citizens.* Cambridge, MA: Harvard University Press.

Inglehart, Ronald. 1990. *Culture shift in advanced industrial society.* Princeton: Princeton University Press.

———. 1997. *Modernization and postmodernization: Cultural, economic, and political change in forty-three societies.* Princeton: Princeton University Press.

Inglehart, Ronald, Miguel Basañez, and Alejandro Moreno. 1998. *Human values and beliefs: A cross-cultural sourcebook. Political, religious, sexual, and economic norms in forty-three societies: Findings from the 1990–1993 World Values Survey.* Ann Arbor: University of Michigan Press.

Huntington, Samuel P. 1991. *The Third Wave: Democratization in the Late Twentieth Century.* Norman: University of Oklahoma Press.

Zimmerman, William. 2002. *The Russian people and foreign policy.* Princeton: Princeton University Press.

CHAPTER 3

Voting and Electoral Behavior

Philip E. Converse and Donald R. Kinder

Few complex social problems lend themselves so obviously to investigation by survey research as the "one-person, one-vote" ethic of democratic theory. A properly devised cross-section sample of the enfranchised adult population is a sample of the electorate, active and otherwise. Not only are researchers able to estimate candidate preferences on an appropriate base before Election Day, but they can also explore the policy concerns that diverse citizens bring to the polling booth, thereby grasping some sense of the underlying substantive "mandate" that hoists winners over losers. More profoundly, such surveys can increase our understanding of the short- and long-term dynamics of public opinion in the democratic process.

In this chapter we review the history of ideas that provides the context for the initiation of the series of National Election Studies carried out at the Institute for Social Research (ISR) since 1948. We then focus upon the evolution of that program, including a summary of its intellectual fruits, and give some attention as well to its organizational innovations that have changed the landscape of survey research more generally.

Background

Not surprisingly, sample surveys first came to the attention of the broad public in the fall of 1936, when the most respected straw polls—cumulations of vote preferences invited from anybody interested enough to supply them—predicted an Alfred Landon victory in the presidential election, just before his landslide defeat by Franklin Roosevelt. George

Gallup, an enthusiast for democratic practice already engaged in more solidly based market surveys of the public, had predicted this fiasco months before the election. His own surveys, while underestimating the ultimate margin, at least had predicted a comfortable victory for Roosevelt. This highly visible coup gave the new survey methods instant credibility within the interested public (Converse 1987).

Paul Lazarsfeld from Columbia University, a friend of Gallup, was the first academically based scholar to use new techniques of market surveys for serious empirical studies of voting behavior. Lazarsfeld in his own market research had become fascinated by the choice processes that led diverse consumers to choose one product over its rivals in the marketplace. He was also enthusiastic about what he called a "panel study design," whereby changes in decisions could be monitored by the clever device of reinterviewing the same panel of respondents at multiple points in time while preferences were being crystallized by the flow of relevant advertising and other communications. These ingredients were brought together in a study of the 1940 presidential election carried out by Lazarsfeld and his colleagues in Erie County, Ohio. The first wave of interviews was conducted in April, well before the summer party conventions would choose candidates to compete in the fall campaign and in a period when it still remained unclear whether Roosevelt would seek an unprecedented third term. The point was to establish a baseline before the race had even begun and then watch how citizens progressively weighed campaign information to make their final vote decisions.

The People's Choice (Lazarsfeld, Berelson, and Gaudet 1948), the primary report of the study, was a classic despite some rather unexpected findings. Most notable was the discovery that the April electorate was not sitting with a mental tabula rasa awaiting the nomination of the candidates. Instead, a remarkable fraction of the sample was already clear about which party they would vote for in the fall. Thus the number of voters displaying basic preference changes as the campaign wore on was nearly inadequate for analysis. The investigators made a brilliant adjustment, focusing on what might be thought of as the "social context" of the vote decision. The best predictor of vote choice in the election was a combination of social niches: those in Erie County who were middle class, Protestant, and of rural residence were very likely to have voted Republican. Those who were working class, Catholic, and urban voted Democratic. These demographic groupings largely accounted for the surprising level of voter certitude as early as April of the election year. To the degree that change did occur during the campaign, it showed up mainly among persons who were cross-pressured by a mix of the traits mentioned, such as middle-class Catholics or farm laborers. These cross-pressures produced tardy vote decisions and, significantly, a decreased probability of voting at all. The interest in social context also focused attention on interpersonal influence within face-to-face groups and on a bold hypothesis (the "two-step flow of communications") whereby many of the voters ignored details of campaign exhortations but were acceptant of grosser judgments formed by local "opinion leaders" who did follow rival campaign events in more detail.

The work at Columbia revolutionized the study of political behavior by harnessing the new survey research methods to investigate the "why" of grassroots voting decisions, a marked departure from commercial political pollsters with their brief and frequent surveys to monitor who was leading in horse-race terms. Lazarsfeld, preoccupied by his many roles in keeping his new Bureau of Applied Social Research funded at Columbia as well as by the intrusions of the war mobilization, did not immediately continue his voting work, although he encouraged the National Opinion Research Center, then at the University of Denver, to mount the first academically based national study of a presidential election in 1944. Unfortunately, no full-dress academic report was made of this project.

By 1948, however, Lazarsfeld had raised funding for a second presidential election study, this time in Elmira County, New York. The choice of a community venue rather than a national sample was partly due to the fact that the Columbia group lacked a national-sample field staff. But it was also true that the most exciting hypotheses from the Erie County project had involved the impact of interpersonal influence on citizen vote decisions. The study in Elmira County was designed for intensive investigation of a voting microcosm where intracommunity influences could be monitored and thus was more appropriate than the "atomization" involved in selecting a thousand or two respondents scattered across a far-flung population. The main report of the study, *Voting* (Berelson, Lazarsfeld, and McPhee 1954), soon became a second classic in this growing field.

The 1948 presidential election became famous for another notorious prediction failure. Harry Truman, who advanced to the presidency at Roosevelt's death in 1945, ran for a second term in his own name. The Republicans had made major inroads on the large New Deal majority of Democrats in the 1946 congressional elections and were optimistic about capturing the White House in 1948 after a sixteen-year absence. The commercial polls generally found the Republican aspirant Thomas Dewey to be winning the horse race in their final October interviews, and early returns on election night were so promising that newspaper "extra" editions reached the street proclaiming Dewey the winner. However, in the end Truman retained the presidency by a narrow popular vote margin.

This failure of the polls led to another round of soul-searching about the validity of the survey method. The influential Social Science Research Council established a blue-ribbon committee of social scientists to diagnose the pollsters' problems. As it happened, the new Survey Research Center (SRC) at the University of Michigan had had a small omnibus survey in the field that October, gathering data for a diverse set of clients, and had included a question on voting intentions in the upcoming presidential election. This tiny sample of 610 respondents had showed a narrow Truman victory. Hence money was quickly found by Angus Campbell, director of SRC, to reinterview the October respondents after the election and to assess actual votes and perceptions of why Truman had won (Converse 1987). These data were welcome fodder for the SSRC committee, which came to see the commercial poll misprediction as due mainly to the use of simple quota sampling instead of strict probability sampling procedures on which the SRC and its chief sampling statistician, Leslie Kish, had been insisting. (Other factors important in deeper hindsight included an unusually undecided 1948 electorate and an early termination of commercial polling in the month of October, before a surge favoring Truman.) Whatever the diagnosis, this sequence of events was the seed from which the SRC Political Behavior Program and the progression of NES took root.

The Early Period: 1950–70

The fortuitous 1948 study produced a short report by Campbell and Kahn (1952) entitled *The People Elect a President,* published by ISR. It also produced the funding contacts and intellectual momentum that made possible a full-dress study of the 1952 presidential election. Face-to-face interviews averaging over an hour with a large national sample (2,021 respondents) were taken in the seven weeks before the election, with a briefer interview just after the election covering most of the same respondents. The aim of the follow-up was to collect reports of final votes cast, although the further half-hour interview added considerable information to the data. The study was reported by Campbell, Gurin, and Miller as *The Voter Decides* (1954).

ISR leaders were partial to "programmatic" studies in which various scientifically worthwhile substantive topics would be pursued through multiple intellectually related projects over extended periods of time. This vision fit neatly with the mandated rhythms of national elections, and, although funding uncertainties were ever present, a Political Behavior Program was created within SRC, which over an evolving sequence of structural arrangements has carried out parallel surveys of every biennial national election (i.e., presidential and off-year congressional elections) since 1952, along with a broader portfolio of complementary investigations into American and foreign political life. The 1956 study produced a report of ambitious proportions, profiting from the embryonic time-series to lay out a theoretical paradigm for the analysis of mass behavior in the election setting. This volume, *The American Voter* (Campbell et al. 1960), with diverse subsequent elaborations, came to define what scholars in the United States and abroad have referred to in ensuing decades as the Michigan Model, a primary contribution to a revolution in the discipline of political science and the study of public opinion and political process.

The Intellectual Evolution

The Columbia studies had primarily been in a sociological tradition, although Lazarsfeld's own interests in individual motivation and decision making drew him toward social psychology. As V. O. Key (Key and Munger 1959), the preeminent student of American elections, famously noted in the 1950s, the Columbia work failed to address the primary interests of political scientists because of the stress on demographic groupings as the main causal agents. The frequently conflicting partisan coloration of these groupings was indeed a capital fact. But political scientists also wanted to understand the short-term dynamics that could change control of the White House, gubernatorial mansions, and legislative bodies from election to election. Demographic groupings, which shifted relative proportions at a glacial pace over decades if at all, manifestly could not account for such short-term dynamism.

The 1952 election study was principally in the hands of two social psychologists—Angus Campbell and Gerald Gurin—and Warren E. Miller, who had a degree in political science from Syracuse University but had also trained with Floyd Allport, another noted social psychologist. The study design, while including modules on voting by demographic groups, partitioned the voter's perceptual field into orientations toward (1) political parties; (2) candidates; and (3) issues. It was thought that such complex preference structures would indeed leave room for substantial change in response to the short-term flow of events.

The 1956 study and *The American Voter* laid out a larger structure for research under the label of the "funnel of causality," which located clusters of variables impinging on the vote decision in two dimensions. The first reflected temporal proximity to the final vote. At the distal end was membership in politically relevant demographic groupings, some of which (ethnicity, gender, age, etc.) were clearly ascribed statuses and hence exogenous. At the proximal end would be comparative evaluations of the candidates in the immediate election situation, from which the actual vote choice is nearly tautological. In between are many determinants ranging from long-term ones like basic political ideology or other social values and interest to more topical, shorter-term bases for evaluation. The second dimension was defined by political relevance. Some galvanizing social events, such as a collapse of farm prices, are not intrinsically relevant to partisan politics until they receive some translation in that direction, typically by the publicizing of differences in party postures on the subject. "Translation" brings such influential events within the funnel metaphor; the funnel narrows as the election approaches because distal events have more time to become politicized than more proximal political events that require less translation. *The New American Voter* (Miller and Shanks 1996) is a noteworthy recent statistical actualization of the funnel structure covering presidential elections since 1980.

Of course, the funnel metaphor is no more than a way of organizing our thinking about vote determinants, although it does contain within it the wisdom that correlations between distal states and a given vote are typically much lower than those for more proximal states. But within such a structure, the early studies began to establish an importance hierarchy of determinants. Most important empirically was party identification. Seen as the affective residue of more complicated orientations to the competing parties, this variable is notably more stable in the public over extended periods of time than any other political attitudes or "predispositions" examined before or since. This is the "standing decision" variable that took the Columbia group by surprise in Erie County in 1940.

At the other extreme, issue orientations play a more dilute role than expected. For diverse reasons, direct comparisons are not easily made here with the importance of party as a determinant. In most political systems, political parties are few in number and usually maintain their general identity for decades at a time. But political issues are nearly uncountable, and they drift in and out of public focus in any intermediate term. So there is no reason to expect any single issue, even an extremely galvanizing one, to compete with party identification over any extended time period, although it is much easier to imagine if all possible issues can somehow be kept in view. More profoundly, ideologies can be seen as huge bundles of specific policy postures, including very basic axes of dispute, that have been rationalized in an overarching structure. For the most politically attentive citizens—say one in five or ten—a sense of ideological location is likely to trump party identification, both in its stability and in its impact on political evaluation. For the less attentive (the vast majority in modern electorates), however, the terms of ideological debate have limited currency and party loyalties (if present at all) become the main frame of reference. More specific issues do not disappear from the equation and can at times and at places be fiercely held, especially when group interests are clearly at stake. But they tend to be narrow-bore and often of only sporadic concern (Campbell et al. 1960; Converse 1964; Converse and Pierce 1986).

Other Research Designs

The designs mentioned in the previous section are a few of the signature elements of the Michigan Model, with respect to the study of elections. These alone have prompted large and prolific cottage industries of research around the country and abroad in the intervening forty years, with many probing fingers of elaboration. At the same time, other designs for the analysis of political behavior have been developed for some of these elaborations. We shall summarize a few of the more important ones developed by the Political Behavior Program within ISR.

At an early point, Warren Miller devised a pregnant expansion of the basic election study in order to examine the broader role of elections in political representation. The design begins with a sample of legislative jurisdictions such as congressional districts. Then proper samples of the public are interviewed in each of these constituencies, with emphasis on their policy preferences and voting intentions. Interviews are carried out with at least the representatives elected by these districts and ideally with all candidates, winning and losing, who were competing for the affections of their constituents. These interviews establish the personal policy postures of competing candidates and also the conceptions these elite personages have of the policy sentiments within their districts. The latter can, of course, be compared for accuracy with the actual constituent interviews. The difference in policy congruence between winners and losers and the constituency is a measure of the importance of popular election outcomes in determining legislation. The roll-call voting of winners in the subsequent legislature can be examined as a means of assessing elite responsiveness to public preferences. This basic design was carried out for the U.S. Congress in the 1958 election and produced several classic essay-level reports (e.g., Miller and Stokes 1963). It is, of course, an expensive design. Nonetheless, it has been replicated in a half dozen industrialized democracies of Western Europe, and an ambitious comparative review of results has recently appeared as *Policy Representation in Western Democracies* (Miller et al. 1999).

Another study launched by the Political Behavior Program was designed to assess the intergenerational transmission of political values, by interviewing in 1965 a national sample of high school seniors and independently interviewing their parents. M. Kent Jennings has followed these teenagers with occasional interviews over the past thirty years, as reported in chapter 4. Other very different designs included a Miller-Stokes study of informal political communication and influence among workers in Detroit auto plants in the late 1950s and studies in the late 1960s canvassing official voting records in the precincts where election study respondents lived, as a means of validating the accuracy of their reports of turning out to vote (Clausen 1966; Traugott and Katosh 1979; Katosh and Traugott 1981).

Collectivizing Research Resources

There had been a conviction within SRC from the early 1950s that data from expensive large-scale sample surveys, paid for by public institutions, were public goods. This posture was contrary to earlier assumptions in academe, often very fiercely held, that data collected by a researcher were private intellectual property that could be permanently shielded from second-party scrutiny, apart from portions that the researcher might choose to publish.

As early as 1954 the Political Behavior Program had hosted more than a half dozen summer fellows, making the 1952 election study data available to them along with training in their use. All were Young Turks eager to prod the discipline of political science to join in the burgeoning postwar emphasis on quantitative empirical work in the social sciences. The seminar sparked a flock of publications and created a voracious appetite among a set of highly prolific researchers for more and newer data. Demand for customized election study tabulations mounted steeply from year to year, and by the late 1950s the time drain on program staff to keep outside access not just a principle but a reality was becoming prohibitive.

Warren Miller devised a radical institutional solution. He reasoned that, if he could convince a large enough set of the nation's universities to join in a subscription consortium to underwrite an appropriate Ann Arbor staff, data could be supplied to member institution scholars at cost, without draining from funds granted for other research purposes. There were many mountains to cross to turn such a vision into reality, not the least of which was deanly horror at a request to send some portion of local research funds to a competing university. Miller first tackled the top research universities and, with the help of the strategically placed 1954 summer fellows, who understood firsthand the need for such a mechanism, soon had a short list of prestigious if initially hesitant university subscribers. Subsequent months of personal travel on Miller's part brought the list to several scores of members, including virtually all of the large research universities. The enterprise was then fiscally viable, and the Inter-university Consortium for Political Research (ICPR) was launched in 1962.

As an idea whose time had come, the fledgling organization expanded rapidly in a number of directions. Although data from the growing series of election studies were briefly the heart of the archive of machine-readable data, the scope grew mightily in the first years. Spreading outward through election surveys done elsewhere and through an archiving of county-level vote returns for the United States back to 1830 (later to 1788), an increasing variety of subject matter became available for secondary access, ranging from all sorts of social surveys conducted by the SRC and other sister institutions to major data collections of the federal government, including the public-use samples from the national censuses and data from other sources such as the Justice Department's Crime Victimization Surveys. As the subject matter expanded, it became appropriate in 1974 to broaden the organization's title to the Inter-university Consortium for Political and Social Research.

Consortium functions were also quickly multiplied, most notably with a summer program to train young social scientists, typically late graduate students and beginning faculty from member institutions across the country and abroad, in quantitative research methods not available at their home institutions. In the early period, when such methods had yet to be taught in some departments of social science or history, the fare was rather elementary. However, the summer program continues to thrive into the present, now serving less for remedial study than as a window on the most advanced topics in methods, taught by a visiting faculty of experts from around the country.

In short, ICPSR now has over 320 subscribing North American members, typically but not exclusively individual universities, as well as roughly 200 further memberships scattered across all populated continents abroad, some being generalized memberships for individual countries that service their domestic universities. The archive is the largest repository of social science data in the world, holding 5,450 study titles embracing some 45,000 data files. Access to these data for researchers worldwide is now entirely via the Internet. In the year ending June 2003, some 768,000 uses were recorded. The NES are still the most frequently sought titles, although the General Social Survey (GSS), conducted periodically at NORC; the Panel Study on Income Dynamics at the SRC, with its thirty-year panel observations of family formation and economics; and Inglehart's World Values Study, with comparative surveys in several scores of countries; are very popular as well. On the pedagogical side, over 200 younger scholars had already taken summer training by 1965; in the current period well over 650 scholars are hosted each year.

Summary: The Impact of the Early Period

Developments surrounding the sequence of election studies launched by the Political Behavior Program at ISR have had a dramatically larger impact on the discipline of political science both in the United States and abroad than any other local chain of events elsewhere in the past half century, impinging vitally on the development of theory, methods, and infrastructure. If we hew to more objective indicators, *The American Voter* has been included on any list of even moderate length as among the most influential social science volumes in these decades. Yet it was but one of a long list of publications that were written on the subject of elections by the authors of that publication before 1967. According to the Social Science Citation Index, this broader corpus of Political Behavior Program work published before 1967 was receiving hundreds of citations annually well into the 1980s.

The impact abroad has also been noteworthy. Before 1960, observers such as the Norwegian sociologist Stein Rokkan and his colleague Henry Valen, Jorgen Westerstahl from Sweden, the French historian Georges Dupeux, and David Butler from Oxford had come to Ann Arbor to inspect the U.S. election studies for inspirations worth transplanting to nascent election studies in their own lands. A much larger number of such pilgrims, from a greater variety of countries, visited for shorter periods. Interest was high on all sides in laying the groundwork for comparative cross-national work assessing the effects of differing regimes and political institutions on the workings of democracies. In ensuing years senior members of the Political Behavior Program staff took sabbaticals abroad to help develop election study traditions. Angus Campbell went to Norway; Philip Converse went to France to collaborate with Dupeux, a relationship that much later produced *Political Representation in France* (Converse and Pierce 1986); and Donald Stokes went to England to collaborate on the study that eventuated in *Political Change in Britain* (Butler and Stokes 1969). Converse also went to Brazil with McDonough before 1970; and somewhat thereafter Warren Miller went to both Sweden and the Netherlands for visits that were crucial in the directions that election studies took in both of those countries. Close contacts were also established before 1970 in West Germany with Rudolf Wildenman, Max Kaase, and others.

The early impact in Western Europe is well exemplified in the fact that by the 1970s Stein Rokkan and the French political scientist Jean Blondel, in close consultation with Warren Miller, had taken the lead in creating a European Consortium for Political Research (ECPR) in the Michigan image. The ECPR, for some time now located at the University of Essex, has become a key component of the social science research infrastructure in the European community, with an archive, a vigorous summer training program, and friendly interchange of both faculty and scholars with Ann Arbor.

Organization of the Election Studies after 1970

The year 1970 serves well as a dividing point in this half century history. In the late 1960s, Campbell and Converse moved off to research projects of another stripe, while Stokes proceeded to administrative roles in Ann Arbor and Princeton. The 1968 election study was the last in which any of them played a major role. This did not mean, however, a shrinking staff. Indeed, the rapid expansion of the consortium itself meant major staff growth. Moreover, steady additions to the senior staff were being recruited from the political science faculty at the University of Michigan, from specialties in international relations and comparative politics, thereby diversifying the local definition of "political behavior" beyond election studies.

Despite this diversification, the election studies remained a major core of SRC activities and the focus of Miller's personal efforts. An enormous amount of attention was required simply to keep the election series funded. As early as 1954, when the 1952 study report was completed and Campbell had begun to seek funds for a large 1956 study, Campbell was asked by potential donors: "Why do you want to study this election? You just studied one." Of course, no question could have been more incompatible with the ISR ethic of "programmatic research," but there was nonetheless a severe problem in finding "programmatic funding" to support it. Indeed, each of the major presidential studies from 1952 through 1968 had been financed by a different donor, and by 1970 the pool of untapped funding sources was wearing very thin. As an emergency measure, the 1972 study had to be made into something of an omnibus study, pooling smaller contributions from several sources, including for the first time the National Science Foundation.

The Election Studies as a "National Resource"

In 1977 Warren Miller, supported by various distinguished colleagues around the country, submitted a proposal to NSF for "Long-Term Support for the American National Election Studies," under an arrangement giving control over study content to students of electoral politics around the country, with immediate access to the data guaranteed not only to the collegium of planners in a given year but to all interested parties. The new proposal was arguably the first "big science" in the social sciences, but NSF officials were hardly strangers to the basic structure of the situation requiring such big science. Elsewhere it had long been recognized that where the proper collection of field data had become inordinately expensive—as with large telescopes, cyclotrons, oceanic research vessels, and the like—such facilities could not be erected anew for each successful investigator-initiated proposal. Obviously, a major facility must maintain some particular locus, with the specifications for, and fruits of, its data collection a matter of shared responsibility. NSF therefore must balance off its award of "plum" facilities to particular locations with stringent requirements that research priorities and data collections be broadly shared.

Part of the willingness of the social science directorate at NSF to accept the radical idea of five-year guaranteed funding for election studies stemmed from the great interest it had earlier taken in the development of the consortium as a data-dissemination device. NSF had in fact nurtured this development with several strategically timed research grants, and by

1977 the mechanisms to ensure data sharing on a large scale across the country had already built an excellent track record. So the main challenge was to design the structure for collective supervision of data priorities and collection. NSF sanctified the new conception by formally recognizing the election study sequence at the Center for Political Studies as a "national resource for the social sciences," its first such designation.

The University of Michigan would host the series with the principal investigator, Warren Miller, and his CPS staff. However, a national board of overseers would set long-range priorities for study content and would review annual budgets, staff performance, and the like. Most notably, the board was expected to find ways to identify the relevant "community" as completely as possible and to update it with a system of "stimulus letters" that would review plans and solicit endorsements or contrary suggestions. This pioneering organizational design has since been replicated in one degree or another by the GSS, launched at NORC in 1972, and the Panel Study of Income Dynamics, begun in 1968, as NSF has come to provide multiyear funding for other "national resource" data collections.

The meta-issue throughout, of course, as for any longitudinal studies, is the amount of precious interview time that can be usurped for emerging theoretical or empirical issues, relative to space for "core" items repeated to maintain the continuity of time-series information. This trade-off was already an issue in preparing the 1956 election study in the wake of the 1952 design; and, of course, it has remained one of the toughest problems for the board of overseers, since the diversity of views in the community is large. Sapiro (1999) provides a detailed discussion of this and other basic dilemmas that constantly shadow discussions among the board.

Warren Miller served as sole principal investigator of the NES through 1988. Donald R. Kinder and Steven J. Rosenstone became co–principal investigators in 1990 and 1992 and Rosenstone again in 1994. Virginia Sapiro of the University of Wisconsin joined Rosenstone as principal investigator in 1998, and Kinder and Nancy Burns, also of the University of Michigan and CPS, became co–principal investigators on site in 1999.

The Later Intellectual Evolution of NES

NES keeps a log of printed materials that make major use of NES data. For rather obvious reasons, this list is surely an undercount, as there is no way to monitor use in detail. Nonetheless, the list by mid-1999 contained over three thousand entries covering the preceding fifty years. It includes diverse genres, ranging from semiformal work such as presentations at professional meetings, doctoral dissertations, and memoranda recounting analyses from the numerous pilot studies testing content and instrumentation, all the way to full-length books and articles in professional journals. Most of the items cited are basically political, typically focused on electoral politics; but some address nonpolitical topics such as female employment rates or church attendance, given the many such items for which the NES time-series is unique.

From this description it is clear that NES data are now used by such an enormous diversity of scholars, covering such a huge waterfront of interests, that it is hard to imagine any adequate intellectual summary here. We shall, however, consider a few recurring themes and provide a sampler of the range of intellectual issues being explored.

The Fundamental Time-Series

A supreme attraction of the NES series, of course, is its time depth. While some publications from it focus on a given election or microperiod, the time-series still provides a rich context. But many uses vigorously exploit the time-series character of the collection. Thus there is great interest in secular trends and diagnosis of large-scale dynamics in the voting system.

Especially in the 1970s, much analytic attention was spent assessing whether the fundamentals gauged in *The American Voter* on the basis of two presidential elections held up in subsequent elections. A spate of publications (the most ambitious being *The Changing American Voter* by Nie, Verba, and Petrocik [1976]) argued that two of the main signature elements of the Michigan Model—party identification and issue orientations—had significantly changed roles by the 1960s and 1970s. Reported strength of party identification had begun to decline early in 1964, and for a decade its durability and impact on voting seemed to be ebbing. In the same general period, more galvanizing (and polarizing) political issues than were typical in the 1950s seemed to arise, and there were signs of this growing resonance, especially around issues of race and moral/cultural divides (e.g., abortion), in the survey response. No sooner had the ink dried on these sharply revisionist accounts in the later 1970s, however, than most of the underlying trends began to reverse. Party loyalties started a sharp upward trend again and by the mid-1990s were (by most indicators) at least back to their impact levels of the 1950s and early 1960s (e.g., Bartels 2000). The situation with issue orientations is, as always, vastly more complicated. On the one hand, it seems true that some of the new "cultural" issues are indeed more resonant than those of the 1950s. On the other hand, some of the apparent gain in the 1960s and 1970s may have more to do with question wording than with objective change in the electorate (Sullivan, Piereson, and Marcus 1978).

It now seems clear that the later 1960s and early 1970s constituted abnormal periods politically relative to what came before and after. But this kind of assessment, bearing on the responsiveness of basic electoral parameters to uncommon events, is the kind of learning that only long time-series can reveal.

Expanding the Model of the Vote

Through a series of new research gambits, the basic model of voting has been considerably expanded in the years since the collective NES has operated. Three examples follow.

Candidate-Centered Voting. In the initial developments of the Michigan Model from the original triad of orientations to party, issues, and candidates, candidates had largely receded into the background. There were occasional exceptions, however, and they seemed to converge on the same point: namely, that citizens vote in overwhelming numbers for the presidential candidate they like better (e.g., Stokes 1966; Kelley and Mirer 1974). This unremarkable observation—one hesitates to call it a "finding"—led eventually to a line of inquiry on candidate-centered voting. The central contention here is that presidential candidates are judged partly by the sort of person they seem to be.

In fact, when asked to describe what they like and dislike about a particular president, or an ideal president, Americans refer frequently to aspects of character. Especially prominent are references to two general traits: competence and integrity. Presidential candidates are judged by their intelligence, knowledge, and experience, on the one hand, and by their honesty, decency, and ability to set a moral example, on the other. Such judgments seem consequential, in that voters' assessments of candidates in just these terms substantially determine the choices they make (e.g., Kinder 1986; Markus 1982; Miller, Wattenberg, and Malanchuk 1986; Miller and Shanks 1996; Rahn, Aldrich, and Borgida 1994). Developed first at NES, instrumentation to assess public perceptions of candidate character has become a regular part of election surveys and electoral interpretation around the world (e.g., Bean 1993; Bean and Mughan 1989; Johnston et al. 1992).

Retrospective Voting. Butler and Stokes (1969), in their famous analysis of political change in Britain, argued that "The preeminent means by which the public simplifies the complexities of government action is by shifting its attention from policies to performance" (285). Are economic conditions improving? Is the government corrupt? Is the nation's defense sound? To answer such questions, voters need not master the rival policies the candidates promote; they only need to take stock of how things are going and then credit or blame the incumbent party accordingly. As Fiorina (1981) has elegantly shown, American national elections are, in important part, referenda on the incumbent party's performance in office.

This result leaves open *how* voters assess a government's record. Self-interest is one lively hypothesis: perhaps voters simply examine their own circumstances, supporting candidates and parties who have advanced their interests. A political calculus based on such homespun calculations would greatly reduce the costs of becoming informed about the world of politics. A second possibility is that voters pay attention not so much to their own problems and achievements in reaching political decisions but to problems and achievements of the country—the "sociotropic hypothesis" (Kinder and Kiewiet 1981). Instead of asking the incumbent, "What have you done for me lately?" sociotropic voters ask, "What have you done for the *nation* lately?" Empirically disentangling these two interpretations is not easy (e.g., Kramer 1983; Bartels and Brady 1993), but taken all around, the evidence suggests that voters follow the sociotropic logic more closely than the self-interest logic, responding to changes in general economic conditions more than to changes in their personal economic lives, in the United States and in Western Europe alike (Feldman 1982; Kinder and Kiewiet 1981; Kinder, Adams, and Gronke 1989; Lewis-Beck 1988; Markus 1988).

The sociotropic result might seem to imply that a significant portion of the electorate is sensible, since they rely on information about the economy as a whole rather than judging entirely from their own, perhaps idiosyncratic, experiences. But given that the broader well-being of the nation cannot be safely deduced from firsthand observation, perhaps voters can be bamboozled about the real state of the country. On this score the available evidence is now on balance rather reassuring. That is, the American public's assessment of the national economy tracks changes in real economic conditions quite faithfully (Haller and Norpoth 1994; MacKuen, Erikson, and Stimson 1992; see also chap. 5, this volume).

Third-Party Voting. At the heart of *The American Voter* is party identification, based on the observation that most voters think of themselves as being either Republican or Democrat, and unless deflected from this basic identification by short-term forces–for example, displeasure over their party's performance in office or disapproval of their party's nominee—they act as loyal Democrats or Republicans come Election Day.

There is evidence that fierce pro-con loyalties in the two-party case suffer some modest dilution in highly multiparty systems (for France, see Converse and Pierce 1986). And even for the United States, the original account ignores the occasional intrusion of significant third parties in presidential voting, as with George Wallace in 1968, John Anderson in 1980 and, most notably, Ross Perot in 1992. What prompts Americans to bolt from their normal attachments and support a third party?

The enormous political variety represented by third parties in the United States would seem to frustrate general answers to these questions. Even though politics can make strange bedfellows, what would Wallace, Anderson, and Perot supporters possibly have in common? According to Rosenstone, Behr, and Lazarus (1996), the differences among them turn out to be superficial. Third-party candidates of whatever political persuasion draw primarily on those Americans who have grown disenchanted with the two major parties. Rosenstone and his colleagues conclude that third-party voting in America can be interpreted principally as a sign of major party failure.

Campaigns and Persuasion

In *The People's Choice,* Lazarsfeld, Berelson, and Gaudet (1948) conclude that presidential campaigns are generally ineffective at persuasion. Rather than converting voters from one side to the other, campaigns *reinforce* the early deciders and *activate* the latent predispositions of the initially uncommitted.

Despite dramatic changes over the last half century in politics and society, this conclusion has stood up very well. As large-scale and extravagantly expensive exercises in persuasion, American presidential campaigns leave a great deal to be desired. We know this from panel studies patterned after the original Lazarsfeld design (e.g., Finkel 1993; Markus 1982) and from aggregate forecasting models that accurately predict the outcome of American presidential elections from information available before the campaign gets under way, including the razor-thin result of 2000 (e.g., Rosenstone 1983; Bartels and Zaller 2001; Gelman and King 1993).

Activation and reinforcement are vital political processes, as Lazarsfeld and his colleagues knew. But acknowledging the importance of these and other processes of influence (on agenda setting, priming, and framing, see Kinder 2003), the main and arresting lesson of more than a half century of empirical research on presidential campaigns is failure. Why are presidential campaigns so ineffective at persuasion?

One answer is that the campaign mounted by one side is "neutralized" by the campaign mounted by the other (Lazarsfeld and Merton 1948; Bartels 1992a; Gelman and King 1993). Under current arrangements—electoral competition dominated by two well-established parties and presidential campaigns funded primarily by public sources—both sides assemble roughly equally capable teams of roughly equal experience and intelligence, who set about spending roughly the same (large) amount of money in roughly the same ways.

Another answer is that presidential campaigns run up against the most basic and enduring of the voters' political predispositions: party identification. For many strong partisans, the details brought forward by any particular campaign merely bolster their enduring sense of political superiority (Bartels 1993, 2000; Campbell et al. 1960; Converse 1966).

And if strong partisans are essentially unmovable because they are so deeply committed, other potential voters are difficult to persuade because they are not paying attention. In the midst of analyzing the flood of political propaganda unleashed by the 1940 presidential campaign, Lazarsfeld, Berelson, and Gaudet (1948, 121) noticed that, far from being drowned in information, most voters "did not even get their feet wet." Lazarsfeld and his associates were referring to presidential campaigns, but their point is a very general one. A major obstacle to persuasion is a habitually inattentive and often distracted audience (Converse 1975).

Finally, if little persuasion usually occurs in the fall presidential campaign season, we should not conclude that other kinds of campaigns necessarily fail. A clear case to the contrary is provided by the sequence of primaries and open caucuses that select our presidential nominees. This current system produces more persuasion first of all because the competition takes place within parties, largely nullifying party attachments. Second, candidates vary in the recognition and resources they command at the start of the process. Finally, and perhaps most significantly, the selection process takes place over time, in a tightly bunched sequence of contests, inviting contamination of later outcomes by earlier ones.

To study such dynamics requires specialized designs. In 1984, NES was structured to monitor the electorate over the entire course of the presidential campaign. This "Rolling Cross-Section" consisted of forty-six independent weekly cross sections, beginning in early January before the formal campaign and ending only in mid-December. Relying primarily upon these data, Bartels (1988) provides an eye-opening analysis of the complex dynamics of presidential nomination politics. In *Presidential Primaries and the Dynamics of Public Choice,* Bartels demonstrates that variation in the outcome of these primaries can be explained by the interplay among (1) differences in voters' political predispositions, which vary from one state to the next; (2) differences in voters' expectations, shaped by short-term fluctuations in electoral fortunes; and (3) differences in voters' uncertainties, which generally diminish over the course of the campaign. To assess the impact of progressive primaries, Bartels compares what actually happened in particular years with a simulation of a one-day national primary, assuming that uncertainty about the candidates and expectations regarding their relative chances would take the values prevailing on the eve of the first primary. This comparison yields stunning results. For example, in 1976, absent the primary campaign, Carter would have been a far weaker candidate; George Wallace would probably have benefited from Carter's decline; and the Democratic convention of that year would probably have had real work to do. Thus primary campaigns can matter, and in a big way. Especially consequential are early and unanticipated outcomes—surprising victories or defeats—that change voters' expectations and, in turn, alter their choices.

Public Opinion

Most Americans glance at the political world bewildered by ideological concepts, without a consistent outlook on public policy, holding real opinions on a limited set of issues, and knowing precious little. So it was in the Eisenhower years (Converse 1964), and so, by and large, it remains today (Kinder 1998). Conceding that ideological abstractions lie beyond what most Americans can or care to manage, and that on any particular matter of political contention not everyone will have a genuine opinion, how can we explain the real opinions that citizens do express?

Group Centrism. One possibility is the group centrism hypothesis: that ordinary Americans organize their opinions around visible social groupings, simplifying complex questions of public policy by turning them into judgments on the deservingness of the social groups who are the policy's apparent beneficiaries. The evidence available for this suggestion was fragmentary twenty-five years ago (Converse 1964); now it seems overwhelming. Research in this vein has turned away from systems of beliefs to take up discrete opinions on specific topics, such as poverty and economic inequality (Bobo and Kluegel 1993; Gilens 1999); U.S. relations with the former Soviet Union (Bartels 1992b); and affirmative action (Kinder and Sanders 1996). In each of these particular domains, public opinion seems rather sturdy. On the one hand, such findings suggest a structure and intelligibility to public opinion perhaps somewhat greater than the analysis of belief systems implied; on the other hand, at least some of the ideas and sentiments providing this structure—racial prejudice, ethnocentrism, indifference to the poor—are not exactly democratically inspiring. In this respect, group centrism carries a decidedly mixed message.

Matters of Principle. To Alexis de Tocqueville, it was "singular stability of certain principles" that defined the essence of American political life (1945). The American people were in constant motion, but the American political mind, Tocqueville thought, remained fixed, committed to a few key ideas. Consistent with Tocqueville's intuition, a considerable and gathering tide of scholarship now shows that public opinion is in important respects rooted in principles. Opinion on particular matters of politics appears to be, in part, a reflection of differences over more general matters: the sanctity of work and effort, the importance of equality, or the proper size and scope of government (e.g., Feldman 1988; Feldman and Zaller 1992; Kinder and Sanders 1996; Kinder and Winter 2001; Markus 2001).

Collective Public Opinion. A primary justification for the election study series is to provide periodic assessments of the public's basic political beliefs. Core questions, posed identically at regular intervals to comparable samples, make research on political change possible. Indeed, NES has protected core questions scrupulously enough over a long enough period that research on such change is not only possible but almost irresistible. The subject here is collective public opinion and its fluctuations over time: shifts in support for government policy (Page and Shapiro 1992); alterations in national priorities (Hibbs 1979; Iyengar and Kinder 1987); changes in assessments of national economic conditions (MacKuen, Erikson, and Stimson 1992); swings in national mood (Stimson 1999); fluctuations in partisanship (MacKuen, Erikson, and Stimson 1989); and oscillations in election outcomes (Kramer 1971; Rosenstone 1983). These investigations produce one result in common: on all these matters, the public as a whole appears to behave as if it were well informed and quite sensible. The analysis of aggregate public opinion suggests that the limitations of individual citizens tend to cancel rather than multiply when put together into the public as a whole (see chap. 5, this volume). Across these diverse investigations, opinion and choice in the aggregate emerge as responsive to broad changes in society, economics, and politics. From this vantage point, public opinion looks sensible, well informed, and perhaps even, as Page and Shapiro (1992) would have it, rational.

Recent work on public opinion in the aggregate is an entirely welcome development, not least for the leverage it provides on enduring questions of democratic responsiveness and political representation (Stimson, MacKuen, and Erikson 1995). But what we make of the rational public hinges on how this rationality is understood to have come about. A major source of this transformation of uninformed and disinterested citizens into an informed and sensible public is simply statistical aggregation, in the course of which the errors and confusions of inattentive individuals cancel one another out. This "magic of aggregation" does not require special institutional design or particular cultural values (Converse 1990).

But the error and confusion suffered by ordinary citizens is not always random; sometimes it is systematic, structured by deliberate programs of misinformation, cynical television advertisements, appeals to racism, and the like. There is no a priori reason to expect that such systematic forces on opinion will neatly cancel out (Bartels 1996). Indeed, Page and Shapiro (1992) provide several compelling cases—the fabricated missile gap that may have helped carry Kennedy into the White House, for one—where the public responded sensibly to the information given, but the information was directly misleading. The statistical account for aggregate rationality is also troubling from the perspective of democratic aspirations, for the directional and sensible signal that emerges from aggregation may be determined disproportionately by the handful of citizens who are paying close attention, at least to the particular issue domain involved (Converse 1975, 1990; Stimson 1999).

Political Participation

Political action usually takes well-defined and well-established forms—a repertoire, in Tilly's (1986) formulation. The contemporary American repertoire includes participating in elections, petitioning government, going out on strike, joining a voluntary association, enlisting in a social movement, or taking to the streets in protest.

That these various forms of action are all included in the same repertoire does not mean that they are all drawn upon equally. On the contrary, some forms—notably, voting for president—are common, while others—boycotting a local business—are rare (Rosenstone and Hansen 1993;

Verba, Schlozman, and Brady 1995). Small numbers of Americans do a lot, larger numbers do nothing, and the rest do one thing or another, depending on timing and circumstance. There is, in short, enormous variation in American participation, and the question is, Why?

Resources and the Price of Participation. Participation in politics is costly. It eats up time and sometimes money; it requires a variety of skills; and it is encouraged by the confidence that taking part will be worthwhile. So if the question is, Who participates in politics? then a good (if partial) answer would seem to be, those who can pay the costs. Political action comes mostly from those citizens who command ample resources: plenty of time, lots of money, training in the skills required for political action, and bold confidence that their efforts will pay off (Verba, Schlozman, and Brady 1995).

One practical implication of the claim that participation is costly and that prospective participants count costs has to do with registration requirements and turnout. In order to vote, Americans must first register. Registration, as Wolfinger and Rosenstone (1980) point out, "is usually more difficult than voting, often involving more obscure information and a longer journey at a less convenient time, to complete a more complicated procedure" (61). Within the United States, registration procedures vary widely (though less now than they did prior to the Voting Rights Acts of 1965 and 1970), and such variation accounts for a substantial share of differences in voter turnout from one jurisdiction to the next (Kelley, Ayers, and Bowen 1967; Nagler 1991; Wolfinger and Rosenstone 1980).

Participation and Mobilization. From the perspective of elites, participation is a resource. That is, public officials and political organizations try to use participation for political advantage. To enhance their chances of winning an election, passing a bill, modifying a ruling, or influencing a policy, officials and organizations attempt to mobilize the public: they sponsor meetings and rallies, circulate petitions, request contributions, instruct citizens about the issues at stake and how and when to act, drive voters to the polls, supply citizens with arguments with which to bombard their representatives, and more (Rosenstone and Hansen 1993).

One extensively researched case of mobilization is the party canvass. During a typical national campaign, representatives of the Democratic and Republican parties contact roughly one out of every four potential voters, talking to them about the candidates and the coming election, and the evidence suggests that they are wise to do so (e.g., Eldersveld 1956; Gosnell 1927; Gerber and Green 2000; Kramer 1970; Rosenstone and Hansen 1993). These results suggest an explanation for the puzzling decline in American turnout over the latter half of the twentieth century (McDonald and Popkin 2001). The decline is puzzling because it coincides with alterations in social structure and registration procedure that together should have substantially increased participation. Over this period, the proportion of Americans having successfully completed a high school diploma almost doubled. In the meantime, the Twenty-fourth Amendment eliminated the poll tax while the Voting Rights Act of 1965 suspended literacy tests. All other things equal, turnout should have increased.

That turnout fell may have to do in part with the transformations that have come to political campaigns. Where mobilization once relied on face-to-face contact between prospective voters and party activists (Gosnell 1937; Wolfinger 1974), mobilization belongs now to "professional campaign consultants, direct mail vendors, and commercial phone banks" (Gerber and Green 2000, 653). As the political parties substituted telephone calls and direct mailings for personal canvassing, more potential voters remained home (Rosenstone and Hansen 1993; Gerber and Green 2000).

Cross-National Coordination

International trade in election studies has led to the recent development of genuinely comparative cross-national studies. Over a quarter of a century ago, Stein Rokkan called for more coordinated cross-national research, recognizing that even creative and opportunistic secondary analysis of independently planned surveys would never be able to provide strictly comparable data resources. In 1994, through the Comparative Study of Electoral Systems (CSES), NES helped to establish a collaborative program for election studies responsive to Rokkan's call.

The overriding purpose of CSES is to provide truly comparable data to assess the interplay between electoral institutions and grass roots political behavior. Toward this end, CSES has begun coordinating the collection of data in more than thirty consolidated and emerging democracies. The data concern institutional arrangements, electoral laws, and survey data on the beliefs and choices of citizens, all provided by indigenous teams of researchers within each nation. CSES offers the opportunity to assess some of the relative consequences due to variation in institutions, all of which in their own way set parameters for various stages of the electoral process and hence reside more or less comfortably within the single grand species of democratic forms.

Summary

This chapter has described an important but tiny sample of the topics addressed with NES data in recent years. With little trouble we could have doubled the length of our chapter without running out of excellent examples: studies of representation that seek to determine the degree to which elected representatives are faithful delegates (e.g., Bartels 1991); studies that examine voting in House elections, where central themes are the advantages of incumbency and the influence of money (e.g., Jacobson 1980); research that marks the return of emotion to theories of public opinion and electoral choice (e.g., Marcus, Neuman, and MacKuen 2000); models of public opinion deriving from current cognitive theory that assumes not well-formed and fixed preferences but rather fluid computations on the fly, developed most elegantly by Zaller (1992); and more.

In these various ways, the program of electoral research begun haphazardly at ISR fifty years ago has broadened into a tradition of systematic measurement that has exceeded the usual bounds of time and space afflicting much social research. The measurements already have exceptional time depth, at least for the United States (and increasingly for most of Western Europe); and the extension of such standardized measurements to a rapidly increasing and culturally diverse set of nations permits, among many other things, the comparative analysis of democratic forms in emergent democracies with their counterparts in the long-established ones. We enter the new millennium with an unprecedented capability for assessing both the microworkings of democratic participation and the impact of popular representation on political decision making.

REFERENCES

Bartels, Larry M. 1988. *Presidential primaries and the dynamics of public choice.* Princeton: Princeton University Press.

———. 1991. Constituency opinion and congressional policy making: The Reagan defense build-up. *American Political Science Review* 85:457–74.

———. 1992a. The impact of electioneering in the United States. In *Electioneering,* ed. David Butler and Austin Ranney, 244–77. New York: Oxford University Press.

———. 1992b. The American public's defense spending preferences in the post–cold war era. *Public Opinion Quarterly* 58:479–508.

———. 1993. Messages received: The political impact of media exposure. *American Political Science Review* 87:267–85.

———. 1996. Uninformed votes: Information effects in presidential elections. *American Journal of Political Science* 40:194–230.

———. 2000. Partisanship and voting behavior, 1952–1996. *American Journal of Political Science* 44:35–50.

Bartels, Larry M., and Henry E. Brady. 1993. The state of quantitative political methodology. In *Political science: The state of the discipline II,* ed. Ada W. Finifter, 121–59. Washington, DC: American Political Science Association.

Bartels, Larry M., and John Zaller. 2001. Presidential vote models: A recount. *PS: Political Science and Politics* 34:9–20.

Bean, Clive. 1993. The electoral influence of party leader images in Australia and New Zealand. *Comparative Political Studies* 26:111–32.

Bean, Clive, and Anthony Mughan. 1989. Leadership effects in parliamentary elections in Australia and Britain. *American Political Science Review* 83:1165–79.

Berelson, Bernard, Paul Lazarsfeld, and W. N. McPhee. 1954. *Voting: A study of opinion formation in a presidential election.* Chicago: University of Chicago Press.

Bobo, Lawrence, and James R. Kleugel. 1993. Opposition to race targeting: Self-interest, stratification ideology, or racial attitudes? *American Sociological Review* 58:443–64.

Butler, David, and Donald Stokes. 1969. *Political change in Britain.* New York: St. Martin's Press.

Campbell, Angus, Philip E. Converse, Warren E. Miller, and Donald E. Stokes. 1960. *The American voter.* New York: Wiley.

Campbell, Angus, Gerald Gurin, and Warren E. Miller. 1954. *The voter decides.* Evanston, IL: Row Peterson.

Campbell, Angus, and Robert Kahn. 1952. *The people elect a president.* Ann Arbor: Survey Research Center, Institute for Social Research, University of Michigan.

Clausen, Aage R. 1966. Response validity: vote report. *Public Opinion Quarterly* 32:588–606.

Converse, Jean M. 1987. *Survey research in the United States.* Berkeley: University of California Press.

Converse, Philip E. 1964. The nature of belief systems in mass publics. In *Ideology and discontent,* ed. D. E. Apter, 206–61. New York: Free Press.

———. 1966. The concept of a normal vote. In *Elections and the political order,* ed. Angus Campbell, Philip E. Converse, Warren E. Miller, and Donald E. Stokes, 9–39. New York: Wiley.

———. 1975. Public opinion and voting behavior. In *Handbook of political science,* ed. Fred I. Greenstein and Nelson W. Polsby, 75–168. Reading, PA: Addison-Wesley.

———. 1990. Popular representation and the distribution of information. In *Information and democratic processes,* ed. John A. Ferejohn and James H. Kuklinski, 369–88. Urbana: University of Illinois Press.

Converse, Philip E., and Roy Pierce. 1986. *Political representation in France.* Cambridge, MA: Belknap Press.

Eldersveld, Samuel J. 1956. Experimental propaganda techniques and voting behavior. *American Political Science Review* 50:154–65.

Feldman, Stanley. 1982. Economic self-interest and political behavior. *American Journal of Political Science* 26:446–66.

———. 1988. Structure and consistency in public opinion: The role of core beliefs and values. *American Journal of Political Science* 32:416–40.

Feldman, Stanley, and John Zaller. 1992. The political culture of ambivalence: Ideological responses to the welfare state. *American Journal of Political Science* 36:268–307.
Finkel, Steven E. 1993. Reexamining the "minimal effects" model in recent presidential campaigns. *Journal of Politics* 55:1–21.
Fiorina, Morris P. 1981. *Retrospective voting in American national elections.* New Haven: Yale University Press.
Gelman, Andrew, and Gary King. 1993. Why are American presidential election campaign polls so variable when votes are so predictable? *British Journal of Political Science* 23:409–51.
Gerber, Alan S., and Donald P. Green. 2000. The effects of personal canvassing, telephone calls, and direct mail on voter turnout: A field experiment. *American Political Science Review* 94:653–64.
Gilens, Martin. 1999. *Why Americans hate welfare.* Chicago: University of Chicago Press.
Gosnell, Howard F. 1927. *Getting-out-the-vote: An experiment in the stimulation of voting.* Chicago: University of Chicago Press.
———. 1937. *Machine politics: Chicago model.* Chicago: University of Chicago Press.
Haller, H. Brandon, and Helmut Norpoth. 1994. Let the good times roll: The economic expectations of U.S. voters. *American Journal of Political Science* 38:625–50.
Hibbs, Douglas A., Jr. 1979. The mass public and macro-economic performance: The dynamics of public opinion toward unemployment and inflation. *American Journal of Political Science* 23:705–31.
Iyengar, Shanto, and Donald Kinder. 1987. *News that matters: Television and American opinion.* Chicago: University of Chicago Press.
Jacobson, Gary C. 1980. *Money in congressional elections.* New Haven: Yale University Press.
Johnston, Richard, Andre Blais, Henry E. Brady, and Jean Crete. 1992. *Letting the people decide: Dynamics of a Canadian election.* Stanford: Stanford University Press.
Katosh, John P., and Michael W. Traugott. 1981. The consequences of validated and self-reported voting measures. *Public Opinion Quarterly* 45:519–35.
Kelley, Stanley, Jr., R. E. Ayers, and W. G. Bowen. 1967. Registration and voting: Putting first things first. *American Political Science Review* 61:359–79.
Kelley, Stanley, Jr., and T. Mirer. 1974. The simple act of voting. *American Political Science Review* 68:572–91.
Key, V. O., Jr., and Frank Munger. 1959. Social determinism and electoral decision: The case of Indiana. In *American voting behavior,* ed. Eugene Burdick and Arthur F. Bradbeck. Glencoe, IL: Free Press.
Kinder, Donald R. 1986. Presidential character revisited. In *Political cognition,* ed. Richard R. Lau and David O. Sears, 233–55. Hillsdale, NJ: Erlbaum.
———. 1998. Opinion and action in the realm of politics. In *The handbook of social psychology,* ed. Daniel T. Gilbert, Susan T. Fiske, and Gardner Lindzey, 4th ed., 2:778–867. Boston: McGraw-Hill.
———. 2003. Communication and politics in the age of information. In *Handbook of political psychology,* ed. David O. Sears, Leonie Huddy, and Robert L. Jervis, 357–93. Oxford: Oxford University Press.
Kinder, Donald R., Gordon S. Adams, and Paul W. Gronke. 1989. Economics and politics in the 1984 American presidential election. *American Journal of Political Science* 33:491–515.

Kinder, Donald R., and D. Roderick Kiewiet. 1981. Sociotropic politics: The American case. *British Journal of Political Science* 11:129–61.

Kinder, Donald R., and Lynn M. Sanders. 1996. *Divided by color: Racial politics and democratic ideals.* Chicago: University of Chicago Press.

Kinder, Donald R., and Nicholas Winter. 2001. Exploring the racial divide. *American Journal of Political Science* 45:439–56.

Kramer, Gerald H. 1970. The effects of precinct-level canvassing on voting behavior. *Public Opinion Quarterly* 34:560–72.

———. 1971. Short term fluctuations in U.S. voting behavior, 1896–1964. *American Political Science Review* 65:131–43.

———. 1983. The ecological fallacy revisited: Aggregate versus individual level findings on economics and elections and sociotropic voting. *American Political Science Review* 77:92–111.

Lazarsfeld, Paul F., Bernard Berelson, and Hazel Gaudet. 1948. *The people's choice.* 2d ed. New York: Columbia University Press.

Lazarsfeld, Paul F., and Robert K. Merton. 1948. Mass communication, popular taste, and organized social action. In *The communication of ideas,* ed. L. Bryson, 95–118. New York: Harper.

Lewis-Beck, Michael S. 1988. *Economics and elections: The major Western democracies.* Ann Arbor: University of Michigan Press.

MacKuen, Michael, Robert S. Erikson, and James A. Stimson. 1989. Macropartisanship. *American Political Science Review* 83:1125–42.

———. 1992. Peasants or bankers? The American electorate and the U.S. economy. *American Political Science Review* 86:597–611.

Marcus, George, W. Russell Neuman, and Michael MacKuen. 2000. *Affective intelligence and political judgment.* Chicago: University of Chicago Press.

Markus, Gregory B. 1982. Political attitudes during an election year: A report of the 1980 NES panel study. *American Political Science Review* 76:538–60.

———. 1988. The impact of personal and national economic conditions in the presidential vote: A pooled cross-sectional analysis. *American Journal of Political Science* 32:137–54.

———. 2001. American individualism reconsidered. In *Citizens and politics,* ed. James Kuklinski, 401–32. Cambridge: Cambridge University Press.

McDonald, M. P., and Samuel L. Popkin. 2001. The myth of the vanishing voter. *American Political Science Review* 95:963–74.

Miller, Arthur H., Martin P. Wattenberg, and Oksana Malanchuk. 1986. Schematic assessments of presidential candidates. *American Political Science Review* 80:522–40.

Miller, Warren E., Roy Pierce, Jacques Thomasson, Richard Herrera, Soren Holmberg, Peter Esaiasson, and Bernhard Wessels. 1999. *Policy representation in Western democracies.* New York: Oxford University Press.

Miller, Warren E., and J. Merrill Shanks. 1996. *The new American voter: Conflict and consensus in American presidential elections.* Cambridge, MA: Harvard University Press.

Miller, Warren E., and Donald E. Stokes. 1963. Constituency influence in Congress. *American Political Science Review* 57:45–56.

Nagler, Jonathan. 1991. The effect of registration laws and education on U.S. voter turnout. *American Political Science Review* 85:1393–1406.

Nie, Norman H., Sidney Verba, and John R. Petrocik. 1976. *The changing American voter.* Cambridge, MA: Harvard University Press.

Page, Benjamin I., and Robert Y. Shapiro. 1992. *The rational public.* Chicago: University of Chicago Press.

Rahn, Wendy M., John H. Aldrich, and Eugene Borgida. 1994. Individual and contextual variations in political candidate appraisal. *American Political Science Review* 88:193–99.

Rosenstone, Steven J. 1983. *Forecasting presidential elections.* New Haven: Yale University Press.

Rosenstone, Steven J., Roy L. Behr, and Edward H. Lazarus. 1996. *Third parties in America: Citizen response to major party failure.* Princeton: Princeton University Press.

Rosenstone, Steven J., and John Mark Hansen. 1993. *Mobilization, participation, and democracy in America.* New York: Macmillan.

Sapiro, Virginia. 1999. Fifty years of the National Election Studies: A case study in the history of "big social science." Paper presented at the annual meeting of the American Political Science Association, August, Atlanta.

Stimson, James A. 1999. *Public opinion in America: Moods, cycles, and swings.* 2d ed. Boulder, CO: Westview.

Stimson, James A., Michael B. MacKuen, and Robert S. Erikson. 1995. Dynamic representation. *American Political Science Review* 89:543–65.

Stokes, D. E. 1966. Some dynamic elements of contests for the presidency. *American Political Science Review* 60:19–28.

Sullivan, John L., J. E. Piereson, and George E. Marcus. 1978. Ideological constraint in the mass public: A methodological critique and some new findings. *American Journal of Political Science* 22:233–49.

Tilly, Charles. 1986. *The contentious French.* Cambridge, MA: Harvard University Press.

Traugott, Michael W., and John P. Katosh. 1979. Response validity in surveys of voting behavior. *Public Opinion Quarterly* 43:359–78.

Verba, Sidney, Kay L. Schlozman, and Henry E. Brady. 1995. *Voice and equality: Civic voluntarism in American politics.* Cambridge, MA: Harvard University Press.

Wolfinger, Raymond E. 1974. *The politics of progress.* Englewood Cliffs, NJ: Prentice-Hall.

Wolfinger, Raymond, and Steven J. Rosenstone. 1980. *Who votes?* New Haven: Yale University Press.

Zaller, John. 1992. *The nature and origin of mass opinion.* Cambridge: Cambridge University Press.

CHAPTER 4

Survey Research and Political Socialization

M. Kent Jennings

Development of the Field

Around the beginning of the twentieth century educators were busy conducting studies of schoolchildren. Such investigations included choices of exemplars, national figures most admired by the children (Greenstein 1965, 128–52). These "surveys" marked the first known empirical study of political socialization, though the practice of political socialization—preparing individuals for their roles in the political world—is as old as political life itself. The precise term apparently made its debut in the first edition of *The Handbook of Social Psychology* (Lipset 1954). However, it was not until Hyman's publication of *Political Socialization* (1959) that the coinage began to gain wide currency. Hyman's book relied very heavily on the extant survey literature of adult political attitudes and behaviors (especially in the area of partisanship) to make informed speculations about the role of preadult learning in shaping later political orientations and in providing a modicum of intergenerational continuity.

Hyman's book coincided with important primary research that helped launch a veritable landslide of inquiry, both in the United States and abroad. Because the general concept of socialization was a well-established one in several disciplines, these inquiries, and later ones as well, could utilize extant theories and substantive knowledge. Unlike much of the previous work, however, the great majority of the political socialization scholarship has been and remains anchored in survey methodology. At the same time, it should be noted that a much thinner, though complementary, strand of research based on different methodologies has also been present. Important examples of exceptions to the dominance of survey research include the informal field studies of children in several countries by Coles (1986) and the semiprojective techniques used by Adelson and his colleagues in studying adolescents in three Western countries (e.g., Adelson and O'Neil 1966).

The first two survey projects to capture the imagination and attention of scholars, especially those in political science, utilized self-administered questionnaires submitted to elementary schoolchildren. Easton and Dennis (1969) and Hess and Torney (1967), working from the same data base of a national, purposive sample of twelve thousand second to eighth graders, authored two books that laid down a foundation for much work to follow. Both volumes emphasized the content and progression of political learning, with Easton and Dennis focusing more on the systemic consequences and Hess and Torney more on individual development. Drawing on a much smaller data base in New Haven, and supplemented by more informal face-to-face interviewing, Greenstein (1965) reached similar conclusions about the content and staging of early political learning. Both projects, by Easton and Dennis and Hess and Torney, emphasized the positive and relatively benign processes and outcomes of political socialization. Children were seen to hold an initially rose-colored view of the political world, inspired in part by benevolent images of the presidency and veneration of patriotic symbols. Although more realistic perceptions and understandings set in with advancing age and cognitive development, the overall effect was viewed as salutary for the successful functioning of the political system as well as the citizenry.

Following in the wake of these pioneering studies came a flood of smaller-scale projects. The initial investigations had utilized primarily white, more or less mainstream subjects. Subsequent studies often aimed at minorities and special populations. These inquiries tended to elaborate upon, modify, and in some instances reject the conclusions of the earlier work. In particular, it was found that various minorities did not necessarily adopt the prevailing views of a benign regime, nor did they necessarily have the political attributes typically associated with the mainstream (e.g., Jaros, Hirsch, and Fleron 1968; Greenberg 1970; Abramson 1972). Other studies, including one dealing with the assassination of President John F. Kennedy (Sigel 1965), looked at the impact of specific events on children's views of the political system. Again, virtually all of these efforts employed survey methods, most commonly self-administered questionnaires.

Political socialization constituted a buzz word within the political science discipline during the 1960s and early 1970s. Conferences and panels abounded, readers were published, and finally came the ultimate sign of status, *The Handbook of Political Socialization* (Renshon 1977). But even as the field was cresting, it was being undermined on several fronts. One reason for this was the dwindling novelty of studying schoolchildren. Political scientists in particular were accustomed to dealing with the "real world" of politics, one where adults ruled. The fascination with preadults began to fade rather quickly.

A second and more immediately relevant source of disenchantment rested in the problematics of using survey methods, especially self-administered forms, on schoolchildren. In addition to all the usual shortcomings associated with self-administration, it was charged that schoolchildren were simply cognitively ill-prepared to address the kinds of topics being presented to them. Critics claimed that misunderstandings of the child's construction of politics were bound to emanate from the use of such methods.

More significantly, and perhaps not unrelated to the methodological qualms, the conclusions of the early studies came under assault from the force of history and, subsequently, further research. A common theme of the pioneering efforts was that the orderliness of the American political system and the perpetuation of the political culture rested in substantial part on successful socialization, in particular the development of diffuse trust in political institutions, the acquisition of civic virtues, and a commitment to the American ethos, however vaguely defined. The early studies of preadults seemed to echo, and in a sense explain, adult America as observed in the 1940s and 1950s. This view of normalcy was rudely interrupted by a series of national tragedies and conflicts during the 1960s and early 1970s, including the assassinations of President Kennedy, Senator Robert Kennedy, and civil rights leader Martin Luther King Jr.; the turmoil surrounding the Vietnam War and the civil rights movement; large-scale riots in several cities; and a flowering of alternative life-styles that challenged traditional thinking.

Thus the image of the cohorts (early baby boomers) as trusting, virtuous elementary schoolchildren was replaced by one characterized by mistrust, defiance, outrage, and occasional violence—in short, the so-called protest generation. In addition, post-Watergate surveys of children showed marked changes (e.g., Dennis and Webster 1975). As compared with same-aged children in the earlier studies, these children were far less trusting of political institutions.

It was argued by some observers that the protesters and their sympathizers were acting on valued American norms acquired in their socialization, including such hallowed norms as freedom of expression, justice, and humanitarianism. Nevertheless, their behavior caused many scholars to question the utility of the early childhood studies and the worth of continued studies. If a cohort could so suddenly deviate from its projected path, it was argued, what was the value of studying children, with their at best nascent political orientations in place? Implicitly, also, the worth of surveying preadults was called into question.

What had once been a bull market became very bearish (Cook 1985; Conover 1991). Ironically, even as fresh research efforts tailed off, the concept of political socialization and the term itself became embedded in a number of subfields, including public opinion, electoral behavior, political culture, and political movements. Political socialization came to be assumed, rather than observed, and was sometimes treated as something captured by what appeared to be persistent adult orientations, presumably originating in preadulthood (Miller and Sears 1986). Nevertheless, empirical research did not disappear completely, and, as the concluding section of this chapter argues, there has been a strong renaissance of research in recent years.

The Michigan Project: Design Elements

A vital link was missing in trying to extrapolate from what was being learned about childhood socialization to the adult world of politics, namely, the late adolescent and early adult years. What kinds of political orientations did late adolescents have as they stood on the brink of political adulthood, and what were the forces shaping their political character? The initial phase of the Michigan political socialization project addressed these questions and stood as a bridge between the early studies and the ongoing work with adult populations, especially as represented by the National Election Studies, then under way at the Survey Research Center (SRC), and culminating in the seminal volume *The American Voter* (Campbell et al. 1960; see also chapter 3, this volume).

In describing what eventually resulted in a long-term, multigenerational investigation, it will be useful to have table 4.1 as a reference point.[1] Shown in the top portion are the key components of the design, organized around the primary sample of high school seniors. Outlined in the bottom half are the three types of analytic units that are made possible by the longitudinal, intergenerational features of the design. Some major results based on these three analytic units will be presented in the next section.

The core of the original study consisted of interviews with a national probability sample of 1,669 twelfth graders from the senior class of 1965, distributed across 97 public and nonpublic schools. Attached to this core were interviews with at least one parent of 1,562 of these seniors and with both parents in 430 instances. Additional data, not shown in table 4.1, consisted of interviews with 317 of the social studies teachers to whom the students had been most exposed in high school, interviews with the prin-

TABLE 4.1. Abbreviated Research Design for National Study of Political Socialization

Primary Sample of High School Seniors				
Survey Year	1965	1973	1982	1997
Age	18	26	35	50
(*N*)	(1,669)	(1,348)	(1,135)	(935)
And Their:				
Parents	x	x	x	
Parent Spouses	x	x	x	
Own Spouses		x	x	x
Own Children				x

Three Analytic Approaches to the Data Sets
(Y = Youth, class of 1965; P = Parent; Sp = Spouse; Ch = Y's Own Child)

Dyadic and Triadic Analysis (Family Units)
A. Contemporaneous P-Y relationships—P65-Y65; P73-Y73; P82-Y82; Y97-Ch97.
B. Lagged P-Y relationships—e.g., P65-Y73, Y82, Y97.
C. Contemporaneous P-Sp and Y-Sp relationships—e.g., P65-Sp65; P82-Sp82; Y73-Sp73; Y97-Sp97.
D. Contemporaneous and lagged triads—e.g., Y82-SP82-P82; Ch97-Y97-Sp97; Y82-Sp82-P65.

Generational Analysis (Aggregate Level)
A. Single generation over time—Y65, 73, 82, 97; P65, 73, 82.
B. Contemporaneous cross-generation comparisons—P65-Y65; P73-Y73; P82-Y82; Y97-Ch97.
C. Lagged cross-generation comparisons—e.g., P65-Y97; Y73-Ch97; P73-Y82-Ch97.

Panel Analysis (Individual Level)
A. Adjacent and nonadjacent waves for Y—i.e., the six pairings built up from 1965, 1973, 1982, and 1997.
B. Same for P, except limited to 1965, 1973, and 1982.

cipals of each school, and self-administered questionnaires completed by all members of each senior class in four-fifths of the schools.

Despite the uniqueness of the 1965 study and its contributions to the understanding of political socialization (Jennings and Niemi 1974), it ultimately constituted a source of frustration when treated as an end in itself. While it provided strong evidence about the nature of the forces contributing to the political makeup of American youth circa the mid-1960s, it could not assess the durability of these orientations in the face of new personal and societal influences.

The pursuit of these and related questions led to the conversion of the original, static inquiry into a longitudinal design. In 1973, 81 percent of the original young adults and 75 percent of the original parents were resurveyed. Data were also collected from spouses. These two-generation panels formed the basis for a dynamic analysis of political attributes, in particular for the young adults, who had aged from eighteen to twenty-six—a critical span in terms of generational theories (Mannheim [1928] 1972).

While generational and historical themes dominated much of the analysis of the 1965 and 1973 panels (Jennings and Niemi 1981), the inexorable aging of both generations led to a third wave that would be especially sensitive to themes of continuities and discontinuities over the life cycle. Subsequently, 68 percent of the original young adults and 57 percent of the original parents were resurveyed, along with their spouses, in 1982. The youths were by then in their mid-thirties, with the angst of young adulthood behind them, while substantial portions of the parent generation, with a mean age of sixty-three, were now entering the retirement years.

The lure of observing the class of 1965 as it reached middle age, plus the potential of creating a three-generational data set, prompted the most recent investigation, in 1997. Remarkably, some 55 percent ($N = 935$) of the original sample was reinterviewed to produce a four-wave, thirty-two-year span panel. Comparisons of panel dropouts with stayers reveal relatively few differences on the variables of interest. Indeed, the 1982 panelists were more representative of the original 1965 sample than were the 1973 panelists. Not surprisingly, however, the four-wave respondents were a shade more politically engaged than were the dropouts. Additional data collection in 1997 included self-administered questionnaires obtained from the spouses ($N = 477$) and the offspring, aged fifteen and above ($N = 778$), of the four-wave panelists. Due to "natural" attrition and incapacitation, no attempts were made to resurvey the original parents, whose mean age would have been seventy-eight.

The timing of the project bears mention because it raises issues of generalizability that the findings may be cohort-centric due to the historical location of the high school class of 1965 (e.g., Sears 1990). For purposes of studying a historically important cohort, the timing of the study was exceedingly fortuitous. For purposes of generalization, it was less so. Lying as it does at the heart of what came to be called the "protest generation," the class of 1965 might well exhibit distributional patterns and developmental trends that set it apart from preceding and succeeding cohorts. Short of having available any prior comparison data sets and only partial replications in subsequent studies, it is technically very difficult to overcome the concern about generalizability. Surely, the distributions of particular measures could, and should, vary across preceding and following cohorts in accordance with changes in the larger environment. On the basis of studies conducted elsewhere and at other times (see subsequent discussion), however, generalizability appears to be warranted with respect to underlying processes and patterns of relationships.

The Michigan Project: Major Conclusions

As noted previously, the lower half of table 4.1 shows the major types of analyses that can be pursued with the rich and rather complex data sets that have been generated by the design. In the following sections, I present some of the highlights emerging from each perspective and how they relate to several themes and issues in the field.

Family Influences as Assessed by Dyads and Triads

One set of findings has challenged a widely accepted model of political socialization, which posited the direct transmission of political orientations from parent to child, mainly via processes of social learning. Although there is virtually always more similarity than dissimilarity between parents and their offspring, the level of congruence tends to run lower than what the conventional view would predict. Using a continuity correlation (r) of .5 as a mark of high congruence, for example, it turns out that most parent-child correlations fall below that criterion. Notwithstanding the strong questioning of the family transmission model generated by the project, the relative influence of parents still looms large compared with other agents such as teachers, curriculum, and peers. Moreover, the transmission model has also proved to be generally more persuasive than a model using family social traits as predictors of offspring political traits (Glass, Bengston, and Durham 1986; Jennings 1984; Niemi and Chapman 1999, 45–56).

The more concrete, visible, and repetitive the orientations in question, the more successful the within-family reproduction. Political objects impregnated with partisan, moral, and religious content stand out in this respect. More abstract, ephemeral, and historically conditioned objects are much less successfully passed on, in part because the parents themselves often exhibit only modest firmness on such attributes. Illustratively, reproduction fidelity runs higher on such measures as party identification and evaluations of party leaders and on such issues as school integration and school prayers than it does on such topics as political trust and the government's role in the economy. Successful transmission generally ranges higher among the more politicized parents and among those who give more consistent political cues. Similarly, the more homogeneous the set of agents acting on the child, as in the case of politically similar versus dissimilar parents, the more predictable are the offspring's orientations. Contrary to past beliefs, the mother's role in intergenerational transmission proves fully as influential as that of the father, if not more so.

Parent-child concordance is at its height just as the child stands ready to leave the family domicile. Congruence of either a contemporaneous or lagged nature recedes in the following years, thus deflating the thesis that latent or "sleeper" effects would bring the young adults into greater alignment with their parents. Testifying to the force of period effects acting on each generation, within-family congruence tends to be highest when assessed contemporaneously. Initial analyses of the new set of parent-child pairs created from the 1997 survey, the erstwhile offspring of 1965 now serving as parents, suggest a continuation of patterns observed for the first set of parent-child pairs.[2] Contrary to expectations based on a weakening of traditional familial structures since the 1950s and 1960s and the emergence of a political culture less explicitly involved with and trusting of political institutions, parent-child concordance in the new set of pairs looks very much like that of the original set (Jennings, Stoker, and Bowers 1999). The very kinds of traits most readily passed on in the earlier era are also those most readily transmitted in the later one. Indeed, on the bellwether trait of party identification, the correlation coefficients for the two sets of parent-child pairs are statistically indistinguishable. And the older "children" in the third generation are somewhat less like their parents than the younger ones, paralleling the lagged results found for the first set of pairs.

The early and intermediate reports regarding transmission provoked further work and some controversy. There have been several replications of the basic design, some of which emphasized the importance of how salient the political orientation was to the socialization agents and perceptual accuracy of those being socialized as key determinants of successful transmission (e.g., Campbell 1980; Tedin 1974; Westholm 1999). A series of partial replications based on national samples in the United States and other countries demonstrated that the findings from the Michigan project were far from unique (e.g., Allerbeck, Jennings, and Rosenmayr 1979; Percheron and Jennings 1981; Niemi and Chapman 1999).

More generally, the study results contributed to subsequent discussions about several key issues in the field. One concerned how the field should be conceptualized, with some writers arguing that distinctions should be made between political learning, civic education, and political socialization (e.g., Conover 1991). Another topic was whether the primacy of early learning with respect to later adult orientations, which was implicit in the political socialization paradigm, was actually justified (e.g., Marsh 1971; Searing, Wright, and Rabinowitz 1976). Issues of design and measurement were also raised, with some questioning the emphasis of the Michigan study on political socialization as a dependent variable (e.g., Weissberg 1976) and others noting that measurement unreliability was contributing to the generally modest to moderate congruence between parent and child appearing in our results (Dalton 1980).

Although used primarily in their roles as parents, the subset of mother-father pairs contained in each survey can also be deployed as husband-wife pairs. Thus an early analysis of parental husband-wife pairs evaluated the distribution of political resources and participation within the marriage and the conditions maximizing the advantage of one spouse compared with the other (Jennings and Niemi 1971). Thanks to the presence of detailed marital histories and panel data for couples in each generation, it became clear that marital partners *tend* to converge over time in terms of political attitudes and participation (Stoker and Jennings 1995; Jennings and Stoker 2000). Similarly, levels of political activity also tend to converge over time, especially for those activities that encourage joint behavior. Reciprocal influences are at work in each case, though with respect to attitudes husbands exert more influence on wives than vice versa, and convergence is more evident if the marriage survives the early years. Convergence on participation is especially likely on activities that put a priority on joint efforts and resources. It is important to note that *any* kind of marital transition, including getting married, works to depress political activity over the short run.

Cross-Generational and Within-Generational Comparisons

As the project metamorphosed into a long-term panel design, the kinds of topics addressed became increasingly germane for other subfields, even though political socialization remained a guiding light. The presence of longitudinal data on two family-linked generations opened up the possibility of observing the development and maintenance of political generations, a much discussed popular and scholarly topic. Despite mainly modest to moderate lineage congruence over time, aggregate congruence between the generations is usually sufficiently high to prevent the appellation of generation gap, all the more remarkable considering that the class of 1965 lies at the heart of the protest generation. Admittedly, the younger generation has been more liberal on social issues and partisanship, but for the most part these are not huge gulfs. It is intriguing that the two generations perceived a much wider gap than in fact existed according to their self-reports. Substantial disparities in political participation and knowledge do emerge, but these could often be explained by life stage developments or peculiarities of the historical periods when each generation came of age (e.g., Jennings 1996). While the younger generation tended to become somewhat more conservative in some respects after the 1973 wave, this movement appears to echo the general drift of American society rather than being a manifestation of aging or life-cycle effects.

The seeming paradox between reasonably high aggregate similarity between the generations coupled with modest lineage (i.e., parent-child) similarity can be resolved in four ways. First, the developing child in complex and transitional societies is exposed to a variety of cues, stimuli, and conditioning effects that are far from uniform; thus the result may be individuals who bear only modest similarity to any particular agent but resemble all in general. Second, as discussed in more detail in the following section, many political orientations are fairly shallow in childhood and adolescence. As such they are subject not only to measurement error but also to factors acting outside the home environment and subsequent to leaving the family domicile. Third, and related, developing children and adolescents must be seen as playing an active, mediating role themselves. The preadult mind is not simply an empty vessel into which the family or other agents can pour political content and expect a uniform product. Finally, both generations in our project have been living through the same historical time. Period effects, while falling more heavily on the younger generation (Beck and Jennings 1991), exert their will on the older one also and helped move the two generations in tandem—nowhere more manifestly so than in growing disenchantment with many politically relevant institutions and groups.

If the gap between the generations has been less dramatic than popular accounts might have us believe, gaps within the class of 1965 have been substantial. As Mannheim ([1928] 1972) noted, differently situated youths may work over the same historical materials in quite different fashions, thus yielding generation units within the same biological generations. The clearest example of this phenomenon in the Michigan project appears in the form of the (mainly) anti–Vietnam War protesters. Given the presence of a panel and repeated measures, one of the great strengths of the project is that it can be utilized in quasi-experimental fashion. Based on the "pretest" of 1965, we established that the eventual college-degree protesters were originally quite similar to college-degree nonprotesters. Subsequent soundings extending as far as the 1997 survey, however, uncovered enduring effects that clearly set off the protesters both behaviorally and attitudinally from other college graduates who did not protest (Jennings 1987, 2002). Protesters remain more liberal and participative throughout the postprotest era. Threads of intergenerational continuity also appear in that the parents and young adult offspring of the protesters are more liberal and participative than are the parents and offspring of the nonprotesters.

Such dramatic personal experiences do not inevitably generate strong political consequences. Although one-half of the young males served during the Vietnam War, their subsequent political attitudes were typically not much different from those who had not served, ceteris paribus (Bachman and Jennings 1975; Jennings and Markus 1977). Three key features distinguish the impact of protesting and military service. First, whereas prior predispositions undoubtedly helped determine who volunteered to become a protester, a majority of the servicemen had been drafted or had volunteered as a preemptive strategy. Hence the initial motivations accompanying the two experiences differed dramatically. Second, the protesters were more socially homogeneous than were the servicemen and responded to their respective experiences in a more homogeneous fashion. Finally, protesting activities tended to be narrowly focused and peaked during a two-year period, whereas military activities not only were quite diverse but were also experienced over a much longer period because men in the sample entered the service at various points throughout the war and were, correspondingly, of different ages when they did so.

Having longitudinal data on hand for two generations has also proved invaluable in assessing the continuity of relationships central to the formation and playing out of political orientations. Of all the predictors associated with political participation and a range of political attitudes, none is more pronounced than that of education. Despite the much higher levels of absolute years of schooling achieved by the class of 1965 than their parents, the role of relative education proves to be quite similar across the two generations, a pattern replicated in a more recent work dedicated to accounting for the rising levels of political tolerance in the American public and the concomitant leveling off or decline of participation (Nie, Junn, and Stehlik-Barry 1996). Thus the educational stratification system, operating through both its pedagogic and credentialing functions, easily transcends the experiential gaps represented by these two generations. Moreover, the stratification sets in well before the attainment of higher education. The availability of the 1965 observations for the younger generation reveals sharp differences according to eventual educational achievements. Higher education is undoubtedly important in helping shape political character, but factors associated with such achievement have already begun to leave their mark well before the actual attainment.

Individual-Level Analysis Based on the Panels

Sorely absent from most socialization inquiries have been repeated measurements of the same individuals over time. Ideally, one would begin these observations before the teenage years. Nevertheless, being able to track eighteen-year-olds as they wend their way through life provides an ideal vehicle for examining individual-level continuity from late adolescence onward. The longitudinal presence of the parental generation supplies a later-stage comparison point.

As noted earlier, a vexing, almost crippling topic attached to the study of political socialization is that of persistence, both in terms of continuity at the individual level and, especially important for political scientists, in terms of continuity of components affecting the operation of the political system. Substantively, as with parent-child transmission patterns, so too with continuity over time: the more concrete, affect-laden, and reinforced the political attributes, the higher the individual-level continuity over time.

Political knowledge and partisan attachments lead the way in this regard, with some long-standing group-related issues also having staying power. It is important to note that these results from the longer-term panels match the patterns generated by the shorter-term panels represented by the two NES panel series during the 1950s and 1970s (Converse and Markus 1979).

Although the two generations displayed similar selectivity in the kinds of traits most highly preserved over time, the shape of the persistence pattern differs in a crucial way. As expected but seldom demonstrated, and in support of the crystallization and immunization models of learning, the stability of orientations at the individual level is universally and substantially higher among parents than among their offspring during the first panel period. Young adults are less stable due in part to the weakly structured nature of many of their preexisting political orientations and also to the new and different perspectives encountered by many of them after leaving home. Parents, by contrast, have had many years in which to become comfortable with their political beliefs and practices and are less likely to be encountering novel situations.

Correspondingly, the younger generation scores very substantial gains in stability during the second panel period, when they age from twenty-six to thirty-five. These gains frequently bring them near or equal to the levels achieved by their parents over the same time span (Jennings and Markus 1984). Those increases remain fairly much in place over the last panel period, as the cohort ages from thirty-five to fifty. As noted earlier, questions have been raised about the cohort-centric nature of the 1965 sample. However, a subsequent replication for a different birth cohort elicited very similar patterns of attitudinal and behavioral strengthening during the mid-twenties to early thirties age range (Jennings 1989).

These findings, coupled with those from studies of more specialized populations as represented by the Bennington College students (Newcomb et al. 1967; Alwin, Cohen, and Newcomb 1991) and the Lewis Terman gifted students project (Sears and Funk 1999), lend considerable support to a combination of the "impressionable years" and lifelong persistence models of political learning. This combination seems especially apt for mid-range political orientations, those more fundamental than transitory political issues and personalities but less central than basic political identities and values. The political importance of this crystallization process lies in the content of what is being crystallized. If the content differs from that for preceding cohorts, then we have the makings of generational, or at least generation unit, differences—as in the case of the student protesters.

Important variations in continuity exist within the younger generation.

It has long been contended, but seldom demonstrated with large-scale or long-term inquiries, that higher education challenges and alters previous political beliefs and practices by exposing students to more novel material and experiences than those encountered by their age peers who have not gone to college. Again, the virtue of the quasi-experimental aspect of the project is apparent. Comparisons of high school only, some college, and college degree or higher members of the class of 1965 do in fact demonstrate an inverse relationship involving educational attainment and continuity between 1965 (prior to any post–high school education) and 1973 (after such attainments), much as traditional theorizing suggests. However, during the second panel period the better educated score large gains in stability, which propel them to levels equal to or surpassing those of the less well educated. Thus the college years are more destabilizing, but once having achieved some solidification of their attitudes, the college-educated hold on to them more determinedly (Jennings 1993).

Similarly, even more striking patterns emerge when looking at those individuals who became politically active most quickly (Jennings and Stoker 1999). Early contact with the political process brings new and additional information not acquired by those who delayed or opted out of political activity. This early contact tended to produce lower stability during the initial panel period. By the second panel period, however, those early engaged individuals achieve remarkable increases in stability, so much so that they surpass the less engaged in stability on virtually all attitudinal measures. This remains true in the third panel stage. Participation itself, then, becomes part of the socialization process.

Stability levels prove useful analytically in other ways as well. One illustration concerns the linkage between subjective social class identification and political involvement. It is primarily among those with stable identifications that the expected advantage in political participation of middle class over working class identifiers emerges (Walsh, Jennings, and Stoker, forthcoming 2004).

Survey Research and Prospects for the Future

Three developments have helped lead to a resurgence of interest in and scholarship about political socialization, even though not always under that explicit heading. One development was the crumbling of the Soviet Union and the appearance of transitional and new democracies around the globe. This has generated numerous surveys emphasizing generational differences and dipping down into the teens for their samples to catch the cohorts coming of age in the postreform era (e.g., Finifter and Mickiewicz 1992). It has also led to studies of efforts by the new regimes to instill in preadults, especially via the educational system, the norms of democracy and marketplace economics (e.g., Slomczynski and Shabad 1998), as well as assessments of basic political norms and their correlates in a number of settings (e.g., Finchilescu and Dawes 1998; Boehnke, Hagen, and Hefler 1998; Macek et al. 1998). Nearly all of these studies rely on survey research as the primary mode of data collection, sometimes in the form of quasi-experimental designs. Deadly outbreaks of ethnic conflicts in the wake of the dissolution of the Soviet-led Eastern bloc, to say nothing of ongoing ones in a number of other sites around the world, have also raised anew the issue of how these hostilities breed and are bred by the political socialization process (e.g., Coles 1987). Thus dramatic events in the political world have provided a natural laboratory for examining the processes and outcomes of political socialization.

A second development, most trumpeted in the United States but said to characterize most Western countries as well, springs from the apparent decline in social capital and civic virtue among upcoming cohorts. Prompted by such markers as lower voting turnout, falling interest in public affairs, and declining civility, a variety of institutions are now turning to the question of education and training of the young, ranging all way from mandatory service learning programs to more opportunities for participation in student affairs, altered curriculums, better teacher training, smaller classroom sizes, more emphasis on morality, and alternatives to the traditional public schools. The American Political Science Association has established a task force on civic education. Books are being devoted to citizenship education (e.g., Ichilov 1990). Assessments dealing with the character and impact of curriculum and school characteristics are appearing (e.g., Niemi and Junn 1998). Surveys based on retrospective reports show that participating in high school government and organizations predicts later real-world political participation (Verba, Schlozman, and Brady 1995, 416–60), a finding congruent with one growing out of the Michigan project based on prospective panel analysis (Beck and Jennings 1982; Jennings and Stoker 2001). The relationship between investments in the social capital of youngsters and their later political and civic behavior is being examined (Smith 1999). Even though the scholarship associated with the concerns about declining civic virtue may fly under various banners, the central concept is political socialization, and the majority of these studies will employ survey methodology.

A third development, and much associated with the first two, is renewed interest in the question of persistence and the dynamics of learning. There would be little interest in the first two topics if some degree or *type* of continuity was not assumed or, from a normative point of view, seen as a desirable goal. Results from the Michigan project as well as other long-term panel studies (Alwin, Cohen, and Newcomb 1991; Sears and Funk 1999) form part of this renewed focus, as do shorter-term studies of children and adolescents (Sears and Valentino 1997; Smith 1999). Other examples include surveys of individuals who have undergone particular kinds of preadult experiences (e.g., Cole, Zucker, and Ostrove 1998) and the generational emphasis found in studies of collective memories (e.g., Schuman, Belli, and Bischoping 1997). Replicated surveys, as represented by such projects as the NES, the General Social Surveys, and the Eurobarometer Surveys, are also important in this respect because they permit the tracing of birth cohorts over extended periods of time. In doing so, they facilitate informed interpretations drawing upon the conditions under which preadult socialization occurred and how these cohorts respond to later developments.

Similarly, the accumulation of longitudinal data based on repeated surveys of special populations—such as those of high school students by the Monitoring the Future project (see chapter 11, this volume) and those of entering college students by the American Council of Education—provides leverage on what the socialization process has rendered up by the time young adulthood is reached. In a related vein, the pooling of youth studies based on large samples permits the tracing of fine-grained, age-graded developments in political orientations in a way typically not possible with single cross-sectional surveys (Watts 1999). In a very real sense, then, the future well-being of political socialization scholarship hinges on the accumulation of longitudinal survey data based on the same individuals or the same populations.

NOTES

1. Funding for the original project came from the Danforth Foundation. Subsequent studies were supported by the Ford Foundation, the National Institutes on Aging, and, most intensively, the NSF. Data files are available from the Inter-university Consortium for Political and Social Research.

2. The third-generation respondents range in age from fifteen to thirty-eight, with a mean age of twenty-three. Consequently, parent-child analysis for this new set of pairs needs to take age into account, unlike the case for the original pairs, where the parents were of variable age but the offspring were of the same age.

REFERENCES

Abramson, Paul. 1972. Political efficacy and political trust among black schoolchildren: Two explanations. *Journal of Politics* 34:1243–75.

Adelson, Joseph, and Robert P. O'Neil. 1966. Growth of political ideas in adolescence: The sense of community. *Journal of Personality and Social Psychology* 4:295–306.

Allerbeck, Klaus, M. Kent Jennings, and Leopold Rosenmayr. 1979. Generations and families: Political action. In *Political action: Mass participation in five Western democracies,* ed. Samuel Barnes, Max Kaase, et al., 487–522. Beverly Hills: Sage.

Alwin, Duane F., Ronald L. Cohen, and Theodore M. Newcomb. 1991. *Political attitudes over the life span: The Bennington women after fifty years.* Madison: University of Wisconsin Press.

Bachman, Jerald G., and M. Kent Jennings. 1975. The impact of Vietnam on trust in government. *Journal of Social Issues* 31:141–55.

Beck, Paul Allen, and M. Kent Jennings. 1982. Pathways to participation. *American Political Science Review* 76:94–108.

———. 1991. Family traditions, political periods, and the development of partisan orientations. *Journal of Politics* 53:742–63.

Boehnke, Klaus, John Hagen, and Gerd Hefler. 1998. On the development of xenophobia in Germany: The adolescent years. *Journal of Social Issues* 54:585–602.

Campbell, Angus, Philip E. Converse, Warren E. Miller, and Donald E. Stokes. 1960. *The American voter.* New York: Wiley.

Campbell, Bruce A. 1980. A theoretical approach to peer influence in adolescent socialization. *American Journal of Political Science* 24:324–44.

Cole, Elizabeth R., Alyssa N. Zucker, and Joan M. Ostrove. 1998. Political participation and feminist consciousness among women activists in the 1960s. *Political Psychology* 19:349–71.

Coles, Robert. 1986. *The political lives of children.* Boston: Houghton Mifflin.

Conover, Pamela. 1991. Political socialization: Where's the politics? In William Crotty, ed., *Political science: Looking to the future,* 3:125–52. Evanston, IL: Northwestern University Press.

Converse, Philip E., and Gregory Markus. 1979. Plus ça change . . . : The new CPS election study panel. *American Political Science Review* 73:32–49.

Cook, Timothy E. 1985. The bear market in political socialization and the costs of misunderstood psychological theories. *American Political Science Review* 79:1079–93.

Dalton, Russell. 1980. Reassessing parental socialization: Indicator unreliability versus generational transfer. *American Political Science Review* 74:421–31.

Dennis, Jack, and Carol Webster. 1975. Children's images of the president, in 1962 and 1974. *American Politics Quarterly* 3:386–405.

Easton, David, and Jack Dennis. 1969. *Children in the political system.* New York: McGraw-Hill.

Finchilescu, Gillian, and Andrew Dawes. 1998. Catapulted into democracy: South African adolescents' sociopolitical orientations following rapid social change. *Journal of Social Issues* 54:563–83.

Finifter, Ada W., and Ellen Mickiewicz. 1992. Redefining the political system in the USSR: Mass support for political change. *American Political Science Review* 86:857–74.

Glass, Jennifer, Vern L. Bengston, and Charlotte Chorn Dunham. 1986. Attitude similarity in three generation families: Socialization, status inheritance, or reciprocal influence? *American Sociological Review* 51:685–98.

Greenberg, Edward. 1970. Children and government: A comparison across racial lines. *Midwest Journal of Political Science* 14:249–75.

Greenstein, Fred I. 1965. *Children and politics.* New Haven: Yale University Press.

Hess, Robert D., and Judith Torney. 1967. *The development of political attitudes in children.* Chicago: Aldine.

Hyman, Herbert. 1959. *Political socialization.* New York: Free Press.

Ichilov, Orit, ed. 1990. *Political socialization, citizenship education, and democracy.* New York: Teachers College Press, Columbia University.

Jaros, Dean, Herbert Hirsch, and Frederic J. Fleron Jr. 1968. The malevolent leader: Political socialization in an American sub-culture. *American Political Science Review* 62:564–75.

Jennings, M. Kent. 1984. The intergenerational transfer of political ideology in eight Western nations. *European Journal of Political Research* 12:261–76.

———. 1987. Residues of a movement: The aging of the American protest generation. *American Political Science Review* 81:367–82.

———. 1989. The crystallization of orientations. In *Continuities in political action,* ed. M. Kent Jennings, Jan van Deth, et al., 313–48. Berlin: de Gruyter.

———. 1993. Education and political development among young adults. *Politics and the Individual* 3:1–24.

———. 1996. Political knowledge over time and across generations. *Public Opinion Quarterly* 60:228–52.

———. 2002. Generation units and the student protest movement in the United States: An intra- and intergenerational analysis. *Political Psychology* 23:303–24.

Jennings, M. Kent, and Gregory B. Markus. 1977. The effects of military service on political attitudes: A panel study. *American Political Science Review* 71:131–47.

———. 1984. Partisan orientations over the long haul: Results from the three-wave Political Socialization Panel Study. *American Political Science Review* 78:1000–1018.

Jennings, M. Kent, and Richard G. Niemi. 1971. The division of political labor between mothers and fathers. *American Political Science Review* 65:69–82.

———. 1974. *The political character of adolescents.* Princeton: Princeton University Press.

———. 1981. *Generations and politics.* Princeton: Princeton University Press.

Jennings, M. Kent, and Laura Stoker. 1995. Life-cycle transitions and political participation: The case of marriage. *American Political Science Review* 89:421–33.

———. 1999. The persistence of the past: The class of 1965 turns 50. Paper presented at the annual meeting of the Midwest Political Science Association, April, Chicago.

———. 2000. Political similarity and influence between husbands and wives. Paper presented at the annual meeting of the American Political Science Association, September, Washington, DC.

———. 2001. Generations and civic engagement: A longitudinal multiple-generation analysis. Paper presented at the annual meeting of the American Political Science Association, September, San Francisco.

Jennings, M. Kent, Laura Stoker, and Jason Bowers. 1999. Politics across generations. Paper presented at the annual meeting of the American Political Science Association, September, Atlanta.

Lipset, Seymour Martin. 1954. The psychology of voting. In *The handbook of social psychology*, ed. Gardner Lindzey, 2:1144–45. Cambridge, MA: Addison-Wesley.

Macek, Petr, Constance Flanagan, Leslie Gallay, Lubomir Kostron, Luba Botcheva, and Reno Csapo. 1998. Postcommunist societies in times of transition: Perceptions of change among adolescents in Central and Eastern Europe. *Journal of Social Issues* 54:547–61.

Mannheim, Karl. [1928] 1972. The problem of generations. In *The new pilgrims*, ed. Philip G. Altbach and Robert S. Laufer, 101–37. Reprint, New York: David Mckay.

Marsh, David. 1971. Political socialization: The implicit assumptions questioned. *British Journal of Political Science* 1:435–65.

Miller, Steven D., and David O. Sears. 1986. Stability and change in social tolerance: A test of the persistence hypothesis. *American Journal of Political Science* 30:214–36.

Newcomb, Theodore, Kathryn Koenig, Richard Flacks, and Donald Warwick. 1967. *Persistence and change: Bennington College and its students after twenty-five years.* New York: Wiley.

Nie, Norman H., Jane Junn, and Kenneth Stehlik-Barry. 1996. *Education and democratic citizenship in America.* Chicago: University of Chicago Press.

Niemi, Richard G., and Chris Chapman. 1999. *The civic development of ninth- through twelfth-grade students in the United States: 1996.* NCES 1999–131. Washington, DC: U.S. Department of Education, National Center for Education Statistics.

Niemi, Richard G., and Jane Junn. 1998. *Civic education: What makes students learn?* New Haven: Yale University Press.

Percheron, Annick, and M. Kent Jennings. 1981. Political continuities in French families: A new perspective on an old controversy. *Comparative Politics* 13:421–36.

Renshon, Stanley, ed. 1977. *The handbook of political socialization.* New York: Free Press.

Schuman, Howard, Robert F. Belli, and Katherine Bischoping. 1997. The generational basis of historical knowledge. In *Collective memory of political events: Social psychological perspectives*, ed. J. W. Pennebaker, D. Paez, and B. Rime, 47–77. Hillsdale, NJ: Erlbaum.

Searing, Donald D., Gerald Wright, and George Rabinowitz. 1976. The primacy principle: Political socialization and belief systems. *British Journal of Politics* 6:83–113.

Sears, David O. 1990. Whither political socialization research? The question of persistence. In *Political socialization, citizenship education, and democracy*, ed. Orit Ichilov, 69–97. New York: Teachers College Press, Columbia University.

Sears, David O., and Carolyn Funk. 1999. Evidence of the long-term persistence of adults' political predispositions. *Journal of Politics* 61:1–28.

Sears, David O., and Nicholas A. Valentino. 1997. Politics matters: Political events as catalysts for preadult socialization. *American Political Science Review* 91:45–65.

Sigel, Roberta S. 1965. An exploration into some aspects of political socialization: School children's reactions to the death of a president. In *Children and the death of a president: Multidisciplinary studies*, ed. Martha Wolfenstein and Gilbert Kliman, 30–61. New York: Doubleday.

Slomczynski, Kazimierz, and Goldie Shabad. 1998. Can support for democracy and the market be learned in school? A natural experiment in post-communist Poland. *Political Psychology* 19:749–79.

Smith, Elizabeth. 1999. The effects of investments in the social capital of youth on political and civic behavior in young adulthood. *Political Psychology* 20:553–80.

Stoker, Laura, and M. Kent Jennings. 1995. Life-cycle transitions and political participation: The case of marriage. *American Political Science Review* 89:421–36.

Tedin, Kent L. 1974. The influence of parents on the political attitudes of adolescents. *American Political Science Review* 68:1579–92.

Verba, Sidney, Kay Lehman Schlozman, and Henry E. Brady. 1995. *Voice and equality.* Cambridge, MA: Harvard University Press.

Walsh, Kath Cramer, M. Kent Jennings, and Laura Stoker. 2004. The effects of social class identification on participatory orientations toward government. *British Journal of Political Science* (forthcoming).

Watts, Meredith. 1999. Are there typical age curves in political behavior? The "age invariance" hypothesis and political socialization. *Political Psychology* 20:477–500.

Weissberg, Robert. 1976. The politics of political socialization. *Youth and Society* 8:117–46.

Westholm, Anders. 1999. The perceptual pathway: Tracing the mechanisms of political value transfer across generations. *Political Psychology* 20:525–52.

PART 2

The Behavioral Study of Economics

F. Thomas Juster

The Survey Research Center's (SRC's) Economic Behavior Program (EBP) represents a unique set of research activities for academic economists. The program's most distinguishing features are, first, the strongly held perception that the measurement of economic behavior, as well as of variables that might influence behavior, is critical to making real progress in improving our understanding of economic processes and outcomes and, second, that multidisciplinary insights are essential to scientific progress. These perceptions are in sharp contrast to the traditional view among academic economists—that the development of theoretical structure and sophisticated econometric models are the key factors in determining the rate of scientific progress and that the administrative data bases produced by government statistical agencies provide a satisfactory empirical base for testing and improving theories and models. The idea that designing and collecting empirical data should be a major concern of academic economists would not find much support among academics in the 1940s and 1950s, although there is some evidence to suggest that this attitude has been changing during recent years—perhaps rapidly.

Studies of economic behavior can be accurately described as the core program when the SRC was formed at the University of Michigan in 1946. The SRC's founding fathers comprised a group of researchers at the Division of Program Surveys in the U.S. Department of Agriculture, headed by Rensis Likert. In 1944, Likert and his colleagues approached the board of governors of the Federal Reserve System to ascertain their interest in supporting a financial survey of consumers. Consumers had accumulated a substantial amount of savings bonds during World War II, and the question was whether consumers were planning to cash in those bonds to purchase goods and services or to retain them as a source of economic security. What consumers chose to do would make a very substantial difference in the types of stresses faced by the economic system during the transition from a wartime to a peacetime economy. The board agreed to carry out a large pilot study in 1945, and the first of these surveys—the Survey of Consumer Finances—was conducted by the Division of Program Surveys in January and February 1946. In July 1946, Likert's group left the federal government and established the SRC at the University of Michigan, and their initial behavioral economics study was the early 1947 version of the SCF.

Although the study was designed as a way to help predict what consumers would do with their accumulated wartime savings, the director of the SCF, George Katona, managed to persuade the Federal Reserve Board (FRB) that trying to extract financial information from consumers would be more successful if the survey instrument had a few "can-opener" questions that would be easy to answer, would make the respondent feel at ease, and might even provide useful information about future behavior. Thus the SCF started off with questions like "Are you better or worse off than you were a year ago?" or "Is this a good or a bad time to buy a car?" or "Do you expect prices to go up, go down, or stay about the same?" Questions of this sort, while being plausibly presented to the FRB as a way to improve response rates for the financial parts of the survey, were seen by researchers like Katona as providing the raw materials for testing theories about consumer behavior in an affluent society, where expectations and attitudes could be thought of as affecting consumers' willingness to spend.

The Survey of Consumer Finances and the Study of Wealth

The SCF, along with the can-opener questions about attitudes and expectations, was conducted annually from 1946 to 1960 with the financial support of the FRB. Dissatisfaction on the part of the FRB with the inability of the SCF estimates of wealth to match up with external control totals (principally, the estimates of aggregate assets and debts produced by the FRB) eventually led the FRB to substantially reduce its support for the continuation of the SCF. From 1960 through the early 1970s, the SCF data series continued to be collected with a diversified funding base that included private foundations (especially the Ford Foundation), federal government agencies, and the FRB. During this period the SCF occasionally included a panel feature, as in the 1967–70 study known as the debt panel.

Although 1971 was the final year in which the original SCF series was collected, interest in obtaining updated measurements of asset holdings and debts among American households continued to surface periodically. In 1977, for example, the FRB financed an abbreviated version of the SCF, which was focused mainly on debt owed and debt burden. As a way to improve the quality of asset surveys by combining a conventional area probability sample with a sample of households known to be in the upper end of the wealth distribution, a 1983 version of the SCF was fielded with a small sample of extremely wealthy households derived from tax files. Even though the response rate for the wealthy tax file sample was extremely low (households had to volunteer to be included in the survey, and only about 9 percent of the selected list sample were willing to volunteer), the survey produced results that were markedly closer to external control totals (again, FRB estimates from aggregate data) than any previous SCF had managed to do. The 1983 survey was followed by a truncated reinterview in 1986 and then in 1989 by a fuller-scale SCF that had a panel component as well as a list sample derived from tax files. A response rate about four times higher was achieved for the wealthy tax file sample by the simple expedient of changing the ground rules for volunteering. In 1983, respondents had to volunteer positively before they would be contacted about participation in the survey, while in 1989 respondents had to opt out or else they would be routinely contacted about participation.

The SCF series now appears to be on a steady three-year cycle, with surveys designed much like the 1989 survey conducted in 1992, 1995, and 1998. Although most of the historic SCF series has been administered by the SRC, the last few observations, starting with 1992, have been conducted by National Opinion Research Center at the University of Chicago. What has been learned from this long history?

First, we have learned quite a lot about how to measure wealth, defined as the total sum of financial assets such as savings accounts, stocks, and bonds and real assets such as a home, investment in real estate, or investment in a business, less debt. (These developments are detailed in the last section of this introduction to part 2.) Second, both from observing the SCF wealth series and from tapping into other surveys that contain wealth data, such as the Panel Study of Income Dynamics and the Health and Retirement Study, we have learned that wealth is a very different phenomenon than income: (1) wealth is more highly skewed; for example, about one-quarter of total national wealth (including both financial wealth and housing equity) is owned by the top one-half of 1 percent of U.S. households, with the majority of households having little or no wealth beyond housing equity (Curtin, Juster, and Morgan 1989); (2) even *within* income deciles, there is enormous variability in wealth; for example, the top decile of wealth holders in the lowest income decile owns more wealth than the median U.S. household, while the bottom decile of wealth in the top income decile has virtually zero wealth holdings (Venti and Wise 1999); (3) the health status of the population, including both husbands and wives in married couple households, is powerfully related to household wealth (Smith 1999); and (4) wealth predicts future saving, income held constant, rather than the reverse, probably because both savings and wealth reflect household tastes and preferences.

Consumer Attitudes and Expectations

As noted earlier, the first consumer attitude surveys came from the introductory questions to the annual SCF. The notion of collecting attitudinal and expectational data as part of the wealth survey continued from 1946 through 1952, when the SRC began to collect these data with greater periodicity than the annual SCF series. Hence, from 1952 through the mid-1960s, consumer attitude surveys were conducted several times a year, depending on the availability of financial support. The attitude surveys grew in content as they became more of a stand-alone rather than an adjunct to the SCF data, and they subsequently moved from an irregular quarterly basis (up to about 1965) to a regular quarterly basis (from 1966 through 1977) and then to a regular monthly basis (from 1978 to the present time). The attitude surveys, and some of the analytic issues involved in the measurement of attitudes and expectations, are discussed in chapter 5 by Richard Curtin, director of the Survey of Consumer Attitudes.

The Dynamics of Income, Poverty, and Aging

While the SCF series, and the associated measures of consumer attitudes and expectations, dominated the early years of the EBP's agenda, recent decades have seen several highly visible and analytically unique behavioral surveys coming from the EBP, along with several important surveys done at NORC and at the U.S. Census Bureau. The most visible of these ongoing SRC studies are the PSID, which started in 1968, and the HRS, which began in 1992. Both studies continue to the present time and are summarized here and discussed at length in chapter 6 and chapter 12. Surveys done elsewhere include the National Longitudinal Surveys done at NORC, focused on labor market behavior, and the Survey of Income and Program Participation (SIPP) done at the U.S. Census Bureau, focused on understanding the role of public programs in alleviating poverty.

Panel Study of Income Dynamics

The PSID—which grew out of the Survey of Economic Opportunity (SEO), conducted in 1966 and 1967 by the Office of Economic Opportunity (OEO) of the Department of Health, Education, and Welfare—was designed to try to understand why there was so much continued poverty in the face of a strong economic expansion. PSID has some very innovative design features due mainly to the persistence and ingenuity of its founding director, James Morgan.

When OEO approached the SRC to continue collecting information on the OEO poverty sample, Morgan persuaded the OEO to combine its poverty sample with a standard probability sample, on the grounds that it was at least as interesting to understand why households that were above the poverty level slipped below from time to time as it was to understand how and why people who were below the poverty level moved above it. In addition, Morgan persuaded the OEO, along with subsequent sponsors, to follow children in sample households who left to head their own households. That made the PSID a fully representative sample (aside from new immigrants) of the dynamics of population change in the United States. In a study lacking the addition of these split-off households, the sample would eventually represent only the upper end of the age distribution and would not have any young respondents representing newly formed households. As discussed in chapter 6, the PSID has gone on to become perhaps the most widely used social science survey in the world, and its general design has been copied by a number of European countries.

Health and Retirement Study

The HRS, detailed in chapter 12, originated from the recognition within the National Institute on Aging (NIA) of the National Institutes of Health (NIH) that the data needed to understand retirement decisions of the emerging baby boom cohort were severely limited as well as outdated—the most recent study with sufficient numbers of older people to entertain detailed analysis was the Retirement History Survey, which started in the late 1960s, terminated in 1978, and studied a single cohort. Thus NIA circulated a request for proposals for a research program aimed at understanding the dynamics of retirement decisions and the evolution of health status and economic status as people aged. The SRC at the University of Michigan was selected as the responsible organization; planning began in 1990, and the first wave of data was collected in 1992 for a sample of households with at least one spouse between the ages of fifty-one and sixty-one (born between 1931 and 1941). New cohorts were added in subsequent years—those born before 1924 were added in 1993; those born between 1924 and 1930 and between 1942 and 1947 were added in 1998; and those born between 1948 and 1953 are scheduled to be added in 2004. The survey content was designed to examine health status and health insurance coverage; family structure and transfers; labor force participation and job characteristics; economic status including both income and wealth; and expectations, attitudes, and preferences.

Unique features of the HRS were the enormous effort put into the development of survey content, including formation of half a dozen multidisciplinary working groups comprising academic experts along with survey measurement specialists, who met regularly over an eighteen-month period; the use of administrative records on earnings (from Social Security files) to greatly enrich the earnings histories of individual respondents; the collection and coding of pension plan documents from the employers of HRS respondents covered by a private pension plan; the commitment to innovate, both in terms of content not ordinarily included in surveys (e.g., probability judgments about survival, job loss, receipt of inheritances, and deteriorating health; measures of risk aversion and time preference; and tests of cognitive functioning) as well as in ways of reducing the measurement error in critical but error-prone variables such as income and wealth; and the planned addition of new birth cohorts every five to six years, making HRS both a genuinely longitudinal study and a representative sample of the U.S. population over age fifty (except for immigration occurring after the various age cohorts entered the HRS sample).

Time Use

A final major research program, cutting across activities in the SRC and the Center for Political Studies at the Institute for Social Research (ISR), studied the use of time among American households. The history of such studies in the United States goes back into the 1920s, and the earliest studies were largely concerned with the behavior of households in relatively isolated rural or small town communities such as Ithaca, New York, where a good bit of substantive and methodological research in the area of time use was directed by Kathryn Walker (1976).

The first comprehensive study of time use in the United States as a whole was part of a cross-national study of urban time use in a number of (mainly) developed countries conducted in 1965–66 by a consortium of scholars headed by the Hungarian sociologist Alexander Szalai (1972). The studies used a common instrument and had a common format, but the sample design was such that people age sixty-five and over were excluded, as were people living in rural areas with populations less than thirty thousand persons.

Interest in time use studies emerged again in the mid-1970s, motivated by concerns over the evolution and importance of unpaid productive uses of time; the impact on child development of time invested in children by parents; and the way in which time use changed over the life cycle as people move from school settings to work settings, formed families, had children, left the work force, and so forth. A 1975–76 Time Use Study was designed and conducted by the SRC (Juster and Stafford 1985). Principal innovations were (1) the inclusion in the sample of both husbands and wives in married couple households; (2) four separate diary observations (two weekdays, one Saturday, and one Sunday) for each respondent; and (3) the testing of several different procedures for collecting time use data that were designed to assess the validity and reliability of the conventional time diary format. Experimental modes of data collection included the use of a randomly programmed electronic paging device to measure activities instantaneously and later convert them to time intervals and the use of a very detailed description of a single hour in the prior twenty-four-hour day, designed to assess the quality characteristics of the conventional time diary data collection format.

There are at least five distinct areas of inquiry in which time use data can make a substantial contribution to our understanding of the way economic and social systems function (Juster and Stafford 1991): (1) understanding the change over time in work and leisure activities and the distribution of work and leisure hours among members of the household; (2) assessing the level of overall well-being; (3) understanding variation in the performance of economic systems characterized by different institutional arrangements; (4) examining a much broader definition of societal investments in the future, particularly investments represented by resources devoted to the education and training of children; and (5) achieving a richer understanding of total product from both market and nonmarket work both among households and among individuals within particular households.

As an illustration of the improved insights associated with the availability of time use data, in the United States paid work hours declined substantially for men from the mid-1960s to early 1980s, while paid work hours for women increased over the same time period. A common inference is that leisure time increased for men but decreased for women. A broader definition of work that includes unpaid household work changes that conclusion: defining work as the sum of paid work hours plus commuting time plus unpaid household work, the data indicate that total work hours *declined* for women (because their market work hours rose by less than their unpaid household work hours decreased), while for men total work hours also *decreased* but for the opposite reason (their unpaid household work hours increased, but by less than their paid work hours declined). Thus leisure time increased for both men and women over this period.

Other Studies

EBP studies that do not meet the longevity criteria but nevertheless have added appreciably to our understanding of important economic and social processes include studies of the distribution of income and wealth and its intergenerational transmission (Morgan et al. 1962); a study of the effects of disability payments on labor force participation (Morgan,

Snider, and Sobol 1958); a study of tort system insurance settlements, which showed very large expenses in automobile accidents and little equity and thus became the basis for no-fault automobile insurance (Conart et al. 1964); a study that showed that high marginal tax rates did not reduce work effort of the affluent (Barlow, Brazer, and Morgan 1966); and studies of charitable giving of time and money, indicating that the two were complements rather than substitutes (Morgan, Dye, and Hybels 1975).

Enhancements in the Measurement of Income and Wealth

As noted previously, a major problem with measuring wealth is that it requires a very special sample to provide an adequate assessment of total national wealth. Until the last decade and a half, survey estimates of wealth, and to a lesser degree income, were suspect because they tended to show very large amounts of item nonresponse. A typical survey respondent to either a wealth or income question would provide a "yes" or "no" answer to whether they possessed a particular asset or source of income, but then a large proportion would say either that they didn't know the value of their asset or income flow or that they were not willing to provide that information to the interviewer. Thus, the frequency of "don't know" or "refused" responses approaches 30–40 percent for many asset types and 15–20 percent for virtually any income flow, a potential source of substantial bias if nonresponders differ significantly from respondents in terms of their income or wealth. A way around this problem, or at least a way to determine whether there is a noticeable bias, was originated in an SRC wealth module developed for the PSID in 1984.

This module was unique in a number of respects. First, it had a very small number of asset categories, compared to the level of asset detail typically asked about on wealth surveys. Second, it had a novel way of handling the missing data problem on asset items: when a respondent reported that they either didn't know or wouldn't tell how much of a particular asset type their household had, they were immediately asked a yes-no question about some rounded dollar amount, for example, "Would it be more than $5,000?" Respondents who said "yes" were then asked a higher amount question, such as "Would it be more than $50,000?" Respondents who said "no" were asked a lower amount question, for example, "Would it be more than $1,000?" This series of unfolding bracket questions was introduced into the PSID wealth module as a way to provide less biased imputations, in the event that respondents unwilling or unable to provide continuous data turned out to have a different distribution of wealth, personal characteristics being equal, than respondents providing continuous data.

It turned out that, although there were some differences in the PSID sample between respondents providing continuous data to the initial questions and those providing bracketed responses after initial nonresponse, the differences were much larger in other data sets where the same technique was applied. PSID, at the time this wealth experiment was conducted, was in its twenty-sixth year of data collection, and respondents who continued to be in the study after that many years were much less likely to be sensitive about providing income or wealth data than were respondents in other studies. For example, HRS, begun in 1992, estimated that mean values for respondents providing bracketed data were, for many assets, more than double the mean values of wealth components for respondents providing continuous data. That is, those who could not or would not answer the initial wealth questions, but then gave bracket responses, tended to be substantially richer than respondents providing continuous data. As a result, aggregate wealth is estimated to be substantially higher when bracketing techniques are used (Juster and Smith 1997).

In addition to the enhancement in the quality of wealth data flowing from the use of these bracketing or unfolding techniques, a number of changes were made in the measurement of income flows that also substantially improved the quality of the income data collected in surveys. Typically, the income and wealth data are produced in separate modules. In contrast, the 1996 HRS developed a merged module in which respondents were first asked whether they had a particular type of asset (e.g., checking account, savings account, or money market fund); if so, they were asked about how much they had altogether in those accounts; then they were asked whether they received any interest or dividend income from these assets; if so, they were asked with what periodicity and, depending on the response, the amount of income received during the most recent month, quarter, or year.

The results of this simple transformation from two separate modules into a single merged module produced dramatic differences in the reporting of income from assets. As an illustration, in the 1994 study using conventional measurement techniques, only about 17 percent of households with financial assets of more than one-quarter of a million dollars reported receiving $5,000 or more in interest and dividend income. In the

1996 survey, using the experimental design with a merged asset-income module, almost five times as many households (over 75 percent) with financial assets of more than one-quarter of a million dollars reported receiving $5,000 or more in interest and dividend income. Overall, the level of income from financial assets was two to three times larger using the experimental methodology than it had been using the conventional methodology. For asset types like rental real estate and business or farm income, the differences were not quite so dramatic but were still extremely large (Hurd, Juster, and Smith 2003; Juster, Lupton, and Cao 2002).

These new measurement methods cannot be used on all survey designs. Obviously, the merged income and wealth approach can only be used if the survey measures both income and wealth. Furthermore, the unfolding or bracketing techniques may not be feasible if a survey includes fifty to one hundred asset categories rather than eight to ten. Finally, much research still needs to be done on these new methods. For example, the distribution of bracketed responses to asset or income questions is strongly related to the initial (entry point) bracket question (Hurd 1999). Methods of adjusting the data for this bias need to be developed. Nevertheless, we see in economics, as in other fields, that the interplay of theory with continually evolving survey methods and data has reshaped and enriched our understanding of major macroeconomic and microeconomic phenomena.

REFERENCES

Barlow, Robin, Harvey E. Brazer, and James N. Morgan. 1966. *Economic behavior of the affluent.* Washington, DC: Brookings Institution.

Conart, Alfred F., et al. 1964. *Automobile accident costs and payments: Studies in the economics of injury reparation.* Ann Arbor: University of Michigan Press.

Curtin, Richard, F. Thomas Juster, and James N. Morgan. 1989. Survey estimates of wealth: An assessment of quality. In *The measurement of saving, investment, and wealth*, ed. Robert E. Lipsey and Helen S. Tice. Chicago: University of Chicago Press.

Hurd, Michael D. 1999. Anchoring and acquiescence bias in measuring assets in household surveys. *Journal of Risk and Uncertainty* 19 (1–3): 111–36.

Hurd, Michael D., F. Thomas Juster, and James P. Smith. 2003. Enhancing the quality of data on income: Recent innovations from the HRS. *Journal of Human Resources* 38 (3): 758–72.

Juster, F. Thomas, Joseph Lupton, and Honggao Cao. 2002. *Ensuring time-series consistency in estimates of income from wealth.* Ann Arbor: Institute for Social Research, University of Michigan.

Juster, F. Thomas, and James P. Smith. 1997. Improving the quality of economic data: Lessons from the HRS and AHEAD. *Journal of the American Statistical Association* 92 (440): 1268–78.

Juster, F. Thomas, and Frank P. Stafford. 1985. *Time, goods, and well-being.* Ann Arbor: Survey Research Center, Institute for Social Research, University of Michigan.

———. 1991. The allocation of time: Empirical findings, behavioral models, and problems of measurement. *Journal of Economic Literature* 29:471–522.

Morgan, James N., Martin H. David, Wilbur J. Cohen, and Harvey E. Brazer. 1962. *Income and welfare in the United States.* New York: McGraw Hill.

Morgan, James N., Richard F. Dye, and Judith Hybels. 1975. *Results from two national surveys of philanthropic activity.* Ann Arbor: Survey Research Center, University of Michigan.

Morgan, James N., Marvin Snider, and Marion G. Sobol. 1958. *Highlights from a study on lump-sum redemption settlements and rehabilitation.* Ann Arbor: Survey Research Center, University of Michigan.

Smith, James P. 1999. Healthy bodies and thick wallets: The dual relation between health and economic status. *Journal of Economic Perspectives* 13 (2): 145–66.

Szalai, Alexander. 1972. *The use of time: Daily activities of urban and suburban populations in twelve countries.* The Hague: Mouton.

Venti, Steven F., and David A. Wise. 1999. Lifetime earnings, savings choices, and wealth at retirement. In *Wealth, work, and health: Innovations in measurement in the social sciences,* ed. James P. Smith and Robert J. Willis. Ann Arbor: University of Michigan Press.

Walker, Kathryn E., and Margaret E. Woods. 1976. *Time use: A measure of household production of family goods and services.* Washington, DC: Center for the Family of the American Home Economics Association.

CHAPTER 5

Psychology and Macroeconomics

Richard T. Curtin

Born for Peace

The Economic Behavior Program at the Survey Research Center (SRC) began in troubled times. Its agenda was focused on understanding the role of the consumer in the transition from a wartime economy to what all hoped would be a new era of peace and prosperity. Many feared that the post–World War II economy would again give rise to the same type of deflationary spiral and mass unemployment that characterized the Great Depression of the 1930s. Press headlines in mid-1945 proclaimed "Government Economists Predict Eight Million Unemployed by 1946." What actually occurred was quite different. In the first half of 1946 the unemployed numbered three, not eight, million, and instead of deflation the economy faced very strong inflationary pressures. Unlike economists, consumers exhibited a great deal of confidence about the postwar economy. Acting on that confidence, consumers spent an increasing fraction of their incomes, as the savings rate plunged from 11.7 percent at the start of 1946 to just 2.2 percent by mid-1947—a low in the savings rate that would not again be recorded for fifty years.

In a postmortem on the forecast error, Nobel laureate Lawrence Klein (1946, 291) noted, "It is immediately obvious where this forecast failed—in the prediction of consumer expenditures. . . . The order of magnitude of the error involved is great, and, what is more serious, it is great enough to lead to disastrous policy recommendations." As might be expected, the forecast error prompted widespread concerns about whether the underlying economic theory or statistical methodology, or both, were wrong. Klein concluded that the fault did not lie in theory or method but rather in implementation. What was needed in his view were models with more detailed equations, fewer exogenous variables, and a more dynamic specification.

This forecast failure clearly suggested that, in addition to information on consumers' financial situation, forecasting models require information on the economic and psychological factors that shape changes in consumers' spending and saving decisions. The economic situation of consumers had undergone sweeping changes from the Depression of the 1930s to the resurgent war economy of the 1940s. Wartime spending had been constrained by rationing, leaving the rising incomes generated by the wartime economy to rebuild the savings depleted by the Depression. Unfortunately, little data existed at that time that could be used to quantify the change in consumers' asset holdings. Just as important, little was known about how consumers would adjust their saving and spending priorities in the postwar economy.

Over fifty years after these issues were first addressed, the national economy recently ended the longest sustained period of economic growth recorded in more than a century and at this writing is in the early stages of a recovery that is of uncertain vigor and duration. The remarkable performance of the economy during the 1990s seemed to suggest that the problems facing the post–World War II economy had all but disappeared. Unfortunately, this was not the case. In many ways the primary concerns about the national economy remain remarkably similar. While fears of mass unemployment on the scale experienced in the 1930s were not present when the 1990s expansion began, apprehensions about future job and income prospects were so widespread in the early 1990s that it was referred to as a "jobless" expansion, and these fears reemerged as the economy and stock market sputtered into the twenty-first century. Concerns about inflation still dominated public policy considerations—with a twist. After World War II policy was tilted against the possibility of renewed *deflation* (incorrectly, since inflation was the greater threat), while in the early 1990s policy was tilted against the possibility of renewed *inflation* (in the midst of strong disinflationary trends).

The prominent role of savings is also similar. The proportion of income saved remained above the 1947 low for fifty years, but by the end of 1999 the savings rate recorded a new low. At the start of the decades of the 1940s and the 1990s, consumers were keenly aware of the inadequacy of their savings and reserve funds. To be sure, the concerns expressed by consumers in the 1990s were more focused on the inadequacy of their savings for retirement, whereas in the earlier period, short-term precautionary motives were more common. What is unchanged, however, is the important and sizable impacts on the macroeconomy that result from the influence those asset holdings have on consumers' economic decisions.

In both periods the sizable increases in wealth resulted from unusual circumstances rather than disciplined long-term savings plans. Just as the wartime restrictions on spending forced greater savings, the bull stock market of the 1990s increased wealth through passive capital gains. The pace and extent of the restoration of savings were as unexpected as they were welcomed. While consumers hesitated to draw on their accumulated investments in both periods, they did not hesitate to spend a larger share of their current income. The bear stock market of the early 2000s, however, created new apprehensions about future consumer spending.

Thus, many of the concerns from fifty years ago still apply to the economy of the twenty-first century. Unlike the 1940s, however, there is now a substantial amount of data on the financial assets held by consumers, including the types, amounts, and distribution across households. Such data still need to be supplemented by information on the attitudes and expectations of consumers to gain a more complete understanding of the potential impact on the macroeconomy. As an increasing share of the population nears and enters retirement, research on income expectations must focus on developments in financial markets as well as labor markets. Moreover, measures of expected risk and uncertainty must be broadened to include not only the health and disability of individuals but also expected changes in private and public health and pension programs.

Method to Substance

> "We are interested in how people are getting along financially these days. Would you say that you are better off or worse off financially than you were a year ago?"

So began the first survey of consumers in 1946. The primary purpose of that first survey was to collect data on household assets and debts. The sponsor of the survey, the Federal Reserve Board, initially had little interest in the attitudes and expectations of consumers. Their goal was a financial balance sheet, the hard currency of economic life, not the soft data of consumer sentiment. George Katona, the founder of the survey program, convinced the sponsor that few respondents would be willing to cooperate if the first question asked was "We are interested in knowing the amount of your income and assets. First, how much do you have in your savings account?" Sound survey methodology required that other, more general and less threatening questions were first asked to build rapport, to establish a sense of trust and confidence with the respondents.

Katona devised a conversational interview that introduced each new area of interest with questions that first elicited respondents' general opinions before asking the detailed questions on dollar amounts. Although the sponsor was convinced that such attitudinal questions were needed for methodological reasons, Katona was told that he did not need to report any of these results since the FRB had no interest in the attitudinal findings. Ultimately, the FRB, as well as many others, became as interested in the findings on consumers' expectations as on consumers' balance sheets. Although the first measures of consumer expectations may seem serendipitous, they were in reality no happenstance. Katona had long been interested in the interaction of economic and psychological factors and seized this opportunity to pursue his innovative research agenda.[1]

Katona contended that the power of the consumer to shape the course of the macroeconomy resulted from two developments in the American economy following World War II. First, growth in consumer incomes as well as asset holdings provided people with greater financial latitude. Income changes could no longer be expected to result in immediate and offsetting changes in consumption. This financial latitude meant that consumers became active decision makers, able to gauge the timing of their spending decisions to best serve their present and future needs. The second change involved the growing importance of consumer "investment" goods—purchases of homes, vehicles, and other large household durable goods (Juster 1966a). These large and infrequent purchases are more likely to be deliberate decisions, whose timing could as easily be advanced as postponed, and the purchases frequently involve the risks associated with the use of credit. As a result, the timing of spending decisions became increasingly dependent on consumers' expectations about future trends in income, employment, prices, and interest rates and correspondingly less dependent on their current and past economic situation.

Although the factors that shaped spending decisions drew most of the attention, research on savings motivations was a central element of the research agenda. Based on research conducted in the late 1940s and 1950s, Katona (1960) documented the widespread prevalence of precautionary savings motives, primarily reflecting concerns about future employment risks as well as the possibility of future illness or disability. Katona also found that savings motivations differed substantially by life-cycle stage. Savings for retirement rose in importance only after age forty-five, while younger families more often cited saving for their children's education or accumulating funds to make a down payment on a house or some other large purchase.

Measurement Issues

The empirical analysis of the relationship between survey measures and subsequent spending behavior has revolved around two major issues. The first issue was whether data on purchase intentions or more general measures of consumer attitudes and expectations were the more effective measures. Interwoven with the issue of the appropriate type of measure was the appropriate methodology for testing. A cross-section analysis relates attitudes and behavior for a given individual, while time-series analysis relates changes in attitudes at the mass level with subsequent changes in aggregate trends. Since the latter are an aggregation of the former, it was assumed that the empirical evidence should be consistent on both the individual and aggregate levels. This was the position advocated by Arthur Okun, James Tobin, and others on the Smithies committee that was established to review the data's predictive performance in the mid-1950s. Tobin's argument was that, if the relationship did not exist on the microlevel, neither would it exist at the macrolevel. Tobin's (1959, 10) initial conclusion was that "Buying intentions have predictive value; other attitudinal questions do not."[2] Katona's (1957) response to the Smithies committee report was that the cross-section tests were not properly specified and that theoretical considerations indicated the relevance of aggregate time-series tests of trends in mass attitudes even if the predictive performance of individual attitude items was inconclusive in cross-section analysis.

The results of additional analyses confirmed some of Tobin's early cross-section conclusions but seemed inconsistent with the presumption that the results would generalize to time-series analysis. For the prediction of a single individual's purchases, the intentions data did perform better than the more general attitudinal measures.[3] At the aggregate level of analysis, however, the results were reversed. Juster (1969) helped to resolve the paradox when he found that the failure of intentions data in time-series analysis was due to the combination of three factors: (1) sampling and measurement errors represented a more serious problem for the time-series analysis; (2) the intentions data contained strong seasonal patterns and the analysis needed to be based on seasonally adjusted series; and (3) differences in expressed intentions should be assigned differential weights that reflect actual subsequent purchase rates for each response category. Each of these factors was found to contribute to the lack of explanatory power of intentions data in time-series models, although the differential weights had the largest impact. The combined time-series and cross-section results indicate that neither the more general sentiment measures nor buying intentions are better per se as a predictive tool but rather that each construct can play a useful role depending on the analytic framework.

The Census Bureau did conduct surveys of sufficient size using detailed probability measures of intended purchases from 1967 to 1973. The surveys were discontinued, however, following an early assessment indicating that the probability measures had poor predictive performance.[4] For a variety of reasons, including the very large sample sizes that would be needed for robust measures of purchase intentions, SRC discontinued the measurement of purchase intentions in the mid-1970s in preference to the more general measures of consumer sentiment.[5]

Consumer sentiment is now one of the most closely watched indicators of future economic trends. The latest figures on sentiment trends are routinely reported in the press and incorporated into many macroeconomic models as well as the Index of Leading Economic Indicators devised by the U.S. Department of Commerce. The inclusion of consumer confidence in the Leading Indicator Composite Index in 1989 was a significant, independent confirmation of its usefulness for understanding and forecasting changes in the national economy. The success of this approach is also attested by the many other organizations that now regularly monitor consumer sentiment at the national, state, and local levels in this country as well as in many others. The Conference Board began measuring U.S. consumer confidence in the late 1960s. Other countries that monitor consumer sentiment include Austria, Australia, Belgium, Canada, China, Czech Republic, Denmark, Finland, France, Germany, Great Britain, Greece, Hungary, Indonesia, Ireland, Italy, Jamaica, Japan, Luxembourg, Norway, Poland, Russia, Spain, South Africa, Sweden, Switzerland, and Taiwan.

The relationship between changes in the Index of Consumer Sentiment and annual growth rates in the gross domestic product (GDP) is shown in figure 5.1, with the shaded areas representing periods of economic reces-

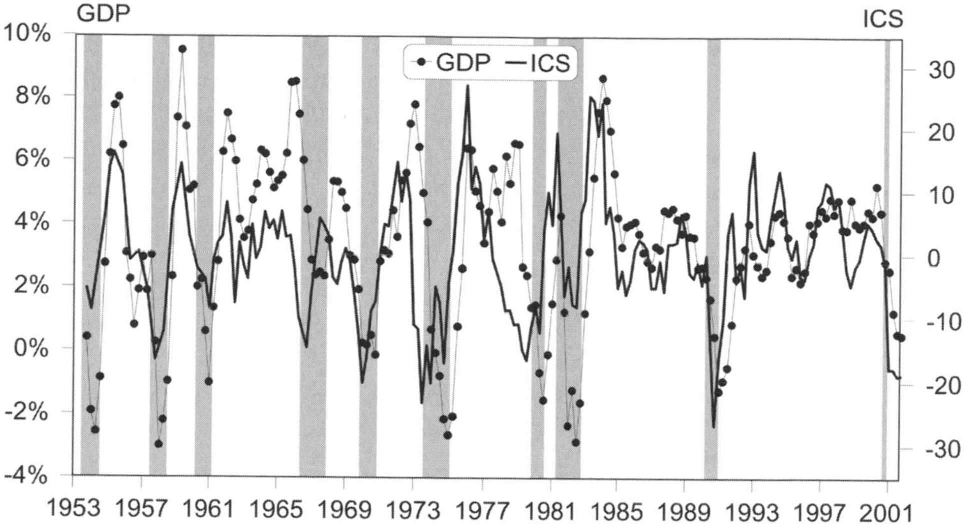

FIG. 5.1. Times-series of Index of Consumer Sentiment and Gross Domestic Product, 1953–2001 (shaded areas = economic recessions)

sion. As the figure clearly demonstrates, changes in the Index of Consumer Sentiment typically precede changes in GDP growth and the onset of recessions. Howrey (2001) found the Index of Consumer Sentiment to be a significant predictor of future trends in GDP, even after controlling for the economic variables typically used to predict GDP.

Convergent Economic Theories

The importance of expectations for the explanation of consumption decisions was also reflected in independent advances in economic theory, sparked by the work of two Nobel laureates. Friedman's permanent income hypothesis (1957) and Modigliani's life-cycle theory (Modigliani and Brumberg 1954) emphasized the role of expectations in determining consumers' current spending and saving decisions. To be sure, these theoretical advances were forged from the traditional assumptions of rational calculation and utility maximization rather than from empirical observations based on population surveys. The driving force of both theories was the assumption that rational consumers would attempt to maximize utility by allocating their lifetime stream of income into an optimal pattern of lifetime consumption.

These theories addressed a major failure of the Keynesian consumption function following World War II. The Keynesian consumption function, which viewed current income as the main determinant of consumer spending, failed as a forecast of economic trends. The Keynesian prediction that the average propensity to consume (the ratio of consumption to income) would fall as income rose was based on the observation that the average propensity to consume was lower at higher income levels. It was this facet of the Keynesian approach that led to the prediction that shortfalls in consumer demand would precipitate another depression following World War II. In fact, the ratio of consumption to income has shown no tendency to decline over time, and it was the constancy of this ratio that became the centerpiece of the permanent income hypothesis.

Numerous empirical studies of the life-cycle permanent income hypothesis, both at the macro- and microlevel, have rejected the general premise that consumption is equal to the annuity value of lifetime resources. This prompted greater attention to potential sources of misspecification, such as the failure to account for liquidity constraints (an inability to borrow against future income) and the presence of myopic or rule-of-thumb consumers (who based their consumption decisions on current rather than permanent income).[6] It is important to note that the usual assumption of additively time-separable utility had the effect of eliminating expenditures on durables from much of the empirical work—the very expenditures that Katona long argued were most susceptible to shifts in expectations and had the most impact on cyclical developments in the economy.

Perhaps the most important enhancement of economic models was the move away from the restrictive assumptions regarding how uncertainty about the future influences decisions about current consumption. The restrictive assumptions only allowed for the effect of the mean of the expected future income stream on consumption. Once uncertainty about future income is incorporated, the variance of future income also has an impact on current consumption decisions, depending on the extent of accumulated assets and the level of current income relative to expected future income. Based on more plausible assumptions about the utility function, Kimball (1990) has shown that consumers could be expected to accumulate precautionary savings as a hedge against uncertainty, and a growing body of empirical evidence supports this contention (Caballero

1991; Carroll 1994, 1997; Carroll and Samwick 1997, 1998). The strength of the precautionary savings motive depends on the variance of consumption and interest rates.

It is interesting that Carroll (1997) indicates the importance of precautionary savings by citing data from a 1983 survey that asked consumers about their primary savings motives. This was the same question developed by Katona in the late 1940s and on which he based his analysis of savings motivations cited earlier. Katona's insights into savings motivations have now been echoed fifty years later in detail: recent research has emphasized that precautionary savings motives are especially important at younger life-cycle stages, while the savings motives among older consumers are focused more on retirement. There was even close agreement on the age at which the shift in savings motives occurred—age forty-five according to Katona and about age fifty according to Carroll. While Katona based his finding on consumers' self-described savings motives, in the theoretical models the shift was related to the growing level of accumulated retirement assets that also serve to buffer against risks prior to retirement. Even Katona's emphasis on taking account of uncertainty about potential future medical expenses and longevity has now also gained widespread acceptance.

Consumer-Led Recessions

There is no consensus among economists on the causes of economic recessions (Christiano and Fitzgerald 1999). As Cochrane (1994, 295) observes, "What shocks are responsible for economic fluctuations? Despite at least two hundred years in which economists have observed fluctuations in economic activity, we still are not sure." Cochrane's analysis concludes that none of the common candidates (monetary, credit, price, and technology shocks) accounts for the bulk of the observed fluctuations. Instead, he finds that "consumption shocks" account for a relatively large share of the variation. This is a troublesome finding for many economists since standard intertemporal models of consumption do not produce consumer-led recessions.

Since consumption is an endogenous variable, the ultimate source of the shock is at the center of the debate. Macromodels already incorporate information on all of the observable exogenous variables that have been hypothesized to shape consumption decisions. Cochrane suggests that the source of the shocks must reflect information about future economic conditions that are known to consumers but are unobserved by economic models. Economists typically assume that consumers base their economic expectations on the public information releases of governmental agencies—that is, on the same sources of information used by economists. Media reports may be the dominant source of information for consumers about some developments, such as prospective changes in government policies or changes in international economic conditions. For many other types of economic developments, however, the mass media are not the most important sources of information for consumers. Personal experience, direct knowledge of changes in local employment conditions, changes in prices and the availability of goods in local markets, and the numerous other direct connections that consumers have with changing economic conditions are often more influential.

As Cochrane (1994, 350) observes, "One might doubt that agents in the economy can forecast so much better than economists. . . . But this argument forgets aggregation." Even if each consumer is assumed to possess only information about his or her own prospects, the aggregation of the idiosyncratic information can provide a robust indicator for future macroeconomic trends. Indeed, if economic fluctuations are primarily driven by private, unobserved information, this would explain the persistent puzzle about the determinants of business cycles. This situation can be corrected by a more detailed specification of what information consumers utilize, how they assess and integrate information from diverse sources, and how the resulting expectations are utilized in making their consumption decisions.

Theory of Expectations

Fifty years ago, Katona challenged the economic profession to include the measurement of economic expectations in models of macroeconomic behavior. By the close of the twentieth century, nearly all macroeconomic models emphasized the role of expectations in shaping economic behavior. Indeed, some observers have identified the incorporation of expectations as the most important innovation in economic theory over the past quarter century. What Katona and other behavioral scientists envisioned, however, was quite different from what actually came to dominate economic theory. To be sure, Katona's view that expectations formed an indispensable component of consumers' decisions has been validated. It was the measurement of expectations that proved to be the crucial divide.

The rational expectations hypothesis (Muth 1961) that now dominates economic theory is quite different from the bounded rationality advocated by other social scientists, most notably by Herbert Simon (1947, 1957, 1978). Despite the lack of convincing empirical evidence, economics views rationality in terms of the choices it produces (substantive or full rationality), whereas other social sciences view rationality in terms of the process that is used to make choices (procedural or bounded rationality).[7] As Mankiw (1988, 440) explains, "Economists routinely assume that firms rationally maximize profits and that consumers rationally maximize utility. It would be an act of schizophrenia not to assume that economic agents act rationally when they form their expectations of the future." But for many social scientists, bounded rationality rather than full or unbounded rationality is the more sensible assumption.[8]

The schism between economics and psychology reflects fundamental differences in how rationality is conceptualized and in the methodology used to test theory. The adequacy of the psychological assumptions that underlie economic theories was as sharply debated at the start of the twentieth century as it was at the start of the twenty-first century (Lewin 1996). While all agree that behavioral choice reflects the use of reason, the crucial difference lies in how rationality is defined. It was Friedman's (1953) celebrated essay on methodology that declared the validity of economic theories to be independent of their psychological assumptions. Ever since, economists have solely focused on whether the postulate of unbounded or bounded rationality was the more productive theoretical construct in terms of the accuracy of its predictions, not with the realism of the embedded behavioral assumptions. From the perspective of psychology, the view that implausible assumptions about psychological processes were acceptable acted to perpetuate the schism.

Why has empirical evidence failed to settle the issue of bounded versus unbounded rationality? Perhaps it is as Lovell (1986, 120) lamented more than a decade ago in his review of empirical tests of the rational expectations hypothesis: "Why should data spoil such a good story?" Indeed, the clear advantage of the rational expectations hypothesis is its theoretical strength. The hypothesis has proved to be enormously productive in transforming macroeconomic theory. While the empirical tests have generally not supported the hypothesis, the rationality assumption enabled the powerful tool of optimization to systematically expand the depth and breadth of economic theories. In contrast, while bounded rationality has frequently been confirmed in empirical studies, research on bounded rationality has not led to an integrated theoretical structure that could spark further advances in economic theory. Indeed, because of the theoretical fragmentation, the divergences attributable to bounded rationality have been generally classified as anomalies rather than being incorporated into mainstream theory. The list of such anomalies is long and growing: the impact of framing, asymmetry of behavioral responses to gains and losses, relative reference points, anchoring, endowment effects, confirmatory bias, failure to ignore sunk costs, overvaluation of out-of-pocket costs relative to opportunity costs, the use of mental accounts as a means to control spending and saving decisions, and so forth (Tversky and Kahneman 1982b; Earl 1990; Thaler 1991, 1992; Rabin 1998; Rabin and Schrag 1999).

Proponents of each side of the debate between bounded and unbounded rationality have often focused on the empirical analysis of inflation expectations.[9] A common element of each view is that economists rather than consumers would hold more accurate year-ahead inflation expectations. While the costs and skills involved made it unlikely that ordinary consumers would form accurate forecasts, professional forecasters could be presumed to have financial incentives to acquire and utilize appropriate information to form accurate expectations. Lott and Miller (1982), Gramlich (1983), Grant and Thomas (1999), and Thomas (1999) compared inflation forecasts made by professional economists (Livingston survey) and by consumers (SRC's Surveys of Consumers).[10] As Thomas (1999, 141–42) summarizes the most recent findings, "consensus household inflation forecasts do surprisingly well relative to those of the presumably better-informed professional economists." Indeed, the median consumer forecasts of year-ahead inflation rates "outperformed all other forecasts in the 1981–97 period on simple tests of accuracy as well as on tests for unbiasedness."[11] Similar comparisons were done for year-ahead forecasts of the national unemployment rate. Curtin (1999) found that consumers' forecasts of the year-ahead unemployment rate outperformed those of professional forecasters as well as forecasts from two prominent macroeconomic models.

While these results do not vindicate either position, they do challenge the underlying assumptions of both views about the process governing the formation of expectations. These findings do underscore Katona's original insistence that nothing would prove as beneficial to the advancement of our understanding as the empirical measurement of expectations.

Measurement of Expectations

Expectations are beliefs about the future. Plato cited this definition more than two thousand years ago, and it remains to this day the generally accepted meaning of the term. From the earliest of times, people have commonly stated their expectations using verbal qualifications to indicate their degree of certainty in their beliefs about the future. It was not until the development of probability theory in the seventeenth century that expectations were quantitatively defined as probabilistic judgments. Although it is still much more common for people to express uncertainty using nonquantitative verbal descriptions, the use of probability statements in everyday conversations has increased over time. People also commonly express their expectations as contingent on the information available to them, consistent with the generally accepted view that expectations are conditional probability statements.

While the economic theorist and the consumer share the same general conceptualization of expectations, theorists have always desired greater measurement precision than was thought attainable in household surveys. Indeed, as expectations have become a more central component of economic models, the theoretical specifications of the desired measures have become more exacting. The ideal measure would specify the characteristics of the complete probability distribution for a precisely defined future event or outcome.

Reliable and valid measures of expectations are subject to all of the problems usually associated with survey design. Aside from the more general issues of survey methodology, the crucial measurement issue has involved judgments about the capacity of individuals to provide meaningful responses. The goal of achieving the greatest possible precision must be balanced against the likely prevalence of measurement and non-response errors. Increasing the precision of the measures also increases the extent of information that respondents must access from memory, the required computational skills, and the motivation of respondents to provide accurate responses.

The choice of response scale has been typically justified by assumptions about the ability of respondents to provide meaningful answers as well as the degree of precision required by the hypothesis under investigation. The presumed trade-off between the greater precision of numeric scales and the reduction in measurement error by using verbal scales has repeatedly been challenged as misguided. The concerns have centered on the imprecision of verbal descriptions compared with numeric scales, and the resulting loss of interpersonal comparability as well as intrapersonal comparability across events or over time. For example, the probabilities associated with the term "almost certain" differed significantly across respondents, extended over a relatively broad range, and overlapped with the range of probabilities assigned to the term "probable." Moreover, the range and overlap of probabilities varied depending on the specific verbal descriptions used in the scale.

Although numeric scales are assumed to facilitate the comparability of responses among people, across situations, and over time, it is not entirely clear that they do so. Just as two respondents may associate different numerical probabilities with a given verbal scale category, so they may well differ in their understanding of the meaning of a given numeric probability. Moreover, methodological research has rarely focused on whether verbal likelihood scales or numeric probabilities show a greater correspondence to behavioral decisions. Another variant of this same issue is the presumption that the algebra of modern probability theory can be used to interpret the results (Dominitz and Manski 1997). As Kahneman and Tversky (1982, 48) have noted, "In making predictions and judgments under uncertainty, people do not appear to follow the calculus of chance or the statistical theory of prediction."

Overall, numeric probability scales have clear comparative advantages for a broad range of research topics and have long been advocated by Juster (1966b), Savage (1971), Manski (1990), and Fischhoff (1994). Although simply shifting from a verbal response scale to a numeric probability scale has considerable merit insofar as the question asks respondents for a single point estimate of the likelihood of an event or outcome, the numeric response may still be vulnerable to misinterpretation.

The resolution to these measurement issues, however, was not the primary motivation to move toward the measurement of the complete probability distribution. The impetus has mainly come from developments in economic theory that have increasingly stressed the importance of the degree of uncertainty associated with consumers' expectations. It is the measurement of uncertainty that requires the specification of the complete probability distribution for each person. Given the entire distribution, measures of central tendency can then be supplemented by measures of dispersion to capture the impact of the uncertainty with which expectations are held.

Researchers have typically focused on two techniques to elicit probabilities to estimate the entire cumulative distribution function (Lichtenstein, Fischhoff, and Phillips 1982). The first asks respondents to attach "values" to various points on the percentile distribution, say, at 1 percent, 25 percent, 50 percent, 75 percent, and 99 percent. The other method asks respondents to attach probabilities to selected values, say, an income of $10,000, $25,000, $50,000, and so forth. Research on these two approaches indicates that the former method yields more narrow interquartile ranges, while the latter is subject to anchoring effects. In a comparison of several variants of each method, Seaver, von Winterfeldt, and Edwards (1978) found that for continuous variables the superior approach was to ask respondents to attach probabilities to selected values. This is the measurement approach that has recently been used by Dominitz and Manski (1997) and Guiso, Japelli, and Terlizzese (1992).

While the overall results of these initial attempts are quite promising, the results are not without some drawbacks. A presumably correctable problem is that the detailed questions prompted unusually large amounts of item nonresponse, and, among those who provided answers, an unusually large number of respondents reported a 100 percent probability for a single value rather than probabilities spread over a range of possible outcomes.[12] In reviewing the results of the survey conducted by Guiso, Japelli, and Terlizzese (1992), Carroll (1994) interpreted the results as an indication that consumers did not understand the survey question rather than as an indication of the absence of uncertainty. Methodological experimentation is likely to provide question sequences that minimize the item nonresponse as well as providing measures that reliably capture variations in uncertainty. Dominitz and Manski (1997) achieved higher response rates by using a computer-assisted approach that tailored questions to each respondent, and their approach holds the most promise for future development. The methodological task is not trivial since overconfidence in probability assessments has been widely documented and is typically measured by the width of the interquartile range, the same metric used by Dominitz and Manski as a proxy for uncertainty.

Another methodological concern involves the issue of question framing. There has been little research on the impact of different frames of reference on measures of economic expectations. It is unlikely that shifting the frame of reference from gains to losses would yield the same probability distributions, for example, when asking about the probability of losing a job versus the probability of keeping a job; the probability of income gains versus losses; or the probability of living to age eighty-five versus dying before age eighty-five. Nor has there been much research on whether expectations measured as gains or losses would show a greater correspondence with subsequent behavior.

A more difficult challenge involves the measurement of expected changes in real rather than just nominal economic variables. Economic theory typically focuses on expected changes in inflation-adjusted measures, such as real income. If changes in income and inflation were independent, separate measures of expected changes in nominal income and inflation would suffice. Such economic variables are rarely independent, however, and combining the separate measures requires assumptions about the covariance of the growth rate of nominal income and inflation expected by each respondent. Although this measurement problem could be avoided by simply asking respondents to state their expected probability distributions in real terms, it is clearly of some interest to distinguish between these two sources of uncertainty. How to best estimate the joint probability distribution underlying real income uncertainty deserves a high priority on future research agendas.

Another measurement challenge lies in the recognition that household income is derived from many different sources and that uncertainty may differ significantly for each income source. Focusing only on the labor income of the respondent may be a reasonable approach for young single adults, but not among older two-earner households with accumulated assets. While it may be more realistic to assume independence between different sources of household income than between each income source and inflation, it still represents a significant task to estimate the uncertainty associated with total household income. Of course, the ideal measure would be of uncertainty about the future lifetime path of human and nonhuman wealth rather than simply focusing on uncertainty about next year's income.

Twenty-first-Century Agenda

Fifty years after the inception of SRC's EBP, the unfounded concerns that the economy would slump into recession were replaced during the late 1990s by the equally unfounded outlook of unending prosperity. The shift toward exuberance at the close of the twentieth century was spawned by the longest economic expansion in more than 150 years. This was not the first time that such notions gained widespread acceptance. In the midst of the long expansion of the 1960s, the death of the business cycle was also declared. Then, as now, the death notices included the same caveats that the maintenance of appropriate economic policies was necessary and that historical experience had repeatedly proved such announcements premature. The only difference was that the recent notices also alleged that fundamental changes in the economy have made the concept of the traditional business cycle obsolete. To be sure, the frequency and severity of cyclical downturns have diminished dramatically in the closing decades of the twentieth century. New technologies have dampened the once volatile swings in inventories, and the ongoing consumption shift from goods to services also acts to diminish the potential for cyclical fluctuations.

Will the twenty-first-century economy also witness a corresponding decline in the importance of consumer expectations as a force in shaping developments in the macroeconomy? While it is likely that in the twenty-first century recessions will be less frequent and less severe, it is highly unlikely that complete immunity will be achieved. While some of the past sources of instability may well disappear, the growing global interdependence of the U.S. economy may elevate what were once minor impacts into more serious concerns for the domestic economy. Moreover, relative to declines in other potential sources, instabilities originating in the consumer sector, which accounts for two-thirds of all spending, may as a result become even more prominent.

To a significant extent, the first half of the twenty-first century will still be shaped by the forces set in motion in the post–World War II era. The baby boom that followed World War II synchronized movements through the economic life cycle for an unusually large proportion of the population. It also synchronized shifts in how people assess their future economic prospects. Over the coming decades, the focus of the baby boom generation will shift from uncertainties about labor market conditions to risks originating in financial markets, starkly highlighted by the first bear market of the twenty-first century. Uncertainty about future rates of return on financial assets plays an important role in consumers' assessments of their lifetime or permanent income regardless of their age. The relative importance of labor income, however, declines as consumers near retirement and become increasingly dependent on realized returns on their accumulated financial assets.

Precautionary savings theories focus on the impact of uncertainty about the future. Once sufficient wealth is accumulated during preretirement years, there is no need for such buffer stocks of savings. Precautionary motives, however, will not disappear in retirement. Uncertainty about future real returns on assets will prompt consumers to engage in precautionary decreases in spending, in much the same manner that precautionary motives act to increase savings prior to retirement. Although uncertainty about future rates of return is incorporated into current theories of consumption, little is known about how consumers form expectations about future real rates of return, especially across their entire portfolio of asset holdings. Research on understanding how people assess uncertainty about future incomes must incorporate information on how people form expectations about future needs and how those expectations change as they age. Expectations about longevity and disability, as well as about in vivo transfers and bequests, will play an increasingly important role in shaping consumer behavior in the twenty-first century. In addition, expectations about changes in the provisions of private and public health and pension programs will also be needed to fully understand how people assess potential future risks.

Given that Social Security and other pension entitlements will represent a major share of incomes in the future, some have contended that there is little reason to expect income uncertainty during retirement to have a significant impact on the macroeconomy. By this same reasoning, it could also be argued that uncertainty about future labor income would not represent a significant problem since even at the worst of times the overwhelming majority remains employed. In addition, this line of reasoning ignores the potential impact of inflation. This is particularly true for changes in relative prices that are to the disadvantage of the elderly, as not all pension entitlements are fully indexed to inflation. Moreover, compared with variations in labor market conditions, valuations of financial assets are likely to exhibit more abrupt and relatively larger changes since shocks in global financial markets are more rapidly reflected in domestic financial markets than in domestic labor markets. To be sure, consumers do not react to every change in stock and bond prices, especially when their investment horizons are long. Little is known, however, about the thresholds or conditions that prompt changes in expectations about future rates of return, whether those factors operate in an asymmetric fashion, how time preferences and risk aversion change as people age, and what sources of information have the most influence on their assessments.

While most changes in consumer expectations are incremental, at times the changes are large and occur abruptly. Over the past fifty years, the sharpest changes in consumer expectations have been associated with the rapid development of unexpected events whose implications are difficult to assess. Whereas slow change allows gradual adaptation, rapid change prompts a disabling sense of uncertainty and disengagement. The inaction caused by such abrupt changes may generate a self-reinforcing process that acts to accentuate rather than mitigate the underlying source of uncertainty. Although each of the sharp declines in consumer confidence during the past fifty years has been explained in retrospect, none has been predicted in advance. Indeed, the more common finding has been that apparently similar economic developments have had quite dissimilar effects on consumers' expectations. Research is needed to understand the conditions under which similar economic shocks produce quite dissimilar results. More generally, attention needs to be given to how consumers evaluate and incorporate information about low probability events that have potentially large consequences. This task is as important as it is challenging since it directly focuses on the extreme tails of probability distributions, where prior research on economic expectations is almost entirely absent.

At the dawn of the twenty-first century, this research program faces as many challenges as opportunities for the scientific advancement in our understanding of the role of the consumer in shaping the macroeconomy. Despite the many changes in the economic environment as well as in the economic situation of consumers, there is no reason to expect the influence of the consumer on macroeconomic trends to wane in the twenty-first century. The strength of the research program is that it is based on the premise that the description and prediction of consumer behavior represent the best means to foster advances in theory. While there is nothing more useful than good theory, there is nothing more productive in generating theoretical advances than good data. The unique contributions of this research program will continue to be built on the collection of data that enables rigorous tests of established theory as well as to allow the unexpected to emerge and energize new theoretical advances. Rather than being confined to the armchair of the theorist, the research program will continue to seek advances from the armchairs of respondents as they explain the factors underlying their economic decisions.

NOTES

1. Katona documented the development of his theories in a series of books: *Psychological Analysis of Economic Behavior* (1951), *The Powerful Consumer* (1960), *The Mass Consumption Society* (1964), and *Psychological Economics* (1975). For an overview of Katona's theoretical contributions, as well as a complete list of his publications and biographical information, see Curtin 1983.

2. It should be noted that Tobin's cross-section analysis as well as the early time-series tests were based on what would now be considered unacceptably small sample sizes on which to base a definitive assessment. Tobin's analysis was based on a cross-section sample of 632 cases, and the early time-series tests were based on between eleven and twenty-two observations.

3. The predictive ability of intentions data in cross-section analysis has been shown by Klein and Lansing (1955), Mueller (1957), Tobin (1959), Juster (1964), Maynes (1967), and Dunkelberg (1972). Time-series tests were conducted by Mueller (1963), Friend and Adams (1964), Adams (1964, 1965), Suits and Sparks (1965), Ferber (1966), Maynes (1967), Dunkelberg (1969), Fair (1971), and Juster and Wachtel (1972). Nearly all of the more recent analyses have focused on aggregate time-series tests, including those by Garner (1981); Curtin (1984); Fuhrer (1988); Praet and Vuchelen (1989); Hall (1993); Blanchard (1993); Acemoglu and Scott (1994); Cochrane (1994); Huth, Eppright, and Taube (1994); Carroll, Fuhrer, and Wilcox (1994); Matsusaka and Sbordone (1995); Abderrezak (1997); Eppright, Arguea, and Huth (1998); Danthine, Donaldson, and Johnsen (1998); and Howrey (2001).

4. The decision was initially based on time-series tests, which included twenty quarterly observations, with another two quarters of data collected before the closure took effect. The addition of those two data points had a large impact on the estimated parameters, turning the probability measure of purchase intentions into a highly significant predictor. Although this could have been interpreted as ample demonstration of parameter instability with sample sizes of twenty, McNeil (1974, 6) interpreted the result as indicating that "any confidence in the predictive value of the [purchase probability] index would have been ill founded." It is interesting that in a report summarizing the reasons for halting the survey, McNeil concluded, "In retrospect, it would seem that the warnings of Katona and Mueller about the limitations of cross-sectional tests were not given adequate attention. . . . In the future we would do well . . . to exercise the utmost caution in using cross-section results to infer time-series performance" (11).

5. For a description of the design and methodology of the survey, including the questionnaire items and formulation of the index of consumer sentiment, see Curtin 1982b. Annual summaries of the survey findings are published by the Department of Economics at the University of Michigan in the proceedings for the Economic Outlook Conference. See also the SCA Web site: <http://www.sca.isr.umich.edu/main.php>.

6. Some of these factors were found to be quantitatively large; for example, Campbell and Mankiw (1989) estimate that about half of all disposable income accrues to rule-of-thumb consumers, with consumption mainly responding to innovations in current income. Based on PSID data, Zeldes (1989) finds the same split between liquidity-constrained and -unconstrained consumers, with the behavior of the latter approximating what would be expected based on the life-cycle permanent income hypothesis.

7. The acceptance of the full rationality postulate would still provide unbiased predictions of aggregate behavior if the departures due to bounded rationality were random. Research by Tversky and Kahneman (1982a), however, has convincingly demonstrated that the departures represent systematic biases. Even with the presence of such systematic bias, some theorists have maintained that markets would effectively act to eliminate the influence of such "quasi-rational" agents. Russell and Thaler (1985) have found, however, that the market conditions necessary to produce this result rarely exist.

8. To be sure, a growing number of economists do advocate bounded rationality. For an overview of research based on bounded rationality, see Conlisk 1996 as well as the collected papers of Simon (1997).

9. There is a rather large literature focused on the inflation expectations series derived from SRC's surveys, including Turnovsky 1970, Carlson and Parkin 1975, Wachtel 1977, Figlewski and Wachtel 1981, Fishe and Lahiri 1981, Curtin 1982a, Gramlich 1983, Bryan and Gavin 1986, Rich 1989, Fishe and Idson 1990, Grant and Thomas 1999, and Thomas 1999.

10. Some have argued that professional forecasters do not provide their true unbiased forecast but act strategically so as to maximize their compensation by publishing distinctive forecasts to generate publicity for their firms (Laster, Bennett, and Geoum 1999). As a result, it is argued that published forecasts are a poor proxy for the economist's true expectations and hence create a bias toward the rejection of the rational expectations hypothesis.

11. The usual test of rational expectations involves testing the relationship between the realized inflation rate in period t as a function of the expected inflation rate for period t formed at $t-1$, usually expressed as $P_t = \alpha + \beta P_t^{e\,t-1}$. For expectations to be unbiased, the appropriate test requires $\alpha = 0$ and $\beta = 1$. The results for the median consumer expectations were nearly identical to the values posited by the rational expectations hypothesis. The estimates (standard errors) were $\alpha = 0.09$ (0.66) and $\beta = 0.99$ (0.18).

12. The frequency of item nonresponse in the Italian Survey of Household Income and Wealth was high by any standard: 55 percent of eligible respondents did not answer the questions, and among those that did provide answers, 63 percent gave a point estimate for expected change in income, inflation, or both (Guiso, Japelli, and Terlizzese 1992). Dominitz and Manski (1997) measured current and expected income levels, taking the difference as a measure of expected change in income. The resulting item nonresponse rate was 47 percent for the measure of expected income change. Calculating the expected change as the difference in levels is likely to yield estimates that are coarse and imprecise compared with direct measures of the expected change in income. This is an especially important problem for time-series analysis since defining income expectations as the difference between two relatively noisy level estimates may lead to high and spurious variability in income expectations.

REFERENCES

Abderrezak, A. 1997. Consumer expectations and cyclical durations. *Quarterly Review of Economics and Finance* 37 (4): 843–54.

Acemoglu, D., and A. Scott. 1994. Consumer confidence and rational expectations: Are agents' beliefs consistent with the theory? *Economic Journal* 104:1–19.

Adams, F. G. 1964. Consumer attitudes, buying plans, and purchases of durable goods: A principal components, time-series approach. *Review of Economics and Statistics* 46 (4): 347–55.

———. 1965. Prediction with consumer attitudes: The time-series—cross section paradox. *Review of Economics and Statistics* 47 (4): 367–78.

Blanchard, O. 1993. Consumption and the recession of 1990–1991. *American Economic Review* 83 (2): 270–74.

Bryan, M. F., and W. T. Gavin. 1986. Models of inflation expectations formation: A comparison of household and economist forecasts: Comment. *Journal of Money, Credit, and Banking* 18 (4): 539–44.

Caballero, R. J. 1991. Earnings uncertainty and aggregate wealth accumulation. *American Economic Review* 81 (4): 859–71.

Campbell, J. Y., and N. G. Mankiw. 1989. Consumption, income, and interest rates: Reinterpreting the time-series evidence. In *NBER Macroeconomics Annual*, ed. O. Blanchard and S. Fischer. Cambridge, MA: MIT Press.

Carlson, J. A., and M. Parkin. 1975. Inflationary expectations. *Economica* 42:123–38.

Carroll, C. D. 1994. How does future income affect current consumption? *Quarterly Journal of Economics* 109 (1): 11–147.

———. 1997. Buffer-stock saving and the life cycle/permanent income hypothesis. *Quarterly Journal of Economics* 112 (1): 1–55.

Carroll, C. D., J. C. Fuhrer, and D. W. Wilcox. 1994. Does consumer sentiment forecast household spending? If so, why? *American Economic Review* 84 (5): 1397–1408.

Carroll, C. D., and A. A. Samwick. 1997. The nature of precautionary wealth. *Journal of Monetary Economics* 40:41–71.

———. 1998. How important is precautionary savings? *Review of Economics and Statistics* 80 (3): 410–19.

Christiano, L. J., and T. J. Fitzgerald. 1999. The business cycle: It's still a puzzle. *Economic Perspectives, Federal Reserve Bank of Chicago* 22 (4): 56–83.

Cochrane, J. H. 1994. Shocks. *Carnegie-Rochester Conference Series on Public Policy* 41:295–364.

Conlisk, J. 1996. Why bounded rationality? *Journal of Economic Literature* 34:669–700.

Curtin, R. T. 1982a. Determinants of price expectations: Evidence from a panel study. In *International Research on Business Cycle Surveys*, ed. H. Laumer and M. Ziegler. Hampshire, UK: Gower.

———. 1982b. Indicators of consumer behavior: The University of Michigan Surveys of Consumers. *Public Opinion Quarterly* 46:340–52.

———. 1983. Curtin on Katona. In *Contemporary Economists in Perspective*, ed. H. W. Spiegel and W. J. Samuels, 1:495–522. New York: Jai Press.

———. 1984. Consumer attitudes for forecasting. In *Advances in consumer research*, ed. T. C. Kinnear, 11:714–17. Provo, UT: Association for Consumer Research.

———. 1999. The outlook for consumption in 2000. *The Economic Outlook for 2000*. Ann Arbor: Department of Economics, University of Michigan.

Danthine, J. P., J. B. Donaldson, and T. Johnsen. 1998. Productivity growth, consumer confidence, and the business cycle. *European Economic Review* 42:1113–40.

Dominitz, J., and C. F. Manski. 1997. Using expectations data to study subjective income expectations. *Journal of the American Statistical Association* 92 (439): 855–67.

Dunkelberg, W. C. 1969. Forecasting consumer expenditures with measures of attitudes and expectations. Ph.D. diss., University of Michigan.

———. 1972. Impact of consumer attitudes on behavior: A cross-section study. In *Human behavior in economic affairs*, ed. B. Strumpel, J. N. Morgan, and E. Zahn. New York: Elsevier.

Earl, P. E. 1990. Economics and psychology: A survey. *Economic Journal* 100 (402): 718–55.
Eppright, D. R., N. M. Arguea, and W. L. Huth. 1998. Aggregate consumer expectation indexes as indicators of future consumer expenditures. *Journal of Economic Psychology* 19:215–35.
Fair, R. C. 1971. *A short-run forecasting model of the United States economy.* Lexington, MA: Heath.
Ferber, R. 1966. Anticipations, statistics, and consumer behavior. *American Statistician* 20 (4): 20 24.
Figlewski, S., and P. Wachtel. 1981. The formation of inflationary expectations. *Review of Economics and Statistics* 63 (1): 1–10.
Fischhoff, B. 1994. What forecasts (seem to) mean. *International Journal of Forecasting* 10 (3): 387–403.
Fishe, R. P. H., and T. L. Idson. 1990. Information-induced heteroscedasticity in price expectations data. *Review of Economics and Statistics* 72 (2): 304–12.
Fishe, R. P. H., and K. Lahiri. 1981. On the estimation of inflationary expectations from qualitative responses. *Journal of Econometrics* 16:89–102.
Friedman, M. 1953. *Essays in positive economics.* Chicago: University of Chicago Press.
———. 1957. *A theory of the consumption function.* Princeton: Princeton University Press.
Friend, I., and F. G. Adams. 1964. The predictive ability of consumer attitudes, stock prices, and non-attitudinal variables. *Journal of the American Statistical Association* 59:987–1005.
Fuhrer, J. C. 1988. On the information content of consumer survey expectations. *Review of Economics and Statistics* 70 (1): 140–44.
Garner, A. 1981. Economic determinants of consumer sentiment. *Journal of Business Research* 9:205–20.
Gramlich, E. M. 1983. Models of inflation expectations formation: A comparison of household and economist forecasts. *Journal of Money, Credit, and Banking* 15 (2): 155–73.
Grant, A. P., and L. B. Thomas. 1999. Inflationary expectations and rationality revisited. *Economics Letters* 62:331–38.
Guiso, L., T. Japelli, and D. Terlizzese. 1992. Earnings uncertainty and precautionary saving. *Journal of Monetary Economics* 30:307–37.
Hall, R. E. 1993. Macro theory and the recession of 1990–1991. *American Economic Review* 83 (2): 275–79.
Howrey, E. Philip. 2001. The predictive power of the index of consumer sentiment. *Brookings Papers on Economic Activity* 2001 (1): 175–207.
Huth, W. L., D. R. Eppright, and P. M. Taube. 1994. The indexes of consumer sentiment and confidence: Leading or misleading guides to future buyer behavior. *Journal of Business Research* 29:199–206.
Hymans, S. 1970. Consumer durable spending: Explanation and prediction. *Brookings Papers on Economic Activity* 2:173–99.
Juster, F. T. 1964. *Anticipations and purchases.* Princeton: Princeton University Press.
———. 1966a. *Household capital formation and financing: 1897–1962.* Princeton: Princeton University Press.
———. 1966b. Consumer buying intentions and purchase probability: An experiment in survey design. *Journal of the American Statistical Association* 61:658–96.

———. 1969. Consumer anticipations and models of durable goods demand. In *Economic forecasts and expectations,* ed. J. Mincer. New York: Columbia University Press for NBER.

Juster, F. T., and P. Wachtel. 1972. Anticipatory and objective models of durable goods demand. *American Economic Review* 62 (4): 564–79.

Kahneman, D., and A. Tversky. 1982. On the psychology of prediction. In *Judgment under uncertainty: Heuristics and biases,* ed. D. Kahneman, P. Slovic, and A. Tversky, 48–68. Cambridge: Cambridge University Press.

Katona, G. 1951. *Psychological analysis of economic behavior.* New York: McGraw-Hill.

———. 1957. Federal Reserve Board committee reports on consumer expectations and saving statistics. *Review of Economics and Statistics* 39 (1): 40–45.

———. 1960. *The powerful consumer: Psychological studies of the American economy.* New York: McGraw-Hill.

———. 1964. *The mass consumption society.* New York: McGraw-Hill.

———. 1975. *Psychological economics.* New York: Elsevier.

Kimball, M. S. 1990. Precautionary saving in the small and in the large. *Econometrica* 58 (1): 53–73.

Klein, L. R. 1946. A post-mortem on transition predictions of national product. *Journal of Political Economy* 54 (4): 289–308.

Klein, L. R., and J. B. Lansing. 1955. Decisions to purchase consumer durable goods. *Journal of Marketing* 20:109–32.

Laster, D., P. Bennett, and I. S. Geoum. 1999. Rational bias in macroeconomic forecasts. *Quarterly Journal of Economics* 114:293–318.

Lewin, S. B. 1996. Economics and psychology: Lessons for our own day from the early twentieth century. *Journal of Economic Literature* 34 (3): 1293–323.

Lichtenstein, S., B. Fischhoff, and L. D. Phillips. 1982. Calibration of probabilities: The state of the art to 1980. In *Judgment under uncertainty: Heuristics and biases,* ed. D. Kahneman, P. Slovic, and A. Tversky, 306–34. Cambridge: Cambridge University Press.

Lott, W. F., and S. M. Miller. 1982. Employers' and workers' inflation expectations: Prediction accuracy and the natural-rate hypothesis. *Eastern Economic Journal* 8:283–88.

Lovell, M. C. 1986. Tests of the rational expectations hypothesis. *American Economic Review* 76 (1): 110–24.

Mankiw, N. G. 1988. Recent developments in macroeconomics: A very quick refresher course. *Journal of Money, Credit, and Banking* 20 (3, pt. 2): 436–49.

Manski, C. F. 1990. The use of intentions data to predict behavior: A best-case analysis. *Journal of the American Statistical Association* 85 (412): 934–90.

Matsusaka, J. G., and A. M. Sbordone. 1995. Consumer confidence and economic fluctuations. *Economic Inquiry* 33:296–318.

Maynes, E. S. 1967. An appraisal of the consumer anticipations approaches of forecasting. Proceedings of the Business Economics Statistical Section of the American Statistical Association,114–23.

McNeil, J. M. 1974. *Census Bureau programs to measure consumer purchase expectations: 1959–1973.* Technical Paper 36. Washington, DC: Bureau of the Census, U.S. Department of Commerce.

Modigliani, F., and R. Brumberg. 1954. Utility analysis and the consumption function: An interpretation of cross-section data. In *Post-Keynesian economics,* ed. K. Kurihara. New Brunswick, NJ: Rutgers University Press.

Mueller, E. 1957. Effects of consumer attitudes on purchases. *American Economic Review* 47 (6): 946–65.
———. 1963. Ten years of consumer attitude surveys: Their forecasting record. *Journal of the American Statistical Association* 53:899–917.
Muth, J. F. 1961. Rational expectations and the theory of price movements. *Econometrica* 29 (3): 315–35.
Praet, P., and J. Vuchelen. 1989. The contribution of consumer confidence indexes in forecasting the effects of oil prices on private consumption. *International Journal of Forecasting* 5:393–97.
Rabin, M. 1998. Psychology and economics. *Journal of Economic Literature* 36:11–46.
Rabin, M., and J. L. Schrag. 1999. First impressions matter: A model of confirmatory bias. *Quarterly Journal of Economics* 114 (1): 37–82.
Rich, R. 1989. Testing rationality of inflation forecasts from survey data: Another look at the SRC expected price change data. *Review of Economics and Statistics* 71:682–86.
Russell, T., and R. Thaler. 1985. The relevance of quasi rationality in competitive markets. *American Economic Review* 75 (5): 1071–82.
Savage, L. J. 1971. Elicitation of personal probabilities and expectations. *Journal of the American Statistical Association* 66 (336): 783–801.
Seaver, D. A., D. von Winterfeldt, and W. Edwards. 1978. Eliciting subjective probability distributions on continuous variables. *Organizational Behavior and Human Performance* 21:379–91.
Simon, H. A. 1947. *Administrative behavior.* New York: Free Press.
———. 1957. *Models of man: Social and rational.* New York: Wiley.
———. 1978. Rationality as process and as product of thought. *American Economic Review* 68 (2): 1–16.
———. 1997. *Models of bounded rationality.* Cambridge, MA: MIT Press.
Suits, D. B., and G. R. Sparks. 1965. Consumption regressions with quarterly data. In *Brookings quarterly econometric model of the United States,* ed. J. S. Duesenberry, G. Fromm, L. R. Klein, and E. Kuh. Chicago: Rand McNally.
Thaler, R. H. 1991. *Quasi-rational economics.* New York: Russell Sage.
———. 1992. *The winner's curse.* Princeton: Princeton University Press.
Thomas, L. B., Jr. 1999. Survey measures of expected U.S. inflation. *Journal of Economic Perspectives* 13 (4): 125–44.
Tobin, J. 1959. On the predictive value of consumer intentions and attitudes. *Review of Economics and Statistics* 41 (1): 1–11.
Turnovsky, S. 1970. Empirical evidence on the formation of price expectations. *Journal of the American Statistical Association* 65:1441–54.
Tversky, A., and D. Kahneman. 1982a. Causal schemas in judgments under uncertainty. In *Judgment under uncertainty: Heuristics and biases,* ed. D. Kahneman, P. Slovic, and A. Tversky, 117–28. Cambridge: Cambridge University Press.
———. 1982b. Judgment under uncertainty: Heuristics and biases. In *Judgment under uncertainty: Heuristics and biases,* ed. D. Kahneman, P. Slovic, and A. Tversky, 3–20. Cambridge: Cambridge University Press.
Wachtel, P. 1977. Survey measures of expected inflation and their potential usefulness. In *Analysis of inflation: 1965–1974,* ed. J. Popkin. Cambridge: Ballinger.
Zeldes, S. P. 1989. Consumption and liquidity constraints: An empirical investigation. *Journal of Political Economy* 97 (2): 305–46.

CHAPTER 6

Evolution and Change in Family Income, Wealth, and Health: The Panel Study of Income Dynamics, 1968–2000 and Beyond

Greg J. Duncan, Sandra L. Hofferth, and Frank P. Stafford

The origins of the Panel Study of Income Dynamics were in Lyndon Johnson's War on Poverty, when the Office of Economic Opportunity directed the U.S. Census Bureau to conduct a nationwide assessment of the extent to which the War on Poverty was affecting people's economic well-being—in short, were we winning or losing? This Census Bureau study, called the Survey of Economic Opportunity, completed interviews with about thirty thousand households, first in 1966 and again in 1967.

An interest in continuing this survey of economic trajectories in a flexible, university-based research environment led James D. Smith and his OEO colleagues to approach James Morgan and his Economic Behavior Program colleagues at the Survey Research Center (SRC) at the University of Michigan. The proposal was to interview for five years a nationally representative subsample of approximately two thousand low-income SEO households. Morgan and his EBP colleagues (Lansing, Katona, Mueller, Stafford, and others) had among them extensive prior experience in economic surveys, especially in the postwar study of income, spending, and wealth; and Morgan, lead author of the 1962 book *Income and Welfare in the United States*, was a natural choice to lead the new study.

Initially, Morgan was reluctant to take the study on because the OEO design called for following only low-income households. He argued for the virtues of complete population representation, pointing out, for example, that understanding why nonpoor households fell into poverty was at least as interesting as knowing why poor households climbed out. Fortunately for scientific progress, he was able to convince OEO to fund a different design. In this new design two thousand randomly chosen OEO households that were in poverty at the time were combined with a fresh cross section of about three thousand households from the SRC national sampling frame. When weighted, the combined sample was representative of the entire population of the United States, including nonpoor as well as poor households. As a further research advantage, the disproportionately large number of low-income households produced large analysis samples of blacks and other disadvantaged groups.

In the Beginning (and Implications Beyond)

The other innovative design element, widely discussed within the EBP and the sampling section of SRC, was the idea of following the children of sample families as they left to form their own households. To follow such "split offs," it was argued, would offset the problem of panel attrition. And by continually adding these young families, a panel study could provide a continuous self-representing sample of the U.S. population. The PSID research planners realized that including the newly formed families of children who left to live on their own would both provide continued representation of such young families and support the study of early adult experiences of children from different economic backgrounds and poverty exposures (Hill 1992). This element of genealogy-based design, which allows the study to maintain the representation of the young (with weights) and to observe the effects of family background, was a momentous event in survey design history. In effect, the PSID follows a bloodline, not a person. Use of this insight opened up the eventual study of intergenerational connections.

When played out over more than thirty years, these design features enable the PSID to provide the following data:

1. Data on a nationally representative cross section of families and individuals in 1968;
2. Data on nationally representative annual cross sections from 1969 through 1999 of families and individuals descended from the original 1968 sample (but excluding effects of immigration, which were corrected for in 2001);
3. Thirty-year-plus longitudinal data on individuals in the initially

representative 1968 sample, including generational outcomes for children observed both when they were living with their parents and long after they struck out on their own in adulthood; and

4. Shorter-run comparative longitudinal data on representative cohorts of individuals at any point between 1968 and 1999.

These design features and other tangible and intangible elements of data quality[1]—response rates have been high and largely random with respect to observable variables (Fitzgerald, Gottschalk, and Moffitt 1998)—have combined to make the PSID one of the most widely used and influential data sets in the social science research community. As of early 2000, over one thousand PSID-based articles have appeared in over one hundred different refereed journals; and the bibliography lists about three thousand publications, dissertations, and working papers. From 1972 to 1999 over 250 Ph.D. dissertations used PSID data. In the period 1995–99 over 325 published papers appeared using PSID data. This represents a significant rise in the rate of publication over prior five-year intervals, indicating that the research value of such a panel can accelerate decades after the initial wave. The uses are so broad that these numbers are surely undercounts. In the 1990s, publication rates were approximately five per year in the top four economics journals, six per year in the top labor-economics journals, and five per year in the top five sociology and family journals.[2] This extensive use of the PSID has led it to be on the National Science Foundation's list of its fifty most significant projects in its fifty-year history. In this group of the "Nifty Fifty," as they are called, the PSID is the only social science project. One cannot hope to present a comprehensive summary of what has been learned from these many studies. Our approach is decidedly selective.

Probably unappreciated at the design phase was the enormous long-run challenge of keeping track of all these family histories that were to accumulate from this genealogical or steady state design. Remember, the study had been established to continue for five years, and continuance beyond that was just the normal researcher's hope of study longevity. The first interview was a simple respondent-friendly thirty-two-page questionnaire, and pages 31 and 32 were done by interviewer observation only.

Elements of the postwar study of consumer behavior were evident. In Section C (on cars), the question "What year model/make is it?" was asked of each car, along with its condition (e.g., good, fair, poor), insurance, car payments, and annual repair costs. Multiple cars, like multiple individuals within a family, give rise to various types of relational data. The learning from earlier efforts to create files (for General Motors and Ford) with cars as the units of observation combined with characteristics of their owners provided important lessons. From this experience the PSID team was able to pioneer the construction of relational data files connecting individual family members and their personal characteristics to the characteristics (such as shared housing or family wealth holdings) of the families to which they belonged.

With time, the instrument grew dramatically longer and more involved. These factors of family evolution and instrument complexity operate multiplicatively in conjunction with temporal accumulation of prior information to challenge both the researcher's imagination and the archiving and processing team. For researchers it is safe to say there are analysis domains that have yet to be explored.

The year 1972 proved momentous for the PSID. Its original five years were coming to an end when President Nixon abolished the OEO virtually overnight. Responsibility for the PSID was transferred to the Assistant Secretary for Planning and Evaluation (ASPE) of the Department of Health, Education, and Welfare (now Health and Human Services), where visionary ASPE officials such as Larry Orr saw the value of continuing to support the PSID.

The year 1972 was also the first of Greg Duncan's twenty-five years with the project. As a second-year economics graduate student at Michigan, he was attracted to work at the SRC by Morgan's mile-a-minute course on survey methods and by the invaluable experience of spending his senior undergraduate year in Costa Rica as part of a field studies program. His first PSID tour of duty was as a data editor, reading the often lengthy interviewer explanations of complications that rendered responses to the PSID's many closed-ended questions problematic. The job required the ability to make sense of the individual family's demographic and economic data, which was done by observing the myriad events behind families' seemingly tumultuous economic fortunes and learning which pieces of data deserved the greatest trust.

The poverty focus of the PSID's early years had led to the inclusion of an eclectic set of supplemental measures that might be expected to differentiate families who climbed out of poverty from those who stayed poor. Thus, the first five annual questionnaires are filled with measures of locus of control, future orientation, achievement motivation, employment barriers, entrepreneurial activity, trust/hostility, avoidance of unnecessary risks, access to sources of information and help, and a short sentence-completion test. Given the short interview length, these measures represented a large share of the early total content.

The inclusion of subjective measures in the PSID had some interesting intellectual history behind it. Some years earlier Milton Friedman had remarked that, for the Michigan EBP group, studying behavior was the most important objective: "Don't ask people what they think, ask them what they do!" The name of the research unit, the Economic *Behavior* Program, has its origins partly in this exhortation. So the use of subjective measurements and assessments had to meet the test of whether these variables could predict interesting economic behavior. The program, as it evolved, acquired a multidisciplinary flavor both from the active involvement of psychologists such George Katona and from the interest of a small but highly effective group of mainstream economic advisors, including Jim Tobin, Larry Klein, and Guy Orcutt (two of whom were Nobel laureates).

In more recent work there are results indicating that some of the social-psychological measures included in the early PSID waves are much more predictive of long-run and intergenerational success than of short-run outcomes. Early analyses of the short-run (i.e., five-year) effects on labor-market earnings of measures such as personal control and achievement motivation failed to show robust and important connections (Duncan and Morgan 1981; Augustyniak, Duncan, and Liker 1985). However, when levels of labor-market success in the early 1990s are related to the early-wave measures of personal control and components of achievement motivation, much more powerful linkages emerge. The collection of twenty-five-year-old social-psychological measures accounted for as much of the variation in current earnings as did completed schooling! Thus, some of the measures have proved quite powerful in differentiating individuals according to their long-run (but not short-run) successes and failures.

While these influences are intriguing, simply populating the PSID instrument with a selection of interesting social-psychological measures would come at the cost of reduced coverage of the current core—a heavy price to pay. However, some measures might be asked for only one or two waves but not included as core variables. An example is the 1996 module on risk tolerance (Barsky et al. 1997). One hint that risk tolerance may matter for the long run comes from recent work on the intergenerational effects of these early-wave measures (Yeung, Duncan and Hill 2000). A boy's future success, as measured by eventual completed schooling and early career attainment, is shown to be enhanced by having a risk-averse father (i.e., reports fastening his seat belt, has car or medical insurance, etc.). Perhaps having a father who dampens rather than reinforces the excesses of youth is beneficial for boys. At any rate, these two sets of long-run results suggest the value for attainment research of taking a very long view.

In the Middle Years, 1980–92

Based on this early lack of predictive power, however, attitudes and aspirations dwindled as a share of the questionnaire content. Other, more manageable analyses led to chapters published in the first of ten *Five Thousand American Families* volumes. By the late 1970s, after a decade of operation, the status of the PSID properly evolved from a poverty study into a unique longitudinal data resource for social scientists from several disciplines. The genealogical design was already paying off. Not only were there panel observations with which analysts could work, but the sample, with weights, could be used to describe the economic circumstances of the full U.S. population, not just the surviving remnant of an initial sample.

The broadening research themes beyond poverty spells, combined with ASPE's declining budget fortunes, led to a transfer of primary funding for the study from ASPE to the NSF. A major threat to the continuation of the PSID emerged when Reagan's first budget proposal for the NSF arrived on the scene: it recommended a 75 percent cut in social and economic science funding, a cut that was seen as a way station toward zero and would have done in the PSID. Had it not been for three years of emergency funding—orchestrated by then ISR director Tom Juster—from the Ford, Sloan, and Rockefeller Foundations, the PSID would have ended. Albert Rees of the Sloan Foundation remained deeply committed to the PSID and was an important sponsor well beyond the financial support that he helped to provide.

The content domains of the PSID data collection have always been twofold. The first is to maintain a clean and consistent time-series of core content—employment, family income, and family structure—based on the study's annual interviews. An example of the long-term payoff of this microdata-based panel is illustrated by work with the PSID to study wage dynamics over the business cycle (Abraham and Haltiwanger 1995). Only micropanel data can be used successfully to show that, net of a composition bias (changes in participation rates by different wage groups over the business cycle and specifically a disproportionate reduction in employment by low-wage workers in recessions), wages of individual workers really are flexible and move in phase with the business cycle.

The second data agenda item, dictated by the desire to maintain the capacity of the PSID to address contemporary research issues and, eventually, by the longer-term funding structure of the study, has been to complement the core with question supplements. Some of these topics, introduced originally as supplements, have proven to be of sufficient and persistent value that they have evolved into core content items. Notable among the components that have achieved the hard-earned right to be core topics are the National Institute on Aging–sponsored modules on wealth (in 1984, 1989, 1994, and every interviewing year starting in 1999—the first year of biennial interviewing). More recently, an enhanced set of health conditions (Section H) has moved to the category of core topics, and automobile ownership and purchases, originally in the PSID to understand transportation as a factor in poverty dynamics, has been reinstated as a core topic after a twenty-seven-year hiatus. The reason for this is to better understand the level and timing of durable expenditures *and* to understand transportation barriers to employment under state-specific limits to vehicle ownership by welfare recipients.

The surge of labor-market research in the 1970s led to the elimination of the PSID gender bias in the detail of questions asked of married women.[3] Question supplements on work histories, labor-market attachment, and on-the-job training were added. In 1980, Morgan anticipated the interest in "social capital" and altruism by leading an effort to develop a question supplement on both past and possible future flows of time and money help between households (see Boisjoly, Hofferth, and Duncan 1995; Hofferth, Boisjoly, and Duncan 1998, 1999; Hofferth and Iceland 1998). These were exciting times because the research team had the freedom to conceive and develop supplements on contemporary topics. Coupled with the ever-expanding PSID time-series of core content, this freedom provided a growing national network of analysts with unique data drawn from a large national sample of households.

The nature of PSID operations changed somewhat when its major funding was taken over in the early 1980s by the NSF. An NSF board of overseers began to review and pass judgment on PSID operations. While many of their suggestions have improved the PSID considerably, the burdens of dealing with academic overseers proved considerable, at least in the initial stages of the arrangement. Perhaps this was because the study team had enjoyed such a high degree of autonomy up to that point. The creative elements of the PSID shifted more to the invention and design of question modules that supplemented the PSID's demographic and economic core. About 70 percent of what it took to collect and process the data was funded by NSF, so the project became increasingly dependent on federal agencies and, occasionally, private foundations to fund question supplements that would help cover the $2.5 million (current dollar) annual cost.

The question supplements developed in the 1980s and early 1990s were funded primarily by the National Institute of Child Health and Human Development (NICHD), the Department of Health and Human Services, and the National Institute on Aging. This funding enabled the PSID to add valuable question supplements on fertility, health, wealth, children's schooling, and intergenerational transfers. A Ford Foundation–funded supplement sample of Latino households was implemented from 1990 to 1995. Funding was also secured for projects establishing links between PSID sample members and the National Death Index and between PSID respondent addresses every year and geographic identifiers. Having geographic identifiers such as census tracts, zip codes, and counties has enabled analysts to match contextual information from the decennial census and other sources to the interview information to explore the nature of neighborhood effects. These efforts have recently been revitalized and improved—to the benefit of the larger research community. Most exciting is that new methodologies are being developed for the analysis of spatial data. These will allow for formal modeling of to-be-estimated spatial aggregates and for modeling of changes in the environment resulting either from persons moving to a different location or from the environment at the location changing through time. This may give a boost to an empirical and theoretical literature in spatial economics, an area long dormant but believed to be due for renewed interest.

Operationally, these supplemental activities required a great deal of proposal writing and other entrepreneurial effort. This was carried out by a group of colleagues, in particular Greg Duncan (PSID codirector at the time), Martha Hill, Dan Hill, Charlie Brown, and Jim Lepkowski. Although burdensome, the process forced the team to branch out and develop a network of contacts in government agencies and to seek occasional private-sector funding. The process was facilitated by a remarkably capable and perceptive set of individuals heading research programs in government agencies, in particular, Richard Suzman in the NIA, Daniel Newlon in the NSF, and Jeffrey Evans in the NICHD, all of whom understood both the scientific issues and the mechanisms for converting research opportunities into funding. In 1994 Sandra Hofferth joined the

PSID as codirector. In 1995 Frank Stafford joined as codirector and serves as director and principal investigator of the PSID today. In 2001, Bob Schoeni became codirector of the study.

Some Lessons from a Long, Genealogical Panel

What a Family's Life Cycle Is Really Like

Despite the study's longitudinal nature, most analysts typically approached the first decade of PSID data as though they were drawn from a cross section. Longitudinal methods were not widely used in the 1970s, and the PSID questionnaire provided many novel measures that, when analyzed using cross-sectional methods, produced interesting and, most important, publishable articles. Many studies were inspired by the active program of research by the community of labor economists and focused on current popular topics, such as earnings differences between men and women and between union and nonunion workers. Many papers were written on the economic rewards of on-the-job training, childcare choices of working parents, and, using retrospective reports, intergenerational models of completed schooling.

Juxtaposed to the cross-sectional patterns, however, were results indicating a striking degree of economic turbulence and perhaps genuine mobility at all income levels (Morgan et al. 1974; Duncan et al. 1984). The hallmark finding, suggested by prior panel studies at EBP and strongly supported by the early panel analysis of the PSID, was great income fluctuation from one year to the next, producing many transitions into and out of both poverty and affluence and onto and off the welfare rolls. Moreover, other important changes frequently took place: roughly one in five families changed composition from one year to the next, and a comparable fraction pulled up stakes and moved from one location to another. These changes in family composition were important for implementing the sample design (which included following geographic movers out of their initial clustered sample design) *and* for understanding income dynamics.

What was going on? Were the income changes merely the result of measurement errors, or were families' economic fortunes really more volatile than previously believed? If the turbulence was real, what caused it and to what extent was it voluntary or at least anticipated? And how much of the turbulence reflected true mobility—permanent changes in economic and, perhaps, social position? The data patterns were in sharp contrast to the prevalent academic conceptions of social and economic position in the 1970s. These views included unchanging social class; the slow, steady building of stocks of economically valuable (human capital) skills; and fairly predictable life-cycle changes experienced by individuals as they age. In the life-cycle view, early adulthood was usually seen as a period of relatively low income as career and marital arrangements were being sorted out. Income was expected to grow as careers stabilized and, in some cases, blossomed and as multiple earners in households increased the household's total income. Retirement was seen as occasioning a drop in real income, cushioned by Social Security and private pension payments and by declines in work-related expenses.

Since that time there have been many conceptions of the need to deal with fluctuating income via the use of buffer stocks of liquid assets or lines of credit (Deaton 1992; Carroll 1994), but this was not a central element in empirical social science of the 1970s. Lenore Weitzman's (1985) sensational but overstated depiction of the dire economic consequences of divorce was still years in the future and had not yet been integrated into life-cycle theories. Elder's landmark studies of the Great Depression (1974) provided a vivid picture of the consequences of severe macroeconomic disruptions, but few thought that these kinds of disruptions were a regular feature of many families' lives in the prosperous second half of the twentieth century.

The prevailing life-cycle view of income evolution, however, conformed closely to (and, indeed, has been developed from) family income data drawn from representative cross sections of the population showing higher levels of household income for older individuals until their late forties and then lower levels at older ages. If we succumb to the temptation to use these cross-sectional data on different families at various life-cycle stages to represent the likely economic path of individuals as they age, we might view individual income trajectories as fairly smooth, with fluctuations occurring infrequently and at discrete points of the life cycle, such as early adulthood and retirement.

PSID as well as subsequent longitudinal household and administrative data reveal economic and social trajectories that are much more disparate and chaotic than those envisioned by early formulations of the life-cycle perspective. An idea of the scope of these fluctuations can be gleaned from table 6.1, which is taken from Duncan's (1988) PSID-based analysis of household income trajectories over the eleven-year period between 1969

TABLE 6.1. Level and Stability of Income, 1969–79, by age and sex

Age in 1969	Mean Income Level[a]	Percent with Income Rising Rapidly	Percent with Income Falling Rapidly	Percent with Big (>50%) Drops in Income at Least Once	Of Those With Drops, Percent Expecting Income Loss	Percent Poor at Least Once	Percent Poor 6 or More Years
25–54 yrs							
Men	$43.1	35	6	18	9	13	2
Women	40.0	32	10	24	6	20	5
46–55 yrs							
Men	38.7	22	13	26	12	14	3
Women	32.3	21	20	33	24	21	6
56–65 yrs							
Men	29.5	7	38	38	34	17	4
Women	22.1	6	35	39	25	27	9

Note: Taken from Duncan 1988. "Rapid rise" in size-adjusted income is an increase greater than 5 percent per year. "Rapid fall" in size-adjusted income is a decrease greater than 5 percent per year. Over an eleven-year period, an annual real growth rate of 5 percent will increase a family's real income by over 70 percent; a negative 5 percent rate will nearly cut it in half.

[a]Mean income level, in thousands of 1985 dollars.

and 1979.[4] Since the longitudinal experiences of men and women are quite different, data are presented separately by gender.

The first column shows the average level of family income over the eleven-year period and displays typical life-cycle patterns. Household incomes are highest for individuals who spent the entire period in their prime earning years; are somewhat lower for those who were initially forty-six to fifty-five years old, some of whom will have retired during the eleven-year period; and are lower still for the next older cohort, who were between the ages of fifty-six and sixty-five when the eleven-year period began. The gap between the family incomes of men and women increases substantially over the life cycle as a result of the increasing proportion of women who are not living with spouses or partners.

To what extent do these averages conceal diverse individual experiences? The second and third columns of table 6.1 show the fractions of the sample in various age and sex groups with either very rapid growth (more than 5 percent per year) or sharp declines (falling by at least 5 percent per year) in inflation-adjusted living standards over the period.[5] Several startling facts emerge, the foremost of which is the prevalence of either large positive or large negative trajectories. With the exception of men aged forty-six to fifty-five, at least 40 percent of all groups displayed either large positive or large negative economic trajectories. Life-cycle average income figures do indeed obscure a great deal of offsetting change at the individual level.

Consistent with early life-cycle theory, the average direction of the trajectories varies predictably across the age groups. Rapid increases are concentrated in the early adult years, while most of the rapidly decreasing average trajectories are experienced by the cohort of retirement age. But there are many exceptions to these life-cycle age patterns. Duncan (1988) also estimated the incidence of adverse income "events," which he defined as instances in which size-adjusted family income fell by 50 percent or more in consecutive years. This yardstick is similar to that employed by Elder (1974) and his colleagues in their studies of the effects of the Great Depression, which found long-lasting effects of income drops of one-third or more.

The incidence of sharp drops in income-to-needs ratios over the life course is shown in the fourth column of table 6.1. The overall risk is high: between 18 and 39 percent of the various groups are estimated to have experienced such a drop at least once during the eleven-year period. Most of these decreases left the individuals involved with, at best, modest incomes. Not shown in table 6.1 is the fact that 87 percent of the individuals experiencing these decreases saw their family incomes fall to less than $25,000. The PSID has questioned respondents about their expectations of future changes in economic status. This makes it possible to calculate what fraction of the 50-plus percent income drops were preceded in either of the previous two annual interviews by a report that the respondent expected his or her family economic status to decline. The fifth column of table 6.1 shows that both a majority of all income declines and the vast majority of preretirement income drops were unexpected.

Taken together, longitudinal PSID data show that it is a mistake to treat the path of average incomes as the typical income course of individuals as they age. Family incomes are quite volatile at nearly every point in the life cycle, making rapid growth or decline in living standards more the rule than the exception. We do not have to look with Elder and his colleagues to the Great Depression to find frequent instances of economic loss and hardship; the risk of sharp decreases in living standards is still significant at virtually every stage of life. Most of the losses are unexpected. These losses occur despite our system of government safeguards (e.g., unemployment insurance and Aid to Families with Dependent Children [AFDC]) and intrafamily transfers that might be expected to reduce or eliminate them.

So What?

Should these newly discovered economic fluctuations be a concern? Elder's (1974) data provide compelling but historical evidence of circumstances in which economic shocks can have devastating effects on both adults and children. In *Falling from Grace,* Katherine Newman (1988) draws data from the 1980s to document the psychological and other damage brought about by downsizing, divorce, and other events. Countless more specialized studies focus on the consequences of individual events such as layoffs, divorce, and widowhood (e.g., Yeung and Hofferth 1998). Perhaps contemporary economic dislocations are even more damaging than those in the 1930s, since there is much less of a sense that these events are shared by others.

On the other hand, some events producing economic losses may have benign or even beneficial effects. For example, when children leave parental homes, older parents decide not to move in with their adult children, despite the financial advantages they would otherwise enjoy, because they value their independence. Although their incomes are lower than before retirement, retired individuals may be better off because they have more leisure time than when they were working and because the predictability of retirement has allowed them time to prepare for its financial and psychological consequences. Similarly, despite their unstable incomes, construction workers may be well off because their higher rates of pay compensate them for the instability of their jobs, and the self-employed may value "being their own bosses" over a stable salary. In short, not all instances of income instability have the same negative implications. Indeed, some have argued explicitly that income variability over the life cycle is of little analytic and policy interest (Murray 1986). Work with the PSID data collected on housing equity, other wealth, and financial flows has been used to assess the ability of families to smooth over periods of income decline.

Research on the consequences of economic fluctuations is difficult because few data sets combine reliable longitudinal information on family income with well-measured subsequent physiological or psychological outcomes. An interesting exception using PSID data related the level and stability of income to mortality. McDonough et al. (1997) treated PSID data as if they were a series of independent six-year panels, the first spanning the calendar years 1972–78, the second spanning 1973–79, and so forth, with the last one spanning the years 1983–89. Within each six-year period they used the first five years to measure the level and stability of household income and the sixth and final year to measure possible mortality.

Key results are presented in table 6.2. They are taken from a logistic regression in which the dependent variable is whether the individual died during the sixth and final year of the given period. Income level and stability over the preceding five-year period are combined into a single classification of families:

1. Low and unstable income (i.e., mean income under $20,000) and at least one big income drop[6] over the given five-year period;
2. Low and stable income;
3. Middle-class (mean income between $20,000 and $70,000) and unstable income;
4. Middle-class and stable income;
5. Affluent and unstable income; and
6. Affluent and stable income (the reference group).[7]

Consistent with a number of other studies, mortality risks fall as income level rises. Individuals with low incomes have three to four times the mortality risk of the affluent individuals in the reference group (see chap. 9, this volume). New in the analysis is the result that *unstable* incomes also contribute to mortality risk, but only among the middle class. When compared with the reference group of the consistently affluent, middle-income individuals with stable incomes had a marginally significant 1.5 times elevation of mortality risk. In contrast, an individual with middle-class but unstable income had a risk ratio that was more than three times that of individuals in the reference group and was almost as high as individuals in the two low-income groups. Instability mattered at neither the low nor the high end of the income distribution, perhaps because the disadvantages of low incomes and the advantages of affluence overwhelm the possible effects of instability. An important item for future research is whether it is the income fluctuations per se or the events (e.g., unemployment or widowhood) producing them that increase the mortality risks.

Poverty and Welfare Dynamics

The book *Years of Poverty, Years of Plenty* (Duncan et al. 1984) was an attempt to summarize the most important lessons from the first ten years of the PSID. It included chapters on family economic and labor-market mobility, labor market differences between blacks and whites and

TABLE 6.2. Odd-Ratios of Mortality for Individuals Aged 45–64 Years, by Income Level and Stability, 1972–89

Five-Year Mean Income Level and Stability	Odds Ratio	95% Confidence Interval
Income <$20,000 and 1+ income drops	3.7*	2.4–5.7
Income <$20,000 and no income drops	3.4*	2.2–5.1
Income $20–$70,000 and 1+ drops	3.2*	1.9–5.5
Income $20–$70,000 and no drops	1.5*	1.0–2.0
Income >$70,000 and 1+ drops	1.4	0.7–2.6
Income >$70,000 and no drops	1.00 (reference group)	—

Note: Taken from McDonough et al. 1997, table 3. "Income drop" is defined as a situation in which size-adjusted family income fell by 50 percent or more in consecutive years.

*Coefficient is at least twice its standard error. Odds ratios are adjusted for age, sex, race, family size, and period.

between men and women, and poverty and welfare dynamics. It was to be an accessible summary of findings, and to a large extent it found its way into classrooms and policy discussions. The interest generated by the book focused overwhelmingly on its findings on the dynamic nature of poverty and welfare use. As with the more general life-cycle results, there was a huge gap between popular perceptions of these phenomena and the data's clear message of turbulence and mobility. When the PSID began, and continuing today, popular perceptions of the permanence of poverty and welfare receipt were widespread. We speak easily of "the poor" as if they were an ever-present and unchanging group. Indeed, the way we conceptualize the "poverty problem," the "underclass problem," or "the welfare problem" seems to presume the permanent existence of well-defined groups within American society. Much of our data on poverty is based on large annual Census Bureau surveys in which family annual cash incomes are compared with a set of "poverty thresholds" that vary with family size. In 1998, a three-person family with an income below $12,802 would be designated as poor; the threshold for a four-person family is $16,400. Although the poverty rates calculated each year by the Census Bureau generate a great deal of publicity, they rarely change by as much as a single percentage point from one year to the next. Longer-run trends show jumps during recessions and a disturbing secular increase in the poverty rate among families with children.

If, let us suppose, one in five children was poor in two consecutive Census Bureau survey "snapshots," and those poor children shared similar characteristics (e.g., half lived in mother-only families), what conclusion should be drawn? The observation would be consistent with an inference of absolutely no turnover in the poverty population and seems to fit the stereotype that poor families with children are likely to remain poor and that there is a hard-core population of poor families with little hope of self-improvement. However, the same evidence is equally consistent with 100 percent turnover—or any other percentage one might pick—assuming only that equal numbers of people with similar characteristics cross into and out of poverty.

In fact, a hallmark finding of the PSID is that a great deal of turnover exists among both the poor and welfare recipients (Duncan et al. 1984). Only a little over one-half of the individuals living in poverty in one year are found to be poor in the next, and considerably less than one-half of those who experience poverty remain persistently poor over many years. Similarly, many families receive income from welfare sources at least occasionally, but relatively very few do so year after year. Many descriptions of poverty experiences are possible with the PSID; perhaps the simplest is a count of the number of years in which an individual lived in a family with total annual income that fell short of the poverty threshold in that year. In the case of the eleven-year period used for table 6.1, if poverty were a persistent condition, then the sample would cluster at one of two points—no poverty at all or poverty in all of the eleven years. If much contact with poverty is occasional, then we would expect that the persistently poor would be a small subset of the larger group that had at least some experience with poverty.

The last two columns of table 6.1 show what fractions of individuals in the various age-sex groups spent at least one of the eleven years below the poverty line and which spent more than half of the time (at least six of eleven years) in poverty. The difference in the sizes of these two groups at all stages of the life cycle is striking. Depending on the life-cycle stage, between 20 and 27 percent of adult women experienced poverty at least once during the eleven-year period. The risk of at least occasional poverty was considerably lower for adult men than for women. Persistent poverty, defined as living in poverty for more than half of the eleven-year period, characterized fewer than one-tenth for any of the subgroups and is usually less than 5 percent. An older woman's chance of experiencing persistent poverty is roughly twice that of a woman between the ages of twenty-five and forty-four and is nearly five times as high as that of a man between the ages of twenty-five and forty-four. Poverty rates for children, especially minority children, are much higher, with nearly one-quarter of black children living in persistent poverty (U.S. Department of Health and Human Services 1997).

Adopting "event history" methods such as the life table and the Cox regression (Tuma and Groeneveld 1979), Mary Jo Bane and David Ellwood (1986, 1994) furthered the transformation in how social scientists and policy analysts viewed poverty and welfare dynamics. These methods enabled them to characterize the nature and determinants of poverty and welfare experiences by the duration of "spells" (i.e., the length in time of continuous periods of poverty or receipt). Essential data from the Bane and Ellwood analyses are presented in table 6.3. In the case of poverty, they use the PSID to estimate what fraction of families who first begin a poverty experience do so for the short run (one to two years), medium run (three to seven years), or longer run (eight or more years). They find that, while a clear majority of poverty spells are short, a substantial subset of poor families have longer-run experiences. Heterogeneity of experiences is thus key.

The original Institute and Center Directors of the Institute for Social Research (from its inception through the late 1960s): Institute Director Rensis Likert *(center)*; Angus Campbell *(left)*, Director of the Survey Research Center; and Dorwin Cartwright *(right)*, Director of the Research Center for Group Dynamics. (Photograph courtesy of the Bentley Historical Library, University of Michigan, University of Michigan News and Information Services, Box A6.)

The Institute for Social Research building in the 1950s—a former hospital building, complete with enclosed patient fire escape slide. (Photograph by Dale Fisher of Dale Fisher Associates.)

Leslie Kish *(center)*, Irene Hess *(right)*, and staff in the SRC Sampling Section (*left to right:* Doris Royster, David Sanchez, and Gilly Aga-Oglu Ludden) work on one of SRC's early area probability samples. (Photograph courtesy of the Bentley Historical Library, University of Michigan, University of Michigan News and Information Services, Box A10.)

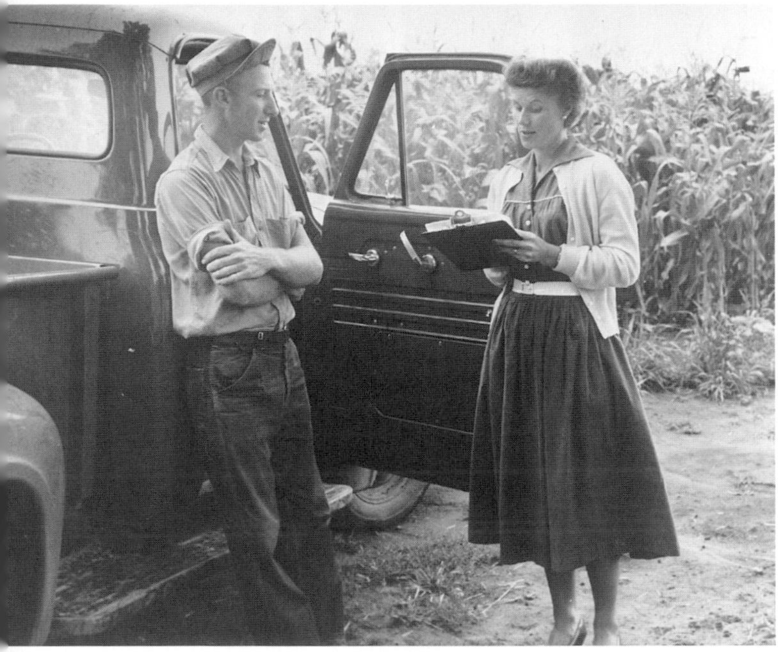

Michigan Survey Research Center interviewer taking an interview with a respondent in the 1950s. (Photograph courtesy of the Bentley Historical Library, University of Michigan, University of Michigan News and Information Services, Box A10.)

At the end of the twentieth century, almost all face-to-face as well as telephone interviewing at the Michigan Survey Research Center was done using computer-assisted-interviewing software operating on laptops carried by field interviewers, with interviews transmitted electronically to Ann Arbor. Interviewers in this study also took electronic blood pressure and direct height and weight measures on respondents in their homes, and blood and saliva samples were collected by medical technicians for a subset of willing respondents. (Photograph courtesy of Ratib Al-Ali.)

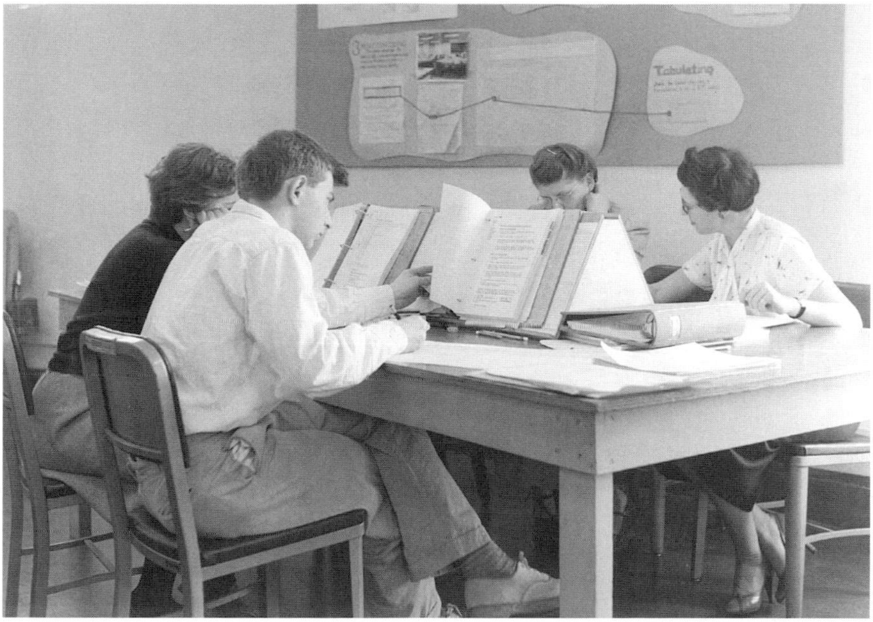

Paper and pencil coding of interviews in the Michigan Survey Research Center in the early postwar period. (Photograph courtesy of the Bentley Historical Library, University of Michigan, University of Michigan News and Information Services, Box A6.)

Computer-assisted coding and telephone interviewing being carried out in Michigan Survey Research Center's Survey Support Laboratory in the late 1990s. (Photograph by Philip Dattilo.)

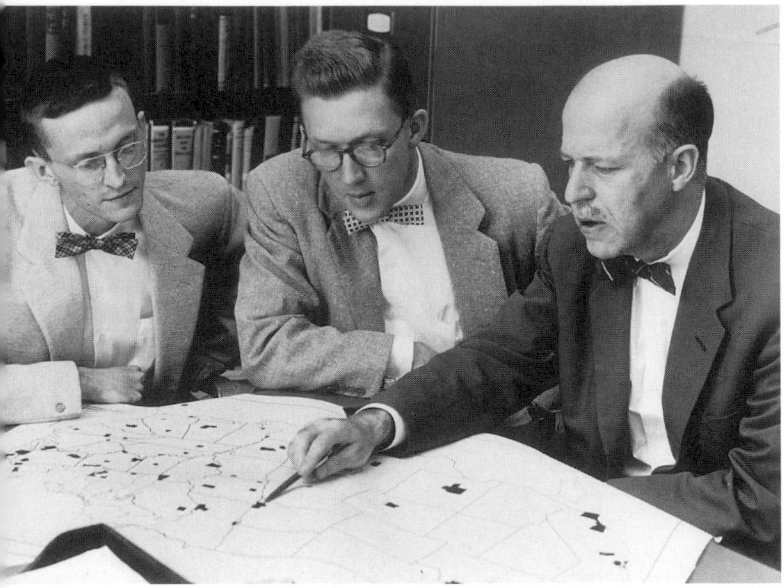

Angus Campbell *(right)*, Warren Miller, and Philip Converse *(left)* plan the sampling for the first of the National Election Studies by the Michigan Survey Research Center in the 1950s. (Photograph courtesy of the Bentley Historical Library, University of Michigan, University of Michigan News and Information Services, Box A10, SRC-16.)

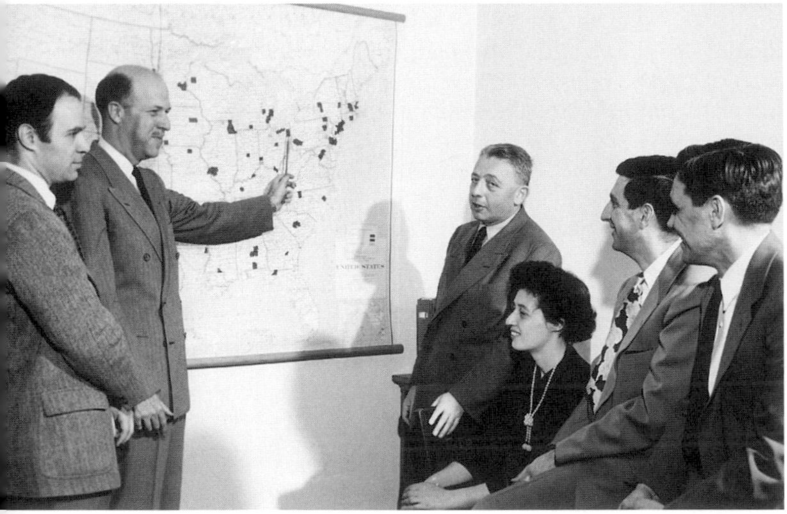

Planning of the sampling and survey design for the Surveys of Consumer Finance and Consumer Attitudes in the 1950s *(left to right):* later Nobel Prize winner Lawrence Klein, Angus Campbell, George Katona, Eva Mueller, James Morgan, and John Lansing. (Photograph courtesy of the Bentley Historical Library, University of Michigan, University of Michigan News and Information Services, Box A10.)

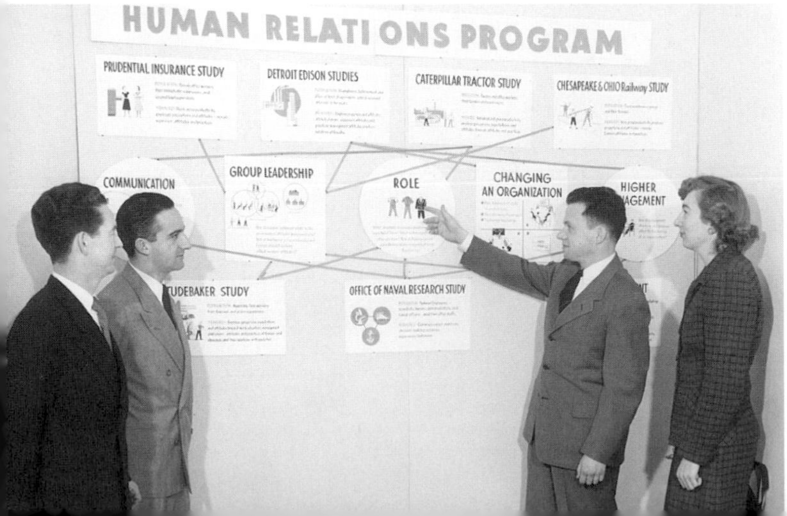

Discussing the conceptual foci and ongoing studies of the Human Relations Program (later Organizational Behavior Program) of the Michigan Survey Research Center in the 1950s *(left to right):* Eugene Jacobson, Robert Kahn, Gerald Mahoney, and Nancy Morse. (Photograph from the Institute for Social Research photo archives.)

Stanislav Kasl *(left)* and Sidney Cobb plan research in the 1960s on the social environment and health (mental and physical). (Photograph from the Institute for Social Research photo archives.)

George Brooks in the biochemical laboratory established in the Social Environment and Health Program in the 1960s. (Photograph from the Institute for Social Research photo archives.)

Stephen Withey and Elizabeth Douvan observe a pilot interview on one of the early studies of youth population, adolescent and later life course development at the Michigan Survey Research Center and Institute for Social Research. (Photograph courtesy of the Bentley Historical Library, University of Michigan, University of Michigan News and Information Services, Box B1, Item 24.)

Reflecting the still growing internationalization of demographic research in the Survey Research Center and Institute for Social Research, an interviewer working for Michigan's Population and Ecology Research Laboratory in Nepal conducts an interview with a Nepalese woman using the Life History Calendar developed for the Intergenerational Panel Study of Parents and Children in the Detroit area. (Photograph courtesy of Dr. Lisa Pearce.)

The staff in 2000 of the Monitoring the Future Study of substance use and abuse and adolescent and early adult development *(left to right):* Lloyd Johnston, John Schulenberg, John Wallace, Jerald Bachman, and Patrick O'Malley. (Photograph by Martin Vloet, University of Michigan Photo Services.)

Robert Willis *(left)*, current director of the Health and Retirement Study, and F. Thomas Juster *(right)*, its founding director, discuss the study with U.S. Representative Vernon Ehlers, congressman from Grand Rapids and leading architect of federal policies supporting scientific research and education, as part of the activities inaugurating the first decade of the twenty-first century as the Decade of Behavior in federal support of the biomedical and social sciences. (Photograph courtesy of Charles Votaw.)

James Jackson *(second from right)*, Director of the National Program of Research on Black Americans, discusses plans for the Survey Research Center's "How America Responds" survey of the American population after September 11, 2001, with Robert Kahn *(center)* and program trainees (*left to right:* Alfred DeFreece, L'Heureux Lewis, and Debbie Coral). (Photograph by Don Goings, courtesy of the Institute for Social Research.)

The Institute and Center Directors of the Institute for Social Research during the celebration of ISR's fiftieth anniversary in 1998 *(left to right):* William Zimmerman, Director of the Center for Political Studies; James House, Director of the Survey Research Center; David Featherman, Director of the Institute for Social Research; James Jackson, Director of the Research Center for Group Dynamics; and David Lam, Director of the Population Studies Center. (Photograph courtesy of the University of Michigan Photo Services.)

The Institute for Social Research building from 1994 to the present, built for ISR in three stages between the mid-1960s and the early 1990s. (Photograph by Philip Dattilo.)

Striving to discover *the* correct characterization of poverty—transitory or persistent—is fruitless, since poverty experiences are always a mixture of transitory episodes and long-term spells. The implications of these data analyses are profound, since the heterogeneous nature of poverty experiences implies that a one-size-fits-all policy approach may be ineffective. The needs arising from short duration spells call for social-insurance approaches in which fears of dependence need not be a concern. Some have argued that such policies need to be designed in ways to encourage financial reserves as a partial substitute for income support (Hubbard, Skinner, and Zeldes 1995). Long-term poverty spells are a different matter and call for policies that address the causes of the longer-run problems of the poor.

In the data presented in the second column of table 6.3, Bane and Ellwood (1994) calculate the likely total number of years of receipt for families just starting to receive AFDC.[8] They find a roughly even distribution of first-time welfare recipients across the three time intervals; roughly one-third have very short welfare experiences, one-third have medium-length experiences, and the final one-third have long-term receipt. With welfare, as with poverty, heterogeneity is a key feature. Prior to the reforms of 1996, AFDC operated simultaneously as a short-term insurance and long-run support program. As shown in table 6.3, many families using AFDC did so for only a few years, received help from it, got back on their feet, and never returned. However, a substantial fraction of recipients was indeed long-term, raising all of the rhetoric that seems to surround contemporary discussions of welfare.

These different patterns figured prominently in the debate over welfare reform. Ellwood (1988) proposed time limits as a means of addressing some of the problems associated with long-run receipt, although in the context of

TABLE 6.3. Distribution of Lengths of Spells of Poverty and AFDC, for Individuals First Beginning Spells of Poverty and AFDC

	Poverty, for Nonelderly Persons Beginning a Poverty Spell, in percentages	AFDC for Women Beginning an AFDC Spell, in percentages
1–2 years	60	36
3–7 years	26	35
8+ years	14	29
Total	100	100

Source: Poverty data taken from Bane and Ellwood 1986, table 2; AFDC data taken from Bane and Ellwood 1994, table 2.3.

a comprehensive package of supports designed to ensure that families who wanted work could get it and that the incomes of working families remain above the poverty line. In fact, welfare reform is now being implemented in fifty different ways across the states, with some incarnations resembling Ellwood's recommended policies but others quite different.

Road Trip

News and use of data from the PSID soon spread to several European countries and generated interest in launching similar studies. The most ambitious and widely used such studies are the German Socio-Economic Panel and the Swedish Household Panel (Huhallens economiska levnadsförhållen, or HUS), both of which collected first-wave data in 1984, and the British Household Panel Survey, which collected its first wave in 1990. Luxembourg, the Netherlands and the Lorraine region of France ran panels in the 1980s; quite comparable household panels in all European Community (EC) countries began in the early 1990s.

Many of these studies were shaped with input from researchers with PSID experience. One surprising result from comparative longitudinal analyses of income data is that the United States is far from alone in its high degree of economic mobility, particularly among the poor. This issue has important implications for the poverty debate in the United States. The Luxembourg Income Study project has documented the much higher rates of poverty that prevail in the United States than in other Western industrialized countries. Conservatives have argued that these uniquely high rates of U.S. poverty are the price we pay for our economic dynamism. Poverty is certainly less a worry if the economy will ensure that prosperity is a year or two away. To what extent are the lower poverty rates of European countries associated with lower amounts of economic mobility? Based on a project that examined poverty dynamics in nine countries, the results of this question are listed in the first column of table 6.4 (Duncan et al. 1995).

Data from Canada, Finland, and Sweden came from administrative records; all other results were from household panel surveys. Considerable effort was expended to ensure that all studies were based on representative and comparable samples and defined income levels and changes in comparable ways. To establish a comparable poverty line across countries, we used a relative threshold—50 percent of the median income of all households in the country.

The first column in table 6.4 presents a cross-sectional snapshot of poverty rates across the countries. Consistent with data from the cross-sectional Luxembourg Income Study, the poverty rate is found to be much higher in the United States, particularly among blacks, than in European countries, with the Canadians somewhere in between.

Poverty dynamics can be gauged by the fraction of poor families (defined as having incomes below 50 percent of the median in year t) that, in year $t + 1$, have income above 60 percent of the median.[9] If one calculates the poverty escape rates based on the entire poor population within each country (data not shown in table 6.4), then the U.S. poor rank near the bottom. However, this is due largely to the fact that the U.S. poor are, on average, much further away from the poverty line than are the poor in other countries. If we take only those families with year t incomes close to the poverty line (i.e., with incomes between 40 and 50 percent of the median), then the poverty escape rates are remarkably similar across the countries (second column of table 6.4). A more direct calculation of the degree of income instability among low-income families (third column of table 6.4) shows, if anything, less instability in the United States.[10]

Thus, the surprising result from this comparative study is that patterns of economic turbulence in other industrialized countries are similar to those in the United States. The extent of genuine economic mobility in

TABLE 6.4. Poverty Rates, Poverty Transitions, and Income Changes of Low-Income Families in Mid-1980s

Country	Percent of Families with Incomes below 50% of Median	Percent of "Near Poor" Climbing Out of Poverty	Typical Percent Income Change for Families in Bottom Decile
Canada	17	23	21
Finland	3	47	28
France-Lorraine	4	32	10
Germany (West)	8	24	18
Ireland	11	22	22
Luxembourg	4	29	10
Netherlands	3	23	8
Sweden	3	45	9
United States	20	22	15
German foreign residents	18	23	12
U.S. blacks	49	15	8

Note: Taken from Duncan et al. 1995, table 11.2. "Poverty" is defined by income less than 50% of median income in given country. "Near poor" are families with incomes 40–50% of median in base year. "Climbing out" is defined as year 1 to year 2 income change from <50% of the median to >60% of the median.

these data is another matter. Most of the families climbing out of poverty do not end up in the middle class, and more than a few return to below-poverty-level incomes from time to time. A companion analysis of welfare dynamics (Duncan et al. 1995) found, if anything, that the U.S. recipients had shorter-term experiences than did recipients in most other countries.

Poverty and Child Development

The fascinating PSID data on family income and poverty dynamics have also begun to be studied. Can we gain understanding of the patterns of change in family economic well-being? Since family structure itself had changed so much and figured so prominently in the income changes, a number of studies were done on the economic determinants and consequences of events such as divorce, widowhood, and out-of-wedlock childbearing. Economists such as Gary Becker had developed interesting models of these kinds of behavior, but so too had sociologists and psychologists. By the mid-1980s, attention turned to the "so what?" questions. PSID analysts were able to provide a detailed description of the dynamic patterns of poverty, family structure, and social conditions. Yet, collectively, little was known of the effects of these changes and events on the psychological and physical health of adults and on the life chances of individuals who experienced these events while growing up.

Addressing the "so what?" questions with the across-generation motion picture of economic, demographic, and social conditions and events had become possible by the late 1980s. Early efforts to link economic and other events in the sample produced a mixed record of success, perhaps because older adults' formative years predated the first PSID waves. Much more promising has been research on child and adolescent development, which has been able to draw upon more complete information, much of it dating from birth and extending to the early adult point at which developmental and labor market outcomes can begin to be assessed.

No single discipline monopolizes theoretical and methodological insights in this field of research, but there has been remarkably little collaboration of the relevant social science disciplines. Consequently, developmental studies designed by psychologists and sociologists attend to neither the economic dimension of family life nor economic aspects of the policy implications of the research. Moreover, economist-driven studies give short shrift to the idea of critical periods and to the careful measurement of outcome and process favored by psychologists and sociologists.

Many studies, books, and reports have demonstrated correlations between children's poverty and various measures of child achievement, health, and behavior (e.g., Duncan and Brooks-Gunn 1997; Brooks-Gunn and Duncan 1997; Children's Defense Fund 1994; Mayer 1997). As summarized in Brooks-Gunn and Duncan (1997, table 1), the strength and consistency of these associations are striking. Relative to nonpoor children, poor children are twice as likely to repeat a grade and to become a high school dropout. The ratio is 1.4 for learning disability; 1.3 for parent-reported emotional or behavior problems; 3.1 for a teenage out-of-wedlock birth; 6.8 for reported cases of child abuse and neglect; and 2.2 for experiencing violent crime.

But literature on the causal effects of poverty on children has major shortcomings, the most important of which is that family income is not reported in many data sources that contain crucial information about child outcomes. As a result, studies using these kinds of data have often used variables such as occupation, single parenthood, or low maternal education to infer family income levels. But income is far from synonymous with these other variables. As we have seen, family incomes are surprisingly volatile, which means that there are only modest correlations between economic deprivation and typical measures of socioeconomic background.

What is the best way to combine the insights from economics and developmental psychology to understand the effects of poverty on children? Psychology emphasizes the importance of conditions surrounding developmental stages and transitions. The greater malleability of children's development and the overwhelming importance of the family (as opposed to school or peer contexts) lead to expectations that economic conditions in early childhood may be far more important for shaping children's ability and achievement than are conditions later in childhood.

The possibility that the effects of economic conditions on children's development depend upon the childhood stage is foreign to most economists, whose developmental models are very simplistic and tend to focus on the role of "permanent" income. It is often assumed that families anticipate bumps in their life-cycle paths and can therefore save or borrow to smooth their consumption across these bumps. But while some economists recognize the potential importance of credit and other constraints faced by poor families, none had attempted to gauge the implications of the bumps in the context of children's development. The long-run scope and careful measurement of PSID income enabled Duncan et al. (1998) to investigate the importance of childhood stage–specific poverty for completed schooling. Their sample consisted of 1,323 children born between 1967 and 1973, who were observed in PSID families for the entire period between birth and age twenty to twenty-five and who constituted a representative sample of children in these birth cohorts. To allow for the differential impact of income by childhood stage, they related years of children's completed schooling to measures of family income averaged over the first, second, and third five-year segments of the children's lives (see table 6.5).[11]

Taken as a whole, the results show that the timing of economic deprivation matters a great deal for the schooling outcomes, with income early in life by far the most important. The coefficients reported in table 6.5 suggest, for example, that, controlling for income in other life stages and other family conditions, children in families with incomes between $15,000 and $25,000 during the birth to age five period average two-thirds of a year more schooling. This is about one-third of a standard deviation more when compared to children in families with income averaging under

TABLE 6.5. Effects of Stage-Specific Parental Income on Completed Schooling and High School Graduation Rates

Income Averaged Over:	Additional Years of Completed Schooling
Age 0–5	
Below $15,000	.00 (reference group)
$15,000–24,999	.66*
$25,000–34,999	.73*
$35,000–49,999	.78*
$50,000 and above	1.41*
Age 6–10	
Below $15,000	.00 (reference group)
$15,000–24,999	.16
$25,000–34,999	.24
$35,000–49,999	.44
$50,000 and above	.33
Age 11–15	
Below $15,000	.00 (reference group)
$15,000–24,999	.34
$25,000–34,999	.41
$35,000–49,999	.36
$50,000 and above	1.08*

Note: Based on Duncan et al. 1998, table 3.

*Coefficient is at least twice its standard error. All regressions include controls for mother's schooling, family structure, race, gender, age of mother at the birth of the child, total number of siblings, whether ever lived in South, number of geographic moves, and number of years mother worked for 1,000+ hours. Parental income is inflated to 1993 price levels.

$15,000. In contrast, income from middle childhood and adolescence failed to predict strongly to the schooling outcomes.[12] In short, economic deprivation occurring early in childhood appears to have the most pronounced and longest-lasting effects on children's achievement. The lens of early childhood as the critical period with respect to economic deprivation has some important policy implications (Duncan and Brooks-Gunn 1997). For example, the five-year time limits in the 1996 welfare reform legislation are not as worrisome as sanctions, since few families hitting five-year limits will contain young children living with them, but many families sanctioned off Temporary Assistance for Needy Families (TANF) programs or who have to work at inflexible jobs without paid leave can have young children placed in a very stressful environment with potential for long-term costs for their schooling and achievement (Hofferth et al. 2000; Hofferth 2002).

Children in PSID families, 1997 and Beyond

In recent years, the PSID has been used to examine the consequences of events and circumstances during the years that children are living with their parents for children's educational and economic successes as young adults (Brooks-Gunn et al. 1993; Duncan, Brooks-Gunn, and Klebanov 1994; Duncan et al. 1998; Haveman and Wolfe 1994; McLanahan and Sandefur 1994). Until 1997, such measures were collected annually from interviews with one adult respondent. For all individuals in the sample under age thirty, these measures are available from birth. Once children become teenagers, information about their marital status, fertility, behavior, and labor force activities is obtained, and, once they form their own household, the outcomes of early events, such as completed schooling, are available. However, the only information on children as children had been limited to age, sex, and race. Therefore, we did not know the mechanisms by which early family, school, and neighborhood experiences facilitate or detract from leading a healthy, productive adult life. In 1995, funding from ASPE at the Department of Health and Human Services permitted the PSID to include a set of questions asked of adults about their own and their young children's school successes and failures. While this was an important first step, the supplement was limited. It contained no direct assessments of children's development and experiences. The Child Development Supplement to the PSID (PSID-CDS) rectified that situation.

With funding from the NICHD, the PSID-CDS collected information in

1997 on up to two randomly selected children between the ages of birth and twelve of PSID respondents both from the primary caregivers and from the children themselves (Hofferth et al. 1999).

Child Outcome Measures

For the most part the study on child outcome measures used existing measures to assess children, age three and older, and their families. Children's well-being was defined in terms of cognitive/academic, socioemotional, and physical development. Outcome measures included (1) school progress, including academic achievement and cognitive ability, grade failure/progression, highest grade completed, verbal and math ability and literacy; (2) socioemotional well-being; and (3) health. Another set of items measured child health and functioning around the time of birth and at the time of the survey.

Child and Family Process Measures

Following these child assessment measures, the primary caregiver answered a set of interviewer-administered questions about each child, for up to two children. These questions were designed to obtain more information about the family and to assess parental functioning and parent-child and parent-parent relations. Measures included a self-esteem scale, a self-efficacy scale, a depression scale, and assessments of economic strain, social support, household tasks, food security, schooling and school progress, and parental engagement in school.

One unique aspect of this study was the collection of information from a second caregiver. While assessment of father involvement in the lives of their children is a key goal, we define the second caregiver quite broadly, since in many low-income households the second caregiver is a grandmother. In addition, father involvement was obtained in 1997, whether or not the father lived with the child.

Parental, School, Community, and Governmental Resources

Through 1997, the PSID core survey collected annual information on the number of parents, number and ages of children, presence of other adults, income, employment, earnings, hours of work, and education of all family members. Measures of parental financial resources are excellent, and all major components of wealth as well as income are assessed. In 1997 a child support supplement was funded for the first time and was included in the core to provide information on fathers' financial contributions to children. However, information about expenditures on children in the core is limited, as are questions about the quantity and quality of time spent with children. The PSID-CDS obtained information about parental expenditures on child care and school and about children's participation in nonparental child care and early childhood programs from birth until school entry and at the time of the survey.

Another unique aspect of the 1997 PSID-CDS was the collection of a time diary of children's activities. Previous national data on children's time use were collected in 1981 by the University of Michigan on a small sample of several hundred middle-class families. Many studies continued to utilize these numbers in the 1990s even though they were outdated (Task Force on Youth Development and Community Programs 1992). Parental time with children is one area in which data reported in stylized (nondiary) form are considered unreliable because of a strong social desirability bias. A study using U.S. data from the 1920s to the 1980s reported that parental time caring for children rose rather than declined over the period, in spite of increased maternal employment (Bryant and Zick 1996). Until 1997 no data were available to document changes since 1981.

Because resources from schools and preschool programs are important to children's lives, the PSID-CDS collected information from the teacher and administrator of the child's school or child care center or program, the family day-care home, or the other day-care provider. The teacher or caregiver provided information on the child, on activities in the classroom, and on his or her own characteristics. The administrator provided information on the characteristics and composition of the school and its student body. The teacher instrument for elementary school included a diary of child and teacher activities during the school day, teaching style, the resources available in the classroom, and the characteristics of students and teacher. Teachers provided information on child behavior using the same measures used by parents.

Finally, the PSID-CDS includes a rich set of measures of the economic, social, and policy characteristics of the community in which the child lives. Questions asked directly of parents include the extent to which parents know their neighbors, participate in community activities, and view their neighborhood as "safe."

What Have We Learned So Far?

In 1981 only about one-half of all PSID-CDS children lived in families with an employed mother, compared with two-thirds in 1997. One-quarter of all the children lived in traditional two-parent families in which the father worked and the mother was a homemaker. In contrast, 42 percent lived in families in which both parents worked. Four percent lived in two-parent families in which the father did not work. A second change between 1981 and 1997 was the increased proportion living with only one parent. Twenty-eight percent lived with a single parent in 1997, compared with only 20 percent in 1981. Parents were better educated in 1997. Twenty-four percent had completed some college, compared with 16 percent in 1981. They also were more likely to have one or two instead of three children in 1997. The median family income for families with children under the age of thirteen was almost $40,000 (Hofferth 1998).

As a result of such demographic changes since the early 1980s, we find that children's activities have changed. Their amount of free time has dropped slightly, leading to reduced time playing, watching television, eating, and just "hanging out" (Hofferth and Sandberg 2001b). Instead, children spend more time in structured activities such as school, day care, sports, and art activities. Mothers have less time for preparing food and clothing at home, so children spend more time accompanying their parents shopping and less time helping with traditional household tasks. Other changes appear to be linked to education-related changes in attitudes and values regarding appropriate activities for children, such as the increase in sports participation, art activities (including music lessons), reading, and personal care and the decline in church-related activities.

Even with these changes, children's lives in 1997 differed only in degree from those of children in 1981. In 1997, children spent 74 hours a week sleeping, 25 hours in school and day care, 9 hours eating, and 9 hours in personal care (Hofferth and Sandberg 2001a). That left about 51 hours of discretionary time. Children spent about one-quarter of that time watching television and another one-quarter playing. Children spent very little time reading for pleasure (1.2 hours per week) or studying (2 hours). In their remaining free time children participated in sports, visited, did household chores, and just "hung out."

Do these changes in children's time matter for children's achievement and adjustment? Family characteristics are most important to children's development. Living with parents who have more schooling, living with two parents, having a mother with higher test scores, having parents who expect their child to complete college, and being from a smaller family are associated with children having higher levels of achievement (Hofferth 1998). Even after adjusting for family differences, however, children's activities are associated with achievement and adjustment. Participation in sports and reading is associated with children's achievement, particularly in problem solving and on verbal tests; spending more time eating, sleeping, and participating in sports is also associated with reduced behavior problems. Active leisure is more valuable for achievement than passive leisure, such as watching television and just hanging out, and participation in family and social activities is associated with better social adjustment.

One of the big questions is whether mothers, when they engage in paid work, lower their investment in children, who may suffer consequent disadvantage in cognitive achievement and adjustment. Research using 1997 PSID-CDS diary estimates of maternal time spent with children found only small differences (2.4 hours per week) between the time children spent engaged in activities with mothers in two-parent dual-earner households and two-parent single-earner households (Hofferth 2001), though there was a larger difference (5.2 hours) in the time employed and nonemployed mothers were available to children. The largest difference in engagement lay between two-parent families and single-parent families, a difference of 9 hours per week for dual-earner two-parent versus employed single-mother families and a difference of 6 hours per week for two-parent versus one-parent nonemployed-mother families.

A major question is whether time with parents has increased or decreased over the past several decades, as women have moved into the work force and as single parents have raised increasing numbers of children. Though there have been major demographic changes in the U.S. population, analyses indicate that changes in population structure between 1981 and 1997 would have decreased children's time with mothers and fathers if the changes had not been offset by positive changes in parental behavior (Sandberg and Hofferth 2001). Considering all types of families, the most important demographic factor affecting children's time with parents between 1981 and 1997 was the increase in single-parent families, not maternal labor force participation. The decline in paternal time due to increasing numbers of parents rearing children without partners shows up as a lack of increase in overall parental time in all families, in spite of an increase in mothers' time. In two-parent families, however, decreased time with mothers because of increasing maternal work was offset by increasing time with mothers and fathers due to behavioral changes. The behavioral changes uncovered here over a period of rapid social change are encouraging signposts for children. They run counter to popular claims that increased maternal employment and paternal indifference have reduced parental time with children in two-parent families, though low parental time is still problematic for children living in single-mother families.

Long-Term Earnings Structure Changes

In addition to the study of family influences on schooling and development, earnings, and adult outcomes, the PSID data can be used to test theories of the changing nature of work and the structure of wages. The availability of a long time-series on labor income in the PSID allows the examination of major changes in the labor market. The mid-1970s to late 1980s were the years of skill-based technical change. Despite the rise in the share of the labor force with higher education, the earnings of these workers continued to rise both in absolute terms and, even more, relative to those with less education. Data from the PSID on the percentile distribution of annual labor earnings for adult men employed at least fifteen hundred hours per year show that, throughout much of the lower part of the earnings distribution, there was a downward slide from 1973 to 1985, which was continued into the Gulf War recession in 1991. Since 1990 (and in many cases since 1985), the Consumer Price Index (CPI) adjusted wages show increases throughout much of the lower part of the earnings distribution (5th–30th percentiles) and the upper part of the earnings distribution (75th–95th percentiles). Only in the middle percentiles was there earnings stagnation during the period 1985–95. When we allow for a 1 percent per year CPI bias, even the middle percentiles experienced a rising standard of living over the period of the mid-1980s to the mid-1990s.

A parallel analysis for adult women shows even better earnings growth between the mid-1980s and the mid-1990s. For women, even in the middle percentiles, earnings rose at a rate above the CPI. At the 50th percentile, earnings rose 13 percent, from $21,627 to $24,280. Allowing for CPI bias, this is in the range of 25 percent per decade. At the upper part of the earnings distribution, the gains net of inflation were higher still. For the 90th percentile the 1985–95 gains were 19.5 percent, and for the 95th percentile the annual earnings of women working fifteen hundred or more hours rose from $47,887 to $60,648, a gain of 26.6 percent above the CPI.

Rising wages and labor income of educated workers, combined with rising relative supply, appear to be explainable by a simple general equilibrium model where skilled and less skilled workers initially trade final or intermediate goods that are more specialized to each. Information technology effects a type of "skill-extensive technical change" that allows the skilled workers to produce things previously in the domain of the less skilled. This technological competition (Gomery 1994) from the skilled workers erodes the economic role of the less skilled workers, reducing their income even as overall GDP rises (Johnson and Stafford 1998). The predicted result is economic growth, but uneven growth in which skilled workers receive more than 100 percent of the rising GDP growth, with redistribution away from the less skilled. Did the low-earner families move up the income scale by also acquiring job skills? Further analysis shows that much of the gain to college-educated workers is among the younger cohorts *and* among those in what the Department of Commerce identified as information technology industries (Kim, Johnson, and Stafford 2001). Additional work shows that beyond these cross-sectional snapshots there has been increased wage mobility, both upward and downward, from the mid-1970s on (Gottshalk and Moffitt 1994). However, much of the increase in intertemporal variability is within the upper decile of earnings.

The 1990s and Beyond

With new technology enhancing the ability to collect, process, and deliver data, what should be asked of whom? The "of whom" part is still heavily shaped by the genealogical structure set out in the design, as discussed earlier, and much of the "what" part is derived from the long continuity of measures on income and employment, housing, and food consumption that are part of the core. In recent years PSID staff have worked closely with the PSID board to redefine the core as part of a special effort to increase information about children living in PSID families. This has given rise to a new and broader set of measures that are considered to be core items—to be asked as part of every biennial PSID interview. Changes to the sample were made in 1997 to control costs (arising from the sample growth resulting from split offs) and to achieve better representation (e.g., of immigrants). Changing to biennial interviewing to reduce costs has led to pressure to increase the interview length to what seems an effective upper limit of seventy-five minutes.

Areas for increased use of the PSID that have led to a redefinition of the research directions include the following:

1. Intergenerational transfers and intergenerational research;
2. Wealth, savings, and consumption;
3. Life-course health and economic status;
4. Child development;
5. New welfare sequences to capture changing welfare policy; and
6. Immigration.

Measuring Wealth and Health

A representative topic of these areas, and one that interacts with many of the long-standing core topics, is wealth. Economic research in the study of wealth seems to have followed the stock market: high and rising to a peak in the mid- to late 1960s and then a long period of stagnation until approximately the last decade. Fortunately, the idea of adding wealth to the PSID came in the early 1980s, when it was decided that enough information on lifetime economic histories was available to make the study of the transitions into retirement a priority area. The first wealth data were collected in the PSID in 1984 with support from the NIA. Then, as now, there was a research interest in household responses to capital gains, particularly those gains from rising equity values. By measuring wealth increases in excess of active savings flows, one could, it was argued, measure and analyze capital gains. It was also decided to add information on prospective retirement plans (for those age forty-five to sixty-four), on global health and health-care utilization, and on pensions of the head of household and wife. To complete the financial picture, a wealth and savings module was designed, which, when combined with the long-standing series on housing and mortgages, would provide a measure of household wealth and active savings. Measuring active savings (money put into or taken out of the various items in a household wealth portfolio) required a sufficient time interval. A very short time interval is problematic since the interviews are not actually collected at uniform one-year intervals but often at shorter intervals as a result of appointments and availability of the respondent and interviewer. A five-year interval was chosen and the companion active savings measures were added in 1989. The wealth and savings measures were asked of all families, not just those nearer to retirement.

The quality of the wealth data was enhanced by the pioneering use, starting with the PSID in 1984, of "unfolding bracket" questions (Juster and Suzman 1995; Juster and Smith 1997; Juster, Smith, and Stafford 1999; Hurd and McFadden 1996; for details about the procedure, see Juster's introduction to part 2, this volume). For those households owning an asset, the proportion not reporting either a dollar amount or a bracket in the PSID wealth categories is surprisingly small, typically in single digits (Hurst, Luoh, and Stafford 1998, table A1).

The main shortcoming of the PSID data for analysis of wealth and saving behavior appears to be at the very upper end of the income and wealth distribution, where PSID coverage is not only sparse but also based on a visibly unrepresentative sample of very wealthy households. However, for the part of the wealth distribution below the top 1 or 2 percent, the PSID data appear to be very comparable to the demonstrably high-quality SCF data (Juster, Smith, and Stafford 1999). Even beyond the 98th percentile, the two surveys diverge greatly only beyond the 99.5 percentile, where SCF has the advantage of a high wealth oversample.

Learning about Wealth

Early work, from 1972 to 1989, demonstrated the impacts of the level and stability of income on odds ratios of mortality for individuals age forty-five to sixty-four. General health status has also been shown to have a strong correlation with household wealth (Smith 1999, table 9). Among the population under age fifty-five, the 1994 wealth ratio of those family heads reporting themselves to be in excellent health compared to those reporting poor health is eight to one for those age twenty-five to thirty-four; six to one for those age thirty-five to forty-four; and about four to one (on a much larger base) for those age forty-five to fifty-four. At this stage the interrelations among income from the labor market, lost income from injury or illness, and health gains from greater resources available to purchase medical care or more nutritious foods are likely elements in an empirical framework to understand the strong relation between wealth and health. Yet both theorizing and empirical work on this process are just beginning. What is the role of community influences? Do those who are healthier expect to live longer and thereby plan to acquire more wealth to support longer consumption streams? If so, do they look to start early in life? Are both health and wealth status driven by a common element such as future orientation, avoidance of unnecessary risk, or planning? How much of the wealth-health relation depends on medical and biological factors? How much depends on social factors and family relations? The timing of medical events as they relate to economic and family outcomes over the life course will become researchable once we accumulate histories, both retrospectively and prospectively, from our recently designed health modules for the PSID.

Conclusion

The PSID began in 1968 as a project with a specific mission: to understand the changing fortunes of lower-income families as part of the War on Poverty. To fulfill this mission several initial design features were implemented. First, a representative national sample was combined with an oversample of initially poor families. Second, to maintain a representative sample of young families, even over the initially planned five-year duration of the study, older children who left home to form their own families were added as new sample members. Third, by combining these three elements (the initial sample, the poverty oversample, and the newly formed families from each) through the use of weights, the resulting data portray the full U.S. population. With time this sample design has a weakness: the absence of new immigrants and the children of new immigrants born after the initial sample was drawn in 1968. By adding in this missing part of the evolving U.S. population in 1997 and 1999, the study continues to provide descriptive and analytic data on the full U.S. population some thirty years after its origin.

The initial content domains of the PSID were quite circumscribed. Besides attitudes and beliefs, the main quantitative elements were the money incomes and other financial resources flowing into the family to each of the individual family members. Expenditures were measured, where practical. The categories were chosen both to facilitate an understanding of the resources needed to participate in labor markets or in other ways to earn income (such as ownership of a functioning car) and to evaluate the real standard of living (housing, food expenditures, and numbers of equivalent adults in the family). The PSID became recognized as a unique resource quite early in its history. The reasons are simple: the strength of the sample design and the success in following split offs and continuing panel families were combined with a growing array of important panel measures of key economic and demographic variables with great analytic potential.

Through time, many of the initial attitudinal measures were curtailed, and an expansion of the initial behavioral content occurred. By continuing to select content that fits together—in the sense of providing a comprehensive set of measures on family well-being, its antecedents over the life course and across generations, and its correlates—the PSID has become perhaps the most widely used research data set in the social sciences. Research use of the PSID data, rather than declining as the "interesting questions" in its focus have been studied, has, to the contrary, accelerated in the most recent decade. There is every reason to believe that this will continue into the future, as analysts begin to examine the clusters of variables measuring health status, wealth levels, intergenerational transfers, child learning environments in the home and in school, and the consequences of new social policy parameters that influence poverty status and eligibility for public transfers.

NOTES

1. At the PSID Web site (http://psidonline.isr.umich.edu) is a feature, PSID Data Quality, that reports on the studies conducted to assess the quality of measures such as wealth, income, health, demographic histories, and new measurement methodologies (Belli, Shay and Stafford 2001).

2. These publication data come from the 2000 PSID bibliography on the Web site.

3. Mary Corcoran, Martha Hill, and Karen Mason spearheaded the effort to establish comparability between the labor market information collected from men and women.

4. An extension of this analysis by Burkhauser and Duncan (1994) shows that the basic patterns changed little between the 1970s and late 1980s.

5. Over an eleven-year period, an annual real growth rate of 5 percent will increase a family's real income by over 70 percent; a negative 5 percent rate will nearly cut it in half.

6. Consistent with table 6.1, an income drop is defined as a situation in which size-adjusted family income fell by 50 percent or more in consecutive years.

7. Control variables include the age of the individual, calendar year, race, and average size of the given person's household over the first five years of the window.

8. In contrast to the poverty data, which are based on single spells of poverty, the welfare-receipt data allow for multiple spells of receipt. Since transitions out of poverty or off welfare are often followed in a year or two by another spell, it is important to attempt to capture multiple spells in these calculations.

9. Sixty percent rather than 50 percent was used to avoid classifying instances of small income changes as transitions out of poverty.

10. The instability measure used here is the median absolute percentage change in income among families in the bottom decile of the income distribution. Note that since data from the Scandinavian countries are based on administrative records, are not sub-

ject to interview response errors, and do not show consistently different patterns, measurement error is not likely to be an overwhelming factor in these relative rankings.

11. The regression models also control for the mother's schooling, family structure, race, gender, age of the mother at the birth of the child, total number of siblings, whether the mother ever lived in the South, number of geographic moves, and number of years the mother worked more than one thousand hours. Parental income is inflated to 1993 price levels.

12. As shown in table 6.5, Duncan et al. (1998) did find that high parental income during adolescence had a strong positive effect on completed schooling. Additional analyses produced the unsurprising result that having affluent parents as a teenager increases your chances of attending college.

REFERENCES

Abraham, Katherine G., and John C. Haltiwanger. 1995. Real wages and the business cycle. *Journal of Economic Literature* 33:1215–64.

Augustyniak, Sue, Greg J. Duncan, and Jeffrey Liker. 1985. Panel data and models of change: A comparison of first difference and conventional two-wave models. *Social Science Research* 14:80–101.

Bane, M. J., and David T. Ellwood. 1986. Slipping in and out of poverty: The dynamics of spells. *Journal of Human Resources* 21:1–23.

———. 1994. *Welfare realities.* Cambridge, MA: Harvard University Press.

Barsky, Robert B., F. Thomas Juster, Miles S. Kimball, and Matthew D. Shapiro. 1997. Preference parameters and behavioral heterogeneity: An experimental approach in the health and retirement study. *Quarterly Journal of Economics* 112:S537–S579.

Belli, Robert F., William Shay, and Frank P. Stafford. 2001. Event history calendar and question list survey interviewing methods: A direct comparison. *Public Opinion Quarterly* 65:45–74.

Boisjoly, Johanne, Sandra L. Hofferth, and Greg Duncan. 1995. Access to social capital. *Journal of Family Issues* 16:609–31.

Brooks-Gunn, Jeanne, and Greg J. Duncan. 1997. The effects of poverty on children. *Future of Children* 7 (2): 55–71.

Brooks-Gunn, Jeanne, Greg J. Duncan, Pamela Klebanov, and Naomi Sealand. 1993. Do neighborhoods influence child and adolescent development? *American Journal of Sociology* 99:353–95.

Bryant, W. K., and C. Zick. 1996. An examination of parent-child shared time. *Journal of Marriage and the Family* 58:227–37.

Burkhauser, R., and Greg J. Duncan. 1994. Sharing prosperity across the age distribution: A comparison of the United States and Germany in the 1980s. *Gerontologist* 34:150–60.

Carroll, Christopher D. 1994. How does future income affect current consumption? *Quarterly Journal of Economics* 109:111–47.

Children's Defense Fund. 1994. *Wasting America's future.* Boston: Beacon Press.

Deaton, Angus. 1992. *Understanding consumption.* Oxford: Clarendon Press.

Duncan, Greg J. 1988. The volatility of family income over the life course. In *Life-span development and behavior,* ed. P. Baltes, D. Featherman, and Richard M. Lerner. Hillsdale, NJ: Lawrence Erlbaum.

Duncan, Greg J., and Jeanne Brooks-Gunn, eds. 1997. *The consequences of growing up poor.* New York: Russell Sage.

Duncan, Greg J., Jeanne Brooks-Gunn, and Pamela K. Klebanov. 1994. Economic deprivation and early childhood development. *Child Development* 65:296–318.

Duncan, Greg J., Richard Coe, Mary Corcoran, Martha Hill, Saul Hoffman, and James N. Morgan. 1984. *Years of poverty, years of plenty: The changing economic fortunes of American workers and families.* Ann Arbor: Institute for Social Research, University of Michigan.

Duncan, Greg J., Bjorn Gustafsson, Richard Hauser, Guenther Schmaus, Stephen Jenkins, Hans Messinger, Ruud Muffels, Brian Nolan, Jean-Claude Ray, and Wolfgang Voges. 1995. Poverty and social-assistance dynamics in the United States, Canada, and Western Europe. In *Poverty, inequality, and the future of social policy: Western states in the new world order,* ed. Katherine McFate, Roger Lawson, and William J. Wilson. New York: Russell Sage.

Duncan, Greg J., and James N. Morgan. 1981. Sense of efficacy and changes in economic status—A replication. *Journal of Human Resources* 16:649–57.

Duncan, Greg J., Wei-Jun Yeung, Jeanne Brooks-Gunn, and Judith Smith. 1998. How much does childhood poverty affect the life chances of children? *American Sociological Review* 63:406–23.

Elder, G. H. 1974. *Children of the great depression.* Chicago: University of Chicago Press.

Ellwood, David. 1988. *Poor support: Poverty and the American family.* New York: Basic Books.

Fitzgerald, John, Peter Gottschalk, and Robert Moffitt. 1998. An analysis of sample attrition in panel data: The Michigan panel study of income dynamics. *Journal of Human Resources* 33:251–99.

Gomery, Ralph E. 1994. A Ricardo model with economies of scale. *Journal of Economic Theory* 62:394–419.

Gottshalk, Peter, and Robert Moffitt. 1994. The growth of earning instability in the U.S. labor market. *Brookings Papers on Economic Activity* 2:217–72.

Haveman, Robert, and Barbara Wolfe. 1994. *Succeeding generations: On the effects of investments in children.* New York: Russell Sage.

Hill, Martha. 1992. *The panel study of income dynamics.* Beverly Hills: Sage.

Hofferth, Sandra. 1998. *Healthy environments, healthy children: Children in families.* Ann Arbor: Institute for Social Research, University of Michigan.

———. 2001. Women's employment and care of children in the United States. In *Women's employment in a comparative perspective,* ed. T. Van der Lippe and L. Van Dijk. New York: Aldine de Gruyter.

———. 2002. Did welfare reform work? Implications for 2002 and beyond. *Contexts: A Journal of the American Sociological Association* 1:45–51.

Hofferth, Sandra L., Johanne Boisjoly, and Greg Duncan. 1998. Parental extrafamilial resources and children's school attainment. *Sociology of Education* 71 (July): 246–68.

———. 1999. The development of social capital. *Rationality and Society* 11:79–110.

Hofferth, Sandra, Pamela Davis-Kean, Jean Davis, and Jonathan Finkelstein. 1999. *The child development supplement of the panel study of income dynamics: 1997 user guide.* Ann Arbor: Institute for Social Research, University of Michigan.

Hofferth, Sandra L., and John Iceland. 1998. Social capital in rural and urban communities. *Rural Sociology* 63:574–98.

Hofferth, Sandra L., and John F. Sandberg. 2001a. How American children spend their time. *Journal of Marriage and the Family* 63 (May): 295–308.

———. 2001b. Changes in American children's time, 1981–1997. In *Children at the millennium: Where have we come from, where are we going?* ed. T. J. Owens and S. L. Hofferth, 193–229. Oxford: Elsevier Science.

Hofferth, Sandra L., Julia Smith, Vonnie C. McLoyd, and Jonathan Finkelstein. 2000. Achievement and behavior among children of welfare recipients, welfare leavers, and low-income single mothers. *Journal of Social Issues* 56:747–74.

Hubbard, R. Glenn, Jonathan S. Skinner, and Stephen P. Zeldes. 1995. Precautionary saving and social insurance. *Journal of Political Economy* 103:360–99.

Hurd, Michael, and Daniel McFadden. 1996. The effects of anchoring on the distribution of consumption and saving. Paper presented at the NBER Summer Institute on Aging, August.

Hurst, Erik, Ming Ching Luoh, and Frank P. Stafford. 1998. The wealth dynamics of American families. *Brookings Papers on Economic Activity* 1:267–337.

Johnson, George E., and Frank P. Stafford. 1998. Technology regimes and the distribution of real wages. In *Microfoundations of economic growth: A Schumpeterian perspective,* ed. Gunnar Eliasson and Christopher Green. Ann Arbor: University of Michigan Press.

Juster, F. Thomas, and James P. Smith. 1997. Improving the quality of economic data: Lessons from the HRS and AHEAD. *Journal of the American Statistical Association* 92:1268–78.

Juster, F. Thomas, James P. Smith, and Frank P. Stafford. 1999. The measurement and structure of household wealth. *Labour Economics* 6:253–75.

Juster, F. Thomas, and Richard Suzman. 1995. An overview of the health and retirement study. *Journal of Human Resources* 30 (Supplement): S7–S56.

Kim, Young-Seong, George E. Johnson, and Frank P. Stafford. 2001. Information technology and income dynamics of American families. Working Paper, University of Michigan, Ann Arbor.

Luwig, Jens, Greg. J. Duncan, and Paul Hirschfield. 1998. Urban poverty and juvenile crime: Evidence from a randomized housing-mobility experiment. Northwestern University/University of Chicago Joint Center for Poverty Research Working Paper No. 2, November.

Mayer, Susan. 1997. *What money can't buy.* Cambridge, MA: Harvard University Press.

McDonough, Peggy, Greg J. Duncan, David Williams, and James House. 1997. Income dynamics and adult mortality in the U.S., 1972–1989. *American Journal of Public Health* 87 (9): 1476–83.

McLanahan, Sara, and Gary D. Sandefur. 1994. *Growing up with a single parent: What hurts, what helps.* Cambridge, MA: Harvard University Press.

Morgan , James N., Martin H. David, Wilbur J. Cohen, and Harvey E. Brazer. 1962. *Income and welfare in the United States.* New York: McGraw-Hill.

Morgan, James N., et al. 1974. *Five thousand American families—Patterns of economic progress.* Vol. 1. Ann Arbor: Institute for Social Research, University of Michigan.

Murray, Charles. 1986. *According to age: Longitudinal profiles of AFDC recipients and the poor by age group.* Prepared for the Working Seminar on the Family and American Welfare Policy.

Newman, Katherine. 1988. *Falling from grace: The experience of downward mobility in the American middle class.* New York: Free Press.

Sandberg, John F., and Sandra L. Hofferth. 2001. Changes in children's time with parents: United States, 1981–1997. *Demography* 38:423–36.

Smith, James P. 1999. Healthy bodies and thick wallets: The dual relation between health and economic status. *Journal of Economic Perspectives* 13:145–66.

Task Force on Youth Development and Community Programs. 1992. *A matter of time: Risk and opportunity in the nonschool hours.* New York: Carnegie.

Tuma, N. B., and L. D. Groeneveld. 1979. Dynamic analysis of event histories. *American Journal of Sociology* 84:820–54.

U.S. Department of Health and Human Services. 1997. *The green book: Overview of entitlement programs, 1997.* Washington, DC: U.S. Government Printing Office.

Weitzman, Lenore. 1985. *The divorce revolution.* New York: Free Press.

Yeung, Wei-Jun J., Greg J. Duncan, and Martha S. Hill. 2000. Putting fathers back in the picture: Parental activities and children's adult attainments. *Marriage and Family Review* 29:97–113.

Yeung, W. Jean, and Sandra L. Hofferth. 1998. Family adaptations to income and job loss in the U.S. *Journal of Family and Economic Issues* 19:255–83.

PART 3

From the Study of Organizations to the Study of Health

Robert L. Kahn

The somber mood and temper of this new millennium, already marked by long-standing wars, unresolved enmities, and newly invented forms of terrorism, stand in sharp contrast to the optimism of the early years after World War II. The victory over Nazi Germany and its allies, the Marshall Plan as a uniquely generous contribution to the rebuilding of Europe, and the emergence of the United Nations organization as an instrument of international cooperation made it seem that many of the historic burdens and blunders that had plagued the world would now be eased and corrected.

The social sciences, perhaps especially the emerging hybrid of social psychology and its accompanying methodology of survey research, shared in this general optimism and developed their own manifestations of it. The uses and usefulness of survey methods during the war were becoming increasingly apparent as their practitioners turned or returned to academic life and authorship. Publication of the multivolume *The American Soldier* by Stouffer and his colleagues (1949) provided perhaps the most prominent wartime example of quantitative social research meeting both national needs and scientific standards.

In founding the Survey Research Center (SRC) at the University of Michigan in 1946, Rensis Likert and his close colleagues were expressing this optimism and hopefulness. By the standards of that time, they were already sophisticated survey researchers, but they almost certainly overestimated the power of survey data to guarantee wise and benign policy decisions. Two of the three original SRC programs—the research program in economic behavior and a looser aggregation of studies in a program called public affairs—were strongly oriented toward issues of national policy. The third, originally called human relations, began the SRC's studies of organizations. It was no less ambitious to become an instrument of policy change as well as scientific discovery, but the implicit targets were more corporate than legislative.

The application of survey methods to research in large-scale organizations was urged both by external factors and by Likert's long-standing interest in organizational issues. In the larger society, the doctrines of Frederick Taylor and the near worship of time study were under attack. Chester Barnard's insightful book on the executive function dates from the late 1930s (Barnard 1938), as does the famous Hawthorne research (Roethlisberger and Dickson 1939). Elton Mayo's critique of contemporary industrial society was still earlier (Mayo 1930). Robert Merton's major analysis of social structure came decades later, but in 1940 he published an influential article on bureaucratic structure and personality (Merton 1940, 1950).

How much of this research had informed the opposition to Taylorism is unclear. The anti-Taylor forces were a loose array of organizations and individuals often referred to as the human relations movement; they included academics, labor unions, and an assortment of social observers and critics. Their alternative principles were less clearly formulated than Taylor's reliance on time study and precise instructions for task performance, but they emphasized participation and flexibility in the work setting rather than unquestioning obedience and rigidity in prescribed task behavior.

Likert's interest in these matters had been apparent well before his years in Washington. Before moving there in 1939 to head the new Division of Program Surveys in the Department of Agriculture, he had directed research on morale and motivation at the Life Insurance Agency Management Association. Shortly after the SRC was established at the University of Michigan, Likert persuaded Daniel Katz, a social psychologist who had worked with the Division of Program Surveys in Washington and had done research on morale and productivity in shipyards during World War II, to join the Michigan group as the director of a new program of organizational studies. With an initial grant from the Office of Naval Research in 1947, Likert and Katz started the Human Relations Program, as it was first called.

Support from the Office of Naval Research was of great importance in getting the new program under way and in getting access to the corporations in which the early studies were conducted. However, the program soon came to depend on support by the organizations in which it was conducting research. These contractual relationships influenced the research in at least two ways: they emphasized single-organization designs rather than populations of organizations, and they involved requests for help in interpreting and implementing the survey findings.

The SRC's program of research on organizational issues thus dates from the Center's earliest years and is now in its sixth decade. Its development over those years is represented in the three chapters that follow. Chapter 7, by Robert L. Kahn, gives the programmatic history of organizational research at the SRC, decade by decade. The first ten years were dominated by cross-sectional surveys of single organizations, which concentrated on the behavior of first-level supervisors and the workers they supervised. Employee satisfaction and productivity were the dependent variables of interest, and the research reflected the hopeful hypothesis that workers who were satisfied with their jobs would express their satisfaction by delivering relatively high performance. By the end of the 1950s, data from the early studies led the researchers to replace this hypothesis with more realistic motivational propositions. The decade of the 1950s also saw the development of survey feedback as a systematic method for the utilization of survey data in large-scale organizations.

By the second decade of organizational studies in the SRC, the accumulation of findings and the experience of the researchers led to efforts at theoretical integration. Major examples are Likert's *New Patterns of Management* (1961) and *The Social Psychology of Organizations* by Katz and Kahn (1966). During the 1960s, organizational research in the SRC also paid increasing attention to structural factors, especially as reflected in the distribution of power and authority. The earlier development of survey feedback as a method of organizational change was tested in a series of field experiments, and the range of organizations under study was expanded to include labor unions and voluntary organizations.

Finally, the 1960s were years of change for the SRC organizational program itself. The early interest in survey feedback as a method of organizational change was enlarged and led to the creation of a new research center in the Institute for Social Research (ISR), the Center for the Utilization of Scientific Knowledge (CRUSK), dedicated to research on the process of data utilization itself. The earlier research on worker satisfaction was also expanded to include a broad array of well-being measures, studied as outcomes of job demands and opportunities. This new research emphasis led to the establishment of a companion program in the SRC. The idea was that the Organizational Behavior Program would continue its concentration on organizational effectiveness as the main outcome of interest. The new program, initially called the Mental Health in Industry Program, would concentrate on the impact of organizational demands and rewards on the well-being of members. It later broadened into the Social Environment and Health Program (SEH), and its parent Organizational Behavior Program slowly dissipated.

In chapter 7, Kahn describes the decades of organizational research at ISR, including its later period of research on sources of stress at work, their effects on mental health and other signs of strain, and the factors that moderate the stress-strain relationship. Current work in the SEH Program is described in chapter 8 by Richard H. Price and in chapter 9 by James S. House and George A. Kaplan. Both of these chapters reflect a strong emphasis on measuring and assessing health—mental health in the Price chapter and physical health in the chapter by House and Kaplan. Both also show a sustained effort to extend and validate survey measures by linking them to criteria beyond self-report.

In his broad review of survey research on issues of mental health over a fifty-year period, Price distinguishes two main lines of development. The first emphasizes concepts and measures of well-being; the second attempts to measure the prevalence of mental disorders as clinically defined. The work of the SRC has contributed to both approaches but has concentrated on the first of them, the measurement of well-being and its social-psychological determinants. Price traces this development from the 1957 study Americans View Their Mental Health (Gurin, Veroff, and Feld 1960) through its 1976 replication (Veroff, Douvan, and Kulka 1981); from the study of well-being and subjective quality of life (Campbell, Converse, and Rodgers 1976; Campbell 1981); and from the National Study of Black Americans (NSBA), which included four waves of data over a thirteen-year period (Jackson et al. 1996). The chapter also includes the three national Quality of Employment (QOE) Surveys as part of this developmental sequence (Quinn et al. 1973; Quinn, Seashore, and Mangione 1975; Quinn and Staines 1979).

Of these studies, only Americans View Their Mental Health, with its use of projective tests and its inquiry into help seeking, reaches toward measuring the prevalence of mental disorders. Kessler and his colleagues, however, in the National Comorbidity Survey (NCS), link survey data directly to the DSM-III-R criteria of mental disorders (Kessler et al. 1994).

Chapter 8 concludes with a discussion of ways of improving the mental health of populations, an aim that is shared by the research both on well-being and on mental disorders.

Chapter 9 begins with a comprehensive review of the gradual entry of social science and survey research into the domain of health, including physical health and illness. The chapter then moves to an assessment of the current orientation of the SEH Program. The authors emphasize the transition of key staff members from researchers trained as social psychologists (with the emphasis on psychology) to those more identified with sociology and epidemiology. The programmatic studies accordingly shift toward investigation of sociological variables, especially socioeconomic status and its ramifications, as hypothesized causes of health or illness. Research on sociological risk factors includes race, ethnicity, socioeconomic status, and the derivative variable of socioeconomic inequality. Health outcomes include the "hard" variables of mortality and morbidity as well as the more familiar measures of self-reported well-being or illness.

The emphasis on populations, on sociological antecedents to health, and on the combination of self-report with other methods of measurement is a welcome development. As a longtime researcher on organizational phenomena, however, I hope to see increasing inclusion of organizational variables in the program's research. Organizations, especially work organizations, are the environments in which stresses are imposed or buffered, in which abilities are utilized or neglected, and in which aspirations are frustrated or fulfilled. They are also the vehicles by which socioeconomic comfort or privation is mediated and by which socioeconomic inequalities are imposed or resolved.

REFERENCES

Barnard, Chester. 1938. *The functions of the executive.* Cambridge, MA: Harvard University Press.

Campbell, Angus. 1981. *The sense of well-being in America.* New York: McGraw-Hill.

Campbell, Angus, Philip E. Converse, and Willard L. Rodgers. 1976. *The quality of American life.* New York: Russell Sage.

Gurin, Gerald, Joseph Veroff, and Sheila Feld. 1960. *Americans view their mental health.* New York: Basic Books.

Jackson, James S., et al. 1996. Racism and the physical and mental health status of African Americans: A thirteen year national panel study. *Ethnicity and Disease* 6:132–47.

Katz, Daniel, and Robert L. Kahn. 1966. *The social psychology of organizations.* New York: Wiley.

Kessler, Ronald C., et al. 1994. Lifetime and twelve-month prevalence of DSM-III psychiatric disorders in the United States: Results from the national comorbidity survey. *Archives of General Psychiatry* 1:8–19.

Likert, Rensis. 1961. *New patterns of management.* New York: McGraw-Hill.

Mayo, Elton. 1933. *The human problems of an industrial civilization.* New York: Macmillan.

Merton, Robert K. 1940. Bureaucratic structure and personality. *Social Forces* 18:560–68.

———. 1950. *Social theory and social structure.* New York: Free Press.

Quinn, Robert P., et al. 1973. *The 1969–70 survey of working conditions: Chronicles of an unfinished enterprise.* Ann Arbor: Institute for Social Research, University of Michigan.

Quinn, Robert P., Stanley E. Seashore, and Thomas W. Mangione. 1975. *Survey of working conditions, 1969–70.* ICPSR computer file. Ann Arbor: Institute for Social Research, University of Michigan.

Quinn, Robert P., and Graham L. Staines. 1979. *The 1977 Quality of Employment Survey: Descriptive statistics with comparison data from the 1969–70 Survey of Working Conditions and the 1972–73 Quality of Employment Survey.* Ann Arbor: Institute for Social Research, University of Michigan.

Roethlisberger, Fritz J., and W. J. Dickson. 1939. *Management and the worker.* Cambridge, MA: Harvard University Press.

Stouffer, Samuel A., et al. 1949. *The American soldier.* Princeton: Princeton University Press.

Veroff, Joseph, Elizabeth Douvan, and Richard A. Kulka. 1981. *The inner American: A self-portrait from 1957 to 1976.* New York: Basic Books.

CHAPTER 7

Survey Research in the Study of Organizations

Robert L. Kahn

In the Survey Research Center (SRC), research on organizations began in 1947, when Rensis Likert and Daniel Katz established a program in what was then called human relations. The program was part of a widespread development in the early years after World War II. Interest in the psychosocial aspects of work was growing, not only among social scientists but also in some labor unions and government agencies. People spoke of the "human relations movement," and the phrase fit well the intellectual excitement and eagerness for change that was characteristic of organizational researchers as well as practitioners.

In the United States, clusters of organizational researchers came together at Yale University (Argyris, Lawler, Hackman, Vroom), Harvard University (Lawrence, Lorsch), the Massachusetts Institute of Technology (McGregor, Bennis, Schein), Carnegie Mellon University (Simon, Cyert, March), Ohio State University (Shartle, Stogdill), and other universities.

During the same years, related work was developing in other countries, especially England, Scandinavia, and the Netherlands. The Tavistock Institute in London was a center of organizational and group research (Trist, Emery, Jaques, Rice). Some years later, the University of Manchester (Cooper, Payne) and the University of Sheffield (Warr) became sources of sustained organizational research. Organizational surveys and experiments were also under way in Norway (Thorsrud) and in Sweden (Gardell, Levi, Frankenhaeuser, Theorell, Johansson). The Tavistock work, especially that of Trist and Emery, was notable for its development of systems theory and the conceptualization of organizations as sociotechnical systems. The Scandinavian research was pioneering in many ways—

especially in mounting large-scale organizational experiments and in the integration of behavioral science with technology and medicine. In addition to the articles and monographs by the aforementioned authors, organizational research in these countries is well described in the *Handbook of Industrial and Organizational Psychology* (Triandis, Dunnette, and Hough 1994).

In the Netherlands, the field of organizational research is called work/organizational psychology, usually abbreviated as W/O. The dual designation reflects the Dutch emphasis on working at two levels, that of the individual and of the organization. W/O research has had substantial support from Dutch industry and government, and concentrations of organizational researchers (Drenth, Thierry, Roe, and others) have come together at different times in Amsterdam, Leiden, and Tilburg. Their work, along with that of other European researchers, is well summarized in the *Handbook of Work and Organizational Psychology* (Drenth 1984).

This chapter traces the development of the SRC's program of research on organizational behavior, as it came to be called, decade by decade. Over time the program evolved from a focus on organizational effectiveness to a focus on health. Current work in the program, now called the Social Environment and Health Program, is described in greater depth in chapters 8 and 9.

Organizational Studies: The First Decade

Four themes dominate the organizational studies of the early years: employee participation in decision making, the delegation of power, the relationship of satisfaction to productivity, and the use of survey feedback as a method of organizational change.

Employee Participation in Decision Making

Employee participation in decision making was perhaps the most important theme in the early years of organizational studies. The concept came in part from the research of Kurt Lewin and his colleagues on the dynamics of small groups, which had demonstrated that group members were more committed to group goals when they had participated in formulating them. The relevance of this principle to industrial work groups had been shown in experiments using as criteria the "hard" variables of productivity, absence, turnover, and rapidity of adapting to new methods (Coch and French 1948). Concentration on employee participation also developed in opposition to the doctrines of Frederick Taylor (1915) and time study, which emphasized fractionation of industrial jobs, conformity to prescribed motions, and unquestioning obedience to supervision.

The earliest organizational studies by the SRC were done entirely in large corporations, most of them industrial—a utility, a railroad, and a large insurance company. Most of the research designs were cross-sectional comparisons of rank-and-file work groups and their first-level foremen or supervisors.

The underlying hypothesis of these studies was that supervisors who showed more consideration for group members, communicated more fully to them, and perhaps even gave them some autonomy on the job and some share in decisions would have better production records as well as more satisfied workers. These supervisory behaviors were at first summarized as a dichotomy, *employee-oriented versus production-oriented supervision.* The hypothesis was borne out in the cross-sectional data: the work groups of employee-oriented supervisors scored higher in both production and job satisfaction (Katz, Maccoby, and Morse 1950; Katz et al. 1951). A similar dichotomous approach, which contrasted supervisory "consideration" with "initiating structure," was developed by Shartle and Stogdill and their colleagues at Ohio State University (Stogdill 1948).

By the early 1950s, data from a large study in heavy industry led to a modification of this dichotomous approach. Questions about the supervisors' emphasis on production and on employee concerns were asked separately rather than as a forced dichotomous choice, and the responses showed a wide scatter. Supervisory concern for employees and emphasis on production goals were thus seen as orthogonal rather than mutually exclusive, with highest performance the result of their combination (Katz and Kahn 1952). A similar schema was proposed by Robert Blake and Jane Mouton (1964) as "the managerial grid," which clarified the conditions under which both satisfaction and productivity could be maximized and was then widely used as a training device.

Findings from the study in heavy industry also modified the human relations hypothesis that cohesive work groups, in which interpersonal bonds were strong, would be more productive than groups in which the peer relationships were weaker. The expectation was that informal assistance among workers would be more frequent in the cohesive groups, which, in turn, would result in higher output. Group cohesiveness, however, turned out to have stronger effects on variance than on level of output. Cohesive groups tended to set informal norms of production for their members, and whether these norms were high or low depended on other factors, including supervision (Seashore 1954).

Delegation of Power

The ramifications of employee-centered supervision were many, and one of the most important involved the distribution of power. Addressing this issue brought the research into the domain of organizational structure, which had been a major topic for sociologists at least since Weber's work became available in English translation (Weber 1947). If workers were to have more say in the methods and pace of their work, a delegation of power from first-level supervision to the rank and file was required. This delegation required a similar award from second- to first-level supervisors, and so on up the managerial hierarchy.

An ambitious field experiment was launched in four divisions of a large insurance company to test this proposition and to determine the causal link between supervisory behavior and performance. In two of the four divisions, first-level supervisors were persuaded to delegate functions of scheduling and oversight that they had previously exercised. They in turn were given functions that had been reserved to the next higher level, and the process of delegation continued up the hierarchy to the vice presidential level. First-level supervisors in the other two divisions were given equally intensive training with the opposite emphasis—retention of all supervisory prerogatives, close oversight, and unwavering insistence on production quotas.

Research findings were mixed; productivity increased in both sets of experimental groups. However, people in the "empowered" work groups were also more satisfied with their work, had fewer absences, and were less likely to be considering other jobs. Yet they were not more productive than the other experimental groups (Morse and Reimer 1956). The researchers came to recognize, with some reluctance, that there was more than one path to productivity.

Satisfaction and Productivity

The failure of this ambitious field experiment to confirm the expected relationship between satisfaction and productivity, a prediction that in retrospect seems theoretically naive and socially overoptimistic, constituted a serious problem at the time. The notion that "satisfied workers were productive workers" had tremendous appeal, both to researchers and to the managements that sponsored the research. "Doing well by doing good" is an almost irresistible slogan. Furthermore, the hypothesis had been given some support by the earlier cross-sectional data. Later work found varying relationships between satisfaction and productivity, from strongly positive to significantly negative, depending on job complexity and many other contextual factors. Meta-analysis, however, put the mean correlation near zero (Vroom 1964). Motivational patterns are complex, and many factors affect productive behavior at work. Georgopoulos and his colleagues developed a more cognitive, "path-goal" approach to the prediction of productivity, which took account of these motivational differences (Georgopoulos, Mahoney, and Jones 1957).

Survey Feedback

From the beginning, researchers at the SRC had been interested in the uses of survey data for policy and practice. For those staff involved in corporate-sponsored organizational research, the use of data was a particularly important issue. The managers of the organizations paying for the research wanted it to make their organizations more effective, and they wanted the researchers to assist in the process. In the beginning, none of the researchers had the skills and experience to do this confidently, and not all of them were interested in acquiring them. The frequently heard motto "let the data speak for itself," while slightly ungrammatical, was extremely popular. If making use of survey data was wholly the responsibility of the sponsoring organization, the researchers could move on to other concerns—scholarly publication and the design of the next project.

Floyd Mann and his colleagues took a more constructive view. They became interested in the process of data utilization, which they regarded as both an area in need of invention and a potential domain of research in its own right. They developed a method of introducing survey data into an organization that brought about significant improvement. Survey feedback, as they called it, involved group discussion of the survey results in "organizational families," each consisting of a supervisor and the people reporting directly to that person. The process began at the top of the organization, with the president and the group of vice presidents, and continued down the hierarchy to first-level supervisors and nonsupervisory workers. All supervisors had thus participated in a feedback discussion before they were required to lead one with their own subordinates. The survey materials for discussion in each group consisted of its own data (without identifying individual respondents), data for other comparable groups (not identified), and data for the company as a whole. One or another of the SRC staff was present to facilitate these discussions but did not lead them.

The SRC members involved in this innovative work regarded the feedback process itself as a research opportunity. Its initial use, in a large public utility, showed positive results on a number of measures of organizational function (Mann 1957). A later and more ambitious test with fourteen thousand people in twenty-three organizations showed positive effects of survey feedback on most of sixteen indexes of organizational climate, leadership, group process, and satisfaction (Bowers 1973).

Organizational Studies: The Second Decade and Beyond

In the 1960s, research on organizations expanded along two different but complementary lines: one continued the emphasis on organizational effectiveness and its determinants; the other investigated the relationship between work and health. The original program, renamed as the Organizational Behavior Program, continued to study the contributions of individuals to organizations; the newer program, called the Mental Health in Industry Program, studied the effects of organizational demands on individuals.

Organizational Behavior Program

Three main lines of development characterized the work in organizational behavior during these years: (1) theoretical integration; (2) intensive pursuit of earlier conceptual leads, especially issues of power, attachment to work, and organizational change; and (3) expansion of the types and numbers of organizations studied.

Theoretical Integration

Likert's *New Patterns of Management* (1961) proposed a typological framework that classified organizations along a number of dimensions derived from the earlier empirical work. The organizational types, designated Systems 1 through 4, were strongly suggestive of a range from autocratic to participative management. For each type, there was a defining profile based on employee responses to survey scales of control, communication, decision making, commitment to goals, and other indicators of managerial orientation and practice. The empirical evidence, summarized by Likert, favored participative (Systems 3 and 4) over autocratic management.

The normative emphasis of Likert's book should not lead readers to ignore its theoretical contributions. His concept of hierarchical organizational structure as a set of overlapping work groups, each consisting of a supervisor and his or her immediate subordinates, linked group phenomena to the structure and effectiveness of the organization as a whole. The structure of overlapping groups was also consistent with the attainment of organizational change by means of survey feedback. Each such group became, potentially, a unit for the receipt and utilization of survey data, a problem-solving unit in its own right. The assumption was that each group would be empowered to act directly on issues that did not affect others. For matters that involved other organizational units, members of each group depended on their supervisor, as a member of the next higher group, to represent their concerns. The success of group leaders in doing so turned out to be a significant factor in the performance of their own groups (Pelz 1951).

In addition to the Likert book, another integrative effort, by Katz and Kahn (1966), treated organizations as open systems, dependent upon an environment composed of other organizations from which they obtained resources and to which they exported their products. Parsons (1956) had taken a similar approach in an influential two-part article that carried the modest title "Suggestions for a Sociological Approach to the Theory of Organizations." This emphasis on each organization's life-giving connectedness to its environment was developed more fully some years later as resource-dependency theory (Pfeffer and Salancik 1978).

The open-system model of Katz and Kahn treated the internal structure of an organization as a set of functionally specialized but interdependent subsystems—one responsible for producing the organization's core commodity or service; others for obtaining the necessary raw materials, selling, or otherwise exporting them; another subsystem for performing the continuing functions of innovation and adaptation; and an additional function of overall management that cut across the others. The findings of organizational research, wherever done, were interpreted in terms of this theoretical approach.

The open system view of organizations, with its emphasis on external as well as internal factors, suggested research on populations of organizations or at least sets of interdependent organizations rather than single organizational units. The work of a few sociologists (e.g., Hawley 1950) and general systems theorists (e.g., Miller 1955, 1965a, 1965b; Campbell 1969) showed that these researchers were already thinking in terms of organizational populations and were pondering, in Darwinian terms, the factors that explained survival or extinction within such populations. But it remained for Hannan and Freeman (1977), Aldrich (1979), and Scott (1992, 2001) to develop more fully the integration of the ecological view with organizational theory. Their work marks the beginning of an important branch of organizational research, now known as population ecology.

Meanwhile, for the SRC in the 1960s and 1970s, research opportunities continued to present themselves one organization at a time. There was a sustained programmatic effort, however, to develop studies of organizational populations and to include a wide range of organizational types—labor unions, voluntary organizations, kibbutz communities, and multidivisional corporations. Local chapters of national voluntary organizations, for example, and local units of a national delivery service provided some approximation to populations of more independent organizations, competing for resources, growth opportunities, and survival.

Pursuit of Earlier Conceptual Leads

Power ~ Social psychologists had been accused of being "soft on power," ignoring it in favor of gentler aspects of group and organizational life (Cartwright 1965). A series of studies initiated by Arnold Tannenbaum concentrated on the exercise of power in organizations. Using questions that asked people at each hierarchical level to estimate the extent to which specific kinds of decisions and activities were controlled at their own level or by those above them, Tannenbaum and his colleagues generated "control curves," profiles that showed both the absolute amount of power exerted at each level of the organization and the relative distribution of power across all hierarchical levels (1968, 1974; Tannenbaum and Kahn 1958). This approach was widely used in the United States and in other countries, including some with an ideological commitment to widely shared power in work settings—for example, workers councils in Yugoslavian industry and work settings in Israeli kibbutz communities. Overall findings indicated that organizational productivity was determined more by the absolute amount of control exerted over workers from all sources; satisfaction and commitment, on the other hand, were more responsive to the relative levels of hierarchical control, with the sharing of power being conducive to more positive responses.

Attachment to Work ~ Some effort to go beyond the concept of job satisfaction came early in the program. By 1960, two studies had explored the meaning of work in people's lives in some depth (Weiss and Kahn 1960; Morse and Weiss 1955). These early studies contradicted the usual economic assumption that work is intrinsically dissatisfying and that it is undertaken only for its extrinsic monetary rewards. Certainly work has negative aspects, most obvious in jobs that are dangerous, monotonous, or isolating. People are well aware of these factors, but many reported that their work itself was a source of satisfaction, and a large majority found the social aspects of work satisfying. Seventy percent of all workers said that they met some of their best friends at their workplaces.

Employment is thus experienced as a mix of positive and negative factors, and research evidence is mixed as to where the balance lies. In an attempt to find that balance, at intervals over a period of several decades we asked employed men and women this highly hypothetical question: "If you were to get enough money to live as comfortably as you'd like for the rest of your life, would you continue to work?" When this question was first asked in the 1950s, the majority of employed women and nearly three-quarters of employed men said that they would prefer to work even if they had no financial need to do so. Those percentages were stable for some time but showed some reduction in the 1970s; the question has not been used in more recent years. A more objective criterion, however—the age at which people retire from paid employment— indicates a lesser attachment to work; most people retire as soon as retirement is economically viable. Recent surveys indicate that people nearing retirement age still express a preference to continue working, but not necessarily at the same job or on a full-time basis (Herzog, House, and Morgan 1991). Such choices are strongly affected by external economic conditions; periods of growth and consequent labor shortage, for example, increase the availability of part-time jobs for older men and women.

During the 1970s, this line of research was greatly expanded in three national surveys on the quality of employment. These studies reflected a growing national and international interest in what were called social indicators. Both the legislative and executive branches of the federal government expressed their realization that conditions at work affected other aspects of life and thus the quality of life for the society as a whole. Accordingly, the Department of Labor sponsored this research.

The main aims of the research were to assess the frequency and severity of work-related problems, to indicate which demographic and occupational groups were most affected by these problems, and to measure their impact in terms of job satisfaction and well-being. Findings from these studies are reported in three published monographs and hundreds of journal articles (Quinn and Shepard 1974; Quinn, Staines, and McCullough 1974; Quinn and Staines 1979). The monographs included an assessment of the frequency and severity of labor standards problems. For example, the percentage of workers who reported discrimination because of their race or nationality was less than 10 percent, but more than half of those who reported it at all rated it as a "sizable" or "great" problem. Only inadequate family income, which was reported by about 20 percent of respondents, was rated as a sizable or great problem by so large a proportion of those who experienced it. How these and other indicators may have changed in more recent years is not known. Certainly changes in the economy and in the technology of work, and increases in national awareness of race and gender as work-related issues, have been great in the decades since the Quality of Employment Surveys were last performed. Whether they will be resumed is more dependent on national policy than on national need and scientific promise. Meanwhile, some questions on the quality of work experience have been included in the General Social Survey of the National Opinion Research Center. The World Health Organization (WHO) has launched a Quality of Life initiative, and the sustained work of the MAPI organization in France incorporates some quality of employment content in its broader research.

Organizational Change ~ Several field experiments in organizational change were conducted during the 1960–1970 decade, all of them involving survey feedback and some of them involving more direct alterations of organizational structure (Seashore 1964; Seashore and Bowers 1963, 1970). They had in common an attempt to induce change in the direction of Likert's System 4: a strongly participative managerial style, a substantial delegation of power, and consequent increases in worker autonomy. Experimental results showed significant increases in both productivity and job satisfaction, but the textbook conditions of experimental control were not met.

Communication between experimental and control groups could not be prevented; indeed, in some cases, the maintenance of isolated control groups was impossible. It is ironic that the spread of innovations in this way is considered desirable and called "diffusion" in everyday organizational life but is highly undesirable and called "contamination" in experimental designs. The experimental groups were also exposed to other external influences. New employees were hired; union contracts were negotiated; pay incentives were altered; in short, the ongoing business of organizational life continued, experiment or no. In retrospect, we do not believe that these intrusions were avoidable; rather, we believe that the protocols and designs of experiments in ongoing organizations need serious rethinking in order to bring them into alignment with the realities of organizational life.

With these and other considerations in mind, Mann and his colleagues in 1970 created a new research center in the Institute for Social Research (ISR), the Center for Research on the Utilization of Scientific Knowledge. This accurately descriptive but awkward title, quickly shortened to its acronym, CRUSK, summarized the rationale for the new center. The founding group, influenced by their experience with survey feedback and sensitivity training (T-groups, encounter groups, and the like), felt that there was a persistent lag between the accumulation of scientific knowledge and its utilization in policy and practice. They were committed to the idea that this lag, which was more conspicuous in the social-psychological than in the technological domain, was itself an appropriate area for research. The new center, therefore, would be involved in facilitating change, but always with accompanying research on the process. It would act on the Lewinian maxim of "no research without action; no action without research" (Lewin 1947). Early work was promising, although there was some difficulty in integrating a staff that consisted partly of "change agents," who were eager to work directly on bringing organizations nearer to the principles of participatory decision making, and partly of researchers who were more comfortable with data than with the quasi-consultative role of facilitating the planned organizational changes.

Despite a number of successful projects and research publications (e.g., Mann 1961; Michael 1973), the new research center had a short lifeline, in part for the reasons mentioned earlier but more because of difficulty in generating sustained funding. In some fields, the task of utilizing the findings of basic research is well recognized. Physicians use the research findings of basic science in biochemistry and related domains. Engineers in their several specialties are essentially the interpreters and appliers of research findings from more basic scientific fields. The founders of CRUSK had comparable aspirations for the social sciences, but their vision was not widely shared. Most leaders of organizations wanted help in using research, not additional research on the process of utilization. Most funding agencies were also less than forthcoming, and CRUSK terminated in the mid-1980s.

Number and Types of Organizations Studied

The earlier organizational studies, as we have seen, were conducted almost entirely in industry, and their designs were limited to single organizations. The variables that are researchable in single organizations are, almost by definition, intraorganizational. The open system view of organizations, with its emphasis on external as well as internal factors, suggested research on populations of organizations or at least sets of interdependent organizations rather than single organizational units. Moreover, researchers were seeking findings that would hold across organizations of all types or that could be systematically modified to take account of typological differences.

For the SRC in the 1960s and 1970s, research opportunities continued to present themselves one organization at a time, primarily from the corporate world. There was a sustained programmatic effort, nevertheless, to develop studies of organizational populations and to include a wide range of organizational types. Accordingly, studies were launched in labor unions, in voluntary organizations (e.g., Girl Scouts, Boy Scouts, League of Women Voters), in government agencies, and in kibbutz communities. The structure of some of these organizations was sufficiently decentralized so that local chapters or divisions could be treated as if they were separate organizations. This meant that the effects of such structural properties as size, number of hierarchical levels, and stability of top leadership could be analyzed while overarching properties of organizational function and technology were held constant.

Late Developments and New Beginnings

The Organizational Behavior Program entered its final phase in the late 1970s and early 1980s, after a series of new developments. Edward Lawler, who joined the SRC from Yale University, and Stanley Seashore launched a set of field experiments in organizational change and methods of measuring it. This work is summarized in *Assessing Organizational Change* (Seashore et al. 1983).

The emphasis on measuring the quality of working life continued, with a combination of intensive organizational studies (Lawler, Nadler, and Cammann 1975) and earlier national surveys (Quinn and Shepard 1974; Quinn and Staines 1979). In a comparative study of thirty community hospitals, Georgopoulos (1975) extended his theoretical work linking organizational structure to problem solving and overall effectiveness. Tannenbaum and his colleagues extended his research on the magnitude and distribution of power in organizations to include international comparisons and the effects of employee ownership (Conte, Tannenbaum, and McCulloch 1981; Rosner, and Tannenbaum 1983; and Tannenbaum and Rozgonyi 1986).

These books and articles were among the last published work of the Organizational Behavior Program. Three of the senior researchers (Seashore, Tannenbauum, and Georgopoulos) were approaching retirement. Lawler moved to the University of Southern California, where, with some of his younger University of Michigan colleagues, he established the Center for Effective Organization (CEO) in 1980. The guiding principle of that center is given in the title of one of its earliest books, *Doing Research That Is Useful for Theory and Practice* (Lawler et al. 1985). The center continues with great success the pattern of survey research in organizations, and it has also been successful in developing a substantial set of sponsoring organizations.

Quantitative survey research in organizations also continued in the work of some private consulting companies. Likert, after retiring as director of the ISR in 1970, founded a survey and consulting group (Rensis Likert Associates [RLA]) that utilized a standardized questionnaire based on Likert's typology of Systems 1 through 4 as measures ranging from authoritarian to participatory practice. Feedback procedures, as described earlier, were then introduced to encourage organizational change toward the System 4 ideal. Other consulting groups have developed similar approaches. Sirota Consulting, founded by a former doctoral student and staff member of the SRC, is a major example.

Social Environment and Health Program

The SEH Program, initially called the Mental Health in Industry Program, began as a spin-off from the Organizational Behavior Program. The researchers who launched the new program—French, Kahn, and Mann—regarded it as complementary to its parent. The emphasis in the parent program, as we have seen, continued to be on the determinants of organizational effectiveness, that is, on the contributions of individuals to organizational outcomes. The thrust of the new program was the reverse, in a sense: organizational factors were to be the independent variables; their effects on individuals, especially on their health and well-being, were the outcomes of interest. The three founding members of the program were soon joined by Sidney Cobb, a physician and epidemiologist, and the interdisciplinary thrust of the new program was further emphasized by the creation of the SRC's first "wet laboratory" for the analysis of saliva, blood, and urine samples.

A second distinctive characteristic of the new program was its commitment to a causal framework that began with independently measured properties of organizations or jobs and ended with health-relevant properties of individuals, also measured independently of self-report. Between these two anchors in "objective reality" were the subjective reports of the individuals themselves, their perceptions of the situation and their responses to it. This hypothesized causal sequence was moderated by two sets of additional variables—personality and other enduring attributes of the individual and interpersonal relationships. This framework is illustrated in figure 7.1. Not all studies in the program met the ideal of measuring both independent and dependent variables by means other than self-report as well as by the usual answers of respondents to survey questions, but the aspiration was explicit, and efforts to realize it were serious.

Early studies in the new program investigated the effects of several hypothesized stressors in the work situation: role conflict and ambiguity (Kahn et al. 1964); shift work (Mott 1965; Mann 1965); and job demands, especially qualitative and quantitative overload (Caplan et al. 1975). Research findings from these studies, which are discussed more fully in chapter 9, led to an elaboration of the theoretical framework that emphasized goodness of fit between the person and the work situation, that is, between job demands and the person's abilities and between the job's opportunity structure and the person's needs and aspirations.

The programmatic emphasis on combining self-reported survey data with more objective measures is well represented in a comparative study of job stress and strain in twenty-three occupations, ranging from blue-collar workers to professionals (French, Caplan, and Harrison 1982). Occupational differences in reported strains, both subjective and objective, were large. Moreover, the source of reported strains differed among occupations in ways that were consistent with their independently assessed characteristics. For example, unskilled blue-collar workers scored high on boredom, while professionals scored low on this variable. Air-traffic controllers were higher than people in any other occupation in the amount of concentration required on their job; assembly-line workers scored lowest on this variable. The effects of these stressors on indicators of strain, both physiological and psychological, were significant. They were moderated or buffered, however, by social support from supervisors and peers. Social support from others at work also had direct effects on a number of strain indicators, including irritation, anxiety, and depression. Findings from these and other studies in the earlier years of the SEH Program are summarized in two books, both published in the same year:

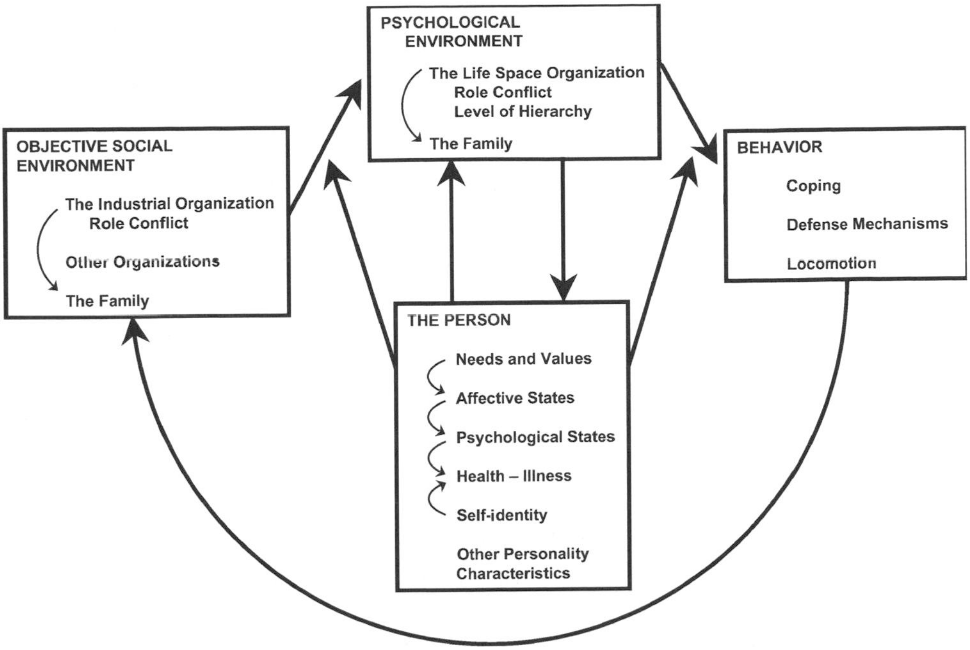

FIG. 7.1. The major foci of the program. The boxes illustrate the main panels of variables, and the arrows show some of the hypotheses. (Redrawn from figure 1 of French and Kahn 1962.)

Work, Stress, and Social Support (House 1981) and *Work and Health* (Kahn 1981).

Both the positive and the negative effects of job characteristics emphasized the importance of work in people's lives. Therefore, in a second generation of studies in the program, the researchers decided to investigate the effects of transitions between work and nonwork status. Research on stress at work was to continue, but the stress of involuntary lack of work was to be added. Researchers planned three sets of studies, each to concentrate on a different life stage. One would follow young men and women as they tried to manage the transition between finishing high school or college and moving full-time into the labor force. A second set of studies would concentrate on job loss, the often unanticipated effect of downsizing, plant closings, and the like. A third set of studies was to follow men and women from work to retirement, voluntary and involuntary. The underlying assumptions were that employment, despite its frequent stresses, has many positive aspects—among them the use of valued skills and abilities and the opportunity to interact with friends. Furthermore, inability to find work as a young person, loss of work in mid-career, and forced retirement all impose economic costs and threats to self-esteem.

These three lines of research developed in different ways. The effects of retirement were never fully investigated within the SEH Program. Other research suggested that retirement itself had no predictable effects on health but that involuntary retirement had some negative effects, at least according to self-report (Morgan 1986). Only years later, with the development of the Health and Retirement Study and the related Asset and Health Dynamics among the Oldest-Old (AHEAD) sample of older cohorts, are the effects of retirement being studied more fully. These projects are discussed in chapter 12.

The intended study of labor force entrance by young people led some colleagues to a broader interest in the transition from late adolescence to adulthood. Thus was spawned a new research program, initially called Youth in Transition (YIT), which has developed into a nationally representative, multicohort study of young people's problems and coping strategies. This study, now called "Monitoring the Future," is a large-scale longitudinal project, and its major focus for many years has been on the use of drugs, legal and illegal, and the longer-term consequences of youthful adventure and addiction. This research is described more fully in chapter 11.

Research on mid-career unemployment has developed in important ways. First in this series was a study of two plant closings in southern Michigan (Slote 1969; Cobb and Kasl 1977). Results of this research, which documented the economic, physiological, and psychological effects of job loss, are described in chapters 8 and 9. Richard Price, Amiram Vinokur, and their colleagues have enlarged the programmatic research on work and health in important ways, substantively and methodologically. They have developed an extensive and highly successful experimental method for moderating the negative effects of unemployment. Their approach, which emphasizes the supportive functions of group process and the importance of role playing and other training for job seeking, has not only reduced the stresses of unemployment; it has also shortened the duration of unemployment and improved the quality of the post-unemployment jobs (Price, van Ryn, and Vinokur 1992; Price and Vinokur 1995). As these findings became known, the experimental work has been emulated in Europe and in Russia and China, where unemployment rates are much higher than in the United States. Thus these and other studies in the SEH

Program have continued and broadened the combination of social psychological and epidemiological research that began in the 1960s and 1970s.

Organizational Research: Present and Future

In recent years the loci of organizational research within universities have developed a different pattern from that described thus far. The University of Michigan is a case in point. The SEH Program continues the experimental work on unemployment and has expanded into other areas of prevention and intervention. However, there is no longer a program of research on organizational behavior in the SRC. With the exception of the experimental work on mitigating the negative effects of unemployment, the emphasis in the SEH Program is on population-based surveys in which the health effects of more sociological causes are investigated.

The rise and fall of university-based research programs is a complex and interesting subject in its own right, one that organizational researchers could well add to their area of interest. Institutional histories, of course, tend to emphasize beginnings rather than endings. An important exception is Herbert Hyman's insightful chapter "The Rise and Fall of the Bureau of Applied Social Research" (Hyman 1991). Many of his observations seem relevant for explaining the gradual demise of the SRC's Organizational Behavior Program. As the years pass, leading figures die, retire, or are lured to other universities. Financial limitations or lack of foresight may hamper recruitment of new talent. Government agencies, foundations, and corporations change their priorities or restrict their funds for external research. And, perhaps most difficult to recognize or admit, lines of research that once generated enthusiasm and new ideas may grow stale or seem to have reached a dead end.

At the University of Michigan and other universities, major growth of sociobehavioral research on organizations has occurred in other units, while it has diminished in the SRC. This development is most prominent in schools of business, but it is also important in other professional schools (e.g., social work, public health, education). Additionally encouraging is the development of sustained interdisciplinary exchange and collaboration among organizational researchers at the University of Michigan and other universities, including Stanford, Carnegie Mellon, and Massachusetts Institute of Technology. The vehicle for this activity at Michigan is the Interdisciplinary Committee for Organizational Studies (ICOS). ICOS conducts a weekly seminar for faculty and doctoral students and also coordinates graduate training for students from various schools and departments who share a concentration on organizational study. Price has described ICOS as a collective good, a commons, as that term was defined in Garrett Hardin's famous article (Hardin 1968). Hardin also emphasized the vulnerability of such shared properties; they depend on the cooperation and restraint of their participants. Like other collective goods, ICOS survives because its participating faculty and students cooperate; they give as well as take. It survives also because the university provides some continuing support. Years ago, we said that the study of organizations, because its content cuts across so many disciplines and professional fields, has many residences but no single home (Katz, Kahn, and Adams 1980). At the University of Michigan, ICOS has become that intellectual home for organizational research and researchers.

Another interdisciplinary unit, the Center for the Study of Complex Systems, has been established more recently. This center brings together for the first time an innovative group of computer experts, economists, mathematicians, psychologists, and others. Their work is not limited to organizations, but they include organizations among the various complex systems, from organisms to nations, whose dynamics they wish to understand.

If we could propose additions to this rich array, our nominations would emphasize the inclusion of architecture and engineering, to acknowledge the sociotechnical facts of organizational life; strengthened links to medicine, to track the ramifications of organizational demands and opportunities; and bold experimentation, to guide the design of organizations that can more fully utilize the abilities and fulfill the aspirations of their members.

REFERENCES

Aldrich, Howard E. 1979. *Organizations and environments.* Englewood Cliffs, NJ: Prentice-Hall.

Blake, Robert R., and Jane S. Mouton. 1964. *The managerial grid.* Houston, TX: Gulf.

Bowers, David G. 1973. OD techniques and their results in twenty-three organizations: The Michigan ICL study. *Journal of Applied Behavioral Science* 9:21–43.

Campbell, Donald. 1969. Variation and selective retention in socio-cultural evolution. *General systems: Yearbook of the Society for General Systems Research* 16:69–85.

Caplan, Robert D., et al. 1975. *Job demands and worker health: Main effects and occupational differences.* Washington, DC: U.S. Government Printing Office.

Cartwright, Dorwin P. 1965. Influence, leadership, and control. In *Handbook of Organizations,* ed. James G. March. Chicago: Rand McNally.

Cobb, Sidney, and Stanislav Kasl. 1977. *Termination: The consequences of job loss.* U.S. . Washington, DC: Department of Health, Education, and Welfare.

Coch, Lester, and John R. P. French Jr. 1948. Overcoming resistance to change. *Human Relations* 1:612–533.

Conte, Michael, Arnold S. Tannenbaum, and Donna McCulloch. 1981. *Employee ownership.* Ann Arbor: Survey Research Center, Institute for Social Research, University of Michigan.

Drenth, Pieter, et al. 1984. *Handbook of work and organizational psychology.* Chichester, West Sussex, and New York: Wiley.

French, John R. P., Robert D. Caplan, and R. Van Harrison. 1982. *The mechanisms of job stress and strain.* New York: Wiley.

French, John R. P., and Robert L. Kahn. 1962. A programmatic approach to studying the industrial environment and mental health. *Journal of Social Issues* 18 (3): 1–47.

Georgopoulos, Basil S. 1975. *Hospital organization research: Review and source book.* Philadelphia: W. B. Saunders.

Georgopoulos, Basil S., Gerald M. Mahoney, and Nile W. Jones. 1957. A path-goal approach to productivity. *Journal of Applied Psychology* 41:345–53.

Hannan, Michael T., and John Freeman. 1977. The population ecology of organizations. *American Journal of Sociology* 82:929–64.

Hardin, Garrett. 1968. The tragedy of the commons. *Science* 162:1243–47.

Hawley, Amos. 1950. *Human ecology.* New York: Ronald Press.

Herzog, A. Regula, James S. House, and James N. Morgan. 1991. The relation of work and retirement to health and well-being in older age. *Psychology and Aging* 2:202–11.

House, James S. 1981. *Work, stress, and social support.* Reading, MA: Addison-Wesley.

Hyman, Herbert H. 1991. *Taking society's measure.* New York: Russell Sage.

Kahn, Robert L. 1981. *Work and health.* New York: Wiley.

Kahn, Robert L., et al. 1964. *Organizational stress.* New York: Wiley.

Katz, Daniel, and Robert L. Kahn. 1952. Some recent findings in human relations research in industry. In *Readings in social psychology,* 2d ed., ed. G. W. Swanson, T. M. Newcomb, and E. L. Hartley. 650–65. New York: Holt.

———. 1966. *The social psychology of organizations.* New York: Wiley.

Katz, Daniel, Robert L. Kahn, and J. Stacy Adams, eds. 1980. *The study of organizations.* San Francisco: Jossey-Bass.

Katz, Daniel, Nathan Maccoby, and Nancy Morse. 1950. *Productivity, supervision, and morale in an office situation.* Ann Arbor: Institute for Social Research, University of Michigan.

Katz, Daniel, Nathan Maccoby, Gerald Gurin, and Lucretia Floor. 1951. *Productivity, supervision, and morale among railroad workers.* Ann Arbor: Institute for Social Research, University of Michigan.

Lawler, Edward E., III, Susan A. Mohrman, Alan M. Mohrman Jr., Gerald E. Ledford Jr., and T. G. Cummings, eds. 1985. *Doing research that is useful for theory and practice.* San Francisco: Jossey-Bass.

Lawler, Edward E., D. A. Nadler, and C. Cammann. 1975. *Organizational assessment: Perspectives on the measurement of organizational behavior and quality of work life.* New York: Wiley.

Likert, Rensis. 1961. *New patterns of management*. New York: McGraw-Hill.

Lewin, Kurt. 1947. Frontiers in group dynamics. *Human Relations* 1:5–41.

Mann, Floyd C. 1957. Studying and creating change: A means to understanding social organization. In *Research in industrial human relations: A critical appraisal*, ed. C. M. Arensberg, S. Barkin, W. E. Chalmers, H. L. Wilensky, J. C. Worthy, and B. D. Dennis, 146–67. New York: Harper Collins.

———. 1961. *Managing major change in organizations: An undeveloped area of administration and social research*. Ann Arbor, MI: Foundation for Research on Human Behavior.

———. 1965. *Hours of work*. New York: Harper and Row.

Michael, Donald N. 1973. *On learning to plan—and planning to learn*. San Francisco: Jossey-Bass.

Miller, James G. 1955. Toward a general theory for the behavioral sciences. *American Psychologist* 10:513–31.

———. 1965a. Living systems: Basic concepts. *Behavioral Science* 10:193–237.

———. 1965b. Living systems: Structure and process. *Behavioral Science* 10:337–79.

Morgan, James N. 1986. Unpaid productive activity over the life course. In *America's aging: Productive roles in an older society*, ed. Institute of Medicine/National Research Council. Washington, DC: National Academy Press.

Morse, Nancy, and Everett Reimer. 1956. The experimental change of a major organizational variable. *Journal of Abnormal and Social Psychology* 52:120–29.

Morse, Nancy C., and Robert S. Weiss. 1955. The function and meaning of work and the job. *American Sociological Review* 20:191–98.

Mott, Paul E. 1965. *Shift work: The social, psychological, and physical consequences*. Ann Arbor: University of Michigan Press.

Parsons, Talcott. 1956. Suggestions for a sociological approach to the theory of organizations. *Administrative Science Quarterly* 1:63–85 (pt. 1), 225–39 (pt. 2).

Pelz, Donald C. 1951. Leadership within a hierarchical organization. *Journal of Social Issues* 7:49–55.

Pfeffer, Jeffrey, and Gerald R. Salancik. 1978. Organizational decision-making as a political process: The case of a university budget. *Administrative Science Quarterly* 19:135–51.

Porter, Lyman W., Edward E. Lawler III, and J. Richard Hackman. 1975. *Behavior in organizations*. New York: McGraw-Hill.

Price, Richard H. 1992. Psychosocial impact of job loss on individuals and families. *Current Directions in Psychological Science* 1:9–11.

Price, Richard H., M. van Ryn, and Amiram D. Vinokur. 1992. Impact of preventive job search intervention on the likelihood of depression among the unemployed. *Journal of Health and Social Behavior* 33 (2): 158–67.

Price, Richard H., and Amiram D. Vinokur. 1995. Supporting career transitions in a time of organizational downsizing: The Michigan JOBS program. In *Employees, careers, and job creation: Developing growth-oriented human resources strategies and programs*, ed. M. London, 191–209. San Francisco: Jossey-Bass.

Quinn, Robert P., and Linda Shepard. 1974. *The 1972–73 Quality of Employment Survey*. Ann Arbor: Institute for Social Research, University of Michigan.

Quinn, Robert P., and Graham L. Staines. 1979. *The 1977 Quality of Employment Survey: Descriptive statistics with comparison data from the 1969–1970 survey of working condi-*

tions and the 1972–1973 Quality of Employment Survey. Ann Arbor: Institute for Social Research, University of Michigan.

Quinn, Robert P., Graham L. Staines, and M. R. McCullough. 1974. *Job satisfaction: Is there a trend?* Manpower Research Monograph, no. 30, U.S. Department of Labor. Washington, DC: U.S. Government Printing Office.

Rosner, Menachem, and Arnold S. Tannenbaum. 1983. *Ownership and alienation in kibbutz factories.* Haifa: University of Haifa, University Center of the Kibbutz, Institute for Study and Research of the Kibbutz and the Cooperative Idea.

Scott, W. Richard. 1992. *Organizations,* 3d ed. Englewood Cliffs, NJ: Prentice Hall.

———. 2001. Institutions and Organizations, 2d ed. Thousand Oaks, CA: Sage.

Seashore, Stanley E. 1954. *Group cohesiveness in the industrial work group.* Ann Arbor: Institute for Social Research, University of Michigan.

———. 1964. Field experiments with formal organizations. *Human Organization* 23:164–70.

Seashore, Stanley E., and David G. Bowers. 1963. *Changing the structure and functioning of an organization.* Ann Arbor: Institute for Social Research, University of Michigan.

———. 1970. The durability of organizational change. *American Psychologist* 25 (3): 227–33.

Seashore, Stanley E., et al. 1983. *Assessing organizational change.* New York: Wiley.

Slote, Alfred P. 1969. *Termination: The closing at Baker plant.* New York: Bobbs-Merrill.

Stogdill, Ralph M. 1948. Personal factors associated with leadership. *Journal of Psychology* 25:35–71.

Tannenbaum, Arnold S. 1968. *Control in organizations.* New York: McGraw-Hill.

———. 1974. *Hierarchy in organizations.* San Francisco: Jossey-Bass.

Tannenbaum, Arnold S., and Robert L. Kahn. 1958. *Participation in union locals.* New York: Row Peterson.

Tannenbaum, Arnold S., and Tamás Rozgonyi. 1986. *Authority and reward in organizations: An international research.* Ann Arbor: Survey Research Center, Institute for Social Research, University of Michigan.

Taylor, Frederick Winslow. 1915. *Scientific management.* New York and London: Harper and Brothers.

Triandis, Harry, Marvin Dunnette, and Leatta Hough, eds. 1994. *Handbook of industrial and organizational psychology.* Vol. 4. Palo Alto, CA: Consulting Psychologists Press.

Vroom, Victor H. 1964. *Work and motivation.* New York: Wiley.

Weber, Max. 1947. *The theory of social and economic organization.* Trans. A. M. Henderson and Talcott Parsons. New York: Oxford University Press.

Weiss, Robert S., and Robert L. Kahn. 1960. Definitions of work and occupation. *Social Problems* 8:142–51.

CHAPTER 8

Understanding and Improving the Mental Health of Populations

Richard H. Price

The last half century of survey research on the mental health of populations has persistently addressed this broad question: "What conditions of mental health are experienced by particular groups in society and what might be done to improve those conditions?" Two arenas of concentrated scientific interest have emerged. First, a lively debate has developed about the appropriate definition and measurement of mental health, focusing on whether mental health should be defined as general psychological well-being or merely the absence of diagnosed mental disorder. Second, mental health population surveys have attempted to increase our understanding of how to improve the mental health of citizens by identifying sociopsychological factors shaping mental health and by understanding naturally occurring patterns of help seeking for personal problems or mental disorder and identifying gaps in available services.

Researchers in the Survey Research Center (SRC) at the Institute for Social Research (ISR) have played important roles in attempts to answer these concerns, working in interdisciplinary teams involving psychiatrists, psychologists, sociologists, epidemiologists, and survey methodologists (Cannell and Kahn 1984; Frantilla 1998). This chapter reviews survey research on mental health of populations conducted over the last fifty years, with an emphasis on surveys that assess the mental health of whole populations. After a brief examination of the early history of mental health surveys immediately after World War II, the chapter will examine two quite different but complementary approaches to assessing the mental health of populations. The first emphasizes the measurement of psychological well-being, while the second focuses on estimating the prevalence of mental disorder. What follows is an examination of the major studies conducted in each of these two research traditions and of how each approach evaluates the mental health needs of populations. Finally, an inventory of promising future directions for improving the mental health of populations will be offered.

Historical Roots of Population Studies of Mental Health

Concern with the mental health of populations in the United States has been most pronounced in times of turbulent social change. As early as 1855, Edward Jarvis's report "Insanity and Idiocy in Massachusetts" devoted special attention to the effects of immigrant status and social class differences on mental health (Vander Stoep and Link 1998). The period during and immediately after World War II also reflected a resurgence of interest in mental health, particularly in the psychological fitness of troops (Star 1950) and the traumatic impact of combat. The social causes of psychological well-being in populations took the center stage in this period, and social psychiatry and social psychology vigorously put forth new ideas about the role of social circumstance and economic deprivation in the development of mental health problems (Hollingshead and Redlich 1958; Faris and Dunham 1939). For example, the Stirling County study (Hughes et al. 1960) assessed the mental health of a rural Canadian community and suggested that the loss of community cohesion eroded individual psychological well-being. The Midtown Manhattan study (Srole et al. 1962; Srole 1975) focused on the impact of urban stress and immigration and revealed relationships between stressful life conditions in urban settings and mental health problems. By the late 1950s a growing interest in psychological well-being in the United States resulted in the Joint Commission on Mental Illness and Health, calling for a large-scale study that would provide broad understanding of the mental health of Americans (Joint Commission 1961).

Even while this line of research on the social roots of mental health problems was expanding, more epidemiological and medical approaches were also gaining favor. The Baltimore study (Pasamanick et al. 1956) was an early attempt to understand the distribution of medical and mental health conditions in poor communities and to identify gaps in the provision of services for the chronically mentally ill. A second study by Tischler et al. (1975) sought to describe the distribution of cases of diagnosed mental illness in a community sample. Still other studies were aimed at explaining the relationship between social class and mental disorder by distinguishing current social causes from predispositions that might lead to "drift" or social selection into circumstances of poverty.

The sophistication of measurement of mental health in populations grew steadily in the post–World War II era for both the well-being and mental disorder approaches. The increasingly powerful tools of modern survey research—including probability sampling methods, interviewer training to increase the reliability and precision of respondent reports, and questionnaire methods for measuring subjective experience—were critical to the development of an epidemiology of mental health and mental disorder. First-generation studies of mental health in populations before World War II had largely been confined to the study of institutional records and were therefore subject to severe sampling biases in estimating the mental health of community populations (Dohrenwend 1998b). A second generation of mental health surveys after the war increasingly relied on personal interviews with representative samples of community respondents, frequently supplemented by expert evaluation of the interview content. Social psychological studies of the mental health of populations also became increasingly sophisticated, developing psychometrically sound rating scales, coding systems, and multi-item indexes using multivariate analytic techniques (Bryant and Veroff 1982). The use of screening scales also became more common, sometimes providing a shorthand method of determining the presence or absence of a mental disorder and in other cases serving simply as a composite assessment of psychological distress (Robins et al. 1981).

But, by the decade of the 1970s, viewpoints had substantially diverged on the proper conceptualization and measurement of mental health. Researchers taking an epidemiological approach to the study of mental health in populations celebrated the growing sophistication in the measurement and diagnosis of cases of mental disorder. As one commentator observed, "One of the most important of these developments in the epidemiologic study of mental disorders was the publication in the *Diagnostic and Statistical Manual* (DSM-III) of specific criteria for the diagnosis of mental disorders to promote more reliable and more specific assessment than had been the case previously" (Regier and Kaelber 1995, 35). At the same time, advocates of the study of psychological well-being in populations were concerned with the distribution of well-being from a very different perspective: "To acknowledge that symptom scales are not adequate as screening devices for mental illness or psychiatric impairment in the community is not to say that they lack significant value as indicators of how Americans *view* their mental health. Symptom patterns are interesting and important indicators of psychological experience in their own right" (Veroff, Douvan, and Kulka 1981, 332).

These two perspectives reflected more than a technical difference of opinion about measurement. They revealed a fundamental difference in theoretical commitment, disciplinary orientation, and preferred research strategy. Contributions to each stream of research have been made by members of the SRC at the ISR.

Population Studies of Well-Being and Life Satisfaction

Theory and research on psychological well-being have benefited from several distinct research traditions. First, research on life satisfaction had its origins in survey research at the ISR (Andrews and Withey 1976; Campbell, Converse, and Rodgers 1978; Gurin, Veroff, and Feld 1960; Veroff, Douvan, and Kulka 1982). This approach emphasized both cognitive elements and affective components of life satisfaction and focused on global indicators of life satisfaction and domain-specific measurements of different aspects of life, such as work and family life. A second approach had its origins in the idea of affect balance (Bradburn 1969). More recently an extension of this tradition (Diener and Diener 1996) has advanced an appraisal-based theory of well-being. Finally, life course developmental approaches to understanding well-being (Ryff and Keyes 1995) have emphasized changes in psychological well-being over the life course and differences that emerge for men and women.

Americans View Their Mental Health

The Joint Commission on Mental Illness and Health was established by Congress in 1957 with the purpose of evaluating the available national resources for coping with the human and economic problems of mental illness (Joint Commission 1961). The SRC at the University of Michigan was asked to conduct an intensive interview survey with a national sample of normal adults to provide information on what the American people thought of their mental health. The ISR researchers believed that a study focusing on the needs of people as they themselves understood them would inform efforts to improve mental health (Gurin, Veroff, and Feld

1960). The study was replicated in 1976 (Veroff, Douvan, and Kulka 1981; Veroff, Kulka and Douvan 1981) and was also designed to assess the subjective mental health and life experience of American adults.

Social Change and Shifts in the Basis of Well-Being

The period marking the two decades between these two surveys of American psychological well-being was a time of great social change and upheaval. As Veroff, Douvan, and Kulka (1982) observe, in addition to changes in communication technologies and transportation, the period was marked by dramatic cultural changes in values, in people's sense of community, and in their attitudes toward authority, as well as by political changes. The period was also marked by a psychological revolution, the beginning of a "therapeutic age" with increased acceptance of professional intervention for psychological problems and a growing belief that organized mental health services could improve well-being (Veroff, Douvan and Kulka 1982).

Comparing the results of the 1957 and 1976 surveys of American mental health provides some striking contrasts. For example, Veroff, Douvan and Kulka (1981) observed a shift from concern about social integration in one's family and community to concern about personal integration and to an increased focus on self-expression in social life. By 1976 these changes permeated the whole society. In the mid-1970s subjective mental health seemed to depend greatly on the nature of interpersonal relationships. While marital relationships were still a powerful source of support and help for married people, Veroff et al. (1982) observed, formal mechanisms for dealing with problems appeared increasingly to supplant more ritualized forms of family and community support.

Patterns of Help Seeking in 1957 and 1976

An innovation introduced in the 1957 survey and carried over in the 1976 replication was inquiry into how Americans sought help in dealing with mental health problems and personal crises. These questions and others linking the two surveys yielded a range of important findings about patterns of help seeking and how they changed over these two decades in American history. For example, Veroff et al. (1982) found that over the twenty-year period between the two studies the proportion of people actually using professional help for personal problems nearly doubled. By 1976 people were much more likely to seek help from a specialized mental health resource such as a psychiatrist, psychologist, marriage counselor, or other mental health professional.

Using results from the 1976 survey, Kulka, Veroff and Douvan (1979) also examined the relationship between social class and the use of professional help for personal problems. Overall, they found that people were much more ready to refer themselves for help by 1976 and that education had become much more influential in shaping people's willingness to define a problem in mental health terms. On the other hand, income continued to be an important influence on help seeking for personal crises and mental health problems. The emphasis on the process of help seeking pioneered in the Gurin, Veroff, and Feld (1960) and Veroff et al. (1982) studies continues to be a critical resource for understanding the use of services and avenues to improvement of psychological well-being today.

Changing Motives in American Men and Women

Forces for social change such as the civil rights movement and the women's movement had a powerful influence on American social history between 1957 and 1976. Among men, the achievement motive remained stable, the motivation for affiliation decreased, and power motives increased. For women, achievement motives increased over the twenty-year period, as did power motives. Veroff et al. (1982) interpreted the results as indicating a change in the interpersonal orientation of American men, reflecting a shift away from interest in affiliative ties and a stronger orientation to seeking influence over others. For women, changes in achievement motivation were thought to reflect an increased sense of identity through achievement, and the increased fear of weakness was thought to reflect women's increasing awareness about their relative status in comparison to men. Recent surveys such as the MacArthur Midlife Development in the U.S. Survey (MIDUS) (Kessler, Mickelson, and Zhao 1997; Lachman and Weaver 1998) may continue to illuminate changes in the motives of American women and men two decades after the Veroff et al. (1982) survey.

National Survey of Black Americans

The National Survey of Black Americans was a landmark survey of African-Americans' mental health (Jackson et al. 1996; Neighbors and Jackson 1996). It drew on the heritage of earlier omnibus surveys of well-being (Campbell and Converse 1978) and the Americans View Their Mental Health Survey (Gurin, Veroff, and Feld 1960) and took a problem-focused approach to understanding how African-Americans cope with stress in their lives. Data were collected on the distribution of personal problems, psychological distress, feelings of happiness and satisfaction, and the way African-Americans cope with life challenges. The survey interviewed African-Americans at four points in time, ending in 1992. This was a period of decreased social and economic resources and increased environmental stress for African-Americans. As Gurin (1996) points out, the study was conceptualized in the late 1970s and did not attempt psychiatric diagnostic classification of its respondents. Rather, it focused on the life experience of the people being assessed and was oriented to mental health needs and patterns of help seeking. The survey relied on a lay black cultural perspective and was innovative in that interviewers themselves were African-American. Neighbors and Jackson (1996) note that most previous epidemiological investigations focused on simple comparisons between black and white populations and that this approach contributed to the mistaken impression that African-Americans were a monolithic group and could only be understood in contrast to a white population.

Results from the NSBA clearly demonstrated that African-Americans varied widely in their outlook and well-being. Neighbors and Jackson (1996) reported a number of important changes in mental health among African-Americans over the course of the study, including decreases in self-esteem and increases in the severity of personal problems, particularly among those with low income and less education. However, measures of life satisfaction did not follow this pattern of decline, and Neighbors and Jackson (1996) suggest that reports of life satisfaction may be part of a self-protective adjustment mechanism to cope with the structural changes they were experiencing at that time.

Quality of American Life and Employment

Omnibus SRC surveys on the quality of American life conducted by Campbell, Converse, and Rodgers (1978) used survey methodology developed in the SRC to assess the quality of life across multiple spheres of experience, including work, family, and community life. In addition to providing an overview of the quality of life as experienced by Americans, these pioneering studies also ushered in major methodological advances in the development of social indicators of psychological and social well-being. One of the most important contributions by Campbell and his colleagues was the decomposition of well-being into cognitive and affective attributes. This development represented both a methodological and a theoretical advance in thinking about the nature of psychological well-being. Based on this study, Andrews and Withey (1976) developed multiple strategies for measuring respondent well-being. Andrews and Crandall (1976) also reported validity studies of well-being that showed high agreement among the multiple formats used for collecting information about well-being. This series of studies provided a powerful portrait of psychological well-being under varying conditions of community life and work. In addition, the studies reflected changes in social conditions from the relatively quiescent 1950s through the turbulent 1960s and their aftermath in the 1970s. As we will see, other traditions of research on psychological well-being have recently emerged to complement these studies, focusing not only on social determinants but also on the personal and biological roots of mental health and disorder.

While not explicitly focused on mental health outcomes, the Quality of Employment Survey (Kahn and Quinn 1970; Quinn et al. 1973; Quinn, Seashore, and Mangione 1975; Quinn and Staines 1979) provided an overview of conditions of employment in the United States in 1969, 1973, and 1977. The study, developed by the U.S. Department of Labor and the SRC, was aimed at understanding the nature and distribution of working conditions and their effect on American workers. The survey was concerned with assessing work-related problems and the degree to which major demographic and occupational groups were affected by those problems. In particular, adequacy of income and fringe benefits, work-related injuries and illness, excessive hours, age, sex and race discrimination, and unpleasant working conditions were inventoried. Declines in life and job satisfaction were detected between 1969 and 1977, but it was unclear whether these were due to changes in the composition of the work force, changes in actual working conditions, or rising expectations in the work force over that period. It is interesting to note that this study was undertaken at the point when women were entering the work force in increasing numbers and when major shifts in family life, leisure, and other activities were also occurring. Dual-earner households were becoming the modal family type, and the QOE investigation was an early indicator of a critical interplay between work and family life, a topic of compelling interest even now.

Population Studies of Mental Disorder

In stark contrast to the studies of psychological well-being just described, population studies of mental disorder strongly emphasized psychiatric diagnosis and represent a second dominant theme in describing the mental health of populations. The disciplines most responsible for developing this approach have been psychiatry and epidemiology and their hybrid subdiscipline, psychiatric epidemiology. Rather than mapping the relationship between the social conditions of family and community life and psychological well-being, population studies of mental disorder have been most concerned with establishing the criteria for defining a diagnostic case and with estimating the prevalence of cases of psychiatric disorder in the population. An important rationale for obtaining accurate measures of prevalence of psychiatric disorder has been to determine the degree to which members of various diagnostic groups have access to and actually use mental health services. The surgeon general's report (Satcher 1999) clearly documents this as a critical gap in mental health services.

These early studies of mental disorder in community populations suggested that the definition of mental disorder itself was a cause for concern. Epidemiological studies yielded substantial differences in prevalence rates of mental disorder from study to study. Kramer (1982) concludes that these differences stemmed less from community differences than from differences in the criteria used for defining a case of mental illness. This concern with case definition ultimately led to the development of a much more detailed and explicit set of criteria for diagnosis and a survey instrument—the Diagnostic Interview Schedule—that would allow lay interviewers to provide reliable diagnoses of survey respondents (Robins et al. 1981).

The Epidemiologic Catchment Area Program

In 1978, the President's Commission on Mental Health (1978) identified the need to document the frequency of specific mental disorders and the use of mental health services in the United States. In response, the National Institute of Mental Health (NIMH) developed a program for the measurement of psychiatric diagnoses based on the criteria published in the Diagnostic and Statistical Manual (DSM-III, American Psychiatric Association 1980) to allow a more accurate estimate of the incidence and prevalence of major psychiatric disorders.

The NIMH Epidemiological Catchment Area (ECA) program (Eaton et al. 1981) was an outgrowth of this new emphasis and a response to the President's Commission on Mental Health. The ECA program required that nonclinicians conduct diagnostic interviews using a highly structured survey instrument. This requirement led to the development of the Diagnostic Interview Schedule (Robins et al. 1981), which could be administered by trained lay interviewers to identify individuals that met the criteria for specific psychiatric disorders. Multiple collaborating sites participated in the ECA study, and individuals both from the community and from institutionalized populations were interviewed.

Findings from the ECA program estimated that approximately 32 percent of adults in the United States reported symptoms that met the criteria for one or more psychiatric disorders during their lifetime (Robins, Locke, and Regier 1991). Approximately 36 percent of men and 30 percent of women met criteria for at least one disorder. Only one-quarter of persons with a disorder sought mental health or addictive services. This clearly represents a major underutilization of existing services by those individuals diagnosed as having a psychiatric disorder or an inadequate supply of affordable and accessible mental health and related services. While the ECA took an important step forward in measuring the prevalence of mental disorder, it was soon followed by other similarly motivated studies.

The National Comorbidity Survey

The National Comorbidity Survey (Kessler et al. 1994) is a landmark diagnostically oriented national survey of mental disorder.[1] The NCS was the first survey to administer a structured psychiatric interview to a national probability sample of adults in the United States using a revised version of the Composite International Diagnostic Interview (CIDI). As Kessler et al. (1994) note, the NCS was designed to take the next step beyond the ECA study and took advantage of three major advances. First, NCS diagnoses were based on the revised version of DSM-III of the American Psychiatric Association, and questions were included that allowed comparison with other diagnostic systems. Second, the NCS not only was designed to estimate the prevalence and incidence of psychiatric disorder but also included a comprehensive risk battery, including family history, questions about childhood and family adversity, measures of social support and social networks, and Research Diagnostic Criteria measures of parental psychopathology. Finally, while the prior ECA study involved collecting data from local samples, the NCS collected data from a national sample and therefore could study regional variations and urban-rural differences in psychiatric disorders as well as the need for services. Such nationally representative samples are clearly of value in policy discussions of service needs for subpopulations within the United States.

Prevalence of Mental Disorder

Nearly 50 percent of respondents to the NCS reported experiencing at least one disorder during their lifetime, and nearly 30 percent reported at least one psychiatric disorder within the last twelve months. These findings suggest a very high national prevalence of mental disorder using DSM-III-R (revised) criteria.

Major depressive episodes, alcohol dependence, anxiety disorders, and simple phobia were among the most common disorders documented in the NCS. One of the most striking findings was the very high concentration of disorders in a small proportion of the population. More than half of all lifetime disorders occurred in the 14 percent of the population who had a history of three or more comorbid disorders. The NCS data also indicated that women had elevated rates of affective disorders and anxiety disorders, while men had elevated rates of substance use disorders and antisocial personality. Finally the NCS also reported low service utilization rates, with less than 40 percent of those with a lifetime disorder ever having received professional treatment.

Comorbidity

As its name implies, the National Comorbidity Survey was particularly focused on identifying individuals with more than one disorder. Kessler et al. (1996) report that the co-occurrence of the addictive and mental disorders is highly prevalent in the general population and is usually due to the association of a primary mental disorder with a secondary addictive disorder. That is, among people with a history of both mental and addictive disorders, the mental disorder usually occurs first. Most typically, the mental disorder is a conduct disorder or an anxiety or affective disorder. Kessler et al. (1996) argue that one implication of these findings is that special assessment and treatment procedures are needed for persons who present co-occurring addictive and mental disorders when seeking treatment.

Childhood Adversity and Subsequent Adult Disorder

One of the most broadly accepted hypotheses in the developmental study of mental health problems is that childhood adversity influences adult mental health. The NCS study collected data on twenty-six forms of childhood adversity, including parental divorce, maternal depression, rape, and other nonpersonal risks such as the experience of natural disasters. Although the NCS is a cross-sectional survey and must rely on retrospective reports, it still provides rich data to evaluate the hypothesis that there is a relationship between early trauma and later mental disorder. Findings from the NCS indicate that, in general, childhood adversity is strongly associated with the onset of disorder, but not with the persistence of disorders into adulthood (Kessler, Davis, and Kendler 1997). The childhood adversities themselves tend to be highly clustered, and, as expected, adult disorders also were clustered and comorbid. These findings suggest that there appears to be little specificity in the relationship between a particular form of childhood adversity and any particular adult disorder.

Patterns of Service Use and Mental Disorder

Both the need for and the use of services by persons with mental health problems were major concerns of the President's Commission on Mental Health (1978) more than two decades ago, and the NCS provides another answer to the question of the underuse of services by persons with mental disorders. Kessler et al. (1999) measured the proportion of respondents who reported a disorder within the previous twelve months and who also obtained some form of outpatient treatment for psychiatric problems in the general medical sector, specialty mental and addictive disorders treatment, help from human service organizations, or assistance from self-help organizations. They were particularly concerned with whether a higher proportion of people entered treatment for disorders than in the earlier ECA study and whether outpatient treatment itself was allocated differently across different service sectors than in the past. The NCS data showed that more serious and complex forms of disorder were more likely to involve service use and that more serious disorders involved treatment in more than one sector.

There is little doubt that the Diagnostic and Statistical Manual (DSM) of Mental Disorders in its successive editions and, in particular, the NCS and its replication both in the United States and internationally establish the study of the prevalence of mental disorder as a prominent approach to understanding the mental health of populations, with further studies ongoing, as discussed at the end of this chapter.

Improving the Mental Health of Populations

The first half of the twentieth century ushered in psychological treatment in the form of psychoanalysis and other "talking therapies" as the recourse of a privileged few. More recently, treatment research has yielded a wide range of pharmacological and behavioral treatments that are effective for a variety of psychological disorders (Nathan and Gorman 1998). But providing access to these treatments on a large scale remains a major challenge, and some observers (Albee and Gullotta 1997) doubt that a large enough group of professionals will ever exist to meet the projected need. The community mental health movement of the 1960s and 1970s in the United States (Denner and Price 1973; Price and Denner 1973) offered new optimism that these benefits could be made available not just to those privileged few but to entire populations, particularly those people made more vulnerable by lack of economic resources or other forms of adversity (Heller, Price, and Hogg 1990). These public health–oriented approaches were aimed at improving community members' access to services and strongly emphasized the value of mutual and social support in families, workplaces, and communities (House 1981; House and Kahn 1985; House, Umberson, and Landis 1988).

Population Needs Assessment to Improve Service Access

A primary goal of nearly every population study of mental health in the last half century has been to assess the mental health needs of the population under study in order to improve mental health. However, these studies have taken two distinctly different approaches to understanding mental health needs. One approach, beginning with the landmark study by Gurin, Veroff, and Feld (1960) described earlier, has been to understand the help-seeking process among persons experiencing a broad range of negative life events and adversity. Any of a variety of personal life events (health, employment, marriage) could trigger a help-seeking effort that went through several distinct stages and might result in an encounter with a professional or nonprofessional. The second approach, primarily adopted by those interested in studying the prevalence of mental disorder and exemplified in the NCS described earlier, has been to ask about service utilization rates among persons with a diagnosed mental disorder. This second approach focuses on a much narrower segment of the population already manifesting a psychological disorder and assumes that a failure to obtain treatment represents a gap in service utilization.

These two approaches provide strikingly different portraits of mental health needs. The approach adopted by those studying the help-seeking process assumes that anyone in the population experiencing a personal crisis is in need of formal or informal help, whether or not they have a diagnosable disorder. The disorder-oriented approach assumes that a diagnosable disorder is a priori an indicator of the need for mental health services.

Stressful Life Events as a Window on Risk Mechanisms and an Opportunity to Improve Mental Health

Both epidemiological and clinical research have demonstrated that a wide range of negative life events such as widowhood, loss of an intimate relationship, job loss, or illness can increase the risk of mental health problems (Kessler, Price, and Wortman 1985). The ISR stress model (Kahn 1981; Kahn and Byosiere 1992; Kahn and Sutton 1983) has emerged as an influential conceptualization of the processes by which social and physical stressors result in short-term responses that, in some cases, may lead to chronic health and mental health problems (see also chap. 9, this volume). The model proposes that the strength of the causal links between initial stressors, short-term responses, and long-term health and mental health consequences can be influenced by social, biological, chemical, and environmental factors. The ISR stress model also provides a framework for conceptualizing the critical leverage points for efforts to improve health and psychological well-being. Indeed, the model has heuristic value both in clarifying the mediating mechanisms linking stressors to poor health and psychological disorder and in identifying potential points of intervention to influence the development of disorder.

Job Loss as a Stressor

The following section focuses on a particular negative life event—involuntary job loss—as an example of the stress process and as an opportunity for intervention both to test hypotheses about risk mechanisms and, at the same time, to reduce the risk of mental health problems. In 1982 researchers at ISR began the Michigan Prevention Research Center (MPRC), a new program of research on stress, coping, and the mental health consequences of conditions of work and unemployment.[2] The continuous program of research conducted over the last two decades has produced information on the problems facing unemployed persons and their families, particularly those problems associated with job search (Caplan et al. 1989), economic hardship (Vinokur, Price, and Caplan 1996), and family difficulties (Howe et al. 1995; Price 1992).

Since the pioneering work of Jahoda, Lazarsfeld, and Zeisel (1933), the psychological and social risks of job loss have been documented for the unemployed person and for the person's family (Dew, Penkower, and

Bromet 1991). Job loss has adverse effects on social and psychological functioning. Research indicates that job loss leads to increased depressive symptoms (Kessler, House, and Turner 1987; Kessler, Turner, and House 1988), increased anxiety, decreased subjective perceptions of competence (Warr, Jackson, and Banks 1988), decreased self-esteem (Jackson and Warr 1984), suicide attempts (Platt and Kreitman 1985), and increased propensity for violent behavior (Catalano et al. 1993).

These outcomes of job loss are well documented, but examining job loss through the lens of the ISR stress model can shed additional light on questions of who might be most vulnerable, the risk mechanisms responsible for adverse mental health effects, and what interventions might reduce the vulnerabilities or alter the risk mechanisms responsible for mental health problems. In addressing the question of moderating influences on the relationship between employment status and mental health problems, for example, Price, van Ryn, and Vinokur (1992) identified elevated but subclinical depressive symptoms and Vinokur et al. (2000) identified low levels of mastery as vulnerability factors predicting later more severe episodes of depression. In addition, Kessler, Turner, and House (1988) and Vinokur, Price, and Caplan (1996) have shown that economic hardship and financial strain are the dominant mechanisms mediating the relationship between job loss and subsequent episodes of depression in individuals and couples. In short, when job loss results in a cascade of secondary economic stressors and strains, it produces negative mental health effects, and these are most severe among those low in mastery or with subclinical symptoms of depression.

Field Experiments to Test Hypotheses about Causal Mechanisms and to Reduce the Risk of Mental Problems

While the risks described previously are formidable to mental health, persons experiencing job loss face yet another coping challenge: to conduct a job search that allows the successful transition to reemployment and a return to economic and family stability. The MPRC developed a program to aid unemployed workers to more effectively seek reemployment and to cope with the multiple challenges and stresses of unemployment and job search (Caplan, Vinokur, and Price 1997; Price and Vinokur 1995). The JOBS program is a five-session group learning experience based on behavioral science principles designed to teach participants job search skills and to cope effectively with the stressors of job search and unemployment. The randomized field experiments designed to examine the impact of the program on unemployed workers may be regarded as experimental tests of hypotheses regarding (1) the causal role of employment status on mental health; (2) the malleability of vulnerability factors such as depressive symptoms; (3) the protective value of coping skills in dealing with the challenges and setbacks in the job search process; and (4) the causal role of economic hardship mediating the relationship between employment status and depression.

The impact of the JOBS program on mental health and other outcomes has been studied in replicated randomized field trials involving unemployed workers and their partners (Caplan et al. 1989; Vinokur, Price, and Schul 1995). The program returns unemployed workers to new jobs more quickly, produces reemployment in jobs that pay more (Vinokur et al. 1991), and reduces mental health problems associated with prolonged unemployment (Vinokur, Price, and Schul 1995). A long-term follow-up study (Vinokur et al. 2000) indicates that the program prevents the occurrence of major depressive episodes up to two years later. These replicated findings strongly support the hypothesis that employment status has a causal impact on mental health. In addition, the program is particularly effective in preventing depression among those most vulnerable to mental health problems (Price, van Ryn, and Vinokur 1992; Vinokur, Price, and Schul 1995), supporting the hypothesis that this vulnerability factor is malleable and that reducing its magnitude is consequential in protecting mental health. In addition, the program has been shown to inoculate workers against the adverse effects of a second job loss (Vinokur and Schul 1997). In comparison to control group counterparts, program participants who regained employment and then suffered a second job loss did not experience the same discouragement and increased depressive symptoms that afflicted control group participants who had the same labor market experience. It appears that the program psychologically inoculates participants against subsequent job loss setbacks because they gain an enhanced sense of mastery over the challenges of job search (Vinokur and Schul 1997). Finally, Vinokur and Schul (1997) have shown that the relationship between reemployment and improved mental health is mediated by reductions in financial strain. That is, in a randomized trial, where causal inference can be more confidently made, regaining employment can be seen to exert its positive effects on mental health through a reduction in financial strain.

It is possible that a wide variety of negative life events is susceptible to field experimentation with theory-driven interventions that can simultaneously illuminate risk mechanisms and provide prototypes for preventive interventions. Indeed, a research program for the development of risk reduction strategies in mental health, with the ultimate aim of large-scale efforts to improve the mental health of populations, has been recommended by the Institute of Medicine (IOM) (Mrazek and Haggerty 1994).

Risk Reduction Strategies to Improve the Mental Health of Populations

In 1992 the IOM convened a Committee on Reducing Risks for Mental Disorders (Mrazek and Haggerty 1994) to assess the feasibility of risk reduction as a means of preventing the development of mental disorders. Its charge was to review the status of current research on the prevention of mental illness, to review existing federal efforts, and to provide recommendations on policies and programs of research support leading to a prevention research agenda. In conducting its study, the committee identified a range of illustrative preventive programs across the life course that had already demonstrated effectiveness in reducing the risk of mental disorder (Price, Hawkins, and Hamburg 1994). Proven risk-reduction strategies included prenatal and early infancy programs, early intervention for preterm infants, programs to improve family management practices, preschool programs to reduce the risk of academic failure, childhood bereavement programs, alcohol education projects for adolescents, programs designed to enhance couple relationships, programs to cope with unemployment, and programs for the elderly aimed at reducing the risk of depression in widowhood. Since the time of the IOM report, additional reviews have been conducted of literature in the field, adding convincing evidence (Durlak and Wells 1997) that preventive interventions aimed at reducing the risk of mental disorder were not only possible but had demonstrated their effectiveness across a wide range of ages and risk groups.

Looking Ahead: Understanding and Improving the Mental Health of Populations in the Twenty-first Century

The last half century of survey research to understand and ultimately improve the mental health of populations has undergone a series of sea changes. Where there once were several competing theoretical paradigms implicating dynamic, social, learning, and biological mechanisms (Price and Lynn 1986) that each claimed etiological preeminence, now many accounts draw on biological explanations. Beginning in a growing postwar awareness of the power of social environments and social change to shape well-being and illness, the century has ended with the biological organism in the foreground (Dohrenwend 1998a). The following sections briefly note emerging developments in the study of the mental health of populations that are likely to influence the next half century of research—in particular, new developments in the measurement of psychological well-being and disorder and research implicating important biological influences on both psychological well-being and disorder.

New Directions in the Measurement of Psychological Well-Being and Mental Disorder

Early studies by Bryant and Veroff (1982) used data from the 1975 Americans View Their Mental Health Survey to conduct studies of the structure of psychological well-being and identified several distinct underlying dimensions. More recently, Ryff (1995) and Ryff and Keyes (1995) have incorporated a number of theoretical traditions into an empirically based model of psychological wellness based on a national probability sample of U.S. adults. Ryff (1995) and her colleagues identified self-acceptance, positive relations with others, a sense of autonomy, environmental mastery, a sense of purpose in life, and a feeling of personal growth as fundamental dimensions of well-being.

Diener and Diener (1996) and Myers and Diener (1995) have asked what research reveals about the characteristics of happy people. They suggest that self-esteem, a sense of personal control, optimism, and extroversion are critical ingredients for happiness. Indeed, Myers and Diener argue that knowing a person's age, sex, race, or income tells us little about their happiness. Better clues come from individual psychological traits and whether people have a supportive network of close relationships. Looking at the question across cultures, they argue that living in a culture that offers positive interpretations of daily events, being engaged by work and leisure, and having a faith that entails hope and purpose are also critical ingredients of happiness.

The last two decades have also produced substantial gains in the measurement of psychological disorder. The instrument developed from the NCS (Kessler et al. 1994), the Composite International Diagnostic Interview (CIDI), is now used in a wide range of international studies. The World Health Organization is sponsoring a general population epidemiologic survey of mental illness, substance abuse, and behavioral disorders in twelve countries, titled the World Mental Health 2000 Study, or

WMH2000. The study, coordinated by Ustun and Kessler (1999), will obtain cross-national information about the prevalence and correlates of mental disorder, substance abuse, and behavioral disorders to improve assessment of the global burden of these disorders, to study patterns of treatment, and to pinpoint modifiable barriers to obtaining treatment. The SRC is conducting a number of these studies and related ones. For example, a new version of the NSBA, called the National Survey of American Life (NSAL), will compare a national sample of non-Hispanic blacks of Caribbean descent and non-Hispanic whites with a national sample of African-Americans. As Jackson observes (Jackson et al. 1996), these samples will allow investigation of racial and ethnic differences using survey instruments measuring psychological distress and mental disorders based on the CIDI. At the same time, international studies are emerging, including a study by Williams and Williams-Morris (2000) on the effect of torture on mental health in South Africa.

Biological Influences on Well-Being and Mental Disorder

While early postwar studies of the mental health of populations emphasized the social determinants of well-being, more recent research has taken possible biological origins of mental health as its point of departure. For example, Lykken and Tellegen (1996) studied the subjective well-being of a birth record–based sample of several thousand middle-aged twins. They report that neither socioeconomic status, family, income, educational attainment, marital status, nor religious commitment accounted for more than 3 percent of the variance in well-being. They concede that, while positive and negative life events do produce changes in happiness, the effects appear as fluctuations around a stable temperamental "set point" for the individual. They note that the well-being of one's identical twin, either now or ten years earlier, is a far better predictor of one's own happiness than one's own educational achievement, income, or status, and they conclude that variations in well-being are determined by "the great genetic lottery that occurs at conception" (189).

Similarly, the biological roots of psychological disorder have been explored in a variety of genetically informative research designs and have begun to change our assumptions about the etiology of important forms of disorder such as depression. Recent twin studies of psychological disorder that directly compare the concordance rates of genetically identical monozygotic with dizygotic twins have produced strong evidence for genetic influences on depression. Kendler et al. (1993) have presented an integrated etiological model for the prediction of episodes of major depression. They report that 60 percent of the explained variance in depression was due to direct effects of genetic factors and that the remaining 40 percent was mediated by the history of prior depressive episodes, stressful life events, and neuroticism. It is interesting to note that negative life events appear to have higher concordance rates in monozygotic than in dizygotic twins, and Kendler and his associates have reported that genetic factors account for 40 to 75 percent of the variation in social support in twin pairs. Although these findings may in part reflect cumulative effects over the life course or could reflect confounding period and genetic effects, these remain striking. They suggest that factors influencing mental health previously thought to be entirely due to the social environment, such as the influence of negative life events and social support, may be determined in part by genetic factors. A great deal of research is needed to unravel these causal strands, with survey research continuing to be central to this effort.

Conclusion

While these studies are only examples from the emerging research evidence, they clearly signal the need for more sophisticated models of the combination of biological factors and environmental adversity in the expression of psychological well-being and disorder (Dohrenwend 1998b; Kendler et al. 1993). It is now increasingly clear that individuals, through their traits and vulnerabilities, evoke responses of support or withdrawal and actively select, and are selected into, niches of adversity or nurturance that are consequential for their well-being and psychological disorder. The causal pathways remain to be understood, and we will need advances in the measurement of life events, in genetically informative designs to study individual and family life course, and in the introduction of biological measures to complement our capacity to measure environmental adversity and support. Beyond these challenges lies the opportunity to design social and biological interventions that can simultaneously clarify the nature of causal pathways between adversity and disorder and offer models of humane intervention to a society continuously in need of them.

NOTES

1. The Web site for the NCS is <http://www.hcp.med.harvard.edu/ncs/indexframe.htm>.

2. The Web site for MPRC is <http://www.isr.umich.edu/src/seh/mprc/>.

REFERENCES

Albee, George W., and T. P. Gullotta, eds. 1997. *Primary prevention works.* Vol. 6. Thousand Oaks: Sage.

American Psychiatric Association. 1980. *Diagnostic and statistical manual of mental disorders.* 3d ed. Washington, DC: American Psychiatric Association.

Andrews, Frank M., and Richard Crandall. 1976. Validity of measures of self-reported well-being. *Social Indicators Research* 3:1–19.

Andrews, Frank M., and Steve B. Withey. 1976. *Social indicators of well-being: Americans' perceptions of life quality.* New York: Plenum.

Bradburn, Norman M. 1969. *The structure of psychological well-being.* Chicago: Aldine.

Bryant, Fred B., and Joseph Veroff. 1982. The structure of psychological well-being—A sociohistorical analysis. *Journal of Personality and Social Psychology* 43 (4): 653–73.

Campbell, Angus, Philip E. Converse, and Willard L. Rodgers. 1978. Quality of American life. 2d ICPSR ed. Computer file. Ann Arbor: Institute for Social Research, University of Michigan, Social Science Archive.

Cannell, Charles F., and Robert L. Kahn. 1984. Some factors in the origins and development of the Institute for Social Research, the University of Michigan. *American Psychologist* 39 (11): 1256–66.

Caplan, Robert D., Amiram D. Vinokur, and Richard H. Price. 1997. From job loss to reemployment: Field experiments in prevention-focused coping. In *Primary prevention works: Issues in children's and families' lives,* ed. G. W. Albee and T. P. Gullotta, 16:341–79. Thousand Oaks: Sage.

Caplan, Robert D., Amiram D. Vinokur, Richard H. Price, and Michelle van Ryn. 1989. Job seeking, reemployment, and mental health: A randomized field experiment in coping with job loss. *Journal of Applied Psychology* 74 (5): 759–69.

Catalano, Ralph, David Dooley, Raymond W. Novaco, Georjeanna Wilson, and Richard Hough. 1993. Using ECA survey data to examine the effect of job layoffs on violent behavior. *Hospital and Community Psychiatry* 44 (9): 874–79.

Denner, Bruce, and Richard H. Price, eds. 1973. *Community mental health: Social action and community reaction.* New York: Holt, Rinehart, and Winston.

Dew, Mary A., Lili Penkower, and Evelyn J. Bromet. 1991. Effects of unemployment on mental health in the contemporary family. *Behavior Modification* 15 (4): 501–44.

Diener, Edward, and Carol Diener. 1996. Most people are happy. *Psychological Science* 7 (3): 181–85.

Dohrenwend, Bruce P. 1998a. Adversity, stress, and psychopathology: Overview of the evidence for the importance of adverse environmental conditions in the causation of psychiatric disorders. In *Adversity, Stress, and Psychopathology,* ed. B. P. Dohrenwend. New York: Oxford University Press.

———. 1998b. A psychosocial perspective on the past and future of psychiatric epidemiology. *American Journal of Epidemiology* 147 (3): 222–31.

Durlak, J. A., and A. M. Wells. 1997. Primary prevention mental health programs for children and adolescents: A meta-analytic review. *American Journal of Community Psychology* 25 (2): 115–52.

Eaton, William W., Darrel A. Reigier, Ben Z. Locke, and Carl A. Taube. 1981. The epidemiologic catchment area program of the National Institute of Mental Health. *Public Health Reports* 96 (4): 319–25.

Faris, Robert E., and Warren H. Dunham. 1939. *Mental disorders in urban areas: An ecological study of schizophrenia and other psychoses.* Chicago: University of Chicago Press.

Frantilla, Anne, ed. 1998. *Social science in the public interest: A fiftieth-year history of the Institute for Social Research.* Ann Arbor: Bentley Historical Library, University of Michigan.

Gurin, Gerald, Joseph Veroff, and Sheila Feld. 1960. *Americans view their mental health.* New York: Basic Books.

Gurin, Patricia. 1996. Forward. In *Mental health in black America,* ed. Harold W. Neighbors and James S. Jackson. Newbury Park, CA: Sage.

Heller, Kenneth, Richard H. Price, and J. R. Hogg. 1990. The role of social support in community and clinical intervention. In *Social support: An interfactional view. Issues in social support research,* ed. B. R. Sarason, I. G. Sarason, and G. R. Pierce, 482–507. New York: John Wiley.

Hollingshead, August B., and Fredrick C. Redlich. 1958. *Social class and mental illness: A community study.* New York: Wiley.

House, James. 1981. The nature of social support. In *Work stress and social support,* ed. James House. Reading, MA: Addison-Wesley.

House, James S., and Robert L. Kahn. 1985. Measures and concepts of social support. In *Social support and health,* ed. S. Cohen and S. L. Syme, 111–51. San Francisco: Academic Press.

House, James S., Debra Umberson, and Karl Landis. 1988. Structures and processes of social support. *Annual Review of Sociology* 14:293–318.

Howe, George W., Robert D. Caplan, David Foster, Mindy Lockshin, and Claire McGrath. 1995. A research strategy for developing preventive interventions. In *Stress in the 90s,* ed. G. Keita and S. Sauter. Washington DC: American Psychological Association.

Hughes, Charles C., Marc-Adelard Tremblay, Robert N. Rapoport, and Alexander H. Leighton. 1960. *People of Cove and Woodlot: Communities from the viewpoint of social psychiatry. Volume II: The Stirling County study of psychiatric disorder and sociocultural environment.* New York: Basic Books.

Jackson, James S., Tony N. Brown, David R. Williams, Myriam Torres, Sherrill L. Sellers, and Kendrick Brown. 1996. Racism and the physical and mental health status of African Americans: A thirteen year national panel study. *Ethnicity and Disease* 6 (1–2): 132–47.

Jackson, Paul R., and Peter B. Warr. 1984. Unemployment and psychological ill-health: The moderating role of duration and age. *Psychological Medicine* 14:605–14.

Jahoda, Marie, Paul F. Lazarsfeld, and H. Zeisel. 1933. *Marienthal: The sociography of an unemployed community.* Chicago: Aldine.

Joint Commission on Mental Illness and Health. 1961. *Action for mental health: Final report of the Joint Commission.* New York: Basic Books.

Kahn, Robert L. 1981. *Work and health.* New York: Wiley.

Kahn, Robert L., and Phillip Byosiere. 1992. Stress in organizations. In *Handbook of industrial and organizational psychology,* 2d ed., ed. M. D. Dunnette and L. M. Hough, 3:571–650. Palo Alto, CA: Consulting Psychologists Press.

Kahn, Robert L., and Robert P. Quinn. 1970. Role stress: A framework for analysis. In *Occupational mental health,* ed. A. McLean, 50–115. New York: Rand McNally.

Kahn, Robert L., and Robert I. Sutton. 1983. Prediction, understanding, and control as antidotes to organizational stress. In *Handbook of organizational behavior,* ed. J. W. Lorsch. Englewood Cliffs, NJ: Prentice-Hall.

Kendler, Kenneth S., Michael C. Neale, Ronald C. Kessler, and Andrew C. Heath. 1993. The lifetime history of major depression in women: Reliability of diagnosis and heritability. *Archives of General Psychiatry* 50:863–70.

Kessler, Ronald C., Christopher G. Davis, and Kenneth S. Kendler. 1997. Childhood adversity and adult psychiatric disorder in the U.S. National Comorbidity Survey. *Psychological Medicine* 27:1101–19.

Kessler, Ronald C., James S. House, and J. Blake Turner. 1987. Unemployment and health in a community sample. *Journal of Health and Social Behavior* 28:51–59.

Kessler, Ronald C., Katherine A. McGonagle, Shanyang Zhao, Christopher B. Nelson, Michael Hughes, Suzann Eshleman, Hans-Ulrich Wittchen, and Kenneth S. Kendler. 1994. Lifetime and twelve-month prevalence of DSM-III-R psychiatric disorders in the United States: Results from the National Comorbidity Survey. *Archives of General Psychiatry* 51:8–19.

Kessler, Ronald C., Kristin D. Mickelson, and Zhao Shanyang. 1997. Patterns and correlates of self-help group membership in the United States. *Social Policy* 27:27–46.

Kessler, Ronald C., Christopher B. Nelson, Katherine A. McGonagle, Mark J. Edlund, Richard G. Frank, and Philip J. Leaf. 1996. The epidemiology of co-occurring addictive and mental disorders: Implications for prevention and service utilization. *American Journal of Orthopsychiatry* 66:17–31.

Kessler, Ronald C., Richard H. Price, and Camille Wortman. 1985. Social factors in psychopathology: Stress, social support, and coping processes. *Annual Review of Psychology* 36:531–72.

Kessler, Ronald C., Blake Turner, and James S. House. 1988. Effects of unemployment on health in a community survey: Main, modifying, and mediating effects. *Journal of Social Issues* 44 (4): 69–86.

Kessler, Ronald C., Shanyang Zhao, Steven J. Katz, Anthony C. Kouzis, Richard G. Frank, Mark Edlund, and Philip Leaf. 1999. Past-year use of outpatient services for psychiatric problems in the National Comorbidity Survey. *American Journal of Psychiatry* 156 (1): 115–23.

Kramer, Morton. 1982. The continuing challenge: The rising prevalence of mental disorders, associated chronic diseases, and disabling conditions. In *Perspectives on public mental health,* ed. Morton O. Wagenfeld, P. V. Lemkau, and B. Justice, 103–30. Los Angeles: Sage.

Kulka, Richard A., Joseph Veroff, and Elizabeth Douvan. 1979. Social class and the use of professional help for personal problems: 1957 and 1976. *Journal of Health and Social Behavior* 20:2–17.

Lachman, Margie E., and Suzanne L. Weaver. 1998. The sense of control as a moderator of social class differences in health and well-being. *Journal of Personality and Social Psychology* 74:763–73.
Leighton, Dorothea C., John S. Harding, David B. Macklin, Allister M. MacMillan, and Alexander H. Leighton. 1963. *The character of danger: Psychiatric symptoms in selected communities.* New York: Basic Books.
Lykken, David, and Tellegen Auke. 1996. Happiness is a stochastic phenomenon. *Psychological Science* 7 (3): 186–89.
Mrazek, Patricia J., and Robert J. Haggerty. 1994. *Reducing risks for mental disorders: Frontiers for preventive intervention.* Washington, DC: National Academy Press.
Myers, David G., and Francine Diener. 1995. Who is happy? *Psychological Science* 6 (1): 10–19.
Nathan, Peter E., and Jack M. Gorman, eds. 1998. *A guide to treatments that work.* New York: Oxford University Press.
Neighbors, Harold W., and James S. Jackson. 1996. *Mental health in black America.* Newbury Park, CA: Sage.
Pasamanick, Benjamin, Dean W. Roberts, Paul V. Lemkau, and Dean B. Krueger. 1956. A survey of mental disease in an urban population. *American Journal of Public Health* 47:923–29.
Platt, Stephen, and Norman Kreitman. 1985. Parsuicide and unemployment among men in Edinburgh, 1968–1982. *Psychological Medicine* 15:113–23.
President's Commission on Mental Health. 1978. *Report to the president from the President's Commission on Mental Health.* Stock No. 040–000–00390–8, vol. 1. Washington, DC: U.S. Government Printing Office.
Price, Richard H. 1992. Psychosocial impact of job loss on individuals and families. *Current Directions in Psychological Science* 1 (1): 9–11.
Price, Richard H., and B. Denner, eds. 1973. *The making of a mental patient.* New York: Holt, Rinehart, and Winston.
Price, Richard H., David Hawkins, and Beatrix Hamburg. 1994. *Illustrative preventive intervention research programs.* Washington, DC: National Academy Press.
Price, Richard H., and S. J. Lynn. 1986. *Abnormal psychology in the human context.* 2d ed. Homewood, IL: Dorsey Press.
Price, Richard H., Michelle van Ryn, and Amiram D. Vinokur. 1992. Impact of preventive job search intervention on the likelihood of depression among the unemployed. *Journal of Health and Social Behavior* 33 (2): 158–67.
Price, Richard H., and Amiram D. Vinokur. 1995. Supporting career transitions in a time of organizational downsizing: The Michigan JOBS program. In *Employees, careers, and job creation: Developing growth-oriented human resource strategies and programs,* ed. M. London, 191–209. San Francisco: Jossey-Bass.
Quinn, Robert P., Stanley E. Seashore, and Thomas W. Mangione. 1975. Survey of working conditions, 1969–1970. ICPSR computer file. Ann Arbor: Institute for Social Research, Social Science Archive, University of Michigan.
Quinn, Robert P., and Graham L. Staines. 1979. *The 1977 Quality of Employment Survey: Descriptive statistics with comparison data from the 1969–1970 survey of working conditions and the 1972–1973 Quality of Employment Survey.* Ann Arbor: Institute for Social Research, University of Michigan.
Quinn, Robert P., et al. 1973. *The 1969–1970 survey of working conditions: Chronicles of an*

unfinished enterprise. Ann Arbor: Institute for Social Research, University of Michigan.

Regier, Darrel A., and Charles T. Kaelber. 1995. The epidemiologic catchment area (ECA) program: Studying the prevalence and incidence of psychopathology. In *Textbook in psychiatric epidemiology,* ed. Tohen A. Z. Tsuang, 135–55. New York: Wiley-Liss.

Robins, Lee N., John E. Helzer, J. Croughan, and Kathyrn R. Ratcliff. 1981. National Institute of Mental Health diagnostic interview schedule: Its history, characteristics, and validity. *Archives of General Psychiatry* 38:381–89.

Robins, Lee N., Ben Z. Locke, and Darrel A. Regier. 1991. An overview of psychiatric disorders in America. In *Psychiatric disorder in America,* ed. L. N. Robins and D. A. Regier, 328–66. New York: Free Press.

Ryff, Carol D. 1995. Psychological well-being in adult life. *Current Directions in Psychology* 4 (4): 99–104.

Ryff, Carol D., and Corey L. M. Keyes. 1995. The structure of psychological well-being revisited. *Journal of Personality and Social Psychology* 69 (4): 719–27.

Satcher, David. 1999. *Mental health: A report of the surgeon general.* Washington, DC: U.S. Department of Health and Human Services (SAMHSA/NIH).

Srole, Leo. 1975. Measurement and classification in socio-psychiatric epidemiology: Midtown Manhattan study (1954) and midtown Manhattan restudy (1974). *Journal of Health and Social Behavior* 16:347–64.

Srole, Leo L. T. S., Stanley T. Michael, Marvin K. Opler, and Rennie Thomas. 1962. *Mental health in the metropolis: The midtown Manhattan study.* Vol. 1. New York: Blakiston Division, McGraw-Hill.

Star, Shirley A. 1950. The screening of psychoneurotics in the Army: Technical development of tests. In *Measurement and prediction,* vol. 4, ed. Samuel A. Stouffer, Louis Guttman, Edward A. Suchman, Paul F. Lazarsfeld, Shirley A. Star, and John A. Clausen. Princeton: Princeton University Press.

Tischler, Gary L., Jerzy E. Henisz, Jerome K. Myers, and Philip C. Boswell. 1975. Utilization of mental health services. I: Patienthood and the prevalence of symptomatology in the community. *Archives of General Psychiatry* 32:411–18.

Ustun, Bedirhan T., and Ronald C. Kessler. 1999. *The World Mental Health 2000 Study: WMH2000.* Geneva: World Health Organization.

Vander Stoep, A., and Bruce Link. 1998. Social class, ethnicity, and mental illness: The importance of being more than earnest. *American Journal of Public Health* 88 (9): 1396–402.

Veroff, Joseph, Elizabeth Douvan, and Richard Kulka. 1981. *The inner American: A self-portrait from 1957 to 1976.* New York: Basic Books.

———. 1982. Americans view their mental health. ICPSR computer file. Ed. Survey Research Center, University of Michigan. Ann Arbor: Inter-university Consortium for Political and Social Research Institute for Social Research.

Veroff, Joseph, Richard A. Kulka, and Elizabeth Douvan. 1981. *Mental health in America: Patterns of help seeking from 1957 to 1976.* New York: Basic Books.

Vinokur, Amiram D., Richard H. Price, and Robert D. Caplan. 1996. Hard times and hurtful partners: How financial strain affects depression and relationship satisfaction of unemployed persons and their spouses. *Journal of Personality and Social Psychology* 71 (1): 166–79.

Vinokur, Amiram D., Richard H. Price, and Yaacov Schul. 1995. Impact of the JOBS intervention on unemployed workers varying in risk for depression. *American Journal of Community Psychology* 23 (1): 39–74.

Vinokur, Amiram D., and Yaacov Schul. 1997. Mastery and inoculation against setbacks as active ingredients in the JOBS intervention for the unemployed. *Journal of Consulting and Clinical Psychology* 65 (5): 867–77.

Vinokur, Amiram D., Yaacov Schul, Jukka Vuori, and Richard H. Price. 2000. Two years after a job loss: Long term impact of the JOBS program on reemployment and mental health. *Journal of Occupational Health Psychology* 5 (1): 32–47.

Vinokur, Amiram D., Michelle van Ryn, Edward M. Gramlich, and Richard H. Price. 1991. Long-term follow-up and benefit-cost analysis of the jobs program: A preventive intervention for the unemployed. *Journal of Applied Psychology* 76 (2): 213–19.

Warr, Peter B., Paul Jackson, and Michael Banks. 1988. Unemployment and mental health: Some British studies. *Journal of Social Issues* 44:47–68.

Williams, David R., and Ruth Williams-Morris. 2000. Racism and mental health: The African American experience. *Ethnicity and Mental Health* 5:243–68.

World Health Organization. 1990. *Composite international diagnostic interview (CIDI, Version 1).* Geneva: World Health Organization.

CHAPTER 9

The Psychosocial Nature of Physical Health

James S. House and George A. Kaplan

The improvement of population health is one of the major achievements of the twentieth century. Life expectancy at birth in the United States has grown from almost fifty years in 1900 to seventy-seven years as we enter the new millennium, an increase greater than that in all of prior human history (cf. Coale 1974). The end of the nineteenth and the first half of the twentieth centuries witnessed dramatic developments in biomedical science, associated with the work of Koch, Lister, Pasteur, Fleming, Salk and others, which focused on the conquest of infectious diseases. This work has been epitomized by the virtual eradication of smallpox and poliomyelitis, with the development and widespread delivery of a safe and effective antipolio vaccine in the 1950s and 1960s perhaps the most dramatic single example.

Social Science, Survey Research, and Health

Social science, survey research, and the University of Michigan Survey Research Center (SRC) played significant roles in some of these developments. The SRC, for example, collected and tabulated the data on the 1953–54 field trials of the Salk polio vaccine, under the overall direction of epidemiologist Thomas Francis Jr. of the University of Michigan School of Public Health, leading to the dramatic announcement on April 12, 1955, that the vaccine was safe and effective. These events marked the high-water mark of the advance of the biomedical doctrine of specific etiology, which saw disease as caused by a specific biological agent and saw disease prevention and control as focusing on the identification and then neutralization of that biological agent via treatment, immunization, or eradication.

Beginning in the same period, however, social science, survey research, and the SRC and Institute for Social Research (ISR), in conjunction with prescient biomedical scientists, developed new and broader perspectives on the nature, course, and etiology of disease. Increasingly, psychosocial models, methods, and data have come to complement, and in certain ways and areas even dominate, biomedical models and data. By midcentury in the developed nations of Europe and North America, and increasingly in the more rapidly developing nations of South America, Asia, and Africa, the nature of the diseases that threatened human health was beginning to change. The new epidemics were chronic diseases such as cancer and, especially, cardiovascular diseases (Omran 1971). Their emergence and spread largely arrested from the late 1950s to the early 1970s the dramatic and steady improvements in life expectancy and population health of the first half of the twentieth century.

The Study of Chronic Disease

Compared to the generally acute infectious diseases, diseases such as cancer and cardiovascular diseases were chronic in both their etiology and their course—developing insidiously over a long period of time and then often having a long course of intermittent stages of activity and remission (House 1987). They were also not amenable to understanding or control within the dominant biomedical paradigm of searching for a single disease-specific etiologic agent and a single "magic bullet" that could roll back, prevent, or eradicate that agent. Rather, the causes and precursors of disease were multifactorial, with none either necessary or sufficient to produce disease (or conversely able to prevent or cure disease by its absence or eradication). A new terminology—"risk factors"—emerged to denote these multiple contingent causes or precursors of chronic disease (Aronowitz 1998).

At first the search for risk factors of chronic disease remained heavily biomedical, focusing on physiologic indicators such as blood pressure and cholesterol in the case of cardiovascular diseases or physical-chemical-biological environmental exposures such as asbestos and coal dust in the case of cancer and chronic respiratory disease. The role of such factors in the etiology and course of chronic disease was suggested by laboratory experiments with animals or case-control studies in humans, in which the characteristics and medical and life histories of cases with given diseases were compared retrospectively to those of similar or matched controls without the disease. These case-control studies relied increasingly on the developing methods of survey research and social statistics.

These social science methods became central, however, to the new gold standard for establishing the etiologic importance of a risk factor—the prospective population or cohort study. Appropriate and sizable samples of populations were selected, assessed via interview and examination for health and putative chronic disease risk factors, and then repeatedly interviewed and examined over time to monitor the onset of mortality or morbidity and its subsequent course. The role of these putative risk factors in predicting the onset and course of disease could then be established. In the 1950s and 1960s a major set of continuing national and community surveys was initiated to monitor the prevalence of chronic and infectious diseases and, more important, to determine the role of various risk factors in their etiology and course—for example, the Framingham (MA), Tecumseh (MI), Evans County (GA), Washington County (MD), and Honolulu (HI) studies of cardiovascular disease; the National Health Interview Surveys (NHIS); and the National Health (and Nutrition) Examination Surveys (NHES or NHANES). They provided the evidence that blood pressure, cholesterol, and smoking were major risk factors for cardiovascular disease. None of these studies or findings would have been possible without the parallel developments in the theory, methods, and practice of survey sampling, interviewing, data processing, and statistical analysis in the social sciences (cf. chap. 2, this volume).

From Biomedical to Psychosocial Models and Data

The impact of social science, survey research, and the SRC and ISR on the science and practice of public health and even medicine went much broader and deeper, altering the very nature of the variables, theories, and data used to understand and improve physical health. The confluence in the 1950s and 1960s of strands of biomedical thinking of ancient origins with newly developed theories and methods of social science gave rise to new psychosocial or biopsychosocial paradigms for the study and improvement of the physical health of individuals and populations (see chap. 8, this volume, for similar developments in the area of mental health).

The germ theory model of specific etiology, which dominated thinking about health in much of the late nineteenth and early twentieth centuries, had its root in ancient times in the Greek goddess Panakeia, one of the two daughters of Asclepius, the Greek god of health. Panakeia was the healing goddess, whose knowledge of natural remedies carries over today in the search for magic bullets or panacea. A parallel framework derives from Panakeia's sister, Hygiea, who saw health as the natural order of things, maintained by living with reason and moderation and proper adaptation to the environment (Renaud 1993). Thus, hygiene or promotion of broadly healthful lifestyles and environment, rather than preventive or therapeutic measures against highly specific agents or diseases, was the avenue to promoting health and preventing disease. These ideas inspired public health efforts in ancient times and again over the past few centuries to promote such measures as clean water supplies, public sanitation, and general reduction of environmental pollutants, programs that were reinforced but not originated by the germ theory of disease. In the 1950s, Dubos (1959) and others argued for renewed emphasis on this view of health as a product of more general organism-environment adaptation, complementary to the late-nineteenth- and early-twentieth-century approaches targeted at very specific etiologic agents.

This more environmental approach to health was given psychosocial form by several specific twentieth-century developments. One was a new body of evidence on the "limits of modern medicine." The work of Thomas McKeown (1976, 1988) and others (McKinlay and McKinlay 1977; Fogel 1994) showed that most of the advance in overall population health and life expectancy of the nineteenth and twentieth centuries occurred prior to the development of the germ theory of disease, much less its widespread application via preventive vaccination or pharmacologic treatment. Even those admiring of the achievements of modern medicine estimate that only about five years of the almost thirty-year increase in life expectancy in the United States in the twentieth century were due to modern preventive or therapeutic medical practice (Bunker, Frazier, and Mosteller 1994), with many more years attributable to a combination of public health and sanitation (increasingly informed by modern medical science but also antedating it) and especially broad patterns of socioeconomic development with associated improvements in nutrition, clothing, housing, and household sanitation (Preston 1977; Wilkinson 1996).

A second major development was the recognition of the impact of individual behavior or lifestyle, most notably the impact of cigarette smoking. The surgeon general's (DHEW 1964) report *Smoking and Health* drew on a broad range of evidence, including that from community epidemiological surveys, to identify smoking as a clear risk factor for all causes of mortality and especially lung cancer and cardiovascular disease. At the same time, Lester Breslow fielded a major continuing probability survey of the adult population of Alameda County, California (Oakland and environs), to understand the role of a broad range of health behaviors or lifestyles in promoting health and preventing disease. Lisa Berkman and Breslow (1983) summarized the results of this and other work, showing that not only smoking but also low levels of physical activity and immoderate levels of body mass and alcohol consumption were all significant and substantial risk factors for mortality (cf. Kaplan 1992). Thus again via the tools of survey research, health behaviors or lifestyles became major risk factors for health and targets for health promotion and disease prevention (DHHS 1990).

Finally, converging evidence from both laboratory psychophysiology and sample survey epidemiology was suggesting that other psychosocial characteristics of individuals and their environments, and the relation between these, were also risk factors for disease. Physiologists Walter Cannon (1932) and Hans Selye (1956) documented a syndrome of physiological responses (including adrenocortical secretions and related neuroendocrine activation, gastric secretions, and elevated heart rate and blood pressure, labeled by Selye as the "general adaptation syndrome," or GAS) to a wide range of environmental stressors and challenges, including infectious agents, heat, cold, physical pressure and restraint, and social psychological threat. Cannon and Selye saw this syndrome as an evolved adaptive response to physical stressors requiring "fight or flight," but one that became maladaptive in the face of modern stressors, many of which are psychosocial in nature and often chronic and inescapable. Thus, in the face of these modern stressors, the GAS may become a prolonged rather than transitory mode of response, giving rise to what Selye termed "diseases of adaptation," such as hypertension, heart disease, ulcers, and arthritis. Thus, there was a plausible basis by which purely social or psychological conditions or stimuli with no obvious connection to health can give rise to physical disease and even death. This physiological explanation for the impact of psychosocial factors on physical health has been deepened and extended into the emerging field of psychoneuroimmunology (Ader, Felten, and Cohen 1991).

This confluence of theoretical and empirical developments, in which survey research and social science had already played a significant role, gave rise to a number of centers of research on the role of psychosocial factors in the etiology and course of physical as well as mental health and illness. Perhaps most notable among these centers in the country were the San Francisco Bay area (including often collaborating researchers at the University of California campuses at Berkeley and San Francisco, Stanford University, the Alameda County Study [aka the Human Population Laboratory of the California Department of Public Health], Stanford Research Institute, and others); the Boston Cambridge area (especially at Harvard); Duke University and the University of North Carolina School of Public Health in the Research Triangle area of North Carolina; Columbia University; the University of Pittsburgh and Carnegie Mellon University; and since 1958 the SRC and ISR at the University of Michigan, in collaboration with researchers in the University of Michigan School of Public Health. Stockholm, Sweden, also became a major center, including the University of Stockholm, Karolinska Institute, and later the National Institute for Psychosocial Factors in Health, which had significant ties to the SRC/ISR group. The work at SRC and ISR played a leading role in, and well exemplifies, the ideas and accomplishments that have made health research and policy increasingly psychosocial in nature over the last several decades.

The Survey Research Center/Institute for Social Research Social Environment and Health Program

As indicated by Robert Kahn in the introduction to part 3 and in chapter 7, the SRC's Organizational Behavior Program began to shift in the late 1950s toward a focus on the impact of the organizational environment on individual satisfaction and well-being. Two researchers from that program, Kahn and Floyd Mann, joined with John R. P. French Jr., a founding member of ISR's then only other center, the Research Center for Group Dynamics, to found a new intercenter program, the Mental Health in Industry Program. With research support from the National Institute of Mental Health and consistent with the SRC and ISR emphasis on programmatic research, French, Kahn, and Mann embarked on a range of research projects on the impact of organizational environments on individual mental health and well-being, collaborating with each other and other colleagues and students. But first they also developed a programmatic statement and theoretical framework that guided and integrated the various research activities (French, Kahn, and Mann 1962).

The Institute for Social Research Model and the Study of Occupational Stress

Perhaps the most enduring legacy of this early period of research was French, Kahn, and Mann's overarching theoretical framework, often just known as the "ISR model" for research on psychosocial factors in health. The work of Cannon, Selye, and others provided a theoretical model for understanding how psychosocial factors and stresses could "get under the skin" to cause physical as well as mental illness. Their work did not, however, explain how the subjective experience of stress, which affects both mind and body, is itself generated. The ISR model (see fig. 7.1) did just this, constituting the first specification of a general theoretical framework that has been utilized in other forms and refinements by themselves (French, Rogers, and Cobb 1974) and by many others (e.g., Lazarus and Folkman 1984; McGrath 1970) under rubrics such as stress and adaptation, stress and coping, or stress-diathesis models. The model in figure 7.1, reflecting its origins in organizational research, did not yet make health the central outcome. However, health became central in later variants of the paradigm, one of which (from House 1981) is shown in figure 9.1.

The key feature of the ISR model and its successors or imitators is that objective social circumstances or potential stressors give rise to variable perceptions of the stressfulness or other characteristics of the situation, depending on characteristics of the environment or the individual that are referred to as conditioning, moderating, buffering, or vulnerability factors. Perceptions of stress or threat then give rise to physiological, psychological, and social responses either that help to reduce the objective stressor or perceived stress and hence protect health or that lead to adverse mental or physical health outcomes via the pathways illuminated by Cannon, Selye, and subsequent psychophysiological research.

The ISR researchers immediately utilized this framework in their research, for example, in Kahn and his colleagues' (1964) seminal volume, *Organizational Stress.* Using a combination of survey studies of both national populations and more focused organizational samples, this work showed that objective role conflict (the conflicting demands of the others who interact with the occupant of an organizational role) is predictive of perceived role conflict, and both of these are associated with greater feelings of tension or stress and decreased psychological well-being. These relationships were moderated, however, by both individual dispositions (e.g., flexibility versus rigidity) and the quality of social relationships with supervisors and coworkers—personal flexibility and/or supportive

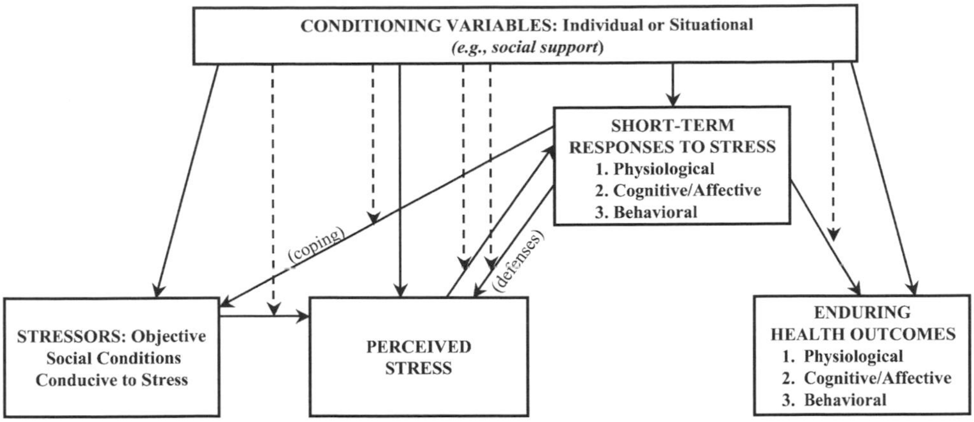

FIG. 9.1. A paradigm of stress research. Solid arrows between boxes indicate presumed casual relationships among variables. Dotted arrows from the box labeled "conditioning variables" intersect solid arrows, indicating an interaction between the conditioning variables in the box at the beginning of the solid arrow in predicting variables in the box at the tip of the solid arrow. (Redrawn from House 1981, 36.)

supervisors and coworkers reducing the amount of perceived role conflict in the presence of a given level of objective conflict or reducing experienced tension and psychological distress in the face of given levels of objective or perceived role conflict. French and his colleagues (Kasl and French 1962; French, Tupper, and Mueller 1965; Caplan et al. 1975) did similar work showing the adverse mental and physical (e.g., blood pressure) health consequences of low occupational status and quantitative and qualitative work overload. For example, the greater workload and responsibility of administrators (versus professors or scientists) in university and federal science and technology organizations was associated with higher levels of blood pressure and cholesterol on average. Again, the effects were moderated or buffered by individual and social factors, including supportive supervision. Mann's interests turned increasingly toward interventions to improve the well-being and health of organizations' members, and he became the founding director in 1964 of the first new ISR center, the Center for Research on the Utilization of Scientific Knowledge (discussed in chap. 7, this volume).

As the Mental Health and Industry Program broadened its staff and its research interests beyond the study of both organizations and mental health, its name changed to the Social Environment and Health Program.

The most important impetus for these changes was the recruitment to SRC and ISR in 1962 of Sidney Cobb, a physician-epidemiologist whose research interests had been moving increasingly in psychosocial directions. Cobb brought with him a biochemist, George Brooks, and a biochemical laboratory was established in the ISR building. The range of outcomes studied broadened beyond mental health to include chronic diseases (e.g., arthritis and cardiovascular diseases) and their biomedical precursors or risk factors (e.g., blood pressure, cholesterol, and serum uric acid). The range of social environments and experiences studied also expanded beyond work organizations to include unemployment, status inconsistency and role conflicts in the family, and relations between work and family.

Cobb converted one of French's social psychology students, Stanislav Kasl, into a social epidemiologist who later helped to develop an important center of social epidemiologic research at Yale. Together with French and Kahn they showed that unemployment due to plant closings had a broad range of deleterious effects on the physical and mental health of workers, including depression, reduced self-esteem, anxiety, resentment, reported insomnia and physical health problems, and elevations in physiological indicators such as blood pressure, cholesterol, and pulse rate. It is interesting to note that the health changes become quite pronounced during the period of anticipation between the announcement of the plant closing and the actual termination, with post-termination effects dependent on the length and severity of the unemployment experience (Cobb and Kasl 1977). Cobb also led a major study of the health impacts of job stress in air traffic controllers (Cobb and Rose 1973); and French, Cobb, and Robert Caplan embarked on a continuing study of role overload and stress among scientists and administrators of the National Aeronautics and Space Administration and later samples of multiple organizations (Caplan et al. 1975). Kahn (1981) summarized the cumulative evidence from this program of research and related work by others, showing that work stress and unemployment were consequential risk factors for physical and mental health.

From Work Stress to Social Support

These and later ISR studies (e.g., House et al. 1979; House 1981; House et al. 1986; House and Cottington 1986) were major contributors to establishing occupational stress as a risk factor for morbidity and mortality from cardiovascular disease and other causes. Although research in the SEH programs and more broadly in SRC and ISR gradually moved away from the initially central focus on work and organizations, these issues remained important in some portions of SEH (cf. chap. 8 by Price) and elsewhere. For example, Karasek and Theorell (1990) and colleagues in the United States and Europe, drawing in part on ISR research, developed new theory and empirical evidence that health outcomes were a joint function of job stress, or demands in their framework, and decision latitude, or control on the job. They and ISR researchers were equally interested in other individual and social factors that could potentially buffer or compensate for the deleterious impact of stress on health. This interest led the ISR researchers to become leaders in theoretically conceptualizing and empirically measuring social relationships and supports and documenting their important beneficial effects on health. Drawing on his work with Caplan, French, Kahn, Kasl, and others, Cobb (1976) authored one of the two foundation papers (the other was Cassel 1976) that pointed to social relationships and support as a major determinant of health and the way stress affects health.

Social relationships and supports became a central research agenda for the SEH Program and other major centers of research on the psychosocial nature of health about the time, in 1978, that House rejoined the program in which he had received graduate training in the 1960s, after spending eight years on the faculty at Duke University and collaborating with John Cassel and other researchers in the Department of Epidemiology at the University of North Carolina. Initial work by Caplan, French, House, and their colleagues showed the important role of social support from supervisors, coworkers, and spouses in promoting mental and physical health and buffering the adverse effects of occupational stress (Caplan et al. 1975; LaRocco, House, and French 1980; House 1981). Following the lead of Berkman and Syme (1979), House and his colleagues broadened the focus to the impact of social relationships on health in general populations, first showing that social relationships were protective against all-cause mortality in the Tecumseh Community Health Study (House, Robbins, and Metzner 1981), even with substantial controls for baseline demographic and biomedical indicators of health or its risk factors, and then showing that these results were part of a broad convergence of prospective epidemiologic research, arrayed in figure 9.2, that showed lack of social relationships to create a risk for all-cause mortality comparable to that of cigarette smoking (House, Landis, and Umberson 1988).

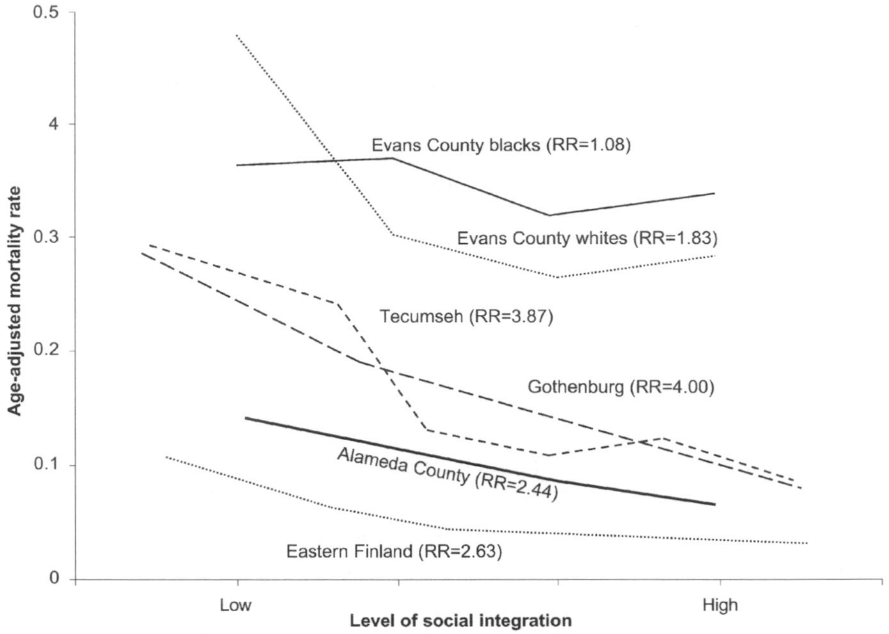

FIG. 9.2. Level of social integration and age-adjusted mortality for males in five prospective studies. RR is the relative risk ratio of mortality at the lowest versus highest level of social integration. (Redrawn from figure 1 of House, Landis, and Umberson 1988.)

A New Focus on Aging

The aging of the population of the United States and the world has posed new issues and problems for science and society. Social science at SRC and ISR, and more generally, has responded to these societal changes with an increased focus on aging. Stimulated by early work at the Duke University Center on Aging and Human Development (Busse and Maddox 1985) and elsewhere, and supported in considerable degree by the establishment of the National Institute on Aging and its strong program of social and behavioral research, this new focus involved growth not only in the fields of gerontology and geriatrics but also in the methods and paradigms of the full range of social sciences being applied to and shaped by the phenomenon of an aging society. Examples of this were evident across most of the major research programs and centers of SRC and ISR (cf. chaps. 4, 10, 11, 12, and 14) and very much within the SEH Program. Kahn and Toni Antonucci initiated a national longitudinal study of the nature, determinants, and health consequences of what they termed "convoys" of social support across middle and later life (Kahn and Antonucci 1981). House, Kahn, and Ronald Kessler joined with Regula Herzog of the SRC Social Indicators Program and James Jackson and Camille Wortman of the RCGD in a major program project proposal centered around two major longitudinal studies: (1) Americans' Changing Lives (ACL), on the role of psychosocial factors in the maintenance of health and effective functioning over the life course in a national sample of 3,617 adults age twenty-five or older, first interviewed in 1986 and reinterviewed in 1989 and 1994; and (2) Changing Lives of Older Couples (CLOC), on the prospective impact of widowhood in a sample of 1,532 members of married couples with husbands age sixty-five or older in the Detroit metropolitan area who were first interviewed in 1987–88, with individuals whose spouses subsequently died reinterviewed (through 1993) at six to nine months, eighteen to twenty-four months, and about forty-eight months after the death of their spouse. Analyses and mortality follow-up of these studies continue, and a fourth wave of interviews of the ACL sample occurred in 2001–2002.

These studies have documented the continuing and growing importance of social relationships and supports in older age (Kahn and Antonucci 1981); the extent, nature, and beneficial health consequences of both paid and unpaid productive activity over the life course (Herzog et al. 1989; Herzog, House, and Morgan 1991; Musick, Herzog, and House 1999); the deleterious health effects of widowhood but also variation in these effects by gender and by the pre- and postbereavement marital and psychosocial characteristics and experiences of the deceased and surviving bereaved spouses (e.g., Umberson, Wortman, and Kessler 1992; Carr et al. 2000); and the considerable role of psychosocial factors, especially socioeconomic status (which seems to influence and shape almost all behavioral and psychosocial risk factors), in the maintenance of health and effective functioning in middle and latter life (House et al. 1990, 1994; House and Williams 1996; Lantz et al. 1998). For example, the data in figure 9.3 shows how the experience of functional limitations varied by age and education in the ACL sample in 1986 (with lower educated persons showing levels of functional limitation in their thirties, forties, and early fifties that are only observed among higher educated persons who are twenty to thirty years older, with the higher educated manifesting almost no limitations prior to age fifty-five). As shown in figure 9.4, those differences were largely eliminated when persons with different levels of education were statistically equated in terms of income and eleven other indi-

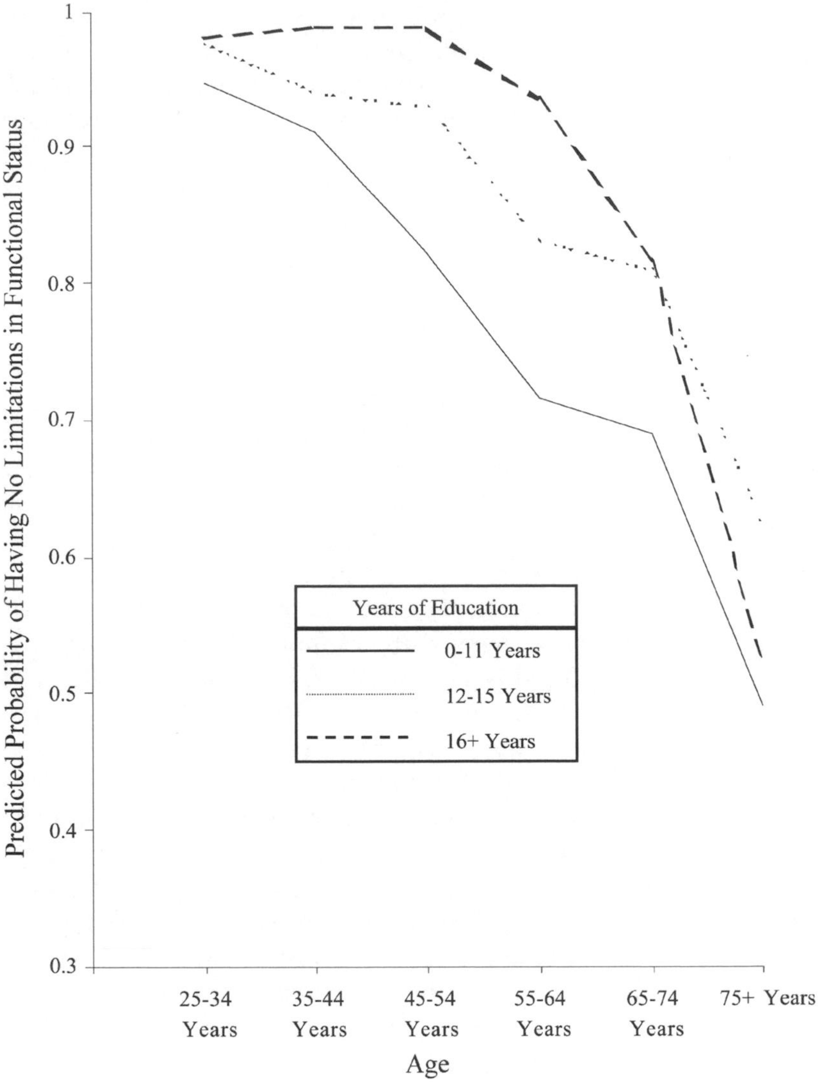

FIG. 9.3. Age by predicted probability of having no limitations in functional status within levels of education, controlling for sex and race. (Redrawn from House et al. 1994, 223.)

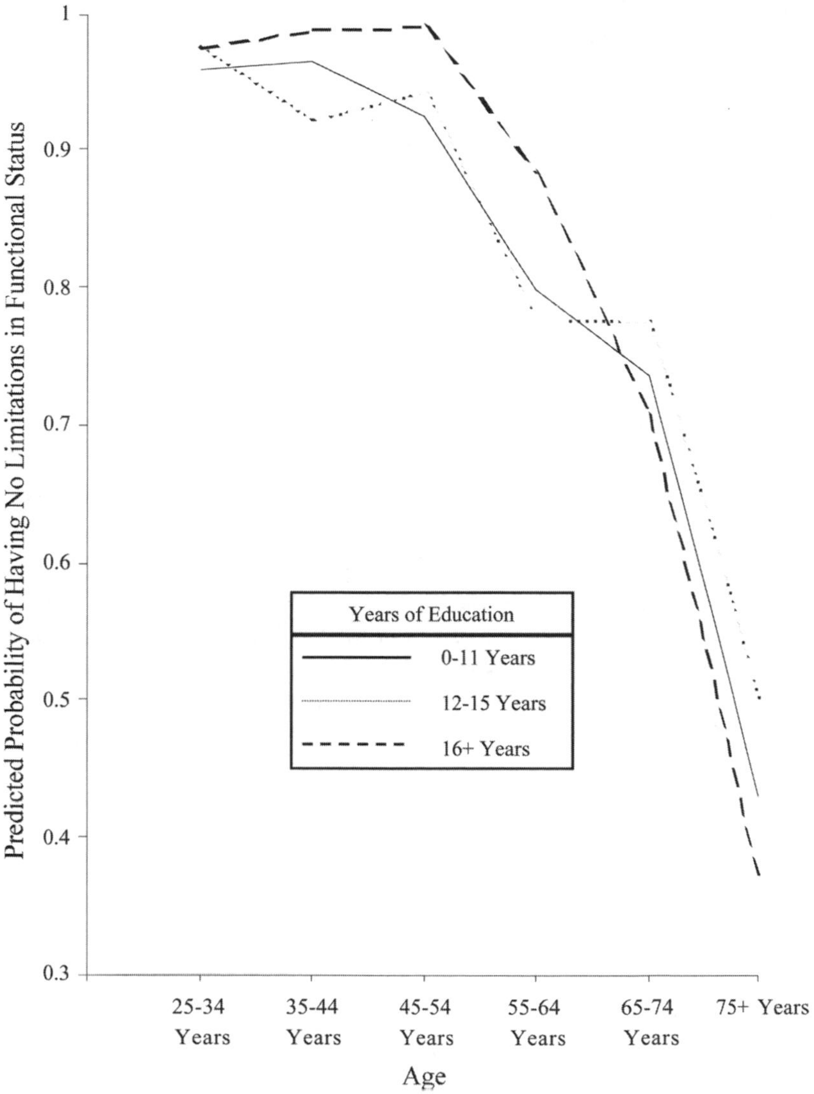

FIG. 9.4. Age by predicted probability of having no limitations in functional status within levels of education, controlling for sex, race, income, the interaction of age times income, and exposure to psychosocial risk factors. (Redrawn from House et al. 1994, 223.)

cators of health behaviors (i.e., smoking, drinking, and weight), acute and chronic stress, social relationships and supports, and psychological dispositions (i.e., self-efficacy).

A Broader Social Focus

In the 1980s and 1990s, the SEH Program continued to evolve toward a broader social focus, as Caplan, Cobb, French, Kahn, and Kasl—who all except Cobb were trained as psychologists—retired or moved elsewhere and were succeeded by sociologists (James House, Ronald Kessler, and David Williams), social epidemiologists (Sherman James, George Kaplan, and John Lynch), and a community psychologist (Richard Price). The program participated and played a lead role in moving toward a new frontier in the study of psychosocial factors in health—understanding and alleviating the large, persistent, and even increasing socioeconomic and racial/ethnic disparities in health in our and other societies. Stimulated by the seminal findings in the United Kingdom that socioeconomic differences in health had persisted and even grown in the several decades following the establishment of the National Health Service (Townsend and Davidson 1982; Marmot, Kogevinas, and Elston 1987), the work of the SEH researchers contributed to the recognition of these disparities as a major public health problem in the United States (Haan, Kaplan, and Camacho 1987; Haan, Kaplan, and Syme 1989; House et al. 1990, 1994; Kessler 1979; James et al. 1987; James 1993; Williams 1990; Williams and Collins 1995). Their reduction has become a major priority of the Public Health Service and National Institutes of Health for national health research and policy (DHHS 2000; Varmus 1999).

The results of the ACL study depicted in figures 9.3 and 9.4 and similar results in other studies (Lynch et al. 1996) focused interest on the role of socioeconomic status as a kind of master status or fundamental cause (House et al. 1990; Link and Phelan 1995) that shapes individuals' experience of and exposure to most all behavioral and psychosocial risk factors in health and hence their ability to maintain health and effective functioning over the life course. Kaplan brought to Michigan in 1997 an even longer history of similar research and findings in the Alameda County Study (e.g., Haan, Kaplan, and Camacho 1987; Haan, Kaplan, and Syme 1989) and a Finnish cohort (Lynch et al. 1996) and a new focus on the role of income inequality in the health of the populations of those areas

(Kaplan et al. 1996; Lynch et al. 2000). Socioeconomic deprivation and unemployment (especially its attendant financial strain) were also major foci of work on mental health by Kessler, House, Price, and Amiram Vinokur (see chap. 8).

James and Williams brought with them in the early 1990s ongoing programs of research on the way race and ethnicity and socioeconomic status combine to influence health. James's work has shown the deleterious health impact of an orientation of striving to achieve in the face of adversity (labeled "John Henryism") among African-Americans, whose combination of racial/ethnic and socioeconomic status poses great obstacles to achievement (James et al. 1987; James 1994). Williams's work showed that, although socioeconomic factors can account for a considerable degree of racial/ethnic disparities in health, the experience of discrimination is one of a number of factors that explain why racial/ethnic disparities in health persist even among persons of equivalent socioeconomic positions (House and Williams 2000; Williams 1997; Williams et al. 1997).

Looking Downstream and Upstream

The research of the members of the SEH Program occupies a unique niche in the burgeoning fields of medical sociology, health psychology, social epidemiology, and behavioral medicine. The research is anchored in survey studies of general national and community populations in the United States and other countries (e.g., Finland and South Africa), increasingly of a longitudinal nature. These surveys provide a continuing record of psychosocial characteristics and experiences of these populations and their reported health status, and they serve in and of themselves as the basis of important analyses of a variety of psychosocial factors in health. However, the SEH researchers seek to link these survey data, on the one hand, to "downstream" biomedical assessments of mortality, morbidity, and psychophysiological risk factors and pathways and, on the other hand, to independently generated "upstream" assessments of the social environments and contexts in which individuals live, work, and play (Kaplan and Lynch 1997, 1999). These emphases resulted in the SEH Program and University of Michigan School of Public Health's being awarded in 1999 one of five NIH-initiated Centers for Mind-Body Research, with the Michigan center focused on understanding socioeconomic and racial/ethnic disparities in health.

The Psychosocial Nature of Physical Health: Looking Backward and Forward

Over the past forty years, survey research and related social science methods and theories have transformed our understanding of the nature and future of individual and population health, with the SEH Program at SRC being a central player and exemplar of this transformation. When the SEH Program began in 1958, the idea that behavioral, psychological, and social factors played a major role in health was regarded skeptically, if at all, by most biomedical and health researchers and practitioners and the general public. Today we know that poor health behaviors, chronic and acute stress, lack of social relationships and supports, and a variety of psychological dispositions (e.g., anger/hostility, lack of self-efficacy, hopelessness, and depression) are major risk factors for morbidity and mortality from most chronic diseases and all causes. We also understand that socioeconomic and racial/ethnic disparities are major public health problems in the United States, which is arguably the reason that the United States lags increasingly behind many developed countries in levels of population health (e.g., life expectancy and infant mortality), despite spending more, absolutely and relatively, on health care and health research than any nation in the world.

Conceptual bases of this new understanding of the psychosocial nature of physical health have derived from long-term interdisciplinary research programs such as the SEH Program, while the empirical foundation is a growing body of longitudinal probability sample survey studies, combining assessment of psychosocial and medical variables in major community and national populations—the so-called prospective epidemiologic study. Thus, the methods of survey research have helped to generate both the data and the theory underlying a new psychosocial conception of the nature and determinants of individual and population health, which must be numbered as one of the significant contributions of social science in the latter half of the twentieth century. The recent revolution in genomics is providing new insights into biological disease processes, but the impact of genomics on the major sources of morbidity and mortality such as heart disease and cancer will be generally to add factors to a multicausal process in which psychosocial variables play an increasingly large role.

There remains a great deal to learn about what psychosocial factors are most consequential for physical as well as mental health and how and why this is the case. Achieving such understanding requires increasing linkage of survey data both to measures of the broader social and physical-chemical-biological environments in which people live, work, and play and to the physiologic and genetic factors that combine with psychosocial factors in producing health outcomes (House 2002). A particularly promising area of investigation lies in the understanding of the sociophysical environments in which people live, work, and learn. As we begin to understand the critical nature of the effects of such environments on risk factors and health outcomes (Kaplan 1996; Sampson, Raudenbush, and Earls 1997; Robert 1998, 1999), the need for the development of techniques that describe such environments, the interactions that occur in them, and the demands and resources that they represent increases. This presents an important opportunity to build intellectual and methodological bridges between similar efforts in urban sociology (Wilson 1987; Sampson and Wilson 1995), child development (Brooks-Gunn, Duncan, and Aber 1997), ethnography (Center for the Ethnography of Everyday Life at SRC/ISR, directed by anthropologist Thomas Fricke; Newman 1999), and medical sociology (Macintyre, Maciver, and Sooman 1993). Survey research will remain central to the population-based research necessary to answer these questions. The Michigan Center for Mind-Body Research has launched a major survey study of the health of adult residents of Chicago in relation to their psychosocial life situations and the social and physical environments in which they live and work.

We also should begin to think more deeply about, and even act on, the policy implications of existing research theories and findings. We need research that evaluates (and even initiates) planned or unplanned social changes or interventions that affect psychosocial risk factors for health—ranging from income and racial/ethnic discrimination to stress and the social and psychological factors that may be protective of health. The work of Price, Vinokur, and colleagues of the Michigan Prevention Research Center in SRC (described in chap. 8) represents one such effort.

In sum, survey-based social science research and the SRC and ISR have played a major role in transforming our understanding of the nature of individual and population health in the United States and in the world in the twentieth century, just as they have transformed our understanding of economics, the life course of individuals and families, politics, and race and ethnicity. In the area of health, the capacity to carry out long-term studies of probability samples of broad general populations has been a sine qua non for generating in a period of forty to fifty years the empirical evidence and theoretical understanding of psychosocial variables as major determinants or risk factors for physical as well as mental health.

The task for the next century is not only to continue to refine our knowledge and understanding of how and why psychosocial factors are so consequential for health but also to begin to understand how this knowledge can be used more effectively to promote and improve individual and population health. Interdisciplinary survey-based research will remain central to that process.

REFERENCES

Ader, Robert, David L. Felten, and Nicholas Cohen, eds. 1991. *Psychoneuroimmunology.* 2d ed. San Diego: Academic Press.

Aronowitz, Robert A. 1998. *Making sense of illness: Science, society, and disease.* New York: Cambridge University Press.

Berkman, Lisa F., and Lester Breslow. 1983. *Health and ways of living: The Alameda County study.* London: Oxford University Press.

Berkman, Lisa F., and S. Leonard Syme. 1979. Social networks, host resistance, and mortality: A nine year follow up of Alameda County residents. *American Journal of Epidemiology* 109:1003–9.

Brooks-Gunn, Jeanne, Greg J. Duncan, and J. Lawrence Aber. 1997. *Neighborhood poverty: Context and consequences for children.* New York: Russell Sage.

Bunker, John P., Howard S. Frazier, and Frederick Mosteller. 1994. Improving health: Measuring effects of medical care. *Milbank Quarterly* 72 (2): 225–58.

Busse, Ewald W., and George L. Maddox. 1985. *The Duke longitudinal studies of normal aging.* New York: Springer.

Cannon, Walter B. 1932. *The wisdom of the body.* New York: W. W. Norton.

Caplan, Robert D., Sidney Cobb, John R. P. French Jr., R. Van Harrison, and S. Richard Pinneau. 1975. *Job demands and worker health.* HEW (NIOSH) Publication No. 75–160. Washington, DC: U.S. Department of Health, Education, and Welfare.

Carr, Deborah, James S. House, Ronald C. Kessler, Randolph Nesse, John Sonnega, Camille Wortman. 2000. Marital quality and psychological adjustment to widowhood among older adults: A longitudinal analysis. *Journal of Gerontology: Social Sciences* 55B (4): S197–S207.

Cassel, John C. 1976. The contribution of the social environment to host resistance. *American Journal of Epidemiology* (104): 107–123.

Coale, Ansley J. 1974. History of human population. *Scientific American* 3 (231): 40–51.

Cobb, Sidney. 1976. Social support as a moderator of life stress. *Psychosomatic Medicine* 5 (38): 300–314.

Cobb, Sidney, and Stanislav V. Kasl. 1977. *Termination: The consequences of job loss.* Washington, DC: U.S. Department of Health, Education, and Welfare.

Cobb, Sidney, and Robert M. Rose. 1973. Hypertension, peptic-ulcer, and diabetes in air-traffic controllers. *Journal of the American Medical Association* 4 (224): 489–92.

DHEW. 1964. *Smoking and health.* U.S. Surgeon General's Advisory Committee on Smoking and Health. Washington, DC: U.S. Public Health Service.

DHHS. 1990. *Healthy people 2000: National health promotion and disease prevention objec-*

tives. Washington, DC: U.S. Department of Health and Human Services. <www.cdc.gov/nchs/about/otheract/hp2000/hp2000htm>

———. 2000. *Healthy people 2010.* Understanding and improving health, 2d ed. Washington, DC: U.S. Government Printing Office. <http://www.healthypeople.gov/Document/pdf/uih/2010vih.pdf>

Dubos, René J. 1959. *Mirage of health: Utopias, progress, and biological change.* New York: Harper.

Fogel, Robert W. 1994. Economic growth, population theory, and physiology: The bearing of long-term processes on economic policy. *American Economic Review* June:369–95.

French, John R. P., Jr., Robert L. Kahn, and F. C. Mann. 1962. A programmatic approach to studying the industrial environment and mental health. *Journal of Social Issues* 3 (18): 1–47.

French, John R. P., Jr., Willard Rogers, and Sidney Cobb. 1974. Adjustments as a person-environment fit. In *Coping and adaptation: Interdisciplinary approaches,* ed. G. V. Coethro, D. A. Hamburg, and J. F. Adams. New York: Basic Books.

French, John R. P., Jr., C. J. Tupper, and Ernst Mueller. 1965. Workload of university professors. Cooperative Research Project No. 2171, U.S. Office of Education. Ann Arbor: University of Michigan.

Haan, Mary, George A. Kaplan, and T. Camacho. 1987. Poverty and health: Prospective evidence from the Alameda County study. *American Journal of Epidemiology* 125:989–98.

Haan, Mary N., George A. Kaplan, and S. Leonard Syme. 1989. Socioeconomic status and health: Old observations and new thoughts. In *Pathways to health: The role of social factors,* ed. John P. Bunker, Deanna S. Gomby, and Barbara H. Kehrer, 76–135. Menlo Park, CA: H. J. Kaiser Family Foundation.

Herzog, A. Regula, James S. House, and James N. Morgan. 1991. The relation of work and retirement to health and well-being in older age. *Psychology and Aging* 2 (6): 202–11.

Herzog, A. Regula, Robert L. Kahn, James N. Morgan, J. S. Jackson, and Toni C. Antonucci. 1989. Age differences in productive activities. *Journal of Gerontology* 4 (44): S129–S138.

House, James S. 1981. *Work stress and social support.* Reading, MA: Addison-Wesley.

———. 1987. Chronic stress and chronic disease in life and work: Conceptual and methodological issues. *Work and Stress* 1 (2): 129–34.

———. 2002. Understanding social factors and inequalities in health: Twentieth-century progress and twenty-first-century prospects. *Journal of Health and Social Behavior* (43):125–42.

House, James S., and Eric M. Cottington. 1986. Health and the workplace. In *Application of Social Science to Clinical Medicine and Health Policy,* ed. L. Aiken and D. Mechanic, 392–416. New Brunswick, NJ: Rutgers University Press.

House, James S., Ronald C. Kessler, A. Regula Herzog, Richard P. Mero, Ann M. Kinney, and Martha J. Breslow. 1990. Age, socioeconomic status, and health. *Milbank Quarterly* 68 (3): 383–411.

House, James S., Karl Landis, and Debra Umberson. 1988. Social relationships and health. *Science* 241:540–45.

House, James S., James M. Lepkowski, Ann M. Kinney, Richard P. Mero, Ronald C.

Kessler, and A. Regula Herzog. 1994. The social stratification of aging and health. *Journal of Health and Social Behavior* 35:213–34.

House, James S., Anthony J. McMichael, James A. Wells, Berton H. Kaplan, and Lawrence R. Landerman. 1979. Occupational stress and health among factory workers. *Journal of Health and Social Behavior* 20 (June): 139–60.

House, James S., Cynthia Robbins, and Helen M. Metzner. 1981. The association of social relationships and activities with mortality: Prospective evidence from the Tecumseh Community Health Study. *American Journal of Epidemiology* 116 (1): 123–40.

House, James S., Victor Strecher, Helen L. Metzner, and Cynthia Robbins. 1986. Occupational stress and health among men and women in the Tecumseh Community Health Study. *Journal of Health and Social Behavior* 1 (27): 62–77.

House, James S., and David R. Williams. 1996. Psychosocial pathways linking SES and CVD. *Report of the Conference on Socioeconomic Status and Cardiovascular Health and Disease,* 119–24. Washington, DC: National Institutes of Health; National Heart, Lung, and Blood Institute.

———. 2000. Understanding and reducing socioeconomic and racial/ethnic disparities in health. In *Promoting health: Intervention strategies from social and behavioral research,* ed. Brian D. Smedley and S. Leonard Syme, 81–124. Washington, DC: National Academy Press.

James, Sherman A. 1993. Racial and ethnic differences in infant mortality and low birth weight: A psychosocial critique. *Annals of Epidemiology* 3:131–36.

———. 1994. John Henryism and the health of African Americans. *Culture of Medicine and Psychiatry* 18:163–82.

James, Sherman A., D. S. Strogatz, S. B. Wing, and D. L. Ramsey. 1987. Socioeconomic status, John Henryism, and hypertension in blacks and whites. *American Journal of Epidemiology* 126:664–73.

Kahn, Robert L. 1981. *Work and health.* New York: Wiley.

Kahn, Robert L., and Toni C. Antonucci. 1981. Convoys of social support: A life course approach. In *Aging: Social change,* ed. S. B. Kiesler, J. N. Morgan, and V. K. Oppenheimer. New York: Academic Press.

Kahn, Robert L., Donald M. Wolfe, Robert P. Quinn, J. Diedrick Snoek, and Robert A. Rosenthal. 1964. *Organizational stress: Studies in role conflict and ambiguity.* New York: Wiley.

Kaplan, George A. 1992. Health and aging in the Alameda County study. In *Aging, health behaviors, and health outcomes,* ed. K. W. Schaie, D. Blazer, and J. S. House, 62–88. New Jersey: Lawrence Erlbaum.

———. 1996. People and places: Contrasting perspectives on the association between social class and health. *International Journal of Health Services* 26:507–19.

Kaplan, George A., and John W. Lynch. 1997. Whither studies on the socioeconomic foundations of population health. *American Journal of Public Health* 87:1409–11.

———. 1999. Socioeconomic considerations in the primordial prevention of cardiovascular disease. *Preventive Medicine* 6 (29): S30–S35, pt. 2.

Kaplan, George A., Elsie R. Pamuk, John W. Lynch, Richard D. Cohen, and Jennifer L. Balfour. 1996. Inequality in income and mortality in the United States: Analysis of mortality and potential pathways. *British Medical Journal* 312:999–1003.

Karasek, Robert A., and Tores Theorell. 1990. *Healthy work: Stress, productivity, and the reconstruction of working life.* New York: Wiley.

Kasl, Stanislav V., and John R. P. French Jr. 1962. The effects of occupational status on physical and mental health. *Journal of Social Issues* 18 (3): 67–90.

Kessler, Ronald C. 1979. Stress, social status, and psychological distress. *Journal of Health and Social Behavior* 20 (September): 259–72

Lantz, Paula M., James S. House, James M. Lepkowski, David R. Williams, Richard P. Mero, and Jieming Chen. 1998. Socioeconomic factors, health behaviors, and mortality: Results from a nationally representative prospective study of U.S. adults. *Journal of the American Medical Association* 279 (21): 1703–8.

LaRocco, James M., James S. House, and John R. P. French Jr. 1980. Social support, occupational stress, and health. *Journal of Health and Social Behavior* 21:202–18.

Lazarus, Richard S., and Susan Folkman. 1984. *Stress, appraisal, and coping*, New York: Springer.

Link, Bruce G., and Jo C. Phelan. 1995. Social conditions as fundamental causes of disease. *Journal of Health Social Behavior* (extra issue):80–94.

Lynch, John W., George Davey-Smith, George A. Kaplan, and James S. House. 2000. Income inequality and health: A neo-material interpretation. *British Medical Journal* 320:1200–1204.

Lynch, John W., George A. Kaplan, R. D. Cohen, J. Tuomilehto, and J. T. Salonen. 1996. Do cardiovascular risk factors explain the relation between socioeconomic status, risk of all-cause mortality, cardiovascular mortality and acute myocardial infarction? *American Journal of Epidemiology* 144:934–42.

Macintyre, Sally, Sheila Maciver, and Ann Sooman. 1993. Area, class, and health: Should we be focusing on places or people? *Journal of Social Policy* 22:213–34.

Marmot, Michael, M. Kogevinas, and M. A. Elston. 1987. Social/economic status and disease. *Annual Review of Public Health* 8:111–35.

McGrath, Joseph E., ed. 1970. *Social and psychological factors in stress.* New York: Holt, Rinehart, and Winston.

McKeown, Thomas J. 1976. *The role of medicine: Dream, mirage, or nemesis?* London: Nuffield Provincial Hospitals Trust.

———. 1988. *The origins of human disease.* London: Blackwell.

McKinlay, John B., and Sonya J. McKinlay. 1977. The questionable contribution of medical measures to the decline of mortality in the twentieth century. *Milbank Memorial Fund Quarterly* 55:405–28.

Musick, Marc A., A. Regula Herzog, and James S. House. 1999. Volunteering and mortality among older adults: Findings from a national sample. *Journal of Gerontology: Social Sciences* 54 (3): 173–80.

Newman, Katherine S. 1999. *No shame in my game: The working poor in the inner city.* New York: Knopf and the Russell Sage Foundation.

Omran, Abdel R. 1971. The epidemiological transition: A theory of the epidemiology of population change. *Milbank Quarterly* 4:509–38, pt. 1.

Preston, Samuel H. 1977. Mortality trends. *Annual Review of Sociology* 3:163–78.

Renaud, Marc. 1993. The future: Hygiea versus Panakeia? *Health and Canadian Society/Sante' et Societe'* 1:2229–49.

Robert, Stephanie A. 1998. Community-level socioeconomic status effects on adult health. *Journal of Health and Social Behavior* 39:18–37.

———. 1999. Socioeconomic position and health: The independent contribution of community socioeconomic context. *Annual Review of Sociology* 25:489–516.

Sampson, Robert, Stephen W. Raudenbush, and Felton Earls. 1997. Neighborhoods and violent crime: A multilevel study of collective efficacy. *Science* 277:918–24.

Sampson, Robert J., and William J. Wilson. 1995. Toward a theory of race, crime, and urban inequality. *Crime and Inequality*, ed. J. Hagan and R. D. Peterson, 37–54. Stanford: Stanford University Press.

Selye, Hans. 1956. *The stress of life*. New York: McGraw-Hill.

Townsend, Peter, and N. Davidson. 1982. *Inequalities in health: The Black Report*. Hammondsworth, UK: Penguin.

Umberson, Debra, Camille B. Wortman, Ronald C. Kessler. 1992. Widowhood and depression: Explaining long-term gender differences in vulnerability. *Journal of Health and Social Behavior* 33:10–24.

Varmus, H. E. 1999. Statement before the House and Senate Appropriations Subcommittees on Labor, Health, and Human Services, and Education, February 23–24.

Wilkinson, Richard G. 1996. *Unhealthy societies: The afflictions of inequality*. New York: Routledge.

Williams, David R. 1990. Socioeconomic differentials in health: A review and redirection. *Social Psychology Quarterly* 2 (53): 81–99.

———. 1997. Race and health: Basic questions, emerging directions. *Annual Review of Epidemiology* 7:322–33.

Williams, David R., and Chiquita Collins. 1995. U.S. socioeconomic and racial differences in health: Patterns and explanations. *Annual Review of Sociology* 21:349–86.

Williams, David R., Yan Yu, James S. Jackson, and Norman B. Anderson. 1997. Racial differences in physical and mental health: Socioeconomic status, stress, and discrimination. *Journal of Health Psychology* 2 (3): 335–51.

Wilson, William J. 1987. *The truly disadvantaged: The inner city, the underclass, and public policy*. Chicago: University of Chicago Press.

PART 4

Developments in the Study of Family and the Life Course

Duane F. Alwin

The scientific study of families and the lives of their members has burgeoned over the past fifty years. Through the application of surveys of human populations, along with other methodological approaches, a great deal of knowledge has been developed concerning the historical, demographic, economic, cultural, and social structural influences on human lives. This section introduces the chapters that follow and places them into a larger framework for the study of family and the life course.

The Life-Course Perspective

The study of lives and the life course focuses on patterns of developmental trajectories, the ways in which events and experiences shape those patterns, the ways in which trajectories across different realms interconnect, and the intersection of development, ecology, and history within social institutions and social structure (see Settersten 1999). Historical factors clearly shape the pathways of individuals in family, education, work, health and well-being, religious, political, and leisure or retirement activities, as well as shaping the institutional contexts in which those developments take place.

The study of the life course gained momentum through the work of some of the twentieth-century giants in the fields of personality and cognitive development, such as Erik Erikson's *Childhood and Society* (1950), Henry Murray's *Explorations in Personality* (1938), and Louis Terman's series *The Genetic Studies of Genius* (1925, 1947). Murray's emphasis on the personality as a constantly changing configuration, as a consequence of the "dynamic transactions between a changing human organism and its changing environment," was especially important (Rabin et al. 1990, 3). One can also locate the study of the life course, and especially its relation to social change, in some of the classic writings in sociology, such as W. I. Thomas and Florian Znaniecki's *The Polish Peasant in Europe and America* (1927), which relied on life histories and other personal documents to track the orientations of individuals and adjustments to biographic and social change.

With roots in classical perspectives in the social and behavioral sciences, the study of biographic chronologies and their impact on development was given a boost by post–World War II developments in theorizing about human lives, society, and their interconnection. C. Wright Mills's critique of functionalist sociology and its search for universals suggested in *The Sociological Imagination* (1959) that sociologists should actively pursue the intersection of *biography* and *history* to examine, for example, the biographic factors that bring the person to the position as well as the set of historical factors that bring the position to the person. And several pathbreaking works in the social sciences—for example, Peter Blau and Otis Duncan's *The American Occupational Structure* (1967), Glenn Elder's *Children of the Great Depression* (1974), and Theodore Newcomb and colleagues' *Persistence and Change* (1967)—indicated that researchers in many subfields of the social and behavioral science disciplines increasingly utilized a life course perspective in the study of social factors that affect the "life chances" and developmental outcomes of individuals.

In the 1960s and 1970s social and behavioral scientists carved out a place for themselves in the study of aging, with people such as Paul Baltes, Bernice Neugarten, Matilda White Riley, Warner Schaie, John Clausen, William Sewell, and Glen Elder leading the way. Human development is a lifelong process, and hence sociologists established an American Sociological Association section called the "Sociology of Aging." Later the National Institute on Aging was founded to provide federal support for research on all aspects of the aging process, including social, cognitive, and biological. Sociologists interested in human development were very much a part of these movements and in the 1970s began to popularize the concept of "life course" to refer to the vastly complex "age-graded life patterns embedded in social institutions . . . [that are] subject to historical change" (Elder 2000, 1614; see also Featherman and Lerner 1985).

We can envision the life course paradigm very broadly, organized so that it reflects the entire life course: beginning with childhood and family experiences, making the transition from dependence on the family to the universalistic standards of the school and other social institutions, and then making the transition through youth and adolescence, to young adulthood and the productive years, to old age and retirement. The topics considered within these broad-gauged life stages could be conceptualized in terms of major trajectories (e.g., education, careers, family relationships) and transitions (e.g., marriage, childbearing, divorce, widowhood). This perspective would also emphasize the interconnections between history, including demographic shifts and social changes over time, and biographical changes in human lives and personal experiences. One of the "discoveries" induced by the interaction of feminist theorizing with developmental studies was the necessity of conceptualizing and researching the life course differently for women and men (see, e.g., Gilligan 1982; Hulbert and Schuster 1993). It is also possible *and necessary* to study these processes across societies and over time within any given society (see chap. 10, this volume).

Approaches to research on lives and the life course can be organized around four distinct research strategies (see Alwin and Campbell 2001, 31–32), some of which are reflected in the following chapters: (1) research concerned with predicting the occurrence of an event or the transition from one state to another, for example, movement from the parental home into marriage or cohabitation (Thornton, Young-DeMarco, and Goldscheider 1993); (2) strategies concerned with determining the consequences of an event or a set of related events, for example, the effects of the death of a spouse on adjustment (Carr et al. 2000); (3) studies of intraindividual change, where change is assessed in terms of growth or development and where the main objective is the prediction of initial levels, trajectories, and rates of change, for example, research on the development of cognitive abilities over the life span (Schaie 1996); and (4) strategies that focus on the change and stability of interindividual differences, their causes, and their consequences, for example, research on the trajectories of the stability of individual differences (Alwin 1994).

Families and Children

Child development and family studies was an interest of social and behavioral scientists in the post–World War II period, with several disciplines playing a role in the development of the National Institute of Child Health and Human Development. In recent years there has been an explosion of concern about the health and viability of the family as the key link between generations. While we can send spacecraft to Mars and Jupiter, the resolution of key social issues arising from widespread changes in family formation and dissolution has proven much less tractable. The Family and Demography Program at Survey Research Center (SRC), headed by Arland Thornton, has actively pursued the study of the family as a unit of social organization. This program of research has articulated historical and cross-cultural views of the family through time and space; it has developed valuable theoretical perspectives on the family, innovative methods of analysis, and research on specific topics, including childbearing, marital formation, cohabitation and dissolution, family structure, and kinship networks. Chapter 10 by Thornton and Axinn illustrates how survey research has been used to understand the context, sources, and consequences of family change in the area of fertility and family growth. They review the history of studies of fertility behavior and transitions in the United States and the development of cross-national studies of fertility but focus primarily on the design and development of studies of fertility initiated by Ronald Freedman, David Goldberg, and their colleagues at the University of Michigan: the Growth of American Family Studies (GAF) and the Intergenerational Panel Study of Parents and Children (IPS). Particular emphasis in this work has been given to the timing and sequencing of changing social contexts, individual and family experience, and behavioral choices over the life course.

The Transition to Adulthood

In virtually all societies, each generation experiences life differently. Each has its "unique themes and problems, [regularly facing] situations vastly different from those that confronted their parents" (Clausen 1986, 7). The parental generation is often responsible for mediating the influences of social change on their children, and the role of the elder generations in promoting adaptation to social change must be acknowledged. However, the generation itself may be viewed as a powerful source of adaptation and change during the period in the life course when young people make the transition to adulthood. Used in this way, the concept of "generation" refers to the intersection of individual lives with historical time, with new generations replacing older ones through time (Mannheim 1952; Alwin and McCammon 2003). While generational replacement is a biological inevitability *within families*, the replacement of generations at the macrosocial level over time does not correspond in any neat manner to the historical process, because the temporal gap between generations is variable across families. Because we typically measure historical placement of lives in terms of year of birth, our analyses of generational replacement are more properly characterized by the terms "cohort effects" and "cohort turnover" (Ryder 1965).

The concepts of "generation" and "cohort" are powerful tools for analyzing social change in Western industrialized societies because of the extended period of adolescence during which time peer behavior and peer influences rival those of the preceding generation. One of the most innovative and important ISR developments that has capitalized on the use of the cohort concept in the study of social change is the Monitoring the Future project in SRC. Funded primarily to monitor drug use and abuse among the high school–age population, the MTF project has employed a cohort-sequential design to study secular trends (period effects), cohort differences, as well as age-related changes in a wide range of developmental outcomes, such as self-esteem, social values, and orientations to work, in addition to drug use. Chapter 11 by O'Malley, Bachman, Johnston, and Schulenberg provides a powerful illustration of the payoffs to both scientific knowledge and policy decision making made by the MTF project. The chapter addresses the issue of the dynamic relationship between attitudes and behavior—a classic topic in the tradition of social psychology—focusing specifically on the link between drug use and attitudes. The authors' discussion raises the questions of whether attitude change is driving behavior change or vice versa, whether there is a causal effect in both directions, or whether both are being affected by prior factors rendering their relationship spurious. Their work shows that people tend to both adjust their behavior to conform to their beliefs and attitudes and change their beliefs (or rationalize) to grow comfortable psychologically with their behavior.

Life-Span Development

Other SRC life-span developmental research using longitudinal designs has focused on the life-span continuity of some of the development outcomes salient during adolescence and young adulthood. One line of research, begun by Theodore Newcomb in the mid-1960s (Newcomb et al. 1967) and carried on more recently by the SRC's Program in Socio-environmental Studies (directed by the present author), has focused on achieving a broad-gauged theoretical understanding of the processes by which attitudes and belief systems change or become stable over the adult life span. Empirical evidence has been sought for three separate, but not mutually exclusive, life course explanations of human stability and change: *generational* or "cohort" explanations, *life cycle* or "aging" explanations, and *historical* or "period" explanations of individual change (e.g., Alwin and Scott 1996; Alwin and McCammon 2003).

A central goal of this research has been to analyze how beliefs and identities acquired early in adulthood persist and/or change over time. These goals were addressed in the 1980s through a follow-up of the women who participated in Newcomb's (1943) classic study at Bennington College. That work employed Newcomb's early theoretical insights into the processes by which individuals' responses to social change are shaped by their immediate environment, ideas that have since become incorporated into social psychological perspectives on human development (see Bronfenbrenner 1979). The follow-up of the Bennington women and related research demonstrated how the individual's reference groups mediate and interpret the influences of social and political events across the life course (see Alwin, Cohen, and Newcomb 1991; Cohen and Alwin 1993; Jennings, chap. 4, this volume) and how the distinct experiences of cohorts shape the developmental trajectories over time (e.g., Alwin 1997, 1998). More recently, this research has focused not only on attitudes and belief systems but on personality, cognitive skills, values, and behavior as well (see, e.g., Alwin 1994, 1995, 1996, 2001; Alwin and McCammon 1999, 2001, 2002).

Aging and Human Development

Traditional studies of aging have focused primarily on the life courses of older people. To be specific, the field of gerontology has focused exclusively on the later segments of the life course, when people are making transitions out of the labor force and other health-related transitions. In addition, a relatively new area called the "demography of aging" explores demographic perspectives on the development of lives and the life course approaches to the study of traditional demographic topics. Connections among demographic processes across the life course have been examined, including connections among migration, marriage, childbearing, marital dissolution, and mortality. To accomplish the goal of understanding the life course, the study of aging integrates research from the fields of demography, economics, epidemiology, psychology, public health, and sociology. Other specific topics include debates concerning the compression of morbidity, mortality-morbidity tradeoffs, cognitive aging, economic status and employment behavior, living arrangements, mental health, social relationships, medical care receipt of the elderly, and the components of "successful" aging (Rowe and Kahn 1998).

There is a virtual consensus that one of the most productive approaches to the study of aging and human development involves the collection and analysis of longitudinal data. This is borne out by the vast number of research projects over the past few decades that pay attention to the location and measurement of events and processes in time (see Alwin and Campbell 2001). In chapter 12, Herzog, Willis, and Weir articulate many of the kinds of substantive issues raised in the study of aging for which longitudinal data are uniquely suited. They focus on two basic questions: (1) To what does research on aging aspire? and (2) What does aging research need in order to realize those aspirations? Many of the examples given and the findings they review are derived from the series of panel surveys known as the Health and Retirement Study, which will provide a series of replicated longitudinal studies of a sequence of birth cohorts currently and in the future. The first of these began in 1992 as a panel survey of persons from cohorts born in 1931 through 1941 and reinterviewed in 1994, 1996, 1998, and 2000 (see Juster and Suzman 1995). The idea of the HRS derived from a growing awareness of the inadequacy of data available from the Retirement History Survey that began in 1969 and that followed a set of cohorts of men and unmarried women born in 1906 through 1911 for ten years. Basing one's inferences about processes of aging on such a limited spectrum of historical cohorts, it was argued, had obvious limitations, given, for example, the growing participation of women in the labor force and related changes in the family. The collection of data on health and other antecedents of work and retirement decisions for more recent cohorts was viewed as essential to understanding experiences related to processes of aging in the more contemporary social context.

Emerging Perspectives

In addition to providing a conceptual apparatus for thinking about human development and human lives, the life course is also a theoretical orientation within contemporary social science. It has established a common field of inquiry by providing a framework that guides research in terms of problem identification and formulation, variable selection and rationales, and strategies of design and analysis (see Giele and Elder 1998). In just the past five years multiple edited volumes and conferences have been dedicated expressly to topics pertaining to the life course, many of which are interdisciplinary in nature. The Sloan Foundation has recently funded several new research and training institutes (e.g., the Cornell Life Course Institute, Tom Fricke's program in the Ethnography of Everyday Life) that focus on life course issues. It is clear from these many indications that this perspective has become a major force within the disciplines of sociology, anthropology, and psychology, and hopefully we will soon see similar developments within economics and related fields as well as continuing interdisciplinary developments.

One outgrowth of this will be increasing attention to comparative studies of aging and human development across the life course, such as the work of Antonucci, Akiyama, and their associates at ISR that focuses on comparisons between and among Asian, European, and North American populations (e.g., Antonucci et al. 2001).

REFERENCES

Alwin, Duane F. 1994. Aging, personality, and social change: The stability of individual differences over the adult life span. In *Life-span development and behavior,* ed. David L. Featherman, Richard M. Lerner, and Marion Perlmutter, 135–85. Hillsdale, NJ: Erlbaum.

———. 1995. Taking time seriously: Studying social change, social structure, and human lives. In *Examining lives in context: Perspectives on the ecology of human development,* ed. Phyllis Moen, Glen H. Elder Jr. and Kurt Lüscher, 211–62. Washington, DC: American Psychological Association.

———. 1996. Parental socialization in historical perspective. In *The parental experience at midlife,* ed. Carol D. Ryff and Marsha M. Seltzer, 105–67. Chicago: University of Chicago Press.

———. 1997. Aging, social change, and conservatism: Linking aging and social change in the study of political identities. In *Conceptual and methodological issues in the study of aging and social change,* ed. Melissa Hardy, 164–90. Beverly Hills: Sage.

———. 1998. The political impact of the Baby Boom: Are there persistent generational differences in political beliefs and behavior? *Generations* 22:46–54.

———. 2001. Parental values, beliefs, and behavior: A review and promulga for research into the new century. In *Children at the millenium: Where have we come from? Where are we going?* ed. Timothy J. Owens and Sandra L. Hofferth, 97–139. New York: Elsevier Science.

Alwin, Duane F., and Richard T. Campbell. 2001. Quantitative approaches: Longitudinal methods in the study of human development and aging. In *Handbook of aging and the social sciences*, ed. Robert H. Binstock and Linda K. George, 22–43. New York: Academic Press.

Alwin, Duane F., and Ryan J. McCammon. 1999. Aging vs. cohort interpretations of differences in GSS vocabulary scores. *American Sociological Review* 64:272–86.

———. 2001. Aging, cohorts, and verbal ability. *Journal of Gerontology: Social Sciences* 56B:S151–S161.

———. 2003. Generations, cohorts, and social change. In *Handbook of the life course*, ed. J. T. Mortimer and M. Shanahan, 23–49. New York: Kluwer Academic/Plenum.

Alwin, Duane F., and Jacqueline L. Scott. 1996. Attitude change: Its measurement and interpretation using longitudinal surveys. In *Understanding change in social attitudes*, ed. Bridget Taylor and Katarina Thomson, 75–106. Brookfield, VT: Dartmouth.

Alwin, Duane F., Ronald L. Cohen, and Theodore M. Newcomb. 1991. *Political attitudes over the life span: The Bennington women after fifty years.* Madison: University of Wisconsin Press.

Antonucci, Toni C., J. E. Lansford, L. Schaberg, J. Smith, H. Akiyama, K. Takahashi, R. Fuhrer, and J. F. Dartigues. 2001. Widowhood and illness: A comparison of social network characteristics in France, Germany, Japan, and the United States. *Psychology and Aging* 16:655–65.

Blau, Peter M., and Otis D. Duncan. 1967. *The American occupational structure.* New York: Wiley.

Bronfenbrenner, Urie. 1979. *The ecology of human development: Experiments by nature and design.* Cambridge, MA: Harvard University Press.

Carr, Deborah S., James S. House, Ronald C. Kessler, Randolph M. Nesse, J. Sonnega, and Camille Wortman. 2000. Marital quality and psychological adjustment to widowhood among older adults: A longitudinal analysis. *Journal of Gerontology: Social Sciences* 55B:S197–S207.

Clausen, John A. 1986. *The life course: A sociological perspective.* Englewood Cliffs, NJ: Prentice-Hall.

Cohen, Ronald L., and Duane F. Alwin. 1993. Bennington women of the 1930s: Political attitudes over the life course. In *Women's lives through time: Educated American women of the twentieth century*, ed. Kathleen D. Hulbert and Diane T. Schuster, 117–39. San Francisco: Jossey-Bass.

Elder, Glen H., Jr. 1974. *Children of the Great Depression.* Chicago: University of Chicago Press.

———. 2000. The life course. In *Encyclopedia of Sociology*, ed. E. F. Borgatta and R. J. V. Montgomery, eds., 3:1614–22. New York: Macmillan Reference USA.

Erikson, Erik H. 1950. *Childhood and society.* New York: W. W. Norton.

Featherman, David L., and Richard M. Lerner. 1985. Ontogenesis and sociogenesis:

Problematics for theory and research about development and socialization across the lifespan. *American Sociological Review* 50:659–76.

Giele, Janet Z., and Glen H. Elder Jr. 1998. *Methods of life course research: Qualitative and quantitative approaches.* Thousand Oaks, CA: Sage.

Gilligan, Carol. 1982. *In a different voice: Psychological theory and women's development.* Cambridge, MA: Harvard University Press.

Hulbert, Kathleen D., and Diane T. Schuster, eds. 1993. *Women's lives through time: Educated American women of the twentieth century.* San Francisco: Jossey-Bass.

Juster, F. Thomas, and Richard Suzman. 1995. An overview of the Health and Retirement Study. *Journal of Human Resources* 30:S7–S56.

Mannheim, Karl. 1952. The problem of generations. In *Essays in the sociology of knowledge,* ed. P. Kecskemeti, 276–320. London: Routledge and Kegan Paul.

Mills, C. Wright. 1959. *The sociological imagination.* New York: Oxford University Press.

Murray, Henry. 1938. *Explorations in personality.* New York: Oxford University Press.

Newcomb, Theodore M. 1943. *Personality and social change: Attitude formation in a student community.* New York: Dryden Press.

Newcomb, Theodore M., Kathryn E. Koenig, Richard Flacks, and Donald P. Warwick. 1967. *Persistence and change: Bennington College and its students after twenty-five years.* New York: Wiley.

Rabin, A. I., Robert A. Zucker, Robert A. Emmons, and Susan Frank. 1990. *Studying persons and lives.* New York: Springer.

Rowe, John W., and Robert L. Kahn. 1998. *Successful aging.* New York: Pantheon Books.

Ryder, Norman B. 1965. The cohort as a concept in the study of social change. *American Sociological Review* 30:843–61.

Schaie, K. Warner. 1996. *Intellectual development in adulthood: The Seattle Longitudinal Study.* Cambridge, UK: Cambridge University Press.

Settersten, Richard A., Jr. 1999. *Lives in time and place: The problems and promises of developmental science.* Amityville, NY: Baywood.

Terman, Louis. 1925. *Genetic studies of genius.* Vol. 1, *Mental and physical traits of a thousand gifted children.* Stanford: Stanford University Press.

———. 1947. *Genetic studies of genius.* Vol. 4, *The gifted child grows up.* Stanford: Stanford University Press.

Thomas, William I., and Florian Znaniecki. 1927. *The Polish peasant in Europe and America.* New York: Alfred Knopf.

Thornton, Arland A., Linda L. Young-DeMarco, and Frances Goldscheider. 1993. Leaving the parental nest: The experience of a young, white cohort in the 1980s. *Journal of Marriage and the Family* 55:216–29.

CHAPTER 10

The Social Demography of Fertility: Some Contributions of American Surveys

Arland Thornton and William G. Axinn

Marriage, family, and the bearing and rearing of children have long been central institutions for human beings. Evolutionary scholars suggest that mating, reproduction, and family life coevolved with many other features of the human condition to form the foundation for current human behavior, ranking with walking upright, language, flexible hands, large brains, and extended youthful dependency in defining the meaning of being human (Buss 1994; Diamond 1992; Hrdy 1999; Daly and Wilson 2000; Broude 1994).

Marriage and family were the institutions of the Western world that organized many of the activities and relationships of women, men, and children. The family unit built around the marital couple and their children was the prime economic unit of society, being the main locus of production and consumption. Marriage defined womanhood, manhood, and adult status. Marriage and family relationships also governed living arrangements and the division of labor and authority within the family and between the sexes. Consequently, the institutions of marriage and family permeated the minds of individual women and men, provided central elements of human identity, and helped to define economic well-being, physical and mental health, and relationships among individuals (Herlihy 1985; Hanawalt 1986; Parsons and Bales 1955; Ogburn and Tibbitts 1933).

From a population perspective, the renewal of the older generation occurs through the bearing, rearing, and socialization of children into adulthood. Fertility is, thus, a central element in the population equation, combining with mortality and migration to define the size, growth, and structure of a population (Ryder 1964).

Many religious institutions have given mating, reproduction, and family life special significance. In the West the Roman Catholic Church endorsed marriage, family life, and childbearing, teaching that they were divine institutions. Catholicism made marriage a sacrament, and while the Protestant reformers rejected the sacramental nature of marriage, they continued to believe that marriage and family life were ordained of God and often viewed marriage as a covenant with God or as a commonwealth with the Church (Phillips 1988; Brundage 1987; Witte 1997).

Early Studies of Marriage, Family, and Childbearing

Given the centrality of marriage, families, and the bearing and rearing of children to human life, it is not surprising that scholars have long been interested in these dimensions of human life. Both Plato and Aristotle gave attention to these central elements of the human condition, as did subsequent generations of scholars (Nisbet 1980). The icons of Western sociology—Max Weber, Karl Marx, and Émile Durkheim—all devoted considerable attention to family issues in their writings, as did other important early sociologists such as Frederick LePlay and Edward Westermarck (Thornton 2001). Marriage and childbearing were also central elements in the writings of Robert Malthus and generations of subsequent demographers (Peterson 1999; Thornton 2001).

Censuses and Vital Statistics

Although the earliest scholars of family, marriage, and childbearing had little systematic information upon which to base their conclusions and speculations, extensive materials began to become available in the eighteenth and nineteenth centuries. Censuses began to be taken on a regular basis in many Western countries, including the United States. Vital registration systems that recorded baptisms, marriages, and deaths were put in place by religious authorities and later evolved into registration systems that are currently administered by civil authorities (Lorimer 1964; Linder 1964). Census materials and vital statistics provided family and demographic scholars the raw materials to describe family and population processes and how they might change across time.

Family and demographic scholars of the eighteenth and nineteenth centuries also utilized numerous other sources of information in their studies. Some European scholars such as Malthus, LePlay, and Westermarck spent extensive time in the field collecting their own information through ethnography, personal observation, and in-depth interviewing (Thornton 2001). LePlay, for example, deployed field-workers who observed individuals and their families, conducted semistructured interviews, and talked with members of the community. Scholars of this era also used the extensive accounts of Western travelers, soldiers, ethnographers, explorers, and colonial administrators to document and compare the family and reproductive systems in numerous non-Western societies (Nisbet 1980; Thornton 2001). These comparative international data were used to construct speculative schemes about the trajectory of family change in the West that were later shown to have no basis in actual Western history (Thornton 2001).

However, by the early twentieth century demographers in the United States and Europe had reliably documented through censuses and vital statistics one of the most dramatic changes in the history of the Western world: the revolution of vital processes through the dramatic decline of both fertility and mortality. Also documented were socioeconomic differentials in childbearing and family size (Notestein 1982; Ryder 1964; Whelpton and Kiser 1945–50). Many scholars, at first, attributed both the decline in childbearing and the existence of differential childbearing to deterioration of physiological capacity associated with urban and industrial life. However, in-depth studies in the first part of the twentieth century using specialized populations such as hospital patients, obstetrical patients, and clients of family planning clinics suggested that both the decline and the differentials in fertility were the result of voluntary use of family planning (Notestein 1982; Whelpton and Kiser 1943–45; Freedman, Whelpton, and Campbell 1959).

These studies of specialized populations, of course, raised additional questions. To what extent could they be replicated in general studies of the population? How widespread were fertility impairments and the use of voluntary family planning in the general population? And, if voluntary family planning was the primary force behind both the fertility decline and the fertility differentials, what were the motivations behind the use of family planning? What social, economic, psychological, and personality characteristics influenced family size desires and the use of contraception?

Indianapolis Fertility Study

By the late 1930s it had become evident that population censuses and vital statistics would not be sufficiently flexible and intensive to provide the data necessary to answer such questions (Whelpton and Kiser 1945–50; Westoff, Potter, and Sagi 1963). A group of distinguished American scholars formed the Committee on the Study of Social and Psychological Factors Affecting Fertility and immediately set themselves the task of designing and implementing a study to match their name (Whelpton and Kiser 1943–45, 1945–50). The study designed by the committee was the Indianapolis Fertility Study, the first large-scale general population survey in the United States devoted to the documentation of fertility and the factors influencing it. Although the goals of the project were aggressive in desiring to explain fertility motivations and behavior, it also saw itself as a project where questions and procedures for future studies could be formulated and evaluated. Consequently, in addition to limiting the study to Indianapolis, the committee interviewed only once-married native white Protestant couples with at least an elementary school education. The committee collected an extensive array of survey data in Indianapolis in 1941 about fertility and the forces influencing it. The results of this study were reported in a series of papers that were subsequently collected into five volumes edited by P. K. Whelpton and Clyde Kiser (1954–56, 1958).

The Indianapolis Fertility Study also set the foundation for three new streams of family and fertility research, two domestic and one international. Each of these three streams of research was to be based on the systematic sample survey, a research tool that substantially enhanced scholarly ability to understand family and demographic motivations and behavior (Hauser and Duncan 1964a, 1964b; Freedman, Whelpton, and Campbell 1959; Ryder 1964; Westoff, Potter, and Sagi 1963). As Bumpass and Westoff (1970) suggest, the two American streams of fertility research divided into a series of repeated national cross-sectional surveys and two long-term panel studies, with Princeton University and the University of Michigan playing key roles in both streams of research.

Cross-Sectional Studies of American Fertility

The first stream of American fertility studies was initiated in 1955 as the Growth of American Families Study (GAF), a nationally representative cross-sectional study of white American women, conducted at the University of Michigan (Freedman, Whelpton, and Campbell 1959). A similar study was conducted in 1960 (Whelpton, Campbell, and Patterson 1966). In 1965 and 1970 similar studies were conducted by Princeton University under the title of the National Fertility Study. This series of cross-sectional national studies of fertility was subsequently institutionalized within the National Center for Health Statistics of the federal government, where they continue to the present as the National Survey of Family Growth (NSFG).

Panel Studies

The second stream of American family and fertility studies were panel studies begun in the late 1950s and early 1960s. These studies were motivated by a growing recognition that panel studies had considerable advantages over cross-sectional studies in evaluating causal influences on family and demographic behavior. One of these panel studies was the Princeton Fertility Study, which began in 1957 and extended through the mid-1960s (Bumpass and Westoff 1970). Another panel study was the Intergenerational Panel Study (IPS) of Parents and Children (described below), which was initiated in 1962 and extended into the 1990s (Thornton, Freedman, and Axinn 2002).

International Studies

The third stream came from the internationalization of family and fertility studies, with numerous family and fertility studies being conducted around the world. These include, but are not limited to, the large comparative projects carried out under the auspices of the World Fertility Survey, the Demographic and Health Surveys, and the Family and Fertility Surveys.

American Cross-Sectional Studies of Family and Fertility

In the subsequent sections of this chapter we discuss the design, implementation, and evolution of the two streams of American family and fertility surveys. Given the focus of this volume, we devote most of our attention to the two studies begun at the University of Michigan in the 1950s and 1960s, the GAF Study and the IPS. We discuss how these studies began, evolved, and relate to the larger body of data and research concerning family and fertility in the United States.

The Growth of American Families Study

The first national sample survey study of fertility in the United States—the GAF Study—was conducted in 1955 by the Survey Research Center (SRC) of the University of Michigan under the direction of Ronald Freedman, Pascal Whelpton, and Arthur Campbell.[1] The study interviewed 2,713 currently married white women ages eighteen to thirty-nine about both the history and the future of the size of their families (Freedman, Whelpton, and Campbell 1959). This was also the first survey to interview Catholic women about their family sizes and fertility regulation behavior.[2] In fact, this national survey of fertility regulation and contraceptive use was considered a pathbreaking effort to interview a nationally representative general population sample of women about such potentially sensitive topics. Although there initially were concerns about women being willing to respond to these questions, the response rate and quality of data were high. The interviewers reported that it was not difficult to ask the respondents to provide information that was so important to them.

The GAF Study took place during a time of tremendous demographic upheaval. Following decades of sustained declines in both fertility and mortality, the period directly following World War II was characterized by unprecedented increases in fertility. As scholars and policymakers alike were aware that fertility was the driving force behind population growth and ultimately population size, a central aim of the 1955 GAF Study was to learn more about fertility behavior with an aim toward forecasting future population growth. So, in addition to documenting trends and socioeconomic differentials in family size and contraceptive methods, this survey also asked women about their attitudes, expectations, and preferences. In summarizing the findings of the study, the study directors concluded with a series of forecasts of future trends in family size and the consequences of those trends for population growth (Freedman, Whelpton, and Campbell 1959).

The effort to measure women's childbearing preferences opened a key new area for social scientific inquiry—unintended pregnancy. Unintended pregnancy is composed of both unwanted pregnancies and mistimed pregnancies. The 1955 GAF was the first survey to provide national estimates of the prevalence of unintended pregnancy, but over time this issue became a central focus of the national fertility surveys (Campbell and Mosher 2000). Moreover, the issue has evolved into a central concern of U.S. public health policy (Healthy People 2000) and as such will probably continue to be an important motivation for national fertility surveys for some time to come.

The second GAF study was fielded in 1960, also by SRC. This time 2,986 women, composing a nationally representative sample of white, currently married women ages eighteen to forty-four, were interviewed. Small samples of previously married white women ages twenty-three to forty-four (n = 66) and currently married black women ages eighteen to thirty-nine (n = 270) were also interviewed (Whelpton, Campbell, and Patterson 1966). An explicit aim of the 1960 survey was to test how well the forecasts based on the 1955 survey predicted what had actually occurred by 1960. Toward this end, the 1960 survey repeated a good deal of the content from the 1955 survey. The 1960 survey was also designed to go beyond the 1955 survey, by breaking new ground in areas such as white-nonwhite differences in fertility and related behaviors, use of family planning services, the effectiveness of contraceptive methods, and analyses of trends using the powerful combination of the two national surveys (Whelpton, Campbell, and Patterson 1966). However, measurement of socioeconomic differentials in family size and contraceptive use, measurement of family size and fertility regulation expectations and preferences, and forecasts of future fertility and population growth trends remained at the heart of the 1960 GAF study (Whelpton, Campbell, and Patterson 1966).

The combination of the two GAF studies in 1955 and 1960 taught the demographic and survey research communities many important lessons. Fertility and related behaviors were changing quickly and not always in ways that were easy to predict. The baby boom was beginning to plateau and decline, an unexpected change motivating more detailed investigation of likely causes of changes in fertility differentials and trends. Race, education, employment, and religion all began to emerge as key socioeconomic determinants of fertility and related behavior. Inconsistencies between socioeconomic differentials in fertility outcomes and socioeconomic differentials in fertility preference also began to point toward the link between preferences and behavioral outcomes as a key explanation for fertility differentials. Just as crucial to the evolution of this stream of research, information about fertility, contraception, and family planning could be successfully collected from a nationally representative sample of the general population. In fact, success with interviews about these potentially sensitive topics had been so great that researchers could begin to imagine more ambitious surveys of potentially even more sensitive, but increasingly crucial topics.

The National Fertility Studies

Between 1960 and 1965 the work to gather national survey data on fertility and related factors moved from the University of Michigan to the Office of Population Research at Princeton University.[3] The National Fertility Study was fielded in 1965 under the direction of Norman Ryder and Charles Westoff. This survey was explicitly designed to build on and expand the work of the earlier GAF Studies of 1955 and 1960 (Ryder and Westoff 1971; Westoff and Ryder 1977). The sample size was increased substantially, the black population was oversampled by a factor of two, and, in 1965 only, women ages forty-five to fifty-four were also interviewed (Westoff and Ryder 1977, 3). In 1970 the Office of Population Research led a second National Fertility Study. This survey, fielded by the Institute for Survey Research at Temple University, included all ever-married women under age forty-five, adding a sample of the previously married to the sample of currently married women (Westoff and Ryder 1977). Together, these two national surveys extended the time-series of U.S. national fertility surveys to four surveys over fifteen years.

The 1965 and 1970 studies were particularly important because of radical changes going on in fertility behavior in the United States at that time. In 1960 the oral contraceptive pill was introduced, and what followed was one of the most remarkable transformations in American family formation behavior in history—what became known as the "contraceptive revolution" (Westoff and Ryder 1977). The 1965 and 1970 surveys revealed dramatic increases in contraceptive use in the United States (Ryder and Westoff 1971). The revolution was a product not only of widespread pill use but also of increased use of IUDs and sterilization (Westoff 1975). This dramatic behavioral shift raised many questions about which contraceptive methods were being used, who in the population was most likely to use these methods, how long methods were being used, and how much unwanted and mistimed fertility was being avoided by using these methods. These were all questions that data from the National Fertility Studies could be used to answer (Westoff 1975; Westoff and Ryder 1977). In fact, estimation of the levels of unwanted and mistimed childbearing continued to be a major focus of these studies, and the new high prevalence of contraception added complexity to this aim and increased the need for precision in these estimates (Campbell and Mosher 2000).

In spite of the dramatic increase in rates of contraceptive use and improvements in the methods of contraception, levels of unintended pregnancy remained high. Concerns about these high rates of unintended pregnancy motivated more detailed investigations of the socioeconomic differentials in related factors—a concern that continues to motivate a good deal of U.S. fertility research to the present day (Hershaw 1998). The detailed measurement and large sample sizes embedded in the 1965 and 1970 survey allowed investigations of socioeconomic differences in fertility preferences and behavior in unprecedented detail (Ryder and Westoff 1971; Westoff 1975). These investigations revealed greater differentials in fertility outcomes than in fertility preferences, suggesting some groups were more able to translate their preferences into behavior than other groups.

Important for the advancement of survey methods, demographers retained a strong spirit of self-criticism toward the measurement of fertility and related topics among the national population throughout this period. This critical perspective focused on issues of sampling and coverage; measurement errors arising from the instrument, interviewer, or respondent; and even the basic design of the repeated cross-sectional survey (Ryder 1973). This ongoing criticism of the specific survey methods and designs used in the National Fertility Studies helped to stimulate the demographic community's interest in new and improved survey methods in general and in applying cutting-edge survey techniques to fertility surveys specifically. As such, it paved the way for future national fertility surveys to include survey methodological advancements directly as part of their scope (as discussed later). Also, partly as a result of work on the National Fertility Studies, the scientific community began calling for longitudinal studies of family formation that could be used to examine issues of cause and consequence, urging that such studies need not be national and multipurpose in nature (Ryder 1973). We take up this topic in greater detail later in the chapter.

The National Survey of Family Growth

By the early 1970s it was broadly recognized that the regular collection of national statistics on fertility and related behaviors was essential to the public interest. As a result, the enterprise was moved from the academic sector to the National Center for Health Statistics, where the first NSFG was conducted in 1973 under the direction of John Patterson and William Pratt (Ryder 1973). This was to be the first of several "Cycles" of the NSFG conducted by the National Center for Health Statistics. After Cycle 1 of the NSFG in 1973, Cycle 2 was fielded in 1976, Cycle 3 in 1982, Cycle 4 in 1988, Cycle 5 in 1995, and Cycle 6 in 2002. Throughout this period the data collection fieldwork was contracted to various survey data collection organizations, but by Cycle 6 the chain had come full circle—the Institute for Social Research (ISR) at the University of Michigan collected Cycle 6.[4] The period from 1973 to the present has been one of regularizing the collection of national survey data on family and fertility but also one of innovation in the populations studied, in the subject matter examined, and in the methods used.

Though all the cycles of the NSFG have interviewed nationally representative samples of the general population of the United States, the scope of the population examined has been continuously expanded throughout the history of the study. Furthermore, the expansion in the population studied reflects the evolution of substantive issues related to family formation processes in the United States. In 1973, "never married women with children in the household" were added to the sampling frame (Westoff and Ryder 1977). By 1982, the sample was expanded to 7,600 women ages fifteen to forty-four, representing both ever-married and never married women (Mosher 1982). This shift to include the never married and the currently unmarried women among those interviewed reflects both a growing substantive interest in marriage and in the contribution of marital processes to family size and a growing methodological confidence in the ability of survey researchers to interview a broad spectrum of the population with regard to potentially sensitive issues. By 1995, Cycle 5 of the NSFG also included significant oversampling of both the black and Hispanic populations, to allow the study of patterns within these groups, as well as more detailed comparisons across groups (NCHS 1997). This expansion reflects the growing interest in variations in family formation patterns across subgroups of the population and in the factors that produce those variations. In Cycle 6, for the first time in the history of national fertility surveys, a full-scale national sample of men as a companion to the national sample of women of childbearing age was included. This latest expansion reflects growing interest in men's roles in family and family formation processes, as well as increased concern about factors related to the spread of sexually transmitted diseases.

The substance studied through the NSFG has also evolved in important ways during this period. All the NSFG surveys extend the focus on measurement of trends in family size, childbearing processes, contraception, use of family planning services, birth preferences and expectations, and intendedness of births forward in time. But new themes also emerged. Marriage and associated behaviors, such as divorce and premarital cohabitation, became an increasingly important focus of NSFG. Reproductive health, particularly impaired fecundity and sexually transmitted diseases, also became an increasingly central topic. And sex, sexuality, and relationships between men and women also became a more important focus of the study. In fact, by Cycle 5 in 1995, the NSFG had evolved into a massive survey investigation of a wide array of factors related to fertility, family growth, and reproductive health. It remains the country's key data source for national measurement of sexual behavior, the use and effectiveness of contraceptive methods, impaired fecundity and infertility, fertility preferences and expectations, unintended fertility, socioeconomic differentials in fertility, adoption, use of family planning services, and prevalence of behaviors that increase the risk of sexually transmitted diseases (Mosher and Bachrach 1996).

Data from the NSFG document many of the key issues in American family and fertility in the 1980s and 1990s. One example is the manyfold growth in the popularity of premarital cohabitation and concurrent delays in entry into marriage in the United States (Mosher and Bachrach 1996). Another example is the stability over time of high rates of unintended childbearing in the United States (Hershaw 1998). A third example is the estimation of the very large number of women seeking to adopt children in the United States (Bachrach, London, and Maza 1991). Together the surveys have produced a myriad of important findings beyond the scope of reporting in this chapter; these are summarized in a series of articles by William Mosher, current director of the NSFG for the National Center for Health Statistics, and his colleagues (Mosher 1982, 1988; Mosher and Bachrach 1996; NCHS 1997).

The NSFG has also been an important laboratory for research on survey methods and improvement in methods of collecting national survey data. Because the NSFG measures many potentially sensitive dimensions of family formation processes, including sexuality, abortion, and sexually transmitted diseases, it has always stimulated innovation in methods of measurement. It was one of the first large-scale, federal sample surveys to use computer-assisted personal interviewing methods and, because of the sensitive material included in the study, one of the first to use audio computer-assisted self-interviewing methods. In fact, Cycle 5 of the NSFG devoted substantial effort to the measurement of abortion and sexual behavior via audio-CASI. The NSFG has also stimulated several important design innovations. Cycle 4 included a telephone reinterview follow-up two years later. Cycle 5 included lengthy event history measures of respondents' life histories and the creation of detailed, multilevel contextual data files (NCHS 1997). Each of these innovations was designed to meet the needs of the scientific and policy-making communities' ongoing efforts to understand the trends in and determinants of behaviors related to the formation and dissolution of American families. The needs of this important program of research are likely to continue to propel significant methodological innovation in this series of national surveys for some time to come.

This series of American fertility surveys has served as a model for numerous fertility surveys in other countries. Many of the leaders of the American studies, including Ronald Freedman, Leslie Kish, Norman Ryder, and Charles Westoff, played key roles in the very large series of surveys conducted under the auspices of the World Fertility Survey and the Demographic and Health Surveys.

American Panel Studies of Family and Fertility

Two of the limitations of the cross-sectional surveys for the study of family and fertility behavior were apparent to the analysts of the Indianapolis Fertility Study (Whelpton and Kiser 1954–56, 1958; Westoff et al. 1961; Westoff, Potter, and Sagi 1963). One was the reliance of the cross-sectional study on the retrospective reporting of behavior. A second was that this study design frequently resulted in analysts trying to explain fertility behavior occurring over several decades with familial, psychological, social, and economic circumstances existing at the time of the survey. This circumstance substantially threatened the ability of analysts to disentangle the causal relationships producing empirical correlations between fertility and the factors believed to influence it.

With this recognition, the scholarly community quickly turned to the design of long-term panel studies—the Princeton Fertility Study in 1957 and the IPS in 1962. Although the two studies had different investigators and different study designs, they grew out of the same research traditions and shared many of the same design features.

Perhaps most important was the fact that the two studies conceptualized family building as a dynamic sequential process that occurred across time (Westoff et al. 1961). Couples made decisions about having a first child, and then when that first child was born they decided about having a second child. This sequential decision-making process suggested a research strategy where investigators identify a group of couples who have either just married or just given birth to a child, interview the couple soon thereafter, and then follow the couple across time to see who had children or additional children. The Princeton Fertility Study implemented this design by sampling a group of couples who had just given birth to a second child in 1956, while the IPS sampled couples who had just married or had a first, second, or fourth child in 1961.

The two panel studies were also similar in that they were conducted in large metropolitan areas—the IPS in Detroit and the Princeton Fertility Study in the largest eight metropolitan areas. Because of financial limitations, neither study had the resources to oversample the nonwhite population and consequently limited the samples to whites. One important difference between the two studies was that the Princeton Fertility Study retained its focus as a one-generation fertility project, whereas the Detroit-based IPS was subsequently transformed into a two-generation study with a broad focus on a range of family issues.

Princeton Fertility Study

The Princeton Fertility Study was explicitly conceptualized as a descendant of the Indianapolis Fertility Study (Westoff et al. 1961; Westoff, Potter, and Sagi 1963; Bumpass and Westoff 1970). The Princeton Fertility Study, like the Indianapolis project before it, was designed to focus on the social and psychological factors affecting fertility. Many of the hypotheses motivating the Indianapolis project also motivated the Princeton study, and certain measures were repeated.

As noted earlier, the Princeton Fertility Study was based on a sample of white couples in eight of the largest American metropolitan areas. The women in these couples (approximately 1,200) had given birth in September 1956 to their second child and were interviewed in 1957, approximately six months after the birth of the child. This initial interview was designed both to ascertain the woman's experience and to serve as a baseline for studying subsequent fertility decisions and behavior.

The women in the Princeton Fertility Study were interviewed again three years later, in 1960, with the focus on the decision to have a third child (Westoff, Potter, and Sagi 1963). The third and final interview of the Princeton project was conducted between 1963 and 1967. This third interview was staggered across time to maximize the possibility of measuring final parity while at the same time limiting the length of recall (Bumpass and Westoff 1970).

Intergenerational Panel Study of Parents and Children

The IPS drew inspiration from both the 1955 and 1960 GAF Studies and the Princeton Fertility Study. It began in 1962 at the University of Michigan under the leadership of Ronald Freedman and David Goldberg.[5] The IPS was initiated at the height of the baby boom and was motivated by an interest in using a panel design to study stability and change in desired and expected family size. Also of interest was how these fertility desires and expectations were translated into realized family size.

The original study was designed to examine the interrelationships of childbearing with the familial, social, and economic institutions in which the couples were embedded. The researchers wanted to know how childbearing was influenced by the economic position and resources of the family, by the family's social mobility, by religious affiliation and commitment, by the internal structure of the family, and by linkages between the family and other kinds of social relationships. Thus, from the beginning the IPS was designed to include a wide range of fertility and family information.

When Goldberg and Freedman conceived the idea of this longitudinal study in 1961, it was convenient to base the research in the Detroit metropolitan area because of the excellent survey capabilities of the Detroit Area Study (DAS).[6] The DAS also bore most of the costs of the initial survey. Basing the initial study in the Detroit metropolitan area also facilitated the matching of marriage and birth records, which was essential for classifying the first births of all respondents by their pregnancy status at marriage. These data have proven to be valuable in predicting other aspects of family building. The decision to base the study in a single metropolitan area was also buttressed by analyses showing that, with appropriate sample definitions, important results from the Indianapolis Fertility Project were very similar to those coming from the nationally representative GAF data (Whelpton and Kiser 1954–56, 1958).

The initial sample of the IPS consisted of approximately 1,100 women selected on a probability basis from the birth records of married white women who had a first, second, or fourth birth in the Detroit metropolitan area in July 1961. Approximately equal numbers of women were selected from each of the parity groups. An additional sample of approximately

200 recently married white women from the Detroit metropolitan area was also included, bringing the total sample to approximately 1,300 women. The original baseline information was collected in January–March 1962 in face-to-face interviews.

The first three follow-up surveys were conducted in the fall of 1962, 1963, and 1966 under the direction of Freedman, with the considerable assistance of Lolagene Coombs. These three interviews were conducted primarily by telephone to minimize costs. Home visits were made for respondents who had no telephones or who could not be reached by telephone. To facilitate the follow-up interviews the baseline survey had obtained the names, addresses, and telephone numbers of three friends or relatives who would know how to reach the respondents if they moved. These follow-up interviews continued the original emphasis on childbearing and its intersection with larger family issues.

The early 1960s brought new opportunities for demographers with international interests in fertility and population growth. Consequently, in the early 1960s—at the same time that Freedman and Coombs were conducting the early waves of the IPS—they became heavily involved in research and consulting about fertility and family planning in Taiwan. The heavy involvement of Freedman and Coombs in research in Taiwan prevented them from conducting follow-up studies with the Detroit sample after 1966.

After a decade-long hiatus the IPS was renewed with a new data collection in 1977 under the direction of Arland Thornton and Deborah Freedman. Consistent with the original purposes of the study, the 1977 data collection maintained a strong interest in childbearing. Because the women participating in the study had begun their childbearing during the central years of the baby boom and had completed their fertility during the "baby bust" years of the late 1960s and 1970s, it was possible to examine how their original plans and preferences had changed over time and how this childbearing was influenced by and influenced other dimensions of family life.

The goals of the 1977 study were also expanded to include several new avenues of research concerning family life, most importantly gender roles and marital instability. It was clear by the 1977 reinterview that a revolution was under way in gender roles. The IPS was in an advantageous position to study the dynamics of changes in women's and men's roles because the original data collections in the 1960s had ascertained extensive information about the division of labor in the family, household decision making, and attitudes toward gender roles. The collection of similar information in the late 1970s would permit documentation of changes in work and family life and how these were interconnected with other family factors such as childbearing and financial well-being.

The IPS was also well positioned to examine another important new phenomenon of the 1960s and 1970s—the dramatic increase in marital instability. The early waves of the IPS contained a wealth of information about the couples that could be used to understand their subsequent experience with divorce. The extension of the study to 1977 provided additional opportunities to examine marital dissolution and its intersection with other important familial, social, and economic factors.

In 1980 the IPS became intergenerational when the children who were born in 1961, and who were then eighteen years old, were added to the study. Interviews were conducted in 1980 with both these children and their mothers. The inclusion of the children added to the power of longitudinal data the strength of interviews with two generations in each family. Both the children and the mothers were interviewed again in 1985, when the children were age twenty-three, and in 1993, when the children were age thirty-one. The IPS now has data from eight waves of interviews, the last three involving two generations.

A major motivation for making the IPS intergenerational in 1980 was the opportunity to study the influence of the parental family on the attitudes and behavior of children. Social scientists had long been interested in the ways in which children are influenced by the parental family, and growing concerns about the effects of parental poverty, marital instability, and female employment on children's well-being had increased interest in these questions. The IPS was particularly well placed to study these issues because it had available a large body of demographic, social, economic, and attitudinal data about these children's families. These family data covered the entire first fifteen years of the children's lives. In addition, this information was not collected retrospectively but at important points in the lives of the families as the children matured. By designing a data collection that included the children, the study could collect extensive information from the children that would permit study of how multiple aspects of life in the second generation are influenced by parents.

The 1980–93 data collections were designed to address three main dimensions of the lives of young people. First was the marriage and childbearing plans and behavior of the young people, dimensions of family life that had changed dramatically during the 1960s and 1970s. A second dimension of inquiry was the socioeconomic aspirations and achievements of the young people, aspects of life that are intricately interwoven with family formation during the young adult years. The third research goal centered on the personal, familial, and social adjustments of the young people and how they were influenced by many dimensions of the parental family.

In 1985 a life history calendar was introduced into the data collection with the young people. The use of the life history calendar was motivated by the increasing interest of social science in the processes that underlie change in the lives of individuals. It had become increasingly clear by 1985 that studies of the dynamics of individual behavior are greatly facilitated by collecting detailed information about the timing and sequencing of events over the life course. However, the imperfections of human memory make the retrospective collection of reliable event history information difficult, and the life history calendar facilitates the collection of such information. The IPS was an ideal place to use a life history calendar because all the children were born in the same year and were only twenty-three years old at the time of the 1985 interview. The 1985 life history calendar ascertained monthly information for the children between the ages of fifteen and twenty-three for residence, marital transitions, cohabitating relationships, births, living arrangements, school enrollment, employment, and military service. A similar life history calendar was used in 1993 to update information between the 1985 and 1993 interviews. The improvements made in calendar procedures in the IPS have contributed to life history calendar methodologies for others (Freedman et al. 1988; Caspi et al. 1996; Belli 1998).

A unique feature of the IPS has been its unusually high response rates (Coombs and Freedman 1970b; Freedman, Freedman, and Thornton 1980; Thornton, Freedman, and Camburn 1982). The study interviewed 92 percent of the target sample in the initial 1962 interview. In 1993—thirty-one years and seven waves of interviews later—84 percent of the mothers who were alive and eligible for reinterview were still participating. Similarly, 83 percent of the children who were still alive participated in the last wave in 1993. Of the original sample families where neither the mother nor the child was known to be dead or seriously ill, interviews were obtained in 1993 from both the mother and the child in 80 percent of the families. These high response rates have minimized the difficulties of attrition, one of the most serious threats to the validity of panel studies.

The IPS has had a rich set of published findings about a broad range of family issues. Publications from the interviews conducted in the 1960s dealt mainly with stability and change in reproductive expectations and preferences and the consequences of premarital pregnancy for subsequent socioeconomic achievement (Coombs and Freedman 1970a; Freedman and Thornton 1979). The study also provided a successful test of a new sophisticated measure of fertility preferences created by Lolagene and Clyde Coombs (Coombs 1979). This measure captures the range of fertility preferences underlying a single number preference. This measure obtained in 1962 helped to predict subsequent fertility, net of the conventional preference measure. This measure was subsequently used in Turkey, Taiwan, Hungary, and Nepal.

One of the central themes of the research findings from the later waves of interviews is the changing nature of family life (Thornton and Young-Demarco 2001; Axinn and Thornton 2000). Over the past several decades there has been a substantial relaxation of the social prescriptions for family behavior and an expansion of the range of permissible individual behavior. The IPS has demonstrated a weakening of the normative imperative to marry, to stay married, to have children, and to maintain a strict division of labor between women and men. The IPS has also been used to document the complexity of contemporary home leaving by the younger generation and new patterns of marriage and cohabitation (Goldscheider, Thornton, and Young-DeMarco 1993; Thornton 1988).

The IPS has shown how young people are influenced by many dimensions of the parental family, including attitudes and values, religious affiliation and commitment, marital experience, socioeconomic position, and maternal employment. Many aspects of children's behavior and attitudes—including sex roles, premarital sex, cohabitation, marriage, divorce, and childbearing—are closely related to the values, attitudes, and behavior of parents (Thornton, Alwin, and Camburn 1983; Thornton 1985; Thornton and Camburn 1987; Axinn and Thornton 1992, 1993; Barber 2000). The transmission of attitudes and values across generations is greater when the children and mothers have close interpersonal relationships (Weinstein and Thornton 1989). Parental religiosity has been shown to be a more important influence on children's attitudes and behavior than has religious affiliation (Thornton and Camburn 1987; Pearce 2002; Thornton, Axinn, and Hill 1992). The IPS has also shown that parental religiosity positively influences the quality of parent-child relationships and that religious commitment not only influences personal and family behavior but is influenced by children's experience with premarital sex and cohabitation (Thornton and Camburn 1987; Thornton, Axinn, and Hill 1992). The data have shown that several dimensions of parental marital and childbearing experience—including age at marriage, a premarital pregnancy, and experience with divorce—are closely associated with the children's own attitudes and experiences with courtship, cohabitation, and marriage (Thornton and Camburn 1987; Axinn and Thornton 1996; Thornton 1991). Research using these data has shown that parental socioeconomic status is positively related to the children's educational attainment but negatively associated with the rapidity of the children's entrance into intimate relationships (Alwin and Thornton 1984; Axinn, Duncan, and Thornton 1997; Axinn and Thornton 1992).

A major motivation of the original data collection in 1962 centered on the idea that the shift of many activities and relationships from the family to nonfamilial organizations would have important implications for family members. Investigations of this hypothesis have shown that young people who grow up in families with many of the activities of life conducted within the family have higher levels of self-esteem than others. In addition, they are more likely to choose marriage over cohabitation as the first type of intimate co-residential union.

Research using the IPS consistently demonstrates the interweaving of the various strands of life during the children's transition to adulthood. Children's attitudes and values concerning cohabitation and marriage in young adulthood consistently predict subsequent cohabitation and marital behavior, while experience with cohabitation modifies attitudes and values (Axinn and Thornton 1993). In addition, home leaving and entrance into cohabiting and marital unions are closely intertwined with educational achievements (Goldscheider, Thornton, and Young-DeMarco 1993; Thornton, Axinn, and Teachman 1995). Children's own religiosity is also associated with their subsequent marital and cohabiting behavior (Thornton, Axinn, and Hill 1992).

Concluding Comment

In recent decades additional data sets have emerged for the study of family and fertility behavior. Some of these studies have been designed explicitly for the study of family and fertility behavior. In addition, because of the central importance of marriage and family issues to other dimensions of life, many data sets designed for other purposes have proven to be valuable for family and fertility studies. Among the currently available data sets useful for the study of family and fertility issues are the National Study of Children, Americans View Their Mental Health, the General Social Surveys, the National Study of Adolescent Males, the

National Study of the High School Class of 1972, High School and Beyond, the National Longitudinal Study of Youth, Monitoring the Future, the National Survey of Families and Households, and the Panel Study of Income Dynamics, including its Child Development Supplement.

Marriage, childbearing, and family life are so central to the fabric of social life that survey research on these topics is likely to be as great in the next fifty years as it has been in the past fifty years. The future of survey research on these topics is likely to hold innovative new designs and new methodological advances. The new designs may include localized smaller-scale studies of specific topics embedded in national sample designs. They may include the use of new technologies such as the Internet, Palm Pilots, and cellular technology to conduct longitudinal panel studies. Or they may include new methods of obtaining biological measures to study genetic, hormonal, or infectious disease dimensions of fertility and family life. Key advancements in scientific knowledge in the areas of family research are likely to come from the close cooperation of substantive experts, methodologists specializing in data collection, and methodologists specializing in data analysis. The ISR aims to build on its contributions to this area of science over the past fifty years by working with other scientists around the country to advance this area throughout the next fifty years.

NOTES

The authors appreciate the comments and suggestions by Ronald Freedman concerning an earlier draft of this chapter. The discussion of the IPS in this chapter draws upon a more extensive discussion of this data set by Thornton, Freedman, and Axinn (2002).

1. Researchers at the Scripps Foundation were also involved in the design of the 1955 GAF.

2. At that time, self-identified Catholics made up more than one-quarter of the white population of the United States (Freedman, Whelpton, and Campbell 1959).

3. Researchers at the University of Wisconsin's Center for Demography and Ecology were also involved in designing and fielding the National Fertility Studies of 1965 and 1970.

4. The ISR currently has a contract from the National Center for Health Statistics to collect Cycles 6, 7, and 8 of the NSFG.

5. Because the IPS began as a project about the fertility behavior of Detroit women in 1962, it was originally titled Family Growth in Detroit. With the widening geographical distribution of the sample and the expansion of the content in 1980, the project was renamed the Study of American Families. However, because the study is not representative of the larger national population, the study directors were not totally

comfortable with this name and more recently have referred to the project as the Intergenerational Panel Study of Parents and Children.

6. The DAS of the University of Michigan conducts sample surveys in Detroit as part of the training in survey research for graduate students in the social sciences. It is at the same time a research facility for social science faculty. The baseline survey for the IPS was the subject of the DAS research in 1961–62. After that, the reinterviews were conducted by SRC field staff. The research for this study was first based at the Population Studies Center and was directed by Ronald Freedman, David Goldberg, and Lolagene Coombs. Since 1975 it has been based at SRC and the Population Studies Center and directed by Arland Thornton, with Deborah Freedman as his research associate from 1975 to 1995.

REFERENCES

Alwin, D. F., and A. Thornton. 1984. Family origins and the schooling process: Early versus late influence of parental characteristics. *American Sociological Review* 49 (6): 784–802.

Axinn, W. G., G. J. Duncan, and A. Thornton. 1997. The effects of parental income, wealth, and attitudes on children's completed schooling and self-esteem. In *Growing up poor,* ed. G. J. Duncan and J. Brooks-Gunn, 518–30. New York: Russell Sage.

Axinn, W. G., and A. Thornton. 1992. The influence of parental resources on the timing of the transition to marriage. *Social Science Research* 21 (3): 261–85.

———. 1993. Mothers, children, and cohabitation: The intergenerational effects of attitudes and behavior. *American Sociological Review* 58 (2): 233–46.

———. 1996. The influence of parents' marital dissolutions on children's family formation attitudes. *Demography* 33 (1): 66–81.

———. 2000. The transformation in the meaning of marriage. In *Ties that bind: Perspectives on marriage and cohabitation,* ed. L. Waite, C. Bachrach, M. Hindin, E. Thomson, and A. Thornton, 147–65. New York: Aldine de Gruyter.

Axinn, W. G., and S. T. Yabiku. 1999. Community change, the social organization of families, and fertility limitation. Paper presented at the annual meeting of the Population Association of America, March, New York.

Bachrach, C. A., K. A. London, and P. A. Maza. 1991. On the path to adoption: Adoption seeking in the United States. *Journal of Marriage and the Family* 53 (3): 705–18.

Barber, J. S. 2000. Intergenerational influences on the entry into parenthood: Mothers' preferences for family and nonfamily behavior. *Social Forces* 79 (1): 319–48.

Belli, R. F. 1998. The structure of autobiographical memory and the event history calendar: Potential improvements in the quality of retrospective reports in surveys. *Memory* 6 (4): 383–406.

Broude, G. J. 1994. *Marriage, family, and relationships: A cross-cultural encyclopedia.* Santa Barbara, CA: ABC-CLIO.

Brundage, J. A. 1987. *Law, sex, and Christian society in medieval Europe.* Chicago: University of Chicago Press.

Bumpass, L. L., and C. F. Westoff. 1970. *The later years of childbearing.* Princeton: Princeton University Press.

Buss, D. M. 1994. *The evolution of desire.* New York: Basic Books.

Campbell, A. A., and W. D. Mosher. 2000. A history of the measurement of unintended pregnancies and births. *Maternal and Child Health Journal* 4 (3): 163–69.

Caspi, A., T. E. Moffitt, A. Thornton, D. Freedman, J. W. Amell, H. Harrinton, J. Smeijers, and P. A. Silva. 1996. The life history calendar: A research and clinical assessment method for collecting retrospective event-history data. *International Journal of Methods in Psychiatric Research* 6:101–14.

Coombs, L. C. 1979. Reproductive goals and achieved fertility: A fifteen year perspective. *Demography* 16 (4): 523–34.

Coombs, L. C., and R. Freedman. 1970a. Premarital pregnancy, childspacing, and later economic achievement. *Population Studies* 24 (3): 389–412.

———. 1970b. Problems and possibilities in conducting panel fertility studies. *Population Et Famille* 20:1–19.

Daly, M., and M. I. Wilson. 2000. The evolutionary psychology of marriage and divorce. In *Ties that bind: Perspectives on marriage and cohabitation,* ed. L. Waite, C. Bachrach, M. Hinden, E. Thomson, and A. Thornton, 91–110. Hawthorne, NY: Aldine de Gruyter.

d'Avray, D. L. 1985. The gospel of the marriage feast of Cana and marriage preaching in France. In *The Bible in the medieval world: Essays in memory of Beryl Smalley,* ed. K. Walsh and D. Wood, 207–24. Oxford: Basil Blackwell.

d'Avray, D. L., and M. Tausche. 1981. Marriage sermons in ad status collections of the central Middle Ages. In *Archives d'histoire doctrinale et littéraire du moyen age,* ed. É. Gilson, G. Théry, M.-T. d'Alverny, and M.-D. Chenu, 71–119. Paris: Librairee Philosophique J. Vrin.

Diamond, J. M. 1992. *The third chimpanzee: The evolution and future of the human animal.* New York: Harper Collins.

Freedman, R., D. S. Freedman, and A. Thornton. 1980. Changes in fertility expectations and preferences between 1962 and 1977: Their relation to final parity. *Demography* 17 (4): 365–78.

Freedman, D. S., and A. Thornton. 1979. The long-term impact of pregnancy at marriage on the family's economic circumstances. *Family Planning Perspectives* 41 (1): 6–20.

Freedman, D., A. Thornton, D. Camburn, D. Alwin, and L. Young-DeMarco. 1988. The life history calendar: A technique for collecting retrospective data. In *Sociological Methodology,* ed. C. C. Clogg, 37–68. San Francisco: Jossey-Bass.

Freedman, R., P. K. Whelpton, and A. A. Campbell. 1959. *Family planning, sterility, and population growth.* New York: McGraw-Hill.

Glendon, M. A. 1977. *State, law, and family: Family law in transition in the United States and Western Europe.* Amsterdam: North-Holland.

Goldscheider, F., A. Thornton, and L. Young-DeMarco. 1993. A portrait of the nest-leaving process in early adulthood. *Demography* 30 (4): 683–99.

Hanawalt, B. A. 1986. *The ties that bound: Peasant families in Medieval England.* New York: Oxford University Press.

Hauser, P. M., and O. D. Duncan. 1964a. Overview and conclusions. In *The study of population: An inventory and appraisal,* ed. P. M. Hauser, and O. D. Duncan, 1–26. Chicago: University of Chicago Press.

———. 1964b. The data and methods. In *The study of population: An inventory and appraisal,* ed. P. M. Hauser and O. D. Duncan, 45–75. Chicago: University of Chicago Press.

Healthy People. 2000. Statistical notes, 1991–2000. Hyattsville, MD: U.S. Department of Health and Human Services, Public Health Service, Centers for Disease Control.

Herlihy, D. 1985. *Medieval households.* Cambridge, MA: Harvard University Press.

Hershaw, S. K. 1998. Unintended pregnancy in the United States. *Family Planning Perspectives* 30 (1): 24–29.

Hrdy, S. B. 1999. *Mother nature: A history of mothers, infants, and natural selection.* New York: Pantheon.

Linder, F. 1964. World demographic data. In *The study of population: An inventory and appraisal,* ed. P. M. Hauser and O. D. Duncan, 321–60. Chicago: University of Chicago Press.

Lorimer, F. 1964. The development of demography. In *The study of population: An inventory and appraisal,* ed. P. M. Hauser and O. D. Duncan, 124–79. Chicago: University of Chicago Press.

Mosher, W. D. 1982. Fertility and family planning in the 1970s: The National Survey of Family Growth. *Family Planning Perspectives* 14 (6): 314–20.

———. 1988. Fertility and family planning in the United States: Insights from the National Survey of Family Growth. *Family Planning Perspectives* 20 (5): 207–17.

Mosher, W. D., and C. A. Bachrach. 1996. Understanding U.S. fertility: Continuity and change in the National Survey of Family Growth, 1988–1995. *Family Planning Perspectives* 28 (1): 4–12.

NCHS. 1997. Plan and operation of the 1995 National Survey of Family and Growth. *Vital and Health Statistics* (series 1) 36.

Nisbet, R. A. 1980. *History of the idea of progress.* New York: Basic Books.

Notestein, F. W. 1982. Demography in the United States: A partial account of the development of the field. *Population and Development Review* 8 (4): 651–88.

Ogburn, W. F., and C. Tibbitts. 1933. The family and its functions. In *Recent social trends in the United States, Report 1,* ed. Presidents Research Committee of Social Trends, 661–708. New York: McGraw-Hill.

Parsons, T., and R. F. Bales. 1955. *Family, socialization, and interaction process.* Glencoe, IL: Free Press.

Pearce, L. 2002. The influence of early life course religious exposure on young adults' dispositions toward childbearing. *Journal for the Scientific Study of Religion* 41 (2): 325–40.

Pearce, L., and W. G. Axinn. 1988. The impact of family religious life on the quality of parent-child relationships. *American Sociological Review* 63 (6): 810–28.

Peterson, W. 1999. *Malthus: Founder of modern demography.* New Brunswick, NJ: Transaction.

Phillips, R. 1988. *Putting asunder: A history of divorce in Western society.* Cambridge: Cambridge University Press.

Ryder, N. B. 1964. Fertility. In *The study of population: An inventory and appraisal,* ed. P. M. Hauser and O. D. Duncan, 400–436. Chicago: University of Chicago Press.

———. 1973. A critique of the National Fertility Study. *Demography* 10 (4): 495–506.

Ryder, N. B., and C. F. Westoff. 1971. *Reproduction in the United States, 1965.* Princeton: Princeton University Press.

Thornton, A. 1985. Changing attitudes toward separation and divorce: Causes and consequences. *American Journal of Sociology* 90 (4): 856–72.

———. 1988. Cohabitation and marriage in the 1980s. *Demography* 25 (4): 497–508.

———. 1991. Influence of the marital history of parents on the marital and cohabitational experiences of children. *American Journal of Sociology* 96 (4): 868–94.

———. 2001. The developmental paradigm, reading history sideways, and family change. *Demography* 38 (4): 449–65.

Thornton, A., D. Alwin, and D. Camburn. 1983. Causes and consequences of sex role attitude change. *American Sociological Review* 48 (2): 211–27.

Thornton, A., W. G. Axinn, and D. Hill. 1992. Reciprocal effects of religiosity, cohabitation, and marriage. *American Journal of Sociology* 98 (3): 628–51.

Thornton, A., W. G. Axinn, and J. D. Teachman. 1995. The influence of school enrollment and accumulation on cohabitation and marriage in early adulthood. *American Sociological Review* 60 (5): 762–74.

Thornton, A., and D. Camburn. 1987. The influence of the family on premarital sexual attitudes and behavior. *Demography* 24 (3): 323–40.

Thornton, A., D. Freedman, and D. Camburn. 1982. Obtaining respondent cooperation in family panel studies. *Sociological Methods and Research* 11 (1): 33–51.

Thornton, A., R. Freedman, and W. G. Axinn. 2002. Intergenerational panel study of parents and children. In *Looking at lives: American longitudinal studies of the twentieth century*, ed. E. Phelps, F. F. Furstenburg, and A. Colby, 315–44. New York: Russell Sage Foundation.

Thornton, A., and L. Young-DeMarco. 2001. Four decades of trends in attitudes toward family issues in the United States: The 1960s through the 1990s. *Journal of Marriage and the Family* 63 (4): 1009–37.

Weinstein, M., and A. Thornton. 1989. Mother-child relations and adolescent sexual attitudes and behavior. *Demography* 26 (4): 563–77.

Westoff, C. F. 1975. The yield of the imperfect: The 1970 National Fertility Study. *Demography* 12 (4): 573–80.

Westoff, C. F., R. G. Potter Jr., and P. C. Sagi. 1963. *The third child: A study in the prediction of fertility.* Princeton: Princeton University Press.

Westoff, C. F., R. G. Potter Jr., P. C. Sagi, and E. G. Mishler. 1961. *Family growth in metropolitan America.* Princeton: Princeton University Press.

Westoff, C. F., and N. B. Ryder. 1977. *The contraceptive revolution.* Princeton: Princeton University Press.

Whelpton, P. K., A. A. Campbell, and J. E. Patterson. 1966. *Fertility and family planning in the United States.* Princeton: Princeton University Press.

Whelpton, P. K., and C. V. Kiser. 1943–45. *Social and psychological factors affecting fertility.* Vol. 1, *The Household Survey in Indianapolis.* New York: Milbank Memorial Fund.

———. 1945–50. *Social and psychological factors affecting fertility*, Vol. 2, *The intensive study: Purpose, scope, methods, and partial results.* New York: Milbank Memorial Fund.

———. 1954–56, 1958. *Social and psychological factors affecting fertility.* Vol. 5, *Concluding reports and summary of chief findings from the Indianapolis study.* New York: Milbank Memorial Fund.

Witte, J., Jr. 1997. *From sacrament to contract: Marriage, religion, and law in the Western tradition.* Louisville, KY: Westminster John Knox Press.

CHAPTER 11

Studying the Transition from Youth to Adulthood: Impacts on Substance Use and Abuse

Patrick M. O'Malley, Jerald G. Bachman, Lloyd D. Johnston, and John Schulenberg

Importance of the Transition from Youth to Adulthood

The processes by which individuals develop and improve themselves have become a major focus for social scientists over the course of the twentieth century. Developmental psychologists took the lead, with an emphasis on development in early life, particularly its first two decades. Sociologists have become conspicuous in life-course studies, emphasizing development and change across the entire life span and placing life-span development in a broader contextual framework including historical period and cohort as well as environmental factors. Emphasis has increasingly shifted from early studies of a young developing organism with little regard for the environment beyond the family to studies of human development across the entire age span and within complex and ever-changing environmental contexts.

Such life-course studies have tended to focus on transitions from one phase of life to another. A variety of transitions occur, but none more important than that from adolescence to adulthood. The concept of adolescence (a period during which a young person has undergone puberty but has not reached full maturity) as a fairly long, well-delineated phase of development is relatively new. In most times and places, the transition from childhood to adulthood was not an extended period. As a consequence of industrialization, however, children began to spend more time in school, and the time from childhood to full adulthood became extended (Crockett 1997). In the twentieth century, adolescence has been studied intensively, and the transition from adolescence to young adulthood is now viewed as a critical developmental transition with major sequelae throughout the life span.

Critical to understanding this or any transition is the distinction between selection and socialization and the closely related concepts of stability and change. By the end of high school, much has already occurred for adolescents that will affect their transition to adulthood. Academically successful college-bound adolescents are different in many ways from their non-college-bound counterparts. Thus, although there are important differences between college graduates and non–college graduates, many of those differences are due to long-standing factors that predate the college experience. In other words, a selection effect occurs such that individuals who select themselves (or are selected by others) into particular environments differ from those who do not select those environments.

Socialization, on the other hand, refers to the process by which an environment (or social role) produces changes in individuals. For example, the college experience and environment may produce changes that would not have occurred otherwise. Selection tends to promote or reflect stability, whereas socialization tends to promote or reflect change.

The study of change was affected by a number of circumstances that emerged shortly after midcentury. One was recognition of the need for the study of the human life course within social and historical context. One of the leaders of the study of life course notes that, while he was in graduate school from 1958 to 1962, the concept of life course had not yet appeared in the scholarly literature (Elder 1998); however, the decade of the 1960s changed that substantially. Another factor was the continuing methodological advances in the social sciences in the study of change (Baltes and Nesselroade 1979). A series of insightful works was published in the 1960s, including Bereiter 1963, Bohrnstedt 1969, Campbell and Stanley 1967, Coleman 1968, Cronbach and Furby 1970, and Lord 1963. Common to all of the methodological advances was the need for carefully designed and executed longitudinal studies.

Another important circumstance affecting the study of change was the willingness of the federal government to sponsor large-scale longitudinal survey research that would investigate the phenomenon of change in individuals' lives. Thus, in 1965 the Department of Labor contracted for studies of four different age-gender cohorts in order to understand better the sources of variation in labor market behavior and experiences. These National Longitudinal Surveys provided a wealth of labor-force-related information that was critical to the development of labor market policies. Initially the focus was much more on labor market variables. Over the years, however, other government agencies have funded components of the surveys that provided data relevant to their missions. As a result, the surveys now include data about a wide range of events such as schooling and career transitions, marriage and fertility, training investments, child-care usage, and drug and alcohol use. The depth and breadth of each survey allow for analysis of a variety of topics, such as the transition from school to work, job mobility, youth unemployment, educational attainment and the returns to education, welfare recipiency, the impact of training, and retirement decisions (Parnes and Sproat 1984; see also <http://stats.bls.gov>).

In 1960, Project TALENT, the largest long-range educational research project ever attempted, began under funding from the Office of Education. The goals of the longitudinal component of this project were to develop a national inventory of human resources, to achieve a better understanding of how young people choose and develop in their careers, and to identify the educational and life experiences that are most important in preparing individuals for their life work. Project TALENT was also an attempt to determine why so much of the nation's human potential was being lost because of a lack of appropriate education, and what schools, counselors, and parents could do to reduce this loss (Steel, Wise, and Abeles 1984). Impetus for this project was provided in part by the successful launching of a satellite into orbit by the Soviet Union in 1957, leading many to question whether the United States was making sufficient use of its human potential.

The NLS and Project TALENT are two of the more ambitious efforts that characterized the field of survey research in the 1960s. Both were conducted under government contracts, which means that there was a considerable degree of control of the research by the federal government. Yet both were also very much embodiments of social scientific research.

A third major study was also initiated in the 1960s, the Youth in Transition project at the University of Michigan Survey Research Center (SRC). The effect of failure to complete high school had become an increasingly important issue for social scientists and society. The YIT project set out to follow a nationally representative single panel of young men from age fifteen to twenty-three. This (and similar other studies, including Project TALENT and the NLS) produced a number of lessons regarding how large-scale survey research could shed new light on the transition from youth to adulthood (Bachman et al. 1997).

First, social scientists saw the critical need for longitudinal designs, which could determine if dropping out of high school led to differences between dropouts and graduates or if it merely maintained long-standing differences that predated the dropping out. Second, nationally representative samples were seen as important for a variety of reasons, especially if the results were to inform national policy. "External validity" had recently been recognized as important for any research, and nationally representative samples have an obvious claim to external validity. Third, scientists also recognized that a large-scale study whose principal purpose was, for example, to examine the effects of dropping out could be a vehicle to address a variety of other purposes as well. (There are significant cost efficiencies when multiple purposes are served in a single survey.) Fourth, the SRC sample of students became the basis for one of the earliest major studies incorporating a contextual approach; in this case the context was the high school. Late in the twentieth century, combining the study of individuals within larger contexts (e.g., family, school, neighborhood, community, and state) emerged as a major research focus.

Finally, one of the most significant lessons learned from the YIT study was the realization that many questions about development and transition could not be answered with just a single cohort. One example occurred with a measure of trust in government. The extent of trust that respondents professed to have in government declined with age in the YIT sample of young men as they matured from age fifteen to twenty-three. But the cohort was age fifteen in the fall of 1966 and twenty-three in the spring of 1974. This was the era of an unpopular war in Vietnam, the revelations of Watergate, the assassinations of Martin Luther King and Robert F. Kennedy, and a great deal of dissatisfaction—perhaps growing dissatisfaction—with government institutions. Thus, one could not know from a single cohort if the decline in trust in government was indeed an age-related phenomenon or if it reflected processes that were occurring across all or most of the age bands in the society as a whole (Bachman and Jennings 1975). That is, consistent with the basic tenets of what was then emerging as the life-span development movement in psychology (e.g., Baltes 1968; Schaie 1965) and the life-course movement in sociology (e.g., Elder 1974; Ryder 1965), it is necessary to distinguish among age-graded effects, history-graded birth cohort effects, and population-level secular trends, or period effects (e.g., Nesselroade and Baltes 1979). In the example of trust in government, other research showed clearly that the decline occurred across all age groups and thus constituted a period effect rather than an age or cohort effect (House and Mason 1975).

Hence, there was and is a need for multiple cohorts, studied across time, with continued additions of new cohorts. Thus was born the Youth and Social Issues program at SRC, centered around a new major study, Monitoring the Future, which incorporated such a design. Initiated at the beginning of the fourth quarter of the century, MTF currently continues to add new cohorts every year. It was initially conceived in part as a broad social indicators study, designed to assess several kinds of changes (and stabilities) that might be occurring among American young people:

- changes from one high school class cohort to another (cohort effects)
- life cycle or maturational changes that appear consistently for all cohorts (age effects)
- changes in particular years reflected across all age groups (period effects, or secular trends)
- changes linked to different environments (high school, college, employment) or role transitions (departure from the parental home, marriage, parenthood)

Despite MTF's potentials for understanding the nature of the transition from youth to adulthood in the rapidly changing context of American society, little enthusiasm was found among potential sponsors for a study with the breadth of content initially envisioned.

At about the time the study was proposed, however, substance use among American youth was emerging as a major social problem. The epidemic of illicit drug use was unprecedented in our society, emerging first among college students and other young adults but soon thereafter spreading to adolescents of increasingly younger ages. Because the use and abuse of substances—both licit and illicit—can have major impacts on the behaviors and attitudes of youth as they make transitions from adolescence to young adulthood, the drug problem became a matter of great concern at all levels of society. That concern led the federal government to provide financial support for the monitoring of these types of problems and for in-depth study of individual and environmental causes and consequences of the various component behaviors. A cohort-sequential design would permit the examination of the effects of age, period, and cohort, as well as different environmental and social role transitions, and thus would facilitate the search for causal explanations (Johnston et al.

1996). The initial support for MTF came from the White House's Special Action Office on Drug Abuse Prevention; within a year it was transferred to the newly established National Institute on Drug Abuse, which has continued funding the study since, under a series of competitive investigator-initiated research grants. Although focused on substance use and abuse since its inception, MTF, in its study of that problem and related aspects of the lives of adolescents and young adults, has contributed to modifying and shaping our understanding not only of substance use but also of more general aspects of development in adolescence and early adulthood.

Substance Use and the Transition from Youth to Adulthood

Substance use and abuse is a particularly important set of health-related behaviors, especially among youth, for a number of reasons. The societal impact of tobacco, alcohol, and illicit drug use is extraordinarily high—a recent study estimates that the economic cost to the nation of alcohol and drug abuse was $246 billion in 1992, the most recent year for which sufficient data were available (Harwood, Fountain, and Livermore 1998). The extraordinary societal costs of tobacco use are well established. In addition to the estimated more than four hundred thousand premature deaths per year attributable to smoking, the costs include those associated with direct health care. These have resulted in a settlement agreement with almost all states, in which the major tobacco companies have agreed to pay the states well over $200 billion through the year 2025 and over $32 billion within the first five years. Additional tobacco costs include those from direct exposure to secondhand smoke, smoking-caused fires, and smokeless tobacco use, as well as costs from lost or reduced work productivity (Warner 1998).

Adolescence and young adulthood are developmental periods of particular importance for understanding and preventing the onset of substance use and abuse problems, because the great majority of substance use begins in adolescence or early adulthood.

Individual differences in the natural history of substance use and abuse are played out for the most part during the second and third decades of life. Some young adults smoke cigarettes, some drink excessively, some use illicit drugs, and some do combinations of these. Many of these behaviors change over time. Why do some individuals substantially change their patterns of drug use after high school, while others do not? In this chapter we focus on this question, considering specifically how the various transitions from adolescence to young adulthood lead to changes in drug use.

Monitoring the Future as an Instrument for Understanding the Drug Problem

The remainder of this chapter focuses primarily on what might be called the drug problem in the mainstream of the population. Findings are based on analyses of the MTF series of surveys that included on an annual basis a national sample of individuals who remained in high school through the end of their senior year and subsamples of those who participated in panel surveys extending into young adulthood. Marginalized individuals (e.g., active criminals, incarcerated persons, homeless persons, hard-core addicts) are less likely to be reached by mail survey attempts and less likely to complete and return questionnaires. Thus the study does not cover all youth and young adults, and most likely the individuals who were omitted were disproportionately involved in heavy drug use and other problem behaviors.

Nevertheless, we believe that the participating respondents constitute a broadly representative sample of high school graduates in the United States. Certainly, the drug-using and drug-abusing behaviors examined here constitute a very important portion of the nation's drug problem, and the processes whereby a great many of the nation's young adults "mature out" of youthful drug use and abuse are important for understanding why others do not. The study includes a substantial proportion of all young adults who are habitual cigarette smokers, as well as many who occasionally drink to excess, some of whom eventually become chronic alcohol abusers. Although the research underrepresents those who are deeply involved in the illicit drug subculture, it does include a great many who use illicit drugs (particularly marijuana but also cocaine) on at least an occasional basis and often on a more than occasional basis.

Secular Trends (Period Effects) in Drug Use

How likely is it that a young adult is a user of a particular drug? The answer to that question depends on several factors: the drug being considered; individual factors such as age, marital status, gender, race; and the historical period in which the question is asked, because dramatic changes in drug use have occurred in the last few decades. As late as 1960, the average young adult was highly unlikely to have ever used marijuana, but that likelihood changed dramatically by 1970, as use of marijuana increased, and increased through the 1970s. As shown in figure 11.1, by 1980 the odds were about two to one that an average young adult between eighteen and twenty-five years old had used marijuana at least once (Substance Abuse and Mental Health Services Administration 1997, 1999). After peaking around 1980, marijuana use declined, so that by 1990 the average young adult was less than half as likely to be a current marijuana user as the average young adult in 1980 (as shown in the lower curve in fig. 11.1).

So one important determinant of drug use among young adults—or adolescents or older adults, for that matter—is simply the historical period in which they live. Especially with respect to illicit drugs, the probability of use is closely related to the type of drugs in vogue. More important for science and social policy is understanding the factors that seem to influence individuals' drug-using behaviors. We focus on age (or maturational) effects—changes with age, and the experiences and transitions cor-

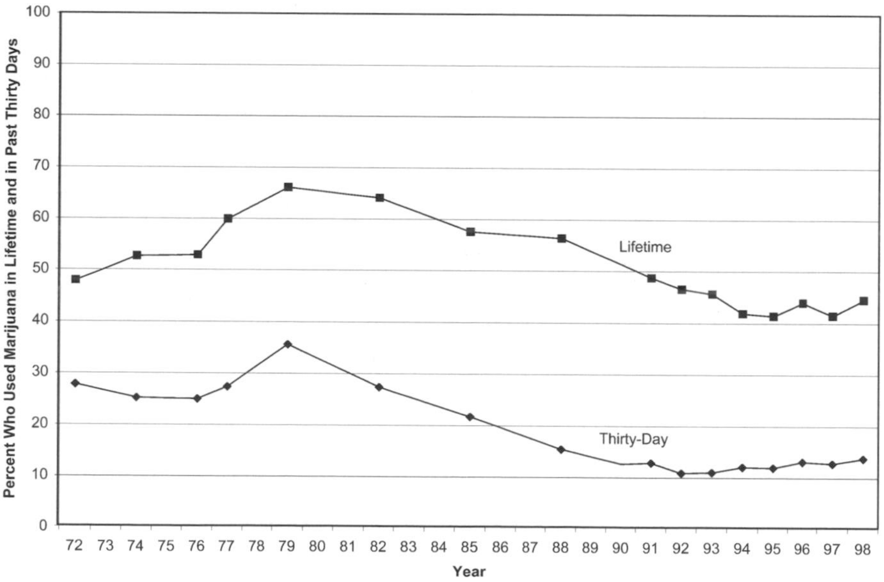

FIG. 11.1. Trends in lifetime and thirty-day marijuana use among young adults, ages eighteen to twenty-five, 1972–98. (Data from Substance Abuse and Mental Health Services Administration 1997, 1999.)

related with aging, that tend to be common across cohorts and across recent historical periods. But it should be clear that changes associated with age are not necessarily fixed; rather, they may vary by cohort and by historical period (O'Malley, Bachman, and Johnston 1988; Schulenberg et al. 2000).

Perceptions and Attitudes about Drugs

Among the most important determinants of the popularity of illicit drugs in recent years has been disapproval of their use and perceptions that their use entails real risks of harm, physical or otherwise. We have tracked these attitudes and perceptions since 1975 and have shown that they correspond very closely with (and sometimes slightly precede) changes in drug use (Johnston 1982, 1985; Johnston, O'Malley, and Bachman 1999a). We have also demonstrated that increased disapproval and perceptions of risk largely account for the overall declines in marijuana use during much of the 1980s and for later declines in cocaine use, and we have shown that declines in disapproval and perceived risk accompany the more recent increases in use (Bachman et al. 1988; Bachman, Johnston, and O'Malley 1990, 1998).

Figures 11.2 and 11.3 show the association between perceived risk of harm and use for marijuana and for cocaine. In contrast, perceived availability of marijuana and cocaine, unlike the measures of perceived risk, show little or no association with use. The effect of these widely disseminated findings has been to help move the national strategy for drug control in the direction of a demand-side approach. This has included substantially increased federal funding for school-based prevention programs and the development of a national antidrug advertising campaign (which was first developed outside of government and now continues with bipartisan federal financial assistance). In addition, the theory of drug epidemics that grew out of these findings (Johnston 1991), along with the study's identification of the emergence of new substances, has guided efforts in the federal public health establishment toward generating as soon as possible clinical and scientific evidence on the adverse consequences of newer drugs, so that those findings may be disseminated to the youth population in order to alter their perceptions of the dangers of those new drugs. These impacts of the study have derived primarily from the repeated cross-sectional results rather than from the individual longitudinal studies looking at developmental change, a subject to which we now turn.

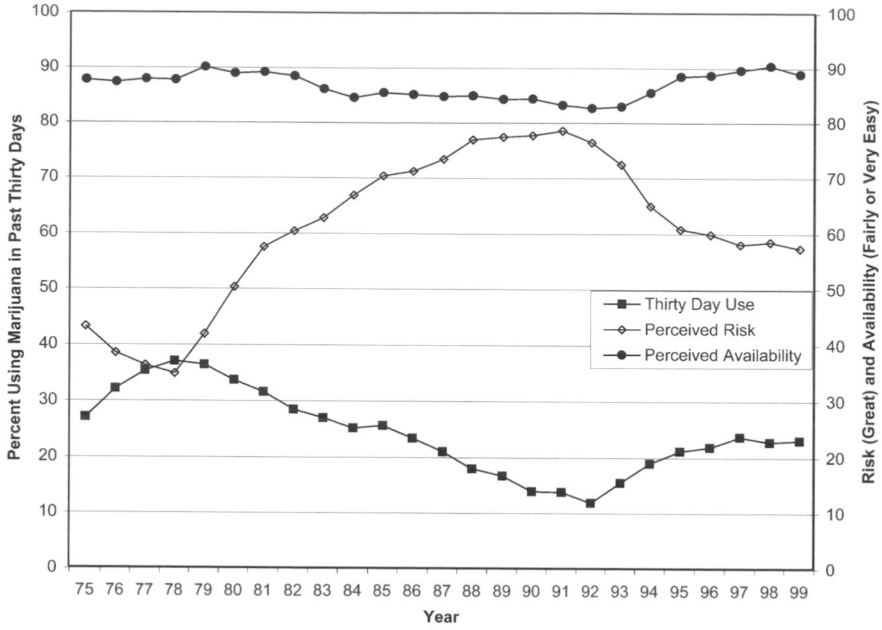

FIG. 11.2. Marijuana: Trends in perceived risk, perceived availability, and prevalence of thirty-day use, high school seniors, 1975–99. "Perceived risk" is percentage saying there is great risk of harm in regular use. "Perceived availability" is percentage saying marijuana is fairly easy or very easy to get. See Johnston, O'Malley, and Bachman 1999a for more details.

Stability of Drug Use during Young Adulthood

The best predictor of a young adult's use of drugs is likely to be that individual's use of the same drug a year or two earlier. We have found high cross-time correlations in drug use, even though such correlations are diminished by unavoidable measurement errors (O'Malley, Bachman, and Johnston 1983), especially when they involve a limited time interval such as two weeks (for a measure of heavy drinking) or thirty days (for the other drugs). Progress in the last quarter-century in estimating and adjusting for measurement errors in longitudinal designs, particularly with three or more time points, has allowed for the estimation of the actual stability of drug use, where stability is defined as the correlation between two true (i.e., error-free) variables assessed at different points in time.

Each of the four substances discussed here (cigarettes, alcohol, mari-

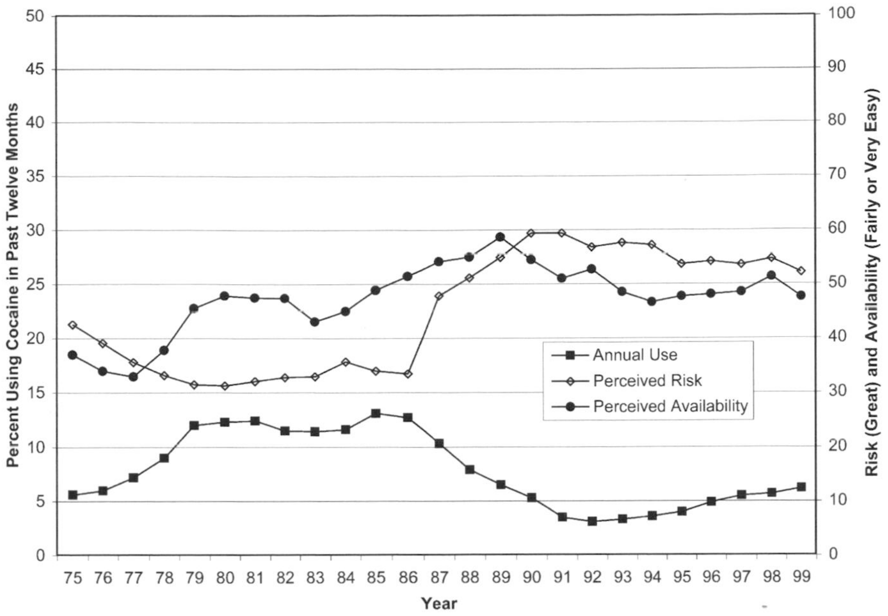

FIG. 11.3. Cocaine: Trends in perceived risk, perceived availability, and prevalence of twelve-month use, high school seniors, 1975–99. "Perceived risk" is percentage saying there is great risk of harm in experimental use. "Perceived availability" is percentage saying cocaine is fairly easy or very easy to get. See Johnston, O'Malley, and Bachman 1999a for more details.

juana, and cocaine) showed very high levels of stability over one-year intervals (Bachman et al. 1997). In the first year after high school stability rates are quite high, ranging from a low of about 0.8 for cocaine to a high of just over 0.9 for cigarettes. The already high annual stability rates increase with age, reflecting fewer environmental and role changes as individuals settle into their adult lives. In spite of the high annual stability rates of these four substances, there is still considerable room for change over an extended period. The cumulative stability rates across the fourteen-year span covered, from age eighteen to thirty-two, are about 0.65 for cigarette use, about 0.45 for alcohol use and marijuana use, and only about 0.25 for cocaine use. Although change during any one year is fairly limited, changes cumulate with each additional year, producing considerable change over the entire period.

For example, many forms of substance use escalate, peak, and decline during the period between late adolescence and young adulthood. Figure 11.4 shows how age (thirteen to thirty-two) is associated with marijuana use (any use in the past twelve months) and with heavy drinking (having five or more drinks in a row at least once in the past two weeks). This figure shows substantial changes associated with age, including in the post–high school years, from ages nineteen to thirty-two. So, while substance use over short periods of time tends to be quite stable in terms of individual differences, important mean level changes in substance use occur during this time. As discussed later, the individual course of substance use in young adulthood depends heavily on post–high school environments and experiences.

Similarities and Differences among Drug-Using Behaviors

Although we often use the term "drug use," there are many distinctions among the various classes of drugs in their use patterns. A major distinction is that the proportions of users, and the amount of use among users, vary greatly by drug. For example, in 1998 two-thirds of young adults

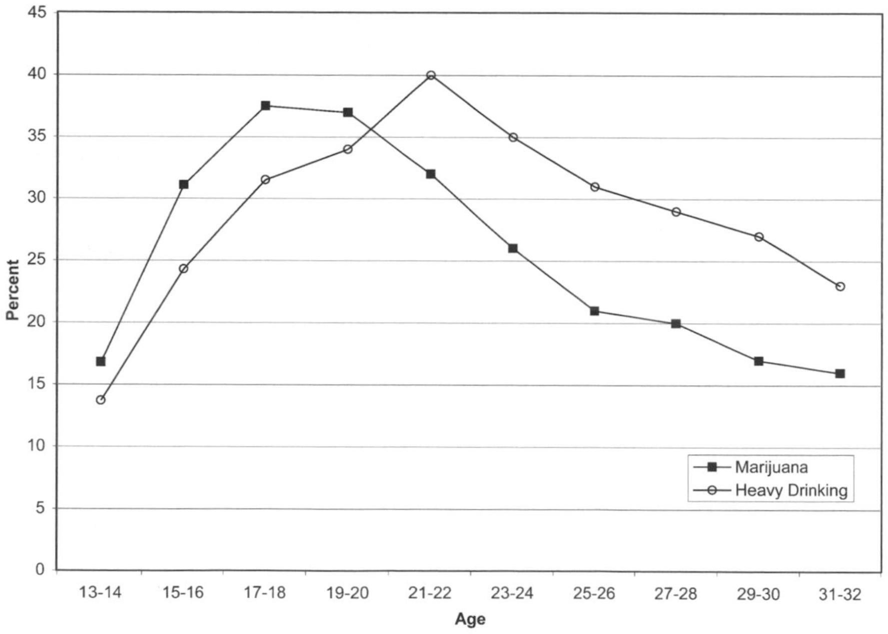

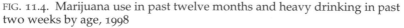

FIG. 11.4. Marijuana use in past twelve months and heavy drinking in past two weeks by age, 1998

were current alcohol users (defined as use in the past month), 13 percent were current marijuana users, and fewer than 2 percent were current cocaine users (Johnston, O'Malley, and Bachman 1999b). Fewer young adults smoke cigarettes than drink alcohol; approximately 30 percent were current smokers in 1998. However, about 21 percent of young adults were daily cigarette smokers, while only about 4 percent of young adults drank on a daily basis. In addition, usage rates of the various drugs have followed very different overall trends, even in the past twenty-five years, and have shown different patterns of age-related change, although all drugs decline in use by the time young adults reach their late twenties and early thirties.

These differences among drug use patterns make it desirable to consider the drugs separately rather than to combine them into a single composite measure of "drug use in young adulthood." Nevertheless, the various drugs have a number of important similarities in the ways that use seems to be linked with post–high school experiences.

Effects of Post–High School Experiences

Changes in roles and experiences contribute to changes in post–high school drug use, with changes in drug use sometimes also preceding and contributing to changes in role status. Nonexperimental studies in natural settings cannot prove causation—even when the analyses employ multiple waves of longitudinal data. Nevertheless, longitudinal panel data can be very helpful in narrowing the range of plausible causal interpretations. Moreover, panel data can play a very important role in sorting out the effects of selection (i.e., preexisting differences) from those of socialization. We will refer to the "impacts" or "effects" of post–high school roles and experiences on drug use, with the proviso that the causal interpretation has not been proved definitively but rather seems to be the most plausible in light of the available evidence.

After graduation from high school, most young adults embark on one of two primary paths—many become full-time college students, and most others enter full-time employment. This key decision has many important correlates; most notably, the full-time college students tend to defer marriage and parenthood, and many of them leave their parents' homes earlier than their age-mates who do not go to college. We believe that the decision of whether or not to attend college is the most fundamental decision. Other decisions then follow from that one, including further decisions having to do with employment, living arrangements, and the timing of marriage. This perspective is similar to the differential socialization hypothesis (cf. Chassin et al. 1992; Schulenberg et al. 1994; Yamaguchi and Kandel 1985b) that early academic success and college attendance represent primary selection factors that channel young adults toward specific socialization experiences. In the following sections we summarize how changes in drug use are linked (bivariately) with a variety of post–high school experiences—college, military service, other employment, engagement, cohabitation, marriage, pregnancy, parenthood, divorce, and other aspects of living arrangements. The details of the complete multivariate analyses can be found in Bachman et al. 1997. In general, those multivariate analyses were linear regressions that included the various post–high school role statuses and experiences, plus a standard set of control variables (race, region of country, high school grade point average, educational aspirations, and urbanicity). Our analyses indicate that the effects discussed here are in fact primarily additive, with just a few exceptions. As might be expected, patterns differ somewhat between men and women, especially the impacts of single parenthood and the distinction between pregnant women and men with pregnant spouses.

Student Status

College attendance has become quite common for young Americans. Among MTF participants, all of whom are high school graduates, a majority were full-time students during the first two years after high school, and many continued to be full-time students after that time period.

One of the largest differences between college students and their noncollege age-mates (i.e., high school graduates one to four years post–high school) is in the rates of daily cigarette smoking: students are much less likely to be daily smokers. This difference is very evident even prior to college attendance. As shown in figure 11.5, high school students who go on to college directly after high school are less likely to be smokers than those who do not go on to college, consistent with a selection effect interpretation. But there is also evidence for some socialization effect because cigarette smoking increased more among nonstudents than among full-time students.

With respect to alcohol use, particularly occasional heavy drinking (sometimes referred to as "binge drinking"), the difference between college students and nonstudents is very different than the pattern for cigarettes. College students show higher rates of alcohol use, particularly heavy drinking, than their noncollege peers. However, the impact of college attendance is greater than would be suggested by a cross-sectional com-

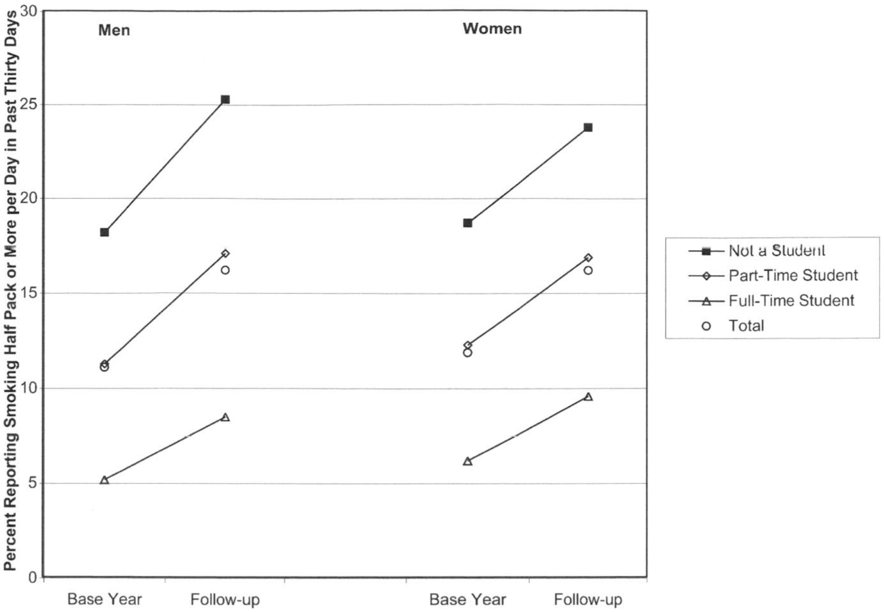

FIG. 11.5. Half pack or more daily smoking by gender and student status. Base year refers to measurement in senior year of high school. Follow-up refers to measurement at ages nineteen to twenty-two (one to four years postgraduation). (Data from the high school classes of 1976–94. See Bachman et al. 1997 for more details.)

parison of the post–high school data, because during high school, those who were college-bound showed lower rates of occasional heavy drinking than the non-college-bound students, as shown in figure 11.6. Thus, the impact of college attendance is to reverse the preexisting difference.

We believe that a major part of the college effect is due to living arrangements. College students are more likely to have moved out of the parental home, to remain single, and to be living in dormitories or other housing involving same-age roommates. When living arrangements are included in multivariate analyses, the impact of student status is reduced. Furthermore, within the student groups, there were also important differences between students who were members of fraternities or sororities and other students, with the fraternity and sorority members being much more likely to engage in heavy drinking (Johnston, O'Malley, and Bachman 1988).

Marijuana use also evidenced a closing of a similar preexisting gap, in

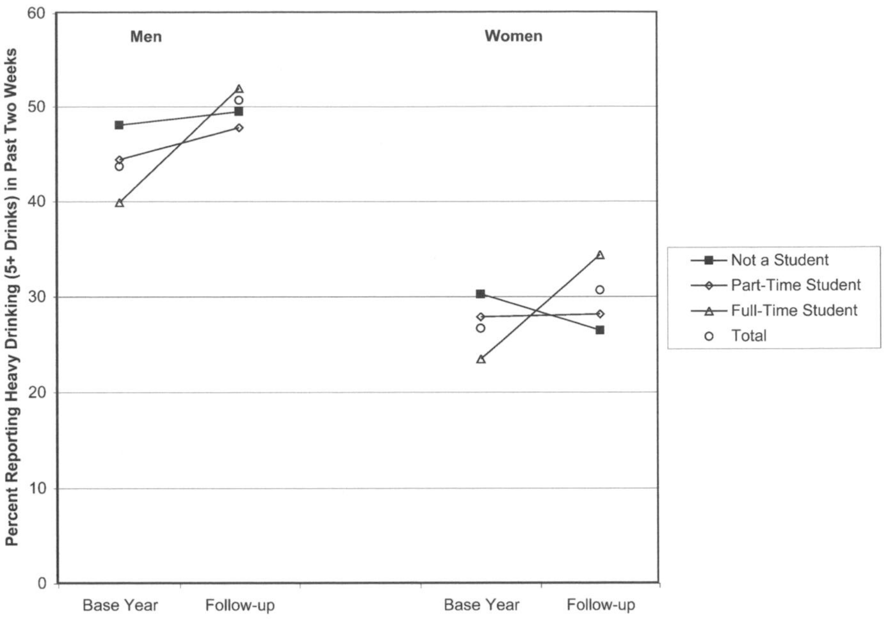

FIG. 11.6. Heavy drinking in past two weeks by gender and student status. Base-year refers to measurement in senior year of high school. Follow-up refers to measurement at ages nineteen to twenty-two (one to four years postgraduation). (Data from the high school classes of 1976–94. See Bachman et al. 1997 for more details.)

which the college-bound individuals were less frequent users. Use rose (slightly) among college students during the first four years after high school but declined (slightly) among nonstudents during this period. In this case there was convergence, but not an actual reversal of the difference, as shown in figure 11.7. Furthermore, multivariate analyses suggest lower than average increases in cocaine use among students, after living arrangements were taken into account. Thus, college attendance appears to have some effect in increasing use of alcohol and marijuana but not cocaine.

Employment and Military Status

After adjustments for student status and marital and living arrangements, the effects of employment status are very slight, including, perhaps sur-

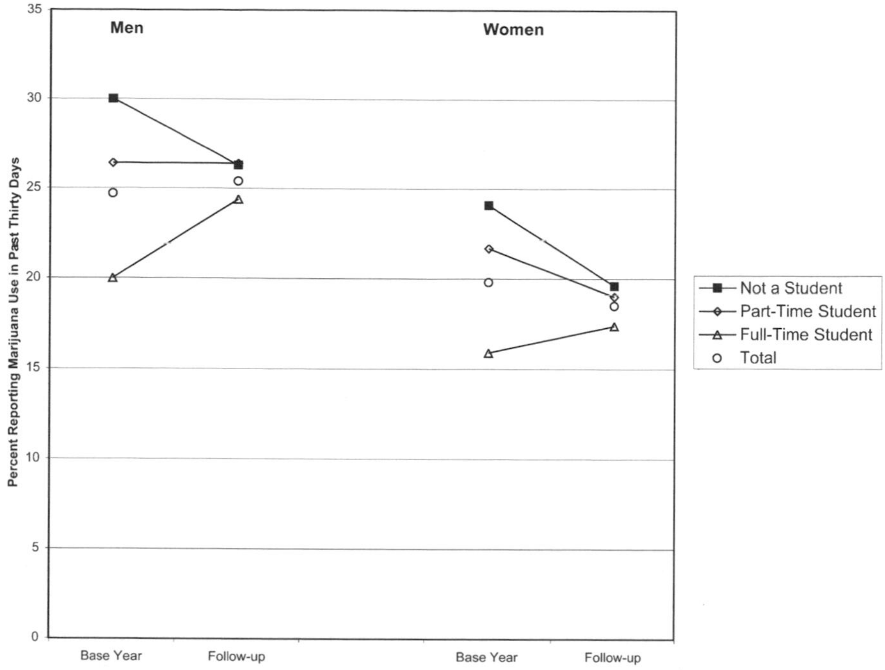

FIG. 11.7. Marijuana use in past thirty days by gender and student status. Base-year refers to measurement in senior year of high school. Follow-up refers to measurement at ages nineteen to twenty-two (one to four years postgraduation). (Data from the high school classes of 1976–94. See Bachman et al. 1997 for more details.)

prisingly, the effects of unemployment. Other longitudinal research also has favored a selection interpretation, linking early drug use to later job instability but finding no causal link from unemployment to adult substance use (Kandel and Yamaguchi 1987; Newcomb and Bentler 1985; Yamaguchi and Kandel 1985b).

Serving in the armed forces was linked with changes in drug use; however, multivariate analyses indicated that the changes were largely independent of other role statuses and responsibilities. In contrast to virtually all other effects found for post–high school experiences and environments, the effects of military service were in opposite directions, with licit drug use (alcohol and tobacco) tending to increase and illicit drug use (particularly marijuana and cocaine) tending to decrease. The differences emerged after high school, for the most part, suggesting the effect of socialization rather than selection. Most likely, the use of random testing for illicit drugs, with immediate severe consequences of testing positive, explains the decline in illicit drug use (Bachman et al. 1999).

Marital Status and Living Arrangements

Perhaps the most fundamental distinction among living arrangements is whether or not an individual is married (and living with a spouse, i.e., not separated). Not surprisingly, then, marriage and the commitment to marriage (engagement) are associated with significant reductions in drinking alcohol and in using marijuana and cocaine. The variety of lifestyle changes that accompany marriage (and engagement)—new responsibilities, mutual caring, intimacy, increased adult contacts, less time spent in singles activities such as bars and parties—seems likely to decrease recreational use of psychoactive substances. The strength of the socialization effects reinforces the importance of the marital relationship in altering behavior.

One living arrangement that has become much more common at the end of the twentieth century compared to the beginning of the century is cohabitation. For respondents in this role status, the data evidence both selection and socialization effects. Those who were cohabiting at the time of a follow-up survey were considerably more likely than average to have been drug users during high school. This was true for both licit drugs and illicit drugs but was particularly so for the illicit drugs. At the time of the follow-up, in general those who were cohabiting were more likely to have increased their use of cigarettes and cocaine, suggesting socialization effects. (These patterns of increased difference were not evident among the cohabiters who were engaged.)

These mixed findings are consistent with earlier studies that provide evidence of selection into cohabitation based on early substance use and unconventional beliefs (Newcomb 1987; Nock 1995; Thornton, Axinn, and Hill 1992; Yamaguchi and Kandel 1985a), as well as socialization influences of cohabitation (Axinn and Thornton 1992; Bachman, O'Malley, and Johnston 1984; Newcomb 1987). The impacts of cohabitation may be quite substantial and may differ depending on how cohabitation fits into the life course. For some individuals, cohabiting may be essentially a short-term precursor to marriage; for others, it may be a long-term alternative to formal marriage; and for others, it may be very different from marriage, reflecting a much lower level of commitment. The effects of cohabitation on substance use will likely vary depending on the different ways that cohabitation fits into the life course.

Young adults who continued to live with their parents showed about average levels of change for all four substances. Basically, these individuals do not experience the greater freedoms associated with moving out and living with age-mates, particularly in college environments, nor do they experience the new commitments and responsibilities of marriage. Thus, their patterns of change fall between the patterns for those who have moved on to other living arrangements.

Among noncollege youth, there were relatively few young adults who reported living alone; they showed slightly greater than average increases in cigarette smoking and alcohol use but no significant differences in changes in marijuana or cocaine use.

Not discussed here is a final residual group, not otherwise classified. The group includes a variety of living arrangements (see Bachman et al. 1997 for details).

Pregnancy, Parenthood, Engagement, and Divorce

One of the clearest effects of a post–high school role on substance use is associated with pregnancy: those who were pregnant reported dramatically lowered levels of alcohol use and marijuana use, and even cigarette use was lowered. Pregnant women were the only group to show an actual reduction between high school and follow-up in the proportion who smoked a half pack or more per day. Becoming pregnant seems to cause women to reduce, and in many cases to cease entirely, their use of all four of the psychoactive substances considered here.

Having a pregnant spouse did not have much effect on drug-using behavior among the men in the study. These men showed no reduction in cigarette use, and changes in use of other drugs disappeared when the effect of marriage was controlled in multivariate analyses.

In general, parenthood, for both the married (the majority) and unmarried (a significant minority), was associated with decreases in the use of alcohol, marijuana, and cocaine. The pattern for cigarette use was different. Single parents, both men and women, were more likely than average to increase their cigarette use, while married women showed some decrease and married men showed no significant change. It is worth noting that, despite the fact that parenthood is often considered a highly stressful role status, there were no increases in substance use among married parents. Among single parents, the only substance showing an increase in use was cigarettes.

Two other aspects of marital status are potentially related to changes in substance use: engagement and divorce. Alcohol, marijuana, and cocaine (but not cigarettes) all showed clear decreases in use among engaged respondents (both cohabiting couples and noncohabiting couples). These effects, which were maintained in multivariate analyses, were similar to marriage effects, although generally smaller. (Similar findings are reported in Yamaguchi and Kandel 1985b.) Divorce, on the other hand, produced clear evidence of an increased use in all four substances. Furthermore, the transition from divorce to remarriage was accompanied by a decrease in the use of all three substances (alcohol, marijuana, and cocaine).

In sum, the several findings on the effects of engagement, marriage, divorce, and remarriage suggest that becoming engaged or married tends to restrain drug use. Remaining married maintains these lowered levels, while becoming divorced removes the restraints. The implication of the finding on engagement (whether or not cohabitation is occurring) is that the mutual commitment in a relationship plus the accompanying changes in social and recreational lifestyle are important causes of sustained decreases in drug use among young adults.

Conclusions and Implications

Stability versus Change and Selection versus Socialization

The findings just described provide evidence for both change and stability in the post–high school years. We have emphasized change—that is, the socialization effects of post–high school environmental and social role transitions. But we saw also some differences that predated the transitions. The most notable is the difference in smoking rates between those who do and do not enter college: these differences were considerable in high school and were maintained (or even enlarged) for years after high school. More generally, there are high levels of stability from one year to the next in all the drug classes considered here. But as individuals make the many important transitions in their young adulthood, they acquire new roles, with accompanying freedoms and responsibilities, and as time goes on, the continuity of youthful patterns of drug use is diminished.

For many, the new freedoms occur immediately after high school graduation, when they go to college or when they move out of the parental home without acquiring the responsibilities of marriage. For others, new responsibilities come shortly after high school graduation, when they marry and become parents. The new responsibilities come later for the increasing numbers of those who attend college or delay marriage. The new freedoms tend to provide more opportunity for drug use, while the new responsibilities tend to provide less opportunity (or motivation) for drug use. Thus, the overall pattern is one of age-related increases in drug use after high school, followed by decreases.

Based on the several patterns for specific substances, we believe the increases in cigarette use observed during the first few years after high school are largely attributable to the absence of restraints that were present when the smokers were in high school. The declines observed beginning in adults' early twenties and continuing into their early thirties in the use of alcohol, marijuana, and cocaine are likely caused to a considerable degree by the increasing extent of responsibilities versus freedoms, as increasing proportions of young adults assume new responsibilities for their spouse, children, and themselves as they move through the third decade of their lives.

Implications of Findings on Age-Related Changes in Drug Use

One of the clearest implications of this study regarding the impact of transition is that drug-using behaviors are highly responsive to social environments. The evidence of the impacts of single life outside of parents' homes (e.g., in college) on increasing some drug use, notably alcohol, and of marriage and pregnancy on decreasing drug use is particularly compelling. The findings regarding cigarette use are at some variance with the general findings. This behavior appears less susceptible to the immediate social environment, though the declines observed among pregnant women indicate that even this behavior can be modified under sufficiently compelling motivation.

The policy implications of many of the findings just described are not particularly specific. Although marriage and pregnancy tend to reduce drug use after high school, we would not advise all high school graduates to marry quickly and to get pregnant as soon as possible. It is, however, very useful to know that the living arrangements typically associated with college tend to produce increases in drinking and marijuana use. This knowledge can be used to justify targeted prevention efforts. And the fact that smoking appears to decline during pregnancy suggests that this is an ideal time for intervention to prevent relapse.

Other findings from the MTF study have influenced policy more directly. A major contribution has been the demonstration of the important role played by attitudes and beliefs in determining trends in drug use and the relatively minor role played by availability of drugs. This demonstration has led to a general acceptance of the importance of demand factors in determining societal levels of drug use. The demonstration of the importance of particular attitudes and beliefs has also provided empirical information that has influenced prevention practices. Indeed, a major government initiative, the antidrug media campaign, and the nation's drug control strategy have embraced the concepts that have emerged from this and related survey-based studies of substance use and abuse in the transition from adolescence to adulthood.

REFERENCES

Axinn, W. G., and A. Thornton. 1992. The relationship between cohabitation and divorce: Selectivity or causal influence? *Demography* 29:357–74.

Bachman, J. G., P. Freedman-Doan, P. M. O'Malley, L. D. Johnston, and D. R. Segal. 1999. Changing patterns of drug use among U.S. military recruits before and after enlistment. *American Journal of Public Health* 89:672–77.

Bachman, J. G., and M. K. Jennings.1975. The impact of Vietnam on trust in government. *Journal of Social Issues* 31:141–55.

Bachman, J. G., L. D. Johnston, and P. M. O'Malley. 1990. Explaining the recent decline in cocaine use among young adults: Further evidence that perceived risks and disapproval lead to reduced drug use. *Journal of Health and Social Behavior* 31:173–84.

———. 1998. Explaining the recent increases in students' marijuana use: The impacts of perceived risks and disapproval from 1976 through 1996. *American Journal of Public Health* 88:887–92.

Bachman, J. G., L. D. Johnston, P. M. O'Malley, and R. H. Humphrey. 1988. Explaining the recent decline in marijuana use: Differentiating the effects of perceived risks, disapproval, and general lifestyle factors. *Journal of Health and Social Behavior* 29:92–112.

Bachman, J. G., P. M. O'Malley, and J. Johnston. 1978. *Youth in transition.* Vol. 6, *Adolescence to adulthood—A study of change and stability in the lives of young men.* Ann Arbor: Institute for Social Research, University of Michigan.

Bachman, J. G., P. M. O'Malley, and L. D. Johnston. 1984. Drug use among young adults: The impacts of role status and social environments. *Journal of Personality and Social Psychology* 47:629–45.

Bachman, J. G., K. N. Wadsworth, P. M. O'Malley, L. D. Johnston, and J. Schulenberg. 1997. *Smoking, drinking, and drug use in young adulthood: The impacts of new freedoms and new responsibilities.* Mahwah, NJ: Lawrence Erlbaum.

Baltes, P. B. 1968. Longitudinal and cross-sectional sequences in the study of age and generation effects. *Human Development* 11:145–71.

Baltes, P. B., and J. R. Nesselroade. 1979. History and rationale of longitudinal research. In *Longitudinal research in the study of behavior and development,* ed. J. R. Nesselroade and P. B. Baltes. New York: Academic Press.

Bereiter, C. 1963. Some persisting dilemmas in the measurement of change. In *Problems in measuring change,* ed. C. Harris. Madison: University of Wisconsin Press.
Bohrnstedt, G. 1969. Observations on the measurement of change. In *Sociological Methodology 1969,* ed. E. Borgatta. San Francisco: Jossey-Bass.
Campbell, D., and J. Stanley. 1967. *Experimental and quasi-experimental design for research.* Chicago: Rand McNally.
Chassin, L., C. Presson, S. J. Sherman, and D. A. Edwards. 1992. The natural history of cigarette smoking and young adult social roles. *Journal of Health and Social Behavior* 33:328–47.
Coleman, J. 1968. The mathematical study of change. In *Methodology in social research,* ed. H. Blalock and A. Blalock. New York: McGraw-Hill.
Crockett, L. J. 1997. Cultural, historical, and subcultural contexts of adolescence. In *Health risks and developmental transitions during adolescence,* ed. J. Schulenberg, J. Maggs, and K. Hurrelmann, 23–53. New York: Cambridge University Press.
Cronbach, L., and L. Furby. 1970. How should we measure "change"—Or should we? *Psychological Bulletin* 74:68–80.
Elder, G. H. 1974. *Children of the Great Depression: Social change in the life experience.* Chicago: University of Chicago Press.
———. 1998. The life course and human development. In *Handbook of child psychology.* Vol. 1, *Theoretical models of human development,* ed. R. M. Lerner, 939–91. New York: Wiley.
Harwood, H., D. Fountain, and G. Livermore. 1998. *The economic costs of alcohol and drug abuse in the United States, 1992.* NIH Publication Number 98-4327. Rockville, MD: National Institute on Drug Abuse.
House, J. S., and W. M. Mason. 1975. Political alienation in America, 1952–1968. *American Sociological Review* 40:123–47.
Johnston, L. D. 1982. A review and analysis of recent changes in marijuana use by American young people. In *Marijuana: The national impact on education,* 8–13. New York: American Council on Marijuana.
———. 1985. Should alcohol epidemiology and drug abuse epidemiology be merged? *Drinking and Drug Practices Surveyor* 20 (March): 11–14.
———. 1991. Toward a theory of drug epidemics. In *Persuasive communication and drug abuse prevention,* ed. R. L. Donohew, H. Sypher, and W. Bukoski. Hillsdale, NJ: Lawrence Erlbaum.
Johnston, L. D., P. M. O'Malley, and J. G. Bachman. 1988. *Drug use among American college students and their noncollege age peers.* Monitoring the Future Occasional Paper No. 25. Ann Arbor: Institute for Social Research, University of Michigan.
———. 1999a. *National survey results on drug use from the Monitoring the Future study, 1975–1998.* Vol. 1, *Secondary school students.* NIH Publication No. 99-4660. Rockville, MD: National Institute on Drug Abuse.
———. 1999b. *National survey results on drug use from the Monitoring the Future study, 1975–1998.* Vol. 2, *College students and young adults.* NIH Publication No. 99-4661. Rockville, MD: National Institute on Drug Abuse.
Johnston, L. D., P. M. O'Malley, J. Schulenberg, and J. G. Bachman. 1996. *Aims and objectives of the Monitoring the Future study and progress toward fulfilling them.* Monitoring the Future Occasional Paper No. 34, 2d ed. Ann Arbor: Institute for Social Research, University of Michigan.

Kandel, D. B., and K. Yamaguchi. 1987. Job mobility and drug use: An event history analysis. *American Journal of Sociology* 92:836–78.

Lord, F. 1963. Elementary models for measuring change. In *Problems in measuring change,* ed. C. Harris. Madison: University of Wisconsin Press.

Nesselroade, J. R., and P. B. Baltes, eds. 1979. *Longitudinal research in the study of behavior and development.* New York: Academic Press.

Newcomb, M. D. 1987. Cohabitation and marriage: A quest for independence and relatedness. *Applied Social Psychology Annual* 7:128–56.

Newcomb, M. D., and P. M. Bentler. 1985. The impact of high school substance use on choice of young adult living environment and career direction. *Journal of Drug Education* 1:253–61.

Nock, S. 1995. A comparison of marriages and cohabiting relationships. *Journal of Family Issues* 16:53–76.

O'Malley, P. M., J. G. Bachman, and L. D. Johnston. 1983. Reliability and consistency of self-reports of drug use. *International Journal of the Addictions* 18:805–24.

———. 1988. Period, age, and cohort effects on substance use among young Americans: A decade of change, 1976–1986. *American Journal of Public Health* 78:1315–21.

Parnes, H. S., and K. Sproat. 1984. The National Longitudinal Surveys of labor force behavior. In *Handbook of longitudinal research.* Vol. 2, *Teenage and adult cohorts,* ed. S. A. Mednick, M. Harway, and K. M. Finello, 99–120. New York: Praeger.

Ryder, N. B. 1965. The cohort as a concept in the study of social change. *American Sociological Review* 30:843–61.

Schaie, K. W. 1965. A general model for the study of developmental problems. *Psychological Bulletin* 64:92–107.

Schulenberg, J. E., J. G. Bachman, P. M. O'Malley, and L. D. Johnston. 1994. High school educational success and subsequent substance use: A panel analysis following adolescents into young adulthood. *Journal of Health and Social Behavior* 35:45–62.

Schulenberg, J., P. M. O'Malley, J. G. Bachman, and L. D. Johnston. 2000. "Spread your wings and fly": The course of health and well-being during the transition to young adulthood. In *Negotiating adolescence in times of social change,* ed. L. Crockett and R. Silbereisen. Cambridge: Cambridge University Press.

Schulenberg, J., P. M. O'Malley, J. G. Bachman, K. N. Wadsworthand, L. D. Johnston. 1996. Getting drunk and growing up: Trajectories of frequent binge drinking during the transition to young adulthood. *Journal of Studies on Alcohol* 57:289–304.

Steel, L., L. L. Wise, and R. P. Abeles. 1984. Project TALENT: A longitudinal study of the development and utilization of individuals' capabilities. In *Handbook of longitudinal research.* Vol. 2, *Teenage and adult cohorts,* ed. S. A. Mednick, M. Harway, and K. M. Finello, 77–98. New York: Praeger.

Substance Abuse and Mental Health Services Administration. 1997. *Preliminary results from the 1996 National Household Survey on Drug Abuse.* DHHS Publication No. (SMA) 97–3149. Rockville, MD: Substance Abuse and Mental Health Services Administration.

———. 1999. *Summary of findings from the 1998 National Household Survey on Drug Abuse.* DHHS Publication No. (SMA) 99–3328. Rockville, MD: Substance Abuse and Mental Health Services Administration.

Thornton, A., W. G. Axinn, and D. H. Hill. 1992. Reciprocal effects of religiosity, cohabitation, and marriage. *American Journal of Sociology* 98:628–51.

Warner, K. 1998. The economics of tobacco and health: An overview. In *The economics of tobacco control,* ed. I. Abedian, R. van der Merwe, N. Wilkins, and P. Jha, 57–75. Rondebosch, South Africa: University of Cape Town.

Yamaguchi, K., and D. B. Kandel. 1985a. Dynamic relationships between premarital cohabitation and illicit drug use: An event-history analyses of role selection and role socialization. *American Sociological Review* 50:530–46.

———. 1985b. On the resolution of role incompatibility: Life event history analysis of family roles and marijuana use. *American Journal of Sociology* 90:1284–1325.

CHAPTER 12

Research on Aging

A. Regula Herzog, Robert J. Willis, and David R. Weir

Older adults represent an ever-growing proportion of the population in the United States as well as in many other developed countries. What are the personal, familial, and societal implications of such an aging society? Gerontological and geriatric research has grown rapidly in recent years to answer some of the pressing questions raised by this development. Researchers in this tradition have paid a great deal of attention to how chronological aging is related to the physical, psychological, and social well-being of individuals, asking the following questions: Do physical health, functioning, and cognition decline uniformly as people age, or is maintenance or even recovery possible? Are change patterns similar for all aging adults? Do political and social attitudes, personality, and psychological well-being change in similar ways? If change patterns vary across domains or individuals, how can differences be explained? If change patterns are similar, which processes are causal and which ones are consequences?

Researchers in the sociology, demography, and economics of aging have addressed how the growth of the aging population impacts on society. Traditionally, support of the aged has taken several forms, including private savings by the aged themselves, financial and in-kind assistance by family members, and public transfer programs such as Social Security, Medicare, and Medicaid. In the face of the increasing societal burden created by the growing proportion of the aged, issues such as these are of concern to researchers: How can public programs be maintained? What are the implications of various modifications of public programs that are currently being discussed? How can private savings be encouraged? How can medical technology be made available on an equitable basis? How can families cope with care of their older members? Which responsibilities fall to society, which ones to the family, and which ones to the individual? And how is all this affected by possible improvement in the health status of older cohorts and by change in the economic situation at large? Aging research helps us sharpen our understanding of the nature of aging and its implications for society.

Researchers also have begun to think about the reverse impact of society on its aging members or the lack of such an impact. In their provocative book *Age and Structural Lag* (1994), Riley, Kahn, and Foner argue that some social structures and opportunities are marked by age constraints that may have been appropriate as long as a century ago but the older population has changed and is now not only larger than it was then but also healthier and better educated. As a result, the social structures and opportunities are lagging behind demographic developments. A specific example in which such a structural lag is evident is the persistence of norms and policies supporting retirement by the age of sixty-five or earlier in the current context of larger numbers of older adults in search of productive contributions and useful roles to fill their long postretirement years.

Although gerontological research is relatively young, the major research issues have been well laid out by several authors. According to Bengtson, Rice, and Johnson (1999), aging research deals with three major sets of research questions: (1) the aged and how they function; (2) aging as a process that happens over time, its variations, and consequences; and (3) how age impinges on social structure and individual behavior. Campbell and Alwin (1999) provide a classification of research questions that is defined primarily in terms of design. These authors propose (1) descriptions at one point in time; (2) aggregate changes over time and their explanations; (3) microlevel changes and their explanations; and (4) methodological issues. Similarly, Baltes (1973, 459) defines the objectives of life-span developmental research as "description, explanation and modification (optimization) of intra-individual change in behavior across the life span, and with inter-individual differences (and similarities) in intra-individual change." Common to the first two classifications is the distinction between one-time description, which may be studied with a cross-sectional design, and change over time, which requires longitudinal studies of cohorts or individuals. Another common thread to all classifications is the emphasis on explanation along with description. Finally, the Bengtson, Rice, and Johnson (1999) classification reminds us of the enormous implications of an aging society for policy, and the Riley, Kahn, and Foner (1994) formulation reminds us of the significance of social structure and policies for older adults.

In this chapter we briefly comment on many of the themes of aging research previously enumerated, indicating how survey research has been central to addressing them. Some of the themes have been well developed and are supported by substantive bodies of research; others are still in a more preliminary state. We will argue that gerontological research by its very nature is complex and challenges research paradigms and methods. It will flourish particularly well in a research environment like the Institute for Social Research (ISR), which is devoted to multidisciplinary research with large longitudinal studies in the context of joint attention to methodology and substance.

Longitudinal Designs

Much of the early aging research addressed changes in personality, intelligence, and physical health that take place as people grow older. The Kansas City Studies (Havighurst, Neugarten, and Tobin 1968), the Seattle Studies (Schaie 1983), and the Baltimore Longitudinal Study of Aging (Shock 1985) are examples. Researchers in the tradition of developmental psychology recognized a long time ago that approximating age changes by observing individuals of different ages in a cross-sectional study confounds cohort differences with age changes and that the description of individual change patterns—or developmental patterns—requires longitudinal or panel information in which individuals or cohorts are observed over time.

One of the prime examples of the erroneous conclusions drawn from cross-sectional age differences was the apparent marked decrease observed in cognitive functioning, particularly in its component of crystallized intelligence. Whereas cross-sectional age differences suggested an age-related decrease in some aspects of crystallized intelligence, such decline was much less obvious in longitudinal studies (Schaie and Willis 1991). What looked like an age-related decline in crystallized intelligence in the cross-sectional data is possibly better explained by a persistent difference between subsequent cohorts: each cohort performed better than the one before it but did not change substantially as it aged. More recently, using thirteen General Social Surveys from 1974 to 1996 to follow longitudinally nineteen similar cohorts, Alwin and McCammon (1999) demonstrated little age-related change, confirming the theoretical prediction of stability of crystallized intelligence across the adult life span. If anything, their results suggest small cohort effects that indicate decreasing crystallized intelligence from earlier to more recent cohorts, a decline that they attributed to the increasing simplicity of textbooks over recent decades.

Another example drawn from economics showed that in cross-sectional data the value of assets increases into high older age. In this case the longitudinal data revealed a selection bias caused by the correlation between mortality and wealth: adults with lower wealth died at earlier ages, leaving a disproportionate number of wealthier adults in the higher age groups (Hurd 1990). However the cohort issues eventually get resolved, it remains clear that panel and repeated cohort studies are able to provide unique and valuable information that cannot be obtained from cross-sectional studies alone. The need for longitudinal surveys to describe individual-level change patterns was recognized in the design of the first Longitudinal Study on Aging (LSOA), which followed longitudinally a national sample of older Americans originally surveyed in the National Health Interview Survey; the original National Long-Term Care Survey (NLTCS), which followed a national sample of disabled older Americans; the Established Populations for Epidemiologic Studies of the Elderly (EPESE), which followed several regional samples of older Americans; and the Retirement History Survey, which followed a national sample of older American males. Data from the LSOA demonstrated, much to everyone's surprise, that health and functioning do not always decline as people progress into old age but may also show improvement and even full recovery (Freedman and Martin 1999). More generally, using longitudinal designs, researchers were able to demonstrate that age-related changes in physical and mental health do not necessarily take place in a discrete, stepwise fashion or follow a monotonically declining path, as suggested by the average patterns (Shock 1985). Rather, a great deal of variability in change patterns was evident, particularly over short time periods (Eizenman et al. 1997; Lang, Featherman, and Nesselroade 1997). Yet, this message has not been fully appreciated by gerontologists, who continue to rely on overall change patterns described by statistical measures of central tendency. Studies in life-course transitions provide yet another example of the need for longitudinal information to understand transitions in education, family, work, health, and leisure that have become more continuous, are less tightly aligned with chronological age, and are more interdependent within and across lives (O'Rand and Campbell 1999). For similar reasons, Nobel laureate Robert Fogel (1994), in his presidential address to the American Economic Association, called for longitudinal designs to better study behaviors related to work, saving, and health.

However, longitudinal research poses formidable methodological challenges over cross-sectional studies, related in part to tracking of individual respondents and adjusting for attrition; to stability of measurement in the context of practice effects and period changes; to the choice of proper time lags between waves; to stability in investigators and infrastructure to guarantee continuity; and, probably most important of all, to the delicate balance between stability of design and methods to allow longitudinal analysis on the one hand and innovation to remain responsive to a changing environment on the other.

The University of Michigan Survey Research Center (SRC) and ISR are home to several long-term and highly successful longitudinal surveys of the adult population. Since its inception in 1968 the Panel Study of Income Dynamics has become the main data source for investigating economic behaviors and outcomes related to labor force and family formation patterns (see chap. 6, this volume). The Americans' Changing Lives survey spans a shorter period of seven and a half years and three waves, with a fourth wave in progress fifteen years after the first wave was conducted. This longitudinal study contains oversamples of older adults and of African-American adults and is a premier data set for studying the psychosocial factors impinging on aging and health (see chap. 9, this volume). Starting in 1992, the Health and Retirement Study and its sister study, the Asset and Health Dynamics among the Oldest-Old study, have followed a middle-aged and an old cohort (with oversamples of African-Americans and Hispanics) for four and three waves respectively and are funded for another three waves. Combined since 1998 into a single survey named HRS, these two studies are designed to investigate the complex interface between health, economic, and family trajectories in the second half of life and to estimate the economic and health implications of an aging American society. All of these longitudinal studies permit tracking individual-level change over time and contain information on major outcomes along with explanatory variables.

Repeated Cohorts

As was quickly recognized by some developmental psychologists as well as others, the longitudinal assessment of a single cohort is confounded by the historical and social context within which its aging takes place. What is needed are different cohorts aging through the same time periods or through the same age ranges. In her 1986 presidential address to the American Sociological Association, Matilda White Riley (1987) emphasized the importance of cross-cohort longitudinal studies, which provide a better basis for researchers to distinguish age, cohort, and period effects.

The decline in disability among older Americans identified by Manton, Stallard, and Corder (1997) is an example of the power of a simple repeated cohort design. Surveying cohorts of identical age in 1982, 1984, and 1989, these authors were able to show that the more recent cohorts reported lower rates of disability at identical ages, potentially signaling a step toward compression of morbidity and mortality and most likely reflecting societal changes in health and preventive care as well as lifestyle changes. Another example of cohort differences is provided by the previously mentioned description of possible cohort patterns in crystallized intelligence.

Many other societal changes suggest that we might find cohort changes in aging patterns. These include changes in the economy such as the rapid changes in values of stocks; changes in health care and economic policies such as the move to defined contribution pension plans and managed health care; changes in medical technology and delivery of care; changes in the level, nature, and environment of work and retirement; changes in lifestyle factors such as smoking, exercise, and diet; decreases in family size; and increases in divorce rates. Repeated cross-sectional surveys such as the Current Population Survey, the decennial census, and the GSS are well positioned to capture the impact of changes in policy, economy, or society on subsequent cohorts by simply describing cohort differences in health status, economic status, or other characteristics. Only a repeated longitudinal design enables researchers to study the effects of those changes on life-cycle dynamics by describing over-time change patterns in characteristics and then investigating the impact of prior choices and behaviors on consequent characteristics.

Recognizing the importance of cohort membership, SRC's HRS program in 1998 added additional cohorts of War Babies (born between 1942 and 1947) and Children of the Depression (born between 1924 and 1930) to its existing HRS cohort (born between 1931 and1941) and AHEAD cohort (born before 1924) and will reinterview all of the cohorts in future HRS waves. In the year 2004 an Early Boomer cohort (born between 1948 and 1953) will be added to the HRS. With this quasi-experimental design it will be possible to study aging in different economic and social contexts and establish the effects of historical, societal, and cultural changes and constraints on human behavior. Early results (Gustman and Steinmeier 2000) of such cohort comparisons already revealed the marked shift from private pensions that provide a certain monthly benefit to retirees (i.e., defined benefit plans) to pensions that provide a certain monthly contribution to a worker's retirement plan (i.e., defined contribution plans). Other aging studies have also added new cohorts. They include the LSOA, designed to measure health, functioning, and disability, and the NLTCS, designed to study disability and functioning.

However, longitudinal studies of several cohorts pose additional challenges over single cohort longitudinal studies, particularly in terms of funding and leadership. Such studies require long-term leadership, which is often incongruous with the career patterns of academic researchers. They also require a stable funding environment in which the long-term investment and the slow payoff of these studies are well understood.

Probability Samples

To capture the diversity in patterns of aging, an accurate description of the older population requires samples representative of the population and its subgroups to which generalizations need to be made. Several authors have noted the age-related increase in variability in physical health and functioning (Dannefer 1988; Rowe and Kahn 1998): some older adults suffer declining health from onsets of chronic disease and impairments, whereas others continue to maintain exceptional health. Capturing such variability and studying its impact on the lives of older Americans require population-representative samples. This is well recognized by the gerontological and geriatric research community but because of cost and logistic constraints is rarely observed. A ten-year-old survey of researchers studying cognition and aging suggested that most samples used in this research domain are convenience samples (Camp, West, and Poon 1989). Likewise, patients from clinical groups tend to reflect the special populations served by a hospital or clinic, as shown in a recent comparison from the Michigan Alzheimer's Disease Research Center (MADRC) with the AHEAD population. MADRC patients were more likely to be male, white, and highly educated and were younger than the nationally representative AHEAD respondents of comparable cognitive impairment. In general, samples used in aging studies probably underrepresent the poorer and sicker part of the population (Herzog and Rodgers 1992).

It is less well recognized that procedures for selecting older and younger adults for cross-sectional comparisons often differ, introducing confounds into age comparisons. Differences in selection procedures may be due to relying differentially on volunteers when recruiting older and younger adults for research, to selecting from specialized but different groups, and to permitting different nonresponse patterns. That such nonrepresentative samples may be consequential was recently suggested by Salthouse (1999) when he speculated that the lack of population-representative samples may contribute to inconsistent findings regarding age patterns in crystallized intelligence.

Population-representative samples are a mainstay for many of the surveys carried out at SRC, such as the already mentioned life span and aging studies ACL, HRS, and PSID as well as several not yet described aging studies, such as the Study of Michigan Generations, designed to investigate methodological issues in survey research with older Americans, and most federal aging surveys (e.g., LSOA and NLTCS). Of course, not all aging studies can be conducted with a nationally representative sample or require such a sample. Exploratory investigations will be done more cheaply on a local sample of sufficient variability. Studies that require intense clinical evaluations, laboratory assessments, or extensive testing are difficult to conduct on a national sample. Typically, these studies have been conducted locally, and national breadth sometimes has been added by involving several centers across the nation in the same research. Examples of such studies are the Epidemiologic Catchment Area studies and the EPESE. Embedding an extensive local data collection in a national sample could provide an attractive combination of the strengths of the two approaches.

Explanation as Well as Description

Some aging researchers are not satisfied with describing the older population or patterns of change across the life span but want to examine the reasons for age-related change patterns. Moreover, the fact that age-related change patterns are not universal but appear to be moderated by historical, social, and individual characteristics has expanded the realm of possible explanations. Baltes (1979) organized causes of developmental changes into the following three groups: (1) normative age-graded influences or effects caused by biological, psychological, and sociocultural factors that are highly correlated with chronological age; (2) normative history-graded influences or effects caused by events that many people experience at the same time; and (3) nonnormative influences or effects caused by factors to which only a subset of all people are exposed. Each group encompasses biological, psychological, and social factors. The rather passive view of the individual assumed by these types of explanations has been noted by theorists of identity, adaptation, and interactionist perspectives. These theorists propose that a further set of possible explanations include the experiences initiated and chosen by the individual and the interpretations given by them to these experiences (Atchley 1999; George 1999; Herzog and Markus 1999).

Because of the nature of the factors thought to be important as explanations of development and because of the individual choice involved, many potential causes cannot be manipulated in the laboratory and thus require observational or quasi-experimental studies. Writing on quasi-experimental designs, Cook and Campbell (1979) pointed out that longitudinal designs were better suited to investigate causation in observational studies than cross-sectional designs because longitudinal designs could establish the time ordering between hypothesized cause and effect and they could control on preexisting differences to mitigate the lack of randomization. More recently, Campbell and Alwin (1999) argued likewise that longitudinal data are needed for explanations of aging phenomena, for which randomized control is often impossible; but these authors also cautioned that not all longitudinal designs are equally powerful for causal inferences by highlighting differences between observational and case-control longitudinal designs. These authors also argued that new analytical techniques such as survival models, multilevel analyses, and structural equation models are able to deal successfully with a number of thorny statistical problems in longitudinal data analysis, contributing greatly to the usefulness of longitudinal data for aging research.

As the cohort study design discussed previously makes clear, biological, psychological, and social causes of aging have to be examined within their historical, societal, and cultural context. Historical context may be studied by examining different cohorts who age through different historical time periods; societal and cultural context may be studied by examining cohorts aging in different societies or social subgroups. The research by House and his colleagues demonstrates that older adults of higher socioeconomic status (SES) report less disability than those of lower SES (House et al. 1990). Liang and his colleagues (Krause et al. 1999; Liang et al. 1999) have developed a research program extending research on stress, social support, religion, and health into Japan and Taiwan. They have shown a good deal of similarity in processes in the different cultures. Likewise, Antonucci and Akiyama have developed in Japan and in the United States surveys addressing social support and mental health across the life span.

To move beyond global historical, societal, and cultural differences to identifying the specific causes, more contextual information is needed than standard epidemiological and survey investigations provide. Residential environment can be a powerful influence on health and behavior as people age. By linking an individual's place of residence (geocode information) to characteristics of places, a wide range of influences can be studied. In the United States, state governments control important policy variables that determine incentives and eligibility for various public programs such as disability insurance or Supplemental Security Income. Economists often use this source of variation to test behavioral responses to policy incentives. The wide local variation in the supply of medical services creates quasi-experimental exogenous differences, or "instrumental variables," from which analysts can infer the effects of treatments such as cardiac catheterization (McClellan, McNeil, and Newhouse 1994). Social conditions such as crime rates, average incomes, or income inequality also vary locally and have been hypothesized to influence health, employment, and geographic mobility. Knowing place of residence can also be a powerful tool to reidentify individuals in anonymized survey data sets like HRS. For that reason, geocode data is only released under restricted conditions to qualified researchers.

Several conclusions may be drawn. First, aging represents a multitude of biological, psychological, and social factors, all of which are possible explanations for the observed age patterns. Second, many of these factors cannot be manipulated in the laboratory and therefore must be investigated in observational or case-control studies. Third, most aging patterns are not universal but conditioned by the historical and societal context within which aging takes place. Therefore, the context provides another set of explanations that must be considered. Data sources that provide a rich set of individual and contextual causal factors in a longitudinal design are rare and so are research teams that are able to bring different disciplines to bear on explaining aging phenomena. Some of the SRC studies such as the ACL, PSID, and HRS represent ambitious efforts to include many of the relevant explanations in a longitudinal quasi-experimental design.

Testing Theories

Theory in the form of "construction of explicit explanations in accounting for empirical findings" (Bengtson, Rice, and Johnson 1999, 5) is considered the ultimate aim of scientific enterprise. Once theories have been formulated, they will generate additional predictions that can be submitted to empirical tests, and thus testing of theories is the ultimate goal of aging-related research. Early work in gerontology focused on describing a wide range of phenomena by age—one of the objectives of gerontological research, according to Bengtson, Rice, and Johnson (1999); Campbell and Alwin (1999); and Baltes (1979). An example is the early work by Nathan Shock and his colleagues at the National Institute on Aging, in which they offer a broad description of age-related changes in biomedical, cognitive, and personality characteristics (Shock 1985). This kind of work has led some to term gerontological research as "data-rich and theory-poor" (Birren 1999, 459) and others to deplore outright the lack of interest in theory building among gerontologists (Bengtson, Rice, and Johnson 1999). In response, volumes edited by Birren and Bengtson (1988) and Bengtson and Schaie (1999) formulated a broad range of midlevel biological, psychological, and social theories to integrate the broad and complex set of findings related to aging.

One of the earliest midlevel social-psychological theories of aging is activity theory (Lemon, Bengtson, and Peterson 1972; Longino and Kart 1982), which postulates that older adults who remain active and involved retain better health and higher well-being. The theory originally grew out of the Kansas City Study and has had a prominent status in aging research ever since, although it was never fully formulated or comprehensively evaluated. More recently, Rowe and Kahn (1998) adopted a form of activity theory when they proposed a beneficial effect of productive activities for older adults. One reason for the lack of conclusive evaluation of the theory relates to the difficulty of addressing the relevant research questions in a methodologically rigorous manner. Because a higher level of activity is more likely to be chosen by healthy than by unhealthy people, the impact of activity is confounded by preexisting health conditions and thus needs to be investigated while controlling for preexisting health status and well-being. The most rigorous design for doing this is a randomized experiment. Such an experiment is difficult to implement for the broad-based and long-term activity levels that are implied by activity theory. We are aware of only one example in the literature where somewhat longer-term involvement in a part-time parks and gardening program among older adults was experimentally manipulated (Soumerai and Avorn 1983). The results showed that older adults involved in the program for six months reported better health and well-being at the completion of the program than older adults who were not enrolled in the program.

A more feasible although methodologically less rigorous approach is represented by longitudinal observational studies. The longitudinal studies of ACL and HRS at SRC have led recently to some of the first evaluations of the impact of activities such as volunteer work on morbidity and mortality of older Americans. Results of these investigations suggest that volunteer work has a beneficial impact on health and mortality, a benefit that is attained with a relatively low level of involvement and does not increase further with additional volunteer work (Luoh and Herzog 2002; Musick, Herzog, and House 1999). Similarly, a recent evaluation of the impact of productive activities on mortality in an older EPESE sample showed a beneficial effect of such activities (Glass et al. 1999). These first rigorous evaluations of activity theory are reasonably promising and suggest further evaluation of a more comprehensive set of activities. They also raise the question of whether the salubrious effect can be attributed to specific activities and their nature or whether the effect is generalizable to any kind of "active" activity. The HRS and ACL studies plan on vigorously pursuing the further evaluation of activity theory.

Economic theories of aging have their origins in the life-cycle model of consumption and saving (Modigliani and Brumberg 1954; Friedman 1957). Put simply, this model asserts that individuals wish to consume at roughly similar levels throughout their lives but are only able to earn income for part of their lives. By saving when young (working) and dissaving when old (retired), individuals can smooth consumption out of a truncated earning period. The model is a rich source of predictions for how past events and future expectations influence savings behavior. Retirement benefits from Social Security or private pensions raise postretirement income and should therefore reduce saving. Longer expected life after retirement should increase saving. Changes in interest rates or the growth rate of wages have more complicated effects. The model is also the basis for important policy concerns about the adequacy of retirement savings (Moore and Mitchell 2000).

Empirical studies of consumption and saving have established important challenges to the life-cycle model. Savings rates are extremely heterogeneous even after controlling for many of the factors that should determine them (Venti and Wise 1998). Although low savers are more of a concern for social welfare and for policy, very high savers are equally difficult for the theory to explain. Similarly, there is substantial evidence that savings are consumed too slowly in retirement. Modifications to the life-cycle model have been proposed to account for these anomalies. Uncertainty about future health, equity values, or entitlement programs has been linked to precautionary saving—holding reserves of wealth beyond what is needed for expected consumption (Hubbard, Skinner, and Zeldes 1995; Deaton 1992). The desire to leave a bequest might also explain high levels of wealth.

SRC researchers are at the forefront of new directions in the economics of the life cycle. Individual heterogeneity in saving or retirement can result from individual differences in preferences such as tolerance for risk, altruism toward parents or children, and preferences for immediate gratification. Experimental modules in the HRS have been designed to elicit these parameters of the utility function so that their role can be tested empirically (Barsky et al. 1997). The standard life-cycle model is a model of individual choice, whereas most people facing retirement are in married couples. Models of joint decision making, including household bargaining, are now being applied to these issues to understand heterogeneity in saving and in preparing for widowhood (Lundberg and Ward-Batts 2000; Weir and Willis 2000).

To study the long-term impact of saving and consumption patterns and the heterogeneity in these processes, longitudinal data containing health, wealth, and labor force information are needed, measuring not only objective characteristics but also subjective perceptions and expectations. The latter are important for the explanation of economic and health decision making and behavior because they reflect the individual decision maker's perspectives. The HRS includes much of this information, and recent research using HRS data has started to test some of the predictions made by the modern life-cycle model. For example, Hurd, McFadden, and Gan (1998) have shown that older adults respond to subjective beliefs about their own mortality in their saving behavior rather than to objective life table probabilities.

Aging Research as Multidisciplinary Research

Although a multidisciplinary perspective benefits the study of all human behaviors, the complex determinants of aging and old age represent a prime example of a research area that can be enriched by the collaboration of researchers from many different disciplinary backgrounds. As noted before, biological, psychological, and social factors and the subjective experience of all of these need to be considered. Moreover, the study of the complex interrelationships between these factors has only just begun and requires active collaboration among the disciplines (Birren 1999). With its multidisciplinary faculty—including sociologists, psychologists, economists, demographers, anthropologists, public health faculty, physicians, and epidemiologists—and with its strong ties to other University of Michigan units, the ISR represents an excellent model for multidisciplinary aging-related research.

As an example, multidisciplinary research on social inequalities across the life span has prospered at SRC and has expanded significantly with the funding of the Michigan Interdisciplinary Center on Social Inequalities, Mind, and Body and the refunding of the HRS and ACL surveys. That higher socioeconomic status is powerfully linked to better health is well established and widely recognized (House and Williams 1996). Many local and regional studies have documented the general relationship, and two nationally representative SRC studies—ACL and HRS—have confirmed the relationship for the entire U.S. population. SRC-based research has taken a distinct life-span approach to this issue in at least two ways. First, House and his colleagues (House et al. 1990, 1994) demonstrated with ACL data representing all American adults that socioeconomic differences in health are most pronounced in middle and early old age (i.e., between forty-five and seventy-five years of age), whereas in young and old adult life the differences are considerably reduced. Second, such health differences are likely to become further magnified in middle age by an increasingly important direction of causation working from health to SES: according to this view, the onset of health problems erodes social standing by reducing productivity and related earnings and by requiring sometimes costly medical treatments. This direction of causation is the focus of some work using the HRS survey of Americans in the second half of life.

Much remains to be learned about the specific processes underlying the relationship between socioeconomic status and health. Most likely, a multitude of processes are involved and a multidisciplinary approach is necessary to provide a comprehensive explanation. One set of likely explanations is the broad set of psychosocial risk factors including stresses, health behaviors, social relationships and supports, activities, and psychological dispositions (Adler et al. 1994; House et al. 1994), requiring collaboration by psychologists, sociologists, social epidemiologists, and public health researchers. Research by House and his colleagues at SRC suggests that such psychosocial factors can explain much of the SES differences in health in cross-sectional studies but perhaps less in longitudinal studies (House et al. 1994). In addition to psychosocial factors, factors related to physical and social environment and family background need to be better evaluated and integrated into the explanation of the development of social inequalities in health across the life span. As part of the Michigan Interdisciplinary Center on Social Inequalities, Mind and Body Research, a project by House and his colleagues will address environmental factors and a project by Kaplan will address childhood background. Furthermore, health trajectories and their impact on labor force participation, economic decision making, and eventually income and assets require collaboration between economists, psychologists, physicians, epidemiologists, and demographers and have seen a burgeoning start in the HRS program. HRS tracks health status with a multidimensional assessment of physical and mental health every two years and at the same time reassesses income and assets in a comprehensive way. Early work using the HRS longitudinal data has demonstrated a decline in income and assets following the onset of major health problems (Smith 1999), possibly via a decline in labor force participation and productivity (Willis 1997). At the same time, use of the HRS longitudinal data has also documented continuing effects of SES differences on health during midlife via the reduction in smoking following a heart attack, which is adopted much more readily by those of higher SES standing (Wray et al. 1998). Finally, medical care utilization needs to be better assessed in surveys in order to evaluate their role in the link between social standing and health. Although existing research has not been able to demonstrate a pronounced effect of medical technology on public health, it has been true that its assessment in population studies has faced severe limitations due to respondents' lack of understanding or recall of specific health care actions. Links of survey responses with clinical data bases and administrative records represent a promising avenue to deal with these limitations and are currently under development in the HRS research program by physicians and health care economists. An important aspect of the link between SES and health is the role played by access to health care and public and private programs to support its use. Health care economists and policy researchers are developing relevant conceptualizations and measures for the HRS in this rapidly changing area.

The experience with interdisciplinary work at SRC and ISR has also taught us the difficulties inherent in such efforts. Difficulties with communication across different terminologies, theories, and methodologies are relatively well understood, and the start-up investments that members in multidisciplinary teams need to make are substantial. Less well recognized may be how multidisciplinary discussions are affected by status differences in disciplines, by relative sizes of disciplinary representation, and by favorite themes and pet ideas. Another less well-recognized difficulty lies in the grants and manuscript review processes that are still largely organized around disciplinary lines. As a consequence, it is often unclear where an interdisciplinary manuscript or proposal should be submitted, and no matter which choice is made, a part of the interdisciplinary product will not be properly evaluated. In specially formed multidisciplinary review groups, experts are sufficiently different in their expertise to defer to other experts except on their own turf.

Methodological Challenges

Survey research with older adults challenges some of the established methodologies and thereby provides new insights into the processes underlying participation in surveys and provision of answers to survey questions. Early on in the development of gerontology as a science, concerns about methods occasionally were raised. Thus, Frances Carp (Carp and Carp 1981) suggested that older adults seemed to be particularly reluctant to confess to a lack of satisfaction in ratings of various domains of life, and Neal Cutler (1979) evaluated the equivalence of multi-item measures such as satisfaction measures for age comparisons. More recently, research methods have been systematically evaluated for data collection from aging populations and for age comparisons by several SRC and ISR researchers. Rodgers and Herzog (Rodgers and Herzog 1987; Rodgers, Herzog, and Andrews 1988; Rodgers, Andrews, and Herzog 1992) conducted a program of research designed to investigate nonsampling errors in surveys of older adults. Although these authors were not overly impressed with the age differences in the quality of survey responses, they cautioned that the small differences could at least in part be due to the nature of nonresponse patterns among older populations (Herzog and Rodgers 1992). They showed that, when no specific efforts are undertaken to enlist older adults' participation, nonresponse tends to be higher among older than younger adults, and they suggest that in older populations nonresponse is related to cognitive and physical impairment, thereby biasing the information from older respondents (Herzog and Rodgers 1988a). Using data from the HRS and AHEAD, such a bias was clearly documented for panel attrition by Dan Hill (1998) and by Herzog and Rodgers (1999).

In an attempt to provide a basis for improving response rates in surveys of older Americans, Groves, Raghunathan, and Couper (1995) proposed a theory of social interaction and environmental constraints and tested it with data from the first observed waves of the AHEAD. These authors demonstrated that different factors relate to the likelihood of making contact and the likelihood of obtaining participation. Contact was increased by whether the interview was conducted face-to-face (instead of by telephone), in an area with relatively small households, and with a household selected by a community sampling frame (versus a list obtained from the Health Care Financing Administration, now the Center for Medicare and Medicaid Services). Cooperation depended on whether questions were raised and on positive comments made by the selected respondent, whether no mention of old age as a barrier was made by the respondent, and whether the household was located in a less densely populated area. Similar factors affected participation in a second wave of the HRS and AHEAD (Couper, Groves, and Raghunathan 1996). One particularly interesting factor affecting nonresponse to the second wave of AHEAD was the identity of the interviewer: older respondents who were approached in the second wave by the same interviewer as in the first wave were more likely to participate than those who faced an unfamiliar interviewer (Hill and Willis 1998).

Schwarz, Knäuper, and Park in SRC and the Research Center for Group Dynamics focused their research on response errors related to the age of the respondent and pursued the particular research question of whether age differences in cognitive functioning translate into age differences in the quality of survey responses. In secondary analyses, the authors found that lower memory performance can actually be advantageous for older respondents: the context of prior questions appears to have less of an effect on older adults' survey responses than on responses of younger adults, presumably because older respondents do not remember the prior survey questions as well (Knäuper 1999a). The apparent inconsistency of this finding with the lack of widespread age differences in survey responses observed by Rodgers and Herzog might possibly be resolved by the different foci of the two research programs: whereas Schwarz, Knäuper, and Park focus on survey questions that have shown large context effects in past research, Rodgers and Herzog selected survey questions to be broadly representative of items used in gerontological research. Further research is required to address this issue.

Reservations among survey researchers about alternative modes of data collection have often arisen from presumed difficulties with older target populations. The HRS program has included experiments on telephone versus face-to-face mode and on between-wave mail surveys. The telephone experiment yielded few mode differences in answers, confirming some earlier findings (Herzog and Rodgers 1988b, 1999). The mail experiment sent in 1999 a self-administered questionnaire to a random subset of all respondents. Analyses are still ongoing, but high response rates have been obtained, and the preliminary assessment of the impact on response rates in subsequent HRS waves reveals little negative effect.

New analytical techniques have been introduced to address methodological issues in aging research. As discussed more fully by Campbell and Alwin (1999), these techniques include survival models particularly well suited to investigating the timing between specific transitions; structural equation models suited to controlling for measurement error across age groups and across longitudinal waves; and multilevel models suited to investigating nested factors such as individual factors nested within community-level or within institution-level factors. The latter technique is pursued by Raudenbush at SRC.

Clearly, the commitment of the research community and SRC to repeated longitudinal studies and to exploring methodologies that address the unique challenges to data collection and data analysis brought forth by such designs has been an integral part of the advancement of gerontology as a science. We believe that a particularly fruitful approach is to address such methodological issues within the context of ongoing longitudinal studies.

Aging Research and Social Policy

Some aging research has its roots in applied and policy issues. For example, the activity and disengagement theories described before were in part born from concrete concerns among caretakers about how to maintain morale among older adults. Similarly, the development of the measures of Activities of Daily Living (ADLs) grew from a need to assess dependency in order to define eligibility for institutionalization. Various reforms of the Social Security and the Medicare systems that are widely discussed today to keep the systems solvent have implications for the behaviors and well-being of the elderly that are as yet incompletely understood. So far, retirement researchers have reached quite different conclusions about whether the preponderance of retirement around the age of sixty-five is due to eligibility for Social Security benefits or to other factors (Gustman and Steinmeier 1986; Lumsdaine, Stock, and Wise 1996; Rust and Phelan 1997). Likewise, health insurance and Medicare are likely to be influential for retirement timing, and there seems to be some consensus that the availability of employer-provided health insurance to workers encourages continued work and that Medicare or the availability of employer-provided health insurance to retirees encourages retirement (Gustman and Steinmeier 1994). One hallmark of the new private pension and health insurance systems is their increased reliance on individual choice and responsibility: defined contribution pension plans require the individual to make investment decisions; cafeteria-type health insurance systems rely on individual choice for the mix of covered services and medications. The success of these plans for the individual would seem to depend on the time and effort that individuals can bring to the decisions and the cognitive resources they can apply (Park et al. 1999). The implications of these recent changes for long-term health and economic well-being are not at all well understood. Finally, eligibility rules for support of long-term care by Medicaid and its relationship to disbursement of wealth are unclear. Some data suggest that eligibility for Medicaid is often already in place upon entry into a nursing home, although the evidence is inconsistent (Carpenter 1988). But whether this fact reflects an impoverishment because of existing health problems that lead eventually to institutionalization or a deliberate passing on of wealth to children in order to achieve eligibility is unclear.

Also, certain subgroups of the population are more directly affected by public policies than others. For example, women represent a large majority of older Americans, and they rely more heavily on Social Security benefits than older men (Smeeding 1999). Women are also more likely to require long-term care than men and to depend on Medicaid for it. The growing proportion of minority older Americans represents other subgroups that are likely to depend more heavily on public programs for old age support. These and other policy issues can be addressed with the data collected as part of the repeated cohort design of the HRS and its oversample of minority Americans.

These examples illustrate the many policy implications of findings about aging processes and the status of the aged. The fact that policy-relevant findings are available, however, does not guarantee that these findings will be used to inform the formulation of policies. Often political exigencies dictate which policies are adopted, and available research is simply used to promote policies considered worth adopting for other reasons. Moreover, the significance of research findings for policy discussions is not always obvious to those concerned, and scientists, policy analysts, and lawmakers have to work together in translating the significance of research findings for policy discussions and in integrating the multitude of relevant scientific information.

Conclusion

Research on aging has grown enormously in recent decades. New editions of the popular *Handbook of Aging and the Social Sciences* (Binstock and George 2001) have been revised every five years over the past decades. The *Journal of Gerontology* has been expanded into four coordinated journals in recent years. It has become clear from this rapidly growing body of research that patterns of aging and the resulting status of the aged in this country are highly variable. Whereas some older Americans are indeed impaired in their physical and mental functioning by acquired chronic conditions and long-standing disadvantages, many older adults maintain a high level of functioning and express a desire to lead an active leisure life or fulfill useful roles in their families and communities. To capture the variability and the patterns that lead to variability, longitudinal research with population-representative samples is required. For example, a recent report by the National Research Council entitled *The Aging Mind* (2000) calls for major longitudinal studies of cognitive functioning and performance. To explain the variability in aging patterns, possible explanatory individual as well as community, cultural, and societal characteristics need to be assessed or intervention studies need to be conducted (Riley, Kahn, and Foner 1994). It has also become clear that aging research is particularly well served by interdisciplinary collaborations and requires considerable methodological innovation and sophistication in order to gain the most from such complex, multifaceted life-span studies. The SRC at ISR, along with similar multidisciplinary research centers elsewhere, will continue to contribute to this knowledge through interdisciplinary and longitudinal aging studies including both substantive and methodological components.

NOTE

The editors and chapter contributors wish to dedicate this chapter to its principal author, Regula Herzog, who died tragically and prematurely shortly before the chapter and volume went to press. Regula made fundamental contributions to the substance and methods for understanding the role of psychosocial factors in human aging, both generally and with respect to specific health problems, especially urinary incontinence. She was a major architect of the health and mental health portions of the HRS, a superb colleague and interdisciplinary collaborator across the social and biomedical sciences, and a beloved mentor of students and early career scientists interested in understanding human aging as a biopsychosocial process.

REFERENCES

Adler, Nancy E., Thomas E. Boyce, Margaret A. Chesney, Sheldon Cohen, Susan Folkman, Robert L. Kahn, and S. Leonard Syme. 1994. Socioeconomic status and health. The challenge of the gradient. *American Psychologist* 49:15–24.

Alwin, Duane F., and Ryan J. McCammon. 1999. Aging versus cohort interpretations of intercohort differences in GSS vocabulary scores. *American Sociological Review* 64:272–86.

Atchley, Robert C. 1999. Continuity theory, self, and social structure. In *The self and society in aging processes,* ed. Carol D. Ryff and Victor W. Marshall, 94–121. New York: Springer.

Baltes, Paul B. 1973. Prototypical paradigms and questions in life-span research on development and aging. *Gerontologist* 13:458–67.

———. 1979. Life-span developmental psychology: Some converging observations on history and theory. In *Life-span development and behavior 2,* ed. Paul B. Baltes and Orville G. Brim Jr., 255–79. New York: Academic Press.

Barsky, Robert B., Miles S. Kimball, F. Thomas Juster, and Matthew Shapiro. 1997. Preference parameters and behavioral heterogeneity: An experimental approach in the Health and Retirement Study. *Quarterly Journal of Economics* 112:S537–S579.

Bengtson, Vern L., Cara J. Rice, and Malcolm L. Johnson. 1999. Are theories of aging important? Models and explanations in gerontology at the turn of the century. In *Handbook of theories of aging,* ed. Vern L. Bengtson and K. Warner Schaie, 3–20. New York: Springer.

Bengston, Vern L., and K. Warner Schaie. 1999. *Handbook of theories of aging.* New York: Springer.

Binstock, Robert H., and Linda K. George. 2001. *Handbook of Aging and the Social Sciences.* San Diego: Academic Press.

Birren, James E. 1999. Theories of aging: A personal perspective. In *Handbook of theories of aging,* ed. Vern L. Bengtson, and K. Warner Schaie, 459–71. New York: Springer.

Birren, James E., and Vern L. Bengtson. 1988. *Emergent theories of aging.* New York: Springer.

Camp, Cameron J., Robin L. West, and Leonard W. Poon. 1989. Recruitment practices for psychological research in gerontology. In *Special research methods for gerontology,* ed. M. Powell Lawton and A. Regula Herzog, 163–89. Amityville: Baywood.

Campbell, Richard T., and Duane F. Alwin. 1999. Quantitative approaches: Toward an integrated science of aging and human development. In *Handbook of aging and the social sciences,* ed. Robert H. Binstock and Linda K. George, 31–51. New York: Academic Press.

Carp, Frances M., and Abraham Carp. 1981. It may not be the answer, it may be the question. *Research on Aging* 3:85–100.

Carpenter, Letty. 1988. Medicaid eligibility for persons in nursing homes. *Health Care Financing Review* 10:67–77.

Cook, Thomas D., and Donald T. Campbell. 1979. *Quasi-experimentation: Design and analysis issues for field settings.* Chicago: Rand McNally.

Couper, Mick P., Robert M. Groves, and Trivellore E. Raghunathan. 1996. Nonresponse in the second wave of a longitudinal survey. Paper presented at the International Workshop on Household Survey Nonresponse, Rome, Italy, October.

Cutler, Neal E. 1979. Age variations in the dimensionality of life satisfaction. *Journal of Gerontology* 34:573–78.

Dannefer, Dale. 1988. What's in a name? An account of the neglect of variability in the study of aging. In *Emergent theories of aging,* ed. James E. Birren and Vern L. Bengston, 356–84. New York: Springer.

Deaton, Angus. 1992. *Understanding consumption.* Oxford: Clarendon Press.

Eizenman, Dara R., John R. Nesselroade, David L. Featherman, and John W. Rowe. 1997. Intraindividual variability in perceived control in an older sample: The MacArthur successful aging studies. *Psychology and Aging* 12:489–502.

Fogel, Robert W. 1994. Economic growth, population theory, and physiology: The bearing of long-term processes on the making of economic policy. *American Economic Review* 84:369–95.

Freedman, Vicki A., and Linda G. Martin. 1999. The role of education in explaining and forecasting trends in functional limitations among older Americans. *Demography* 36:461–73.

Friedman, Milton. 1957. *A theory of the consumption function.* Princeton: Princeton University Press.

George, Linda K. 1999. Social perspectives on the self in later life. In *The self and society in aging processes,* ed. Carol D. Ryff and Victor W. Marshall, 42–66. New York: Springer.

Glass, Thomas A., Carlos Mendes de Leon, Richard A. Marottoli, and Lisa F. Berkman. 1999. Population based study of social and productive activities as predictors of survival among elderly Americans. *British Medical Journal* 319:478–83.

Groves, Robert M., Trivellore E. Raghunathan, and Mick P. Couper. 1995. Evaluating statistical adjustments for unit nonresponse in a survey of the elderly. Paper presented at the International Workshop on Household Survey Nonresponse, Helsinki, Finland, October.

Gustman, Alan L., and Thomas L. Steinmeier. 1986. A structural retirement model. *Econometrica* 54:555–84.

———. 1994. Employer-provided health insurance and retirement behavior. *Industrial and Labor Relations Review* 48:124–40

———. 2000. Retirement outcomes in the Health and Retirement Study. *Social Security Bulletin* 63:57–71.

Havighurst, Robert J., Bernice L. Neugarten, and Sheldon S. Tobin. 1968. Disengagement and patterns of aging. In *Middle Age and aging,* ed. Bernice L. Neugarten, 161–72. Chicago: University of Chicago Press.

Herzog, A. Regula, and Hazel R. Markus. 1999. The self concept in life span and aging research. In *Handbook of theories of aging,* ed. K. Warner Schaie and Vern L. Bengtson, 227–52. New York: Springer.

Herzog, A. Regula, and Willard Rodgers. 1988a. Age and response rates to interview sample surveys. *Journal of Gerontology: Social Sciences* 43:S200–S205.

———. 1988b. Interviewing older adults: Mode comparison using data from a face-to-face survey and a telephone re-survey. *Public Opinion Quarterly* 52:84–99.

———. 1992. The use of survey methods in research on older Americans. In *The epidemiologic study of the elderly,* ed. Robert B. Wallace and Robert F. Woolson, 60–90. New York: Oxford University Press.

———. 1999. Cognitive performance measures in survey research on older adults. In *Cognition, aging, and self-reports,* ed. Norbert Schwarz, Denise Park, Bärbel Knäuper, and Seymour Sudman, 327–40. Philadelphia: Psychology Press.

Hill, Daniel. 1998. Differential attrition and declining health. Memorandum to the HRS/AHEAD Steering Committee, Ann Arbor, MI.

Hill, Daniel, and Robert J. Willis. 1998. Reducing panel attrition: A search for effective policy instruments. Paper presented at the Conference on Data Quality Issues in Longitudinal Surveys, Ann Arbor, MI, October.

House, James S., Ronald C. Kessler, A. Regula Herzog, Richard P. Mero, Ann M. Kinney, and Martha J. Breslow. 1990. Age, socioeconomic status, and health. *Milbank Quarterly* 68:383–411.

House, James S., James M. Lepkowski, Ann M. Kinney, Richard P. Mero, Ronald C. Kessler, and A. Regula Herzog. 1994. The social stratification of aging and health. *Journal of Health and Social Behavior* 35:213–34.

House, James S., and David R. Williams. 1996. Psychosocial pathways linking SES and CVD. In *National Institutes of Health, National Heart, Lung, and Blood Institute's Report of the Conference on Socioeconomic Status and Cardiovascular Health and Disease,* 119–34. Bethesda, MD: National, Heart, Lung, and Blood Institutes.

Hubbard, R. Glenn, Jonathan Skinner, and Stephen P. Zeldes. 1995. Precautionary saving and social insurance. *Journal of Political Economy* 103:360–99.

Hurd, Michael. 1990. Research on the elderly: Economic status, retirement, and consumption and saving. *Journal of Economic Literature* 28:565–637.

Hurd, Michael, Daniel McFadden, and Li Gan. 1998. Subjective curves and life cycle behavior. In *Inquiries in the economics of aging,* ed. David Wise, 259–305. Chicago: University of Chicago Press.

Knäuper, Bärbel. 1999a. The impact of age and education on response order effects in attitude measurement. *Public Opinion Quarterly* 63:347–70.

———. 1999b. Age differences in question and response order effects. In *Cognition, aging and self-reports,* ed. Norbert Schwarz, Denise Park, Bärbel Knäuper, and Seymour Sudman, 341–63. Washington, DC: Psychology Press.

Krause, Neal, Berit Ingersoll-Dayton, Jersey Liang, and Hidehiro Sugisawa. 1999. Religion, social support, and health among the Japanese elderly. *Journal of Health and Social Behavior* 40:405–21.

Lang, Frieder R., David L. Featherman, and John R. Nesselroade. 1997. Social self-efficacy and short-term variability in social relationships: The MacArthur successful aging studies. *Psychology and Aging* 12:657–66.

Lemon, Bruce W., Vern L. Bengston, and James A. Peterson. 1972. An exploration of the activity theory of aging: Activity types and life satisfaction among in-movers to a retirement community. *Journal of Gerontology* 27:511–23.

Liang, Jersey, Joan M. Bennett, Neal M. Krause, Ming-Cheng Chang, Huie-Sen Lin, Yi Li Chuang, and Shwu-Chong Wu. 1999. Stress, social relations, and old age mortality in Taiwan. *Journal of Clinical Epidemiology* 52:983–95.

Longino, Charles F., Jr., and Cary S. Kart. 1982. Explicating activity theory: A formal replication. *Journal of Gerontology* 37:713–22.

Lumsdaine, Robin L., James H. Stock, and David A. Wise. 1996. Why are retirement rates so high at age sixty-five? In *Advances in the economics of aging,* ed. David A. Wise, 11–82. Chicago: University of Chicago Press.

Lundberg, Shelly, and Jennifer Ward-Batts. 2000. Saving for retirement: Household bargaining and household net worth. Paper presented at the annual conference of the Social Security Retirement Research Consortium. Washington, DC, May.

Luoh, Ming-Ching, and A. Regula Herzog. 2002. Individual consequences of volunteer and paid work in old age: Health and mortality. *Journal of Health and Social Behavior* 43:490–519.

Manton, Kenneth G., Eric Stallard, and Larry Corder. 1997. Changes in the age dependence of mortality and disability: Cohort and other determinants. *Demography* 34:135–57.

McClellan, Mark, Barbara J. McNeil, and Joseph P. Newhouse. 1994. Does more intensive treatment of acute myocardial infarction in the elderly reduce mortality? Analysis using instrumental variables. *Journal of the American Medical Association* 272:859–66.

Modigliani, Franco, and Richard Brumberg. 1954. Utility analysis and the consumption function: An interpretation of cross-section data. In *Post-Keynesian economics,* ed. K. K. Kurihara, 388-436. New Brunswick, NJ: Rutgers University Press.

Moore, James F., and Olivia S. Mitchell. 2000. Projected retirement wealth and saving adequacy. In *Forecasting retirement needs and retirement wealth,* ed. Olivia Mitchell, P. Brett Hammond, and Anna Rappaport, 68–94. Philadelphia: University of Pennsylvania Press.

Musick, Mark A., A. Regula Herzog, and James S. House. 1999. Volunteering and mortality among older adults: Findings from a national sample. *Journal of Gerontology* 54B:S173–S180.

National Research Council. 2000. *The aging mind: Opportunities in cognitive research.* Washington, DC: National Academy Press.

O'Rand, Angela M., and Richard T. Campbell. 1999. On reestablishing the phenomenon and specifying ignorance: Theory development and research design in aging. In *Handbook of theories of aging,* ed. K. W. Schaie and Vern L. Bengtson, 59–78. New York: Springer.

Park, Denise C., Christopher Hertzog, Howard Leventhal, Roger W. Morrell, Elaine Leventhal, Daniel Birchmore, Mike Martin, and Joan Bennett. 1999. Medication adherence in rheumatoid arthritis patients: Older is wiser. *Journal of the American Geriatrics Society* 47:172–83.

Riley, Matilda White. 1987. On the significance of age in sociology. *Annual Sociological Review* 52:1–14.

Riley, Matilda White, Robert L. Kahn, and Anne Foner. 1994. *Age and structural lag.* New York: Wiley.

Rodgers, Willard L., Frank M. Andrews, and A. Regula Herzog. 1992. Quality of survey measures: A structural modeling approach. *Journal of Official Statistics* 8:251–75.

Rodgers, Willard L., and A. Regula Herzog. 1987. Interviewing older adults: The accuracy of factual information. *Journal of Gerontology* 42:387–94.

Rodgers, Willard L., A. Regula Herzog, and Frank M. Andrews. 1988. Interviewing older adults: Validity of self-reports of satisfaction. *Psychology and Aging* 3:264–72.

Rowe, John W., and Robert L. Kahn. 1998. *Successful aging.* New York: Pantheon.

Rust, John, and Christopher Phelan. 1997. How Social Security and Medicare affect retirement behavior in a world of incomplete markets. *Econometrica* 65:781–832.

Salthouse, Timothy A. 1999. Pressing issues in cognitive aging. In *Cognition, aging, and self-reports,* ed. Norbert Schwarz, Denise C. Park, Bärbel Knäuper, and Seymour Sudman, 185–98. Philadelphia: Psychology Press.

Schaie, K. Warner. 1983. *The Seattle Longitudinal Study: A twenty-one-year exploration of psychometric intelligence in adulthood.* New York: Guilford Press.

Schaie, K. Warner, and Sherry L. Willis. 1991. *Adult development and aging.* New York: HarperCollins.

Shock, Nathan W. 1985. Longitudinal studies of aging in humans. In *Handbook of the biology of aging,* ed. Caleb E. Finch and Edward L. Schneider, 721–43. New York: Van Nostrand Reinhold.

Smeeding, Timothy M. 1999. Social Security reform: Improving benefit adequacy and economic security for women. Syracuse University Aging Studies Program Policy Brief 16. Syracuse: Maxwell School of Citizenship and Public Affairs, Center for Policy Research, Syracuse University.

Smith, James. 1999. Healthy bodies and thick wallets: The dual relation between health and socioeconomic status. *Journal of Economic Perspectives* 13:145–66.

Soumerai, Stephen B., and Jerry Avorn. 1983. Perceived health, life satisfaction, and activity in urban elderly: Controlled study of the impact of part-time work. *Journal of Gerontology* 38:356–62.

Venti, Steven F., and David A. Wise. 1998. The cause of wealth dispersion at retirement: Choice or chance? *American Economic Review* 88:185–91.

Weir, David R., and Robert J. Willis. 2000. Prospects for widow poverty in the finances of married couples in the HRS. In *Forecasting retirement needs and retirement wealth,* ed. Olivia Mitchell, P. Brett Hammond, and Anna Rappaport, 208–34. Philadelphia: University of Pennsylvania Press.

Willis, Robert J. 1997. Theory confronts data: How the HRS is shaped by the economics of aging and how the economics of aging will be shaped by the HRS. Paper presented at the Conference on Economics of Aging International Health and Retirement Surveys, Amsterdam, August.

Wray, Linda A., A. Regula Herzog, Robert J. Willis, and Robert B. Wallace. 1998. The impact of education and heart attack on smoking cessation among middle-aged adults. *Journal of Health and Social Behavior* 39:271–94.

PART 5

Surveying the Subtleties and Complexities of Race

Maria Krysan

What do people think and how do they feel about people of different races and racial issues? What is the basis for these thoughts and feelings? How have attitudes changed—or not changed—over time? And why? How does one's race influence life chances and experiences? How does the social category of race play itself out in American society? The two chapters in this section provide an overview of the impressive array of insights that survey research has provided in answer to these and other questions about how race is "lived" in America. In the case of chapter 13, by Kinder and Schuman, the survey data provide at once a social telescope that reveals the broad patterns of racial attitudes and a detailed examination of the causes underlying these attitudes. Chapter 14, by Jackson and Williams, demonstrates how surveys can be used as something of a social microscope, serving to bring into focus the particular experiences, nuances, and heterogeneity of African-Americans.

The Complexity of Race in America

One conclusion both chapters make clear is the complexity of race in America—both what people think about it and how it influences people's lives. Chapter 13 traces the history of survey data on racial attitudes in the United States, noting that the topics of the questions asked parallel key moments in the history of U.S. race relations. When Jim Crow was being dismantled, Americans were asked about segregated streetcars and integrated schools. When civil unrest was at its height, questions emerged about the causes of riots, the wisdom of violent protest, and reactions to black militancy. When affirmative action moved onto the political scene—and later came under attack—questions about racial policies and perceptions of reverse discrimination began to appear. By tapping public sentiment about such issues, surveys provide one—though by no means the only—tool for interpreting and understanding race relations. And by tracking these sentiments over time, we learn something about what has and has not changed in American race relations. Later in chapter 13, Kinder and Schuman turn to the question of what underlies what is arguably the most contested dimension of contemporary racial attitudes: what should be done to ameliorate racial inequality. They review and critique the theories of group conflict, ideology, "new" racism, and politics, each of which has been offered to explain the pattern of attitudes toward racial policies.

More generally, Kinder and Schuman make it abundantly clear that describing and explaining the patterns and trends of racial attitudes is not a simple task. They highlight how the issues that are contested today are different—at least to some degree—from those that were important more than a half century ago, when racial attitude questions were first posed to large survey samples of Americans. Moreover, they demonstrate the complexity of racial attitudes: different kinds of survey questions tell different stories about racial attitudes in America.

As we move forward in our attempt to understand and track racial attitudes, it is critical that survey researchers retain old measures of racial attitudes but also continue to develop new measures to create a survey record that reflects the complexity of contemporary race relations. The major ongoing surveys, which will allow for tracking change—or stagnation—over time, have begun to do this, by including questions on such topics as affirmative action, affect toward racial groups, modern stereotypes, perceptions of discrimination, and reverse discrimination. However, a review of the recent surveys suggests that the main contributors (ISR's National Election Studies and the General Social Survey) seem to have an increasing overlap in the questions they ask about race—an overlap that was not true in past decades (see Schuman et al. 1997; cf. Hyman and Sheatsley 1956; Hyman 1964). While a replication across different survey organizations provides valuable information about the reliability of the results, it also means that the survey record on racial attitudes we are constructing may be more narrow and, therefore, less able to reflect the complexity of racial attitudes. In addition, as our country becomes increasingly multiracial/multiethnic, there is a serious need to incorporate questions that are asked of—and about—other racial/ethnic groups, such as Latinos and Asians. Without such inclusion, we run the risk of creating a less complete record for the future about how race has mattered in the hearts and minds of Americans. (For examples of work that moves in this direction, see Bobo and Hutchings 1996; Bobo and Johnson 2000; Bobo and Suh 2000; Charles 2000a, 2000b; Forman, Martinez, and Bonilla-Silva forthcoming; Hughes and Tuch 2000.)

Chapter 14 provides an overview of an ISR research initiative—the Program for Research on Black Americans—that is an exemplar of how surveys can generate systematic and theory- and policy-relevant research to shed light on the intricacies of a particular topic or population. In the case of PRBA, the topic is the experiences and lives of African-Americans. As Jackson and Williams describe in detail in chapter 14, this research has addressed such issues as an elaboration of the concept of social support, a detailed examination of religious participation in its different forms, analyses of the relationship between socioeconomic status and mental health, and assessments of the association between racial discrimination and health. The PRBA has also included methodological innovations about how to draw samples of "rare" populations, how to design multigenerational samples, and how to measure discrimination. These studies have brought into focus the experiences and lives of African-Americans, but their accomplishments and insights extend beyond this to more general insights on social processes and methodological techniques.

Through a focus on African-American experiences across a range of domains, Jackson and Williams also highlight the complexity of race as it is lived in America. Indeed, one of the key observations from their work is the heterogeneity of the African-American population, a heterogeneity that is overlooked when surveys do not intentionally take steps—methodologically and substantively—to incorporate African-Americans in substantial numbers and African-American perspectives in sufficient complexity. This complexity is revealed in their research on such questions as how social class interacts with race to shape individuals' experiences; how aging is experienced by African-Americans; and how different sources of social support become more and less important over the life span. Their studies of the effect of racial inequality on psychological and social resources demonstrate that the relationships are not always straightforward; for example, racial inequality may affect blacks' personal efficacy but not their self-esteem (Williams and Williams-Morris 2000).

More recently, the PRBA has undertaken an impressive set of international and comparative studies, arguing that we need to understand how race, prejudice, and discrimination operate across societies and cultures. This not only will shed light on the more general features of dominant/subordinate relations but will also bring into clearer focus the dynamics, commonalities, and idiosyncrasies of race as it is experienced in the United States (Jackson, Brown, and Kirby 1998). At the same time, PRBA has also turned its attention to ethnic groups within the U.S. black population—specifically Caribbean blacks. This recognition of subgroups within the black population reflects a more general and greater need within social surveys both for attitudinal studies and for studies like this that seek to tap experiences pertaining to race. Specifically, there is a need to increase the diversity of people of and about whom we ask questions. As the U.S. population becomes more racially/ethnically diverse, these comparative models—both across nations and also within our population—become critical. For example, to date, few studies have investigated the attitudes of and about Asians and Latinos. The PRBA's National Survey of American Lives, which includes samples of Latinos and Asians, is a step in the right direction. However, just as it is important to examine diversity within the black population, so too is it important to do this for the range of populations that are subsumed under the social categories of "Asian-Americans" and "Hispanics" (e.g., Barringer, Gardner, and Levin 1995; Bean and Bell-Rose 1999; Rumbaut and Portes 2001; Tuan 1998; Zhou and Bankston 1998; Raijman and Tienda 2000).

The Subtlety of Race in America

A second major theme alluded to—directly or indirectly—in chapters 13 and 14 is the subtlety surrounding some aspects of race as it is lived in America today. For example, this subtlety is reflected in attitude studies where there are concerns about "social desirability" pressures that motivate individuals to keep certain "blatant" racial attitudes to themselves (Krysan 1998; Berinsky 1999). It is also revealed in the very ways in which racial bias or negative racial attitudes are expressed—respondents may now talk less about how blacks are innately inferior but more about how they need to "work harder" (e.g., Bobo, Kluegel, and Smith 1997; Schuman et al. 1997). In the same vein, some types of discriminatory behaviors may have gone underground—instead of signs in store windows indicating "Negroes need not apply" or "Whites Only," bias and discrimination may be more indirect and fueled by more subtle types of racial attitudes, including unconscious stereotyping and implicit attitudes (e.g., Wittenbrink, Judd, and Park 1997; McConnell and Leibold 2001; Devine 1989). Though perhaps this behavior is more subtle, the consequences—in the form of substantial racial inequality and persistent discrimination in housing, jobs, and other social institutions—are far from subtle.

In light of these shifts, those interested in using survey research as a tool for understanding the new and more subtle dynamics of race face a challenge. Surveys are by and large a "blunt instrument," in part because they rely on self-reports of attitudes and behaviors and also because they tend toward breadth and generalizability rather than depth and detail. For example, in the case of attitudinal research, we know that the social context—such as the race of the interviewer or the privacy of the setting—matters (Anderson, Silver, and Abramson 1988; Davis 1997; Schuman and Converse 1971; Hatchett and Schuman 1976; Krysan 1998). And it matters in part because social desirability pressures work against self-reports of negative racial attitudes. In addition, self-reports of experiences with discrimination may be difficult where the manifestations of it are subtle (Schuman et al. 1983).

In fact, some social scientists interested in race and racial issues have lodged criticisms against survey research, asking such questions as, Do people tell the truth when answering racial attitude questions? Do their attitudes have any bearing on their behaviors? Have people really changed their attitudes? What implications do their attitudes have? Can surveys measure experiences of discrimination? Are individual attitudes and experiences, as measured by survey research, the relevant unit of analysis? Clearly, surveys cannot answer all of the important questions we have about racial issues. But, as they have since LaPiere (1934) conducted his vivid demonstration questioning the validity and utility of surveys, survey researchers have weathered these criticisms, and one response has been to develop survey techniques that overcome some of the problems of traditional methods and more successfully measure those aspects of race that *can* be tapped using survey methodology. Such approaches include the use of self-administered questionnaires that increase respondent privacy (Krysan 1998), split ballot experiments that allow for more rigorous and sometimes more subtle tests of hypotheses (Schuman and Bobo 1988), questions that measure stereotypes in a more subtle manner (Bobo and Massagli 2001), surveys that ask more detailed questions of experiences with discrimination in all areas of life (Forman, Williams, and Jackson 1997), and, more recently, technology that allows for the incorporation of videos that manipulate subtle racial cues (Hutchings, Valentino, and Rusch 2001). In short, the increasing complexity and subtlety calls for increased methodological savvy on the part of those interested in using surveys to shed light on race and race relations. To a great degree, research conducted by the Institute for Social Research (ISR)—and by the authors of the two chapters in this part—has been at the forefront on this score. Much of this research is alluded to in chapter 13 and highlighted in chapter 14. However, one particular source of these innovations has been another ISR-affiliated institution: the Detroit Area Study.

The Contributions of the Detroit Area Study to the Methods and Meaning of Race in America

DAS is a graduate training program at the University of Michigan that, since 1952, has launched an annual (usually face-to-face) survey of the Detroit metropolitan area. Though each year's study topic varies, a review of the questionnaires used in the first fifty years reveals that it has routinely collected data that speak to issues of race and race relations. Indeed, the first racial attitude question to appear in a DAS was in 1956, and asked respondents whether "Negro children should be allowed to attend white schools" and whether the respondent would "approve of a six year old white child playing in their home with a Negro child."

About one-quarter of the extant DAS surveys included at least one timely race-related question (and often several questions) on such issues as school and neighborhood integration, affirmative action, and the government's role in eliminating racial discrimination. In another 25 percent of the studies, race or race relations was the key focus, exploring such topics as black and white racial attitudes (1968, 1969, 1971), employer attitudes toward and implementation of affirmative action programs (1972), racial residential preferences (1976, 1992), race and politics (1989), environmental racism (1990), the role of education in shaping racial attitudes (1994), effects of racism on health (1995), the level of interracial contact in everyday life (1996), the structure of white racial ideology (1998), and the influence of race in political advertising (2000). These DAS data collection efforts have led to numerous journal articles, dissertations, and books that have made important substantive contributions to our understanding of race in America (for a compilation of DAS-based publications, see Clemens, Couper, and Powers 2002).

In addition, and equally important, is the long history in DAS of methodological innovation. These innovations have contributed to how we should ask and measure issues related to race, but they have also shown us how to use such methodological "artifacts" to shed light on substantive conclusions. For example, in the 1960s, Schuman and his colleagues (Schuman and Converse 1971; Hatchett and Schuman 1976) assessed the effects of race of interviewer on white and black reports of racial attitudes. The studies used random assignment of interviewer to respondent (something rare in such investigations even today), the goal of which was not simply to reduce the "error" associated with race of interviewer but also to use such effects to reveal something about how race works in America. The respondent-interviewer interaction was treated as a microcosm of interracial interaction in the real world, and its effects were used as an indirect measure of topics that created interracial tension.

In the area of racial residential segregation, DAS studies have been influential by providing, among other things, a methodological innovation that has proven to be both subtle and flexible. In the mid-1970s, Farley and his colleagues (1978) designed a way to measure how people felt about living in neighborhoods with people of different races by using show cards with diagrams of neighborhoods showing varying degrees of racial integration. The results have been frequently cited in the literature on residential segregation, and the approach has been widely replicated—in studies of Atlanta, Detroit, Boston, and Los Angeles in the mid-1990s and in the GSS in 2000—and also modified for use in a multiethnic setting (Charles 2000a, 2000b).

Finally, in the mid-1990s, several DAS studies included survey designs using multiple methods; this multimethod approach has helped extend the utility of survey research for tackling the complex and subtle character of racial issues. Investigations have, for example, used experimental and quasi-experimental designs to compare responses to face-to-face versus more private mail or self-administered questionnaires (Steeh 1994; Krysan 1995); complemented structured face-to-face interviews with depth interviews (Krysan 1995; Bonilla-Silva 1998); incorporated health measures and innovative ways to conceptualize and measure "major experiences" versus "everyday" discrimination (Jackson and Williams 1995); and most recently embedded subtle racial cues in a computer-assisted self-administered instrument (in the context of a face-to-face interview) to assess—indirectly and through experimental manipulation—the effect of race in political campaign advertising (Hutchings, Traugott, and Valentino 2000). The latter is a particularly interesting innovation that combines the power of technology with survey research to help illuminate the subtle influences of race on people's attitudes in the context of a general population survey.

Each of these recent studies, in one way or another, tackles challenges facing survey researchers interested in understanding race in the twenty-first century. DAS has served as something of a laboratory—as well as an important training mechanism—within the ISR. And with respect to understanding race in America, DAS has made significant methodological and substantive contributions to our understanding of race in the wider research literature, viewed through the lens of survey research. The following two chapters provide a valuable gateway to that wider literature.

REFERENCES

Anderson, Barbara A., Brian D. Silver, and Paul R. Abramson. 1988. The effects of the race of the interviewer on race-related attitudes of black respondents in SRC/CPS National Election Studies. *Public Opinion Quarterly* 52:289–324.

Barringer, Herbert, Robert W. Gardner, and Michael J. Levin. 1995. *Asians and Pacific Islanders in the United States.* New York: Russell Sage Foundation.

Bean, Frank D., and Stephanie Bell-Rose, eds. 1999. *Immigration and opportunity: Race, ethnicity, and employment in the United States.* New York: Russell Sage Foundation.

Berinsky, Adam J. 1999. The two faces of public opinion. *American Journal of Political Science* 43:1209–30.

Bobo, Lawrence, and Vincent Hutchings. 1996. Perceptions of racial group competition: Extending Blumer's theory of group position to a multiracial social context. *American Sociological Review* 61:951–72.

Bobo, Lawrence, and Devon Johnson. 2000. Racial attitudes in a prismatic metropolis: Mapping identity, stereotypes, competition, and views on affirmative action. In *Prismatic metropolis: Inequality in Los Angeles,* ed. Lawrence Bobo, Melvin L. Oliver, James H. Johnson Jr., and Abel Valenzuela. New York: Russell Sage Foundation.

Bobo, Lawrence, James R. Kluegel, and Ryan A. Smith. 1997. Laissez-faire racism: The crystallization of a kinder, gentler, antiblack ideology. In *Racial attitudes in the 1990s: Continuity and change,* ed. Steven A. Tuch and Jack K. Martin. Westport, CT: Praeger.

Bobo, Lawrence, and Michael P. Massagli. 2001. Stereotyping and urban inequality. In *Urban inequality: Evidence from four cities,* ed. Alice O'Connor, Chris Tilly, and Lawrence D. Bobo. New York: Russell Sage Foundation.

Bobo, Lawrence, and Susan A. Suh. 2000. Surveying racial discrimination: Analyses from a multiethnic labor market. In *Prismatic metropolis: Inequality in Los Angeles,* ed. Lawrence Bobo, Melvin L. Oliver, James H. Johnson Jr., and Abel Valenzuela. New York: Russell Sage Foundation.

Bonilla-Silva, Eduardo. 1998. *Detroit Area Study: White racial ideology.* DAS #212–468718. Ann Arbor: University of Michigan, Department of Sociology, Detroit Area Studies.

Charles, Camille Z. 2000a. Neighborhood racial composition preferences: Evidence from a multiethnic metropolis. *Social Problems* 47:379–407.

———. 2000b. Residential segregation in Los Angeles. In *Prismatic metropolis: Inequality in Los Angeles,* ed. Lawrence Bobo, Melvin L. Oliver, James H. Johnson Jr., and Abel Valenzuela. New York: Russell Sage Foundation.

Clemens, Judi, Mick Couper, and Kathy Powers. 2002. *The Detroit Area Study: Celebrating fifty years: A record of research conducted by the Detroit Area Study, 1952–2001.* Ann Arbor: University of Michigan, Department of Sociology.

Davis, Darren W. 1997. Nonrandom measurement error and race of interviewer effects among African Americans. *Public Opinion Quarterly* 61:183–207.

Devine, Patricia G. 1989. Stereotypes and prejudice: Their automatic and controlled components. *Journal of Personality and Social Psychology* 56:5–18.

Farley, Reynolds, Howard Schuman, Suzanne Bianchi, Diane L. Colasanto, and Shirley Hatchett. 1978. Chocolate city, vanilla suburbs: Will the trend toward racially separate communities continue? *Social Science Research* 7:319–44.

Forman, Tyrone, Gloria Martinez, and Eduardo Bonilla-Silva. Forthcoming. Latinos' perceptions of blacks and Asians: Testing the immigrant hypothesis. In *Race struggles,* ed. Sundiata Cha-Jua, Ted Koditschek, and Helen Neville. New York: Routledge.

Forman, Tyrone, David Williams, and James S. Jackson. 1997. Race, place, and discrimination. *Perspectives on Social Problems* 9:231–61.

Hatchett, Shirley, and Howard Schuman. 1976. White respondents and race-of-interviewer effects. *Public Opinion Quarterly* 39:523–28.

Hughes, Michael, and Steven A. Tuch. 2000. How beliefs about poverty influence racial policy attitudes: A study of whites, African Americans, Hispanics, and Asians in the United States. In *Racialized politics: The debate about racism in America,* ed. David O. Sears, Jim Sidanius, and Lawrence Bobo. Chicago: University of Chicago Press.

Hutchings, Vincent, Michael Traugott, and Nicholas Valentino. 2000. *Detroit Area Study: Campaign advertising: How it affects voters' attitudes.* DAS #485722. Ann Arbor: University of Michigan, Department of Sociology, Detroit Area Studies.

Hutchings, Vincent L., Nicholas Valentino, and Lara Rusch. 2001. What have you done for my group lately? The effects of subtle racial cues in campaign ads. Paper presented at the annual meeting of the American Association for Public Opinion Research, May, Montreal, Canada.

Hyman, Herbert H. 1964. Attitudes toward desegregation. *Scientific American* 211:16–23.

Hyman, Herbert H., and Paul B. Sheatsley. 1956. Attitudes toward desegregation. *Scientific American* 195:35–39.

Jackson, J. S., K. T. Brown, and D. Kirby. 1998. International perspectives on prejudice and racism. In *Racism: The problem and the response,* ed. J. L. Eberhardt and D. T. Fiske, 101–35. Newbury Park, CA: Sage.

Jackson, J. S., and D. Williams. 1995. Detroit Area Study: Social influences on health: stress, racism, and health protective resources. DAS #491452. Ann Arbor: University of Michigan, Department of Sociology, Detroit Area Studies.

Krysan, Maria. 1995. White racial attitudes: Does it matter how we ask? Ph.D. diss., University of Michigan, Ann Arbor.

———. 1998. Privacy and the expression of white racial attitudes: A comparison across three contexts. *Public Opinion Quarterly* 62:506–44.

LaPiere, Richard T. 1934. Attitudes vs. actions. *Social Forces* 13:230–37.

McConnell, Allen, and Jill Leibold. 2001. Relations among the implicit association test, discriminatory behavior, and explicit measures of racial attitudes. *Journal of Experimental Social Psychology* 37 (5): 435–42.

Raijman, Rebecca, and Marta Tienda. 2000. Immigrants' pathways to business ownership: A comparative ethnic perspective. *International Migration Review* 34 (3): 682–706.

Rumbaut, Rubén G., and Alejandro Portes. 2001. *Ethnicities: Children of immigrants in America.* Berkeley: University of California Press.

Schuman, Howard, and Lawrence D. Bobo. 1988. Survey-based experiments on white racial attitudes toward residential integration. *American Journal of Sociology* 94:273–99.

Schuman, Howard, and Jean M. Converse. 1971. The effects of black and white interviewers on black responses in 1968. *Public Opinion Quarterly* 35:44–68.

Schuman, Howard, Eleanor Singer, Rebecca Donovan, and Claire Selltiz. 1983. Discriminatory behavior in New York restaurants: 1950 and 1981. *Social Indicators Research* 13:69–83.

Schuman, Howard, Charlotte Steeh, Lawrence Bobo, and Maria Krysan. 1997. *Racial attitudes in America: Trends and interpretations.* 2d ed. Cambridge, MA: Harvard University Press.

Sniderman, Paul M., and Edward G. Carmines. 1997. *Reaching beyond race.* Cambridge, MA: Harvard University Press.

Steeh, Charlotte. 1994. *Detroit Area Study: Impact of education on attitudes.* DAS #135791. Ann Arbor: University of Michigan, Department of Sociology, Detroit Area Studies.

Tuan, Mia. 1998. *Forever foreigners or honorary whites? The Asian ethnic experience today.* New Brunswick, NJ: Rutgers University Press.

Williams, D. R., and R. Williams-Morris. 2000. Racism and mental health: The African American experience. *Ethnicity and Health* 5 (3–4): 243–68.

Wittenbrink, Bernd, Charles M. Judd, and Bernadette Park. 1997. Evidence for racial prejudice at the implicit level and its relationship with questionnaire measures. *Journal of Personality and Social Psychology* 72:262–74.

Zhou, Min, and Carl L. Bankston III. 1998. *Growing up American: How Vietnamese children adapt to life in the United States.* New York: Russell Sage Foundation.

CHAPTER 13

Racial Attitudes: Developments and Divisions in Survey Research

Donald R. Kinder and Howard Schuman

Beginning in the 1930s, carefully selected samples of Americans were asked their opinions on a remarkably wide range of subjects, such as capital punishment, foreign affairs, and the minimum wage. But race was not among the issues posed. Indeed, in Cantril's (1951) massive compendium of survey results from 1935 to 1946, only a single question can be found that refers directly to black Americans (an item prompted by Eleanor Roosevelt's resignation from the Daughters of the American Revolution when it denied the use of its concert hall to Marian Anderson). Struck by the virtual absence of racial questions from the early surveys, Paul Sheatsley noted, "The polls, for obvious reasons, tend to ask their questions about the issues that are hot, and it is clear that, during the decade preceding World War II, race relations did not qualify on that basis. . . . Negroes had their place, and it was a rare American white who became exercised over this fact of life" (1966, 217).

All this was soon to change. Black Americans began to organize and press their demands for equal rights; segregation and discrimination moved onto the nation's agenda; and survey research responded accordingly. Our purpose in this chapter is to recount the various ways that race became and remains a major focus for survey research across the social sciences.[1] We will see that what might be termed Sheatsley's "thermodynamic" thesis about how public events and survey content are linked has considerable—though not complete—validity for surveys of racial attitudes over the rest of the twentieth century.

Origins and Continuities

First Stirrings

World War II stimulated the start of survey research on racial issues, both in the country at large and within the military. In 1942 the Office of War Information sponsored a National Opinion Research Center survey that put the first questions on race to a national sample of white Americans, and at about the same time the Office of War Information carried out separate surveys of black Americans in New York City and Memphis. These government initiatives were apparently stimulated by concern over racial tensions that could interfere with the war effort. Indeed, a year later a large "race riot" occurred in Detroit, a major center for military production, when hostilities involving recent black and white migrants from the South erupted in violence, mostly by whites against blacks. (For a general review of social science research at this same point in time, see Horowitz 1944.)

The questions NORC asked of whites dealt mainly with broad principles of segregation, for example, whether buses and streetcars should have separate sections for blacks and whites: 56 percent of white Americans favored separate sections and 44 percent opposed them, with the North/South dividing line an important factor, as it remains, though to a decreasing extent, even today (Schuman et al. 1997). The New York City survey of blacks found that "42 percent felt that it was more important to make democracy work at home than to defeat Germany and Japan when questioned by a black interviewer . . . 34 percent when the interviewer was white" (Wynn 1975, 100).

Questions about white racial attitudes were asked again by NORC in 1944 and 1946. But then there was a hiatus of ten years before NORC again focused on racial issues, despite such important race-related events as the 1948 official desegregation of the military by President Truman. However, when race became a salient public concern as a result of both the 1954 Supreme Court school decision and the larger effort by blacks to end segregation in some Southern localities, Hyman and Sheatsley (1956) repeated several of the earlier questions. They found clear trends toward liberalization of white attitudes; for example, 60 percent now opposed segregated transportation, and support for the principle of school integration had risen from 48 percent to 61 percent.

The other World War II effort to study racial attitudes was reported by

Stouffer and his colleagues as part of their wide-ranging research on *The American Soldier* (1949). One chapter described the attitudes of both blacks and whites toward the practice of racial segregation, which was then standard policy within the military, and it provided encouraging evidence on acceptance by white soldiers of the first small steps toward integrating the Army. Stouffer and his colleagues (1950) also included an experimental study on race of interviewer effects, which showed that "Negro interviewers tended more than white interviewers to elicit responses [by blacks] reflecting . . . pessimistic views of postwar conditions, unfavorable reports on the Army, and manifestations of low personal esprit" (721).

Institute for Social Research's Early Studies of Racial Attitudes

The Survey Research Center (SRC) was not established until shortly after World War II, and there were no surveys on racial attitudes during its first years. The closest the SRC had to an omnibus vehicle that could incorporate questions dealing with race were the political surveys that evolved into the National Election Studies. The best known product of these early surveys, *The American Voter* (Campbell et al. 1960), indexes a number of references to "race" and "Negroes," but the emphasis in such cases was on black electoral behavior.

Questions on racial attitudes were included in election studies in 1958 and 1960, however, and they played a role in Converse's influential study "The Nature of Belief Systems in Mass Publics" (1964). This work is known best for challenging the assumption that most Americans think about politics in broad ideological terms, but it also makes an important point about racial attitudes. After demonstrating that correlations ("constraint") among responses to abstract issues are greater in an elite sample (candidates for Congress in 1958) than in a cross section, Converse shows that, when the attitude object is a familiar population grouping like blacks, the reverse occurs: constraint is higher for the mass sample than for the elite. Even though the racial questions could be said to differ along various nonracial dimensions, he argues that to the general public all the items came down simply to whether one was sympathetic or not toward blacks. As part of the same analysis, Converse shows that the stability of racial attitudes over time (1958–60) is also noticeably greater than for items dealing with more abstract issues—a finding he and Markus (1979) replicated more than a decade later. Thus, the measurement of racial attitudes was already important in ISR research by the late 1950s but in a context—Converse's concern with the fundamental nature of public opinion—that did not make it salient to those interested in racial attitudes per se.

In 1964 the NES asked a new set of questions of both blacks and whites that became important for later time trends, as well as for other types of analysis. Previous questions in NORC and Gallup surveys had mainly concerned the principle of segregation or the personal willingness of whites to accept some degree of integration in their own neighborhoods or schools, but the NES focused on government policy and its new questions dealt with the role of the federal government in advancing civil rights. For example, here is an abbreviated version of one such policy question: "Should the government in Washington see to it that black people get fair treatment in jobs, or should the government in Washington leave these matters to the states and local communities?"

The questions address difficult political issues of *implementing* broad principles of integration, and probably for that reason they have shown less support than have the questions on principles of desegregation or on personal social distance. Yet the wording of the NES implementation questions has had its own limitations for charting trends over time. In earlier years, "fair treatment in jobs" could be taken by almost everyone, white or black, to refer to preventing discrimination against African-Americans. Today the words "fair treatment" may well suggest, at least to a number of black and white respondents, affirmative action in the form of some degree of preference to blacks (Krysan 1999). These kinds of shifts in meaning, some of which are likely whenever we write questions intended for both the present and the future, must be kept in mind when interpreting attitude change over time.

From Civil Rights to Civil Disorders

By the mid-1960s white attitudes toward integration appeared to be moving in a strongly positive direction, prompting Hyman and Sheatsley to write in a second article on trends that "In the minds and hearts of the majority of Americans the principle of integration seems already to have won" (1964, 23). Although this conclusion was doubtless too optimistic, the March on Washington in 1963 brought a quarter of a million people to rededicate themselves to the goals of the civil rights movement and to hear Martin Luther King's eloquent speech "I Have a Dream" about the bright future of integration. In the next year, major civil rights legislation began to make its way through Congress, culminating in the 1965 Voting Rights Act, which altered the long-term political nature of the electorate.

Yet the future of the nonviolent civil rights movement symbolized by King was called into question in 1967 by riots in many American cities, the largest in Detroit, just fifty miles east of ISR's campus setting in Ann Arbor. Unlike Newark, the location of the largest previous riot a month earlier, Detroit had been regarded—at least by many white political figures—as a model city in terms of race relations, with high-wage working-class employment, considerable home ownership by blacks, and some efforts at inclusion of African-Americans in the city government. (Relations between the police and the black community, however, were little different from Newark and other cities.) If Detroit could explode, no city seemed immune, and it became evident that, in the urban centers of the nation, a great many black Americans were far from satisfied with their lot in life. At that point, to use Sheatsley's word, the issue was truly "hot." Furthermore, race involved not only white attitudes but also black attitudes, beliefs, and aspirations, which could no longer be taken for granted as supporting patient steps toward the distant goal of racial equality.

The National Advisory Commission on Civil Disorders was created in 1967 by President Johnson to discover what had happened in the riots, why it had happened, and what could be done to prevent it from happening again. Among other data-gathering efforts, the commission initiated two substantial ISR survey efforts: one by Caplan and Paige, the other by Campbell and Schuman. Caplan and Paige's primary aim was to determine the types of individuals who participated in the riots in Detroit and Newark. Their main findings were included in the commission's final report (1968), as well as published separately in *Scientific American* (1968). Contrary to widely held assumptions that the rioters were mainly riffraff consisting largely of an underclass of social deviants or, in another version, of unassimilated recent migrants from the South, the individuals Caplan and Paige identified as rioters were more likely to be long-term residents, had somewhat higher education than nonrioters, and did not differ from nonrioters importantly in either employment experience or income. Nor were there differences on variables such as church attendance, family composition, or belief in the importance of personal ability for reaching life goals. How they did differ was in a greater emphasis on having been blocked by racial discrimination and in a greater sense of black consciousness and of pride in being black.

Paige argued in two subsequent articles for a reconceptualization of the nature of black militancy. In one (1970) he saw the increasingly visible antiwhite militancy of blacks in the late 1960s as due to changes in their historical situation rather than as a result of underlying psychological traits. In earlier years, militancy had been oriented toward achieving integration. By the later 1960s, however, militancy was increasingly associated not only with black pride but also with antiwhite attitudes. In a second article, Paige (1971) characterized rioters as individuals weak in their trust of the city government but strong in their sense of personal efficacy to create political change.

In the second survey effort stimulated by the National Advisory Commission on Civil Disorders, Campbell and Schuman (1968) interviewed probability samples of both whites and blacks in fifteen major northern cities in 1968. Their report in the commission's volume of *Supplemental Studies* addressed four main issues. First, on the issue of calls by new black leaders for separatism, the authors found it useful to distinguish an emphasis on black culture, which was considerable (42 percent of black respondents favored having black children study an African language), from a rejection of integration, which was rare (only 13 percent preferred to live in a mostly black neighborhood). Although younger blacks were especially likely to reject integration, possibly presaging change in the years to come, trends in recent surveys on residential and school preferences indicate integration to have strong support still among black Americans (Schuman et al. 1997). (For a fully developed ISR program of research on black attitudes and beliefs, see chap. 14, this volume.)

The second issue was how the riots were viewed by each race. A large majority of blacks saw the riots as spontaneous protests against unfair treatment, economic deprivation, or both. The white population was more divided. A little more than one-third agreed with the predominant view among black Americans, but almost as many viewed the riots as conspiratorial assaults on law and order by criminal or demagogic elements, with the rest taking a middle position that the riots were a mixture of protest and looting. For *both* blacks and whites, it was especially young male respondents who condoned the use of violence—rioting in the case of blacks, counterrioting in the case of whites. One other finding of importance was that one-third of the white sample indicated that they saw little difference between blacks rioting and blacks demonstrating nonviolently

The third concern of the fifteen-city study was to compare black and white perceptions of the services provided by their city. Although blacks in 1968 were less satisfied than whites across the board, the most important difference involved the police. Blacks were quite likely to believe that they were treated unfairly by the police, in terms of both not receiving help when needed and being frequently harassed for no good reason. Whites seldom believed that either form of poor treatment was common.

The data on city services were analyzed further by Schuman and Gruenberg (1972), who found that dissatisfaction varied more by city of residence than by race—so that blacks in some cities (e.g., San Francisco) were more satisfied with their city services than were whites in other cities (e.g., Boston). Moreover, within cities it was not the color of individual skins that mattered most but rather the color of areas: the greater the proportion of whites in a neighborhood, the more satisfied *both* whites and blacks were with city services, consistent with the assumption that actual services did indeed vary by neighborhood.

The remaining chapter of the fifteen-city report focused on white attitudes toward blacks and was later expanded into a monograph by Campbell (1971). Liberal racial attitudes were more frequent among younger whites and among better educated whites, but it was the interaction of age and education that proved especially revealing. Among older whites who had finished their education prior to World War II, there was little sign that higher educational attainment was associated with more liberal racial attitudes. But among whites who had gone to college in the two decades following World War II, the college-educated held much more liberal attitudes than others of the same age. Evidently, college experience after World War II had a liberalizing effect on white Americans, in part, Campbell suggests, because of the growing importance on campuses of the social sciences. Another unexpected finding was that few white respondents attributed black socioeconomic disadvantage to an inherent lack of ability. Much more frequent was the claim that blacks "don't try hard enough"—what Schuman (1969) called an explanation in terms of "free will." This notion that blacks could succeed if only they applied themselves more diligently plays a key role in important theoretical interpretations of contemporary racial attitudes, as discussed in the second part of our chapter.

Events and Changes into the Present

In the 1980s ISR investigators undertook a study of changes in racial attitudes for the series "Social Trends in the United States," sponsored by the Social Science Research Council. The study drew on NORC, ISR, Gallup, and other available data, and the results were first reported by Schuman, Steeh, and Bobo in 1985; it was revised and expanded in 1997, with the addition of a fourth author, Krysan; and subsequently it is being updated on a public Web site, <tigger.uic.edu/~krysan/index2.html>.

Five major types of questions were analyzed in the study. Questions on broad *principles* of desegregation show the largest changes in a liberal direction. Indeed, for a question about whether black and white "students should go to the same schools or to different schools," the change for whites has been characterized as "the largest for any policy preference of any kind among the thousands . . . examined" (Page and Shapiro 1992, 69). The trend for this question, shown in figure 13.1, is nearly linear over five decades, as illustrated by the straight line, with no hint of a white "backlash" at any point.

Similar trends occur for a second set of questions on *social distance,* though not reaching the ceiling of nearly 100 percent shown in figure 13.1. However, the level of white support also varies considerably when measures of attitude strength are built into a question (e.g., *intensity* of support for integration) or when different amounts of integration are specified (e.g., different proportions of blacks moving into a school). More generally, the trend in figure 13.1 points to the rejection by most whites of segregation as a principle but cannot be taken as a literal prediction of the *amount* of integration that whites favor or accept, as will be discussed later in the chapter.

A third type of question concerns the *implementation* of principles of desegregation through government enforcement, as mentioned earlier,

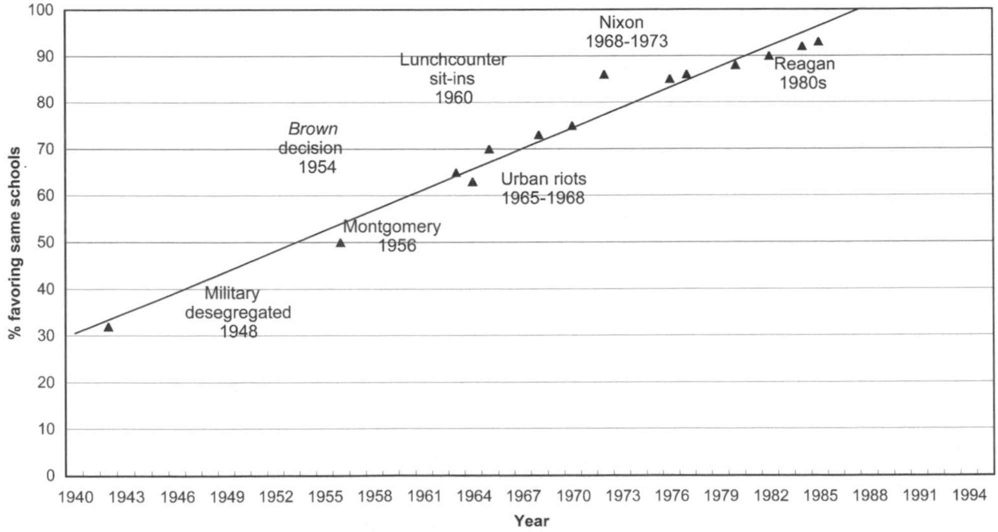

FIG. 13.1. Trend in white attitudes toward integrated schools. (From Schuman et al. 1997, 109, based on data points, shown in triangles, from the General Social Survey.)

and here the results are different. Support by whites is markedly less, and in one case (federal enforcement of school integration) the overall trend has been negative, with less support for implementation after 1970 than earlier. There are not many classic implementation items—questions where government action is proposed to prevent discrimination in a color-blind way—so data on this basic issue could not be fully explored. But if we are searching for signs of continued resistance to ending discrimination, it can be found with regard to government *enforcement* of principles of equal treatment rather than to principles as such. The principles and their implementation *do* appear to be linked in another way: those who indicate stronger feelings about equal treatment in principle are also more apt to support its implementation in practice (Schuman et al. 1997, 134–36).

A fourth type of question about *affirmative action* has tended in recent years to replace implementation questions about color-blind treatment, consistent with Sheatsley's premise that survey research often responds to societal issues that become prominent. The new questions—whether put in terms of compensatory preferences for blacks or of government expenditures to improve the conditions of blacks generally—have received little support from whites at any point in time. Two examples of the low and unchanging levels of white support for compensatory preferential treatment are shown in figure 13.2. Moreover, although increases in respondent education are ordinarily associated with more liberal racial attitudes, the association in the case of preferential treatment is reversed, and it is more educated white respondents who are most opposed to giving preferences to African-Americans in college admissions and employment.

Finally, on a set of questions concerning *beliefs* about black disadvantage, whites have continued to stress lack of motivation by African-Americans to succeed rather than either past or present discrimination. (Blacks, on the other hand, are much more likely to emphasize racial discrimination as pervasive.) Schuman and Krysan (1999) also explored data from the early 1960s, when the civil rights movement led by Martin Luther King Jr. was at its peak. During that brief period, when the focus was on Southern white resistance of a visible and violent nature, the national white population tended to blame whites themselves for black disadvantage. At still earlier points in the 1940s and before, lack of motivation by blacks was probably the predominant white explanation for black disadvantage (Cantril 1951; Katz and Braly 1933), just as it is today. Such nonlinear shifts over time point to the value of collecting frequent trend data on important attitudes.

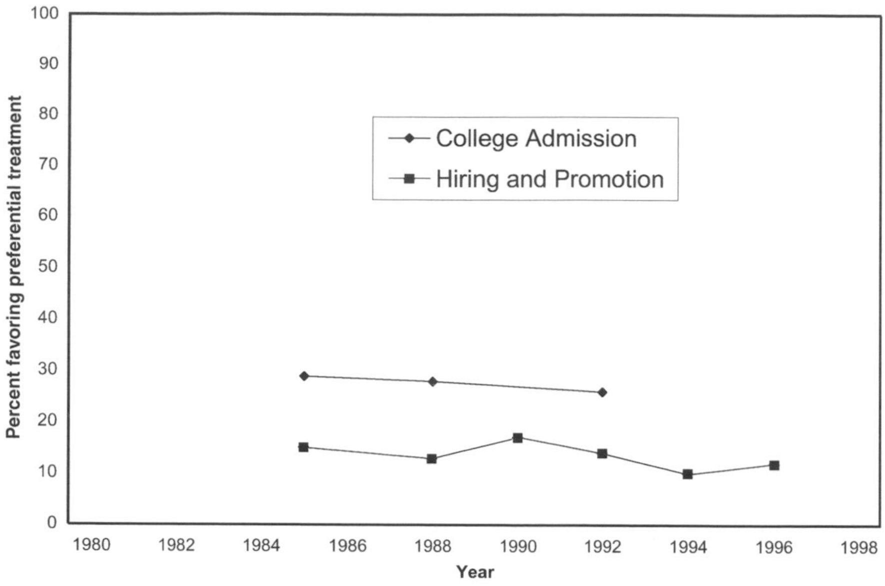

FIG. 13.2. White support for affirmative action for African-Americans (Adapted from Schuman et al. 1997, 179, based on data from the National Election Study.)

How Meaningful Are Trends in Racial Attitudes?

Long ago LaPiere (1934) questioned the degree to which attitudes are related to actions. This issue is difficult to study directly with surveys, but one experiment through the Detroit Area Study showed reasonable accuracy when using survey responses to predict willingness to sign later petitions on open housing (Brannon et al. 1973). More common is an indirect approach that compares aggregate attitude trends over time with overall societal change: at this level the broad picture reported by surveys since the 1940s of shifts from majority support of segregation and discrimination toward current attitudes supporting nondiscrimination and integration is consistent with the fact that the United States today is vastly different on matters of race from a half century ago. To cite just one example, virtually all blacks were once kept at the lowest occupational levels, but today there are nontrivial numbers of African-Americans in high government, educational, and business positions. Yet at the same time, affirmative action policies have been voted down in most states where they have reached the ballot, which is also consistent with survey evidence that white support for affirmative action policies has been and remains very low.

Yet if one takes at face value the kind of results presented in figure 13.1, there is an apparent contradiction between, on the one hand, the claim by almost all whites to favor "same schools" for black and white children and, on the other hand, the continued existence of very substantial amounts of de facto segregation of schools and residential areas. There are several explanations for this apparent contradiction. In part it comes from the very extent of the normative change, which leads some respondents to disguise or suppress their attitudes so as to present a more socially desirable face of tolerance to interviewers (Krysan 1998; Berinsky 1999). A larger part is due to overinterpretation of isolated survey questions. For example, the trend in figure 13.1 tells us simply that when forced to choose between two extreme positions—acceptance of racial integration in principle and of racial segregation in principle—most Americans choose the former. But we know from other survey data that, given the opportunity, most whites distinguish between acceptance of different degrees of integration (e.g., Farley et al. 1978, 1994). Furthermore, white support for integration in schools in real situations is likely to be balanced against other values, such as concerns about educational quality, and the latter (whether correctly perceived or not) can outweigh the former. In addition, Schuman and Bobo (1988) found evidence in randomized experiments and quasi-experiments that opposition to federal enforcement of desegregation has some basis in distrust of federal intrusion into local affairs unrelated to race, though the effect does not seem to be large. In sum, knowing these various qualifications, we should interpret the results in figure 13.1 as reflecting a real and important change in American norms, but not as a literal embracing of all forms of and steps toward school integration.

There is also one special complication in surveys of racial attitudes that can limit their applicability to other contexts: the individual who asks the questions can have large effects on answers (Hyman 1954). Schuman and Converse (1971) reviewed an entire 1968 Detroit Area Study (DAS) questionnaire and found that black respondents expressed substantially more negative feelings toward whites when interviewed by black rather than by white interviewers, and in a later study Hatchett and Schuman (1975–76) showed similar effects of interviewer's race on white respondents. The authors interpret their findings in terms of the norm of politeness: to indicate to a pleasant-appearing interviewer that "you neither trust nor feel friendly toward people of his race probably takes more chutzpah than the average respondent possesses" (Schuman and Converse 1971, 58). They also draw the broader conclusion that the interviewer effect should be regarded not as an artifact of surveys but as a fact of life in America, since the same effect is likely to occur in other spheres when blacks and whites interact (see also Schuman and Hatchett 1974 on political symbols). This methodological problem becomes more acute when studying change over time, for what appears to be a trend in racial attitudes may be due to systematic variations in the composition of interviewing staffs. Anderson, Silver, and Abramson (1988b), for example, documented shifts of 14 to 43 percent between 1964 and 1986 in the proportion of black respondents interviewed by black interviewers in the NES. Nor is it always clear that matching interviewer and respondent by race leads to greater validity (Anderson, Silver, and Abramson 1988a). Thus it is important that race of interviewer be controlled where possible and that readers be aware of this potential problem, which holds even for telephone surveys, since voice can also be a racial marker (e.g., Cotter, Cohen, and Coulter 1982).

Finally, there is the issue of the unique contribution that trend analysis of surveys makes to studying racial change generally. A careful analysis of an array of different kinds of attitude data from different times provides a picture of racial change or stasis that is systematic and that can help in identifying turning points—or in rejecting announcements of turning points that are not really there. Along with demographic and social data on aggregate patterns of behavior (for example, indices of segregation), attitude surveys provide a rich and relatively objective set of indicators with which to compare the more subjective and anecdotal accounts that figure in the rush of daily news. Surveys of racial attitudes should never be treated in a vacuum, but they contribute a perspective on what is happening that is not duplicated by any other form of evidence available to social science, to policymakers, or to the general public.

Competing Interpretations

So far we have emphasized the role played by sample surveys in documenting change and stability in racial attitudes over time. Surveys have also been designed and analyzed for a second purpose: to test alternative theories of racial attitudes. Much of this work takes off from the aforementioned observation that white Americans are more enthusiastic about equality and integration in principle than they are about the policies that would put such principles into effect (Schuman et al. 1997; Jackman 1978; Prothro and Grigg 1960). What are we to make of this?

One answer, as we will see, emphasizes group conflict as the primary source of racial attitudes. Another interprets white support for principles of equality and integration as hypocritical. A third suggests that the gap between principle and policy can be accounted for by the emergence of a new kind of racism. We will take up each of these arguments in turn, thereby clarifying the major ideas that have guided empirical research on racial attitudes over the last three decades. Along the way we hope to demonstrate that the sample survey is valuable not only in describing historical change but also in subjecting alternative explanations to demanding empirical test.

Racial Attitudes as an Expression of Group Conflict

Realistic group conflict theory was introduced to the social sciences at the turn of the century by William Graham Sumner in his famous book, *Folkways* (1906). The theory begins with the assertion that antagonism between groups is rooted in actual conflict: groups have incompatible goals, and they compete for scarce resources. In this analysis, racial groups are participants in the ongoing struggle for economic, political, and social assets. Conflicts of interest cause intergroup conflict, and conflicts are most intense where the real conflicts of interest are greatest, where opposing groups have the most at stake (Coser 1956; LeVine and Campbell 1972; Olzak 1992).

With the gap between principle and policy at least partly in mind, Lawrence Bobo (1988a) set out to develop and apply group conflict theory to contemporary American racial attitudes. In Bobo's account, the protests by black Americans that marked the 1950s and 1960s triggered a realistic sense of threat among white Americans regarding their own group's interests and privileges, which in turn generated opposition to policies promising change in the racial status quo. Whites may genuinely favor equality and integration in principle, but when faced with particular policies that challenge their position—integration of schools or affirmative action at work—principles give way to interests.

This is a plausible argument, and there is a good bit of evidence for it (e.g., Bobo 1983, 1988b; Bobo and Smith 1994; Kinder and Sanders 1996). An important early example of the relevance of realistic group conflict theory to American race relations we owe to V. O. Key. In *Southern Politics in State and Nation* (1949), Key argued that political life in the American South through the middle of the twentieth century was most reactionary in the so-called black belt: an arc of rich soil cutting through the Deep South, where the plantation system and slavery had flourished, where African-Americans continued to reside in concentrated numbers, and where, as Key put it, whites possessed "the deepest and most immediate concern with the maintenance of white supremacy" (5). Key's thesis grew out of a deep acquaintance with Southern history and a flair for maps, census information, and aggregate voting statistics. Sample surveys were generally unavailable to Key, and in any case, as we noted earlier, survey investigators at the time displayed no interest in the topic of race. But Key was right, as scores of subsequent survey-based investigations have confirmed: when the proportion of blacks living nearby increases, whites' racial attitudes harden (e.g., Black and Black 1987; Glaser 1994; Taylor 1998).

One limitation of the empirical literature motivated by realistic group conflict theory is that it has been preoccupied with the response of whites. The vocabulary of realistic group conflict theory is oriented to threat and harm, not to advantage and gain, and so adopts the perspective of whites threatened by blacks. But as a purely theoretical matter, among black Americans, *support* for racial policies should be driven by the perception of group *gain.* And it is: African-Americans are consistently more likely to support government policies on race insofar as they believe such policies will enhance opportunities for their racial group, not for themselves necessarily but for blacks as a whole (Kinder and Sanders 1996).

So group conflict would appear to play a part in the story of racial attitudes—group conflict, yes, but not, or so it would seem, *realistic* group conflict. Contrary to the standard theory, there appear to be only fragile connections between whites' sense of racial threat, on the one hand, and the actual conditions they face, on the other (Kinder and Sears 1981; Kinder and Sanders 1996). Unrealistic, exaggerated threat is typical, and on both sides of the color line (e.g., Aberbach and Walker 1973; Rieder 1985; Sears and McConahay 1973). Conflict between blacks and whites appears to be rooted both in real inequalities and in imagined fears, a potent combination.

Racial Attitudes as Ideological Weapons

Many analysts were impressed with the dramatic postwar transformation in whites' views on integration and equality as matters of principle, but

Mary Jackman was not among them. She suspected that white Americans had learned only to pay lip service to principles, while their real and much less generous racial views were revealed on matters of policy, where "racial attitudes and democratic principles are tested on an everyday basis" (1981a, 162). Originally set out and defended in a series of papers (Jackman 1978, 1981a, 1981b; Jackman and Muha 1984), this argument reached full form in *The Velvet Glove* (1994), Jackman's stimulating analysis of the ideological correlates of social inequality.

There Jackman builds a case for reconceiving intergroup attitudes as political communications, ideological weapons in the struggle for group advantage. In modern capitalist societies, so goes the argument, dominant groups control the means of ideological as well as material production and, through the former, supervise the creation and distribution of "an interpretation of reality and a set of normative prescriptions that serve their interests" (Jackman and Muha 1984, 759). Insofar as subordinate groups accept such interpretations and principles as their own, conflict is managed before it begins and material advantages are preserved without resort to violence.

Jackman argues further that, where inequalities are challenged and contested by the subordinate group, individualism becomes an important element in the dominant group's response and that American race relations supplies just such a case. Whites come to champion the idea of individualism—that citizens should be judged entirely on their individual merits, that the rights and claims of groups are much less legitimate—because it provides them with a principled and apparently neutral justification for opposing policies that favor black Americans. Individualism fits white Americans' political interests perfectly: whites wish to appear both reasonable and responsive, while at the same time making as few real concessions as possible.

Jackman is especially interested in explaining the racial divide, why blacks and whites differ so substantially on matters of politics. Based largely on an analysis of a national survey carried out in 1975 through the SRC at ISR, Jackman concluded that racial differences over such matters as school integration and employment discrimination are a direct reflection of group interest. Black and white Americans both seek to protect and enhance their own group's resources. Black Americans gravitate naturally to federal policies that dismantle segregation and prohibit discrimination, while white Americans move just as inevitably in the opposite direction. Jackman argues that group interests are neither simple nor straightforward. Such interests are constrained by practical considerations (both whites and blacks recognize that they cannot get all that they want) and by ethical commitments (American values such as individualism). But in the end, the racial divide comes down to group interest.

If the racial divide is more complicated than Jackman implies (Kinder and Winter 2001), her account is surely part of the story, and her analysis is appealing not least because it anchors intergroup attitudes in social inequality. As Geertz (1964) observed some years ago, this is an advantage enjoyed by "interest theories" of ideology generally, and the gain that such theories thereby provide to an understanding of ideology is substantial. All this is worth mentioning because psychologically oriented scholars of racial attitudes, taken up next, have not always been scrupulous about situating their analysis within a broader framework of politics and society (Blumer 1958).

A New Racism?

A third reaction to the gap between white support for egalitarian principles and egalitarian policies was the conjecture that a new variety of racism had emerged, one capable of simultaneously accommodating egalitarianism in principle while justifying opposition to particular initiatives designed to alter the racial status quo.

One version of this argument originated out of an analysis of a pair of racially charged campaigns for the mayor's office in Los Angeles in 1969 and 1973 (Kinder and Sears 1981). White voters generally rejected segregation and discrimination in principle, but they found much to disapprove of in black Americans' character and conduct. In their view, blacks were too demanding and outspoken, they were getting more than they were entitled to, and they were insisting on government assistance that they didn't really deserve. Such complaints and resentments formed a coherent point of view that Kinder and Sears named "symbolic racism." Symbolic racism was based not in direct and contemporary racial experiences of any sort—white suburbanites in Los Angeles had virtually no personal contact with blacks—but in deep-seated feelings of morality and in early-learned racial fears and stereotypes. Unconnected to the experiences of everyday life, symbolic racism appeared to be in part the expression of a moral code, a sense of how people should behave and how society should work, and it predicted the white vote more powerfully than did partisanship, conservatism, the personal threats that blacks might pose to whites' private lives, or indeed anything else.

From these relatively humble beginnings in a particular place and a specific time, the notion of symbolic racism—also known as modern racism (McConahay 1982), racial resentment (Kinder and Sanders 1996), or laissez-faire racism (Bobo and Smith 1998)—has come to occupy a prominent position in contemporary scholarship on race relations. Applied to various political settings and measured in somewhat different ways, symbolic racism has turned out over the last thirty years to be a powerful explanation for white opinion on matters of race. White Americans who subscribe to symbolic racism—who believe that discrimination has been eliminated, that blacks have only themselves to blame for their problems, that they spend too much time complaining about their situation and demanding special treatment—are much more likely than those who do not to vote against black candidates, to oppose school integration, to reject affirmative action, to support cutbacks in welfare, and more (e.g., Kinder 2002; Kinder and Mendelberg 2000; Kinder and Sanders 1996; Kluegel and Smith 1986; McConahay 1982; Sears 1988; Sears and Allen 1984; Sears et al. 1997). Furthermore, a close cousin to symbolic racism appears to lie behind recent Western European opposition to colored immigration (e.g., Pettigrew and Meertens 1995).

This new racism emerged, or so it is argued (Kinder and Sanders 1996), out of the turbulent events that constituted the racial crisis of the 1960s. The conspicuous and hard-earned successes of the civil rights movement led many whites to conclude that the obstacles standing in the way of black Americans had been successfully removed. The legal foundations for segregation had been demolished. Discrimination was illegal. Voting rights were being enforced. In the view of many white Americans, the problem of race had been solved and the nation could now move on to more pressing business. Yet glaring racial differences persisted. Whites saw evidence of this everywhere (or at least they thought they did): in crime, poverty, idleness, welfare, and, not least, the epidemic of violence and rioting that raced through American cities. Taking their cues from the egalitarian turn in scientific and elite circles (Degler 1991), white Americans were reluctant to explain what they saw by invoking the idea of biological racism that was so prominent in the nineteenth century: the doctrine that blacks constitute a separate and permanently inferior race. Instead, whites pointed to defects of temperament and character—that blacks disdained hard work and refused to take advantage of the ample opportunities that were now open to them. The new racism is preoccupied with black Americans' putative failure to display the virtues of work and self-sacrifice that white Americans claim as central to their own lives and to the life of their society.

It became possible by the mid-1980s to examine the empirical merits of this argument, thanks in part to new instrumentation introduced into the NES intended to assess symbolic racism. These questions make no reference to genetic inferiority, white supremacy, or racial segregation. Rather, they express a variety of individualistic and moralistic resentments: the sense that blacks have been handed advantages; that government has caved in, showering blacks with special favors; that hard work, self-discipline, and personal sacrifice no longer count for much. Formulated in such terms, symbolic racism turns out to be both quite popular and very powerful. Indeed, to predict white opinion on issues of race, nothing works as well.

But not everyone agrees. Over the years, Paul Sniderman and his colleagues (Sniderman et al. 1997; Sniderman, Crosby, and Howell 2000; Sniderman and Carmines 1997; Sniderman and Piazza 1993; Sniderman and Hagen 1985) have mounted an energetic challenge to the conclusion that racism plays a primary role in white opinion on matters of race today. We take up this challenge in a moment, but first we want to accentuate the positive, to identify points on which practically all analysts of racial attitude agree.

First, policy in the realm of race is complex, and public opinion takes such complexity into account. White and black Americans are not simply for or against all manner of racial policies. Their views depend importantly on details. Does the particular policy require federal intervention? Is it aimed at children or adults? Does it apply to schools or work? Is it about prohibiting discrimination or requiring affirmative action? All these details matter to opinion (Kinder and Mendelberg 1995; Kinder and Sanders 1990, 1996; Schuman et al. 1997; Sears et al. 1997; Sniderman and Piazza 1993).

Second, principles (or values) are indispensable to an adequate comprehension of American public opinion, both in general and on issues of race in particular (Kinder 1983, 1998; Sniderman and Piazza 1993; Sniderman and Carmines 1997). Opinions on policies that are explicitly about race cannot be reduced to expressions of racism alone (symbolic or otherwise). Public opinion in the affairs of race is partly a matter of principle as well. In particular, differences among Americans—black and white—over the importance and desirability of equality of opportunity and limited government predict corresponding differences on specific matters of policy (Feldman 1988; Feldman and Zaller 1992; Gross and Kinder 1998; Kinder and Sanders 1996; Kinder and Winter 2001; Kluegel and Smith

1986; Markus 2001; Schuman and Bobo 1988; Sears, Huddy, and Schaffer 1986).

Third, public opinion depends importantly on how issues are framed and choices are formulated—or, as Sniderman, Crosby, and Howell (2000, 266) put it, on "rhetorical environments." Elites are constantly bombarding citizens with suggestions about how issues should be understood, and these frames alter citizens' understandings and shape their opinions (Bobo and Kluegel 1993; Gilens 1996; Kinder and Sanders 1990, 1996; Nelson and Kinder 1996; Mendelberg 1997, 2001). For example, when frames suggest to whites that the issue in question is really a matter of whether blacks are deserving, racism becomes the dominant ingredient in opinion, while other considerations are shunted to one side. But under frames that suggest that race policies should be thought of as conflicts of interest, as assistance to minorities in general, or as help to the poor, the power of racism is diminished, while principles, interests, and the claims of other groups all come more visibly into play (Kinder and Sanders 1996).

Agreement among racial attitude analysts is not complete, of course, and the differences are sharpest over the political power of racism. Bobo, Kinder, McConahay, and Sears conclude that racism is the most important force behind white opinion on matters of race; Sniderman and his associates say that it is just one of many, and a not very important force at that (e.g., Sniderman and Piazza 1993, 4–5, 19, 28; Sniderman, Crosby, and Howell 2000). They suggest that Kinder and Sanders—and, by implication, Sears, Bobo, McConahay, and the others—have measured something other than racism. According to Sniderman, white Americans answer the symbolic racism questions by calling up general principles that are themselves racially neutral. If Sniderman is correct here, then the way is open to his conclusion that "The contemporary politics of race is at its core driven by a clash between liberal and conservative values and presumptions, not by racism—old or new" (Sniderman et al. 1997, 28).

As we have said, there is room enough in politics for principles and ideas, but the specific contention that, although they intended to measure racism, Kinder and Sears and the rest measured general egalitarianism instead collides with a complement of well-established results. First, the large impact of racism on whites' views on racial policies is over and above the effects due to other plausible explanations, *including egalitarianism.* White Americans disagree over the importance of various kinds of equality to society and politics, and these differences of principle have strong effects on policy opinions, in the domain of race as in others. But taking egalitarianism into account, the impact of racism remains enormous (Kinder 2002; Kinder and Sanders 1996).

Second, the impact of racism is most pronounced on policies that deal explicitly and unambiguously with race (such as school desegregation, fair employment, and affirmative action); is modest though still sizable on what might be called "covert" racial issues (policies such as welfare reform or capital punishment that do not explicitly refer to race but may be widely understood to have racial implications); and vanishes altogether on broad social programs (federal support for public education and national health insurance). This pattern makes perfect sense if symbolic racism is racism and makes no sense if symbolic racism is really values.

Third, symbolic racism is a powerful predictor of other varieties of racism, including racial stereotyping. White Americans who endorse symbolic racism are also inclined to endorse denigrating stereotypes: that, compared to whites, blacks are lazy, dangerous, and stupid (Kinder 2002; Kinder and Sanders 1996; Sears et al. 1997; Wittenbrink, Judd, and Park 1997).

Taken all around, these results make trouble for the claim that racial politics today is only (or even primarily) about values. White Americans oppose policies such as fair housing or affirmative action importantly, though not exclusively, for reasons of race.

Attitudes and Social Change

Not so long ago white Americans defended racial segregation and supported racial discrimination as matters of principle. Now, majorities say that blacks and whites should attend school together, that blacks should have an equal chance to compete for jobs, and that blacks have a right to live wherever they wish. This is an entirely welcome development, but it is not the whole story. As we have seen, white Americans express considerably more enthusiasm for the principles of equality and integration than they do for policies that are designed to bring these principles to life. Government intervention to ensure that black and white children attend school together is unpopular. Affirmative action is *very* unpopular. Why this is so—why it is that many white Americans object to such policies (while black Americans largely embrace them)—has been an abiding preoccupation of recent research. The answers we have reviewed—one emphasizing group interest, another interpreting white support for principles of equality and integration as mere hypocrisy, a third suggesting that the gap between principle and policy can be accounted for by a new racism, and a fourth arguing that white opinion on matters of race is an expression of race-neutral values—are sometimes presented as if they were mutually exclusive, each intended as a single and sovereign explanation. They need not be, however. And although it may not be altogether intellectually satisfying to say so, each probably provides a helpful if partial picture of the ways things really are.

In any event, however carefully they are sampled and assessed, attitudes, of course, cannot tell the full story of race relations in America. The complete story requires attention to economic, social, and political conditions. We take some reassurance from the fact that the picture of change and continuity in racial attitudes that we have tried to sketch here seems broadly consistent with evidence on change and continuity in American race relations in this more material sense.

For example, over the last fifty years or so, black Americans have made significant inroads into the middle class, sharing in the economic prosperity and educational upgrading that came to all of American society following World War II. Since the 1964 Civil Rights Act, discrimination by race has been illegal, and surely it is neither as flagrant nor as pervasive today as it once was. At the same time, important racial differences in employment, income, and especially wealth remain (Farley 1996; Farley and Allen 1987; Jaynes and Williams 1989). Affirmative action programs, which many regard as essential to narrowing these inequalities, are being challenged in the courts and overturned in state referenda. And it is not as if discrimination has disappeared: blacks are still steered away from white neighborhoods when looking to purchase homes, still face discrimination on the job, and still endure racist insults on the streets (Feagin and Sikes 1994). While white Americans tend to believe that discrimination is a problem of the past, black Americans see it as pervasive in society and as a demoralizing presence in their own lives (Sigelman and Welch 1991).

Likewise, while the legal foundations for segregation have been dismantled, universities compete fiercely over the most talented black students, and few whites today are prepared to defend segregation in principle, American cities are more segregated now than they were at the turn of the century (Massey and Denton 1993). And in a detailed examination of Detroit neighborhoods, Farley and his colleagues (1994) show how residential segregation is sustained in part by racial stereotyping: the widespread conviction among whites that blacks are less intelligent, harder to get along with, and less self-reliant than white people.

Also worth noting are the striking transformations that have taken place in the politics of race. On the positive side of the ledger, black participation in political life towers over what it was just a generation or two ago and the number of black elected officials has risen dramatically. Despite these impressive gains, however, black citizens remain substantially underrepresented: altogether, less than 2 percent of elected officials in the United States are black (Bositis 2000), and this condition may worsen in the future, not improve. Recent increases in black representation have been due in large measure to the creation of favorable districts through reapportionment or court order, since it remains today difficult for black candidates to succeed outside black majority districts, and such districts are currently under challenge in the courts. In the meantime, race has altered the nature of party competition in the United States, not necessarily in a wholesome direction. In *Issue Evolution,* Carmines and Stimson (1989) show that the presidential contest between Goldwater and Johnson in 1964 set in motion a fundamental rearrangement of partisan attachments, pivoting on race. In short order, the Democratic party became home to racial liberals; racial conservatives fled to the Republican party; black Americans moved quickly and almost unanimously into the Democratic column; and the South, for one hundred years solidly Democratic, became solidly Republican (Black and Black 1987, 1992; Sundquist 1983). One consequence of these transformations of the electoral landscape was the creation of unhealthy incentives: for Republican candidates to make coded racist appeals to whites and for Democratic candidates to ignore the interests of blacks (Kinder and Sanders 1996; Mendelberg 2001). In short, taken all around, in matters of attitude *and* in matters of material condition, we have come a fair ways, but we have a fair ways yet to go.

In *An American Dilemma,* Gunnar Myrdal (1944) took public opinion on race as a window onto American democracy, the single best way to gauge the extent to which America was living up to its democratic aspirations. It may prove instructive as a final point to reflect for a moment on the primitive tools that were available to Myrdal as he undertook his famous and influential assessment. In the fall of 1938, Myrdal prepared for his massive study with a tour of the American South. Myrdal went, often unchaperoned, to tobacco factories and textile mills, churches and farms, bars and nightclubs, talking to blacks and whites from all walks of life. Myrdal was perceptive, and he threw himself into the work. But he was innocent of probability sampling. He had no way of taking into account the color of his skin in the interviews he conducted. The modern technology of opinion assessment had not yet been invented. Experiments and statistical inference were of no use to him. Myrdal's brilliance and energy were considerable compensations, but it seems obvious to us that the social sciences are much better equipped methodologically at the beginning of the twenty-first century than they were in Myrdal's time and that credit for this improving state of affairs must go, in some large part, to the sample survey. Thank goodness for it, for surely we need all the methodological sophistication we can muster if we are to come to grips with as complex and subtle and persistent a problem as race in America.

NOTES

The authors' names at the beginning of the chapter are listed alphabetically. Howard Schuman had primary responsibility for the section "Origins and Continuities," and Donald Kinder had primary responsibility for the section "Competing Interpretations."

1. Attitudes toward and by Hispanic and other minorities are not included because thus far there has been little such direct research at ISR. Others have drawn on ideas developed in part at the ISR, expanding them in a more "prismatic" direction than the black and white focus here. See, for example, Zubrinsky and Bobo 1996 and Bobo and Hutchings 1996.

REFERENCES

Aberbach, Joel D., and Jack L. Walker. 1973. *Race in the city.* Boston: Little Brown.

Anderson, Barbara A., Brian D. Silver, and Paul R. Abramson. 1988a. The effects of the race of the interviewer on measures of electoral participation of blacks in SRC National Election Studies. *Public Opinion Quarterly* 52:53–83.

———. 1988b. The effects of the race of the interviewer on race-related attitudes of black respondents in SRC/CPS National Election Studies. *Public Opinion Quarterly* 52:289–324.

Berinsky, Adam J. 1999. The two faces of public opinion. *American Journal of Political Science* 43:1209–30.

Black, Earl, and Merle Black. 1987. *Politics and society in the South.* Cambridge, MA: Harvard University Press.

———. 1992. *The vital South: How presidents are elected.* Cambridge, MA: Harvard University Press.

Blumer, Herbert. 1958. Race prejudice as a sense of group position. *Pacific Sociological Review* 1:3–7.

Bobo, Lawrence. 1983. Whites' opposition to busing: Symbolic racism or realistic group conflict? *Journal of Personality and Social Psychology* 45:1196–1210.

———. 1988a. Group conflict, prejudice, and the paradox of contemporary racial attitudes. In *Eliminating racism: Profiles in controversy,* ed. Phylis Katz and Dalmas A. Taylor. New York and London: Plenum.

———. 1988b. Attitudes toward the black political movement: Trends, meaning, and the effects on racial policy attitudes. *Social Psychology Quarterly* 51:287–302.

Bobo, Lawrence, and Vincent Hutchings. 1996. Perceptions of racial group competition: Extending Blumer's theory of group position to a multiracial social context. *American Sociological Review* 61:951–72.

Bobo, Lawrence, and James R. Kluegel. 1993. Opposition to race targeting: Self-interest, stratification ideology, or racial attitudes? *American Sociological Review* 58:443–64.

Bobo, Lawrence, and Ryan A. Smith. 1994. Antipoverty policy, affirmative action, and racial attitudes. In *Confronting poverty,* ed. Sheldon H. Danziger, Gary D. Sandefur, and Daniel H. Weinberg, 365–95. Cambridge, MA: Harvard University Press.

———. 1998. From Jim Crow racism to laissez-faire racism: The transformation of racial attitudes. In *Beyond pluralism: The conception of groups and group identities in America,* ed. Wendy F. Katkin, Ned Landsman, and Andrea Tyree. Urbana and Chicago: University of Illinois Press.

Bositis, David A. 2000. Black elected officials 2000. Report prepared for the Joint Center for Political and Economic Studies, Washington, DC.

Brannon, Robert, Gary Cyphers, Sharlene Hesse, Susan Hesselbart, Roberta Keane, Howard Schuman, Thomas Viccaro, and Diana Wright. 1973. Attitude and action: A field experiment joined to a general population survey. *American Sociological Review* 38:625–36.

Campbell, Angus. 1971. *White attitudes toward black people.* Ann Arbor: Institute for Social Research, University of Michigan.

Campbell, Angus, Philip E. Converse, Warren E. Miller, and Donald E. Stokes. 1960. *The American voter.* New York: Wiley.

Campbell, Angus, and Howard Schuman. 1968. Racial attitudes in fifteen American cities. In *Supplemental Studies,* National Advisory Commission on Civil Disorders, 1–67. Washington, DC: U.S. Government Printing Office.

Cantril, Hadley. 1951. *Public opinion: 1935–1946.* Princeton: Princeton University Press. Prepared by Mildred Strunk.

Caplan, Nathan S., and Jeffery M. Paige. 1968. A study of ghetto rioters. *Scientific American* 219:15–21.

Carmines, E. G., and J. A. Stimson. 1989. *Issue evolution: Race and the transformation of American politics.* Princeton: Princeton University Press.

Converse, Philip E. 1964. The nature of belief systems in mass publics. In *Ideology and discontent,* ed. David E. Apter, 206–61. New York: Free Press.

Converse, Philip E., and Gregory B. Markus. 1979. Plus ça change . . . : The new CPS election study panel. *American Political Science Review* 73:32–49.

Coser, Lewis A. 1956. *The functions of social conflict.* Glencoe, IL: Free Press.

Cotter, Patrick R., Jeffrey Cohen, and Philip B. Coulter. 1982. Race-of-interviewer effects in telephone interviews. *Public Opinion Quarterly* 46:278–84.

Degler, Carl N. 1991. *In search of human nature.* New York: Oxford University Press.

Farley, Reynolds. 1996. *The new American reality: Who we are, how we got here, where we are going.* New York: Russell Sage Foundation.

Farley, Reynolds, and Walter R. Allen. 1987. *The color line and the quality of life in America.* New York: Russell Sage.

Farley, Reynolds, Howard Schuman, Suzanne Bianchi, Diane Colasanto, and Shirley Hatchett. 1978. Chocolate city, vanilla suburbs: Will the trend toward racially separate communities continue? *Social Science Research* 7:319–44.

Farley, Reynolds, Charlotte Steeh, Maria Krysan, Tara Jackson, and Keith Reeves. 1994. Stereotypes and segregation: Neighborhoods in the Detroit area. *American Journal of Sociology* 100:750–80.

Feagin, Joe R., and Melvin P. Sikes. 1994. *Living with racism: The black middle-class experience.* Boston: Beacon Press.

Feldman, Stanley. 1988. Structure and consistency in public opinion: The role of core beliefs and values. *American Journal of Political Science* 32:416–40.

Feldman, Stanley, and John Zaller. 1992. The political culture of ambivalence: Ideological responses to the welfare state. *American Journal of Political Science* 36:268–307.

Geertz, Clifford. 1964. Ideology as a cultural system. In *Ideology and discontent,* ed. David E. Apter. Glencoe, IL: Free Press.

Gilens, Martin. 1996. Race coding and white opposition to welfare. *American Political Science Review* 90:593–604.

Glaser, James M. 1994. Back to the black belt: Racial environment and white racial attitudes in the South. *Journal of Politics* 56:21–41.

Gross, Kimberly A., and Donald R. Kinder. 1998. A collision of principles? Free expression, racial equality, and the prohibition of racist speech. *British Journal of Political Science* 28:445–71.

Hatchett, Shirley, and Howard Schuman. 1975–76. White respondents and race-of-interviewer effects. *Public Opinion Quarterly* 39:523–28.

Horowitz, Eugene L. 1944. "Race" attitudes. In *Characteristics of the American Negro,* ed. Otto Klineberg, 141–248. New York: Harper.

Hyman, Herbert H. 1954. *Interviewing in social research.* Chicago: University of Chicago Press.

Hyman, Herbert H., and Paul B. Sheatsley. 1956. Attitudes toward desegregation. *Scientific American* 195:35–39.

———. 1964. Attitudes toward desegregation. *Scientific American* 211:16–23.

Jackman, Mary R. 1978. General and applied tolerance: Does education increase commitment to racial integration? *American Journal of Political Science* 22:302–32.

———. 1981a. Reply: Issues in the measurement of commitment to racial integration. *Political Methodology* 8:160–72.

———. 1981b. Education and policy commitment to racial integration. *American Journal of Political Science* 25:256–69.

———. 1994. *The velvet glove: Paternalism and conflict in gender, class, and race relations.* Berkeley and Los Angeles: University of California Press.

Jackman, Mary R., and Michael J. Muha. 1984. Education and intergroup attitudes: Moral enlightenment, superficial democratic commitment, or ideological refinement? *American Sociological Review* 49 (December): 751–69.

Jaynes, Gerald David, and Robin M. Williams Jr. 1989. *A common destiny: Blacks and American society.* Washington: National Academy Press.

Katz, Daniel, and Kenneth W. Braly. 1933. Racial stereotypes of one hundred college students. *Journal of Abnormal and Social Psychology* 28:280–90.

Key, V. O., Jr. 1949. *Southern politics in state and nation.* New York: Knopf.

Kinder, Donald R. 1983. Diversity and complexity in American public opinion. In *Polit-*

ical science: The state of the discipline, ed. Ada Finifter. Washington, DC: American Political Science Association.

———. 1998. Opinion and action in the realm of politics. In *Handbook of social psychology,* 4th ed., ed. Daniel Gilbert, Susan Fiske, and Gardner Lindsey, 2:778–865. Boston: McGraw-Hill.

———. 2002. Whitewashing racism: Principles versus prejudice in American political life. Center for Political Studies, University of Michigan. Manuscript.

Kinder, Donald R., and Tali Mendelberg. 1995. Cracks in American apartheid: The political impact of prejudice among desegregated whites. *Journal of Politics* 57:401–24.

———. 2000. Individualism reconsidered. In *Racialized politics,* ed. David O. Sears, Jim Sidanius, and Lawrence Bobo, 44–74. Chicago: University of Chicago Press.

Kinder, Donald R., and L. M. Sanders. 1990. Mimicking political debate with survey questions: The case of white opinion on affirmative action for blacks. *Social Cognition* 8:73–103.

———. 1996. *Divided by color: Racial politics and democratic ideals.* Chicago: University of Chicago Press.

Kinder, Donald R., and David O. Sears. 1981. Prejudice and politics: Symbolic racism versus racial threats to the good life. *Journal of Personality and Social Psychology* 40:414–31.

Kinder, Donald R., and Nicholas Winter. 2001. Exploring the racial divide. *American Journal of Political Science* 45 (2): 439–56.

Kluegel, James R., and Elliot R. Smith. 1986. *Beliefs about inequality: Americans' views of what is and what ought to be.* Hawthorne, NY: Aldine de Gruyter.

Krysan, Maria. 1998. Privacy and the expression of white racial attitudes. *Public Opinion Research* 62:506–44.

———. 1999. Qualifying a quantifying analysis on racial equality. *Social Psychology Quarterly* 62:211–18.

LaPiere, Richard T. 1934. Attitudes vs. actions. *Social Forces* 13:230–37.

LeVine, Robert A., and Donald T. Campbell. 1972. *Ethnocentrism: Theories of conflict, ethnic attitudes, and group behavior.* New York: Wiley.

Markus, Gregory B. 2001. American individualism reconsidered. In *Citizens and politics,* ed. James Kuklinski, 401–32. Cambridge: Cambridge University Press.

Massey, Douglas S., and Nancy A. Denton. 1993. *American apartheid: Segregation and the making of the underclass.* Cambridge, MA: Harvard University Press.

McConahay, John B. 1982. Self-interest versus racial attitudes as correlates of anti-busing attitudes in Louisville. *Journal of Politics* 44:692–720.

Mendelberg, Tali. 1997. Executing Hortons: Racial crime in the 1988 presidential campaign. *Public Opinion Quarterly* 61:134–57.

———. 2001. *The race card.* Princeton: Princeton University Press.

Myrdal, Gunnar. 1944. *An American dilemma: The Negro problem and modern democracy.* New York: Harper and Row.

National Advisory Commission on Civil Disorders. 1968. *Report.* Washington, DC: U.S. Government Printing Office.

Nelson, Thomas E., and Donald R. Kinder. 1996. Issue frames and group-centrism in American public opinion. *Journal of Politics* 58:1055–78.

Olzak, Susan. 1992. *The dynamics of ethnic competition and conflict.* Stanford: Stanford University Press.

Page, Benjamin I., and Robert Y. Shapiro. 1992. *The rational public: Fifty years of trends in Americans' policy preferences.* Chicago: University of Chicago Press.

Paige, Jeffery M. 1970. Changing patterns of anti-white attitudes among blacks. *Journal of Social Issues* 26:69–86.

———. 1971. Political orientation and riot participation. *American Sociological Review* 36:810–20.

Pettigrew, Thomas, and R. W. Meertens. 1995. Subtle and blatant prejudice in Western Europe. *European Journal of Social Psychology* 25:57–75.

Prothro, James W., and Charles M. Grigg. 1960. Fundamental principles of democracy: Bases of agreement and disagreement. *Journal of Politics* 22:276–94.

Rieder, Jonathan. 1985. *Canarsie: The Jews and Italians of Brooklyn against liberalism.* Cambridge, MA: Harvard University Press.

Schuman, Howard. 1969. Free will and determinism in public beliefs about race. *Trans-Action* (December): 44–48.

Schuman, Howard, and Lawrence Bobo. 1988. Survey-based experiments on white racial attitudes toward residential integration. *American Journal of Sociology* 94:273–99.

Schuman, Howard, and Jean M. Converse. 1971. The effects of black and white interviewers on black responses in 1968. *Public Opinion Quarterly* 35:44–68.

Schuman, Howard, and Barry Gruenberg. 1972. Dissatisfaction with city services: Is race an important factor? In *Urban affairs annual review: Urban politics and people,* ed. Harlan Hahn 6:369–92. Thousand Oaks, CA: Sage.

Schuman, Howard, and Shirley Hatchett. 1974. *Black racial attitudes: Trends and complexities.* Ann Arbor: Institute for Social Research, University of Michigan.

Schuman, Howard, and Maria Krysan. 1999. A historical note on whites' beliefs about racial inequality. *American Sociological Review* 64:847–55.

Schuman, Howard, Charlotte Steeh, and Lawrence Bobo. 1985. *Racial attitudes in America: Trends and interpretations.* Cambridge, MA: Harvard University Press.

Schuman, Howard, Charlotte Steeh, Lawrence Bobo, and Maria Krysan. 1997. *Racial attitudes in America: Trends and interpretations.* Rev. ed. Cambridge, MA: Harvard University Press.

Sears, David O. 1988. Symbolic racism. In *Eliminating racism: Profiles in controversy,* ed. Phylis Katz and Dalmas A. Taylor. New York and London: Plenum.

Sears, David O., and Harris M. Allen Jr. 1984. The trajectory of local desegregation controversies and whites' opposition to busing. In *Groups in contact: The psychology of desegregation,* ed. Norman Miller and Marilyn Brewer. New York: Academic Press.

Sears, David O., Leonie Huddy, and L.G. Schaffer. 1986. A schematic variant of symbolic politics theory, as applied to racial and gender equality. In *Political cognition,* ed. Richard R. Lau and David O. Sears. Hillsdale, NJ: Erlbaum.

Sears, David O., and John B. McConahay. 1973. *The politics of violence: The new urban blacks and the Watts riot.* Boston: Houghton Mifflin.

Sears, David O., Colette Van Laar, Mary Carillo, and Rick Kosterman. 1997. Is it really racism? *Public Opinion Quarterly* 61:16–53.

Sheatsley, Paul B. 1966. White attitudes toward the Negro. *Daedalus* 95:217–38.

Sigelman, Lee, and Susan Welch. 1991. *Black Americans' views of racial inequality: The dream deferred.* Cambridge: Cambridge University Press.

Sniderman, P. M., and Edward G. Carmines. 1997. *Reaching beyond race.* Cambridge, MA: Harvard University Press.

Sniderman, P. M., Edward G. Carmines, William G. Howell, and Will Morgan. 1997. A test of alternative interpretations of the contemporary politics of race: A critical examination of *Divided by color.* Paper presented at the annual meeting of the Mid-West Political Science Association, Chicago, April.

Sniderman, P. M., Gretchen C. Crosby, and William G. Howell. 2000. The politics of race. In *Racialized politics,* ed. David O. Sears, Jim Sidanius, and Lawrence Bobo, 236–79. Chicago: University of Chicago Press.

Sniderman, P. M., and M. G. Hagen. 1985. *Race and inequality: A study of American values.* Chatham, NJ: Chatham House.

Sniderman, P. M., and Thomas Piazza. 1993. *The scar of race.* Cambridge, MA: Harvard University Press.

Stouffer, Samuel A., Louis Guttman, Edward A. Suchman, Paul F. Lazarsfeld, Shirley A. Star, and John A. Clausen. 1950. *Measurement and prediction.* New York: Wiley.

Stouffer, Samuel A., Edward A. Suchman, Leland DeVinney, Shirley A. Star, and Robin M. Willins Jr. 1949. *The American soldier: Adjustment during army life.* New York: Wiley.

Sumner, William Graham. 1906. *Folkways: A study of the sociological importance of usages, manners, customs, mores, and morals.* Boston: Athenaeum Press.

Sundquist, James L. 1983. *Dynamics of the party system: Alignment and realignment of political parties in the United States.* Washington, DC: Brookings.

Taylor, Marylee C. 1998. How white attitudes vary with the racial composition of local populations: Numbers count. *American Sociological Review* 63:512–35.

Wittenbrink, Bernd, Charles M. Judd, and Bernadette Park. 1997. Evidence for racial prejudice at the implicit level and its relationship with questionnaire measures. *Journal of Personality and Social Psychology* 72:262–74.

Wynn, Neil A. 1975. *The Afro-American and the Second World War.* New York: Holmes and Meir.

Zubrinsky, Camille L., and Lawrence Bobo. 1996. Prismatic metropolis: Race and residential segregation in the City of the Angels. *Social Science Research* 25:335–74.

CHAPTER 14

Surveying the Black American Population

James S. Jackson and David R. Williams

This chapter focuses on the challenges and scientific opportunities involved in conducting household sample surveys of the American black population. The history and ongoing research within the Program for Research on Black Americans, and other research projects within the Survey Research Center (SRC) and Institute for Social Research (ISR) more broadly, provide a local context for discussing a set of principles needed for an appropriate empirical, social science approach to the design and implementation of sample surveys among black Americans (Clark 1964; Du Bois 1899; Drake and Cayton 1947; Frazier 1932; Schuman and Hatchett 1974; Stanfield and Dennis 1993). Although we primarily review research and findings conducted within the PRBA, findings from other studies conducted at ISR and elsewhere are noted in the context of discussing substantive issues in the areas selected for review.

Consistent with the important theoretical and substantive contributions of Du Bois (1899), Frazier (1932) and Drake and Cayton (1947), to name a few, three major themes or principles have been consistently emphasized in the history and growth of interdisciplinary social sciences focused on the study of black Americans: (1) research strategies that proceed from real-life needs rather than from purely theoretical imperatives; (2) collaborative relationships with black communities; and (3) new research competencies and roles that will facilitate the advancement of collective black interests (Akbar 1985; Boykin and Toms 1985; Boykin, Franklin, and Yates 1980; Du Bois 1899; Frazier 1932; Gordon 1973; Heller 1984; Jackson 1985; Jones 1980; Myers 1985; Smith 1993; Stanfield and Dennis 1993).

The Program for Research on Black Americans

Three major assumptions contributed to the development of the PRBA: (1) a long history of inadequately conceptualized, conducted, and interpreted research on blacks; (2) subjugation of much of what is unique to black Americans to deficit and "culture of poverty" theorizing; and (3) the lack of empirically trained social scientists sensitive to these issues (Stanfield 1993). Studies of black American adults have typically been restricted to limited and special populations. National and regional data on blacks have usually been gathered in the course of surveys of the general population, a procedure that potentially introduces serious biases in the representation of the full range and diversity of the black population, because the latter is distributed geographically very differently from the general U.S. population (Caldwell et al. 1999). An oversampling approach to national surveys has also meant that concepts, measures, and methods developed in the study of the largely white general population have often been employed in the study of black Americans without appropriate modification. There has been little theoretical or empirical concern with the appropriateness of this relatively simple comparative approach (Jackson 1991; Neighbors 1985). Thus, for the most part, national and regional studies have not been informed by an awareness of or an appreciation for the unique cultural experiences of black Americans (Jackson, Tucker, and Bowman 1982; Caldwell et al. 1999).

Partly because of the small and often nonrepresentative samples of blacks, most national surveys have not gone beyond superficial analyses of gross black-white comparisons (Jackson 1991). This cursory treatment has served to perpetuate an overly simplified scientific and policy view of the black experience (Jackson 2000; Jones 1983; Stanfield 1993). Thus, scientific deficiencies dictated the need for data from large, well-designed national probability sample surveys that address, in a culturally sensitive manner, major areas of the life experiences of black Americans (Caldwell et al. 1999; Jackson 1991; Jackson, Tucker, and Gurin 1987; Jackson, Tucker, and Bowman 1982).

A number of historically important events, including a critical mass of graduate students of color and a receptive environment, culminated in 1975 in the formation of the PRBA at the University of Michigan ISR. The PRBA was intended to provide an interdisciplinary, basic social science research group that was sensitive to cultural and systemic factors in the social, psychological, economic, and political behaviors of black Americans. The sample survey was selected as the basic empirical research vehicle. This was due not to its scientific preeminence over other empirical research methods but rather to its ability to generate large quantities of representative data (Schuman and Kalton 1985); its potential link to public policy formulation; and its affinity to the experiences and backgrounds of the program founders at the ISR (Jackson 1991; Jackson, Tucker, and Bowman 1982; Caldwell et al. 1999).

The PRBA has attempted to develop and implement a programmatic embodiment of the philosophical and conceptual principles guiding historically important research on the black population (e.g., Du Bois 1899; Frazier 1932; Schuman and Hatchett 1974). There has been a long history of survey research at ISR and elsewhere using both probability and nonprobability approaches to sampling black populations (Smith 1993). In addition to the pioneering work of Du Bois (1899) and Frazier (1932), there is the work in the 1960s and 1970s by Gurin and Katz (1966) and Gurin and Epps (1975) on black college students; by Marx (1967) on black political attitudes and voting behavior; by Gurin and Gurin (e.g., Gurin, Miller, and Gurin 1980) on politicized racial identity; by Schuman and Hatchett (1974) on black racial attitudes; as well as long-standing research based upon the Panel Study of Income Dynamics (e.g., Hill, Duncan, and Gurin 1985), the decennial censuses, and the monthly Current Population Surveys (e.g., Farley and Allen 1987; Farley 1996). In addition to important secondary analyses of existing long-term data sources (e.g., Schuman, Belli, and Bischoping 1995), more recent research has featured regional surveys by Bobo and colleagues (Bobo et al. 1992) on racial attitudes, as well as a set of large surveys that address specialized interests, such as family dynamics (e.g., Orbuch, Veroff, and Hunter 1999) and socioeconomic, mental health, and physical health statuses (e.g., House et al. 1986).

Major PRBA Studies

Over the past twenty-five years, members of the PRBA have been engaged in the development, collection, and analysis of data from several major national and regional probability surveys that have attempted to address limitations in the existing literature. The National Survey of Black Americans, initiated in 1977 with funding from the Ford Foundation and the Center for the Study of Minority Group Mental Health of the National Institute of Mental Health, was a national probability household survey of 2,107 black Americans eighteen years of age and older, conducted over a seven-month period in 1979 and 1980 (Jackson, Tucker, and Gurin 1987).

The size and representativeness of the sample permit systematic investigation of the heterogeneity of the adult black population. Substantively, this omnibus survey was concerned with major social, economic, and psychological aspects of black American life. The survey questionnaire included items on family and friend relationships, community and neighborhood life, religion, racial identity, political attitudes and participation, informal and formal help resources, and job and employment history. The face-to-face household interviews were conducted by an all-black, male and female, professional interviewing staff, trained and supervised by the PRBA and SRC of the ISR. The existence of a large high-quality sample also made follow-up studies on these same individuals possible and cost-effective. The four-wave panel study of the NSBA—from 1979–80 to 1992–provides a unique perspective on intra-individual change over an important period of history for black Americans.

The national NSBA cross-section survey served as the parent study for the National Three-Generation Family Study (TGFS), conducted in 1980 and 1981 and funded by the NIA and the Ford Foundation. When the respondents in the original NSBA had living family members from two adjacent generations, one randomly selected representative from each lineage position was also interviewed (Jackson and Hatchett 1986). Thus, the TGFS is based upon a national probability sample of black American three-generation lineage family members. In addition, as a part of the TGFS, a reinterview questionnaire was administered to the original cross-section respondents who were members of three-generation families (Jackson and Hatchett 1986; Jackson, Jayakody, and Antonucci 1995).

The reinterview questionnaire, in conjunction with the three-generation instrument, permitted the intensive examination of topics relevant to two major groups of the black population, youth and the elderly. For the elderly, the additional items in the reinterview survey included a focus on such issues as age identification, life review, attitudes toward age-based housing discrimination, institutionalization and the role of the federal government, collective action strategies of older Americans, functional disability, health programs, medical regimen adherence, family interaction patterns, and work-related and retirement concerns. For youth, issues relevant to educational aspirations and expectations; job experiences; cigarette, alcohol, and drug use; family relationships; and leisure time use were the object of study.

Possessing parallel data on individuals in different lineage positions provides the opportunity to test the similarities and differences in attitudes, values, and life experiences across three generations of black American families. The literature records few three-generation lineage family studies of any population, certainly none of the scope and national representation encompassed by this project (Jackson and Hatchett 1986). From a scientific point of view, the study offers unique possibilities to explore assumptions and hypotheses in the literatures on socialization, intergenerational mobility, and a host of other social science issues, as well as social policy and practical implications. Many public policies and programs devoted to economically disadvantaged groups are based on the assumption that the objective problems of poverty and discrimination are exacerbated by family socialization patterns that transmit attitudes, values, and behaviors that are dysfunctional for achievement in this society. Thus, many of these program regulations focus on resocializing individuals, often involving interventions aimed at, or circumventing, the family. The three-generation lineage study provides an opportunity to examine the reasonableness of these basic underlying assumptions.

A third major data collection effort related to both the NSBA and the TGFS was completed in 1984, under a contract from the Department of Health and Human Services (Bowman, Gurin, and Howard 1984). The purpose of this contract was to investigate black youth motivation and mobility using telephone reinterviews of 229 male and female youth (ages fourteen to twenty-four) in the TGFS regarding their educational and occupational attainments. The results of this two-wave panel study suggested that structural features of business cycle unemployment, lack of job training and opportunities, and employment discrimination seemed to be causal factors in the high unemployment and loss of work motivation among black youth rather than the often expressed lack of interest in seeking employment.

A fourth major data collection effort of the PRBA was also completed in 1984. Funded by the Ford, Rockefeller, and Carnegie Foundations, the National Black Election Study (NBES) was designed to assess the attitudes and behaviors of a national sample of the black electorate during the 1984 national campaign and elections (Jackson, Gurin, and Hatchett 1984; Gurin, Hatchett, and Jackson 1989). A random-digit-dial telephone survey of 1,150 black adults was completed prior to the election, and 866 respondents in this sample were reinterviewed immediately following the election. The design was comparable to the pre- and postelection National Election Studies and permits comparisons between the black and general population on many items of common interest (Brown and Wolford 1994; Dawson 1994; Tate 1993). A follow-up of these respondents was completed pre- and postelection in 1988, providing a four-wave panel study of black electoral behavior over the critical political years in the 1980s. The results of the NBES have been important and instructive. Brown (e.g., Brown and Wolford 1994) has shown church-based political behavior to be a very important source of traditional political participation for black Americans. Dawson (1994) has argued the existence of a coherent and important black political belief and ideology system that serves as an important organizing schema in black political behavior (Dawson, Brown, and Allen 1990).

The 1988 International Perspectives on Racism (IPR) survey in the then twelve-country Western European Economic Community (EEC) arose from a concern with the need to understand the nature of racism and its consequences in a cross-national perspective. A subset of the 1988 IPR done in the four countries of Great Britain, France, the Netherlands, and West Germany was designed to replicate items from the 1986 NES that assessed white racial attitudes. In each country respondents were randomly assigned to one of two target groups (France: Southeast Asians and North Africans; Britain: West Indians and South Asians; the Netherlands: Turks and Surinamers), except in Germany, where all respondents received Turks as the targeted out-group. This provided a unique set of data that permit cross-national and cross-cultural analyses of racism and discrimination toward multiple groups of color within and across countries that differ in sociohistorical and cultural national contexts (Jackson, Brown, and Kirby 1998). Follow-up studies of the original 1988 IPR were conducted across the European Community (EU) in 1997 and 2000, and a few monitoring items were included in Eurobarometer Surveys in 1992–2002.

The Future of Black Civil Rights Study (FBCR) was undertaken in 1992 as part of a contract with the Gannett Newspaper Corporation. This study formed an objective, empirical basis regarding black adult sentiments and attitudes for a series of newspaper articles on "Who Speaks for Black America" (*Detroit News,* February 1992). The broader data set contains items that assess a wide array of indicators, many of these replicating items used on earlier PRBA surveys. Analyses on these data (collected by the Gordon Black Corporation) examine the correlates of perceived black attitudes toward multiple institutions, reflections on the past, and expectations for the future of equal opportunity and civil rights in the context of individual and group interests.

PRBA research on physical health, mental health, employment, family life, individual and group identification, and political behavior provided the first in-depth investigation of these issues in large representative samples of the entire black population (Jackson 1991). Scientifically, the results of these surveys are having significant influence on current theorizing about blacks as well as on the content and direction of future research. The inclusion of many policy-relevant questions provides, for the first time, individual and group opinions and feelings that fully represent the breadth and diversity of black people located in all walks of life across the entire United States.

Methodological Innovations

Common to these major data collections in the PRBA are a number of special methodological features, including the investigation of perceived race of interviewer effects (Hatchett 1986). One notable feature of the data collection efforts of the PRBA has been the extensive use of both qualitative and quantitative methods, treated as integrally related. Thus, unique features of all the PRBA data collection efforts have been extensive pilot studies and pretesting of instruments to ascertain cultural sensitivity and meaningfulness of the instruments for black Americans (Caldwell et al. 1999; Chatters 1986; Jackson 1991; Jackson, Tucker, and Bowman 1982).

Novel and unique geographical-area and telephone-sampling methods provided the first opportunity to generalize survey research findings confidently to the entire adult black population, the black elderly population, and black three-generation lineage families. Instrumental in the success of these surveys were four novel developments in screening techniques: (1) the Wide Area Sampling Procedure (WASP); (2) the Standard Listing and Screening Procedure (SLASP) (Jackson, Tucker, and Bowman 1982); (3) the Multiplicity Sampling Procedure (Jackson and Hatchett 1983, 1986); and (4) the disproportionate random-digit-dial telephone sampling procedure (Inglis, Groves, and Heeringa 1987). Each makes important methodological contributions to the general social and behavioral sciences.

Blacks are geographically distributed in two distinct ways in the United States: either they are highly clustered, in urban locations, or they are widely distributed, for example, in broad areas of the western part of the United States or in suburban areas. In the former situation we run the risk of overrepresenting blacks and having unacceptable clustering; in the latter we run the risk of underrepresenting blacks who live in areas of low density. SLASP was applied in both mixed and mostly black areas and provided a unique method of identifying black eligible households by using reference housing units within clusters. WASP was developed for use in areas (clusters or groups of clusters) with suspected few or no black-occupied households. This procedure employed the reference housing unit approach used in SLASP but in a less predetermined manner. In SLASP the interviewer is told explicitly which household units (HUs) to contact for screening the cluster. This procedure minimizes clustering effects, due to taking too many interviews within high-density black areas, across *all* segments selected in the national study. In WASP, the number and location of these reference HUs depend on the interviewers' assessment of the number and distribution of black HUs in the area. The SLASP interviewers listed and classified each HU in a cluster by using the reference HUs. Using procedures that were extensively pretested, the white WASP interviewers asked the reference HUs about blacks in the area and listed only the black HUs. SLASP reduced the costs of screening high-density black clusters, and WASP minimized the cost of screening in geographical areas of low-density black population (no more than three HUs were ever needed to identify all blacks in average sixty-HU low-density black clusters).

Twenty percent of the WASP clusters were selected for intensive screening of households to estimate the extent of undercoverage, if any. The procedure proved even more effective than originally anticipated. Only eight black households in the sampled WASP clusters across the United States were missed. The majority of these were in one particular cluster, and, because of the selection procedures, none would have been selected for the study (Jackson 1991). The WASP procedure permitted the NSBA sample to be obtained with clustering and precision equal to the SRC household samples of comparable size, for a fraction of the cost. It also appears to be an effective and generally useful screening method for future sample surveys of blacks and other rare population groups (Jackson 1991; Hess 1985).

To obtain the samples of elderly, youth, and three-generation family members, special multiplicity sampling procedures (Jackson 1991) had to be developed to garner the relevant information from the original cross-section respondents. A special section of the questionnaire permitted the interviewers to determine with a few simple questions whether the respondent was a member of an existing three-generation lineage (or more) family. If so, the interviewer ascertained the nature of the particular family configuration. The three-generation family type—parent/respondent/child, grandparent/parent/respondent or respondent/child/grandchild—was selected using a predetermined sampling table. The eligible individuals in the adjacent generation positions—that is, the multiplicity sample framework—were then listed, and a random selection table was used to obtain the appropriate two family members. A reinterview with the original respondent provided information on the nature and distribution of all family members that could have potentially generated the family members (e.g., the number of siblings each respondent had who were eligible for the cross-section study) who had a probability of selection equal to the respondent and, if selected, could have provided the same information about the adjacent generations that was ascertained by the interview with the selected respondent. Once the potential eligible respondents/informants were ascertained for each family in the study, appropriate probability weights of selection could be generated and applied to the members of the resulting three-generation, elderly, and youth samples (Jackson, Jayakody, and Antonucci 1995).

The methodological techniques used in constructing the questionnaires, designing and obtaining the samples, as well as training interviewers provide new approaches to survey research generally and particularly to the problems of studying racial-ethnic groups (Jackson 1986b). This work has provided the basis for drawing relatively lower-cost national household samples of black Americans in subsequent studies.

The content of the questionnaires and the quality of the national samples and data collection techniques promise that the studies carried out under the auspices of the PRBA will stand for many years as sources of high-quality data for scientists and policymakers in the broad areas of physical health, employment, family relationships, political behavior, personal adjustment, and mental health. While the investment costs were high in conducting these novel sample surveys, the results have had important scientific and practical consequences and demonstrate the potential to influence the nature of future social and behavioral science research on black Americans.

Conceptual Framework for PRBA Research

The PRBA has used a broad conceptual framework—the life-stress paradigm—for understanding the distribution of distress and disorder among ethnic and racial groups that have experienced discrimination (Jackson, Chatters, and Neighbors 1986; Jackson and Sellers 2001; Pearlin 1989; Pearlin et al. 1981). This has involved focusing on how both diffuse and specific symptom reactions are defined by the general public (lay diagnostic inference) and how these definitions of personal problems influence the nature of coping and responses. The paradigm focuses on how structural and sociodemographic factors influence exposure to life stressors, and on the roles of psychological and social resources (e.g., mastery, self-esteem, job mentors, informal emotional and instrumental support, and religious involvement) in buffering the effects of stress on physical and psychological health (see also chaps. 7, 8, and 9, this volume).

Stress and adaptation are viewed as arising from discrepancies between the demands impinging upon a person and the capacity of that person to cope effectively with those demands (Myers 1982; Cohen, Kessler, and Gordon 1995). High levels of discrepancy are commonly associated with the onset of psychological distress. This orientation places equal emphasis on environmental/situational and individual factors as explanations for possible causes of psychological distress (Neighbors et al. 1983) and also focuses attention on one of the more positive aspects of ethnic and racial minority health—successful problem solving.

Our particular formulation of this framework combines aspects of the Michigan Model (e.g., House 1981; chaps. 7 and 8, this volume), Karasek's Job Strain Model (1979), and the African-American Stress-Coping and Help-Seeking Model (Jackson et al. 1999). Specifically, this work focuses on the relative importance of race, ethnicity, socioeconomic position (SEP), wealth, and gender as antecedents for understanding the nature of stress and its impact on mental and physical health. For example, we recognize that the effects of SEP must be assessed not only at the level of the individual and household but also at the level of the neighborhood and other macrocontexts (e.g., Krieger, Williams, and Moss 1997), which capture important aspects of the physical and social contexts that may adversely affect health over and above the effects of individual characteristics (Williams and Collins 1995). Regardless of individual or household characteristics, black and white neighborhoods differ dramatically in the availability of jobs, predominant family structure, opportunities for marriage, and exposure to conventional role models (Wilson 1996). These demographic and aggregate characteristics are also expected to directly influence stressors across broad domains of work, family, and leisure activities.

There is little information from national studies concerning the impact of life events on the distribution of ill health and psychopathology among racial/ethnic minorities. Chronic stressors (e.g., lack of income, marriage problems, and goal striving) may be equally important determinants of mental health as acute life events (Pearlin 1989; Sellers and Neighbors 1999). Recent developments in the measurement of stress highlight the need to broaden the assessment of stress beyond life events and chronic stressors. Childhood and adult traumatic events, daily hassles, and the absence of desired events have effects on health beyond those of life events and chronic stressors (Wheaton 1994). This comprehensive approach to the measurement of stress accounts for substantially more variability in health status than previous work has suggested (Turner, Wheaton, and Lloyd 1995). Unfortunately, prior studies have not assessed the relationship between comprehensive measures of stress and the health of most ethnic minority groups.

We argue that job and nonjob stressors combine and interact to influence physical and mental health (Jackson and Sellers 2001). These sources of stress in turn affect strains (or short-term responses) and more enduring long-term physical and psychological health outcomes. Stress engenders strain and is associated with a variety of psychological, physiological, and behavioral outcomes (see chaps. 7, 8, and 9, this volume).

Exposure to stress does not always adversely affect health (Cohen, Kessler, and Gordon 1995). Social and psychological resources that can mitigate the impact of stress on health include social relationships, self-esteem, perceptions of mastery or control, anger or hostility, feelings of helplessness or hopelessness, and repression or denial of emotions (House, Landis, and Umberson 1988; Kessler, Little, and Groves 1995; Mirowsky and Ross 1980, 1989; Rogler, Malgady, and Rodriguez 1989; Williams 1990; Williams and Fenton 1994). For example, analyses of data from the 1995 Detroit Area Study highlight the importance of understanding coping processes (Williams et al. 1997). In this study, the mental health of blacks exceeded that of whites, when adjusted for the effects of race-related stress. This pattern is consistent with the suggestion that stressful experiences may more adversely affect the mental health of whites than blacks. Kessler (1979) documented a similar pattern for the relationship between stressful life events and psychological distress for nonwhites (mainly blacks). While blacks were more likely to be exposed to stressful life events, comparable stressful events more adversely affected the mental health of whites. Kessler (1979) suggested that, compared to whites, African-Americans may have earlier and more frequent exposure to adversity, which lessens the impact of stress; greater emotional flexibility, which facilitates recovery; and access to culturally based psychological coping resources. In a recent prospective study, Breslau and colleagues (1991) found that blacks are nearly twice as likely as whites to experience a traumatic event, while the black/white odds ratio for retrospective reporting of lifetime traumatic events was only 1.22, suggesting that blacks may have lower rates of recall or reporting of negative events.

A broad range of other coping resources, including family support and religious involvement, may also play an important role in buffering ethnic and racial populations from the negative effects of stress.

Substantive Themes and Findings

The surveys conducted by the PRBA have made significant contributions to research on mental health, aging, family support networks, religious participation, quality of life and the health consequences of discrimination, racial group consciousness, intergroup relationships, black politics, retirement, and marriage/romantic relationships. We highlight here some selected findings.

Social Support

A major theme that serves to integrate the different parts of the NSBA interviews is social support (Taylor, Jackson, and Quick 1982; Taylor 1986). This is a concept particularly relevant in a study of black Americans. Some writers have pointed to the breakdown of the black family and social networks; others have commented on the strength of the black extended family and have pointed to family and friendship networks as providing major support to black Americans facing the difficult conditions of their lives (Taylor 1985). Social support not only is the subject of the section of the interviews specifically devoted to family and friendships but appears as an aspect of other sections as well: the support provided by people in one's church (Taylor and Chatters 1986); the availability of informal support for help when one is ill (Chatters, Taylor, and Jackson 1985a, 1985b); the people one depends upon in dealing with the stresses of everyday life; the use of informal resources when faced with major personal problems in one's life (Neighbors and Jackson 1984). Analyses of these data have provided invaluable input to the ongoing debate on the black family and the functions that family and social networks perform in black life in America (Jackson 1986a; Hatchett and Jackson 1983; Hunter 1997).

Taylor, Chatters, and Jackson's research investigates the informal social support networks of the black population in general (Chatters, Taylor, and Jackson 1985a; Taylor 1986; Taylor, Chatters, and Jackson 1997), as well as specific subgroups of the black population, such as single mothers (Jayakody, Chatters, and Taylor 1993), elderly blacks (Antonucci, Fuhrer, and Jackson 1990; Chatters, Taylor, and Jackson 1985a, 1985b; Taylor 1985; Taylor and Chatters 1991b), and three-generation black families (Jackson, Jayakody, and Antonucci 1995; Taylor, Chatters, and Jackson 1993). Several general conclusions can be drawn from this body of work.

First, despite major demographic changes in black family structure in the last twenty-five years, social support networks of black Americans continue to be strong and viable (Taylor, Chatters, and Jackson 1997). Second, informal social support networks comprise extended family members (Chatters, Taylor and Jayakody 1989; Taylor 1986) and non-kin, such as church members (Taylor and Chatters 1986, 1988), best friends (Taylor and Chatters 1986; Taylor, Chatters, and Jackson 1997), and fictive kin (Chatters, Taylor, and Jayakody 1994). Church members, in particular, were found to be critical, yet little-researched sources of informal assistance. Third, black adults who do not have any surviving family members or who are estranged from their family tend to rely on non-kin for assistance. Fourth, although the majority of black adults receive assistance from at least one of these groups, there is a small group of black adults who are socially isolated and do not have a viable support network (Taylor 1990; Taylor and Chatters 1986). Finally, differences in reports of the most important type of support received tend to correspond to the needs and challenges facing a specific subpopulation (Jayakody, Chatters, and Taylor 1993; Taylor, Chatters, and Jackson 1993).

In sum, notable among these results have been the findings that point to a very effective, interrelated set of support systems encompassing friends, family, and the church (Taylor and Chatters 1986). These three sources of support wax and wane over the individual life course (Antonucci 2001). Family and friends appear particularly important in earlier years, with an increase in the importance of the church as people age and as family and friendship connections are depleted (Gibson 1986). In addition, Antonucci and Jackson (1990) show that socially supportive processes of reciprocity among blacks may be more similar to those of the French than they are to those of American whites. Both the French and blacks in the United States seem to be more concerned with maintaining reciprocity of socially supportive assistance over the life course than are whites in the United States.

Religion and Religious Participation

Prior research suggests that religion can have a positive impact on psychological well-being by providing systems of meaning that help make sense of stressful experiences. In addition, involvement in religious communities can be an important source of social integration and social support (Taylor and Chatters 1986; Williams 1994). Furthermore, it is possible that individuals who use prayer as a coping strategy have better health outcomes. The NSBA data have facilitated systematic, quantitative research on religious participation among black adults. Several conclusions can be drawn from this body of research. First, two multisample analyses found that, among the elderly (Levin, Taylor, and Chatters 1994) and adults in general (Taylor et al. 1996), blacks exhibit significantly higher levels of religious participation than whites. Second, NSBA respondents generally regard the role of black churches as positive and recognize the diverse functions (e.g., social, religious, material support) of black churches (Taylor, Thornton, Chatters 1987). Third, African-Americans exhibit fairly high levels of religious involvement. In particular, they attend religious services on a frequent basis, have high rates of church membership, characterize themselves as being religious, and are extensively involved in private religious activities (e.g., prayer, reading religious materials, watching or listening to religious programs) (Taylor 1988a; Taylor and Chatters 1991a). Fourth, despite generally high levels of religiosity, there is considerable heterogeneity in religious involvement. Age (Chatters and Taylor 1989), gender (Levin and Taylor 1993), and region (Taylor 1988a) exert pervasive influences, while marital status, socioeconomic status, and urbanicity also have important effects on religious involvement. Fifth, poorer blacks do not exhibit significantly higher levels of religious participation than their higher-income counterparts. Sixth, prayer is an important form of coping with serious personal problems (Ellison and Taylor 1996; Neighbors et al. 1983). Ellison and Taylor (1996) found that, while religious participation is an important predictor of the use of prayer in coping, this practice is also most likely among persons dealing with a health problem or bereavement, persons with low personal mastery, and women. Finally, work exploring various psychosocial functions of religion indicates that religion is an important determinant of life satisfaction (Levin, Chatters, and Taylor 1995) and that, in the face of stress, religious attendance reduces the adverse consequences of these stressors on psychological distress (Williams et al. 1991).

Mental Health Status

One of the major research thrusts of PRBA has been the investigation of socioeconomic influences on mental health. Our work indicates that this relationship is much more complex than previously thought. Neighbors (1988) found that personal income, family income, and an index of poverty were all negatively related to distress—but only among respondents who indicated that they were upset because of an economic or physical health problem. Kessler and Neighbors (1986) demonstrated that the previously well-established relationship between race and psychological distress was not due exclusively to social class but that effects of race and social class are interactive—that is, race differences are significantly more pronounced among those at lower levels of social class. They concluded that, in models that fail to take the interaction into consideration, the effects of race are suppressed and the effects of social class are magnified. Williams, Takeuchi, and Adair (1992) examined the relationship between socioeconomic status and current and lifetime rates of psychiatric disorder in the Epidemiological Catchment Area study. Overall, SES was inversely related to psychiatric disorder for both racial groups, but the association was weaker for black males than for their white peers. In contrast to prior research, they found that among males lower SES whites had higher rates of psychiatric illness than lower SES blacks.

The analyses of Williams, Takeuchi, and Adair (1992) documented that there were distinctive patterns to the distribution of psychiatric disorders in the ECA among blacks and whites. All forms of marital dissolution (separation, divorce, and widowhood) were associated with an increased risk of psychiatric illness for blacks of both sexes and for white males, but the association was stronger for white men than for their black peers. The finding that never married black women did not have higher rates of psychiatric illness than their married peers was especially noteworthy and underscores the need for research efforts that focus explicitly on identifying the health-enhancing cultural strengths and resistance resources in the African-American community. Highlighting the differences between psychiatric disorders and psychological distress, Jackson and Neighbors (1989) found that, among black women of similar ages, those who were divorced or widowed reported higher psychological well-being in comparison to those who were never married.

Help Seeking

Using a problem-focused approach to help seeking, the NSBA found that 55 percent of respondents sought some form of professional help and more than 87 percent contacted at least one member of their informal network (Neighbors et al. 1983). Most respondents used informal help only

(43 percent), or they used informal help in combination with professional help (44 percent); rarely was professional help used in isolation (Neighbors and Jackson 1984). Among those respondents with physical health problems, the informal network channeled blacks to physicians. African-Americans with emotional problems were, on the other hand, least likely to seek any form of assistance. Although grief reactions were very upsetting, respondents reported that ministers rarely referred them for additional counseling. Regardless of the type or severity of the problem, those who contacted clergy first were less likely to seek help from other professionals (Neighbors and Jackson 1996).

African-Americans were unlikely to consult a mental health specialist (Neighbors et al. 1994). Only 9 percent of the respondents who sought professional help contacted a community mental health center, psychiatrist, or psychologist (Neighbors 1985); 14 percent contacted a social service agency (Neighbors and Taylor 1985). Those with mental health insurance were more likely to utilize private psychotherapists. The majority of those who utilized social services, community mental health centers, or private mental health therapists were referred by family members or friends. Taylor, Neighbors, and Broman (1989) found that, among those who contacted a social service agency, most indicated that a friend or relative was instrumental in facilitating use of the agency. A follow-up investigation of NSBA respondents, employing the depression section of the Diagnostic Interview Schedule, revealed that 17 percent of the sample met criteria for major depression. An exploration of help seeking among the depressed showed that 62 percent contacted family or friends and 37 percent sought some form of professional help (only 7 percent contacted a mental health professional). Related analyses from the 1995 DAS found that 14 percent of African-Americans met criteria for major depression. Help seeking among those meeting criteria for depression revealed that 38 percent contacted a family member, 24 percent went to a primary care physician for help, and 15 percent contacted a mental health professional (Neighbors 1997b).

We conducted six focus groups with African-Americans in Detroit to gain a better understanding of how mental health issues are understood and interpreted within the community (Neighbors 1997b). The groups uncovered four key issues: (1) African-Americans are incarcerated for behavior that would send whites to outpatient mental health services; (2) the poor are more likely to be institutionalized for mental health problems than those who are better off; (3) strong feelings of mistrust of whites is a major reason for not considering professional help; and (4) men are more likely to mention their reluctance to admit to a personal weakness (an inability to "handle their own business") as an important reason for their negative attitudes toward going to a psychologist, psychiatrist, or other mental health professional. This male reluctance was also found in the NSBA, where men were much more likely than women to report never having had a serious personal problem in their lives (Neighbors and Jackson 1996).

Psychological Resources and Social Resources

Several studies utilizing data from the NSBA have underscored the importance of psychological resources to African-Americans. These include John Henryism (James 1994), interracial contact (Rosenberg 1979), racial self-esteem (Terrel and Taylor 1980), internalized racism (Thornton et al. 1990), and system blame (Neighbors et al. 1996). Racial self-concept and identity is a neglected resource that can buffer the relationship between stress and health. We recently documented that keeping group identity salient protected African-Americans from some of the adverse effects of discrimination on their health (Williams et al. 1997).

Prior research has given insufficient attention to the potential health consequences of personality dispositions. For example, the John Henryism scale measures an active predisposition to master environmental challenges (James 1994). Research documents that John Henryism is unrelated to the blood pressure levels of whites or blacks of higher SEP. There is, however, a strong positive relationship between John Henryism and blood pressure among lower SEP blacks.

The possible health consequences of buying into the dominant society's stigma of inferiority of one's group are also important to study. For example, research across a broad range of societies (in the United Kingdom, Japan, India, South Africa, and Israel) indicates that groups of low social and economic status perform more poorly on standardized tests (Fischer et al. 1996). One possible mechanism proposed to account for this poorer performance is the existence of group stereotypes that interfere with cognitive functioning in test situations. This phenomenon has been referred to as stereotype threat. Research on stereotype threat has been largely confined to intellectual test performance (Steele 1997). It is conceivable that the salience (and persistence) of negative racial stereotypes may have effects beyond this domain. For example, research by Taylor and his colleagues has found that blacks who score high on internalized racism—that is, they believe blacks are inferior—have higher levels of psychological distress and alcohol use (Taylor, Chatters, Jackson 1997; Taylor and Jackson 1991). A similar pattern of results was found in the NSBA (Williams and Chung in press).

Social scientists have long speculated about the protective implications of system blame for blacks as an explanation for their relative disadvantaged status. The presumed benefit to African-Americans of recognizing themselves as victims of oppression and not holding themselves fully responsible for their low status has led social psychiatric epidemiologists to employ the system-blame concept to explain the lack of racial differences in mental health status (Neff 1985; Veroff, Douvan, and Kulka 1981). Unfortunately, there has been no direct test of this hypothesis to date. In fact, under conditions yet to be fully elucidated, the opposite may be true; system blame may actually diminish individual feelings of self-efficacy, leading to a fatalistic attitude that reduces coping effort in the face of adversity (Jones and Matsumoto 1982; Neighbors et al. 1996; Wheaton 1980). In other research that has illuminated some of the social bases of these psychological resources, Hughes and Demo (1989) found that personal self-esteem, racial self-esteem, and personal efficacy are interrelated and anchored in interpersonal relations with family and friends. These three psychological resources, however, are produced by fundamentally different processes. Hughes and Demo (1989) argue that black self-esteem is insulated from racial inequality, while personal efficacy is not, which may explain why black Americans, who suffer daily and acute episodes of racial inequality (Williams et al. 2000), have relatively high self-esteem but relatively low personal efficacy. We have speculated that, in a racially segregated society, those sources of self-esteem that are related strongly to family, friends, and direct socialization processes may be unaffected by contacts, either symbolically or tangibly, with the white out-group. On the other hand, racial inequality, either chronically or acutely, is related to contact with the white out-group and is more likely than not associated with the blocking of some desired goal (e.g., purchasing a house, going to college, or getting a job). The presence of racial barriers to desired ends would conceivably have direct effects on reducing one's belief that these goals can be achieved, leading to a lowered sense that one can influence outcomes in one's environment (Jackson, Williams, and Torres 2002). Tran, Wright, and Chatters (1991) found that health difficulties tended to erode feelings of personal efficacy, whereas stress from life problems depressed self-esteem. Finally, Krause and Tran (1989) found that aspects of religious involvement are positively associated with self-esteem and personal mastery. Although stress tended to erode feelings of self-worth and mastery, negative effects were offset by increased religious involvement.

Stress and Race-Related Stressors

One critical issue is the extent to which minority status per se increases risk for health and mental health problems (Vega and Rumbaut 1991; Williams and Fenton 1994; Aneshensel 1992). Our research has attempted to identify the types and amounts of discrimination that affect health, allowing us to begin to explain how racial bias combines with other types of stress (e.g., job or family) to affect physical and psychological health between and among ethnic minority groups. Previous research has long argued that discrimination adversely affects the mental health of African-Americans (McCarthy and Yancey 1971). However, stressors that may be unique to, or more prevalent among, ethnic minorities have not been incorporated into the assessment of stress (McLean and Link 1994; Pearlin 1989; Essed 1991; Feagin 1991). Several studies indicate that racial discrimination, as measured by subjective reports, adversely affects the emotional well-being (and physical health outcomes such as blood pressure) of African-Americans and other minorities (Noh et al. 1999; Jackson et al. 1996; Williams and Chung in press; James et al. 1984; Krieger 1990, 1999; Krieger and Signey 1996; Williams and Williams-Morris 2000; Williams and Neighbors 2001; Williams, Neighbors, and Jackson 2002). Other evidence suggests that the experience of unfair treatment, irrespective of race or ethnicity, may have negative consequences for health (Harburg et al. 1973; Kessler, Mickelson, and Williams 1999; Williams et al. 1997). While additive controls for personal control, self-esteem, race/group identity, interracial contact, and social support did not reduce the association between discrimination and health, interaction or moderating analyses revealed that, at higher levels of self-esteem, black identity and family closeness reduced the adverse health impact of discrimination (Williams et al. 1997).

Other analyses have explored the cumulative effects of exposure to discrimination among African-Americans using all four waves of panel data in the NSBA. Reports of racial discrimination over the thirteen-year period were weakly predictive of lower subjective well-being in 1992 (Wave 4). A general measure of racial beliefs (perceiving that whites want to keep blacks down) was related to poorer physical health at Wave 1 and predicted increased psychological distress and lower levels of subjective well-being in 1992 (Wave 4) (Jackson et al. 1996). The association between discrimination and health has also been examined in a sample of 2,398 respondents in Wave 3 of data collection (1994) in the ACL study. About 40 percent of nonwhites reported that they had been treated badly because of their race or ethnicity. These rates of perceived discrimination for the nonwhite groups were substantially higher than for whites. Analyses also found that reports of discrimination were related to lower levels of life satisfaction and higher levels of depression, chronic health problems, and self-rated ill health (Jackson, Williams, and Torres 2002).

In the 1995 DAS (n = 1,139) we developed multiple measures of acute, major life experiences of discrimination and an everyday discrimination scale. About 10 percent of whites report discrimination in employment and harassment by the police compared to about 35 percent of African-Americans. Blacks are about three times more likely than whites to report everyday discrimination as "very often" or "fairly often." Both measures of discrimination are adversely related to psychological distress and psychological well-being (Williams et al. 1997). The association with health status, however, is stronger for the everyday discrimination measure than for the major experiences of discrimination. Some researchers are concerned that perceptions of discrimination may be a consequence of mental health problems. However, recent analyses of multiple waves of data from the NSBA documented that being psychologically distressed and/or meeting criteria for major depression at Wave 2 was unrelated to Wave 3 reports of racial discrimination (Brown et al. 2000). It should also be noted that, although there are important commonalities in the African-American experience, there is also considerable ethnic variation *within* the black population. Blacks from the Caribbean constitute the largest subgroup (Williams, Lavizzo-Mourey, and Warren 1994). But prior studies of minority health have not addressed the consequences of this within-group ethnic variation. The results may not be obvious. One national study with a small sample of persons of Caribbean ancestry found that Afro-Caribbeans reported higher levels of stress, especially financial stress; higher levels of psychological distress; and lower levels of life satisfaction than native-born blacks (Williams 2000). It has been suggested that job stress, frustrated ambitions, discrimination from whites and other blacks, immigration status, and demands from relatives still residing in the Caribbean have negative affects on the health of Caribbean subgroups (Allen 1988; Gopaul-McNicol 1993).

International Perspectives on Prejudice and Racism

A fundamental and overarching PRBA concern is with the ways in which race, ethnicity, socioeconomic level, gender, and minority status per se all might interactively and additively influence risks for exposure to environmental and social stressors, the experience of stress, and the coping and adaptation responses of black Americans. To address these issues, we suggested that cross-national comparative analyses were needed (Jackson and Inglehart 1995), and thus we embarked upon a set of interrelated international studies. Most of these studies have involved European–U.S. comparisons. Additional and related work is ongoing in Japan, Brazil, and South Africa (under the direction of David Williams). In Japan we have been interested in the ways in which the dominant Japanese relate to both immigrants (e.g., Chinese and Koreans) and internal ethnic minority groups (e.g., Burakumin). In Brazil we are participating in a large study under way in Belo Horizonte to examine the ways in which skin color, race, and socioeconomic status work additively and interactively to influence mobility and health outcomes among different "color" groups in a purported "racial democracy." Finally, in South Africa a large study is examining the epidemiology of mental disorders within a society faced with a recent history of group-based torture and attempts at national reconciliation. This latter survey is part of the larger world mental health study designed to investigate the prevalence and correlates of mental disorders in nearly thirty countries across the world. For the purposes of this chapter we focus upon our cross-national European work as illustrative of the general set of international concerns (see chap. 13 for a discussion of some of the same issues in the American context).

The basic assumption of our international work has been that understanding the nature of discrimination and racism, and their psychological and social consequences in the United States, can only be accomplished by studying similarities and differences between dominant and subordinate groups in comparative, cross-national, multiple out-group contexts. Comparative cross-national studies and analyses of dominant and subordinate groups are necessary to understand those aspects of social psychological intergroup relations, (e.g., discrimination and racism) that are nation-state and target-group specific, as well as those components that are common across national boundaries and groups (Jackson, Brown, and Kirby 1998; Pettigrew et al. 1997). For the most part, research on prejudice and racism has been largely target-group specific. Prior research has generally focused on understanding prejudiced reactions toward one specific group, such as whites' reactions to blacks in the United States (Pettigrew and Meertens 1995). We have attempted to go beyond this narrow focus in two ways. First, we have studied the responses of randomly selected dominant group members in five different nations and compared reactions toward different, specific, target groups within these countries. Second, we have asked general questions of respondents about reactions toward persons from other nationalities, religions, races, cultures, and social classes (Inglehart and Yeakley 1993).

Based upon our research over the last fifteen years or so (Jackson, Kirby, et al. 1993; Jackson, Brown, and Kirby 1998; Pettigrew et al. 1997), we suggest that a synthesis may be emerging in the intergroup relations area (see also chap. 13) regarding the importance of individual-level threat based upon the perceptions of basic value differences among dominant and subordinate groups; upon perceived threats to individual and family stability; and upon the threats to the social, political, and economic status of the in-group (Pettigrew et al. 1997). Several theoretical models of intergroup relations and research are couched in these terms—for example, symbolic racism, aversive racism, relative deprivation, belief congruity, scapegoating, real group conflict, and social identity theories (Kinder 1986; Kohn 1987; Meyers 1984; Stephan, Ybarra, and Bachman 1996; Stephan et al. 1996; Ybarra and Stephan 1994). The underlying theme in all of these models is conflict and perceptions of threat, although the kind of perceived threat differs dramatically dependent upon historical circumstances, cultural considerations, and the economic, social, and political context. Threat to self-identity (Allport 1958; Dovidio and Gaertner 1986; Stephan and Stephan 1985) in person-centered models, threat to position dominance (Bobo 1987; Nielsen 1985; Yinger 1985; Giles and Evans 1985; Sidanius, Pratto, and Bobo 1994) in group conflict models, and threat to group identity (Milner 1981; Tajfel and Turner 1979) in value-congruity models provide the motivation for overt out-group reactions. Some recent work by Walter Stephan and his colleagues has reached similar conclusions about the central importance of intergroup anxiety and perceived threat. Under circumstances of constrained resources, real group conflict may be operative (Sherif and Sherif 1953), resulting in perceived threat (e.g., in Britain). Under conditions of relatively rich resources and a relatively tight status hierarchy among different racial and ethnic groups (e.g., in the Netherlands), social identity may be more salient, resulting in threat and group anxiety (Tajfel 1982). Under conditions in which long-term ethnic and racial divisions and conflict demarcate the status hierarchy among some groups (e.g., in France and the United States), socialization theories, symbolic concerns, and basic value differences may provide a more parsimonious explanation of group conflict (Dovidio and Gaertner 1986; Sears and Jessor 1996). Regardless of the specific theoretical model, threat, especially to the hierarchically dominant group and individual, is what accounts for the proximate immediate orientation, feelings about, and actions toward individuals in the groups lower in the status hierarchy (Jackson and Inglehart 1995).

Empirical Approach to Western Europe and United States Comparisons

In 1988 we conducted national household surveys among citizens in the twelve EU countries, with a specific focus on four major Western European countries: France (N = 1,001), Great Britain (N = 1,017), West Germany (N = 1,051), and the Netherlands (N = 1006). These international surveys were on intergroup attitudes, beliefs, and reported behaviors toward specific ethnic immigrant groups (Jackson, Kirby, et al. 1993; Pettigrew et al. 1997). A subset of the questions asked in these surveys replicated part of the special module of intergroup questions included in the 1986 NES in the United States (Kinder and Sanders 1986). This study was replicated in the fifteen EU countries in 1997 (Lemaine et al. 1998) and in 2000 by the EU; a few outcome items (immigration attitudes and orientations) were included in annual surveys in 1992, 1993, 1995, 1996, and 1998.

Similar to racial attitudes research conducted in the United States in 1988, we preselected two country-specific subordinate group(s) to which dominant-group respondents reacted. This provided two randomly drawn samples within three of the four nations so that we could examine the relationships among the constructs, not only across countries but also within countries for different groups. For some purposes, the data for the two groups within each country may be combined to provide larger sample sizes. The selection of the relevant group(s) within each country was done with the assistance of coinvestigators who were knowledgeable about the status and situations of these groups within their respective countries. Analyses conducted by members of the research group (Jackson, Brown, and Kirby 1998; Pettigrew et al. 1997) reflect our interest in four interrelated areas: psychological processes and behavioral intentions; the structure of racial attitudes; cognitive distortions and racial attitudes; and threat, stress, and racism.

Psychological Processes and Behavioral Intentions

One group of analyses focused on differences and similarities of psychological processes and their relationship to endorsement of government help and positive immigration policies among the different countries. Results suggest consistent differences across countries in the levels of affective, racial, and policy positions toward government action and immigration (Jackson, Brown, et al. 2001; Leach 1995), as well as differences in the reactions toward different groups within countries. In general, our findings strongly indicate the presence of negative racialized attitudes among dominant group members in both the United States and our selected European countries and, more important, an influence of these attitudes on government and immigration policy positions related to out-group members (Jackson, Kirby, et al. 1993; Jackson, Brown, and Kirby 1998; Pettigrew et al. 1997). Analyses among four of the major Western European publics (Britain, France, West Germany, the Netherlands) indicate significant overall resistance to government interventions; a small but significant proportion in favor of removing immigrant groups; and a small, but significant proportion unequivocally opposed to any punitive action against out-groups. Policy orientations regarding government help and immigration policies toward out-groups can largely be accounted for by a combination of modern and traditional out-group prejudice or racism (see Pettigrew and Meertens 1995), perceived economic threat from out-groups, and negative feelings toward out-group members (Jackson, Brown, et al. 2001). The rank ordering of the most important factors is highly similar across all countries and target groups (Jackson, Kirby, et al. 1993). Thus, while there may be vast differences in social, historical, economic, and political relations among dominant and subordinate groups across countries, the most immediate cause of prejudicial and discriminatory beliefs, feelings, and behaviors toward out-groups among dominant group members is the perception of threat, regardless of its source (Blumer 1958; Bobo and Hutchings 1996).

However, we have also found instances of strong differences across nations. The 1988 study attempted to examine social cognitions (e.g., stereotypes and prejudices) and affective reactions regarding persons from another nationality, religion, race, culture, or social class. Holmes and Inglehart (1994) showed that, while the overall level of prejudice in these different countries might be similar, there are clear differences in who will be chosen as a target of prejudice. France and Britain are high in their negative reactions toward persons from another race, while Germans' reactions toward members of another race are comparatively the least negative. However, Germans score highest in religious intolerance. Thus, dominant groups in some nations focus their out-group hostility and atrocities toward persons from another race (e.g., Britain and France), while others may focus it on persons from another nationality or religion (e.g., Turks in Germany) (Holmes and Inglehart 1994).

Structure of Prejudice and Racism

A second group of analyses has attempted to disentangle different forms of racism (Pettigrew and Meertens 1995) and to understand how prejudice and racism might be embedded in more general values and beliefs about the world (Jackson and Inglehart 1995). From twenty items traditionally associated with the measurement of racism, five groupings (or factors) emerged as cohesive scales: a four-item factor focusing on intimacy with an out-group; a six-item grouping pertaining to threat and rejection of the out-group; a four-item index of traditional values not to be violated by the out-group; a four-indicator cultural differences factor assessing the degree of difference between the majority and the out-group; and a two-item grouping measuring negative emotions evoked by the out-group. These factors assess various aspects of what have been conceived as both more subtle and more blatant manifestations of racism (Pettigrew and Meertens 1995). Pettigrew and his colleagues (Pettigrew 1989; Pettigrew and Meertens 1995; Pettigrew et al. 1997) developed the two ten-item scales of blatant and subtle prejudice. The Blatant scale has two dimensions: four items measuring intimacy and six threat and rejection items. The Subtle scale contains three dimensions: four items measuring traditional values, four cultural difference items, and two affective prejudice items. As with other work on the structure of racial attitudes (Dovidio and Gaertner 1986; Sears and Jessor 1996), the dimensions of the Subtle and Blatant scales were stable with similar reliability across countries and target groups (Brown et al. 1996; Brown, Torres, and Jackson 1996; Pettigrew and Meertens 1995). In addition, research on the scales suggests that blatant and subtle prejudice are not simple polar opposites but instead represent different types of prejudicial reactions of dominant groups toward subordinate target groups.

In their research, Pettigrew and Meertens (1995) have found three major trends: (1) large differences within two nations, France and the Netherlands, indicating much greater French prejudice toward North Africans than Southeast Asians and significantly greater Dutch prejudice against Turks than Surinamers; (2) a notable pattern in the Netherlands of lower blatant but higher subtle prejudice toward both groups; and (3) much higher subtle than blatant prejudice across all countries and target groups. Pettigrew and Meertens (1995) suggest that these findings indicate normative pressures, especially among the Dutch, to control blatant expressions of prejudice but that these same normative pressures do not operate against the expression of more subtle forms of out-group prejudice. Pettigrew and Meertens (1995) refer to those individuals who score low on both scales as *equalitarians,* those who score high on both as *bigots,* and those who score low on the blatant and high on the subtle as *subtle* racists. Those respondents who scored high on the Blatant scale but low on the Subtle scale were too few to analyze (2 percent). *Bigots* favor sending all immigrants home, regardless of their immigrant status; *equalitarians* generally prefer to send none of the immigrants home, regardless of their status; and *subtles* favor sending immigrants home only when there is a seemingly nonprejudicial reason to do so; for example, they have committed crimes or do not have their documents (Pettigrew et al. 1997).

Normative Analyses

Pluralistic ignorance, broadly construed, is the shared erroneous belief, either over- or underestimated, of the extent to which others in a given population hold the same views as the believer. Recent writings have emphasized errors of overestimation, but the general concept of pluralistic ignorance refers to any such errors. Prior studies on this topic (e.g., Allport 1958; Banton 1986; Katz 1991; Fields and Schuman 1976; O'Gorman 1986) have all found the tendency for dominant group members who are positive toward subordinate out-groups to overestimate the proportion in the dominant group population who hold negative views and for those who are negative to overestimate the proportion in the majority population who are negative, even more so than those who are positive. It is possible that this phenomenon may play a role in contributing to and maintaining institutionalized forms of racism and anti-immigrant sentiments. By "institutionalized" we refer to the established laws, customs, and practices that systematically reflect and produce racial and ethnic inequities, regardless of the level of individual racism that exists (Jones 1997). Even in the absence of strong personal antipathies toward immigrant groups, many Europeans, based upon their distortions of the beliefs about the views of "others like themselves," may not support positive public immigration policies (Jackson, Kirby, et al. 1993). More than "simple" racism may be operating to influence the negative positions that many European citizens hold toward immigration policies.

In our studies, pluralistic ignorance variables were formed by crossing self-perceptions of willingness to have an out-group member as a boss or a close family member by marriage with perceptions of the willingness of others, like themselves, in the country to do the same. The results substantially replicate the major findings of previous work, largely done in the United States and Great Britain (Miller and McFarland 1987; Leach, Kirby, and Jackson 1996), showing that people who are positive tend to overestimate the numbers in the population who are negative and that those who are negative overestimate even more than the positive the numbers in the population who are negative. However, there is one notable exception in the major trends—West Germany, where the negative pluralistic ignorance effect is weaker than in other countries. The lack of a full effect in West Germany may reflect the effects of high mean levels of personal negativity toward having an out-group member as a boss or close family member by marriage, higher than any country or target group. Finally, there is some cross-national variation by country with respect to out-group targets and to whether the issue is about having a boss or a close family member by marriage. The West Germans are much more negative toward Turks in their country than is any other country by group combination. The French are especially negative toward North Africans in both employment and marriage domains in comparison to Southeast Asians; the Dutch tend to be more negative toward Turks than Surinamers, especially in the marriage domain; and the British are slightly more negative toward South Asians in the marriage domain and slightly less negative toward this same group in the employment situation.

Threat, Racism, Stress, and Health

We have proposed (Jackson and Inglehart 1995) that the concept of perceived threat (Stephan and Stephan 1985) is theoretically related to the concept of stress. For example, political, social, and economic changes in the "real" world might lead to high rates of unemployment and inflation, crime, and violence. These are structural factors that clearly cause stress both on a community and on an individual level and that might prime and enhance negative appraisals of social situations. For example, affirmative action provides a timely illustration of this. In the United States, blacks constitute only 12–15 percent or so of the total population and an even lower proportion of those who are adult, able bodied, and capable of work. If all blacks were simply given jobs, it is not clear, given the size of the American population and economy, whether this would pose a significant risk of preventing other Americans from obtaining gainful employment. Yet, the perceptions of threat to jobs among whites certainly contribute to opposition to affirmative action and to stated fears of either loss of opportunity or blocked opportunities for advancement in careers and jobs (Sidanius, Pratto, and Bobo 1994; Dovidio and Gaertner 1986).

It is obvious that individual, cultural, and institutional racism can be, and are, interpreted as stressors for the targets of discrimination and can thus negatively affect social, economic, psychological, and health outcomes (Jackson et al. 1996; Ruggiero and Taylor 1995). However, the significance of understanding the effects of racism and intergroup conflict on the dominant groups' stress level and individual psychological and physical health status has been a neglected topic. Being a bigot may be "dangerous to one's health" (Jackson and Inglehart 1995, 360).

We have proposed that stressors, such as unemployment and downturns in economic conditions, will influence the perceptions of both dominant and subordinate group members in a given community, country, or other defined geographical area. Among dominant group members, we suggest that stress will directly lower psychological well-being and lead to increased racist sentiments toward subordinate groups. Among subordinate groups, we argue that these same negative macroeconomic conditions will contribute to the experiences of stress that, in turn, will lower well-being. In addition, we hypothesize that the racism directed toward subordinate groups by dominant groups will also be experienced as stressful and will contribute independently to lowering well-being even further. Thus, community-level stressors enhance individual-level stress among both dominant and subordinate group members. We tested these relationships among dominant (white) and subordinate (African-American) groups in the United States and among dominant groups (Europeans) in Western Europe. We lacked the data to test these predictions among subordinate groups in Western Europe. The data are from the National Panel Survey of Black Americans (1979–80 and 1987–88), the 1984 GSS, and the 1988 Eurobarometer Survey, using the selected countries of France, Great Britain, Germany, and the Netherlands. Details on the samples and measures are presented in Jackson and Inglehart 1995.

Overall, the results provided strong preliminary evidence for our Reverberation Model of Stress and Racism. Increased stress, represented by perceived financial strain due to unemployment and poor job prospects, is associated with increased negative antipathy toward out-groups. These relationships were found in national samples from the United States among whites and within and across national samples of the four Western European countries. It is also clear that, while perceived economic stress directly reduces well-being, racism also has direct negative effects on well-being. Thus, there are costs associated with holding racist beliefs. While lower levels of well-being might lead to increased racism, the pattern of relationships and the direction of the stress effects argue against this interpretation.

Conclusions

The PRBA is the oldest currently operating social science research team devoted to the collection, analysis, and interpretation of data based upon national and regional probability samples of black Americans. The work completed thus far suggests that findings from analyses of the original 1979–80 NSBA and subsequent data sets continue to be of major scientific value and relevance to social policy issues. The adult cross-section data permitted, for the first time, national estimates of the status and life situation of black Americans across the entire range of socioeconomic and other demographic groupings in the population. Issues of coping and adaptation (Bowman 1984; Neighbors et al. 1983), family structure (Hatchett and Jackson 1983; Hunter 1997; Taylor 1986), educational experiences (Hatchett and Nacoste 1985), race attitudes and identity development (Allen and Hatchett 1986; Jackson, McCullough, and Gurin 1981; Bowman and Howard 1985), social support (Jackson, Chatters, and Neighbors 1982, 1986), and nontraditional economic networks (Jackson and Gibson 1985) are only some of the areas that have been addressed in analyses of the NSBA data sets. PRBA research on physical health, mental health, employment, family life, individual and group identification, and political behavior provided the first in-depth investigation of these issues in large representative samples of the entire black population (Jackson 1991). The inclusion of many policy-relevant questions provides, for the first time, individual and group opinions and feelings that fully represent the breadth and diversity of black people located in all walks of life across the entire United States.

Complementing the types of analyses possible in the cross-section NSBA data set, the three-generation data provided an opportunity to more fully analyze two important at-risk subpopulations—the black elderly and black youth. Analyses of this sample have permitted an assessment of family socialization patterns, economic and social transmission across generations, generational similarity and change, and, for the first time in a data set of national scope, parental and family social and economic contributions to the growth and development of children and grandchildren (Jackson and Hatchett 1986).

Although the National Black Young Adults (NYBA) study (Bowman, Gurin, and Howard 1984), NBES (Gurin, Hatchett, and Jackson 1989; Jackson, Gurin, and Hatchett 1984), ACL, DAS, the Prevalence of Mental Disorders in Michigan Prisons, the NCAA Study of Social and Group Experiences (Jackson, Kiper, et al. 2001), and the new National Survey of American Life (NSAL) were not detailed fully in this chapter, their development and execution share the values, assumptions, and procedures described for the NSBA and other studies. Large studies of political participation, racism and health, religion, physical and metal health, and life-course development have emanated from the pathbreaking NSBA longitudinal panel project (Jackson et al. 1996).

PRBA research continues to make major contributions to the general investigation of how social, cultural, and other contextual factors relate to the ways in which racial status and racialized treatment affect the behavior, physical and mental health, attitudes, and values of blacks in the United States. This is evident in the latest and largest of PRBA's studies. The NSAL, with fieldwork completed in 2003, both differs from and extends earlier national epidemiologic studies of mental health, as well as prior PRBA studies. First, the survey contains a large, nationally representative sample of African-Americans (about 3,600), something neither the ECA studies nor the National Comorbidity Survey of the early 1990s was able to do. Moreover, the NSAL sample also represents Caribbean blacks (about 1,600) and important demographic subgroups within both the African-American and Afro-Caribbean populations (for example, 1,200 African-American and Afro-Caribbean adolescents ages thirteen to seventeen) and smaller samples of adult non-Hispanic whites (about 1,000), Latinos (about 500), and Asian-Americans (about 500). As a result, this project will permit the exploration of similarities and differences in and among various subgroups within the black American population, as well as comparisons with non-Hispanic whites and limited but important comparisons with other major groups of color. These types of analyses are critical because of the major changes that have occurred in black family structure over the last twenty years (Farley 1996; Jackson 2000).

Second, the use of multiple, theoretically driven measures of SES (e.g., Krieger, Williams, and Moss 1997) will result in better measures of SES being available for data analyses. Even when racial differences are "explained" by statistical adjustment for SES, the nature of SES differences across groups makes the interpretation of such findings difficult (Kaufman, Cooper, and McGee 1997).

Third, the NSAL employed successfully the novel geographical screening procedures developed in the NSBA. Once again, these methods assured that every black American household in the continental United States had a known probability of selection (Hess 1985; Jackson, Tucker, and Bowman 1982).

Fourth, this study addresses the *heterogeneity of experience* across ethnic groups within the black population. Most prior research on African-Americans has lacked adequate sample sizes to systematically address this ethnic variation. For example, the NSAL's incorporation of blacks of Caribbean descent will allow empirical analyses of issues never before addressed.

Fifth, the NSAL not only assesses the presence of physical health and mental disorders but also examines levels of impairment, improving upon a major limitation of the data gathered in previous national mental health surveys.

Sixth, all respondents of the survey were selected from segments chosen in proportion to the African-American and Afro-Caribbean population, making this the first national sample of peoples of different race and ethnic groups who live in the same contexts and geographical areas as blacks are distributed.

Survey research focusing on racial and ethnic disparities in health and psychopathology and on within-group differences among black Americans remains important because of the precarious economic and social situations of many Americans of color. In addition, there are differences across racial/ethnic groups over and above considerations of socioeconomic status. Explorations of these additional differences (e.g., acculturation, values, unequal treatment, and health behaviors) can underscore just how much race and ethnicity matter in terms of explaining differences in outcomes at every level of SES (Williams and Jackson 2000). Moreover, not all of these disparities are in the direction of showing a disadvantage for ethnic groups of color. These patterns are not well understood. Despite the impressive advances in knowledge concerning the assessment of national distributions of health and mental health disparities, the prevalence of psychological distress, and help-seeking behavior, much remains to be learned about African-Americans and other black subgroup populations. Through research projects like the NSAL, PRBA and the growing number of PRBA-trained colleagues and collaborations in academic research centers across the United States and the world will continue to lead in explorations of this important frontier of survey research and social science.

REFERENCES

Abramson, P. R. 1986. Who overreports voting? *American Political Science Review* 80:613–24.

Akbar, N. 1985. Our destiny: Authors of a scientific revolution. In *Black children,* ed. H. McAdoo and J. McAdoo. Beverly Hills: Sage.

Allen, A. E. 1988. West Indians. In *Clinical guidelines in cross-cultural mental health,* ed. L. Comas-Diz and E. E. H. Griffith. New York: Wiley.

Allen, R. L., and S. J Hatchett. 1986. The media and social reality effects: Self and system orientations of blacks. *Communication Research* 13:97–123.

Allport, G. W. 1958. *The nature of prejudice.* Reading, MA: Addison-Wesley.

Alpern, D. 1995. Why women are divided on affirmative action. *Working Women* 20:18.

Anderson, B. A., and B. D. Silver. 1987a. Measurement and mismeasurement of the validity of the self-reported vote. *American Journal of Political Science* 30:771–85.

———. 1987b. The validity of survey responses: Insights from interviews of married couples in a survey of soviet emigrants. *Social Forces* 66:537–54.

Anderson, B. A., B. D. Silver, and P. R. Abramson. 1988. The effects of race of the interviewer on measures of electoral participation by blacks in the National Election Studies. *Public Opinion Quarterly* 52:53–83.

Aneshensel, C. 1992. Social stress: Theory and research. *Annual Review of Sociology* 18:15–38.

Antonucci, T. C. 1990. Social supports and social relationships. In *The handbook of aging and the social sciences,* 3d ed., ed. R. H. Binstock and L. K. George. Orlando: Academic Press.

———. 2001. Social relations: An examination of social networks, social support, and sense of control. In *Handbook of the psychology of aging,* 5th ed., ed. J. E. Birren and K. W. Schaie. New York: Academic Press.

Antonucci, T. C., R. Fuhrer, and J. S. Jackson. 1990. Social support and reciprocity: A cross-ethnic and cross-national perspective. *Journal of Social and Personal Relationships* 7 (4): 519–30.

Antonucci, T. C., and J. S. Jackson. 1989. Successful aging and life-course reciprocity. In *Human ageing and later life: Multidisciplinary perspectives,* ed. A. M. Warnes. London: Hodder and Stoughton Educational.

———. 1990. The role of reciprocity in social support. In *Social support: An interactional view,* ed. I. G. Sarason, B. R. Sarason, and G. R. Pierce. New York: Wiley.

Aquilino, W. S. 1994. Interview mode effects in surveys of drug and alcohol use. *Public Opinion Quarterly* 58:210–40.

Baker, E., B. Israel, and S. Schurman. 1996. Role of control and support in occupational stress: An integrated model. *Social Science and Medicine* 43:1145–59.
Banton, M. 1986. Pluralistic ignorance as a factor in racial attitudes. *New Community* 8 (1): 18–25.
Belli, R. F., and J. M. Lepkowski. 1995. *Behavior of survey actors and the accuracy of response.* Ann Arbor Survey Methodology Program, Institute for Social Research, University of Michigan.
Bhagat, R., M. O'Driscoll, E. Babakus, L. Frey, J. Chokkar, H. Ninokumar, L. Pate, P. Ryder, M. Fernandez, D. Ford, and M. Mahanyele. 1994. Organizational stress and coping in seven national contexts: A cross-cultural investigation. In *Job stress in a changing workforce,* ed. G. Keita and J. Hurrell. Washington, DC: American Psychological Association.
Blumer, H. 1958. Race prejudice as a sense of group position. *Pacific Sociological Review* 1:3–7.
Bobo, L. 1987. Group conflict, prejudice, and the paradox of contemporary racial attitudes. In *Eliminating racism: Means and controversies,* ed. P. A. Katz and D. A. Taylor. New York: Plenum.
Bobo, L., and V. L. Hutchings. 1996. Perceptions of racial group competition: Extending Blumer's theory of group position to a multiracial social context. *American Sociological Review* 61:951–72.
Bobo, L., J. H. Johnson, M. L. Oliver, J. Sidaneus, and C. Zubrinsky. 1992. *Public opinion before and after a spring of discontent: A preliminary report on the 1992 Los Angeles County Survey.* Los Angeles: UCLA Center for the Study of Urban Poverty.
Bowman, P. J. 1983. Significant involvement and functional relevance: Challenge to survey research. *Social Work Research* 19:21–27.
———. 1984. Provider role strain, coping resources, and life happiness: A national study of black fathers. In *Empirical research in black psychology,* ed. A. W. Boykin. Rochester, MI: Oakland University.
Bowman, P. J., G. Gurin, and C. Howard. 1984. *A longitudinal study of black youth: Issues, scope, and findings.* Ann Arbor: Institute for Social Research, University of Michigan.
Bowman, P. J., and C. Howard. 1985. Race-related socialization, motivation, and academic achievement: A study of youth in three generation families. *Journal of the American Academy of Child Psychiatry* 24:134–41.
Bowman, P. J., J. S. Jackson, S. J. Hatchett, and G. Gurin. 1982. Joblessness and discouragement among black Americans. *Economic Outlook USA* autumn:85–88.
Boykin, A. W., A. J. Franklin, and F. Yates, eds. 1980. *Research directions of black psychologists.* New York: Russell Sage Foundation.
Boykin, A. W., and F. D. Toms. 1985. Black child socialization: A conceptual framework. In *Black children,* ed. H. McAdoo and J. McAdoo. Beverly Hills: Sage.
Breslau, N., G. C. Davis, P. Andreski, and E. Peterson. 1991. Traumatic events and post-traumatic stress disorder in an urban population of young adults. *Archives of General Psychiatry,* 48:216–22.
Brislin, R. W. 1990. *Applied cross-cultural psychology.* Newbury Park, CA: Sage.
Broman, C. L., H. W. Neighbors, and J. S. Jackson. 1986. *Racial group identification among black adults.* Ann Arbor: Institute for Social Research, University of Michigan.
Brown, K. T., M. Torres, and J. S. Jackson. 1996. Structure of racial attitudes in Western European nations. Manuscript. University of Michigan, Ann Arbor.

Brown, R. E., and M. L. Wolford. 1994. Religious resources and African American political action. *National Political Science Review* 4:30–48.

Brown, T., J. Crocker, J. S. Jackson, T. Lightbourn, and M. Torres. 1996. What drives the bus: Modeling the causal linkages among prejudice, affect, and beliefs toward ethnic and racial out-groups in Western Europe. Manuscript. University of Michigan Press, Ann Arbor.

Brown, T. N., J. S. Jackson, K. T. Brown, R. M. Sellers, S. Keiper, and W. J. Manual. 2003. There's no race on the playing field: Perceptions of racial discrimination among white and black athletes. *Journal of Sport and Social Issues.*

Brown, T. N., D. R. Williams, J. S. Jackson, H. W. Neighbors, M. Torres, S. L. Sellers, and K. T. Brown. 2000. Being black and feeling blue: The mental health consequences of racial discrimination. *Race and Society* 2 (2): 117–31.

Caldwell, C. H., J. S. Jackson, M. B. Tucker, and P. J. Bowman. 1999. Culturally competent research methods in African American communities: An update. In *Advances in African American psychology: Theory, paradigms, methodology, and reviews,* ed. R. L. Jones. Hampton, VA: Cobb and Henry.

Chatters, L. C. 1986. *Health satisfaction or satisfaction with God: Results of a random probe in the National Survey of Black Americans.* Boston: Brandeis University.

Chatters, L. M., and J. S. Jackson. 1989. Quality of life and subjective well-being among black Americans. In *black adult development and aging,* ed. R. Jones. Hampton, VA: Cobb and Henry.

Chatters, L. M., and R. J. Taylor. 1989. Age differences in religious participation among black adults. *Journal of Gerontology: Social Sciences* 44 (5): S183–S189.

Chatters, L. M., R. J. Taylor, and J. S. Jackson. 1985a. Aged blacks' choices for an informal helper network. *Journal of Gerontology* 41:94–100.

———. 1985b. Size and composition of the informal helper networks of elderly blacks. *Journal of Gerontology* 40:605–14.

Chatters, L. M., R. J. Taylor, and R. Jayakody. 1994. Fictive kinship relations in black extended families. *Journal of Comparative Family Studies* 25 (3): 297–312.

Clark, K. C. 1964. *Dark ghetto: Dilemmas of social power.* New York: Harper and Row.

Clark, M. L. 1985. *Racial stereotypes and self-esteem in black Americans.* Winston-Salem, NC: Wake Forest University.

Cohen, S., R. C. Kessler, and L. U. Gordon. 1995. *Measuring stress: A guide for health and social scientists.* New York: Oxford University Press.

Connor, J. H., and S. G. Heeringa. 1992. Evaluation of two cost efficient RDD designs. Paper presented at the annual conference of the American Association for Public Opinion Research, St. Petersburg, FL, May.

Davis, D. W. 1995. *The depth and direction of race of interviewer effects: Donning the black mask.* East Lansing: Michigan State University.

Dawson, M. C. 1994. *Behind the mule: Race and class in African American politics.* Princeton: Princeton University Press.

Dawson, M. C., R. E. Brown, and R. L. Allen. 1990. Racial belief system, religious guidance, and African-American political participation. *National Political Science Review* 2:22–44.

Dillman, D. A., E. Singer, J. R. Clark, and J. B. Treat. 1996. Effects of benefits appeals, mandatory appeals, and variations in statements of confidentiality on completion rates for census questionnaires. *Public Opinion Quarterly* 60:376–89.

Dovidio, J., and S. L. Gaertner, eds. 1986. *Prejudice, discrimination, and racism.* San Diego: Academic Press.

Drake, S. C., and H. Cayton. 1947. *Black metropolis: A study of Negro life in a northern city.* New York: Academic Press.

Du Bois, W. E. B. 1899. *The Philadelphia Negro.* Philadelphia: University of Pennsylvania Press.

Ellison, C. G., and R. J. Taylor. 1996. Turning to prayer: Social and situational antecedents of religious coping among African Americans. *Review of Religious Research* 38 (2): 111–31.

Essed, P. 1991. *Understanding everyday racism: An interdisciplinary theory.* Newbury Park, CA: Sage.

Farley, R. 1996. *The new American reality: Who we are, how we got here, where we are going.* New York: Russell Sage Foundation.

Farley, R., and W. Allen. 1987. *The color line and the quality of life in America.* New York: Russell Sage Foundation.

Feagin, J. R. 1991. The continuing significance of race: Antiblack discrimination in public places. *American Sociological Review* 56:101–16.

Fields, J. M., and H. Schuman. 1976. Public beliefs about the beliefs of the public. *Public Opinion Quarterly* 40:427–48.

Fischer, C. S., M. Hout, M. S. Jankowski, S. R. Lucas, A. Swidler, and K. Voss. 1996. Race, ethnicity, and intelligence. In *Inequality by design: Cracking the bell curve myth,* ed. C. S. Fischer. Princeton: Princeton University Press.

Frazier, E. F. 1932. *The Negro family in Chicago.* Chicago: University of Chicago Press.

Freidenberg, J., M. Mulvihill, and L. R. Caraballo. 1993. From ethnography to survey: Some methodological issues in research on health seeking in east Harlem. *Human Organization* 52:151–61.

French, J. R. P., Jr., and R. L. Kahn. 1962. A programmatic approach to studying the industrial environment and mental health. *Journal of Social Issues* 18 (3): 1–47.

Gaertner, S. L., and J. F. Dovidio. 1986. The aversive forms of racism. In *Prejudice, discrimination and racism,* ed. J. Dovidio and S. L. Gaertner. San Diego: Academic Press.

Gibson, R. C. 1986. Older black Americans: Relationships and coping. *Generations* 10 (4): 11–34.

Gibson, R., and J. S. Jackson. 1992. The black oldest old: Informal support, physical, psychological, and social functioning. In *The oldest old,* ed. R. Suzman and D. Willis. New York: Oxford University Press.

Giles, M. W., and A. S. Evans. 1985. External threat, perceived threat, and group identity. *Social Science Quarterly* 66:51–66.

Gopaul-McNicol, S. A. 1993. *Working with West Indian families.* New York: Guilford Press.

Gordon, T. 1973. Notes on white and black psychology. *Journal of Social Issues* 29:87–96.

Gurin, P., and E. Epps. 1975. *Black consciousness, identity, and achievement.* New York: Wiley.

Gurin, P., S. Hatchett, and J. S. Jackson. 1989. *Hope and independence: Blacks' reactions to part and electoral politics.* New York: Russell Sage Foundation.

Gurin, P., and D. Katz. 1966. *Motivation and aspirations in the Negro college.* Ann Arbor: Institute for Social Research, University of Michigan.

Gurin, P., A. R. Miller, and G. Gurin. 1980. Stratum identification and consciousness. *Social Psychology Quarterly* 43:30–47.

Harburg, E., J. C. Erburt, L. S. Hauenstein, C. Chape, W. J. Schull, and M. A. Schork. 1973. Socio-ecological stress, suppressed hostility, skin-color, and black-white male blood pressure: Detroit. *Psychosomatic Medicine* 35:276–96.

Hatchett, S. J. 1986. Race of interviewer effects in telephone surveys. Paper presented at the annual meeting of the American Association for Public Opinion Research, St. Petersburg, FL, May.

Hatchett, S. J., and J. S. Jackson. 1983. Black extended kin systems: Correlates of perceived family solidarity, geographical propinquity of kin, interaction with kin, and aid received from kin. Paper presented at the Groves Conference on Marriage and the Family, Freeport, Bahamas, November.

Hatchett, S. J., and R. W. Nacoste. 1984. *Exposure to desegregated schooling: Profiling the experience of black Americans.* Ann Arbor: Institute for Social Research, University of Michigan.

Heller, K. 1984. *Psychology and community change.* Homewood, IL: Dorsey Press.

Hess, I. 1985. *Sampling for social research surveys, 1947–1980.* Ann Arbor: Institute for Social Research, University of Michigan.

Hill, M. S., G. Duncan, and P. Gurin. 1985. *Motivation and economic mobility.* Ann Arbor: Institute for Social Research, University of Michigan.

Holmes, S., and M. Inglehart. 1994. The contents of prejudice: A cross-cultural analysis. Paper presented at the annual meeting of the International Society of Political Psychology, Santiago de Compostela, Spain, June.

House, J. 1981. *Work stress and social support.* Reading, MA: Addison-Wesley.

House, J. S., J. M. Lepkowski, A. M. Kinney, R. P. Mero, R. C. Kessler, and A. R. Herzog. 1994. The social stratification of aging and health. *Journal of Health and Social Behavior* 35:213–34.

House, J., V. Strecher, H. Metzner, and C. Robbins. 1986. Occupational stress and health among men and women in the Tecumseh community health study. *Journal of Health and Social Behavior* 27:62–77.

House, J. S., K. Landis, and D. Umberson. 1988. Social relationships and health. *Science* 241:540–45.

Hughes, M., and D. H. Demo. 1989. Self-perceptions of black Americans: Self-esteem and personal efficacy. *American Journal of Sociology* 95 (1): 132–59.

Hunter, A. G. 1997. Living arrangements of African-American adults: Variations by age, gender, and family status. In *Family life in black America,* ed. R. J. Taylor, J. S. Jackson, and L. M. Chatters. Thousand Oaks, CA: Sage.

Inglehart, M. R., and A. Yeakley. 1993. Differences in content—Similarities in reactions: A cross-cultural analysis of responses to out-groups. Paper presented at the annual meeting of the Society for Cross Cultural Research, Washington, DC, June.

Inglis, K. M., R. M. Groves, and S. G. Heeringa. 1987. Telephone sample designs for the U.S. black household population. *Survey Methodology* 13:1–14.

Israel, B., J. House, S. Schurman, C. Heaney, and R. Mero. 1989. The relation of personal resources, participation, influence, interpersonal relationships, and coping strategies to occupational stress, job strains, and health: A multivariate analysis. *Work and Stress* 3:163–89.

Jackson, J. S. 1985. Community surveys of black mental health. Invited address presented at the annual meeting of the American Psychological Association, Los Angeles.

———. 1986a. Survey research on black aged populations. In *Research on black aged populations*, ed. J. S. Jackson. New York: Springer.
———. 1986b. Research on minority aged: Sample surveys of older blacks. In *Research methods in gerontology*, ed. M. P. Lawton and A. R. Herzog. New York: Baywood Press.
———. 1988a. Survey research on aging black populations. In *The black American elderly: Research on physical and psychosocial health*, ed. J. S. Jackson. New York: Springer.
———. 1988b. Methodological issues in survey research on older minority adults. In *Research methods in gerontology*, ed. M. P. Lawton and A. R. Herzog. Farmingdale, NY: Baywood Press.
———. 1996. Survey instruments in national studies of blacks. In *Handbook of tests and measurements for black populations*, ed. R. L. Jones. Hampton, VA: Cobb and Henry.
———. 2001a. Changes over the life-course in productive activities: Black and white comparisons. In *Productive aging: Perspectives and research directions*, ed. N. Morrow-Howell, J. Hinterlong, and M. Sherraden. Baltimore: Johns Hopkins University Press.
———. 2001b. Social gerontology and the black aged. In *The encyclopedia of aging*, ed. G. L. Maddox. New York: Springer.
———, ed. 1991. *Life in black America*. Newbury Park, CA: Sage.
———. 2000. *New directions: African Americans in a diversifying nation*. Washington DC: National Policy Association.
Jackson, J. S., and T. C. Antonucci. 1994. Survey methodology in life-span human development research. In *Life-span developmental psychology: Methodological interventions*, ed. S. H. Cohen and H. W. Reese. New York: Erlbaum.
Jackson, J. S., K. T. Brown, and D. Kirby. 1998. International perspectives on prejudice and racism. In *Racism: The problem and the response*, ed. J. L. Eberhardt and D. T. Fiske. Newbury Park, CA: Sage.
Jackson, J. S., K. T. Brown, T. N. Brown, and B. Marks. 2001. Contemporary immigration policy orientations among dominant group members in Europe. *Journal of Social Issues* 57 (3): 431–56
Jackson, J. S., T. N. Brown, D. R. Williams, M. Torres, S. L. Sellers, and K. B. Brown. 1996. Racism and the physical and mental health status of African Americans: A thirteen year national panel study. *Ethnicity and Disease* 6 (1–2): 132–47.
Jackson, J. S., L. C. Chatters, and H. W. Neighbors. 1982. The mental health status of older black Americans: A national study. *Black Scholar* 13:21–35.
Jackson, J. S., L. M. Chatters, and H. W. Neighbors. 1986. The subjective life quality of black Americans. In *Research on the quality of life*, ed. F. W. Andrews. Ann Arbor: Institute for Social Research, University of Michigan.
Jackson, J. S., and R. Gibson. 1985. Work and retirement among black elderly. In *Work, leisure, retirement, and social policy*, ed. Z. Blau. New York: JAI Press.
Jackson, J. S., P. Gurin, and S. J. Hatchett. 1984. The national black election study. Manuscript. University of Michigan, Ann Arbor.
Jackson, J., and S. Hatchett. 1983. *Finding black respondents in low density areas: The Wide Area Screening Procedure*. Ann Arbor: Institute for Social Research, University of Michigan.

———. 1986. Intergenerational research: Methodological considerations. In *Intergenerational relations,* ed. N. Datan, A. L. Greene, and H. W. Reese. Hillsdale, NJ: Erlbaum.

Jackson, J. S., and M. R. Inglehart. 1995. Reverberation theory: Stress and racism in hierarchically structured communities. In *Stress and communities: Moving beyond the individual,* ed. S. E. Hobfoll and M. deVries. Norwell, MA: Kluwer Academic.

Jackson, J. S., R. Jayakody, and T. C. Antonucci. 1995. Exchanges within black American three generation families: The family environment context model. In *Aging and generational relations,* ed. T. K. Hareven. Berlin: Walter de Gruyter.

Jackson, J. S., S. Keiper, K. T. Brown, T. N. Brown, and W. Manuel. 2001. Athletic identity, racial attitudes, and aggression in first-year black and white intercollegiate athletes. In *Paradoxes of youth and sport,* ed. M. Gatz, S. Ball-Rokeach, and M. Messner. New York: SUNY Press.

Jackson, J. S., D. Kirby, L. Barnes, and L. Shepard. 1993. Racisme institutionnel et ignorance pluraliste: Une comparison transnationale. In *Racisme et modernite,* ed. M. Wievorka. Paris: Editions La Decouverte.

Jackson, J. S., G. Lemaine, J. Ben Brika, and D. Kirby. 1993. Individual out-group rejection: Western European and United States comparisons. Manuscript, University of Michigan, Ann Arbor.

Jackson, J. S., W. McCullough, and G. Gurin. 1981. Group identity development within black families. In *Black families,* ed. H. McAdoo. Beverly Hills: Sage.

Jackson, J. S., and H. W. Neighbors. 1989. Sociodemographic predictors of psychological distress in black adults. In *Proceedings of the Eleventh Conference on Empirical Research in Black Psychology,* ed. A. O. Harrison. Washington, DC: National Institute of Mental Health.

Jackson, J. S., H. Neighbors, R. Taylor, D. Williams. 1999. National Survey of African American Mental Health. Manuscript. University of Michigan, Ann Arbor.

Jackson, J. S., and S. L. Sellers. 2001. Health and the elderly. In *Health and the elderly,* 2d ed., ed. R. Braithwaite and S. E. Taylor. San Francisco: Jossey-Bass.

Jackson, J. S., M. B. Tucker, and P. J. Bowman. 1982. Conceptual and methodological problems in survey research on black Americans. In *Methodological problems in minority research,* ed. W. Liu. Chicago: Pacific/Asian American Mental Health Center.

Jackson, J. S., M. B. Tucker, and G. Gurin. 1987. *National Survey of Black Americans.* Ann Arbor: Inter-university Consortium for Political and Social Research, University of Michigan.

Jackson, J. S., D. R. Williams, and E. S. Gomberg. 1998. A life course perspective on aging and alcohol use and abuse among African Americans. In *The epidemiology of elderly drinking problems: The backdrop of aging,* ed. E. S. L. Gomberg, A. M. Hegedus, and R. A. Zucker. NIAAA Research Monograph. Washington, DC: U.S. Government Printing Office.

Jackson, J. S., D. R. Williams, and M. Torres. 2002. Perceptions of discrimination: The stress process and physical and psychological health. In *Socioeconomic conditions, stress and mental disorders: toward a synthesis of research and public policy.* ed. A. Maney. Internet: www.mhsip.org. Rockville, MD: SAMSHA Science Information Office.

James, K. 1994. Social identity, work stress, and minority workers' health. In *Job stress in a changing workforce,* ed. G. Keita and J. Hurrell. Washington DC: American Psychological Association.

James, S., A. Lacroix, D. Akleinbaum, and D. Strogatz. 1984. John Henryism and blocked pressure differences among black men: The role of occupational stressors. *Journal of Behavioral Medicine* 7:259–75.
Jayakody, R., L. M. Chatters, and R. J. Taylor. 1993. Family support to single and married African American mothers: The provision of financial, emotional, and child care assistance. *Journal of Marriage and the Family* 55:261–76.
Jenkins, A. H. 1984. *The psychology of the Afro-American: A humanistic approach.* New York: Pergamon Press.
Jones, E., and D. Matsumoto. 1982. Psychotherapy with the underserved: Recent developments. In *Reaching the underserved: Mental health needs of neglected populations,* ed. L. Snowden. Beverly Hills: Sage.
Jones, J. M. 1983. The concept of race in social psychology. In *Review of personality and social psychology,* vol. 4, ed. L. Wheeler and P. Shaver. Beverly Hills: Sage.
———. 1997. *Prejudice and racism.* 2d ed. New York: McGraw-Hill.
Jones, R., ed. 1980. *Black psychology.* 2d ed. New York: Harper and Row.
Karasek, R. 1979. Job demands, job decision latitude and mental strain: Implications for job redesign. *Administrative Science Quarterly,* 24; 285–308.
Kaufman, J. S., R. S. Cooper, and D. L. McGee. 1997. Socioeconomic status and health in blacks and whites: The problem of residual confounding and the resiliency of race. *Epidemiology* 8:621–28.
Katz, I. 1991. Gordon Allport's "The Nature of Prejudice." *Political Psychology* 12 (1): 125–57.
Kessler, R. C. 1979. Stress, social status, and psychological distress. *Journal of Health and Social Behavior* 20:259–72.
Kessler, R. C., R. J. A. Little, and R. M. Groves. 1995. Advances in strategies for minimizing and adjusting for survey nonresponse. *Epidemiologic Reviews* 17:192–204.
Kessler, R. C., D. K. Mroczek, and R. F. Belli. 1994. *Retrospective adult assessment of childhood psychopathology.* Ann Arbor: Survey Methodology Program Institute for Social Research, University of Michigan.
Kessler, R. C., K. D. Mickelson, and D. R. Williams. 1999. The prevalence, distribution, and mental health correlates of perceived discrimination in the United States. *Journal of Health and Social Behavior* 40 (3): 208–30.
Kessler, R. C., and H. W. Neighbors. 1986. A new perspective on the relationships among race, social class, and psychological distress. *Journal of Health and Social Behavior* 27 (2): 107–15.
Kinder, D. R. 1986. The continuing American dilemma: White resistance to racial change forty years after Myrdal. *Journal of Social Issues* 42:151–72.
Kinder, D. R., and L. M. Sanders. 1986. *Revitalizing the measurement of white Americans' attitude: A report to the NES 1985 Pilot Study Committee and NES Board.* Ann Arbor: Institute for Social Research, University of Michigan.
Kish, L. 1965. *Survey sampling.* New York: Wiley.
Knauper, B. 1996. *Age and response effects in attitude measurement.* Ann Arbor: Survey Methodology Program Institute for Social Research, University of Michigan.
Knauper, B., R. F. Belli, D. H. Hill, and A. R. Herzog. 1995. *Question difficulty and respondents' cognitive ability: The impact on data quality.* Ann Arbor: Survey Methodology Program Institute for Social Research, University of Michigan.

Kohn, M. L. 1987. Cross-national research as an analytic strategy. *American Sociological Review* 52:713–31.

Krause, N., and T. V. Tran. 1989. Stress and religious involvement among older blacks. *Journal of Gerontology: Social Sciences* 44 (1): S4–S13.

Krieger, N. 1990. Racial and gender discrimination: Risk factors for high blood pressure? *Social Science and Medicine* 30 (12): 1273–81.

———. 1999. Embodying inequality: A review of concepts, measures and methods for studying health consequences of discrimination. *International Journal of Health Services* 29:295–352.

Krieger, N., and S. Signey. 1996. Racial discrimination and blood pressure: The CARDIA study of young black and white adults. *American Journal of Public Health* 86:1370–78.

Krieger, N., D. R. Williams, and N. Moss. 1997. Measuring social class in U.S. public health research: Concepts, methodologies, and guidelines. *Annual Review of Public Health* 18:341–78.

Krysan, M., H. Schuman, L. J. Scott, and P. Beatty. 1994. Response rates and response content in mail versus face-to-face surveys. *Public Opinion Quarterly* 58:381–99.

Lemaine, G., J. Ben Brika, J. S. Jackson, and F. Wittek. 1998. Racism and xenophobia in Europe: Eurobarometer Opinion Poll No. 47.1. First results presented at the closing conference of the European Year against Racism, Luxembourg, December 18–19, 1997.

Leach, C. W. 1995. *Ethnic prejudices as attitudes: An eco-phenomenological view.* Ph.D. diss., University of Michigan.

Leach, C. W., D. C. Kirby, and J. S. Jackson. 1996. *Prejudice and pluralistic ignorance in Western Europe.* Ann Arbor: University of Michigan.

Levin, J. S., L. M. Chatters, and R. J. Taylor. 1995. Religious effects on health status and life satisfaction among black Americans. *Journal of Gerontology* 50B (3): S154–S163.

Levin, J. S., and R. J. Taylor. 1993. Gender and age differences in religiosity among black Americans. *Gerontologist* 33 (1): 16–23.

Levin, J. S., R. J. Taylor, and L. M. Chatters. 1994. Race and gender differences in religiosity among older adults: Findings from four national surveys. *Journal of Gerontology: Social Sciences* 49 (3): S137–S145.

Mangione, T. W., F. J. Fowler, and T. A. Louis. 1992. Questions characteristics and interviewer effects. *Journal of Official Statistics* 8:293–307.

Markides, K. S., J. Liang, and J. S. Jackson. 1990. Race, ethnicity, and aging: Conceptual and methodological issues. In *Handbook of aging and the social sciences,* 3d ed., ed. R. H. Binstock and L. K. George. San Diego: Academic Press.

Marx, G. T. 1967. *Protest and prejudice: A study of belief in the black community.* New York: Harper and Row.

Mays, V. M., and J. S. Jackson. 1991. AIDS survey methodology with black Americans. *Social Science and Medicine* 33:47–54.

McCarthy, J. D., and W. L. Yancey. 1971. Uncle Tom and Mr. Charlie: Metaphysical pathos in the study of racism and personal disorganization. *American Journal of Sociology* 76:648–72.

McCullough, W. R. 1982. *The development of group identification in black Americans.* Ph.D. diss., University of Michigan.

McCullough, W. R., G. Gurin, and J. S. Jackson. 1981. Racial identity and consciousness:

The socialization of ingroup and out-group orientations. Paper presented at the annual meeting of the American Psychological Association, Los Angeles, August.

McLean, D. E., and B. G. Link. 1994. Unraveling complexity: Strategies to refine concepts, measures, and research designs in the study of life events and mental health. In *Stress and mental health: Contemporary issues and prospects for the future,* ed. W. R. Avison and I. H. Gotlib. New York: Plenum Press.

Meyers, B. 1984. Minority group: An ideological formulation. *Social Problems* 32:1–15.

Miller, D. T., and D. McFarland. 1987. Pluralistic ignorance: When similarity is interpreted as dissimilarity. *Journal of Personality and Social Psychology* 53 (2): 298–305.

Milner, D. 1981. Racial prejudice. In *Intergroup behavior,* ed. J. C. Turner and H. Giles. London: Blackwell.

Mirowsky, J., and C. Ross. 1980. Minority status, ethnic culture, and distress: A comparison of blacks, whites, Mexicans, and Mexican-Americans. *American Journal of Sociology* 86 (3): 479–95.

———. 1989. *Social causes of psychological distress.* New York: Aldine de Gruyter.

Myers, H. 1982. Stress, ethnicity, and social class: A model for research on black populations. In *Minority mental health,* ed. E. E. Jones and S. J. Korchin. New York: Praeger.

Myers, L. J. 1985. Transpersonal psychology: The role of the Afrocentric paradigm. *Journal of Black Psychology* 12:31–42.

Myers, V. 1977. Survey methods in minority populations. *Journal of Social Issues* 33:11–19.

Neff, J. 1985. Race and vulnerability to stress: An examination of differential vulnerability. *Journal of Personality and Social Psychology* 49:481–91.

Neighbors, H. W. 1984a. The distribution of psychiatric morbidity: A review and suggestions for research. *Community Mental Health Journal* 10:5–18.

———. 1984b. Professional help use among black Americans: Implications for unmet need. *American Journal of Community Psychology* 12:551–66.

———. 1985. *Comparing the mental health of blacks and whites: An analysis of the race difference tradition in psychiatric epidemiological research.* Ann Arbor: Institute for Social Research, University of Michigan.

———. 1988. The help seeking behavior of black Americans: A summary of findings from the National Survey of Black Americans. *Journal of the National medical Association* 80 (9): 1009–12.

———. 1997a. The (mis)diagnosis of mental disorder in African Americans. *African American Research Perspectives* 3 (1): 1–11.

———. 1997b. Husbands, wives, family, and friends: Sources of stress, sources of support. In *Family life in black America,* ed. R. J. Taylor, J. S. Jackson, and L. M. Chatters. Thousand Oaks, CA: Sage.

Neighbors, H. W., C. H. Caldwell, E. Thompson, and J. S. Jackson. 1994. Help-seeking behavior and unmet need. In *Anxiety disorders in African Americans,* ed. S. Friedman. New York: Springer.

Neighbors, H. W., and J. S. Jackson. 1984. The use of informal and formal help: Four patterns of illness behavior in the black community. *American Journal of Community Psychology* 12:629–44.

———. 1987. Barriers to medical care among adult blacks: What happens to the uninsured? *Journal of the National Medical Association* 79:489–93.

———. 1996. Mental health in black America: Psychosocial problems and help-seeking behavior. In *Mental health in black America,* ed. H. W. Neighbors and J. S. Jackson. Thousand Oaks, CA: Sage.

———. In press. Uninsured risk groups in a National Survey of Black Americans. *Journal of the National Medical Association.*

Neighbors, H. W., J. S. Jackson, P. J. Bowman, and G. Gurin. 1983. Stress, coping, and black mental health: Preliminary findings from a national study. *Prevention in Human Services* 2:5–29.

Neighbors, H. W., J. S. Jackson, C. L. Broman, and E. Thompson. 1996. Racism and the mental health of African Americans: The role of self and system blame. *Ethnicity and Disease* 6 (1–2): 167–75.

Neighbors, H. W., and R. J. Taylor. 1985. The use of social service agencies by black Americans. *Social Service Review* 59 (2): 258–68.

Nielsen, F. 1985. Toward a theory of ethnic solidarity in modern societies. *American Sociological Review* 50:133–49.

Noh, S., M. Beiser, V. Kaspar, F. Hou, and J. Rummens. 1999. Perceived racial discrimination, depression, and coping: A study of Southeast Asian refugees in Canada. *Journal of Health and Social Behavior* 40 (3): 193–207.

O'Gorman, H. 1986. The discovery of pluralistic ignorance: An ironic lesson. *Journal of the History of the Behavioral Sciences* 22:333–47.

Orbuch, T., J. Veroff, and A. G. Hunter. 1999. Black couples, white couples: The early years of marriage. In *Coping with divorce, single parenting, and remarriage: A risk and resiliency perspective,* ed. E. M. Hetherington. Mahwah, NJ: Lawrence Erlbaum.

Painton, P. 1991. Quota quagmire, *Time,* 27 May, 20–22.

Parrott, A. 1995. Stress modulation over the day in cigarette smokers. *Addiction* 20:233–44.

Pearlin, L. I. 1989. The sociological study of stress. *Journal of Health and Social Behavior* 30:241–56.

Pearlin, L. I., E. G. Menaghan, M. A. Lieerman, and J. T. Mullan. 1981. The stress process. *Journal of Health and Social Behavior* 22:337–56.

Pettigrew, T. F. 1989. The nature of modern racism in the United States. *Revue Internationale de Psychologie Sociale* 2:291–303.

Pettigrew, T. F., J. S. Jackson, J. Ben Brika, G. Lemaine, R. W. Meertens, U. Wagner, and A. Zick. 1997. Out-group prejudice in Western Europe. *European Review of Social Psychology* 8:241–73.

Pettigrew, T., and R. W. Meertens. 1995. Subtle and blatant prejudice in Western Europe. *European Journal of Social Psychology* 57:57–75.

Rex, J., and D. Mason. 1986. *Theories of race and ethnic relations.* New York: Cambridge University Press.

Rogler, L. H., R. G. Malgady, and O. Rodriguez. 1989. *Hispanics and mental health: A framework for research.* Malabar, FL: Robert E. Krieger.

Rosenberg, M. 1979. *Conceiving the self.* New York: Basic Books.

Ruggiero, K. M., and D. M. Taylor. 1995. Coping with discrimination: How disadvantaged group members perceive the discrimination that confronts them. *Journal of Personality and Social Psychology* 68:826–38.

Schuman, H. 1966. The random probe: A technique for evaluating the validity of closed questions. *American Sociological Review* 41:224–35.

Schuman, H., R. F. Belli, and K. Bischoping. 1995. The generational basis of historical knowledge. In *Collective memory of political events: Social Psychological perspectives*, ed. J. W. Pennebaker, D. Paez, and B. Rime. Hillsdale, NJ: Lawrence Erlbaum.

Schuman, H., and S. Hatchett. 1974. *Black racial attitudes: Trends and complexities.* Ann Arbor: Institute for Social Research, University of Michigan.

Schuman, H., and G. Kalton. 1985. Survey methods. In *Handbook of social psychology*, vol. 3, ed. G. Lindzey and E. Aronson. New York: Wiley.

Schwarz, N. 1995a. *Cognition, communication, and survey measurement: Some implications for contingent valuation surveys.* Ann Arbor: Survey Methodology Program Institute for Social Research, University of Michigan.

———. 1995b. *What respondents learn from questionnaires: The survey interview and the logic of conversation.* Ann Arbor: Survey Methodology Program Institute for Social Research, University of Michigan.

Schwarz, N., and H. Bless. 1995. Mental construal processes and the emergence of context effects in attitude measurement. *Bulletin de Methodologie Sociologique* 48:101–19.

Schwarz, N., and H. J. Hippler. 1995a. Subsequent questions may influence answers to preceding questions in mail surveys. *Public Opinion Quarterly* 59:93–97.

———. 1995b. The numeric values of rating scales: A comparison of their impact in mail surveys and telephone interviews. *International Journal of Public Opinion Research* 7:72–74.

Schwarz, N., and H. Schuman. 1995. *Political knowledge, attribution, and inferred interest in politics: The operation of buffer items.* Ann Arbor: Survey Methodology Program Institute for Social Research, University of Michigan.

Schwarz, N., and T. Wellens. 1997. Cognitive dynamics of proxy responding: The diverging perspectives of actors and observers. *Journal of Official Statistics* 13:159–79.

Sears, D. O., and T. Jessor. 1996. Whites' racial policy attitudes: The role of white racism. *Social Science Quarterly* 77 (4): 751–59.

Sellers, S. L., and H. W. Neighbors. 1999. Goal-striving stress, socioeconomic status, and the mental health of black Americans. *Annals of the New York Academy of Sciences* 896:469–73.

Sherif, M., and C. W. Sherif. 1953. *Groups in harmony and tension.* New York: Harper.

Sidanius, J., F. Pratto, and L. Bobo. 1994. Social dominance orientation and the political psychology of gender: A case of invariance? *Journal of Personality and Social Psychology* 67:1–13.

Silver, B. D., P. R. Abramson, and B. A. Anderson. 1986. The presence of others and overreporting of voting in American national elections. *Public Opinion Quarterly* 50:228–39.

Smith, A. W. 1993. Survey research on African Americans. In *Race and ethnicity in research methods*, ed. J. H. Stanfield II and R. M. Dennis. Newbury Park, CA: Sage.

Stanfield, J. H., II. 1993. *A history of race relations research: First generation recollections.* Newbury Park, CA: Sage.

Stanfield, J. H., II, and R. M. Dennis, eds. 1993. *Race and ethnicity in research methods.* Newbury Park, CA: Sage.

Steele, C. M. 1997. A threat in the air: How stereotypes shape intellectual identity and performance. *American psychologist* 52 (6): 613–29.

Stephan, W. G., and C. W. Stephan. 1985. Intergroup anxiety. *Journal of Social Issues* 41 (3): 157–75.

Stephan, W. G., O. Ybarra, and G. Bachman. 1996. A threat model of prejudice: The case of immigrants. *Personality and Social Psychology Bulletin* 29:2221–37.

Stephan, W. G., O. Ybarra, C. M. Martinez, J. Schwarzwald, and M. Tur-Kaspa. 1996. Prejudice toward immigrants to Spain and Israel: An integrated threat theory analysis. *Journal of Cross-Cultural Psychology* 4:559–76.

Tajfel, H., ed. 1982. *Social identity and intergroup relations.* Cambridge: Cambridge University Press.

Tajfel, H., and J. C. Turner. 1979. An integrative theory of intergroup conflict. In *The social psychology of intergroup relations,* ed. W. C. Austin and S. Worchel. Monterey, CA: Brooks/Cole.

Tate, K. 1993. *From protest to politics: The new black voters in American elections.* New York: Russell Sage.

Taylor, J., and B. B. Jackson. 1991. Evaluation of a holistic model of mental health symptoms in African American women. *Journal of Black Psychology* 18 (1): 19–45.

Taylor, R. J. 1985. The extended family as a source of support to elderly blacks. *Gerontologist* 25:488–95.

———. 1986. Receipt of support from family among black Americans: Demographic and familial differences. *Journal of Marriage and the Family* 48:67–77.

———. 1988a. Structural determinants of religious participation among black Americans. *Review of Religious Research* 30 (2): 114–25.

———. 1988b. Correlates of religious non involvement among black Americans. *Review of Religious Research* 30 (2): 126–39.

———. 1990. Need for support and family involvement among black Americans. *Journal of Marriage and the Family* 52:584–90.

Taylor, R. J., and L. M. Chatters. 1986. Church-based informal support among elderly blacks. *Gerontologist* 26 (6): 637–42.

———. 1988. Church members as a source of informal social support. *Review of Religious Research* 30:193–203.

———. 1991a. Nonorganizational religious participation among elderly black adults. *Journal of Gerontology: Social Sciences* 46 (2): S103–111.

———. 1991b. Extended family networks of older black adults. *Journal of Gerontology: Social Sciences* 46 (4): S210–S217.

Taylor, R. J., L. M. Chatters, and J. S. Jackson. 1993. A profile of familial relations among three generation black families. *Family Relations* 42:332–41.

———. 1997. Introduction. In *Family life in black America,* ed. R. J. Taylor, J. S. Jackson, and L. M. Chatters. Thousand Oaks, CA: Sage.

Taylor, R. J., L. M. Chatters, R. Jayakody, and J. S. Levin. 1996. Black and white differences in religious participation: A multi-sample comparison. *Journal for the Scientific Study of Religion* 35 (4): 403–10.

Taylor, R. J., J. S. Jackson, and A. D. Quick. 1982. The frequency of social support among black Americans: Preliminary findings from the National Surveys of Black Americans. *Urban Research Review* 8:1–4.

Taylor, R. J., H. W. Neighbors, and C. L. Broman. 1989. Evaluation by black Americans of the social service encounter during a serious personal problem. *Social Work* 34 (3): 205–11.

Taylor, R. J., and W. H. Taylor. 1982. The social and economic status of the black elderly. *Phylon* 42:295–306.

Taylor, R. J., M. C. Thornton, and L. M. Chatters. 1987. Black Americans' perception of the sociohistorical role of the church. *Journal of Black Studies* 18 (2): 123–38.

Terrell, F., and J. Taylor. 1980. Self-concept of juveniles who commit black on black crimes. *Corrective and Social Psychiatry* 20:107–9.

Thoits, P. A. 1995. Stress, coping, and social support processes: Where are we? What's next? *Journal of Health and Social Behavior* (extra issue):53–79.

Thornton, M. C., L. M. Chatters, R. J. Taylor, and W. R. Allen. 1990. Sociodemographic and environmental correlates of racial socialization by black parents. *Child Development* 61 (2): 401–9.

Tran, T. V., R. Wright, and L. M. Chatters. 1991. Health, stress, psychological resources and subjective well-being among older blacks. *Psychology and Aging* 6 (1): 100–108.

Triandis, H. C. 1990. Theoretical concepts that are applicable to the analysis of ethnocentrism. In *Applied cross-cultural psychology,* ed. R. W. Brislin. Newbury Park, CA: Sage.

Turner, K. J., B. Wheaton, and D. A. Lloyd. 1995. The epidemiology of social stress. *American Sociological Review* 60:104–25.

Vega, W. A., and R. G. Rumbaut. 1991. Ethnic minorities and mental health. *Annual Review of Sociology* 17:351–83.

Veroff, J., E. Douvan, and R. A. Kulka. 1981. *The inner American: A self-portrait from 1957 to 1976.* New York: Basic Books.

Wanke, M., and N. Schwarz. 1996. Reducing question order effects: The operation of buffer items. In *Survey processing and measurement quality,* ed. L. Lyberg. Chichester, UK: Wiley.

Weiss, C. H. 1977. Survey researchers and minority communities. *Journal of Social Issues* 33:20–35.

Wheaton, B. 1985. Models for the stress-buffering functions of coping resources. *Journal of Health and Social Behavior* 26:352–64.

———. 1994. Sampling the stress universe. In *Stress and mental health: Contemporary issues and prospects for the future,* ed. W. R. Avison and I. H. Gotlib. New York: Plenum Press.

Williams, D. R. 1990. Socioeconomic differentials in health: A review and redirection. *Social Psychology Quarterly* 53 (2): 81–99.

———. 1994. The measurement of religion in epidemiologic studies: Problems and perspectives. In *Religion in aging and health: Theoretical foundations and methodological frontiers,* ed. J. S. Levin, 125–48. Thousand Oaks, CA: Sage.

———. 2000. Race, stress, and mental health: Findings from the Commonwealth Minority Health Survey. In *Minority health in America: Findings and policy implications from the Commonwealth Fund Minority Health Survey,* ed. C. J. R. Hogue, M. A. Hargraves, and K. S. Collins. Baltimore: Johns Hopkins University Press.

Williams, D. R., and A-M. Chung. In press. Racism and health. In *Health in black America,* ed. R. C. Gibson and J. S. Jackson. Thousand Oaks, CA: Sage.

Williams, D. R., and C. Collins. 1995. U.S. socioeconomic and racial differences in health: Patterns and explanations. *Annual Review of Sociology* 21:349–86.

Williams, D. R., and B. T. Fenton. 1994. The mental health of African Americans: Findings, questions, and directions. In *Handbook of black American health: The mosaic of conditions, issues, policies, and prospects,* ed. I. L. Livingston. Westport, CT: Greenwood Press.

Williams, D. R., and J. S. Jackson. 2000. Race/ethnicity and the 2000 census: Recommendations for African American and other black populations in the United States. *American Journal of Public Health* 90 (11): 1728–30.

Williams, D. R., J. S. Jackson, T. N. Brown, M. Torres, T. A. Forman, and K. Brown. 2000. Traditional and contemporary prejudice and urban whites' support for affirmative action. *Social Problems* 46 (4): 503–27.

Williams, D. R., D. B. Larson, R. E. Buckler, R. C. Heckman, and C. M. Pyle. 1991. Religion and psychological distress in a community sample. *Social Science Medicine* 32 (11): 1257–62.

Williams, D. R., R. Lavizzo-Mourey, and R. Warren. 1994. The concept of race and health status in America. *Public Health Reports* 100:26–41.

Williams, D. R., and H. W. Neighbors. 2001. Racism, discrimination, and hypertension: Evidence and needed research. *Ethnicity and Disease* 11:800–816.

Williams, D. R., H. Neighbors, and J. S. Jackson. 2003. Racial/Ethnic Discrimination and Health: Findings from Community Studies. *American Journal of Public Health* 93 (2): 7–15.

Williams, D. R., D. T. Takeuchi, and R. K. Adair. 1992. Socioeconomic status and psychiatric disorder among blacks and whites. *Social Forces* 7 (1): 179–94.

Williams, D. R., and R. Williams-Morris. 2000. Racism and mental health: The African American experience. *Ethnicity and Health* 5 (3–4): 243–68.

Williams, D. R., Y. Yu, J. S. Jackson, and N. B. Anderson. 1997. Racial differences in physical and mental health: Socio-economic status, stress, and discrimination. *Journal of Health Psychology* 2 (3): 335–51.

Willimack, D. K., H. Schuman, B. Pennell, and J. M. Lepkowski. 1995. Effects of a prepaid nonmonetary incentive on response rates and response quality in a face-to-face survey. *Public Opinion Quarterly* 59:78–92.

Wilson, K. R., and W. R. Allen. 1987. Explaining the educational attainment of young black adults: Critical familial and extra-familial influences. *Journal of Negro Education* 56 (1): 64–76.

Wilson, W. J. 1996. *When work disappears.* New York: Knopf.

Word, C. O. 1977. Cross-cultural methods of survey research in black urban areas. *Journal of Black Psychology* 3:72–87.

Ybarra, O., and W. G. Stephan. 1994. Perceived threat as a predictor of prejudice and stereotypes: Americans' reactions to Mexican immigrants. *Boletin de Psicologia* 42:39–54.

Yinger, J. M. 1985. Ethnicity. *Annual Review of Sociology* 11:151–80.

CHAPTER 15

Survey Research and Social Science: Retrospect and Prospect

James S. House, Eleanor Singer, Robert L. Kahn, Howard Schuman, and F. Thomas Juster

The previous fourteen chapters suggest the broad and in many ways transformative impact that survey research has had on intradisciplinary and especially interdisciplinary social science and also on social science's contribution to understanding major issues of social and policy concern. These developments were summarized in the previous chapters, albeit selectively in terms of topics and in the focus on research based at the University of Michigan Survey Research Center (SRC) and Institute for Social Research (ISR); therefore, we will not reiterate them here. Rather, looking across all of this work, this chapter focuses on a number of general lessons we draw from the past and for the future. We believe these lessons are critical to the advances made over the twentieth century in survey research and will remain critical to further advances in the twenty-first century. We also believe they have relevance beyond survey research to the broader development of science in general and social science in particular.

Lessons from the Past for the Future

Lesson 1: The Interplay of Theory, Substance, and Methods

Too often scientists tend to place in opposition theory versus empirical data and methods versus substance. While these distinctions can be valid and useful, highlighting and reifying them are deleterious to the overall development of science. It is increasingly difficult for one individual to be simultaneously an outstanding theoretician, methodologist, and empirical researcher, but it is crucial that all these competencies be represented in the research enterprise, with the appropriate mix varying across given research projects or domains. Positive synergies can be achieved when all are fostered in appropriate balance within a single research institution or organization.

These assertions reflect our claim in chapter 1 that new methods produce new data that lead to new theory just as much as the reverse. Theoretical problems stimulate empirical and methodological research and vice versa. Similarly, basic science yields knowledge critical to understanding applied problems, and attempting to solve applied problems can lead to developments and advances in basic science. At their best, survey research organizations have involved and made contributions to all of these areas, perhaps epitomized in the collaborations between Robert Merton and Paul Lazarsfeld in the halcyon days of the Columbia University Bureau of Applied Social Research in the 1950s and 1960s, when social science also engaged heavily with issues of applied practice and policy.

Theory and Data

The necessary engagement between theory and empirical data seems a truism, but one that needs to be continually recognized in the social sciences, which still have tendencies to privilege theoretical work as "higher" or "more valuable or fundamental" than empirical research. The distinction between theoretical and empirical work is most clearly recognized and realized in physics, but the necessary value and complementarity of theory, empirical/experimental research, and methodological and instrument development are also well recognized and institutionalized. SRC and ISR are heavily oriented to empirical work and associated methodological development, but that work has been and must be both guided by and generative of theory. Each of the research programs discussed in chapters 3 through 14 began from existing theory but has significantly revised that theory. Similarly, the methodological developments described in chapter 2 often derive from, and contribute to, theoretical developments in statistics, social psychology and sociology, and cognitive science.

One of the major contributions of survey-based social science has been to incorporate the full range of human populations into social science research (and hence theory) rather than relying only on deductive theory or on observation, surveys, or experimentation on highly selected populations (e.g., college students or other, often well-educated, volunteers or informants). In so doing, survey-based research has repeatedly demonstrated that human behavior and social life are substantially affected by considerations other than pure rationality or at least the deductively imputed constructions of it used in much social science theory (cf. Massey 2001). For example, the research on political and electoral behavior described in chapter 3 demonstrated that voters do not totally "rationally" analyze the characteristics or issue positions of candidates or parties vis-à-vis the voter's logical self-interest. Rather, voting decisions are most heavily governed by the enduring and not easily changed inertial factor of party identification. Both voting behavior and economic behavior are substantially influenced by overall assessments of whether times are "good" or "bad." Thus, Katona's simple initial ice-breaking questions as to whether respondents thought things were getting better or worse economically for them and the larger society evolved into important leading indicators of macroeconomic performance and helped spawn new theories about the role of psychological expectations in individual and aggregate economic functioning (cf. chap. 5). In these and other instances, empirically exploring the thoughts, feelings, and behaviors of representative population samples has significantly altered the nature of theories about politics and economics, and such creative tensions between theory and data must and will continue to be central to progress in survey-based social science and in social science more generally.

Methods versus Substance

Although we have separated survey methodology in chapter 2 from substantive areas of research in chapters 3 through 14, method and substance are directly connected in terms of ideas: substantive problems stimulate new methodological developments, and methodological issues can lead to substantive insights. Individual scientists and research projects and programs will of necessity tend to focus more on substance or more on methods, but the creative tensions and synergies between them are crucial.

Thus, the substantive problems of how to understand intergenerational transmission of, and change in, income, attitudes, and behavior have given rise to new longitudinal intra- and intergenerational sample designs. For example, Jennings (chap. 4) found differences in later political attitudes and behavior between individuals in a sample who had engaged in protest during the Vietnam period and individuals who had not. The differences could have arisen because protesting produced lasting changes in those involved or because those drawn to protest were already distinctive prior to the Vietnam period. Fortunately, the sample that Jennings was studying had also been interviewed at an earlier point in time, and he was able to show that protesters and nonprotesters had revealed little difference originally, thus supporting the conclusion that protesting itself was a cause of enduring change. Similarly, longitudinal designs have become central to all of the studies on the life course and aging discussed in part 4 and create new challenges for methodological development in the analysis of longitudinal data.

Even repeated surveys of the same individuals cannot distinguish effects tied closely to a particular historical period from those that transcend that period. Thus, in addition to longitudinal designs that interview a single sample through time, more complex designs have been developed that follow a succession of cohorts through time, as exemplified by the SRC program Monitoring the Future (chap. 11) and the more recent Health and Retirement Study (chap. 12), while the Panel Study of Income Dynamics (chap. 6) not only follows a sample of original respondents but extends its repeated surveys to the descendants of that initial sample. Still a different type of expansion beyond a single cultural context calls for comparing findings for the United States with those from parallel inquiries in other countries (e.g., Converse and Pierce 1986 on the importance of party identification, as noted in chap. 3, and the cross-national comparisons of poverty dynamics noted by Duncan in chap. 6).

One criticism of surveys, especially those dealing with political issues, is that by treating all bearers of attitudes in a sample as equal they ignore power differentials that make the views of some people much more influential than others. The criticism led Stouffer (1955) to create as part of his classic study of civil liberties a sample of "community leaders," along with a more typical cross section of the American population, and to compare the two samples throughout his analysis. A similar expansion of the traditional cross-section survey was undertaken by Miller and Stokes (1963) (see chap. 3) by interviewing both those running for congressional office and cross-section samples of their constituents, in part to learn whether the views of the latter are reflected in the policy sentiments of the former. Moreover, the subsequent votes of the elected congressional representatives could be examined as well.

Substantive and theoretical questions also generate new methods of sampling and data collection as well as research designs. The increasing need and desire to study relatively small racial-ethnic populations more intensively have stimulated developments in the statistics of sampling and data analysis with differential selection probabilities or weights and have led to new methods of population sampling such as the snowball methods developed by Jackson and his colleagues (cf. chap. 14) to ensure inclusion of the full range of the African-American population, especially those living in areas with heavily nonblack populations. Similarly, the need to understand better the life-course determinants of attitudes and behavior led Thornton, Axinn, and their colleagues (cf. chap. 10) to generate a new method for retrospective reporting of life events via the life history calendar as a means of improving life event data in both cross-sectional and longitudinal research on the life course.

Methodological developments or results also give rise to substantive applications. From the early years of survey research in the 1940s, Gallup divided samples into random halves to carry out what were called "split ballot" experiments in order to determine whether political preferences were biased by peculiarities of question wording or order. Such survey-based experiments have continued as an essential methodological tool, as described in chapter 2, but they are also now introduced to study substantive issues as well. In chapter 13 one experiment is reported that compared opposition to federally imposed open housing laws and opposition to the same laws imposed by local referendum, and another experiment dealt with framing issues in a way that emphasizes their relevance only to helping blacks versus framing them to stress principles of fairness to minorities more generally.

Even the limitations of the survey method have been shown to have substantive implications. As discussed in chapter 2, refusals to be interviewed are an important and growing problem for the use of sample surveys. House and Wolf (1978) saw that such rates could serve as indicators of trusting and helpful behavior on the part of citizens, and they used them to study variations across cities differing in size and age. In this way, survey research drew on its own methodological problems to generate substantive insights. More generally, we expect both survey methodology and substantive survey research to continue to interact not only as means and ends but as fruitful sources of ideas in the future.

Lesson 2: Synergies between Basic and Applied Research

Basic and applied research are also often opposed to each other and often differently valued. Yet they are more often than not complementary and synergistic. The whole development of survey research as a science and minor industry is grounded on advances in the basic social and statistical sciences of sampling, measurement, and analysis. However, it is equally important to recognize that applied research has also been a major stimulus to basic science. Nowhere is this clearer than in the formative and generative role that the needs of government and society (e.g., good unemployment count or success in World War II) have had on scientific developments generally and certainly on survey research and social science specifically (cf. chap. 1; Cartwright 1979). Just as natural scientists pooled their efforts in various projects to aid the war effort (from developing atomic bombs to improving treatment of wounds), social scientists were brought together in teams to study war-related problems, and in the course of doing so they developed new methods, theories, and organizational bases for the postwar development of social science. Similarly, the social science developments in research on health detailed in chapters 8 and 9 have been driven by increasing recognition of health as a societal problem, embodied in the NIH, which are the largest funders of basic research in the social as well as biomedical sciences. And the behavioral studies of politics, economics, and aging were all stimulated by pragmatic desires to understand and improve the functioning of democratic politics, market economics, and individuals and society in an aging population. As Featherman stresses in the foreword, survey research and social science at SRC/ ISR and more generally have benefited from a dual commitment to advancing not only basic social science but also the public interest and the amelioration of social problems.

Lesson 3: The Value of Problem-Centered, Interdisciplinary, Programmatic Research

The mutually constructive interplay of theory, methods, and data and between basic and applied research is facilitated by scientific work that is interdisciplinary, programmatic, and problem centered. This lesson, as its title implies, has three parts. Each element—problem-centered research, interdisciplinarity, and programmatic organization—is significant in itself and has effects independent of the others. But there is an interdependence among the three, and their combined effect is more than their sum.

As we have seen, scientifically generative problems may be social or applied as well as basic or theoretical in nature. Significant scientific problems almost always have important (even if somewhat remote) social or applied implications, and major social or practical problems almost always involve basic scientific issues. Focusing on a significant scientific or social problem in turn highlights the need for interdisciplinary involvement and long-term programmatic research. Few important social problems are the province of a single discipline or field, and scientific problems increasingly demand the crossing of disciplinary boundaries for their solution. Sometimes the potentialities of interdisciplinary work become most apparent when outsiders address the focal problems of a discipline. The development of survey-based social science at SRC and ISR was initially fostered largely by psychologists who had already helped to create a hybrid discipline of social psychology. They chose to work on problems central to the disciplines of economics, political science or government, sociology, and organizational management. This crossing of disciplinary boundaries led to major reorientations within all these fields. More recently, interdisciplinary research programs have brought together researchers from several fields—for example, psychologists, sociologists, and biomedical scientists from public health and medicine to understand the psychosocial nature of physical and mental health or, in another area, economists, epidemiologists, demographers, sociologists, and psychologists to understand the nature of human development and aging. Similar interdisciplinary influences occur in more basic areas of theory and research: psychometrics and econometrics have major impacts on theory and research in sociology and political science, and evolutionary biology exerts influence on the social sciences through studies of evolution and adaptation in complex systems.

Thus, the value of interdisciplinary research, long in dispute, is now widely recognized in the physical and life sciences, as well as the social and behavioral sciences. These developments, welcome as they are, do not imply that interdisciplinary research is an alternative to research within disciplines or an intellectual competitor with such research. The history of science shows a number of moments in which a new discovery or theoretical perspective within a discipline generates new intellectual excitement and sets the research agenda for years to come. Physicists in the early twentieth century experienced such a surge, as have geneticists in more recent years. But perhaps especially in the social sciences, the large questions about human behavior are seldom contained within the boundaries of single disciplines, and that fact has become increasingly clear and widely accepted.

Lesson 4: Factors Facilitating Interdisciplinary Work

Less often recognized, little understood, and still less often fulfilled are the requirements for successful interdisciplinary work. Recognition of the need for getting beyond one's own discipline and therefore a readiness to explore the potential for interdisciplinary collaboration are necessary, but they only begin the collaborative process. There is a need for sustained interaction, some of it in person rather than only by computer and telephone. Collaborating scientists must develop a shared conceptual language, and each must learn enough of the other's discipline to enable the development of specific research aims and joint work. Only then does active involvement in joint research projects become feasible (Kahn 1993).

It takes time, therefore, for interdisciplinary research efforts to get under way and more time for them to fulfill their promise and effect major reorientations of science within or across disciplines. Solo research investigators and isolated research projects cannot suffice. The work cited in this book, like that in the natural and biomedical sciences, involves long-term programmatic efforts by groups of scientists working together across disciplinary lines. Major developments and payoffs are the products of work over decades rather than months or even years, though extreme crises such as wars can accelerate this pace. Within SRC and ISR the most successful and influential research programs have continued over a quarter to a half century or more, often integrated and sustained by major continuing projects such as the Survey of Consumer Attitudes, National Election Studies, PSID, Survey of Consumer Finances, MTF, National Survey of Black Americans, HRS, and national and regional surveys of family growth and development. Core continuing surveys underlie major research programs elsewhere such as the California Human Population Laboratory/Alameda County study, the National Longitudinal Surveys at Ohio State, or the Duke University Center for the Study of Aging and Human Development. Other research programs involve less continuous but nevertheless linked and progressively developing sets of studies or surveys, such as the SRC/ISR Social Environment and Health Program. The increasing tendency is for all such programs of research to involve surveys that are longitudinal in nature in order to better understand processes of change and to strengthen causal inferences.

An important feature of successful interdisciplinary research with a programmatic flavor has to do with the scale and continuity of the planning activities involved in major longitudinal studies. Two recent illustrations make the point. In the late 1980s, a major concern developed at the National Institute on Aging about a serious gap in the availability of data needed to understand the retirement and aging process that was clearly becoming a critical policy issue, not only in the United States but also in much of the world. The NIA provided substantial support for what was probably the most extensive planning process ever undertaken in the social sciences, involving the sustained efforts of half a dozen scientific working groups whose objectives were to specify the types of measures that needed to be obtained in order to understand the interplay among health status, economic status, family structure, and decisions to leave the work force by way of retirement. These working groups for the new HRS included a substantial array of disciplines—economists, demographers, sociologists, epidemiologists, psychologists, statisticians, and survey methodologists.

The continued interaction of these planning groups was essential to the design of the study, and the influence of these scientific working groups continues to be substantial, taking the form of numerous enhancements to the quality of the data as well as designing the introduction of important new content. The result is a rich and widely used database with enormous scientific potential, well justifying the very large amount of resources put into the total planning activity and into attracting the attention of a substantial array of research scientists.

A second illustration is the evolution of both the NES and the PSID, which in their early days were designed by an interdisciplinary group of researchers in the SRC but in later years have come to be substantially influenced by a scientific oversight group selected by the National Science Foundation as part of its funding of each study as a national data resource. In the case of PSID, this heavily interdisciplinary group has transitioned the study into a unique study of generational influences on economic outcomes. NES, PSID, HRS, and other long-term studies such as MTF have not only had a major influence on social science research in the United States but have been widely emulated in the developed world. Hence it will be possible in the future to do comparative studies among many of the developed countries of the world with a base of measurements that have substantial elements of commonality, a potentiality already being realized in collaborative ventures such as the Comparative Study of Electoral Systems (cf. chap. 3), the Luxembourg Income Study (cf. chap. 6), and the English Longitudinal Study on Aging being developed along the lines of the Health and Retirement Study.

Lesson 5: The Necessity of Institutional Infrastructures and Support

Long-term interdisciplinary research requires an infrastructure that can bring together and sustain large groups of researchers over long periods of time. This involves creating and maintaining an organizational context that provides professional and technical support, methodological tools or instruments, and access to the objects of study. Examples include the NIH intramural research programs, the major medical research centers, and the national laboratories and observatories in physics, biology, and astronomy. What needs to be recognized is that social science, especially interdisciplinary social science, has similar needs. Survey-based social science research centers and institutes such as SRC, ISR, the National Opinion Research Center, the Research Triangle Institute, and others have met these needs to some extent and will continue to do so.

Experience in these organizations poignantly shows, however, that to provide support these organizations also require support. Potential sources of such support include the universities or private organizations of which survey organizations are a part, as well as private foundations and state, regional, and national governmental agencies. The growth and development of SRC and ISR over a half century have frequently been contrasted with the productive but shorter life of the Columbia Bureau of Applied Social Research. Converse (1987) attributes these differences to the differing degree to which the leaders of SRC/ISR and the Columbia Bureau of Applied Social Research focused their energies on institutional growth and development, as well as the degree to which their host institutions nurtured and supported them.

Clearly in the social sciences, as in the natural sciences, investments in infrastructure must be selective and strategic. But they must be made. Certainly SRC and ISR and their major research projects and programs have been sustained by cooperative efforts among themselves, the University of Michigan, and funding sources in the government, for-profit, and nonprofit sectors. The same is true of other long-term centers of social science research, such as NORC and the Brookings Institution.

Current Frontiers and Future Prospects and Challenges

As we enter the twenty-first century, survey-based social science is extending itself over time, space, and the diversity of human populations, suggesting that this century may be at least as challenging and generative as the previous one. Here we highlight some of the major ongoing developments and future challenges, many of which are discussed more fully in preceding chapters.

The Extension of Surveys in Time: Cross-Sectionally and Longitudinally

Across its history of the last half century, survey research has evolved from taking snapshots to making motion pictures, that is, from conducting single cross-sectional surveys to doing repeated cross-sectional surveys of a given population and, increasingly, conducting true longitudinal surveys of the same individuals over substantial time periods. The General Social Survey, conducted by NORC, and the Current Population Survey, conducted by the Bureau of the Census, are major examples of repeated cross-sectional surveys. The census itself, now a repeated cross-sectional survey, may evolve into an almost continuous series of repeated cross sections, perhaps with longitudinal components, now being piloted as the America Community Survey. Longitudinal studies of the same individuals over time are exemplified by PSID and HRS, both conducted by SRC; NLS, based at Ohio State University and conducted by NORC; and the Survey of Income and Program Participation of the Bureau of the Census. Such studies require the development of infrastructures for archiving and linking repeated surveys over decades, for tracking individuals over time, and for refreshing samples to maintain their representativeness. They also require computer-intensive methods for linking and analyzing information on the same individuals or cohorts over time. These demands are substantial, but the rewards are great. Longitudinal studies allow improved understanding of processes of change, feedback, and reciprocal causation in individuals and populations. For example, they enable us to address such questions as how the availability and demand for illicit substances affect each other and how the rates of use of these substances are changing or how health and wealth are reciprocally related to each other and shape decisions about retirement, migration, and lifestyle in the later years of life. Such issues have begun to be addressed intensively only over the last two decades, and they form a major agenda for the twenty-first century.

Extending Surveys in Space: Linkage with Other Forms of Data

Survey research is sometimes criticized for focusing only on aggregates of atomized individuals. However, the sampling, interviewing, coding, and data processing and analysis methods of surveys can be utilized to gather, organize, and analyze information on geographical, organizational, or administrative units and even whole societies. More important and powerful, survey data on individuals can be linked with data on the households, organizations, communities, political units, and nations of which they are a part. Such linkages allow multilevel and spatial analyses of the impact of broader forms of social organization on individuals, as well as of the effect of individual behavior on successive levels of social organization. Again, adequate methods for collecting, linking, and analyzing such cross-level data have become available only in the last couple of decades, opening new horizons for understanding how properties of communities, political jurisdictions, and even societies combine with individual characteristics and more proximal influences on individuals to affect economic and political behavior, delinquent and criminal behavior, racial/ethnic relations, and health and well-being (Raudenbush and Bryk 2002).

Ethnographic and physical-chemical-biological data can also be linked with survey data to allow better understanding of processes of economic and environmental development and change. The creative use of survey data in conjunction with other social and environmental data is another of the major challenges and opportunities for twenty-first-century survey research and social science, greatly facilitated by new methods of mapping various forms of data onto one another via Geographic Information and Global Positioning Systems and analyzing them spatially.

Comparative Cross-National Studies

The globalization of survey research as well as business and commerce creates the opportunity for comparative and multilevel research on the grand scale of nations or societies. The study of income dynamics, voting, and racial/ethnic attitudes and behaviors in the United States is evolving toward the comparative study of social welfare and electoral systems and of societal patterns of racial/ethnic relations. To understand how and why socioeconomically similar societies vary substantially in their levels of poverty, income inequality, population health, crime, expenditures and saving, political participation, racial/ethnic conflict, and the like, researchers have previously relied on historical and qualitative analysis. Adding comparative survey-based data to the analysis of such issues can yield more precise and reliable answers to questions of great scientific and social importance.

Studies of Special Populations

As surveys have expanded their scope in both time and space, we have also gained increasing facility for surveying more intensively special subpopulations such as racial/ethnic minorities, immigrants, drug users, and entrepreneurs. Thus we can understand the nature and dynamics of such subgroups as well as comparing them with other groups and with the larger society. Studies of this kind have already deepened and altered in many ways our understanding of the racial/ethnic diversity of American society and promise to do the same for the new diversity being created by the largest influx of immigrants in over a century.

Surveys and Experiments

Surveys are often compared unfavorably to laboratory experiments in terms of their ability to study causal processes. However, we have greatly improved our ability to study causal processes in nonexperimental data, especially when such data are longitudinal. We have also come to recognize that surveys and experiments can be combined, either by embedding experimental manipulations of question wording and modes of administration within surveys or by using surveys to track and evaluate the results of experimental social programs or innovations. The increasing articulation of surveys with experimental methods, as well their articulation with organizational, environmental, and ethnographic data, promises to enhance the scientific and social value of both surveys and experiments.

In his presidential address to the American Psychological Association, Donald Campbell (1969) spoke of the United States at its best as an experimenting society. The phrase "experimenting society," which thus far expresses aspiration more than accomplishment, envisions a society in which major policy proposals are tested before their enactment on a national scale. The experimental tests would necessarily be done on a scale large enough to represent the populations affected and long enough to evaluate intended and unintended effects. Survey methods are a major part of social experiments and their evaluation on this scale, as in the income maintenance experiments of the 1970s (Hum 1993; Munnell 1987).

Computerization and the Internet

The nature of survey-based social science in the twenty-first century will continue to be altered, enlarged, and refined by the ongoing computer revolution. Since survey research is a data-intensive method, its possibilities and potentials expand directly with the growth of computing power. The power of former mainframe computers now sits on desktops and even in the laps of interviewers and analysts. These computers can be linked via the Internet and parallel processing to create options for study design, data collection, data processing, storage, transfer, retrieval, and analysis that were unimaginable only a few decades and even years ago. The spread of telephones created a whole new basis of survey sampling and data collection as an addition to rather than a replacement for area sampling and face-to-face interviewing. Similarly, the World Wide Web has created the Web survey as a complement and, in some circumstances, an alternative to face-to-face, telephone, and mail methods of data collection.

At the same time, the development of the Internet and of readily accessible data archives from afar allows individual social scientists in virtually any physical location to apply their personal creativity to the formulation of new theoretical problems and the discovery of new findings. Scientific knowledge and research are inherently based on shared information about methods and findings; the computer, the Internet, and the creation of vast electronically accessible data archives transform the magnitude and rapidity of that sharing. Thus the development of a large and complex infrastructure does not prevent continued creativity at the individual level but indeed facilitates it by enhancing the quantity and quality of data available to individuals anywhere in the world.

Challenges to Survey Methods

As indicated in chapter 2, survey methods, like any other scientific method or instrument, must continually evolve and adapt in response to changes in the nature of the empirical world they are attempting to observe or measure. Self-critical methodological research probes for and tries to alleviate sources of error in sampling, data collection, data processing, or data analyses. These tasks are especially difficult because the social world is more reactive than the physical or biological world to attempts to measure it. Surveys rely, as noted in chapter 1, on the willing cooperation of the public. The norms of cooperation have been threatened over time by social and political changes, by the use of the telephone for marketing appeals, and by the growth of the survey industry itself. Response rates to surveys declined steadily from the 1950s to the late

1960s and early 1970s. Analysis of these trends indicated that they reflected changes in the population and in the social fabric of society: increased female labor force participation, making individuals less likely to be home and more likely to be busy; urbanization and deterioration of urban areas, making respondents more fearful and less trusting (House and Wolf 1978; Groves and Couper 1998); and security and screening systems, making access more difficult, whether in person or by telephone. Lowered expectations among survey scientists and lowered performance among interviewers undoubtedly also played a role in the decline.

Recent analyses paint an even gloomier picture. Noncontact rates, which had been declining over time as a result of greater efforts to reach respondents, appear to have been rising in recent years, dramatically so in the case of telephone surveys, and refusal rates have continued to increase. Despite methodological research and attendant improvements in survey practice—including more sophisticated call-back and refusal conversion algorithms, intensive interviewer training and supervision, and increased use of respondent monetary incentives—response rates have continued to decline even as costs have continued to rise.

Moreover, new challenges continue to emerge in the form of increased concerns about respondent burden, privacy, and confidentiality related to the proliferation of surveys and the increased use of computers and the Internet for data collection and dissemination. Many of the developments already referred to that enhance the information value of surveys—for example, linkage across time, linkage with other data sources, and linkage with contextual information—also may be seen as intrusions into respondent privacy and as threats to the confidentiality of the data collected. These concerns represent a major challenge for survey research in the twenty-first century.

Conclusion

In sum, survey research is arguably the single most important methodological development and contribution of twentieth-century social science. Like telescopes, microscopes, particle accelerators, and chemical analysis methods in the natural sciences, it will remain a pillar of twenty-first-century social science, while also evolving to open up new insights into the nature of social life and the social problems that confront human societies across the globe. Like other innovative and powerful scientific instruments, from radioactive imaging to coding of genetic markers, survey research continues to face scientific, political, and ethical challenges to its use and validity. These challenges will continue to be addressed by methodological research, by studies in the sociology of science, and by ethical analysis. We expect that, in the twenty-first century as in the twentieth, addressing such challenges will continue to improve the scientific quality of surveys and their contribution to human science and wellbeing.

REFERENCES

Campbell, Donald T. 1969. Reforms as experiments. *American Psychologist* 24:409–29.

Cartwright, Dorwin. 1979. Contemporary social psychology in historical perspective. *Social Psychology Quarterly* 42:82–93.

Converse, Jean M. 1987. *Survey research in the United States: Roots and emergence.* Berkeley: University of California Press.

Converse, Philip E., and Roy Pierce. 1986. *Political representation in France.* Cambridge, MA: Belknap Press.

Groves, Robert M., and Mick P. Couper. 1998. *Nonresponse in household interview surveys.* New York: Wiley.

House, James S., and Sharon Wolf. 1978. Effects of urban residence on interpersonal trust and helping behavior. *Journal of Personality and Social Psychology* 36:1029–43.

Hum, Derek. 1993. Economic response to a guaranteed annual income: Experience from Canada and the United States. *Journal of Labor Economics* 11:S263–S296.

Kahn, Robert L. 1993. The MacArthur Foundation program in mental health and human development: An experiment in scientific organization. Occasional Paper. Chicago: MacArthur Foundation.

Massey, Douglas S. 2002. A brief history of human society: The origin and role of emotion in social life. *American Sociological Review* 67:1–29.

Miller, Warren E., and Donald E. Stokes. 1963. Constituency influence in Congress. *American Political Science Review* 57:45–56.

Munnell, Alicia H. 1987. Lessons from the income maintenance experiments: An overview. *New England Economic Review* (May/June): 32–44.

Raudenbush, Stephen W., and Anthony S. Bryk. 2002. *Hierarchical linear models: Applications and data analysis methods.* 2d ed. Thousand Oaks, CA: Sage.

Stouffer, Samuel A. 1955. *Communism, conformity, and civil liberties: A cross-section of the nation speaks its mind.* Garden City, NY: Doubleday.

Contributors

DUANE F. ALWIN is the McCourtney Professor of Sociology, Demography, and Human Development at Pennsylvania State University. Prior to moving to Penn State he spent twenty-three years at the University of Michigan, where he held appointments in the Survey Research Center of the Institute for Social Research and in the Department of Sociology. From 1983 to 1995 Alwin directed the SRC Summer Institute in Survey Research Techniques, and from 1998 to 2000 he chaired the Department of Sociology at Michigan. The focus of his research and teaching includes families and children, aging and the life course, and the linkages between processes of individual development, history, and social change. He is coauthor of *Political Attitudes over the Life-Span: The Bennington Women after Fifty Years* (1991) and has authored or coauthored more than one hundred scholarly articles and chapters on topics related to human development and aging. He is past chair of the Section on Social Psychology of the American Sociological Association.

WILLIAM G. AXINN is professor of sociology at the University of Michigan, where he is also research professor in the Survey Research Center and the Population Studies Center. Prior to coming to the University of Michigan in 1998, he was on the faculty in sociology and demography at the University of Chicago and Pennsylvania State University. His research focuses on the relationships among social change, family organization, intergenerational relationships, marriage, cohabitation, and fertility in the United States and Nepal. His research also includes the development of new methods for collecting social science data and investigations of the relationships between population change and the environment. He directs the Population and Ecology Research Laboratory in Nepal and is deputy director of the National Survey of Family Growth in the United States.

JERALD G. BACHMAN is research professor and Distinguished Research Scientist at the Survey Research Center of the Institute for Social Research at the University of Michigan. For nearly four decades he has directed a program of research on youth and social issues, beginning with the Youth in Transition project in 1964 and continuing with the Monitoring the Future project. His many publications include five books in the *Youth in Transition* series (1967–78); one book on *The All-*

Volunteer Force (1977); and two books based on Monitoring the Future findings, *Smoking, Drinking, and Drug Use in Young Adulthood* (1997) and *The Decline of Substance Use in Young Adulthood: Changes in Social Activities, Roles, and Beliefs* (2002). Current research interests focus on causes, correlates, and consequences of smoking, drinking, and drug use among youth and young adults, as well as on issues related to youth and military service.

PHILIP E. CONVERSE received his doctorate from the social psychology program at the University of Michigan in 1958. He spent most of his career at the Institute for Social Research, first in the Survey Research Center and later in the Center for Political Studies, serving as director of CPS from 1982 to 1986 and director of ISR from 1986 to 1989. He was also the Robert Cooley Angell Distinguished University Professor of Political Science and Sociology. He is author or coauthor of some dozen books, including *The American Voter* (1960), *Elections and the Political Order* (1966), *The Human Meaning of Social Change* (1972), *The Quality of American Life* (1976), and *Political Representation in France* (1986), along with numerous articles, including "The Nature of Belief System in Mass Publics" (1964). A member of the American Academy of Arts and Sciences and the National Academy of Sciences, and a past president of the American Political Science Association, Converse left ISR in 1989 to serve five years as director of the Center for Advanced Studies in the Behavioral Sciences in Stanford, California, before retirement.

RICHARD T. CURTIN has been the director of the Surveys of Consumers in the Survey Research Center at the University of Michigan since 1976. His research has focused on the economic expectations of consumers, including the formation, accuracy, and the impact of economic expectations on consumers' spending and saving decisions. Curtin's monthly outlook reports on prospects for consumer spending as well as the data drawn from his survey program are widely published and utilized by business, governmental agencies, and academic researchers. He has consulted on the establishment of consumer surveys in a number of countries, including China, Hungary, Indonesia, Jamaica, and Russia. He is the author of *Income Equity among U.S. Workers: The Bases and Consequences* (1977) and numerous articles in economic and social science journals and has served as coeditor of the *Journal of Economic Psychology* (1980–92) and as a member of the editorial boards of *Economic Outlook USA* (1970–90) and the *Review of Income and Wealth* (2001–).

GREG J. DUNCAN is the Edwina S. Tarry Professor of Education and Social Policy and a faculty associate at the Institute for Policy Research at Northwestern University, where he is director of the Northwestern University/University of Chicago Joint Center for Poverty Research. Duncan received his Ph.D. in economics in 1974 from the University of Michigan, working on and later directing the Panel Study of Income Dynamics from 1972 until he joined the faculty at Northwestern University in 1995. Duncan's research has focused on issues of economic mobility both within and across generations. He is the author of *Years of Poverty, Years of Plenty* (1984), which documented the surprising degree of economic mobility in the United States, and the coeditor of *Consequences of Growing Up Poor* (1997) about the impacts of poverty on child development. More recently, his research has focused on how welfare reform affects families and children. He was awarded an honorary doctorate degree at the University of Essex in 1999 and was elected into the American Academy of Arts and Sciences in 2001.

David L. Featherman, professor of both sociology and psychology, has directed the University of Michigan Institute for Social Research since 1995. He is an expert on human development throughout the life span, and his most recent book is *Social Science and Policy-Making: A Search for Relevance in the Twentieth Century*, coedited with University of Michigan historian Maris Vinovskis. Before coming home to Michigan, where he received his Ph.D. degree, he served as president of the Social Science Research Council in New York City for six years. He began his academic career at Princeton University and then served with distinction for twenty-one years on the faculty of the University of Wisconsin–Madison as the John Bascom Professor of Sociology.

Robert M. Groves is research professor and director of the Survey Research Center at the Institute for Social Research, as well as professor of sociology, all at the University of Michigan, and research professor at the Joint Program in Survey Methodology at the University of Maryland. He is the author of *Survey Errors and Survey Costs* (1989), *Nonresponse in Household Interview Surveys* (with M. Couper, 1998), and *Surveys by Telephone* (with R. Kahn, 1979); is chief editor of *Telephone Survey Methodology* (1988) and *Survey Nonresponse* (2002); is a coeditor of *Measurement Errors in Surveys* (1991); and is the author of many journal articles on survey methodology. His current research interests focus on theory building in survey participation and models of nonresponse reduction and adjustment.

Steven G. Heeringa is a research scientist in the Survey Methodology Program, the Director of the Statistical and Research Design Group in the Survey Research Center, and the Director of the Summer Institute in Survey Research Techniques at the Institute for Social Research. He has over 25 years of statistical sampling experience directing the development of the SRC National Sample design, as well as sample designs for SRC's major longitudinal and cross-sectional survey programs. During this period he has been actively involved in research and publication on sample design methods and procedures such as weighting, variance estimation, and the imputation of missing data. He is coeditor (with Graham Kalton) of *Leslie Kish: Selected Papers* (2003).

A. Regula Herzog was, until her death in July 2002, senior research scientist in the Institute for Social Research and the Institute of Gerontology and adjunct professor in the department of psychology, all at the University of Michigan. She obtained her M.A. (1975) and Ph.D. (1976) in psychology from the University of Michigan. Her primary research interests were in aging and survey methodology, patterns of productive activities and of health and well-being across the life span, urinary incontinence, cognitive functioning and dementia, and identity formation and maintenance. She played a pioneering role in helping to design and implement the Health and Retirement Study and Asset and Health Dynamics of the Oldest Old, large, ongoing, interdisciplinary, longitudinal studies of older Americans. Herzog authored or coauthored over eighty papers in scientific journals spanning psychology, survey methodology, gerontology, and biomedical fields such as geriatrics and urology. She also authored or edited several books, including *Special Research Methods for Gerontology* (with M. P. Lawton, 1989) and *The Health and Economic Status of Older Women: Research Issues and Data Sources* (with K. C. Holden and M. M. Seltzer, 1989). Just prior to her death she was selected to receive the University of Michigan Distinguished Research Scientist Award, which was awarded posthumously.

Sandra L. Hofferth is a professor in the Department of Family Studies at the University of Maryland at College Park. She received her Ph.D. in sociology from the University of North Carolina in 1976. From 1983 to 1988 Hofferth served as health scientist administrator in the National Institute of Child Health and Human Development (NICHD). From 1977 to 1983 she was research associate and from 1988 to 1994 senior research associate at the Urban Institute in Washington, DC, where she directed the National Child Care Survey 1990 and collaborated on A Profile of Child Care Settings. From 1994 to 2001 she was senior research scientist at the Institute for Social Research, where she codirected the Michigan Panel Study of Income Dynamics and directed its Child Development Supplement. She has researched family issues in the context of public policy for more than twenty years. She has published three books, including *Risking the Future: Adolescent Sexuality, Pregnancy and Childbearing, Vol. II* (coedited with C. Hayes, 1987), and more than seventy articles and book chapters. She was awarded the 1991–92 Jensen Lectureship, jointly sponsored by the American Sociological Association and Duke University, for research contributing to the goal of providing social action with a more rational grounding in tested knowledge and has been a member of the board of the Population Association of America and the NICHD Family and Child Well-Being Research Network.

James S. House is research professor and former director of the Survey Research Center in the Institute for Social Research and professor and former chair of the Department of Sociology at the University of Michigan. He received his Ph.D. in social psychology from the University of Michigan in 1972 and served as instructor, assistant professor, and associate professor in the Department of Sociology at Duke University from 1970 to 1978. Throughout his career his research has focused on the role of social and psychological factors in the etiology and course of health and illness, initially on occupational stress and health, later on social relationships and support in relation to health, and currently on the role of psychosocial factors in understanding and explaining social inequalities in health and the way health changes with age. He is an elected member of the American Academy of Arts and Sciences and the Institute of Medicine of the National Academies of Science; author of *Work Stress and Social Support* (1981); coeditor of *Aging, Health Behaviors, and Health Outcomes* (with Schaie and Blazer, 1992) and *Sociological Perspectives on Social Psychology* (with Cook and Fine, 1995); and an associate editor (for health entries) of the *International Encyclopedia of the Social and Behavioral Sciences* (2001).

JAMES S. JACKSON is the Daniel Katz Distinguished University Professor of Psychology, director of the Research Center for Group Dynamics, research professor and director of the Program for Research on Black Americans at the Institute for Social Research, and director of the Center for Afroamerican and African Studies, all at the University of Michigan. He is Chair of the Section on Social, Economic, and Political Sciences (K) of the American Association for the Advancement of Science (2003–4). He was elected in 2002 as a member of the Institute of Medicine of the National Academies of Science. He was the recipient of a Fogarty Senior Postdoctoral International Fellowship, in 1993–94, for study in France and held for many years the position of *Chercheur Invite, Groupe d'Etudes et de Recherches sur la Science, Ecole des Hautes Etudes en Sciences Sociales.* He is former national president of the Black Students Psychological Association and the Association of Black Psychologists. He has conducted research and published in the areas of international, comparative studies on immigration and race and ethnic relations, health and mental health, adult development and aging, attitudes and attitude change, and African-American politics.

M. KENT JENNINGS is professor of political science at the University of California, Santa Barbara, and professor emeritus and senior research scientist emeritus at the University of Michigan. While at the University of Michigan he initiated and continued a long-term, multigenerational study of political socialization. He has also carried out research in the areas of gender and politics, political elites, and political participation in the United States, several Western European countries, and China. He is a member of the American Academy of Arts and Sciences, served as president of the American Political Science Association, and was a recipient of fellowships from the Guggenheim Foundation, the Center for Advanced Studies in the Behavioral Sciences, and the Netherlands Institute for Advanced Studies in the Humanities and Social Sciences. In addition to numerous articles and book chapters, he has authored or coauthored several books, including *Governing American Schools* (1974), *The Political Character of Adolescence* (1974), and *Generations and Politics* (1981).

LLOYD D. JOHNSTON is research professor and Distinguished Research Scientist in the Survey Research Center of the University of Michigan Institute for Social Research. As principal investigator of the Monitoring the Future study since its inception in 1975, he has conducted research on substance abuse and other behaviors and attitudes of American young people for over three decades. A social psychologist by training, he has served as advisor to the White House, Congress, and many other national and international bodies and has conducted research on a wide range of issues, including the use of alcohol, tobacco, and various illicit drugs; institutional trust; policy evaluation; and the functioning of American high schools. His research interests also include international comparative studies and the application of survey research to social problems generally. Among his books and monographs are *Drugs and American Youth* (1973); *Conducting Follow-Up Research on Drug Treatment Programs* (1977); and a forty-two-volume series of monographs, the latest of which are entitled *Monitoring the Future National Survey Results on Drug Use, 1975–2001, Volumes I and II* (2002).

F. THOMAS JUSTER received his Ph.D. from Columbia University. Prior to joining the Institute for Social Research (ISR) and the faculty of the University of Michigan in 1973, he was on the research staff of the National Bureau of Economic Research. He was director of the ISR from 1976 to 1986 and is currently senior research scientist emeritus at ISR and professor emeritus of economics. His research interests include the analysis of savings and wealth accumulation among U.S. households; the analysis of time allocation among households; the determinants of retirement; and the interrelations between health status, labor force status, and economic status. His current research activities reflect all of these interests. Juster has been an active participant in the national scientific community. He has chaired an American Economic Association Committee on the Quality of Economic Statistics; has been a member of several National Academy of Sciences committees, including the Committee on National Statistics; has served on the Brookings Panel as a senior advisor; has frequently served on American Statistical Association advisory committees; and is a fellow of the American Statistical Association and of the National Association of Business Economics. His publications include four books, including *Time, Goods, and Well-Being* (with Stafford, 1985), six volumes edited or coedited, and numerous journal articles and book chapters.

ROBERT L. KAHN is a social psychologist at the University of Michigan, where he is a professor emeritus of psychology and public health. He is a former director of the Survey Research Center and is now senior research scientist emeritus at the Institute for Social Research, of which he was a founder. His research has concentrated for many years on two main areas: organizational behavior and aging. His early work dealt with organizational effectiveness and its determinants; his later work was more concerned with the impact of organizational demands on health. His research on aging investigates the importance of life-style choices and behavior for minimizing the risk of disease and disability. Among his numerous books are *Organizational* Stress (with Wolfe, Quinn, Snoek, and Rosenthal, 1964), *The Social Psychology of Organizations* (with Katz, 1966 and 1978), and *Successful Aging* (with Rowe, 1998). He is a fellow of the Institute of Medicine of the National Academies of Science, the American Academy of Arts and Sciences, and the American Association for the Advancement of Science.

George A. Kaplan is professor and former chair of the Department of Epidemiology in the School of Public Health; research professor in the Survey Research Center at the Institute for Social Research; and director of the Michigan Initiative on Inequalities in Health, of the Michigan Interdisciplinary Center on Social Inequalities, Mind, and Body, and of the Center for Social Epidemiology and Population Health, all at the University of Michigan. He is an associate in the Population Health Program of the Canadian Institute for Advanced Research and also director of the new Robert Wood Johnson Foundation Health and Society Scholars Program at the University of Michigan. A social epidemiologist, he has published over two hundred papers on the role of behavioral, social, psychological, and socioeconomic factors in disease prevention and health promotion; the cumulative cost of socioeconomic disadvantage on health and functional outcomes in the elderly; the role of socioeconomic status and economic equity on the overall health of populations; the impact of neighborhood and community factors on health; and the impact of life-course trajectories on a variety of health outcomes in adulthood. Kaplan has received numerous honors, including president of the Society for Epidemiologic Research (2002), election to the Institute of Medicine of the National Academies of Science (2001), and the Nobel Forum Lecture (first ever by a researcher in public health sciences, 2000).

Donald R. Kinder is the Philip E. Converse Collegiate Professor of Political Science at the University of Michigan. Kinder has been a fellow at the Center for Advanced Study in the Behavioral Sciences, a Guggenheim fellow, and is a member of the American Academy of Arts and Sciences. He is currently a principal investigator of the National Election Study. He is completing a book on the role of principles and prejudice in American political life (Myrdal's Prediction) and is beginning one, with Nancy Burns, on the politics of gender and race in Atlanta and Detroit. His publications include *News That Matters* (with Shanto Iyengar), *Divided by Color* (with Lynn Sanders), and "Opinion and Action in the Realm of Politics" in the current edition of the *Handbook of Social Psychology.*

Maria Krysan is associate professor of sociology at the University of Illinois at Chicago and a faculty fellow at its Institute for Research on Race and Public Policy. She received her Ph.D. from the University of Michigan in 1995. Her recent research focuses on the factors underlying racial residential preferences, trends in racial attitudes, and the sources of racial policy attitudes. Her investigations of these substantive issues often connect to methodological questions about how to study this sensitive area of social life, combining standard closed-ended survey analysis with mode of administration experiments, analyses of open-ended survey questions, and depth interviews. She is coauthor of *Racial Attitudes in America: Trends and Interpretations* (with Schuman and Bobo, 1997) and is responsible for a Web site that updates the data from that book, <http://tigger.cc.uic.edu/~krysan/racialattitudes.htm>. Her recent work has appeared in *Social Psychology Quarterly, Annual Review of Sociology, Demography, and Social Problems,* and other journals, and she was a visiting scholar at the Russell Sage Foundation in 1998–99.

JAMES M. LEPKOWSKI is research professor at the Institute for Social Research and associate professor of biostatistics at the University of Michigan. He is also a research professor in the Joint Program in Survey Methodology at the University of Maryland. He directs the Michigan Program in Survey Methodology. He has written extensively in the survey methodology research literature on the design of telephone samples, compensating for missing data, and the nature of interviewer and respondent interaction in survey data collection. He is a fellow of the American Statistical Association and was elected to membership in the International Statistical Institute.

PATRICK M. O'MALLEY is research professor at the Survey Research Center of the Institute for Social Research at the University of Michigan. His principal research activity has been with the Monitoring the Future project, which provides annual reports on trends in the use of tobacco, alcohol, and illicit drugs, and related attitudes and beliefs, among American secondary school students, college students, and adults through age forty. His interests include the epidemiology and etiology of the use and abuse of psychoactive drugs, including the policy implications of the research. He is coauthor of three recent books: *Smoking, Drinking, and Drug Use in Young Adulthood* (1997); *The Decline of Substance Use in Young Adulthood* (2002); and *Selecting Statistical Techniques for Social Science Data: A Guide for SASR Users* (1998).

RICHARD H. PRICE is professor of psychology and research professor in the Survey Research Center of the Institute for Social Research at the University of Michigan and director of the Michigan Prevention Research Center and the Interdisciplinary Program on Organizational Studies. His research is focused on social organization, mental health, and the prevention of disorder and disability. His books include *Person-Environment Psychology* (with Walsh and Craik, 1992), *Fourteen Ounces of Prevention* (with Cowen, Lorion, and Ramos-McKay, 1988) and *Evaluation and Action in the Social Environment* (with Politser, 1980). Price has received the Lela Rowland Award for Prevention Research from the National Mental Health Association, the Distinguished Contribution Award from the Society for Research and Community Action of the American Psychological Association, and the Award for International Research from the Society for Prevention Research. He served as president of the Society for Community Research and Action and holds an honorary appointment as professor of psychology at the Institute of Psychology at the Chinese National Academy of Sciences.

JOHN SCHULENBERG is research professor in the Survey Research Center of the Institute for Social Research and professor of developmental psychology at the University of Michigan. He has published widely on several topics concerning adolescent development and the transition to adulthood, focusing particularly on how developmental transitions and tasks relate to health risks and adjustment difficulties. His recent research, published in such journals as *Applied Developmental Science, Developmental Psychology, Journal of Health and Social Behavior, Journal of Studies on Alcohol,* and *Prevention Science,* focuses on the etiology and prevention of substance use, on continuity and discontinuity in overall adjustment during the transition to adulthood, and on the conceptualization and analysis of developmental change. He is a co–principal investigator of the NIDA-funded national Monitoring the Future study and recently completed an NIAAA-funded investigation of the long-term effects of a school-based alcohol misuse prevention program.

HOWARD SCHUMAN is emeritus professor of sociology, emeritus senior research scientist, and former director of the Survey Research Center in the Institute for Social Research at the University of Michigan. His degrees are from Antioch College (B.A. in philosophy), Trinity University (M.S. in psychology), and Harvard University (Ph.D. in Sociology/Social Relations). He is a fellow of the American Academy of Arts and Science and a past president of the American Association for Public Opinion Research. His own research has been mainly within four areas: the question-answer process in surveys; changes in racial attitudes; attitudes toward war; and, most recently, issues involving national and cross-national collective memories. The author of *Questions and Answers in Attitude Surveys: Experiments on Question Form, Wording, and Context* (with Presser, 1981) and *Racial Attitudes in America: Trends and Interpretations* (with Steeh, Bobo, and Krysan, 1997), he now lives on the coast of Maine but continues his research through ISR.

ELEANOR SINGER is research professor in the Survey Research Center of the Institute for Social Research at the University of Michigan, where she served as associate director of SRC from 1998 to 2002. Prior to coming to the University of Michigan in 1994, she was senior research scholar at the Center for the Social Sciences at Columbia University, where she received her Ph.D. in sociology in 1966. She is the recipient of numerous NSF and NIH grants and has written and published widely in two main areas: survey methodology, especially survey participation; and ethical issues in survey research, especially those involving informed consent. She is a former editor of *Public Opinion Quarterly* and a past president of the American Association for Public Opinion Research as well as a recipient of its Lifetime Achievement award.

FRANK P. STAFFORD is professor of economics and research professor in the Survey Research Center, where he serves as director of the Panel Study of Income Dynamics. In May 2000 the PSID was selected as one of the fifty projects that the NSF identified as most interesting or significant in its fifty-year history. He also serves as principal investigator of the National Institute on Aging project "Wealth and Health over the Life Course in the PSID." This project substantially expands the topics studied in the PSID to include pension wealth of families, their health conditions, medical care costs, out-of-pocket medical expenses, and related domains. A third main activity is as principal investigator of the Child Development Supplement of the PSID, a project funded by the National Institute of Child Health and Human Development. He is the author of *Time, Goods, and Well-Being* (with Juster, 1985).

ARLAND THORNTON is professor of sociology at the University of Michigan, where he is also research professor in the Survey Research Center and in the Population Studies Center of the Institute for Social Research and is currently director of the Population Studies Center. His research focuses on trends, causes, and consequences of marriage, cohabitation, divorce, fertility, gender roles, adolescent sexuality, and intergenerational relationships. He is interested in behavioral, attitudinal, and cultural elements of these dimensions of family life and their intersections with economic, educational, and religious institutions, and he conducts research on these topics in Taiwan, Nepal, and the United States. In addition, he is director of the eight-wave, thirty-one-year Intergenerational Panel Study of Parents and Children. He is coauthor of *Social Change and the Family in Taiwan* (with Lin 1994), joint editor of *Ties That Bind: Perspectives on Marriage and Cohabitation* (with Waite et al., 2000), and editor of *The Well-Being of Children and Families: Research and Data Needs* (2001).

DAVID R. WEIR is research professor and associate director for finance in the Survey Research Center and associate director of the Health and Retirement Study. His current research interests include the use of longitudinal data to study chronic disease processes, especially diabetes; the changing relationship of health insurance, economic status, and health over the life course; joint planning by couples for risks of old age including retirement, widowhood, and disability; the measurement of health-related quality of life; and the use of cost-effectiveness measures in health policy and medical decision making. He has published widely in these areas and also in economic history, serving on the editorial board of the *Journal of Economic History* and having twice received the Cole prize for the best paper in that journal.

DAVID R. WILLIAMS is the Harold W. Cruse Collegiate Professor of Sociology, research professor in the Survey Research Center at the Institute for Social Research, and faculty associate in the Center for Afroamerican and African Studies, all at the University of Michigan. His previous academic appointment was at Yale University. His research has focused on social influences on health, and he is centrally interested in the trends and determinants of socioeconomic and racial differences in mental and physical health. He is the author of more than one hundred scholarly papers in scientific journals and edited collections. He is a member of the editorial board of five scientific journals and serves as a member of the board of directors of AcademyHealth and the MacArthur Foundation's Research Network on Socioeconomic Status and Health. In 2001 he was elected as a member of the Institute of Medicine of the National Academy of Sciences.

Robert J. Willis is professor of economics at the University of Michigan, where he is also research professor in the Survey Research Center and research associate of the Population Studies Center in the Institute for Social Research. Before coming to Michigan in 1995, he served on the faculties of the University of Chicago, SUNY at Stony Brook, and Stanford University. Willis is currently principal investigator on a large longitudinal survey, the Health and Retirement Study, which is collecting data on Americans over age fifty. He is an authority on the economics of the family, marriage, and fertility; labor economics; human capital; and population and economic development. Most recently, he has begun exploring the relationship between cognitive aspects of probabilistic thinking and economic behavior. He is the 2002 recipient of the Mindel C. Sheps Award, given for outstanding contributions to mathematical demography or demographic methodology.

William Zimmerman is professor of political science and research professor and former director of the Center for Political Studies at the University of Michigan's Institute for Social Research. His work over the years has focused on Russia, the former Soviet Union, and Yugoslavia. A winner of the Helen Dwight Reid and Pi Sigma Alpha Awards of the American Political Science Association, he has published widely in political science journals. Among his books are *Soviet Perspectives on International Relations* (1969 and 1973); *Open Borders, Nonalignment, and the Political Evolution of Yugoslavia* (1987); and *The Russian People and Foreign Policy: Elite and Mass Perspectives, 1993–2000* (2002). The last is based on mass and elite surveys conducted in Russia in 1993, 1995–96, and 1999–2000.

Index

abortion, 83. *See also* contraception
Abramson, Paul R., 376
academic survey research centers, 9–10, 21. *See also specific research centers*
Achen, Christopher H., 54
achievement motive, 160, 227. *See also* motivation
ACL. *See* Americans' Changing Lives
Activities of Daily Living (ADL), 347
activity theory, aging and, 340–41
Adair, R. K., 407
adolescence, 12–13, 17, 305–6, 310. *See also* adulthood, transition to
adoption, 291
adulthood, transition to, 274–75, 299, 305–10; adolescence and, 12–13, 17, 305–6, 310; trust in government, 308–9; YIT project, 307–8. *See also* drug and substance abuse
advertising campaign, antidrug, 313, 325
affective disorders, 232. *See also* mental disorders; mental health
affirmative action, 89, 368, 373, 374–75, 381, 384, 385, 419. *See also* racial attitudes
affluent society, 120
AFL-CIO (labor organization), 7
African-Americans, 18–19, 31, 157, 263, 355, 443; aging studies of, 334; children of, 172; mental health of, 227–28; social support and, 357–58. *See also* black Americans; racial and ethnic factors; racial attitudes
African-American Stress-Coping and Help-Seeking Model, 402
Afro-Caribbeans, 358, 412, 423
Age and Structural Lag (Riley et al.), 331
aggregation, 90, 140
aging, 4, 12, 17–18, 330–49, 446–47; activity theory and, 340–41; context of, 338–39; demography of, 277; functional limitations of, 259–61; health and, 333, 334, 337, 339, 343; human development and, 276–77; life course and, 272–73, 333; longitudinal designs, 17, 332–34, 336, 338; methodological challenges, 334, 345–47; multidisciplinary research on, 342–45, 349; opportunity structure and, 68; patterns of change, 330, 333, 335, 337–38, 339; policy and, 331, 347–49; probability samples, 336–37; psychosocial nature of health and, 258–62; psychosocial risk factors in, 18, 334, 343–44; repeated cohorts, 333, 334–36, 338, 348; testing theories of, 340–42
Aging Mind, The (National Research Council), 349
Agriculture, Department of. *See* U.S. Department of Agriculture
AHEAD. *See* Asset and Health Dynamics among the Oldest-Old
Aid to Families with Dependent Children (AFDC), 168, 173
air traffic controllers, 214, 256
Akiyama, H., 278, 339
Alameda County, California, 252
alcohol abuse, youth and, 310, 311, 315–16, 317, 324; student status and, 318–19, 320, 325
alcohol consumption, 252
Aldrich, Howard E., 208

Allport, Floyd, 74
alternative lifestyles, 100
altruism, 162
Alwin, Duane F., 43, 271, 455; aging studies by, 331, 332, 338, 340, 347
America Community Survey, 449
American Council of Education, 112
American Dilemma, An (Myrdal), 386
American Political Science Association, 66, 112
American Political Science Review, 67
American Psychiatric Association, 231
Americans' Changing Lives (ACL), 259, 262, 334, 337, 341, 343
American Soldier, The (Stouffer et al.), 195, 367
Americans View Their Mental Health Survey, 198, 239
American Voter, The (Campbell et al.), 74–75, 79, 83, 85, 367
analytic statistics, 23, 27
Anderson, Barbara, 376
Anderson, John, 86
Andrews, Frank M., 44, 53, 229
antidrug advertising campaign, 313, 325
antisocial personality, 232
Antonucci, Toni C., 259, 278, 339
anxiety disorders, 232. *See also* mental disorders; mental health
Aristotle, 282
"Art of Asking Why, The" (Lazarsfeld), 42
Asclepius, 251
Asian-Americans, 422
Asians, 357, 358
Assessing Organizational Change (Seashore), 212
Asset and Health Dynamics among the Oldest-Old (AHEAD), 216, 334, 335, 336, 346
Assistant Secretary for Planning and Treatment (ASPE), 159, 161, 180
attitudes: and behavior, 65, 67, 68, 134; and beliefs, 89, 275, 276, 299, 326. *See also* racial attitudes
audio-CASI (audio computer-assisted self-interviewing), 51, 52, 291
autocratic management, 206–7
Automatic Interaction Detector (AID), 53
automobiles, 158, 162
Axinn, William G., 16, 274, 281, 443, 455

baby boom and baby boomers, 100, 124, 147. *See also* class of 1965; protest generation
Bachman, Jerald G., 275, 305, 318, 455–56
Baltes, Paul B., 331, 337, 340
Baltimore Longitudinal Study of Aging, 332
Baltimore study, 223
Bane, M. J., 172–73
Barnard, Chester, 196
Bartels, Larry M., 88
Becker, Gary, 176
behavior: attitudes and, 65, 67, 68, 134; coding of, 45–46; individual, 297, 298, 310; interviewer, 47, 48, 346, 361; patterns of, 376; permissible, 298. *See also* political behavior
behavioral treatment, 234
Behr, Roy L., 86
Bengston, Vern L., 331, 340
Bennington College study, 110, 276
Berkman, Lisa F., 252, 257
Bershad, M. A., 49
biblical census, 5
biomedical theories, 3–4
Birren, James E., 340
black Americans, 18–19, 288, 290, 365, 393–424; Caribbean, 358, 412, 422, 423; election study, 397–98; help-seeking behaviors of, 407–9; and international perspectives, 413–19; mental health surveys of, 402–4, 406–7; militancy of, 369–70; National Study of Black Americans and, 198; National Survey of Black Americans and, 227–28; religious participation by, 405–6, 410; social support for, 404–5; socioeconomic status of, 402, 406–7, 409, 423; stress and, 401–4, 411–12, 419–21; three-generation family study, 396–97, 400–401. *See also* African-Americans; Program for

Research on Black Americans; racial and ethnic factors; racial attitudes
black representation, 386
Blair, Johnny, 46, 48
Blake, Robert R., 203
Blatant scale of prejudice, 417, 418
Blau, Peter, 272
Blondel, Jean, 80
Bobo, Lawrence, 371, 377, 383, 395
boredom at work, 214. *See also* work
bracket questions, 127–29
Bradburn, Norman M., 40, 52
Brazil, race in, 413
Breslau, N., 403
Breslow, Lester, 252
British Household Panel Survey, 174
Broman, C. L., 408
Brookings Institution, 448
Brooks, George, 256
Brooks-Gunn, Jeanne, 177
Brown, Charlie, 163
Brown, R. E., 398
Brunner, G. A., 37
Bryant, Fred B., 238
Bryk, Anthony S., 54
Bulmer, M., 5
Bumpass, L. L., 284
bureaucratic structure and personality, 196
Bureau of Applied Social Research, 6, 72, 440, 448
Bureau of the Census. *See* U.S. Bureau of the Census
business cycle and expansion, 146–47
Butler, David, 79, 80, 85
buying intentions, 136. *See also* consumers

calculus of chance, 144
campaign advertising, race and, 362
campaign consultants, 92
Campbell, Angus, 8, 9, 73, 80, 228, 367; surveys of, after 1968 riots, 369, 370, 371
Campbell, Arthur, 286
Campbell, Donald T., 338, 451
Campbell, Richard T., 331, 340, 347
cancer, 252, 264
candidate-centered voting, 84. *See also* electoral behavior; voters and voting
candidates' policy postures, 76
Cannell, Charles F., 8, 9, 36, 42, 47, 48
Cannon, Walter, 252, 254
can-opener questions, 120
Cantril, Hadley, 365
canvassing, 91–92
CAPI. *See* computer-assisted personal interviewing
Caplan, Nathan S., 369
Caplan, Robert, 236, 256, 257, 262
cardiovascular disease, 252, 257
career choice, 307
Caribbean blacks, 358, 412, 422, 423
Carmines, E. G., 386
Carnegie Foundation, 397
Carnegie-Mellon University, 201
Carp, Frances, 345
Carroll, C. D., 139, 145
Carroll, S. J., 37
Carter, James Earl, 88
Cartwright, Dorwin, 8, 9
CASI. *See* audio-CASI; computer-assisted self-interviewing
Cassel, Robert, 257
Catholicism, 282, 286
caucuses and primaries, 87–88
causality, funnel of, 75
Cayton, H., 393
census data, 5, 16, 26, 78; aging and, 335; black Americans and, 395; on fertility and family, 282–83. *See also* U.S. Bureau of the Census
Center for Effective Organization, 213
Center for Political Studies (CPS), 67, 125
Center for Research on the Utilization of Scientific Knowledge (CRUSK), 197, 211, 255
Center for Study of Complex Systems, 218
Center for the Study of Minority Group Mental Health, 395
Centers for Mind-Body Research, 263, 265
central tendency, measures of, 144

change patterns: in aging, 330, 333, 335, 337–38, 339; youth and, 306, 309. *See also* social change
Changing American Voter, The (Nie, Verba, and Petrocik), 83
Changing Lives of Older Couples (CLOC), 259
Chatters, L. M., 404–5, 410
childbearing, fertility research and, 283, 288, 291, 294, 295, 300
Child Development Supplement to the Panel Study of Income Dynamics (PSID-CDS), 180–83. *See also* children; Panel Study of Income Dynamics
children: adoption of, 291; adversity and mental health of, 232–33; Child Development Supplement on income and, 180–83; development of, 125; early learning in, 106; fertility studies and, 274, 281, 296–97, 299; life course of, 12–13; Panel Study of Income Dynamics and, 157, 176–79; parents and, 12, 105, 274–75, 298; political socialization and, 99–101, 107–11. *See also* adulthood, transition to
Church, Allan H., 38
cigarette smoking, 311, 317, 323, 324, 325; psychosocial impact of, 250–53, 257, 262; stability rates, 315; student status and, 318, 319
citizen preferences, 66
city services, race and, 371
civil liberties, 442
civil rights movement, 48–49, 368, 373, 381
class of 1965, 102–6; generational comparisons and, 107–9; individual-level analysis of, 109–11
clustering, 29–30
Cobb, Sidney, 213, 256, 257, 262
cocaine use, 313, 315, 317, 320, 324
Cochrane, J. H., 139–40
cognitive function, 47, 228; aging and, 332–33, 335, 336, 346, 349; in black Americans, 409
cohabitation, 322; premarital, 291, 298, 299. *See also* marriage
cohort studies, 68, 275, 276, 277, 309, 442; aging and, 333, 334–36, 338, 348. *See also* class of 1965
Coleman, L., 36
Coles, Robert, 99
college experience, 306, 317, 318–20, 325, 371
color line, 18
Colton, Timothy, 68
Columbia University, 10; Bureau of Applied Social Research, 6, 440, 448
combat trauma, 223. *See also* military
Commerce Department. *See* U.S. Department of Commerce
commercial polls, 11
Committee on Reducing Risks for Mental Disorders, 238
communications, two-set flow of, 72
communications technologies, 66
community mental health movement, 234
community venue, choice of, 72
comorbidity, 232–33. *See also* National Comorbidity Survey
Comparative Study of Electoral Systems (CSES), 67, 92, 447
Composite International Diagnostic Interview Schedule (CIDI), 231, 239, 240
computer-assisted interviewing, 11, 362, 449
computer-assisted personal interviewing (CAPI), 51–52, 291
computer-assisted self-interviewing (CASI), 51
computers, 2, 451–52; software, 31–32, 55
conceptual frameworks, 24–25
Conference Board, 136
consistency effects, 41, 44
Consumer Price Index (CPI), 184
consumers: attitudes of, 122; behavior of, 120; buying intentions of, 136; expectations of, 122, 134, 137; future income and, 138; measurement analysis of, 133–35; recessions led by, 139–40; saving behavior and, 131–33, 341–42

contraception, 284, 287, 288. *See also* family planning
contractibility, 34. *See also* nonresponse error
controlled selection, 28–29
Converse, Jean M., 5, 12, 39, 49
Converse, Philip E., 228, 367, 375, 448, 456; electoral study by, 65, 67, 69, 80
Cook, Thomas D., 338
Coombs, Clyde, 298
Coombs, Lolagene, 295, 298, 301n. 6
cooperation rates, 35, 36–37, 346. *See also* nonresponse error
Corder, Larry, 335
core questions, 89
Corning, Amy, 35, 38
correlations: in election study, 367; questionnaire wording and, 40, 43–44
Couper, Mick P., 33, 36, 37, 49, 52, 346
covariance properties, 43–44
coverage error, 25, 26, 27, 28
Cox regression, 172
CPS. *See* Center for Political Studies
Crandall, Richard, 229
credit, 134, 165
Crime Victimization Surveys, 78
Crosby, Gretchen C., 383
Crossley Organization, 6
cross-national studies, 67, 450
cross-sectional studies, 44, 135–36, 197; of fertility, 284–85
CRUSK. *See* Center for Research on the Utilization of Scientific Knowledge
crystallization model of learning, 110
crystallized intelligence, 332–33, 335. *See also* cognitive function
CSES. *See* Comparative Study of Electoral Systems
cumulative distribution function, 145
Current Population Survey (CPS), 4, 335, 395, 449
curriculum assessments, 112
Curtin, Richard T., 13, 122, 456
Cutler, Neal, 345

data: failure of, 135–36; longitudinal series of, 113, 157, 158; quality of, 158; relational files of, 159; utilization of, 197, 205
data processing and analysis, 53–55, 150; diary format for, 125–26; experimental modes of, 125; innovation in, 442–43; linkages, 449–50; theory and, 149, 440–41
Dawson, M. C., 398
debt panel, 121
deflation, 132
Demo, D. H., 410
democracies, 66, 68–69, 80, 92–93, 112
Demographic and Health Surveys, 285, 292
demographic research, 74
demography, 16; of aging, 277
Dennis, Jack, 99
depression (mental), 15, 236–37, 240–41. *See also* mental disorders; mental health
desegregation, 372. *See also* integration; racial attitudes; segregation
design effect, 30. *See also* survey design
Detroit Area Study (DAS), 294, 301n. 6, 360–62, 374, 403, 412
Detroit auto workers, 77
Detroit race riots, 366, 369
developed world, research in, 447. *See also specific countries*
Dewey, Thomas, 11, 25, 72–73
Diagnostic and Statistical Manual (DSM-III) (American Psychiatric Association), 198, 224, 230–33
Diagnostic Interview Schedule, 230–31, 408
Diener, Edward and Mary, 238
disability, 148
discrimination, racial, 359, 360, 361, 369, 373, 385; stress and, 411, 412
disease: cancer, 252, 264; chronic, 249–50; etiology of, 248–50; psychosocial nature of health and, 248–53; risk factors for, 15–16; sexually transmitted, 290, 291. *See also* health; *and specific disease*
Division of Program Surveys, 8, 119, 196

divorce, 165, 291, 296, 324. *See also* marriage
Doing Research That Is Useful for Theory and Practice (Lawler), 213
Dominitz, J., 145
"Don't Know" option, 40, 44, 45
Douvan, Elizabeth, 226–27
Drake, S. C., 393
drug and substance abuse, 4, 17, 232, 275, 309–26, 449; college experience, 317, 318–20, 325; employment and military status, 320–22; living arrangements and, 319, 322–23; marital status and, 322, 323–24; Monitoring the Future and, 311, 325; policy implications for, 325–26; post–high school experience, 317–18; prevention programs, 313; secular effects in, 311–13; single parenting and, 318, 323; socialization effects, 306, 317, 318, 321, 322, 324–25; stability of, 314–16; usage patterns, 316–17. *See also specific drugs*
Du Bois, W. E. B., 4, 18, 393, 395
Duke University Center on Aging and Human Development, 258
Duncan, Greg J., 156, 159, 163, 170, 177, 456–57
Duncan, Otis, 14, 272
Dupeux, Georges, 79, 80
durable goods, 134, 138
Durkheim, Émile, 282

Eastern Bloc, 112
ecological view of organizations, 208. *See also* organizational studies
econometric models, 119
economic behavior, 13–14, 119–29; measurement of income and wealth in study of, 127–29; studies of, 123–27; Survey of Consumer Finances and, 120–22. *See also* macroeconomic psychology
Economic Behavior Program (EBP), 119, 122–23, 126, 131, 146; Panel Study of Income Dynamics and, 156–57, 164
economic opportunity. *See* Office of Economic Opportunity; Survey of Economic Opportunity
economics, 3, 112; aging and, 334, 341–42
economic security, 68, 120
economic well-being, 348. *See also* socioeconomic status
economy, 4; peacetime, 120, 131–33; voter assessments of, 85
ECPR. *See* European Consortium for Political Research
educational achievement, 299, 306, 307, 309; liberal racial attitude and, 371, 373. *See also* college experience
educational system, 112
Edwards, W., 145
egalitarianism, race and, 380, 381, 383–84
Eisenhower years, 88
Elder, Glenn H., 165–68, 272
elderly, 17–18; black American, 396, 422. *See also* aging
election polls, 6, 11, 12
election studies, 367–68; of black Americans, 397–98; presidential, 71–73, 75, 81, 86–87. *See also* National Election Studies
electoral behavior, 70–93; collectivizing resources on, 77–79; expanding the model of, 84–86; history of research in, 70–73; incumbency and, 93; persuasion and, 86–88; political participation and, 90–93; postwar research in, 73–76; presidential elections, 71–73, 75, 81, 86–87; public opinion and, 88–90; studies after 1970 on, 80–84
electronic paging devices, 125
Ellwood, David T., 172–73
Elmira County, New York, 72
Emery, Fred E., 201
empirical research, 1–2. *See also* methodology
employees: ownership, 213; participation in decision making, 202–5; satisfaction and productivity, 197, 204–5
employment, 24, 209, 368, 397, 420; statistics, 4, 7; youth, 317, 320–21. *See also* unemployment; work

English Longitudinal Study on Aging, 447
environment, 207, 241, 249
EPESE. *See* Established Populations for Epidemiologic Studies of the Elderly
Epidemiologic Catchment Area (ECA), 230–31, 337, 407
epidemiology, 3, 15, 199, 224, 230, 256. *See also* disease
Epps, E., 395
equality/inequality: as principle, 89; racial, 18, 359
Erie County, Ohio, 71, 75
Erikson, Erik, 272
errors, 48, 53, 55, 56, 361; measurement, 38–39, 42, 43–44, 45, 289, 314; reductive, 24–25; standard, 28, 30, 31. *See also* nonresponse error
Established Populations for Epidemiologic Studies of the Elderly (EPESE), 333, 337, 341
ethnic and racial groups, 4, 18–19, 56, 112, 357, 411. *See also* racial attitudes; *and specific ethnic or racial group*
ethnography, 265
Eurobarometer Surveys, 113, 420
Europe, rebuilding of, 195
European Community, 174
European Consortium for Political Research (ECPR), 80
European Union (EU), 398, 415. *See also specific countries*
Evans, Jeffrey, 163
event history methods, 172
expansion and business cycles, 146–47
expectations: consumer decisions and, 137; consumer surveys on, 133–34, 139–41; measurement of, 143–45
experiment design, 211
experimenting society, 451
Explorations in Personality (Murray), 272
expression, freedom of, 101

face-to-face interviews, 11, 52, 361; nonresponse to, 33, 35; telephone surveys compared to, 26–27, 50–51
Falling from Grace (Newman), 168
families, 157, 159; black American, 396–97, 400–401, 404, 405; development of, 4, 274; generational replacement in, 275; income of, 210; influence of, 102–4, 106–8; life course and, 16–18; structure of, 105, 124; transmission model, 102–4, 106–8. *See also* children; intergenerational comparisons; Intergenerational Panel Study of Parents and Children; intergenerational surveys; intergenerational transfers
families, fertility research and, 281, 290, 300; census and vital statistics, 282–83; Intergenerational Panel Study and, 284, 292–93, 294, 295–99
Family and Demography Program, 274
Family and Fertility Surveys, 285
family planning, 283, 287, 295. *See also* childbearing; contraception
Farley, Reynolds, 361, 385
Featherman, David L., 444, 457
federal government: agencies, 7–8; data collections of, 78; on drug use and youth, 309–10; funding by, 20, 313; racial integration and, 368, 372, 375; statistical agencies for, 119; trust in, 308–9. *See also specific agency or department*
Federal Reserve Board, 119, 120, 121, 133–34
feedback, in surveys, 42, 47, 48
Feld, Sheila, 227, 234
feminist theory, 273
fertility, social demography of, 4, 16, 274, 281–301; censuses and vital statistics, 282–83; Detroit Area Study, 294; Growth of American Families study, 274, 284–85, 286–88, 294; Indianapolis Fertility Study, 284, 292, 293; Intergenerational Panel Study, 274, 285, 286, 292, 293, 294–99; National Survey of Family Growth, 285, 289–92; other data sets, 299–300; Princeton Fertility Study, 285, 292, 293–94. *See also* families, fertility research and
Field, Harry H., 9
financial markets, 133, 147–48

Finnish cohort, 262
Fiorina, Morris P., 85
Fischoff, B., 144
Five Thousand American Families (Morgan et al.), 161
flexibility, 56; interviewer, 48; in question wording, 42–43; vs. standardization, 23–24
Fogel, Robert, 333
Folkways (Sumner), 377
Foner, Anne, 331
Ford Foundation, 121, 161, 163, 395, 396, 397
Ford Motor Company, 159
forecast errors, 131–32
formal assumptions, 23
foundations, 163. *See also specific foundations*
France, racism in, 398, 415, 416, 417, 419
Francis, Thomas, Jr., 248
Frankel, Lester, 7
Frankel, Martin R., 31, 48
Frazier, E. F., 393, 395
Freedman, Deborah, 295, 301n. 6
Freedman, Ronald, 292, 294, 295, 300, 301n. 6; Growth of American Family studies and, 274, 286
freedom and responsibility, 324–25
Freeman, John, 208
French, John R. P., Jr., 213, 253–57, 262
Friedman, Milton, 137–38, 141, 160
functional limitations, 259–61
Future of Black Civil Rights Study (FBCR), 398

Gallup, George, 6, 70–71, 443
Gallup polls, 6, 368, 371
Gan Li, 342
Gannett Newspaper Corporation, 398
Gaudet, Hazel, 71, 86–87
Geertz, Clifford, 380
gender, 162; division of labor, 295, 298; drug use patterns and, 318. *See also* men; women
genealogy-based design, 157, 158
generalized variance functions, 30
General Motors Corporation, 159
General Social Surveys (GSS), 79, 113, 210, 332, 335, 449
generational theories, 103, 107
generation concept, 275
generation gap, 107
genomics, 264
geocode data, on aging, 339
Georgopoulos, Basil S., 205, 212–13
Germany, racism in, 398, 415, 416–17, 419
germ theory model, 250–51
gerontology, 258, 276, 330, 332, 340, 345, 347. *See also* aging
Glassman, Marc B., 48
globalization, 69, 450
God, marriage and, 282. *See also* religious institutions; religious participation
Goldberg, David, 274, 294, 301n. 6
Goldstein, K., 37
Goodman, Roe, 28
government, trust in, 308–9
government funding, 20, 313. *See also* federal government
Gramlich, Edward M., 142
Grant, A. P., 142
grassroots politics, 72, 92
Great Britain, racism in, 398, 415, 416, 419
Great Depression, 7, 131–32, 165–68
Green, N., 52
Greenstein, Fred J., 99
gross domestic product (GDP), 136–37, 185
group centrism, 88–89
group cohesiveness, 203
group conflict, race and, 377–78, 379–80, 414
Groves, Robert M., 11, 21, 38, 50, 457; on coverage error, 27; on interviewer behavior, 35, 36–37; on response rates, 33, 346
Growth of American Family Studies (GAF), 274, 284–85, 286–88, 294
Gruenberg, Gary, 371
GSS. *See* General Social Surveys
Guiso, L., 145
Gulf War recession, 184. *See also* recession

Gurin, Gerald, 73, 227–28, 234
Gurin, P., 395

Handbook of Aging and the Social Sciences (Binstock and George), 349
Handbook of Industrial and Organizational Psychology (Triandis, Dunnette, and Howe), 202
Handbook of Political Socialization (Renshon), 100
Handbook of Social Psychology (Lipset), 98
Handbook of Work and Organizational Psychology (Drenth), 202
Hannan, Michael T., 208
Hansen, M. H., 49
Hardin, Garret, 218
Harvard University, 28
Hatchett, Shirley, 49, 375, 395
Hawthorne research, 196
health, 3–4, 16, 198–99, 444; black Americans and, 357, 403; health insurance and, 124; measurement of, 186–90; populations and, 122, 124; psychosocial nature of, 248–53; public, 250–51, 287, 313; racial and ethnic factors in, 262–66; spending on, 263; stress and, 254–58, 411; well-being and, 15; work and, 217. *See also* disease; medicine
health, aging and, 258–62, 333, 334, 337, 339, 341; social status and, 343, 344
health, psychosocial factors and. *See* mental disorders; mental health; psychosocial nature of health
Health and Human Services, Department of. *See* U.S. Department of Health and Human Services
Health, Education, and Welfare, Department of. *See* U.S. Department of Health, Education, and Welfare
Health and Retirement Study (HRS), 17, 216, 446, 447, 449; aging theories and, 341, 342; economic behaviors in, 121, 123–25, 128; methodology of, 346, 347; multidisciplinary research and, 343, 344; repeated cohorts, 277, 334, 335, 442
health insurance, 348
help-seeking behavior, 222, 228; of black Americans, 407–9
Herzog, A. Regula, 17, 259, 277, 330, 350, 457–58; on nonresponse patterns, 345, 346
Hess, I., 26, 28
Hess, Robert D., 99
higher education, 111
high school: dropout rate, 309; governments, 112; graduation rates and parental income, 179
Hill, Dan, 163, 346
Hill, Martha, 163
Hispanic populations, 290. *See also* Latinos
Hofferth, Sandra L., 14, 156, 163, 458
Holmes, S., 416
hospitals, 212
House, James S., 1, 15, 198, 215, 236, 439, 443, 458; aging studies by, 338, 343, 344; health studies and, 248, 257, 259, 262, 263
household surveys, 30, 32, 143; inflation forecasts for, 142; low-income surveys of, 156; nonresponse in, 33–35; poverty and, 123; survey samples of, 121; time use in, 125–26; two earners in, 146, 229; wealth of, 122
household units (HUs), 400
Howell, William C., 383
Howrey, Philip E., 137
HRS. *See* Health and Retirement Study
Hughes, M., 410
human development, 12, 16
humanitarianism, 101
human relations hypothesis, 203
human relations movement, 196, 201
Human Relations Program, 196
human service organizations, 233
Huntington, Samuel P., 67
Hurd, Michael, 342
Hurwitz, W. N., 49
Hygeia, 251
hygiene, 251
Hyman, Herbert H., 8, 98, 217, 366, 368; on interviewer effects, 48, 49

ICPR. *See* Inter-university Consortium for Political Research
ICPSR. *See* Inter-university Consortium for Political and Social Research
ideology, race and, 378–80
illicit drugs. *See* drug and substance abuse; *and specific drugs*
immunization, 249
immunization model of learning, 110
incentives, 37–38
income: consumer behavior and, 133–35, 138; distribution of, 126; electoral behavior and, 89; graduation rates and, 179; measurement of, 127–29, 146; permanent, 137–38, 147; poverty and, 13–14; study of, 122. *See also* Panel Study of Income Dynamics; poverty; wealth
Income and Welfare in the United States (Morgan), 156
Income Survey Development Program, 54
Index of Consumer Sentiment, 136–37
Index of Leading Economic Indicators, 136
Indianapolis Fertility Study, 284, 292, 293
individual behavior, 54, 297, 298, 310
individualism, race and, 379, 382
inequality, racial, 18, 359. *See also* racial attitudes
inflation, 132, 142, 146
infrastructure, institutional, 5, 447–48
Inglehart, M., 416, 420
Inglehart, Ronald, 68, 79
innovations, 451; methodological, 6, 8, 53, 56, 291–92, 357; in natural sciences, 2; in scientific method, 4–5; in screening techniques, 31
"Insanity and Idiocy in Massachusetts" (Jarvis), 223
Institute for Social Research (ISR), 1, 10, 16, 67, 439, 440, 448; aggregated data and, 54; aging studies and, 332, 334, 343, 349; black American surveys, 19, 367, 393, 396; cohort effects and, 275; fertility studies, 290, 300; interdisciplinarity in, 446; methodological innovation at, 53, 56; origins of, 8–9; OSIRIS statistical software and, 31–32; racial attitude studies and, 367, 371; stress model of, 235–36, 254–56. *See also* Detroit Area Study; *and specific studies and projects*
Institute for Survey Research at Temple University, 288
Institute of Medicine, 238
institutional infrastructure, 5, 447–48
institutional investments, 20
institutions, emerging, 68
instrumentation, 4–5
instrument complexity, 159
insurance, 126–27, 348
integration, 361, 368, 370, 372–73. *See also* racial attitudes; segregation
intentions data, 135–36, 150
interdisciplinarity, 12, 344–45, 444–47. *See also* multidisciplinary research
Interdisciplinary Committee for Organized Studies (ICOS), 218
interest rates, 139
intergenerational comparisons, 103, 107
Intergenerational Panel Study of Parents and Children (IPS), 274, 286, 294–99, 300n. 5; Princeton study compared to, 285, 292, 293
intergenerational surveys, 102–4, 107–11, 160
intergenerational transfers, 77, 441
International Perspectives on Racism (IPR), 398
Internet, 451–52. *See also* Web sites
interpersonal influence, 72
Inter-university Consortium for Political and Social Research (ICPSR), 12, 78–79, 112n. 1
Inter-university Consortium for Political Research (ICPR), 67, 78
interviewers: behavior of, 47, 48, 346, 361; nonresponse and, 35–37, 443; race of, 375–76
interviewing, 11, 46–50, 283; computer-assisted, 2, 11, 51–52, 291, 362, 449, 451–52; face-to-face, 11, 26–27,

33, 35, 50–51, 52, 361. *See also* telephone sampling and surveys
investment goods, 134
Iowa State University, 28
IPS. *See* Intergenerational Panel Study of Parents and Children
ISR. *See* Institute for Social Research
Israel, kibbutz communities in, 208
issue orientations, 75, 83–84
Issue Revolution (Carmines and Stimson), 386
Ithaca, New York, 125
IVEWare software, 32, 55

Jackman, Mary, 379–80
Jackson, James S., 19, 259, 355, 420, 443, 458–59; on social support, 357, 404–5
Jackson, Paul, 228
Jahoda, Marie, 235
James, Sherman A., 263
Japan, 339, 413
Japelli, T., 145
Jarvis, Edward, 223
Jennings, M. Kent, 12, 65, 67, 69, 77, 98, 441–42, 459
job loss, 235–36. *See also* unemployment
jobs, fair treatment in, 368. *See also* employment
job satisfaction, 209–10
JOBS program, 236–37
Job Strain Model, 402
John Henryism, 263, 409
Johnson, Lyndon B., 156, 369
Johnson, Malcolm L., 331, 340
Johnston, Lloyd D., 275, 305, 459
Joint Commission on Mental Illness and Health, 223, 225
Journal of Gerontology, 349
Juster, F. Thomas, 1, 13, 17, 119, 161, 439, 460; measurement analysis and, 135, 144
justice, 101. *See also* inequality

Kaase, Max, 80
Kahn, Robert L., 1, 14, 215, 439, 460; aging studies of, 331, 340; health studies of, 253–54, 257–59, 262; on interview methods, 48, 50; organizational studies of, 195–96, 198, 207, 213
Kahneman, D., 144
Kalton, Graham, 40, 49, 54
Kansas City Studies, 332, 340
Kaplan, George A., 15, 198, 248, 344, 460–61
Karasek, R., 257, 402
Karolinska Institute, 253
Kasl, Stanislav, 256, 257, 262
Katona, George, 8, 9, 13, 138–40, 142, 441; consumer surveys and, 120, 133–35; Panel Study of Income Dynamics and, 160; works of, 149
Katz, Daniel, 8, 196, 201, 207, 395
Kendler, Kenneth S., 241
Kennedy, John F., 90, 99, 100
Kennedy, Robert F., 100
Kessler, Ronald C., 403, 407; health studies of, 259, 262, 263; mental health studies of, 232, 233, 240
Key, V. O., 74, 377–78
Keyes, Corey L. M., 238
Keynesian Consumption Function, 138
kibbutz communities, 208
Kimball, M. S., 139
Kinder, Donald R., 12, 18, 461; on electoral behavior, 65, 67, 69, 70; on racial attitudes, 355, 356, 365, 380, 383
King, Martin Luther, Jr., 100, 368, 369, 373
Kiser, Clyde, 284
Kish, Leslie, 8, 9, 26, 28, 31, 73; on error, 55; on fertility surveys, 292; on interviewer variance, 49; software developed by, 30
Klein, Lawrence, 131, 160
Knäuper, Bärbel, 346
Koch, Robert, 248
Kohnke-Aguirre, Luane, 48
Kramer, Morton, 230
Krause, N., 410
Krauss, Elissa, 41
Krosnick, J. A., 43
Krysan, Maria, 49, 355, 371, 373, 461
Kulka, Richard A., 226–27

labor: division of, 295, 298; market behavior of, 123
Labor Department. *See* U.S. Department of Labor
labor force participation, 124, 126
labor income, 148
labor market policies, 307
labor standards problems, 210
labor unions, 7, 201
Landon, Alfred, 6, 11, 70
LaPiere, Richard T., 359, 374
large-scale sample surveys, 77
Latinos, 163, 357, 358, 422
Lawler, Edward E., 212–13
Lazarsfeld, Paul F., 39, 42, 74, 235, 440; presidential election studies, 6, 71, 72, 86–87
Lazarus, Edward H., 86
Leading Indicator Composite Index, 136
learning: early, 106; programs in, 110, 112. *See also* schooling
leisure time, 126
Lepkowski, Charlie, 163
Lepkowski, James M., 21, 27, 37, 50, 461–62
LePlay, Frederick, 282, 283
leverage-saliency theory, 35, 38
Lewin, Kurt, 202, 211
Lewis Terman gifted students project, 110
Liang, Jersey, 338
life course, 12–13, 16–18, 271–74, 278, 443; aging and, 272–73, 333; strategies for, 273; transition to adulthood and, 305, 306
life-cycle model, 165; aging and, 341, 342
life-cycle stage, 135, 139
life events, negative, 237
life expectancy, 248–49
life history calendar, 297, 443
Life Insurance Agency Management Association, 196
lifelong persistence models of political learning, 110
life-span development, 276, 308, 331, 343
life-stress paradigm, 401–4
lifestyle, 100
Likert, Rensis, 6, 8–9, 39, 119–20, 206; organizational studies of, 195–97, 201, 207; typology of Systems 1–4, 210, 213
Lister, Joseph, 248
literacy tests, 92
Literary Digest poll of 1936, 6, 11
Little, R. J., 55
living arrangements, 319, 322–23, 325. *See also* cohabitation
Locander, William, 52
longevity, 139. *See also* aging; life expectancy
longitudinal panel studies, 14, 44, 82, 113, 277, 449; of aging, 17, 332–34, 336, 338; on drug use by youth, 317; on labor market, 306–7; methodology and, 442. *See also* Panel Study of Income Dynamics; *and specific longitudinal studies*
Longitudinal Study of Aging (LSOA), 333, 336
"Long-term Support for the American National Election Studies" (proposal), 81
Lott, W. F., 142
Lovell, M. C., 141
Lowi, Theodore, 66
Luxembourg Income Study, 174, 175, 447

MacArthur Midlife Development in the U.S. Survey (MIDUS), 227
macroeconomic psychology, 131–51; economic theories in, 137–42; future study of, 146–51; measurement of expectations in, 143–46; peacetime economy and, 131–33; survey methods of, 133–37. *See also* economic behavior
Magilvay, Lou L., 50
Mahalanobis, P. C., 49
Maher, Mary P., 37
Malthus, Robert, 282, 283
management styles, 206–7
managerial grid, 203
mandatory service, 112
Mangione, Thomas W., 229
Mankiw, N. G., 141
Mann, Floyd C., 205, 211, 213, 253–55
Mannheim, Karl, 108

Manski, C. F., 144, 145
Manton, Kenneth G., 335
March on Washington (1963), 368
marijuana use, youth and, 312, 313, 314, 321, 324; stability rates, 315–16; student status and, 317, 319–20, 325
marketplace economics, 112. *See also* financial markets
Markus, Gregory B., 367
Marquis, Kent H., 48
marriage, 17, 281; cohabitation and, 291, 298, 299, 322; divorce and, 165, 291, 296, 324; drug abuse and, 318, 325; fertility surveys and, 290, 291, 296, 298, 299, 300; religious institutions and, 282
Marshall Plan, 195
Martin, Elizabeth, 41
Marx, G. T., 395
Marx, Karl, 5, 282
Massachusetts Institute of Technology, 201
Mayo, Elton, 196
McCammon, Ryan J., 332
McConahay, John B., 383
McDonough, Peggy, 80
McFadden, Daniel, 342
McGonagle, Katherine A., 37
McKeown, Thomas J., 251
measurement: consumer analysis and, 133–35; forms of, 144, 146; of mental health, 222, 224
measurement errors, 25, 38–39, 42, 43–44, 45, 124, 143; in drug use studies, 314; in fertility studies, 289; time-series analysis and, 136
media reports, 140
medical expenses, 139
medical sociology, 263
Medicare and Medicaid, 347, 348
medicine, 202
Meertens, R. W., 417, 418
men: drug use by, and marriage, 323; fertility surveys and, 290; help-seeking behavior of, 408–9; life course and, 273. *See also* gender; women
mental disorders, 198–99, 222, 229–31; biological explanations for, 239; childhood adversity and, 232–33; pharmacological treatment of, 234. *See also* mental health
mental health, 15, 413; black Americans and, 402–4, 406–7, 408–9, 411; epidemiology of, 224, 230; history of survey research in, 222–25; improvement of, 234–39; mental disorders and, 229–33; new developments in, 239–41; populations and, 222–41; services for, 226; well-being and, 225–29
Mental Health in Industry Program, 198, 206, 213, 253, 255
merged-asset income module, 127, 129
Merton, Robert, 196, 440
methodology, 10–11, 21–57; in aging research, 334, 345–47; black American research, 399–401; challenges to, 452–53; clustering, 29–30; conceptual frameworks for, 24–25; data processing and analysis, 53–55, 440–43, 449–50; in fertility studies, 289, 291–92; innovation in, 6, 8, 53, 56, 291–92, 357; interviewing, 46–50; longitudinal studies, 306; measurement error, 25, 38–39; models and survey design, 22–23; on nonresponse, 33–38, 443; population coverage, 25–28; questioning modes, 50–53; questionnaire research, 39–46; question wording, 39–42; racial attitudes and, 359–60, 361–62; reliability and validity in, 43–45; sampling methods, 28–33; size and stratification, 28–29, 31; standardization vs. flexibility in, 23–24, 39; vs. substance, 441–43; telephone sampling, 32–33; theory and, 440
Mexican-Americans, 31
Michigan Alzheimer's Disease Research Center (MADRC), 336
Michigan Center for Mind-Body Research, 265. *See also* Centers for Mind-Body Research
Michigan Interdisciplinary Center on Social Inequalities, Mind, and Body, 343, 344
Michigan Model, 74, 76, 83–84, 402

Michigan Population Studies Center, 16
Michigan Prevention Research Center (MPRC), 235–36, 265
Michigan Project, 101–6, 108, 112, 113; conclusions, 104–6; design elements, 101–4
middle class, race and, 385
Midtown Manhattan study, 223
military: drug abuse and, 320–22; psychological fitness of, 223; racial segregation of, 49
Miller, Peter V., 42, 48
Miller, Warren E., 73, 74, 75, 76–78, 80–81, 442
Miller-Stokes study, 77
Mills, C. Wright, 272
minorities, 19, 30–31, 411. *See also* black Americans; *and specific minority*
misinformation, 90
missile gap, 90
monetary incentives, 37–38
money, influence in elections of, 93
Monitoring the Future (MTF), 17, 113, 216, 275, 442, 446, 447; and drug abuse by youth, 309–10, 311, 325
Moon, Y., 52
moral code, race and, 380
Morgan, James N., 14, 53, 123; income study and, 156, 159, 161, 162
mortality: morbidity and, 4, 15; risk of, 170; wealth and, 333
Mosher, William, 291
mother-father pairs, 106–7. *See also* families; marriage; parenthood
motivation, 139, 160, 227; patterns of, 204
Mouton, Jane S., 203
MTF. *See* Monitoring the Future
multidisciplinary research, 332; on aging, 342–45, 349. *See also* interdisciplinarity
multiparty systems, 86
Multiple Classification Analysis (MCA), 53
multiple imputation, 55
multiple-wave re-interview, 45
multitrait-multimethod (MTMM) design, 44
Murray, Henry, 272
Myers, David G., 239
Myrdal, Gunnar, 386–87

Nass, C., 52
National Advisory Commission on Civil Disorders, 369, 370
National Aeronautics and Space Administration, 256
National Black Election Study, 397–98
National Black Young Adults (NBYA), 422
National Center for Health Statistics, 285, 289
National Comorbidity Survey, 198, 231–32, 232–34, 239
National Crime Victimization Survey, 27
National Death Index, 163
national elections, 65. *See also* election studies
National Election Studies (NES), 12, 67–68, 87, 415, 446, 447; cross-national coordination of, 92; long-term time-series of, 65, 81–84; political socialization and, 110, 112; public opinion and, 89, 93; racial attitudes and, 367–68, 382
National Fertility Studies, 285, 288–89
National Health Service, 262
National Industrial Conference Board, 7
National Institute for Psychosocial Factors in Health, 253
National Institute of Child Health and Human Development, 163, 274
National Institute of Mental Health, 230, 253
National Institute on Aging (NIA), 124, 258, 340, 396, 446; Panel Study of Income Dynamics and, 162, 163, 186
National Institute on Drug Abuse, 310
National Institutes of Health (NIH), 16, 124, 262, 263, 444, 448
nationalism, 66
National Longitudinal Studies (NLS), 14, 307, 449
National Longitudinal Studies of Youth (NLSY), 17

National Longitudinal Surveys, 123. *See also* longitudinal panel studies
National Long-Term Care Survey (NLTCS), 333, 336, 337
National Opinion Research Center (NORC), 9–10, 17, 48, 121, 123, 448; election study by, 72, 79; General Social Surveys by, 79, 210, 449; on racial attitudes, 10, 366, 371
national priorities, 89
National Research Council, 349
National Science Foundation (NSF), 12, 14, 81, 113, 158, 161–63, 447
National Study of Adolescent Males (NSAM), 51, 299
National Study of Black Americans (NSBA), 198
National Survey of American Life, 240
National Survey of American Lives (NSAL), 358, 422, 423
National Survey of Black Americans (NSBA), 227–28, 240, 395, 410, 421, 423, 446; on help-seeking behavior, 407–9; on social support, 404, 406; on stress, 411, 412, 420
National Survey of Family Growth (NSFG), 285, 289–92
natural sciences, 1–2
"Nature of Belief Systems in Mass Politics, The" (Converse), 367
Neighbors, Harold W., 228, 407, 408
NES. *See* National Election Studies
Netherlands: organizational research in, 202; racism in, 398, 415, 417, 418
New American Voter, The (Miller and Shanks), 75
Newcomb, Theodore, 272, 276
New Deal majority, 72
Newlon, Daniel, 163
Newman, Katherine, 168
New Patterns of Management (Likert), 197, 206
New York City, 223, 366
Neyman, J., 7, 31
Nie, Norman H., 83
NIH. *See* National Institutes of Health
1965, class of. *See* class of 1965
Nixon, Richard M., 159
NLS. *See* National Longitudinal Studies
NLTCS. *See* National Long-Term Care Survey
nonresponse error, 25, 33–38, 48, 54, 145, 443, 452–53; in aging research, 345–46; design for reduction of, 37–38; interviewer behavior and, 35–37; theory construction to explain, 33–35
NORC. *See* National Opinion Research Center
norms, 100, 101, 112
North Africans, 417, 419
NSBA. *See* National Survey of Black Americans
NSF. *See* National Science Foundation
NSFG. *See* National Survey of Family Growth
numeric scales, 144

occupational status, 255. *See also* labor; work
Office of Economic Opportunity, 123, 156–57, 159. *See also* Survey of Economic Opportunity
Office of Naval Research, 196–97
Office of Population Research at Princeton University, 288
Office of War Information, 366
Ohio State University, 17, 201, 203, 449
Oksenberg, Lois, 36, 42, 48
Okun, Arthur, 135
oldest-old, study of, 216. *See also* aging
O'Malley, Patrick M., 17, 275, 305, 462
one-person, one-vote ethic, 70
open systems, 207
opportunity structure, 68
Orcutt, Guy, 160
Organizational Behavior Program, 198, 206, 213, 217, 253
Organizational Stress (Kahn), 254
organizational studies, 14–15, 195–99, 201–18; conceptual developments in, 208–11; ecological view of, 208; employee participation studies in, 202–5; health studies and, 195–99; recent developments in, 212–17;

organizational studies (*continued*)
survey feedback and, 205–7; systems theory and, 3, 201, 208, 218; theories of, 3; types of organizations in, 212
Orr, Larry, 159
OSIRIS Statistical Software System, 31–32

Page, Benjamin I., 90
Paige, Jeffrey M., 369, 370
Panakeia, 251
panel studies, 71, 113
Panel Study of Income Dynamics (PSID), 14, 156–90, 395, 442, 449; aging and, 334; child development and, 176–81; conclusions of, 182–85; early generations of, 156–61; economic behavior and, 121, 123, 127–28; electoral behavior and, 79; evolution of (1980–92), 161–64; international influence of, 174–76, 447; measuring health and wealth with, 186–90; poverty and welfare in, 170–74; recent developments of, 182–85; results of genealogical panel of, 164–69
parental psychopathology, 232
parent-child relationship, 12, 105, 274–75, 298. *See also* families
parenthood, 318, 323, 404. *See also* childbearing
Park, Denise P., 346
Parsons, Talcott, 207
participative management, 206–7
party identification and partisanship, 68, 75–76, 83–85, 87, 89; political socialization and, 105, 107, 109. *See also* political parties
Pasteur, Louis, 248
Patterson, John, 289
pension plans, 124, 148, 348. *See also* aging
People Elect a President, The (Campbell and Kahn), 73
People's Choice, The (Lazarsfeld, Berelson, and Gaudet), 71, 86–87
Perot, Ross, 86
personal control, measures of, 160
personal efficacy, 358, 410
personal experience, 140
personal problems, 401, 406. *See also* life-stress paradigm
persuasion of voters, 86–88
Petrocik, John R., 83
Pettigrew, T. F., 417, 418
plant closings, 256
Plato, 143, 282
policy. *See* social policy
Policy Representation in Western Democracies (Miller et al.), 77
polio vaccine, 15, 248
Polish Peasant in Europe and America, The (Thomas and Znaniecki), 272
political behavior, 11–13; of black Americans, 398; racial attitudes and, 386; and systems, 65–69; Vietnam period, 441–42. *See also* electoral behavior; political socialization
Political Behavior Program, 73–74, 76–77, 79, 80
Political Change in Britain (Butler and Stokes), 80
political participation, 90–93, 111. *See also* protest generation
political parties, 75, 91, 92. *See also* party identification and partisanship
political representation, 76–77, 80, 90, 93
Political Representation in France (Dupeux), 80
political science, 3
political socialization, 65, 67, 98–113; development of study of, 98–101; future study of, 111–13; generational comparisons of, 107–11; individual level analysis of, 109–11; Michigan project on, 101–6; subfields of, 101
Political Socialization (Hyman), 98
political systems, 68. *See also* democracies
political tolerance, 109
political values, 77
politics, 3; grassroots, 72, 92
polling firms, 6. *See also specific firm*
poll tax, 92
population, 23; change in, 123; coverage of, 25–28; growth of, 286; health status

of, 122; of organizations, 207–8; surveys based on, 218
population ecology, 208
poverty, 13–14, 397; electoral behavior and, 89; Panel Study of Income Dynamics and, 156–57, 159, 161, 170–74; public programs and, 123; study of, 123. *See also* income; Panel Study of Income Dynamics; wealth
power, 204, 208, 212
Pratt, William, 289
PRBA. *See* Program for Research on Black Americans
precision, indices of, 47
prediction, statistical theory of, 144. *See also* probability
pregnancy, 286–87, 289, 297; drug use and, 323, 325
prejudice, 413–15, 416. *See also* racism
presidential election polls, 6, 11, 12, 25
presidential elections, 71–73, 75, 81, 86–87
Presidential Primaries and the Dynamics of Public Choice (Bartels), 88
President's Commission on Mental Health, 230, 233
Presser, Stanley, 39, 40, 41, 46
Price, Richard H., 15, 198, 216, 222, 236, 462; health studies and, 262, 263, 265
primaries and caucuses, 87–88, 98. *See also* electoral behavior
Princeton Fertility Study, 284, 285, 292, 293–94
Princeton University, 288
principles, 89. *See also* moral code
principle vs. policy, race and, 377–78, 379, 384–85
privacy, in interviews, 51, 359
probability, 73, 143–45, 149
probability sampling, 7, 11, 22–23; aging, 336–37; clustering and, 29–30; population coverage and, 25–26
problem-centered research, 444
processing error, 25
productivity, 197, 203
Program for Research on Black Americans (PRBA), 19, 357, 393, 394–404, 406; conceptual framework for, 401–4; cross-national comparison and, 413; methodological innovations in, 399–401; other research data compared to, 421, 422
Program in Socio-environmental Studies, 276
programmatic organization, 444
programmatic studies, 74, 81
Project TALENT, 307
prosperity, 146. *See also* wealth
protest generation, 100, 107, 108, 111. *See also* political participation
PSID. *See* Panel Study of Income Dynamics
psychiatric epidemiology, 230
psychological well-being, 15, 223, 264; black Americans and, 402–4, 406, 409, 412, 420. *See also* mental health
psychology, 3, 308
psychometric theory, 42, 43–44, 445
psychoneuroimmunology, 252
psychosocial factors, 15–16; in aging, 18, 334, 343–44. *See also* socialization
psychosocial nature of health, 248–66; aging and, 258–62; disease and, 248–53; racial and ethnic factors in, 262–66; stress and, 254–58
public health, 250–51, 287, 313. *See also* health
Public Health Service, 16, 262
public information, 140
public opinion, 65, 70, 93; electoral behavior and, 88–90; on race, 382–83, 386; support of, 5. *See also* racial attitudes
public policy. *See* social policy
public programs, poverty and, 123. *See also* welfare

qualitative method, vs. quantitative, 23–24
Quality of Employment Surveys (QOE), 198, 210, 229
quality-of-life goals, 68
quality of working life, 212, 228–29

questioning modes, 50–53, 89, 145. *See also* interviewers; interviewing
questionnaire research, 39–46; black Americans and, 396, 401; correlations in, 40, 43–44; "Don't Know" option, 40, 44, 45; measurement errors in, 43–44, 45; on question wording, 39–42, 66; self-administered, 51, 52, 347, 359, 361; validity and reliability in, 43–45, 46
Quinn, Robert P., 229
quota sampling, 11, 73

race riots (1960s), 366, 369, 370
racial and ethnic factors, 83; electoral behavior and, 89, 90; psychosocial nature of health and, 262–66. *See also* African-Americans; black Americans
racial and ethnic groups, 4, 18–19, 56, 357, 411. *See also specific groups*
racial attitudes, 365–87, 398; affirmative action, 373, 374–75, 381, 384, 385; black militancy and rioting, 369–71; civil rights movement and, 48–49, 368, 373, 381; competing interpretations, 376–77; complexity of, 355–58; Detroit Area Study, 294, 301n. 6, 360–62, 374, 403, 412; egalitarianism and, 380, 381, 383–84; as ideological weapons, 378–80; methodology, 359–60, 361–62; National Election Studies and, 367–68, 382; principle vs. policy in, 377–78, 379, 384–85; social change and, 384–87; stereotyping, 359, 360, 380, 384, 385; subtlety of, 358–60; symbolic racism, 380–84. *See also* black Americans; segregation
racial inequality, 356, 359
racial integration, 361, 368, 370, 372–73
racism, 18, 409
racism, international studies of, 398, 413–19; immigration policy and, 416, 418–19; intergroup anxiety and, 415; normative analyses, 418–19; psychological aspects and policy, 416–17; structure of prejudice and racism, 417–18
Raghunathan, Trivellore E., 55, 346
rational calculation, 137
rational choice, 66, 90
rationality, bounded forms of, 141–42
rational public, 65
Raudenbush, Stephen W., 54, 347
Reagan, Ronald, 161
recession, 136–37, 139–40, 146–47, 184
Rees, Albert, 161
Reeves, B., 52
refusal rates. *See* nonresponse error
relational data files, 159. *See also* data
relationship continuity, 108–9
reliability, in methodology, 43–45, 46
religious institutions, 282, 298
religious participation, 298, 299; by black Americans, 405–6, 410
Rensis Likert Associates, 213. *See also* Likert, Rensis
repertoire, 90. *See also* political participation
replicated surveys, 113
reproductive health, 291. *See also* fertility
research, basic vs. applied, 443–44
Research Center for Group Dynamics (RCGD), 8, 9, 19, 67, 253, 346
Research Diagnostic Criteria, 231
research instruments, 2. *See also* survey research
residential segregation, 361, 375, 385
resource-dependency theory, 207
respondents, 30, 134. *See also* interviewing; nonresponse error
response effects/rates, 40–41, 143, 157, 297; decline in, 452–53; quality of, 47; surveys on aging, 346, 347. *See also* nonresponse error
retirement, 209, 215, 348; Panel Study of Income Dynamics and, 165; saving and, 147–48, 341–42
retirement-age cohort, 167
Retirement History Survey, 124, 277, 333
retrospective voting, 85. *See also* electoral behavior; voters and voting
Reverberation Model of Stress and Racism, 420
Rice, Cara J., 331, 340
Riley, Mathilda White, 331, 335

"Rise and Fall of the Bureau of Applied Social Research, The" (Hyman), 217
risk: aversion to, 148; of disease, 15–16; factors, 249–50, 261; mechanisms, 235–38; tolerance of, 160
risk battery, 232
Rockefeller Foundation, 161, 397
Rodgers, Willard L., 228, 345, 346
Rokkan, Stein, 79, 80, 92
role conflict, 214, 254–56
rolling cross-section studies, 87
Roosevelt, Franklin D., 6, 7, 11, 70–71, 72
Roper Poll, 6
Rosenstone, Steven J., 86, 91
Rowe, John W., 340
Rubin, D. B., 55
Russell, B., 55
Russia, Duma election of 1999, 68
Ryder, Norman, 288, 292
Ryff, Carol D., 238
Ryn, Michelle van, 236

Salk, Jonas, 248
Salk polio vaccine, 15
Salthouse, Timothy A., 337
sample surveys, 12, 21, 70, 377; life course and, 16; as telescope on society, 3
sampling and data collection, 442–43
sampling error, 25. *See also* errors
Sampling Error Program Package, 31
sampling methods, 6, 28–33; quota, 11, 73. *See also* probability sampling; telephone sampling and surveys
Sanders, L. M., 383
Satcher, David, 230
satisficing, 41–42, 345
Savage, L. J., 144
saving: consumer behavior and, 131–35; decisions about, 137; longevity and, 139; motivations for, 139; precautionary theories of, 147; rate of, 131–33; retirement and, 147–48, 341–42
savings bonds, 120
SCF. *See* Survey of Consumer Finances
Schaie, K. Warner, 340
Schoeni, Robert, 164
schooling, completion of, 160
school integration, 375
school prayer, 105
Schul, Yaacov, 237
Schulenberg, John, 275, 305, 462
Schuman, Howard, 1, 18, 375, 439, 463; on question wording, 39–40, 41, 42; on racial attitudes, 49, 355, 356, 365, 373, 395; surveys of, after 1968 riots, 369, 370–71
Schwarz, Norbert, 41, 346
Scientific American (magazine), 369
scientific methods, 4–5, 11. *See also* methodology
Sears, David O., 380, 383
Seashore, Stanley E., 212, 213, 229
seasonally adjusted series, 136
Seattle Studies, 332
Seaver, D. A., 145
segregation, 366, 368; in military, 49; residential, 361, 375, 385. *See also* integration; racial attitudes
SEH. *See* Social Environment and Health Program
self-administered questionnaires, 51–52, 347; racial attitudes and, 359, 361
self-esteem, 228, 299, 358, 410–11
self-expression, 226
self-help organizations, 233
self-interest, 85
Selye, Hans, 252, 254
semiprojective techniques, 99
sensitivity training, 211
SES. *See* socioeconomic status
sexually transmitted diseases, 290, 291
Shapiro, Robert Y., 90
Shartle, Carroll Leonard, 203
Sheatsley, Paul B., 365, 366, 368, 369, 373
Shively, W. Phillips, 54
Shock, Nathan, 340
short-term dynamics, 74–75
Silver, Brian D., 376
Simon, Herbert, 141
Singer, Eleanor, 1, 21, 48, 52, 439, 463; response rates and, 35, 37, 38
single-organization designs, 197
single parenthood, 318, 323, 404

Sirota Consulting, 213
Sloan Foundation, 161, 278
Smith, James D., 156
Smith, Tom W., 51
Smithies Committee, 135
Smoking and Health (surgeon general's report), 251
Sniderman, Paul M., 382, 383
social change, 222, 227, 276; agents of, 211; generation concept and, 275; life course and, 272; racial attitudes and, 384–87. *See also* change patterns
social context, 359. *See also* socialization
social distance, race and, 372
social environmental variables, 15
Social Environment and Health Program (SEH), 198–99, 202, 213, 216, 217, 446; physical health and, 255, 257–58, 262–64
social epidemiology, 256
social experiments, 451
social indicators, 209
Social Indicators Program, 259
socialization, 258; black families and, 397; and drug use of youth, 306, 317, 318, 321, 322, 324–25; preadult, 113. *See also* political socialization
social niches, 71
social policy: aging and, 331, 339, 347–49; drug use, 325–26; race and, 19, 378
social psychology, 12, 18, 445. *See also* psychosocial factors
Social Psychology of Organizations, The (Kahn and Katz), 197
social relationships, 264. *See also* socialization
Social Science Citation Index, 79
Social Science Research Council, 73, 371
social sciences, 1, 10, 19–20, 53; fertility studies and, 278, 297; infrastructure for, 448; interdisciplinarity and, 445; theory vs. data debate in, 440–41
social scientists, 8, 305, 410, 444; youth studies by, 309. *See also specific scientists*
Social Security, 124, 148, 165, 341, 347, 348
social status. *See* socioeconomic status
social support: African-Americans and, 357–58, 404–5; aging and, 330–31
socioeconomic deprivation, 263
socioeconomic differences, in fertility studies, 287, 289, 296, 299
socioeconomic status (SES), 199; aging and, 338, 343, 344; black American, 402, 406–7, 409, 423
Sociological Imagination, The (Mills), 272
sociologists, life course and, 272–73
sociophysical factors, 222
sociotechnical systems, 201
sociotropic hypothesis, 85
software, 31–32, 55. *See also* computers
Sonquist, John A., 53
South (U.S.), racial attitudes in, 378, 386
South Africa, 240, 413
Southern Politics in State and Nation (Key), 377–78
Soviet Union, 89, 111. *See also* Russia
special populations, 450–51
"split ballot" experiments, 443
SRC. *See* Survey Research Center
stability of orientations, 110
Stafford, Frank P., 14, 156, 164, 463
Stallard, Eric, 335
standard errors, 28, 30, 31
standardization, 39, 56; vs. flexibility, in methodology, 23–24; in interviewing, 48
Standard Listing and Screening Procedure (SLASP), 399–400
standing decision variable, 75
statistical computing, 31–32
statistical theory, 7, 144
statistics, 3, 22
status, 255. *See also* socioeconomic status
steady state design, 158. *See also* genealogy-based design
Steeh, Charlotte, 371
Steiger, Darby Miller, 52
Stephan, Walter, 414
stereotyping, racial, 359, 360, 380, 384, 385, 409
Stimson, J. A., 386
Stirling County study, 223
Stock, J. Stevens, 7

Stogdill, Ralph M., 203
Stokes, Donald E., 77, 80, 85, 442
Stouffer, Samuel A., 49, 195, 367, 442
stratification and size, 28–29, 31
stress, 198; black Americans and, 401–4, 411–12, 419–21; mental health and, 235–36; psychosocial nature of health and, 254–58. *See also* mental health
stress-diathesis models, 253
student status, drug use and, 317, 318–20. *See also* college experience
Study of Michigan Generations, 337
substance abuse. *See* drug and substance abuse
substance vs. method debate, 441–43
Subtle scale of prejudice, 417, 418
Sudman, Seymour, 40, 48, 52
"Suggestions for a Sociological Approach to the Theory of Organization" (Parsons), 207
Sumner, William Grant, 377
supervisors, 197, 203–5
Supplemental Studies (Campbell and Schuman), 370
surgeon general's reports, 230, 251
survey data. *See* data
survey design, 35, 44–45, 289
survey feedback, 197, 205–7, 211
Surveying Subjective Phenomena (Martin), 41
Survey Methodology Program, 56
survey methods, 2–3. *See also* methodology
Survey of Consumer Attitudes (SCA), 13, 37, 122, 446
Survey of Consumer Finances (SCF), 13, 120–22, 446
Survey of Economic Opportunity, 123, 156. *See also* Office of Economic Opportunity
Survey of Income and Program Participation, 449
survey research, historical developments, 5–8
Survey Research Center (SRC), 1, 10, 53, 67, 367, 439, 448; aging studies by, 334, 349, 446–47; black American surveys, 19, 393, 396; on coverage error, 26; election prediction by, 11, 25; Family and Demography Program, 274; Growth of American Families Study, 286–88; life course studies, 16, 17; longitudinal studies of, 449; on measurement error, 45; nonresponse research in, 33, 54; organizational research by, 14; origins of, 8–9; political research and, 11, 12; Program in Socio-environmental Studies, 276; questionnaire research, 39–40; research methodology and, 21, 22, 39; Sampling Section at, 28; Survey Methodology Program in, 56; surveys of well-being, 15; survey stratification and, 28–29, 31; theory testing by, 27–28, 440; wealth module of, 127; YIT project, 307–8. *See also* Health and Retirement Study; Monitoring the Future; Survey of Consumer Attitudes; *and specific studies*
survey research design, 65. *See also* methodology
Survey Sampling (Kish), 28
Suzman, Richard, 163
Swedish Household Panel, 174
symbolic racism, 380–84. *See also* racial attitudes
Syme, S. Leonard, 257
symptom patterns, 225, 231
system-blame concept, 410
systems theory, 201, 208, 218
Szalai, Alexander, 125

tailoring behavior, 37
Taiwan, 295, 339
Takeuchi, D. T., 407
talking therapies, 233
Tannenbaum, Arnold S., 208, 213
Task Force on Youth Development and Community Programs, 181
Tavistock Institute, 201
tax file sample, 121
Taylor, Frederick Winslow, 14, 196, 203
Taylor, R. J., 404–5, 408, 409
Tecumseh Community Health Study, 257

telephone sampling and surveys, 11, 32–33, 347, 452; of black Americans, 397, 399; face-to-face interviews compared to, 26–27, 48, 50–51; on family issues, 291, 295; nonresponse to, 34, 35–36
telescope analogy, 3
television advertisements, 90
Temporary Assistance for Needy Families (TANF), 180
Terlizzese, D., 145
Terman, Louis, 272
test-retest (panel design), 45
Theorell, Tores, 257
theory, 20, 22, 56, 439–41; data and, 149–50, 440–41; empirical research and, 1–2; and frameworks for aging, 340–42; of nonresponse error, 33–35, 38; of organizational systems, 3, 201, 208, 218; psychometric, 42, 43–44, 445; statistical, 7, 144; testing of, 27–28, 440
Theory of Expectations, 140–41
therapeutic age, 226
thermodynamic thesis, 365
third-party voting, 85–86. *See also* electoral behavior; voters and voting
Third Wave of democratization, 67
Thomas, L. B., 142
Thomas, W. I., 272
Thornton, Arland, 281, 301n. 6, 443, 463–64; fertility studies of, 16, 274, 281, 295
Three-Generation Family Study (TGFS), 396
Tilly, Charles, 90
time diaries, 126
time-separable utility, 138
time-series analysis, 83–84, 135–36, 195; longitudinal data in, 113, 157, 158; National Election Studies and, 81–84
time use studies, 125–26
Tischler, Gary L., 223
tobacco use, youth and, 310. *See also* cigarette smoking
Tobin, James, 135, 160
Tocqueville, Alexis de, 89
Torney, Judith D., 99
tort system insurance settlements, 127
torture, in South Africa, 240
total survey error paradigm, 24–25
Tourangeau, Roger, 51, 52
Tran, T. V., 410
transitional societies, 107
Traugott, Michael W., 37
traumatic events. *See* stress
Trist, Eric, 201
Truman, Harry S., 11, 25, 72–73, 366
trust, in government, 308–9
Turner, Charles F., 41, 51
Tversky, A., 144
Twenty-fourth Amendment (U.S. Constitution), 92
two-earner households, 146, 229

uncertainty, measurement of, 144, 146. *See also* measurement
unemployment, 235–37, 420; mass fears of, 131–32; rate of, 142; statistics, 4, 7. *See also* employment
unemployment insurance, 168
unfolding techniques, 127–29
United Nations, 195
United States, health-care spending in, 264
university degree programs, 57
University of Chicago, 10, 121
University of Denver, 9, 72
University of Essex, 80
University of Michigan, 1, 10, 67; fertility research by, 284, 285, 294; School of Public Health, 253, 263; survey methodology program at, 11. *See also* Detroit Area Study; Institute for Social Research; Survey Research Center
University of North Carolina, Department of Epidemiology, 257
urban sociology, 265
urban time use, 125
U.S. Bureau of the Census, 4, 7, 28, 449; consumer survey by, 123, 136; poverty data and, 156, 171. *See also* census data
U.S. Congress, 225; elections of, 77, 93
U.S. Constitution, Twenty-fourth Amendment, 92

U.S. Department of Agriculture, 6, 39, 119, 196
U.S. Department of Commerce, 13, 185
U.S. Department of Health and Human Services, 163, 190, 397
U.S. Department of Health, Education, and Welfare, 123, 159
U.S. Department of Labor, 209, 229, 306–7
U.S. House of Representatives elections, 93
Ustun, Bedhiran, 240
utility maximization, 137

Valen, Henry, 79
validity, in methodology, 43–45, 46, 52, 308
Van Hoewyk, John, 37
variance, interviewer, 31–32, 49
Velvet Glove, The (Jackman), 379
Verba, Sidney, 83
verbal descriptions, 144
Veroff, Joseph, 226–27, 234, 239
Vietnam period, 441–42
Vietnam War, 100, 108
Vinokur, Amiram D., 216, 236–37, 263, 265
violence, race and, 370. *See also* race riots
volunteering rules, 121
Voter Decides, The (Miller, Campbell, and Gurin), 73
voters and voting: electoral behavior and, 12, 441; models of, 84–86; persuasion of, 86–88; registration requirements, 91; turnout of, 91–92, 112. *See also* election polls; electoral behavior; National Election Studies
Voting (Berelson, Lazarsfeld, and McPhee), 72
Voting Rights Act of 1965, 91–92, 368

Walker, Kathryn, 125
Wallace, George, 86, 88
War on Poverty, 156
wartime economy, 131–32
wealth: distribution of, 126; measurement of, 121, 122, 127–29, 186–90
Weber, Max, 14, 204, 282
Web sites, 32, 371, 451–52; Web-based surveys, 11, 52. *See also* computers; Internet
Weir, David R., 17, 277, 330, 464
Weitzman, Lenore, 165
welfare, 164, 170–72; reform of, 173–74
well-being, mental health and, 225–29. *See also* health; mental health
Westermarck, Edward, 282, 283
Western Europe, racism in, 416, 420. *See also* European Union; *and specific countries*
Westerstahl, Jorgen, 79
Westoff, Charles F., 284, 288, 292
Whelpton, Pascal K., 284, 286
White House Special Action Office on Drug Use Prevention, 310
whites, race and. *See* racial attitudes
"Who Speaks for Black America," 398
Wide Area Sampling Procedure (WASP), 399, 400
Wildenman, Rudolf, 80
Williams, David R., 19, 240, 263, 407, 464; on African-Americans, 355, 357, 393
Williams-Morris, Ruth, 240
Willis, Robert J., 17, 277, 330, 464
Wilson, Woodrow, 66
Winterfeld, D. von, 145
Withey, Steve B., 229
within-subjects framework, 43–44
Wolf, Sharon, 443
Wolfinger, Raymond E., 91
women: in Bennington College study, 276; fertility surveys and, 286, 288, 290, 293, 294–95; life course and, 273; as majority of elderly, 348. *See also* childbearing; gender; pregnancy
work, 126; attachment to, 209; boredom at, 214; health and, 217; problems related to, 209; quality of life at, 212, 228–29; unpaid, 125–26. *See also* labor
Work and Health (Kahn), 215
work/organizational psychology, 202. *See also* organizational studies
Works Progress Administration (WPA), 7

Work, Stress, and Social Support (House), 215
World Fertility Study, 285, 292
World Health Organization, 210, 239
World Mental Health 2000 Study, 239
World Values Study (Inglehart), 79
World War II, 7–8, 120, 366
World Wide Web, 452. *See also* Web sites
Wortman, Camille B., 259
Wright, R., 410

Yale University, 201, 212
Years of Poverty, Years of Plenty (Duncan), 170
youth, black American, 422
youth, studies of. *See* adulthood, transition to; children; drug and substance abuse
Youth and Social Issues program, 309
Youth in Transition (YIT) project, 216, 307–8
Yugoslavian industry, 208

Zaller, John, 93
Zeisel, H., 235
Zimmerman, William, 65, 465
Znaniecki, Florian, 272